Close Shave

Close Shave

The Life and Times of Baseball's Sal Maglie

by James D. Szalontai

McFarland & Company, Inc., Publishers
Jefferson, North Carolina, and London

Library of Congress Cataloguing-in-Publication Data

Szalontai, James D., 1974–
    Close shave : the life and times of baseball's Sal Maglie / by James D. Szalontai.
    p.   cm.
    Includes bibliographical references and index.

    ISBN 0-7864-1189-9 (softcover : 50# alkaline paper)

    1. Maglie, Sal, 1917– . 2. Baseball players—United States—Biography. I. Title.
GV865.M24S92   2002
796.357'092—dc21   2002006338

British Library cataloguing data are available

©2002 James D. Szalontai. All rights reserved

No part of this book may be reproduced or transmitted in any form or by any means, electronic or mechanical, including photocopying or recording, or by any information storage and retrieval system, without permission in writing from the publisher.

Manufactured in the United States of America

Cover: Sal Maglie sitting in the dugout. (George Brace Photo) Stan Musial lies on the ground after being nailed with a pitch. (National Baseball Hall of Fame Library, Cooperstown, N.Y.)

McFarland & Company, Inc., Publishers
  Box 611, Jefferson, North Carolina 28640
    www.mcfarlandpub.com

Contents

Preface		1
1	Trials and Triumphs of a Bush League Pitcher	3
2	Return to the International League	26
3	Wartime Ball, "Wartime" Pitcher?	37
4	The Baseball War, the Black List, and the Mexican Jumping Beans	50
5	Back With the Giants	74
6	The American Aristocracy and the Miracle Finish	116
7	Pitching in Pain	182
8	A Season to Forget	218
9	Return to Glory	243
10	Banished to Cleveland	281
11	The Barber Joins the Enemy	303
12	From Dodger Blue to Yankee Pinstripes	336
13	The End Is Near	349
14	The Old Warrior Fades Away	364
Chapter Notes		373
Bibliography		385
Index		391

PREFACE

Sal Maglie was a feared, hated, and respected craftsman of pitching who symbolized the rough era in which he played. He is perhaps best remembered for his vicious knockdown pitches that made batters tremble, but his career was much more. It was about courage, fortitude, and resilience. He was written off countless times but always came back to prove the prognosticators wrong. There were many players throughout the history of major league baseball who had great natural talent but squandered it because they didn't apply themselves and take care of their bodies. Maglie was never burdened with such thoughts; he gave everything he had to the game, making the most out of his abilities, and never cheating himself or his team. Sal didn't know what the word quit meant; he overcame a blacklist, crippling injuries, and advanced age to become one of the finest pitchers in the major leagues. Lesser men would have wilted under the arduous conditions that Maglie faced. When things looked bleak he didn't give up and continued to work tirelessly towards his goals. He was a "money pitcher," taking the ball when his team needed a victory and handling the immense pressures that surround him like a true professional.

Maglie had an unspectacular minor league career before debuting with Mel Ott's New York Giants in 1945. His career subsequently spiraled downward as he played in Cuba, Mexico, Canada, and barnstormed around the U.S., after being blacklisted by organized baseball for jumping to Jorge

Pasquel's Mexican League. In 1950, he returned to the Giants and at the age of thirty-three proved he was a bona fide big league hurler. He went on to have a stellar major league career that included stints with the Cleveland Indians, Brooklyn Dodgers, New York Yankees, and St. Louis Cardinals. Maglie had a great curveball and pinpoint control to go along with his intimidating presence. He was a perceptive student of the art of pitching as well: pitching with his arm and his head. In his hands, the baseball was transformed into a weapon as he intimidated countless nervous batters. On the field, he was a ferocious competitor and viewed as dangerous, while off the field he was paradoxically amiable.

Close Shave is not merely a biography of Maglie but also an examination of the teams and players he played with and against. It would be difficult to understand Maglie's career without first understanding those coaches, managers, teammates, and rivals who influenced him. Therefore, biographical sketches are provided of individuals such as Leo Durocher, Dolf Luque, Frank Shellenback, Jackie Robinson, Carl Furillo, Willie Mays, and many others. Baseball as it was played during the 1940s and 1950s was a violent, dangerous, and manipulative sport. This book is an unromanticized look into that game, which avoids quixotic hyperbole and deals with the unsavory aspects of the national pastime in an honest manner. This "golden age" of baseball was replete with intense rivalries that cultivated "beanball" wars, fights, riots and memorable arguments.

The foundation of this work consists of a game-by-game analysis of Maglie's professional career which was compiled using the newspapers of the day. The bulk of the microfilm research was completed at the Alexander Library at Rutgers University and at the New York Public Library. This comprehensive analysis of Maglie's career is interspersed with intriguing stories of the general era, including the teams and players he encountered. It expands greatly on Milton Shapiro's short but insightful biography of Maglie that was published in 1957 by Messner. Like the varying emotions that people felt towards Maglie, this book should cultivate visceral reactions in those who read it. Sal Maglie left an indelible mark on the game and to those who saw him pitch he is not easily forgotten.

Trials and Triumphs of a Bush League Pitcher

Sal Maglie's knees were shaking as he walked to the center of the diamond on August 13, 1938, to make his professional debut. A sizable Offermann Stadium crowd watched intently to see how the local kid from Niagara Falls, now wearing the hometown uniform of the Buffalo Bisons, would fare against the mighty Newark Bears. It was the second game of a doubleheader and the situation would make any pitcher tremble, particularly a raw busher. The Bears had a reputation that paralleled that of the their parent club, the New York Yankees. They were the class of the International League, the most envied team in the bushes. Their 104–48 record in '38 was daunting. They destroyed the circuit, and would have been competitive in the American League. Future major leaguers filled the roster such as regulars Mike Chartak, Buddy Rosar, and Charlie (King Kong) Keller. The pitching staff was just as formidable with future big leaguers Marius Russo, Ernie Bonham, Nick Strincevich, Atley Donald, Joe Beggs and John Lindell on the squad. Steve O'Neill, the Buffalo skipper, gave the pill to Maglie with the bases loaded and two out in the third. Buddy Rosar stepped into the box. The petrified hurler's first offering sailed over his catcher's head to the backstop, a wild pitch. Maglie walked Rosar on four pitches and then walked Keller. After he walked his third consecutive batter, O'Neill gave him a reprieve and took him out. Before the twenty-one year old Maglie left the hill, O'Neill tried to console him: "Better luck next time, kid."[1] Maglie was starting his professional career at an advanced age and that hit song "It's Later Than You Think" would prove applicable to him later in his career.[2] Sal had a confidence problem that August day; he was unsure if he belonged, unsure he could make it. He didn't know how to pitch, how to control his nerves, and how to intimidate batters as of yet, but he would learn. It would be a tortuous professional career, with vast peaks and expansive valleys, but he would survive and strive in the face of the most difficult odds. He would be written off countless times, considered washed up and useless, but Maglie would show courage and prove the prognosticators wrong time after time. The baseball world would come to know him as "The Barber," "Sinister Sal," and the "Renaissance Assassin," while batters called him countless names which are inappropriate to mention in front of children.[3] However on that August day in '38, there were few who knew how far he would go.

The small mill town of Manchester in Western New York would struggle to find its identity in the nineteenth century and soon changed its name to Niagara Falls. Augustus Porter was its most famous citizen and he had first viewed the great cataract in 1795 while on his way to survey the terrain of the Ohio Territory and chart the new American wilderness. By the turn of the twentieth century, Niagara Falls was a thriving industrial city of twenty thousand citizens. The cataract provided a natural geographic border for the United States and Canada, and while Niagara Falls, New York, became a sober industrial city, Niagara Falls, Ontario, became a haven for tourists and for those seeking a good time. The cataract was much more majestic on the Canadian side of the border, much to the chagrin of those who lived in New York. The great "Falls" dominated both communities, like the Dodgers once dominated Brooklyn. The American community developed into a gloomy industrial city which author Pierre Berton called "a welter of grime-coated factories, railroad tracks, telephone poles, and coal piles."[4] The primary entrance was through Buffalo Avenue, and the visitor observed dusky chemical factories and tall smoke stacks. It was a place of lunch-pail blue-collar workers and their places of employment included the Olin Corporation, Union Carbide, Du Pont, and Hooker Chemical. Pollution became a major problem. As World War II approached, carbon was used to churn out new products, but the waste and residue were difficult to break down in the environment. So it was in this rugged, blue-collar community that Sal Maglie came into this earth and left this earth. It was a tough, gritty place to grow up and it helped shape Maglie into what he was.

Salvatore Anthony Maglie was born on April 26, 1917, in Niagara Falls, New York. It was a chaotic time as the country mobilized for war. The

United States Congress had recently declared war on Germany and entered World War I. Sal was the son of Joseph and Mary Maglie. Their neighborhood was a haven for immigrants. Italians, Poles, and Jews were among those who lived in this tough community. Maglie's parents and those of other immigrants wanted their kids to make good in the new country and eventually many of them grew up to be doctors, dentists, and other contributing members of society. Joseph Maglie was originally from Foggia in southern Italy, in the region known as Puglia. He brought a belief in hard work and honesty to America, and found work as pipefitter. Later he owned a grocery store.

Sal was a competitive youth, always playing sports. He was a position player on the sandlot team but wasn't good enough to pitch. His career as a catcher ended when he neglected to wear a mask one day and a foul tip smashed him in the mouth. "I'm at the wrong end of the business," he said to himself.[5] He played the outfield and first base while carrying a capable stick. However he stubbornly stuck by his intention to pitch until given the opportunity. It was his calling. His mother worried because he was constantly playing ball. After dinner he would sneak out the front door when convenient, and if necessary climb out through the window in the bathroom. If his friends were not around he would throw rocks in the Niagara River behind the power plant. Maglie had two sisters, but he was the only boy in the family. After school, his father would often insist that he work in the grocery store. Sal often resisted, insisting that he should go play ball with his friends. When he worked in the store he made some money by delivering orders with a three-wheeled grocery wagon. As a teenager, Joseph got Sal a job working in Dominick's barber shop on East Falls Street. It was an apprenticeship and Joseph thought that Maglie should learn a trade. He was supposed to clean up the store and watch the barbers work but Sal had other ambitions. His employment there lasted for only one day, and he never came back. Later he would be known as "The Barber," a distinction given to him for his ability to throw close to a batter. To give close shaves, and throw at the jugular. Not only was he proficient in baseball but also basketball. It was his basketball talents that garnered most of his attention as a youth.

Maglie went to the Thirteenth Street School, then to South Junior High and finally to Niagara Falls High School. He made the baseball team in high school and through his persistence and hard work became a pitcher. In addition to his school team, Maglie earned five to ten dollars a game by playing for a semi-pro team. After one game a scout from the Dodgers approached and asked him, "Kid, you going to school?" Maglie replied in the affirmative to which the scout said, "Keep going."[6] If his prospects as a ballplayer seemed tenuous, then it was completely the opposite when it came to his abilities on the hardwood. Several college scouts were in attendance for his final high school games. In his senior year he averaged twenty-five points a game and was named captain of the Niagara Falls-Buffalo all-scholastic all-star team. Taps Gallagher, the coach at Niagara University, was impressed with what he saw and offered Maglie a scholarship. However, Maglie did not think college was for him, knowing his parents could use the income he could earn working in the factory. He didn't think that he belonged on a college campus, cogitating some erudite theory, and struggling to get by. He knew that the university only wanted him for his basketball skills. His father was not happy when he found out that Sal was turning down the scholarship. Joseph thought it was a great opportunity for his son to go to college. It was the American dream. However, his son couldn't stand the idea of going to college and not earning a dime for four years. Sal was a pragmatist and a realist; he always knew his limitations and what was needed to become successful. When Sal reminded him that they could use the money around the house, Joseph became angry. He was a proud man, the family had refused to take government handouts during the depression, and he believed that he provided for his family in more than an adequate way. Sal had a job set up in the shipping department of Union Carbide, an electro-metallurgical company. On weekends he would earn extra money by pitching for the company team. His mother cringed at the thought of a future in baseball. His father was reluctant, but gave in, and would become a supporter and fan of Sal's pitching career, especially later when he earned good money. Sal graduated from high school in 1936 and went off to Union Carbide, to follow in the tradition of the blue-collar, working class factory ethic.

In 1936 and '37, Sal was content to earn his five to ten dollars a game on weekends for the company team to supplement his regular salary. The competition was weak, and he got by with a live fastball and an occasional curve. In 1937 when Union Carbide was not scheduled to play on weekends, he moonlighted with the Zito Realtors. The team toured Northwestern New York, visiting towns such as Lackawanna, Lockport, Kenmore, and Gasport. Sal also went to a tryout camp for the Rochester Red Wings of the International League in '37. He threw only three pitches, but that was apparently enough for the person in charge who promptly yelled, "Next."[7] Maglie quickly exited the mound, his confidence shattered. Jack Egan, a scout for the Boston Red Sox, saw Maglie pitch but was dissuaded from signing him for fear that his herky jerky motion would lead to arm trouble. He had a snapping motion towards the elbow when he delivered a pitch. Maglie's pitching motion would change very little over the years and he avoided a serious arm injury, even when the rest of his body was disintegrating. Finally in 1938, Sal caught his break. A local semi-pro team was assembled in Niagara Falls and Maglie found a spot for himself on the roster. The team was called the Cataracts, no doubt named for the great waterfall which hovered over the area, and played its home games in Hyde Park. The park had a good baseball field. Sal's salary called for a significant increase compared to the company team. He was promised twenty-five dollars a game for every game he pitched and fifteen dollars for showing up when he didn't pitch. Joseph was impressed. The Cataracts had an ambitious plan for bringing quality baseball to Niagara Falls. They played a highly competitive and talented brand of semi-pro ball and recruited players from out of state for their team. The schedule was ambitious and they had lofty expectations. However, not many of the local citizenry showed up at Hyde Park and they soon had trouble covering expenses. The venture inevitably folded, and with the money left over the recruited players were paid off first while local players such as Maglie failed to receive their full salary. Maglie benefited greatly from the endeavor. He played against top-notch competition including some Negro League teams. Before one contest Josh Gibson of the Homestead Grays predicted he would hit a homer and he did. Years later, Maglie said, "I guarantee that later on when I knew more about pitching he would have been in the dirt."[8] Steve O'Neill, the manager of the Buffalo Bisons, came to many of the Cataracts games, searching for local talent. He saw promise in the right arm of the young Maglie. O'Neill arranged a meeting with Sal and offered a contract to play with the Bisons. Maglie had expected to be offered an opportunity to play in the low minor leagues. He was mildly surprised to find out that the Bisons were interested. He eagerly accepted the Bisons' offer of $250 a month and a $275 bonus. Salvatore Anthony Maglie was not only a professional pitcher, but only one step removed from the major leagues. If it seemed too easy, it was, and there was a reason for Maglie's advancement to such a high level of competition.

Buffalo had its own industrial revolution in the nineteenth century as immigrants (the Irish in particular) flocked to the city, to become part of the burgeoning American experience. The opening of the Erie Canal served as the impetus for the city's first economic boom. Buffalo was an inland port and was accessible to Lake Erie, Lake Ontario, and the Niagara River. Railroad tracks, factories, and salons sprang up everywhere. The immigrants fueled the industrial giant but they were considered to be at the bottom rung of the social ladder, and faced harsh discrimination. It wasn't long before the residents of Buffalo found their recreation in baseball. The city had a strong baseball history, fielding their first professional team in 1877. From 1886 to 1970 (excluding 1899 and 1900) the Buffalo Bisons played in the International League. Offermann Stadium, which was originally called Bison Stadium, opened in 1924 on the intersection of Michigan and Ferry. It was a cozy ballpark that held about 14,000 people in a single decked grandstand. The grandstand had a roof that covered most of the seats and extended down the foul lines. There was a small bleacher section in left field in foul territory. Patrons watched games for free in left field on rooftops until a 32-foot fence ceased such activity. The scoreboard in center rose to 60 feet with the advertising on top of it. Dimensions were 321 feet down the left field line, 400 feet to center, and 297 feet down the right field line. It was a hitter's park because of the short right field porch, the prevailing winds, and the short distance (33 feet) between home plate and the backstop. Dallas Green had pitched for Buffalo in 1959 and once said, "Offermann was one of the great minor-league ballparks of all time. The people were right on top of you, and it had the same feeling you get in Fenway. And those Buffalo fans knew their baseball."[9] Some of the future major leaguers who played there included Bill Dickey, Rip Sewell, Connie Mack, Jimmy Collins, Joe McCarthy (manager), Bucky Harris, Paul Richards, Lou Boudreau, Fred Hutchinson, Jim Bunning, Billy Pierce, Chris Short, and Bobby Wine.

When Maglie joined the Buffalo Bisons in '38 they were in fourth place and that is precisely where they would finish with a 79–74 record. This qualified them for the playoffs. In 1933, Frank Shaughnessy, business manager of the Montreal Royals, had his idea of a four-team postseason playoff implemented. Previously the league champion was decided solely on the standings at the end of the season. The new system kept fans interested and helped struggling minor league franchises earn extra money which they sorely needed during the depression. By 1936 Shaughnessy became the International League president. Steve O'Neill, the Bisons' manager, was a respected and well liked man who had put together a solid major league career as a catcher. Previously he had managed the Cleveland Indians (1935–37) and would later manage the Detroit Tigers, Boston Red Sox, and Philadelphia Phillies. In addition, he coached in the majors and served as skipper of several minor league teams. Baseball ran in his blood. He had three brothers who also played in the majors. O'Neill was like a second father to Maglie as he tried to develop him in his three years with the squad. The 1938 Bisons were led by Ollie Carnegie (.330, 45 homers, 136 RBIs), James Oglesby (.319, 13 homers, 90 RBIs), Joseph Martin (.331, 10 homers), and Woody Abernathy (.323, 21 homers). Abernathy's season ended prematurely when he was skulled by Syracuse pitcher Johnny Gee on August 6. Buffalo's .284 batting average ranked second to Newark (.301) and they led the league with 149 homers. The pitching staff was led by Ken Ash (15–8, 3.90 ERA) and Fabian Kowalik (15–13, 3.77 ERA).

1. Trials and Triumphs of a Bush League Pitcher

The home run outburst was attributed to the small man who rose above all others in '38, Ollie Carnegie. Carnegie stood at 5'7" and 165 pounds, and was a proficient line drive hitter. Similar to Ted Williams he made contact with the ball just before it smacked into the catcher's mitt. He was a "late hitter" and waited for the last possible moment to pull the trigger. He was a short, powerful man, bowlegged, and did not look like a home run hitter. Carnegie was from rugged western Pennsylvania, playing on a company team in Pittsburgh for eight years before he got a job with the Pennsylvania Railroad. He lost his job, as many did during the Great Depression, and took a shot at professional baseball. In 1922 he had played a couple of games in the Michigan-Ontario League and not until the age of 32 did he return to professional ball in 1931 with Hazelton of the New York-Pennsylvania League. From 1932 to 1941 he was a fixture for the Bisons in left field and perhaps the most popular player in their history. His 1938 season was his best. He led the league in homers (45) and runs driven in (136) while finishing sixth in batting (.330). He was a right-handed hitter who swung a 38-ounce bat and had terrific eyesight. During World War II, with organized baseball short of bodies, he reemerged with the Bisons as a part-time player and coach. He hit 258 homers and drove in 1,044 runs in his International League career, which are both records. Carnegie never got the opportunity to play in the big show. Major league scouts were scared away by his age, lack of speed and weak throwing arm.

In that first game against Newark on August 13, Maglie headed straight to the mound without warming up. He was a thrower, not a pitcher, and his introduction in professional baseball was a harsh lesson. Maglie had never witnessed a professional game until he joined the Bisons. On August 20 he made his second appearance and pitched two scoreless innings in relief in a mop up role as the Jersey City Giants defeated Buffalo by a 12–2 score at Offermann Stadium. Babe Herman, who had once doubled into a double play with Wilbert Robinson's Brooklyn Dodgers, well known as "The Daffiness Boys," hit a homer for Jersey City. Herman was trying to extend his major league career, while batting .324 with 18 homers for Jersey City in '38. He would not make it back to the majors until 1945, when teams were desperate for players because of the war time shortage. Herman batted .279 (380 at-bats) with the Cincinnati Reds in 1936 and an even .300 (20 at-bats) with the Detroit Tigers in 1937. Although on the down side of his career, he was representative of the high quality of talent found in the International League.

A crowd of about 6,000 Buffalo fans showed up in the frigid cold on September 2 to watch the Bisons play host to the Brooklyn Dodgers in an exhibition game. They were not necessarily there to watch the stumbling Brooklyn National League ballclub who were destined for a seventh place (69–80) finish in the senior circuit. They showed up to watch the deity, but they found out that Babe Ruth had become mortal. Larry MacPhail, president of the Dodgers, had brought Ruth in to become a first base coach on the '38 team. However he was actually hired so he could boost attendance and give the people a show by trying to hit homers in batting practice. Burleigh Grimes, the old spitballer, was the manager but his departure seemed inevitable and Ruth yearned for his job. However Leo Durocher, a scrappy, crude infielder, was given the job at season's end. Ruth proved incompetent as a coach and his home run exhibitions were impotent, with the struggling Ruth desperately trying to knock balls over the fence. Durocher had played with Ruth on the Yankees and incessantly mocked the man. Leo allegedly stole his watch in one incident, and derided Ruth's intelligence and his dark complexion, suggesting he was a "negro."[10] In August of '38 Leo humiliated Ruth in the locker room after a game when the Babe botched the signs. A fight broke out and Leo quickly shoved Ruth into a locker before he could get to him. Leo made a living at provocation and humiliation and would later manage Sal Maglie in the baseball wars of the '50s.

The Bisons won the game by a 7–5 score as the Dodgers lost their eleventh contest on their Western swing that included two exhibition games. Ruth hit a couple of homers before the game. His last year as a major league player was in 1935 with the Boston Braves. He was a shell of his former self at that time and thus when he took the field in the exhibition game in '38 he was outclassed. He committed an error, struck out and grounded out twice. Old timers such as O'Neill and George Uhle also played in the game. Maglie was the third Bisons hurler and he surrendered a homer to Goody Rosen in the ninth. It sailed over the right field wall. Maglie remembered that incident till the end of his career, although he would get the year wrong. "I was in the International League and the Dodgers came to play an exhibition. I threw Goody Rosen an inside curve and he hit a homer. A few years later when he was with Syracuse I had to pitch against him again. I kept my curves outside and I always had pretty good luck with him."[11] Maglie had a great ability to recall what he threw to a particular batter in a certain situation so he could change his strategy the next time he faced him. Dan Carnevale (batted .216 in '38) was Maglie's roommate when he broke in with Buffalo and also played with him in 1940. Years later as a Cleveland Indian scout he described Maglie as follows: "He was fearless, highly competitive, had a photographic memory for batters' weaknesses and was a master at pitching."[12] There might have been some hyperbole in that statement because Maglie was anything but a master of pitching during his three years in Buffalo but he did possess a great memory.

On September 4 the Bisons spilt a doubleheader with the Toronto Maple Leafs in Buffalo. Ollie Carnegie hit a walk off, two run homer in the bottom of the ninth in the opener to lead them to a 6–5 win. It was his 45th tater as he broke the Buffalo record of 44 homers achieved by Bill Kelly in 1926. The Maple Leafs bounced back and won the second game, 12–3. Maglie pitched the final three innings but was hammered and gave up eight runs. Five days later, Steve O'Neill allowed Sal to start a game against Montreal. He pitched well in the opening game of a doubleheader but lost 4–1. Sal worked all nine innings, gave up six hits, walked three and hit a batter while striking out two. At the plate he hit a triple off Montreal starter Ed Chapman. Maglie pitched 5 games for the Bisons in '38. He had a 0–1 record with a 3.75 ERA. Sal pitched 12 innings, gave up 5 earned runs, 12 hits, 8 walks, and struck out 4. The Bisons won the opening playoff series against Syracuse, winning four games and losing one. The Newark Bears won their series from Rochester in seven games and defeated Buffalo in five games for Governor's Cup championship and a chance to play in the Little World Series. The Bears were a juggernaut ever since 1932 when Yankees owner Jacob Ruppert hired George Weiss to build up the farm system. Their success came from their ability to find talent by hiring excellent scouts, Paul Krichell in particular, and having the ability to pay for such talent. Ruppert's goal was to develop talent for the Yankees while simultaneously providing Newark with a great team. David Chrisman, a minor league researcher and author, observed that "Ruppert fell in love with Newark and was determined to field a representative minor league club there even at the risk of not always winning the American League pennant at the parent level."[13]

After his shaky debut in the International League, Maglie was not expecting to return. In later years Sal admitted "I thought sure I'd be farmed out to a lower league next season, but they kept me around all year and I didn't get very much work."[14] If the Bisons did not take him back he was content on returning to Union Carbide and pitching semi-pro instead of going to a lower level minor league. For the talented International League batter, Maglie was not difficult to figure out and they hit him hard in 1939. He pitched in 39 games and started 8 of them. His 3–7 record with a 4.99 ERA left much to be desired. Maglie pitched 101 innings, allowed 56 earned runs, 102 hits, 42 walks and struck out 62. At the plate he batted .143. It was a competitive race in '39. Jersey City took the early lead and held on to finish in first place. Billy Southworth's Rochester Red Wings finished second, four games behind Jersey City. Buffalo, Newark, and Syracuse competed down to the wire for the final two playoff spots. The Bisons finished in third place at 82–72 while Syracuse and Newark tied each other with identical 81–73 records and had a one game playoff to determine who would finish in fourth place. The Bears pulled out a 9–6 victory and then defeated Jersey City in the first round of the playoffs. Rochester defeated Buffalo in seven games and then defeated Newark in seven games for the Governor's Cup championship. Offensively the Bisons were led by James Oglesby (.327, 16 homers and 91 RBIs), future Hall of Famer Lou Boudreau (.331, 17 homers, 7 triples), Joseph Martin (.321, 23 homers, 93 RBIs), John Tyler (.288 and a league leading 124 runs scored) and Ollie Carnegie who once again led the league in homers (29) and RBIs (112). He batted .294. Alfred Smith was Buffalo's best pitcher (16–2, 3.26 ERA) while Clay Smith (13–11, 2.94 ERA) and Ken Ash (10–9, 3.94 ERA) also had good years. It was a competitive year in the International League and the fight for the final playoff spot brought interest from fans, which was precisely what the Shaughnessy playoff system was designed to do.

April 20 was replete with the pageantry of opening day as the Bisons opened the season against Jersey City at Roosevelt Stadium before an overflow crowd of 45,112 (paid attendance). It was a momentous day as the attendance was the largest in minor league history. The grandstand and bleachers were packed while thousands of other fans stood behind the outfield fence. It was about 15,000 more fans than had showed up for the New York Yankees opener and the second largest crowd in baseball only to the 47,000 that made their way into Briggs Stadium for the Tigers' opening game. Al Schacht, the "Clown Prince of Baseball," entertained the crowd before the contest with one of his patented exhibitions. Then the Jerseys went out and dropped a 3–2 decision as they made a couple of fielding mistakes that cost them the game. They appeared tense as if they were trying too hard to please the crowd. Fabian Kowalik (6–8, 5.17 ERA on the year) started for Buffalo and went the distance for the victory. The Giants bounced back the next day, 6–2, as Alfred Smith took the loss for the Bisons. Jersey City also took the final game, which included a spree of violence in the ninth inning. A fan took exception to the umpires' ruling on the legality of Bob Carpenter's stance and delivery on the pitching rubber. He then rushed the field and exchanged punches with umpires Roy Van Graflan and Joe Schroeder. The umpires reinforced their ruling on the Jersey City hurler with their fists when the fan attacked them. The fan got the worst of the exchange before the police took him away. It was an ugly scene but one which was not uncommon in baseball. Umpiring was a thankless profession, which was extremely dangerous, particularly in the

1. Trials and Triumphs of a Bush League Pitcher

minor leagues. They had to bear the brunt of physical and verbal abuse, such as fans throwing objects at them or attacking them. National Association president William Bramham frowned on such activities but could not curtail them, although he was successful in allowing the minor leagues to survive and grow during the depression.

Maglie's first game was as a starter against Newark on April 23 at Ruppert Stadium. He was knocked out of the box in the fourth inning after giving up eight baserunners and a couple of runs. However the Bisons scored twice in the ninth inning and pulled out a 7–5 win. After two short relief outings Sal got his first win on May 10. He pitched a scoreless seventh inning in a seven-inning game against Syracuse. Buffalo scored two in the bottom of the seventh to win 5–4. In International League competition if there was a doubleheader scheduled, they would play nine innings in the opener and seven frames in the second game or vice versa.

Against Baltimore on May 13, Maglie lost a 9–5 decision as his record fell to 1–1. He pitched eight innings as the starter but each of his seven base runners (3 hits, 3 walks, 1 hit batter) scored as he served up three homers. Lou Boudreau collected two hits and scored three runs. He was a surehanded shortstop who had played one game with the Cleveland Indians in 1938. In 1939 he would split his time between Buffalo and Cleveland, playing 115 games with the Bisons and 53 with the Indians (.258). The Indians had talent under manager Oscar Vitt and were led by young flamethrower Bob Feller. The roster also included such undesirables as Ben Chapman, Jeff Heath, and Johnny Allen. In 1939 they finished in third place and in 1940 they lost the pennant by a single game to Detroit. The 1940 team was infamous, known as the "Crybaby Indians" when their players asked team president Alva Bradley to fire the intense and combative Vitt towards the middle of the season. Soon American League fans, particularly in Detroit were mocking the players and throwing pop bottles and baby bottles in their direction among other objects. While the pennant race went down the stretch the Indians and Tigers fans declared war on the each other. Then on September 27, the Indians fans threw a crate of tomatoes on the head of Birdie Tebbetts from the upper deck. Tebbetts' Tiger teammates thought he was dead.[15] On the season's final day Bob Feller lost to Detroit's Floyd Giebell. Floyd played with Maglie in Buffalo in 1940 and would collect only two more major league wins. The Indians were anxious to cleanse themselves of the 1940 disaster, as Vitt left after the season and by 1942 Cleveland's twenty-four year old shortstop Lou Boudreau was named manager. Lou was well respected during his tenure in Cleveland and was the Indians' manager through the 1950 season while also being a top rate shortstop.

On May 21 against Toronto, Maglie worked six innings as the starter in the second game of the day. He allowed three runs on seven hits, one walk, and one hit batter while striking out four. The Bisons scored a run in the bottom of the seventh to win, 4–3. Al Smith, who was recently acquired from the Philadelphia Phillies and would be Buffalo's ace hurler during the season, made his first start in the opener and came out on top of a 13–5 victory. Sal's performance in the second game was typical of many of his early starts. He had a decent fastball and a big curveball, which he was able to use and survive with in the early innings, but after the hitters were able to gauge his pitching delivery they hit him hard. Maglie started on the 27th once again versus the Toronto Maple Leafs but he was hammered for five runs in the third inning. Art Jacobs (5–3, 4.86 ERA) relieved him and won the game with a two run single in the seventh inning for an 8–6 victory. Toronto's lineup which included future major leaguers Mayo Smith and Bob Elliott had no problem against Maglie after seeing him for the second time in a week.

The Bisons were victorious in two close battles with the Montreal Royals on May 30 by scores of 22–19 and 7–6 at Offermann Stadium. The first game was an ugly affair in which both teams combined to use thirteen pitchers and hit six homers (five of the six were from Bison hitters). Buffalo committed five errors while second baseman Ray Mack (.293 in '39) committed three of them. Maglie managed to record only two outs and give up five baserunners in the slugfest. The day concluded on a somber tone as Montreal first baseman Gene Hasson was skulled with a pitch. Batters did not wear protective helmets during the times which made the possibility of death on the diamond all too real. Raymond Roche (2–1, 4.79 ERA in '39), a southpaw with a live fastball and a propensity towards wildness, unleashed a heater at the batter's head. Hasson, with only split seconds to react, tried to duck the pitch but it nailed him in the back of the head and he fell to the ground with a sickening thud. The ball rolled towards first base coach Red Rollings while the crowd suddenly ceased all activities and became fixated on the stricken figure that remained limp on the ground. The batter's life was in doubt for he had a severe fracture of the skull and for two days lay in the hospital in critical condition before showing improvement. Doctors predicted it would take ten days before he was "out of the woods," and his future baseball career was in doubt.[16] Hasson's parents rushed to Buffalo and when they arrived on June 4 it was their wedding anniversary. Burleigh Grimes' Montreal club was destined for a seventh place finish as he continuously dumped ineffective talent from the previous year. Hasson played in only those forty-one games on the year and batted .328. The threat of death on the diamond was exacerbated by lack of protective headgear, beanball artists, wildness, poor lighting and several other factors. Young Sal Maglie would witness many more skullings in his career.

On the final day of May, the Bisons swept the three game series from Montreal with a 6–3 victory. They moved into fourth place. Maglie closed out the game for Smith in relief. Maglie had to wait nine days before his next appearance, which came against Syracuse on June 9 in the first game of a doubleheader. Sal worked five innings as the starter in the seven inning affair which the Chiefs won by a 7–6 score. He looked good until the fifth inning when he allowed two runs. He gave up six hits, one walk and hit one batter. He collected two hits, a run and a RBI at the plate. Smith took the loss. Maglie pitched one game in relief before starting again on June 14 versus Jersey City where he allowed three runs in seven innings. It was a quality start but the Giants took three out of four in the series at Roosevelt Stadium as they won 5–3. Once again the Bisons bullpen failed late in the game after Maglie had started. Afterwards Sal was relegated to the bullpen and he ended June with four short relief appearances. He gave up several runs and was hit hard in two of them. On the 16th he lost his second game of the year as the Bisons dropped a 13–8 decision in the second game of a doubleheader.

Maglie had no set role with the ballclub. He had been used as a starter, in mopup situations, in middle relief, and had two long stretches of inactivity where he saw no action for eight and nine days respectively. Towards the midway point of the season he summoned up the courage to have a talk with Steve O'Neill concerning his position with the ballclub. Maglie was upset since he wasn't given the opportunity to pitch regularly and saw a plethora of short relief roles. He admitted that he probably was inclined to be hit hard when he did pitch but argued that he wouldn't become better unless he pitched regularly. O'Neill tipped Maglie off that one of the main reasons he was on the club was because he was well known in the area from his days as a high school basketball star in Niagara Falls and pitching semi-pro.[17] Many of the fans came to Offermann Stadium in hopes of seeing the local kid get into the game. Thus when Maglie pitched poorly in the International League, the Bisons' organization was more inclined to be patient with Sal and not send him down to a lower league. After talking with his manager, Sal was resigned to accept his fate at least for now. Danny Carnevale was another example of a local kid who was given every opportunity to succeed. In 1938 Carnevale batted .216 in Buffalo in 375 at-bats and in 1940 he batted .225 in 258 at-bats. In 1937 he batted at a .354 clip and drove in 100 runs for Perth-Cornwall of the Canadian-American League. He did perform well in the low minors but struggled with the Bisons when Maglie was there. Carnevale was a local kid from Buffalo, went to Canisius College where the Bisons signed him in his sophomore year. Local talent translated into increased sales at the gate and thus were scouted actively.

After struggling early in the season, the Bisons became the hottest team in the circuit during the final two weeks of June as they won 11 of 14 games. On June 21 they were in seventh place (26–33) but by the end of the month they were threatening Newark for fourth place. The pitching staff was bolstered by recent acquisitions Earl Cook (8–7, 4.07 ERA with Buffalo in '39) and Tom Drake (3–5). Veteran Bison hurlers Al Smith, Clay Smith, Ken Ash, Fabian Kowalik, and Bob Kline (6–10, 3.50 ERA) led the staff. The offense hit 22 homers in a 10 game stretch towards the end of June and had accumulated 80 homers by month's end which was 18 more than Baltimore who was the nearest team in the home run category. Just when many fans were questioning the managerial skills of Steve O'Neill they turned the season around. It reminded fans of the 1936 Bisons team, managed by Ray Schalk, that won the International League pennant. After completing a tour of the northern cities to begin July they would return to Buffalo for their longest homestand of the year, which would last nineteen days. They were scheduled to play every team in the circuit except Rochester. O'Neill felt that the team's fate rested in their performance over that stretch and it would determine whether they would be serious pennant contenders.

Maglie was used frequently in July, making eleven appearances, all of them in relief. A crowd approximated at 10,000 showed up at the start of July to celebrate Dominion Day at Maple Leafs Stadium in Toronto with a doubleheader. Clay Smith scattered eight hits for a 2–0 victory in the opener while the Maple Leafs bounced back in the second game behind Phil Marchildon for a 4–1 win. Maglie relieved Kline in the third inning of the second contest and pitched scoreless relief the rest of the way. The Bisons were second in the league in batting (.281) but were seventh in fielding (.954 Pct.) where they had their problems. Instead of having an afternoon doubleheader on July 4 at Offermann Stadium they opted for a twi-night bargain bill so that the citizenry could enjoy the afternoon conducting other activities. Toronto and Buffalo split two games and Maglie pitched two scoreless innings of relief. Two days later Sal won a game against Newark with two scoreless frames while striking out four. Against Baltimore he recorded only two outs and surrendered a couple of runs and in another game against the Orioles he pitched a solid three and two-thirds innings. Sal was hitting a lot of batters and hit yet another one in this game. Buffalo had moved into third place at 47–38 while Rochester and

Jersey City were tied for first at 48–33. Clay Smith won his eighth consecutive game on the 14th and Buffalo won its twelfth straight as an overflow Offermann Stadium crowd of about 15,000 watched the Bisons defeat Syracuse 3–2. However, Syracuse won the second game of the day in which Maglie made a brief appearance in the ninth inning. Smith's eight game winning streak ended on the 18th with a 13–6 loss to Jersey City. Maglie was ineffective in relief, allowing five baserunners including one hit batter. He pitched well in his next four appearances, and won a game on the 24th against Newark with four scoreless innings to improve his record to 3–2.

In Baltimore on August 1, the Bisons dropped a 10–8 decision as the Orioles took three of the four games in the series. Carnegie hit a two run homer in the ninth and Boudreau went 4 for 4. Maglie was the losing pitcher (3–3) as he allowed three runs on four hits and two walks in two-thirds of an inning of relief. He pitched well against Syracuse in his next outing and then blew up on August 7 versus Newark. An estimated crowd of 9,500 showed up at Offermann Stadium to honor Ollie Carnegie on his night. Before the game Carnegie was paraded through the streets of Buffalo and IL president Frank Shaughnessy presented him with the Most Valuable Player award. The game also marked the debut of James (Skeeter) Webb who had been sent down from the Cleveland Indians where he batted a respectable .264 but his 27 errors (.932 fielding average) in 81 games at shortstop prompted a change. Webb batted only .238 for Buffalo while twenty-one year old Lou Boudreau headed to the big show in Cleveland. Maglie replaced Al Smith in the third inning when Newark scored four runs and looked shaky before pitching four scoreless innings after the disastrous third frame. Sal allowed two hits, walked one, hit two batters, and threw a wild pitch. He became unnerved when he came into a tight spot in the third inning. Buffalo won the game 8–7 as Bill Zuber (5–4, 4.44 ERA) won in relief. Maglie tossed four scoreless innings of mopup relief in a 13–8 loss to Newark on the 9th but showed his wildness throwing two wild pitches. On August 14 Maglie made his first start in exactly two months in front of the home fans but was the loser in a 7–3 defeat to Jersey City. He allowed four runs on eight hits and one walk in four innings of work. Against Jersey City on the following day he allowed five base runners, surrendered a couple of runs and recorded five outs. The two teams split a doubleheader but the Giants protested when the lights were turned on in the middle of a Carnegie at-bat in the opener and he promptly hit a grand slam homer. Sal made two more short relief appearances to end the month.

The Bisons swept a series in Rochester with a 9–4 victory on September 2. Earl Cook started but left after he was struck in the pitching arm with a line drive in the sixth inning. Maglie finished out the ballgame allowing one run in the process. Two days later the Montreal Royals gave the Bisons a double setback by scores of 5–4 and 10–5 to drop Buffalo into third place. Maglie was the loser in the second game as his record fell to 3–5 allowing seven baserunners and a couple of runs in three and one-third innings. The following day Maglie lost yet another game as he surrendered a grand slam homer to Lindsey Deal of Montreal at Montreal Stadium, which was most commonly known as Delorimier Downs. Four days later he lost his third game within a week. It was the final game he pitched during the regular season. The Bisons lost to Rochester in the first round of the playoffs in seven games. In the third game John Tyler hit a two run homer but his costly error allowed two runs to score and Rochester won 5–3 to take a 2-to-1 edge in the playoffs. Maglie pitched a scoreless ninth inning in relief of Zuber. Rochester won the final contest by an 8–6 score as Harry Davis batted home four runs. Sal was called to pitch in the eighth inning of this critical game seven but gave up two runs in one inning of work and took the loss. The Bisons' season ended along with Maglie's first full year in professional ball which had been rough.

The 1940 season was a rough year for Steve O'Neill and his Bisons as the team finished in sixth place with a 76–83 record. They were nineteen games behind first place Rochester. The offense was led by catcher Clyde McCullough (.324, 27 homers, 89 RBIs), Les Scarsella (.289, 10 homers, 10 triples), James Outlaw (.309, 14 homers), Pat Mullin (.273, 11 triples, 15 homers, 18 stolen bases), Mayo Smith (.281) and Ollie Carnegie, whose numbers slipped considerably (.281, 15 homers, 64 RBIs). The pitching staff was led by Hal White (16–4 with a league leading 2.43 ERA), Earl Cook (15–12, 3.85 ERA), Floyd Giebell (15–17, 3.73 ERA), James Trexler (8–7, 3.95 ERA) and Fred Hutchinson (7–3, 2.49 ERA). Maglie's 1940 season with Buffalo was a complete disaster as he lost all confidence when it came to getting International League batters out. Sal had a 0–7 record with a 7.17 ERA. He appeared in 23 games (5 starts), pitched 54 innings, allowed 43 earned runs, 80 hits, and 24 walks while striking out 22. His pride was hurt and by season's end he was willing to relinquish his roster spot, no longer tolerating his position to appease the local fans who watched him get hammered on a consistent basis.

Maglie's first appearance of the year was a harbinger of things to come as he surrendered several runs to Syracuse on April 24 in an inning and a third of relief. The Chiefs were outhit 17 to 10 but won by a 9 to 7 margin. The Bisons were off to a bad start and dropped a doubleheader to Jersey City on April 28 before 17,171 fans. The Little Giants broke the minor league attendance record on opening day for the fourth year in a row with

1. Trials and Triumphs of a Bush League Pitcher 19

50,529 paid admissions which was larger then the highest major league opener of 49,417 in Detroit. Maglie was the fourth Buffalo pitcher in the opener and recorded one out in the bottom of the twelfth inning before he allowed a single to Glen Stewart that brought home the winning run. The Bisons started the year by winning only two of ten games on the road. On May 2, firmly entrenched in last place, they played their home opener before about 11,500 (9,995 paid) fans. It was a cold, dreary day, but the Bisons fans treated their team like champions and gave them a huge parade before the contest. However in the rainy weather the Baltimore Orioles pulled out a 14–6 victory and the Bisons lost yet another game. Clyde McCullough reported to the Bisons from the Chicago Cubs where he had made his big league debut. He batted .154 in 26 at-bats for Chicago that year but would later go on to have a long big league career. McCullough was a quality backstop and hit the long ball to left field, which made him ideal for Offermann Stadium.

The Bisons tried to dig themselves out of the cellar in May, but the damage was already done and making the playoffs would be an arduous task. Maglie saw little action and made five short relief appearances during the month. Maglie walked two batters and recorded one out in a wild game on May 11 in Buffalo as the Jersey City Giants trounced the home team by a 21–8 score. Sal rode the pine for fourteen days before his next opportunity to pitch. He failed to get the job done and gave up two baserunners in two-thirds of an inning. Sal pitched two scoreless innings the following day in a loss against Rochester. On May 28 he allowed two runs in three innings as he lost his first game of the year. He allowed five hits, hit one batter and threw a wild pitch. Two days later Sal worked one scoreless inning as Toronto went on to sweep the Bisons in a doubleheader. It's frustrating for a pitcher to wait long periods of time in between outings and is representative of his stature on the ballclub. It wasn't until June 9 that Maglie pitched another game as he relieved Giebell in a six run fifth inning and then pitched the final three frames allowing a run in the ninth. The Orioles swept the doubleheader in Baltimore by 12–6 and 12–4 scores. O'Neill called on Maglie to start on June 14 but he was hammered as the Orioles won 10–0. He allowed seven hits, four walks, and a couple of runs in five and a third innings. Two days later, he allowed one run in three innings of relief. The Newark Bears hit five homers in a doubleheader on June 27 as they took both games from Buffalo by scores of 8–4 and 4–2. Maglie once again gave up a run in three innings of relief. As the month was coming to a close the Bisons ranked sixth in team batting (.255) and only two pitchers were off to excellent starts: Hal White (4–0) and Earl Cook (6–3).

July started inauspiciously with a double defeat to Toronto on the lakefront of Lake Ontario at Maple Leafs Stadium before a large Dominion Day holiday crowd. Maglie gave up three baserunners and the go ahead run in two-thirds of an innings as he took the loss in a 10–9 defeat. He worked a scoreless inning in the second game, a 4–1 loss. Hal White continued to prove he was one of the better pitchers in the league and ran his winning streak to seven games to begin the season before losing. He credited his new found success to not worrying too much on the ball field. In Montreal on July 11, Maglie was hit hard and allowed three runs in the eighth inning in a 9–4 loss. Three days later the Bisons and the Royals split a doubleheader and once again he pitched poorly. Sal allowed three base runners in a third of an inning in the 18–10 Bisons victory in the opener. He pitched a shaky middle relief stint on July 20 as the Maple Leafs emerged victorious at Maple Leafs Stadium by a 7–5 score. Maglie worked out of trouble all day as he allowed two runs on eight hits and struck out three in five innings. The Bisons' record stood at 39–52 in seventh place. However from this point till the end of the season they played at a good 37–31 clip. Fred Hutchinson had compiled a 7–3 record in 12 games but the Tigers called him up and he posted a 3–7 mark with a 5.58 ERA down the stretch. Detroit was in a tight pennant race with Cleveland and New York and would call on players like Hutchinson and Giebell to help them win a pennant. On July 24 Maglie started against Baltimore in the second game of a doubleheader but lost a 10–1 decision to give the Orioles both games. He allowed two runs on eight hits and two walks in four innings as he lost his fourth straight game to begin the year. Three days later the Bisons offense overcame poor pitching by Maglie and came from behind to win an 8–6 decision from Syracuse. Maglie allowed four runs in three innings as the starter. On July 30 Baltimore collected 33 hits in a doubleheader as they won both games by scores of 6–3 and 13–11. Maglie was charged with both losses as his record fell to 0–6. The Chiefs hit him freely in the opener, collecting ten hits and two walks off him in four and a third innings as the starter. Sal nailed one batter with a pitch. In the second contest, with the score knotted at eleven, Maglie allowed two runs to score in the tenth which proved to be the winning margin. It had become more and more apparent to Sal Maglie and spectators in Buffalo that he had no business pitching in the International League and a change needed to be made. However the Bisons' organization was content with his position as a crowd drawer.

The Bisons started August by winning the first game of a doubleheader from Newark at Offermann Stadium by a 2–1 score. Earl Cook tossed a one-hitter and would have had a shutout if Ollie Carnegie hadn't lost two balls in the setting sun. Hal White dropped his record to 8–4 as Newark bounced back in the second contest and won 6–1. Maglie worked the final inning and allowed two runs on three hits and one walk. O'Neill had seen enough and for the rest of August, Maglie would merely wear out the pine on the Buffalo bench. It was well over a month before he was given the opportunity to pitch again. On September 7 against Toronto at Maple Leafs Stadium he toed the slab and pitched an excellent ballgame. The time off had apparently done him some good. He had the opportunity to think about his baseball future and was already planning his next move. He allowed one run on seven hits and one walk while going the distance but lost a close 2–1 decision in the second game of a doubleheader. It was back to the bullpen on September 13 as he allowed two runs in the ninth inning against Rochester in a 13–0 loss. The Red Wings clinched first place with the victory before a Buffalo crowd. Their team was loaded with former and future big leaguers such as position players Harry Davis, Whitey Kurowski, and Ray Mueller. The pitching staff included Mike Ryba, Henry Gornicki, Preacher Roe and John Grodzicki. The Bisons closed out their season in sixth place. It was a disappointing year as far as the weather, bad breaks, injuries, and the lukewarm enthusiasm from the crowd. Towards the end of the season they sold off their two best pitchers, Earl Cook and Hal White, to the Detroit Tigers for about $30,000. The ivory hunters had been following the two pitchers closely since July and the Tigers got the inside track because of their close relationship with Buffalo. The two teams did not have a working agreement but they often acted as if they did. Cook pitched his first and last big league game in 1941 while White would pitch in twelve big league seasons, predominantly in relief and compile a 46–54 record with a 3.78 ERA.

Maglie felt that his ineffectiveness during the season was directly correlated to the lack of work he received. He experienced long periods of idleness and most of the time when he did pitch it was in short relief. Maglie was inexperienced and the Bisons were unwilling to give him too much work and jeopardize their chances of winning ball games which he already did. He was a bush league hurler who did not know much about the art of pitching. Although Sal lacked the confidence and the ability to pitch well in the International League the experience had not scared him so badly that he wanted to go back to Union Carbide right away. His innings dropped from 101 in 1939 to only 54 in 1940. In later years Sal attributed his ineffectiveness to a lack of work. "I had good stuff for 4 or 5 innings.... I'd weaken after that and give away the game," he recalled.[18] He wanted to be given an opportunity to improve and be more than the token local kid on the Bisons. Once again Maglie wanted to talk with O'Neill. Despite a good salary, and a roster position in an excellent league, he demanded to be sent down so he could work regularly and learn how to pitch. He had received a great break going from the semi-pro ranks straight to the International League but it had come at a price. O'Neill warned him that he might never return to this level, but acknowledged that he had courage, and said he would talk to the front office. Shortly after Sal was sent to Jamestown of the Pony League.

The Jamestown franchise had actually started the season in Niagara Falls but relocated on July 13. They were destined to finish in fifth place with a 48–55 record, sixteen and a half games behind first place Olean. For the tailend of the season, Maglie was placed in the rotation and compiled a 3–4 record with a good 2.73 ERA. He pitched in seven games, completed six of them, worked 56 innings, allowed 17 earned runs on 54 hits, 15 walks while fanning 41. It was a good way to end the year after his disastrous International League campaign. Asking to be sent down was a courageous act but it would not be his last. Sal was competitor, a student of the game, and wanted to learn how to pitch which was not something he could do with the Bisons while he got his ears pinned back. When Maglie was sent down he told O'Neill that he would later return to the International League. O'Neill's tenure in Buffalo ended with the 1940 season for in 1941 he was a coach with the Detroit Tigers and became their manager two years later. Maglie's time in Buffalo had toughened him although it was a harsh introduction to professional baseball. Many of the players in the league were better then some major leaguers and were merely waiting for a roster spot to open up in the big leagues. Major league baseball was a fixed entity, with sixteen teams, eight in each league; all the teams were located in the northeast and the Midwest with St. Louis representing the furthest southern and western regions of the majors. The players were predominantly tough white southerners. There was only a sprinkling of players of color in the majors, mostly players from Latin America, and nobody with a dark hue. Some great players would get stuck with a franchise like the Yankees and never get an opportunity because of the surfeit of talent in the organization. With Buffalo, Maglie played with several players who had major league careers including Joe Martin, Eddie Phillips, John Tyler, George Uhle, Ken Ash, Bill Harris, Art Jacobs (1 game with Cincinnati in 1939), Herman Fink, Fabian Kowalik, Lou Boudreau, Henry Helf, Al Smith, Clay Smith, Bill Zuber, James (Skeeter) Webb, Earl Cook (1 game), Thomas Drake, Pat Mullin, Mayo Smith, Clyde McCullough, Greg Mulleavy, John Kroner, Hal White, Floyd Giebell, Fred Hutchinson and James Outlaw.

Maglie pitched in Class A in the Eastern League in '41 with the Elmira Pioneers. The minor leagues were classified as AAA, AA, A, B, C, and D.

Triple-A was the highest classification (e.g., the International League was AAA). In rare circumstances were leagues rated E or A-1. The Eastern League was originally named the New York-Pennsylvania League and changed its name to the Eastern League in 1938. Its second president, Perry Farrell, guided the league through the tough depression years of the early '30s. In November of '37, Thomas Richardson, a businessman and humorist, became president and soon served as the impetus in changing the league's name. In 1939 he watched as the eight team circuit went over the million mark in paid attendance for the first time. Since 1937 the league used the Shaughnessy playoff system. Many other minor leagues used it, ever since the idea became well known and popular. The Elmira franchise had a proud history and was a charter member of the league in 1923. By 1941, Jack Ogden, a former big league pitcher, became the owner and soon hired Ray Brubaker to be his manager. In 1941 the other teams in the circuit included: Williamsport, Wilkes-Barre, Binghamton, Scranton, Hartford, Albany, and Springfield. They played a 140 game schedule. The Eastern League was one of those durable minor leagues that represented the best of Americana when baseball was truly the national pastime. In the *Silver Anniversary Eastern League Record Book: 1923–1947* it says "The Eastern League, nee the New York-Pennsylvania (Nypen) has come a long way the past 24 seasons, whipping depressions and the bloodiest global conflict ever known to mankind, and if its present set of officers and directors has its say, it will continue for as long as baseball exists, and that will be as long as there is an America, for the national pastime is as American as Uncle Sam himself."[19]

Elmira got off to a strong start in their first 31 games as they sported a 17–14 record in third place. The Pioneers had the league's oldest middle infield combination with 37-year-old shortstop Buster Chatham and 36-year-old second baseman Andy Cohen. On May 19, about 4,000 fans showed up on Booster night as the Pioneers defeated Albany 1–0 on Cohen's RBI double in the ninth. They would have a great year at the gate and Elmira's attendance of 124,384 was second to Scranton (171,042) in '41. Maglie defeated Springfield's Early Wynn on May 28 in a 1–0 pitcher's duel. After starting the season with seven straight wins, Wynn lost his first game. Sal allowed only three hits in the contest. Maglie was off to a terrific start as well, and the win was his seventh of the year and placed the Pioneers into first place. By June 18, Pioneers first baseman Ed Kobesky was third in the league in batting at .354 with 40 RBIs in 53 games. In Maglie's first 19 games he had already pitched 106 innings and had a 10–4 record. A typical minor league promotion event, American Legion Night, was held in Albany on July 15 with the Pioneers as the opposition. Before the game players competed in a 50-yard dash, infielders relay competition, fungo hitting contest, and accuracy throwing. It was Railroad Night at Elmira on July 10 as 5,520 fans showed up and watched the Pioneers defeat Scranton 6–4. As the season progressed Elmira became firmly entrenched in third place with a 59–46 record. Rabbit Maranville, who had an exceptional major league playing career and was now manager at Springfield, was honored with his own night at Dunn Field in Elmira on August 3. He had managed the '36 Elmira club that won the second half pennant but lost to Scranton in the playoffs. He batted .323 in 123 games that year. Elmira qualified for the playoffs by finishing in third place at 71–67 in '41. Wilkes-Barre finished first at 87–51.

It had been an excellent year for Maglie. He pitched in 43 games and completed 22 of them, while compiling a 20–15 record and a 2.67 ERA. He pitched 270 innings, allowed 80 earned runs on 231 hits, 107 walks while striking out 148. Maglie became the iron man of the league, leading the circuit in innings and games pitched. Along with Wilkes-Barre's Red Embree (21–5) they were the only twenty game winners. His 270 innings was well over the aggregate 223 professional innings he pitched from 1938 to 1940. Frank Madura of Elmira led the league in batting at .321. Maglie's fast start had given him the fortitude to rush back to Niagara Falls towards the end of May and marry his high school girlfriend, Kathleen Pileggi on May 31. Kay would be a stabilizing force in the Maglie household in the years to come and help hold Sal together during the tough times. In later years Sal said she "knows baseball like her own name."[20] In the first round of the playoffs, Elmira defeated Wilkes-Barre three games to none while they tied one. On September 3, in the first game of the series, Red Embree pitched no-hit ball for nine innings but lost it in the tenth when he allowed his only hit, a homer to Jesse Pike. Maglie recorded the final out in the bottom of the tenth to preserve the 1–0 victory. Williamsport defeated Scranton in their semi-final playoff matchup and they played Elmira for the championship. The series went seven games but Elmira won the closely fought series. Maglie won a close 2–1 decision in the second game. He went the distance, allowing six hits, no walks and fanning seven. Sal lost the sixth game by a 2–1 score as he allowed the two runs on five hits in eight innings. Raymond Roche, who had played with Maglie at Buffalo, won the final game over veteran knuckleballer Roger Wolff, 3–1.

It was a great year for Sal and his baseball career finally looked bright. In later years he would explain his success at Elmira saying, "I got to pitch. In Elmira they let me play, that was all."[21] In Buffalo he felt added pressure pitching in front of the home folks, however in Elmira this problem was alleviated. He was also comforted in the knowledge that if he had a bad game he would still take his regular turn in the rotation. The Eastern League was a good circuit for Maglie. He played against solid competition and future major leaguers such as Early Wynn, Thomas de la Cruz, Bob Lemon, Jim Konstanty, Roger Wolff, Red Embree, Mel Queen and Ralph Kiner who played in the circuit that year. Future National League umpire Art Gore was in the circuit and in August he was knocked cold when a fan threw a pop bottle from the grandstand and nailed him in the head. It was an ugly incident but not infrequent. It had been a great year for baseball in general; a nation became captivated by the game, as it became more and more apparent that the United States would enter the war. Joe DiMaggio's 56 game hitting streak held the attention of the nation before it was broken by two Cleveland pitchers: Al Smith (who had played with Maglie in Buffalo in '39) and Jim Bagby. On September 28 in Philadelphia, Boston Red Sox manager Joe Cronin told Ted Williams that he could take the day off. If he sat he would be assured of a .400 season but he refused and showed great courage saying, "If I couldn't hit .400 all the way I didn't deserve it."[22] He went 6 for 8 in the day's doubleheader and finished at .406. It was a majestic season.

2

RETURN TO THE INTERNATIONAL LEAGUE

During the fall of 1941 it became painfully evident to many Americans that the United States would ultimately have to join the growing war which was rapidly spreading around the world. Despite the fact that President Roosevelt had not promulgated a declaration of war, we were already shooting down Axis ships off our coast that had attacked our vessels. Sal Maglie's future looked auspicious just at the time the stability of the world began to disintegrate. He had gained confidence by pitching regularly at Elmira and had excelled in the Eastern League. Eddie Ainsmith, a New York Giants scout, had noticed Sal's ability during the season. When he provided a report to the Giants braintrust he issued the following caveat: "He hasn't much of a curve, but he could develop."[1] That curve would ultimately develop into his most productive weapon and possibly the best in the game. In possession of Ainsmith's lukewarm endorsement, the New York Giants drafted Maglie during the winter baseball drafts.

Maglie's entrance into the Giants organization came at a time when the team had fallen from its eminent position into mediocrity. John J. McGraw had managed the ballclub with an iron fist from 1902 to 1932. The results were impressive, including ten pennants and three World Series championships in his first twenty-one years as field general. By June of 1932, McGraw's health was failing and his players began to rebel against his Napoleonic ways. Bill Terry had not been on speaking terms with McGraw for two years, and was shocked when the skipper offered him the manager's job. A dumbfounded Terry accepted immediately. The Giants won the World Series in 1933 and brought home pennants in 1936 and '37. The success did not last as the club finished third in 1938 and followed that with fifth, sixth, and fifth place finishes. The Giants had become a second division ballclub. The newspapers predicted Terry's departure, anticipating that Dick Bartell or Billy Jurges would be his successor.

While in Jacksonville, Florida, for the minor league meetings, team owner Horace Stoneham and club treasurer Leo Bondy met with Terry to decide which direction the club should take. A disgruntled Mel Ott also traveled there from his home in Metairie, Louisiana, to discuss his 1942 contract. Ott anticipated a pay cut and thought the team was rushing young Babe Barna to be his replacement. When Stoneham offered him the manager's position, Ott almost fell over. Ott stood in front of them in disbelief just as Terry stood in front of McGraw a decade earlier. Terry became general manager, a position that would put him in charge of the farm system.

The organization's future was uncertain, as was the world's, and Maglie would have to make a name for himself in these chaotic times. Japanese bombers attacked Pearl Harbor five days after Ott became the new manager. Baseball's future was jeopardized until President Roosevelt issued his famous "green light letter," sanctioning the continuation of the game.

Sal Maglie participated in a major league training camp in 1942, although he was used primarily as a batting practice pitcher. On February 14, the Giants headed south to Florida for spring training. This would be the only year during the war in which teams could train in the south or out West. Twelve clubs chose locations in Florida, and four in California. Maglie arrived on the sixteenth and signed his contract three days later. The club's young leader, Mel Ott, found the conditions to be more than adequate. The weather was warm for the first day of practice, the ballpark was improved, and the players were in good condition. Sixteen pitchers were expected in camp but Ott wanted more. He wanted to implement his own system of batting practice with exhaustive batting sessions when the regular players arrived. John McGraw and Bill Terry relied heavily on defense; Ott yearned for a blistering offense.

As the regulars were slowly trickling into camp, Ott put together two teams for an intrasquad game. Carl Hubbell and Hal Schumacher chose the clubs. Hubbell's infield was almost entirely left-handed. In this awkward contest, pitchers played regular positions. Maglie played right field for Schumacher's club which lost 2–1 in ten innings. On the same day Bill Terry picked up another slugger for Ott, Willard Marshall from the Atlanta Crackers.

A few days later Billy Jurges, the captain, signed his contract. It was ironic that Jurges, a combative man known for fighting and vicious takeout slides would become the captain of the Giants. Mel Ott was regarded as one of the nicest players in the rough and tumble game of baseball. Once the regular exhibition tilt began, Maglie spent most of his time riding the pine. New York lost their first two exhibition games to the Brooklyn Dodgers in Havana, Cuba. Maglie was knocked around in an intrasquad contest when the team returned to Florida.

New York defeated the Boston Red Sox on March 7 for their first win against big league competition. Five days later they left their headquarters in Miami and traveled to the Naval Air Station in Opa-Locka to provide some moral support for Uncle Sam's boys by playing a ballgame. Considering that baseball was not the most important thing on the minds of the sailors, it was impressive that they held the lead for seven innings. Planes roared overhead throughout the contest as enthusiastic sailormen cheered pitcher Elmer Stevens till their hero tired in the ninth. Maglie relieved Jesse Danna in the sixth and gave up three runs in four innings of work. He was the beneficiary of a ten run ninth inning as the Giants pulled away with an 18–5 win.

Things quickly went south for New York as the hitting was inept and the overall play sloppy. Ott's reliance on offense may have neglected the defensive game. After a 6–1 loss to Washington on March 22, the Giants found themselves with two wins and eleven loses in Grapefruit League competition. Two youngsters who had played together in Atlanta were the lone bright spots: Willard Marshall and Connie Ryan. The Giants improved as the season approached going 7–5 against major league competition.

Maglie's luck ran out on April 13, when he received news that he was being optioned to Jersey City along with Rube Fischer. He did pitch one more service game against Army at West Point, New York. Maglie started and received his second victory against military competition, allowing two runs in five innings. At the plate he contributed with a double.

While Mel Ott was having difficulty with the big club, the situation in Jersey City was not much better. The minor leagues would be hit particularly hard by the labor shortage as men were brought into the military at an accelerated pace. Frank "Pancho" Snyder, the manager of Jersey City, was handed an exceptionally young squad. He had been named manager in January succeeding Tony Cuccinello, because Terry felt he would do a better job handling an inexperienced International League team. Snyder had played in the big leagues with the Cardinals and Giants and proved himself as a capable major league backstop. With the Jerseys he would successfully mold a spirited young squad while having an acrimonious relationship with International League President Frank Shaughnessy and Mel Ott.

As training commenced in Jacksonville, Snyder attempted to prepare his club for the regular season despite his meager resources. Warren Pickell, a pitcher, and first baseman Norman Jaeger were the only players assured of a regular position. Many observers blamed Ott for keeping players such as Maglie, who saw little action with the big club but could have coalesced with Snyder's team. The Jerseys finished their exhibition season with an 11–6 record. The opening roster consisted of only five players with solid experience in the minor leagues: catcher Hugh Poland, the multi-dimensional Sid Gordon, center fielder Johnny Rucker, and pitchers Bobby Coombs and John Witting.

Maglie, Fischer, and Danna reported late to Jersey City as the trio lingered around the Polo Grounds to watch the first game of the National League campaign. New York played host to their hated rivals, the Brooklyn Dodgers. Before the game Mel Ott and Dodger manager Leo Durocher met at home plate to shake hands with photographers. Mayor Fiorello LaGuardia presented war bonds to the two managers. After the opening ceremonies, Ducky Medwick's bases loaded double and Pee Wee Reese's homer propelled Brooklyn to a 7–5 victory.

The little Giants opened their 1942 campaign at their home park, Roosevelt Stadium, against the Montreal Royals before 55,218 spectators. There were about 13,000 more fans at the Jersey City opener than had attended the Polo Grounds opener. The previous year they drew 61,164. For the first time since the park opened in 1937 they did not lead the minors in opening day attendance despite another large crowd. The political boss of the Democrats, Mayor Frank Hague, threw out the first ball. He had been instrumental in bringing baseball back to Jersey City in 1937 when he persuaded the Giants to purchase the Albany franchise and move it south. The city had a proud minor league history dating back to 1886 when they had a team in the Eastern League.

The crowd went home happy as Jersey City won a thrilling 3–2 contest when Buster Maynard drove home Joe Orengo with two out in the tenth. Bobby Coombs allowed two runs in eight innings as the starter. George Bausewein and Rube Fischer followed him to the hill with Fischer earning the win in relief. Buddy Kerr, Austin Knickerbocker, and Bob Westfall contributed offensively. Knickerbocker pinch-hit for Norman Jaeger in the ninth and electrified the crowd with a homer to knot the game at two. Rucker and Gordon batted one and two in the lineup and each went hitless in four at-bats. These two older players would prove instrumental as the season progressed. Bob Westfall's flashy play at short evoked comparisons to Dick Bartell, the big club's shortstop.

Austin Knickerbocker was representative of a lot of the players on the Jersey City roster. In 1941, he led the Class C Canadian-American League with a .406 average, adding 12 homers and 135 runs driven in. What he lacked was high-level minor league experience. He had been drafted over the winter, similar to Maglie, and quickly became a fan favorite during his short time with the Jerseys. Knickerbocker recalls, "I was there a month, and I went into the service and didn't play ball again for four years. In other words, from 23 to 27, I was out of baseball entirely."[2] He had a cup of coffee with the Philadelphia A's when he returned, but his career ended at 29. Due to military conscription the turnover rate was very high in baseball during the war.

After losing the first two games of the season, Montreal salvaged the third game of the series defeating Jersey City 5–3 before a meager crowd of 1,480. Maglie saw his first action of the year allowing a run in two innings of relief. While the Giants and Dodgers had a ferocious rivalry in the big leagues their two respective IL clubs, Jersey City and Montreal also harbored animosity towards each other.[3] Twenty-one year-old Warren Pickell and Rube Fischer hurled complete game performances to lead Jersey City to a doubleheader win over Burleigh Grimes' Toronto Maple Leafs. The club subsequently lost four in a row, culminating in a 7–5 loss to Buffalo in which the Bisons rallied for five runs in the ninth inning. Maglie recorded the last two outs in the ninth but not before issuing a walk and a hit in the process. Against Rochester he worked a scoreless inning. On April 30, the Jerseys began a road trip on a good note as Maglie earned his first win in a 6–3 victory over Toronto at Maple Leafs Stadium. He relieved Fischer in the fourth and worked out of trouble the rest of the way. Snyder was fuming when he learned that the next day's game would be canceled, setting up consecutive doubleheaders for his squad.

When the New York Giants moved into their first extended road trip, Snyder had hoped he would receive some players to bolster the local attack. Ott would not be obliging, putting the burden on Terry to find talent elsewhere. The main problem for Snyder was pitching. Fischer and Witting had each notched three wins and Coombs had pitched well despite no run support. Pickell had pitched reasonably well but had not proved himself at this level. Neither had Maglie. Sid Gordon replaced Buddy Kerr at third. The hitting was poor, posting a .236 batting average towards the end of April. Only Knickerbocker, Jaeger, and Maynard were hitting over .300.

As baseball pushed on, the war began to penetrate every aspect of American life. Early on the news was not good as the Japanese captured strategic islands and the casualty rate was growing. On April 28 a "dim out" was put in effect along a 15-mile strip of the Atlantic coast. This would have repercussions on baseball. Early in the season Army officers anchored themselves in the Atlantic Ocean to determine if the lights from the Polo Grounds and Ebbets Field would silhouette ships making them easy targets for German submarines. The U-boats had already sunk about 300 U.S. ships off our coastline during the first six months of the year. The glare was deemed unacceptable and night games were canceled.[4] Twilight games would be scheduled throughout the season.

May started on a bad note when Buster Maynard was recalled to New York to replace Hank Leiber who injured his leg. The Jerseys' leading hitter in batting average, hits and homers was gone. Norbert Barker, Rucker, and Knickerbocker would form the new outfield. Fischer was trying to work through a sore arm and Gordon jammed his finger early in the month. Maglie continued to work often in relief, appearing in eight games during May. In the second game of a doubleheader Maglie relieved Fischer after he recorded only one out and worked the final five and two-thirds innings as Montreal defeated Jersey City 5–2 in the seven-inning contest on the 3rd. Weekend games were often doubleheaders and homestands were long. Montreal won the six game series four games to two. Catcher Floyd Beal and pitcher Hugh East joined the squad. On the 9th Maglie shut the door on a 3–2 Giant victory against Rochester. East was the winner. Sal's next two appearances were short as Jersey City lost both of them. It became apparent that Terry's effort to find talent from the big league club had been stymied, he would now try to deal with IL clubs. On May 12, Jersey City was in third place with a 12–13 record.

A night game on May 14 was watched closely by Commissioner Daniel Casey and City Engineer Hugh Clarke to determine if night games could be played at Roosevelt Stadium. The glow was not as great as initially expected, and the go ahead was temporarily given for night baseball. Roosevelt Stadium stood 15 feet above sea level in a hollow. Eventually the club would be forced to play twilight games. The little Giants won the night game, 5–4, as Maglie won his second game with a scoreless inning of relief. Joe Orengo drove home the winner in the ninth. Maglie then worked six innings of relief against the Newark Bears as the Giants lost 13–3. In his next two outings he helped stem the tide in middle relief against Syracuse, and received his third win in one of the contests. In between those outings, Bobby Coombs hurled a six hit shutout against the Chiefs beating Ewell Blackwell. Bobby was thirty-three years old and had been playing professional ball since 1933. On May 30 the league leading Newark Bears disposed of the Jerseys in a doubleheader. Maglie worked an inning in the second game.

The call for healthy bodies to military service hurt the minor leagues to a greater extent then the major leagues. The Florida State League, the Evangeline, Kitty, West-Texas, and California leagues would disband during the '42 season. The railroads were packed and nonessential travel was discouraged so that troops could travel to points of embarkation. Hotels were difficult to find. A decent meal was becoming rare. Fans found it cumbersome to attend games in many cities due to travel restrictions. The government issued a ban on both crude and scrap rubber so that they could be used by the military. The material used to make balls and bats was no longer available. Initially the manufacturer waited until supplies ran out and then were forced to develop an ersatz baseball. The 1943 major league season opened with an inferior "balata ball," which brought baseball back to the dead ball era for a short time. Ballparks were imbued with patriotism, as baseball became a pageantry which propagandized the war effort. The playing of the "Star Spangled Banner" became a fixture before games. Servicemen were admitted free and honored before contests.

Connie Ryan was sent down to Jersey City, which posed a problem for Snyder. Ryan had lost his batting eye by sitting on the bench with New York. Ott expected him to play every day in the minors, but Snyder felt satisfied with the performance of Napoleon Reyes at second. The New York manager would win this battle while Reyes saw playing time at first base. The Jerseys took two from Buffalo on June 3rd as Maglie won his fourth straight in the second game working two innings of solid relief. The pitching staff was overworked and Snyder tried to get the most out of each pitcher. Sid Gordon was beginning to hammer the ball. The following day Maglie ate up seven and two-thirds innings as Rochester won 4–1. East, Witting, Coombs and Maglie had accounted for eighteen of the Giants' twenty-five wins. Despite their shortcomings the Jerseys were hustling and playing excellent baseball. Maglie won his fifth game on the 6th with four scoreless innings to give the team eighteen wins in their last twenty-six games. Rucker, Ryan, and Reyes continued to play well despite a 6–3 loss to Toronto on the 9th. Maglie ate up over six innings.

The twilight affairs that were scheduled around baseball proved controversial in many ways. The games were played under a deadline and the final score would revert back to the last completed inning that encouraged delaying tactics and chaos. On June 12 with the Jerseys playing host to Montreal, the game was scheduled to end at 9:24 P.M. The Royals rallied to take the lead in the top of the ninth and pitcher Hugh East began to stall by throwing nothing close to the strike zone hoping he could reach the deadline and the Jerseys could win since they had finished the previous inning with the lead. The Royals eventually swung at everything and a 3–2 Jersey City deficit was now a 10–3 Montreal lead. In the bottom of the ninth the game was called and the Giants declared the winners. Frank Shaughnessy would have none of it and fined Snyder $100 for turning the game into a "farce." He ordered that the game resume at the interrupted point at a later date. Bill Terry and the Giants braintrust blasted Shaughnessy for acting arbitrarily and not attending the first twilight contest in the league. Terry wired Shaughnessy with a statement that was also printed in the Jersey City paper: "Your telegram addressed to Frank Snyder received. Evidently the decision made by you in last night's game was of your own volition and not governed by the rules concerning baseball games. Since baseball began there has always been stalling tactics when time limits were in effect that benefited the club ahead when the opportunity of winning a ball game was in sight...."[5] In addition Montreal had used delaying tactics on the Jerseys the previous year. Shaughnessy made his ruling before allowing Jersey City a hearing.

Maglie worked in six more games during the month. He worked in long relief, short relief, and as a starter. His record was bolstered to 6–1 as he added a win and a loss to his total. In the longer outings, Maglie was knocked around and his control began to falter. Maglie, Coombs, East, Poland, Gordon, and Orengo were elected to represent the Giants in the first International League All-Star game. Snyder again clashed with the IL president over Shaughnessy's order to rest All-Star hurlers before the big contest.

Jersey City began July by winning two consecutive doubleheaders to give them a six game winning streak. They had creeped within a half game of the first place Newark Bears. Maglie worked three innings against Newark on the 4th of July. Two days later he took the loss as Buffalo defeated the Jerseys, 4–3. Maglie went the distance allowing the four runs on seven hits and ten walks. He gave up gopher balls to Jack Redmond and his former teammate with Buffalo, Jimmy Outlaw. Despite the loss, Snyder's club backed into first place as they had won thirty-four games while losing eighteen since May 14. The All-Star game was a fine success for Maglie's Southern squad as they took a 6–1 decision. The crowd of 5,434 was a disappointment at Buffalo's Offermann Stadium as the proceeds were earmarked for the American and Canadian baseball equipment fund. Coombs, Red Barrett, and Maglie pitched three innings each for the Southern club. Coombs was the winner as Barrett issued the lone run while the Jersey City hurlers held them scoreless. George Stirnweiss and Hank

Majeski of Newark along with Hank Edwards of Baltimore were the hitting stars for the Southern team.

After the All-Star break things went south as Jersey City lost eight of nine games. They showed their inexperience by allowing the close ones to slip away. Maglie worked well in his first five appearances after the break in short relief. Terry pulled off a coup when he wrangled Adrian Zabala from the Jacksonville Tars of the Sally League where he had already won sixteen games. As Montreal came to Jersey City for a six game series the fans lined up for tickets in large numbers to watch the two hated rivals play. Their last contest had ended when Joe Orengo nailed Les Burge on the chin to end the game. Burge lay on the ground unconscious as he was knocked out cold. In that same contest Warren Sandel had skulled Jack Graham with a vicious heater. On the 23rd Jersey City won the first game 9-4 and tied the second. Montreal manager Clyde Sukeforth protested the opener when a field umpire asked for help from the home plate umpire on a close play at first. He was banished from both games for arguing. Maglie made a brief appearance in the opener and worked eight and two-thirds innings of solid relief the following day but the offense produced a mere run as Jersey City lost 2-1. Three days later Dave Koslo won his first game with the club as Maglie recorded the final three outs. His final game of the month was a complete game effort against Toronto that ended in a 1-1 tie.

Newark had pulled away from International League teams by August. Jersey City was anchored in second place when Maglie started the opener of a doubleheader on August 2nd working eight innings with mixed results before yielding to Koslo. Bill Harris took the loss when Rochester won 8-6. Three days later Maglie worked four scoreless innings in their last game at Rochester to win his seventh. A thirty-minute blackout had stiffened the arm of Zabala allowing Maglie to take over. They were 6-5 on the trip with each victory earned by a different pitcher: Maglie, Zabala, Coombs, Ken Jungels, East, and Koslo. A few days later Hugh East lasted eighteen and a third innings before allowing a Russ Derry homer which gave Newark a 3 to 2 win at Ruppert Stadium. The game was the longest ever played at Newark although these combatants had battled to a nineteen-inning stalemate in 1908. Newark took a doubleheader the following day to extend their lead to eleven games over Jersey City. Maglie gave up two gopher balls in the first inning of the opener and scattered two hits the rest of the way to lose 2-1. Koslo pitched respectably in the second game but lost 5-1. A fan climbed over the railing in this game to argue a strike call to Johnny Wittig. Others followed but the police broke up the hostilities before they could spread. Ryan and Snyder were kicked out for arguing during the heated contest. All the proceeds from the game went to the Navy Relief Society and the Army Emergency Fund.

Maglie worked eight innings against Syracuse but lost a tough 2–0 contest. The Giants had fallen to fourth place, fourteen and a half games behind Newark. Sal pitched well in four innings against Buffalo but was knocked out of the box as the starter in his next game. On the 23rd he allowed a run in two innings as he was beginning to be roughed up by the competition. Congresswoman Mary T. Nortan was given her own day at Roosevelt Stadium on August 27 as a crowd of 25,853 including 19,865 women watched the proceedings. The ladies failed to bring the boys luck as they lost 4–0 to Baltimore. Despite the loss the Jerseys had played well at home with a 42–27 record. Maglie worked two-thirds of an inning. His last game of the month was ineffective, three runs in five innings.

The little Giants began the final month in a battle for a playoff spot. On September 2 they were in a tenuous second place position with a two game lead over fifth place Toronto. They played three consecutive doubleheaders against Baltimore to begin the month and split the six games. Maglie lost a game and added a win to improve his record to 8–5. Sid Gordon and Red Howell led the offensive surge. A hard fought win over Newark on September 6 by a 9–8 score assured them of a playoff spot as Snyder used six pitchers including Maglie to ensure the victory. Maglie's final game was a route going performance against the Bears for his ninth win. During World War II several contests and exhibitions took place to stimulate interest from the crowd. The real story on this day was not Maglie's pitching but Johnny Rucker's disputed victory over George Stirnweiss in the 100-yard dash. They finished the race in a virtual dead heat but two judges ruled in favor of Johnny while one of the four judges declared a tie. Nonetheless the Jersey partisans suggested that Stirnweiss had jumped the gun. Rucker had approached the event spontaneously while Stirnweiss had trained for two weeks. Sal Maglie's 400 hundred-foot poke helped the Jerseys win the fungo hitting contest. Jersey City finished the year in fourth place at 77–75.

The war had not discouraged fans from attending games at Roosevelt Stadium. A total of 269,017 (198,412 paid) customers watched the action, an increase of nearly 40,000 from the year before. The national pastime was an essential diversion for Americans during the war. Newark finished in first place, followed by Montreal, Syracuse, Jersey City, Baltimore, Toronto, Buffalo, and Rochester. Bobby Coombs led the league in ERA, 1.99. Red Barrett of Syracuse paced the circuit with twenty wins. Newark's Hank Majeski led in average (.345) and RBIs (121), while Lester Burge of Montreal hit 28 homers.

Maglie finished the year at 9–6 with a 2.78 ERA. He appeared in fifty games, pitching 165 innings, allowing 142 hits and walked 74. He struck out 92. Coombs finished at 17–11, Wittig 11–10, East 10–10, and Fischer 8–7 as the top hurlers. Sid Gordon was the only player with over 100 games played to hit .300. Rucker batted .285 with a team leading 26 steals.

Snyder's club surprised everyone by winning four in a row from Newark in the first playoff round after they had dropped their first two games. Maglie was hit hard in the second game, allowing ten runs on ten hits and four walks in four and one-third innings. Jungels, Wittig, Koslo, and East earned victories. In the Governor's Cup championship, they took on Syracuse who had disposed of Montreal. Syracuse swept the series to earn a right to play in the Little World Series. Maglie appeared in three games pitching an inning apiece. He allowed one run on four hits.

In New York, Mel Ott found that being a player-manager was taxing physically and mentally. He was the first to hold the title from the outfield position since Ty Cobb and Tris Speaker attempted it. Often in the middle of an inning he had to trot in from right field on his bad wheels to make a pitching change. He began to lose concentration and even took Pee Wee Reese out at second with a menacing slide during a game. The Dodgers retaliated under the guidance of Durocher with their own aggressive base running. Hugh Casey and Larry French cut loose with fastballs at Ott's head. Even with the added pressure, Ott rallied the squad to a third place finish. It was their first appearance in the first division since 1938. Mize, Witek, Jurges, and Willard Marshall led the offensive surge. Ott hit .295 with a league high 30 homers and 118 runs. He recorded his 2,500th hit. The quality of play was not diminished, as it would be later during the war.

WARTIME BALL, "WARTIME" PITCHER?

Sal Maglie had climbed his way back to the International League as he had promised Steve O'Neill and had excelled at his craft. He was becoming a more refined hurler, but any immediate plans in organized ball would have to be put on hold. The war effort was becoming more acute. Maglie was called up to his draft board but deemed unfit for military service because of a chronic sinus condition. He was advised to go into defense work. For 1943 and '44 he was placed on organized baseball's "voluntary retired list," and worked as a pipefitter in a defense plant. His employers included International Paper and Union Carbide and later Atlas Steel in Welland, Ontario. Sal and his wife Kay got the opportunity to live like a normal married couple in Niagara Falls without having to travel six months out of the year. In addition, Maglie kept his skills sharp by managing and pitching for Canadian amateur teams on weekends in Niagara Falls and Welland. His 1944 Welland team compiled a 24-1 record as they took the championship. The curveball in particular was developing into a more effective weapon. The last year of the war was a good one for Salvatore Anthony Maglie. Towards the end of the summer he would be wearing a big league uniform pitching for the New York Giants.

As the war progressed the tide was clearly turning in the Allies' favor. Ironically as the Allies victory march advanced, the need for young, physically fit men in the military became more pressing. In 1942–43 the quality of play on big league diamonds remained relatively high. By 1944 major league clubs bore little resemblance to prewar teams. Clubs sought players who were outside the prime draft age — teenagers, old-timers, and the disabled. Some of the kids who suited up during the war included fifteen year old Joe Nuxhall with the Cincinnati Reds and sixteen year old Carl Scheib with Connie Mack's Athletics. The old-timers who returned for another day in the sun included Pepper Martin, Hod Lisenbee, Jimmie Foxx, Babe Herman, and Paul and Lloyd Waner. The 4-F players included Pete Gray (one arm), Dick Sipek (deaf), Tom Sunkel (blind in one eye), Lou Boudreau (bad knees) and Hal Newhouser (bad heart).

Beginning with the 1943 season, Commissioner Landis ordered major league teams to locate their spring training sites east of the Mississippi River and north of the Ohio River. The two St. Louis clubs were given the opportunity to train in Missouri. An informal spring training circuit called the Limestone League was established in Indiana as six teams chose to train in the state. The Boston Red Sox trained at Tufts College in Massachusetts. The Braves chose the Choate Prep School in Wallingford, Connecticut. The Giants chose Lakewood, New Jersey. The Dodgers were located at Bear Mountain, near West Point. The conditions were usually poor, as were the facilities and the weather. Many clubs were unable to have the customary forty players in camp and brought twenty-five or thirty questionable recruits. Some locations were better than others, particularly if the site had a batting cage. Despite the miserable conditions the players did not complain knowing the boys overseas were in a much worse predicament.

The Giants had trained at Lakewood in 1895–96 and were greeted as heroes as they returned nearly fifty years later. The old John D. Rockefeller estate was used as the headquarters. The temperature was reportedly ten degrees higher then the city but a snow plagued 1944 allowed them to play only eight exhibition games and led to Mel Ott's proclamation that they were "the worst conditioned club in Giant history."[1] As the 1945 spring training commenced, Ott greeted the players at the Mansion house. Ernie Lombardi arrived on time instead of his customary late arrival as did Bill Voiselle, the ace who had won twenty-one games in '44. Van Lingle Mungo, a former Brooklyn castoff, signed his contract and boastfully declared he would win twenty games. The pitching staff was the most abundant in baseball with Rube Fischer, Ewald Pyle and Harry Feldman also competing for jobs. Offensively the lineup was similar to '44: the outfield trio of Joe Medwick, Johnny Rucker and Ott. Infielders Phil Weintraub, George Hausmann, Buddy Kerr, and Napoleon Reyes. Lombardi was the backstop. As the training schedule progressed, exhibition games were canceled due to transportation restrictions. Intrasquad and service games would replace them. On March 24 they played the Bainbridge Commodores, an outfit with big leaguers Stan Musial, Earl Naylor, Dick Sisler, and Eddie Miksis. They fought to a 6–6 stalemate. Their subsequent contests were against the Curtis Bay Coast Guard, the New York Yankees, the Jersey City Giants, and the Newark Bears. Before the season opened about 12,000 fans showed up at Ebbets Field as the proceeds of the game between the Giants and Dodgers went to benefit the Red Cross. It was a typical war relief game as they raised $27,409.70.

The nation was in mourning over the death of President Roosevelt as the baseball season commenced. New York got off to a fast start in 1945 as Mel Ott received strong pitching, good defense, and power hitting. On opening day they defeated the Boston Braves by an 11–6 score as Lombardi and Weintraub hit homers. The Giants won eight out of their first nine games as Mel Ott began his fourth season as the skipper. Voiselle, Mungo, and Feldman were pitching well as starters while Ace Adams was backing them up in the bullpen. They were hitting the long ball; even Ott joined in with two homers against Philadelphia on April 24. They ended the month by losing two straight to Brooklyn at the Polo Grounds.

While the Giants were tearing up the league the power structure of baseball was also shifting as Albert B. "Happy" Chandler was named commissioner to succeed the deceased Judge Landis. New York regained its winning ways by taking eight consecutive games to begin May. Adams won his second game in relief of Voiselle on the 2nd as he continued his progression into an ace reliever. On May 5, the Giants were second in the NL in batting with a .265 average and first in club fielding. Voiselle was 3–0 while Feldman, Adams, and Andy Hansen each had two wins. Ott, Hausmann, Weintraub, and Lombardi were hitting well. Throughout the month they thrilled the crowds by winning in dramatic fashion. The war in Europe ended on May 7 as Germany surrendered unconditionally. President Harry S Truman proclaimed May 8, V-E day.

In June the bottom dropped out as the New Yorkers failed to produce clutch hits and lost the close ones. The pitching collapsed. They began the month winning two out of their first twelve and finished June with a 10–19 record. The first day of the month was a harbinger of things to come as they lost a 4–3 decision to the Cardinals. Voiselle lost his third straight after winning his first eight. In the ninth he threw a 0 and 2 pitch to Johnny Hopp who hit it for a triple and propelled St. Louis to victory. Ott had a rule that if a pitcher did not waste such a pitch he would be fined $100.

He stormed in from right field and caught up with Voiselle in the dugout and informed the hurler that the pitch had cost him not $100 but $500.² Ott carried some blame for the loss as he left his pitcher in after a long rain delay. Both Voiselle and Hopp confirmed years later that the pitch was out of the strike zone. The clubhouse felt like a morgue afterwards. Voiselle's spirits were crushed and the Giants went in the tank. The following day they squeaked out a 3–2 win as Mungo won his fifth. The club committed four errors. On June 6, Brooklyn committed eight errors to allow the Giants to win. This was representative of wartime play, from 1942–45, 9,474 errors were committed, an average of 1,500 more than the prewar years. A Brooklyn doubleheader sweep on June 14 dropped them from first to third place. Not even General Eisenhower's appearance at the Polo Grounds on June 19 could bring them luck.

July proved only slightly better as they weighed in with a 14–17 record. On July 3 they showed a glimpse of their early season performance as Feldman tossed a three-hitter and Weintraub hit a homer to lead New York to a 3–2 win. In the 4th of July doubleheader St. Louis took both games as they blasted thirty-six hits and twenty-six runs against Giant pitching. The two starters Voiselle and Dale Emmerich lost and they each shared their frustration by hitting a batter. In the middle of the month New York dropped consecutive doubleheaders to the Cubs. Ott was desperate. Weintraub was benched and replaced by Danny Gardella. Mungo, Voiselle, and Feldman were being knocked around.

With the war coming to an end, Sal Maglie returned to professional baseball with a good conscience in the middle of June. He had missed two and a half years but had tried to stay sharp pitching against Canadian amateurs. Maglie joined Gabby Hartnett's Jersey City Giants in Buffalo. Hartnett had hit 236 big league homers for the Chicago Cubs as a player and was in his second stint as a bush league manager. His club was in first place with a 31–16 record on June 18. Even though Sal was in good shape he soon found out that pitching on weekends against amateurs was unlike pitching against International League competition. Hartnett had heard a lot of good things about Maglie and was happy he joined the club. Sal also sounded excited. "We had a strong team at Welland ... but there's nothing like organized baseball. I'm ready any time Mr. Hartnett wants me to pitch and I'm looking forward to getting a starting assignment sometime this week." A couple of nights earlier Maglie had shutout Satchel Paige and his Kansas City Monarchs by a 1–0 score. Cy Kritzer, a local Buffalo writer wrote concerning Maglie, "He's finally getting that curve ball where he wants it," adding "and you know that kind of a curve he has."³

Maglie debuted at Offermann Stadium as the Jerseys won a doubleheader 2–0 and 9–6. Mike Mellis outlasted seventeen-year-old Art Houtteman in the opener for his ninth win. Graybeards and youngsters were dispersed around the IL during the war similar to the majors. The old-timers included Alfred Todd of Montreal who caught 100 games during the '45 season at the age of 43. Ollie Carnegie returned to Buffalo and batted .301 in 93 at-bats. Teenagers such as Houtteman, Walt Pierce, and Joe Nuxhall pitched in the league that year. Maglie earned the win in the second game despite a shaky performance, allowing three runs on thirteen hits and four walks while driving in a couple at the plate. Maglie recalls, "it was like starting over again I was rusty."[4] The team was in the process of playing a plethora of doubleheaders, as the nine man staff was led by Adrian Zabala (9–2) and Mellis (9–1). Poor hitting cursed the team in late June as they lost seven of ten. Mellis and Maglie lost games on the 24th. Maglie had tossed a no-hitter through four innings before a four run fifth did him in. On the 28th he lost the second game of a doubleheader, 3–0, to Montreal as the Jerseys suddenly found themselves in third place. They were beginning to fade at almost the same time the big club was headed south. Their road trip ended with a 5–12 record.

On the first day of July, Maglie closed the door for Lou "Crip" Polli in the second game of the day. He recorded the five outs in succession. On the 4th of July, 10,164 spectators packed their way into Roosevelt Stadium as the Bears and the Giants split a twinbill. Maglie won the opener 7–3 to improve his record to 2–2. He continued to hit well at the plate getting two hits, one RBI, and scoring a run. On the hill he was wild, walking four but worked out of tough jams with help of seven strikeouts. He won his third game with a solid performance against Baltimore in his next start going the distance. On the 10th he lost his third game getting touched up in relief, although he scored a run and hit a triple at the plate. His first seven appearances came during doubleheaders.

(The newspaper report of the game credited the loss to Maglie but the boxscore inaccurately gave the loss to Frank Rosso which went down in the permanent record. Maglie allowed two runs in the fifth, which put Baltimore up for good. The official record erroneously gives him a 3–7 record for the year when it should be 3–8. Also for some reason virtually every article gives him a 6–7 record).

The Newark Bears continued their domination over the Jerseys with a 7–5 win on the 14th. Roy Zimmerman paced the Bears with his twenty-fourth homer giving Johnny Maldovan the win. Maglie lost his fourth allowing seven runs in eight innings. While he left his fastball and curve at home he did bring his stick going three for four with a homer and two

RBIs. Hartnett's squad had lost ten of twenty-three. Whitey Lockman took his .341 average to the Giants while Les Layton took off for the navy with his .318 average. The outfield was a liability but was bolstered by the acquisition of Eddie Kobesky from the Milwaukee Brewers where he had slumped. The previous year he tore up the IL with 26 homers and 129 RBIs.

During Maglie's final seven outings he lost five games but pitched well. The offense became anemic. On July 22nd he helped the Jerseys win in relief as he stranded eight in the last three innings. Three days later he lost his sixth, working nine innings, giving up four runs on eight hits and four walks while hitting a batter. He lost a 2–1 game to Toronto on July 30. On August 3, he was slugged for nine runs in eight innings against Buffalo. They collected fourteen hits, including four homers against him. If Maglie and the other pitcher of the day, Zabala, were not concentrating, they had an excuse. Mel Ott had sent out a call for arms, and the two Jersey City pitchers were on their way to the big show. Reporters told Ott that Maglie had not torn up the IL, the skipper responded, "True enough, but he's had a lot of experience in the minors. He's twenty-eight and he knows his way around a ball field. He may not be spectacular, but you don't have to worry about his making too many mistakes, either."[5] Another factor was that Maglie had flunked his army physical and therefore was not likely to be drafted. In fourteen games in Jersey City he had compiled an unimpressive 3–8 record with a 4.09 ERA. In 88 innings he allowed 91 hits, 33 walks while fanning 41. He batted .313. The record is misleading since he did not receive much run support. Maglie noted that in Jersey City, "I felt stronger and my control was much better, but I wasn't getting the hitters out at the right time."[6]

Maglie was mildly surprised to get the call because of his difficulties over the last month. Mel Ott put the twenty-eight year old at ease when he informed him of his own problems. The manager was confident Maglie could do a good job. He particularly liked the fact that Sal had a good head on his shoulders and would not get rattled in tight spots. If Maglie pitched well in relief he would get the opportunity to start and join Voiselle, Mungo, and Feldman in the rotation. Before Ott walked away from his desk and shook Sal's hand, he informed him that baseball was a player's market with players constantly coming and going from the military. "You've got the best chance in the world to stick up here now. Make the most of it."[7]

A throng of 22,098 persons attended the grand cathedral, the majestic Polo Grounds, on the first day of August to watch the Braves and the Giants clash. In the third inning Melvin Thomas Ott strode to the plate against reliever Johnny Hutchings. The great Giant was playing out the string of an exceptional, meritorious career. The spring in his legs were fading quickly, the end was in sight. McGraw had first seen him take batting practice as a callow 16 year old youth, and signed him on the spot declaring Ott the "most natural hitter" he'd ever seen.[8] He kept the boy close by and refused to send him to the bushes where managers could tinker with his unorthodox stance. As Hutchings pitched the ball to the plate, Ott lifted his front leg in his patented style and sent the ball hurtling toward right field where it ricocheted off the stands. It was his 500th career homer, making Ott only the third man to accomplish this grand feat behind Babe Ruth (714) and Jimmie Foxx (527). The Giants' manager had made a living at the Polo Grounds, an ideal park for left-handed pull hitters with its short porch down the line. Hutchings plunked Ott his next time up. The youngster Lockman also went deep in the game. The Braves rekindled memories of an old Brooklyn tradition from Uncle Robbie's daffiness boys. Braves manager Del Bissonette was familiar with the proceedings for he had played with the Dodgers from 1928–33. In the second inning two Braves found themselves occupying third base at the same time. New York won the game 9–2 as Emmerich won in relief of Mungo. Ott celebrated his milestone at Toots Shor's restaurant in the evening.

New York won three out of their next four. On August 9, Harry Brecheen pitched the St. Louis Cardinals to a 5–3 win before a modest Polo Grounds crowd of 9,936. New York took a one run lead in the second and could have got more but Hausmann grounded out meekly with the sacks full. In the fourth, Feldman was knocked out of the box as he allowed four runs. With one out, Sal Maglie was summoned from the bullpen to put out the fire. He toed the slab wearing the stylish white, black and gold uniform of the National League Giants. Sal walked a batter before recording the final two outs of the inning. Thus began the career of Sal Maglie in a quiet way.

A screeching contingent of 2,319 women showed up on ladies day to watch New York lose 5–2 to St. Louis the following day. A group of war veterans watched Voiselle get knocked around in the green pasture. Johnny Hopp gave him trouble again by hitting a double. The $500 fine had taken its toll on the pitcher although it was later rescinded. Maglie and Adams did a good job after Voiselle exited. Lombardi accounted for the New York runs with a homer and a sacrifice fly. Rucker was back in center field as Lockman was gobbled up by the army. Lockman hit .341 with 3 homers and 18 RBIs in his short stint with the big club. Adrian Zabala salvaged the third game of the series, pitching a six-hitter in his major league debut.

On August 9, the U.S. dropped a second atomic bomb on a Japanese city, a blow that would end the war. "V-J" day arrived on August 14, victory over Japan. Americans poured out into the streets to celebrate as President Truman announced the news to a jubilant nation just after seven at night EWT. Sal Maglie had earned a start with two solid relief appearances and he toed the rubber before 3,038 fans as New York hosted the seventh place Cincinnati Reds. When the Giants won 5–2 to sweep the four game series, the Reds' losing streak extended to seven. Sal went the distance allowing the two runs on eight hits and four walks for his first big league victory. The competition was less than stellar as Mike Modak also made his first big league start and was relieved by 46 year old Hod Lisenbee. Maglie got his first big league hit as well. New York played sloppy defense but Gardella, Lombardi and Mike Schemer led the way with the bat. The team was in fourth place (59–50), three games behind their hated rivals the Dodgers who were in third place.

Against Pittsburgh, Maglie proved that his first win was no fluke as he applied the whitewash in a 6–0 victory. The Polo Grounds crowd was just settling in when New York scored six runs in the first to make Maglie's job easy. Pittsburgh's starter Xavier Rescigno retired Rucker to start the game. Hausmann beat out a bunt and scored when Ott hit his 18th homer. Gardella singled. Lombardi reached on an error, Schemer doubled scoring Gardella. Kerr was walked intentionally to load the bases and Reyes drove in two with a single. Maglie hit a sacrifice fly before relief pitcher Art Cuccurullo got out of the inning. Sal got another hit, gave up three hits and three walks while striking out six on the mound. He nailed Frankie Gustine in the contest.

On Thursday, the Giants hosted the Dodgers. Third place was up for grabs. The New Yorkers were winding up a successful homestand in which they were currently 15–8. In three weeks they had picked up five games on Brooklyn who had gone 8–9 versus the Western clubs. Sal got the call and began his indoctrination into the Giant/Dodger rivalry before 39,694 Polo Grounds fans. These games often became wars with headhunting and take-out slides the norm. Maglie recalls, "When I first joined the Giants, the manager was Mel Ott. He had a talk with me and told me he wanted me to pitch high inside and low and away. 'And if you want to make money,' Ott added, 'you've got to beat the Dodgers.'"[9] In the bottom of the first while Major General Edgar E. Glenn was being introduced, Eddie Stanky broke into an argument with the first base umpire and was kicked out. The rhubarb was precipitated over Stanky's objection to the arbiter's decision in a game against the Cubs the previous Friday and the $25 fine he received. Maglie was not sharp; Mike Sandlock drove home a Brooklyn run in the second, and Dixie Walker and Ed Stevens drove in runs during the following frame. Ott badly bruised his left hip as he crashed into the right field wall on Stevens' double but refused to exit the game. Voiselle worked five effective relief innings for Sal before Adams made his 54th appearance in the ninth. Ralph Branca, the kid who grew up as a Giant fan, tossed a four-hitter for Brooklyn. Maglie left after three innings, allowing three runs.

After a rainout, the teams traveled to Ebbets Field where the Dodgers humiliated their rivals by sweeping a doubleheader. Maglie made a brief appearance as a pinch runner. New York bounced back the following day as Jack Brewer scattered seven hits to give New York a 6–2 win. People were flocking to the ballparks as the millionth cash customer made their way through the Ebbets Field turnstiles. In Philadelphia a meager crowd showed up at Shibe Park as the Giants swept a doubleheader 4–0, 6–2. Voiselle got back on track by tossing a shutout in the opener for his thirteenth win. The great "Double X," Jimmie Foxx, had a pinch-hit single and pitched a scoreless ninth. At the age of thirty-seven he would have one more day in the sun, hitting .268 with 7 homers and compiling a 1–0 record with a 1.59 ERA as a pitcher for the Phils. Maglie improved to 3–1 in the second game. He scattered ten base runners in the route going performance, had two hits including a double and drove in a run. The hapless Phillies were in the process of finishing last for the seventh time in eight years. In fact the entire history of the ballclub was abysmal. When they played in the dilapidated Baker Bowl they had a sign in right field that advertised "The Phillies Use Lifebuoy," and underneath someone had written in "and they still stink."[10] The park was a subject of ridicule similar to its occupants. The Phillies joined the Athletics in the use of Shibe Park since 1938 when they abandoned the decaying Baker Bowl. Like many of the concrete and steel stadiums built in the early 20th century, Shibe Park would ultimately become antiquated and represent the deteriorating urban city in which it was located.

The Giants and the Dodgers resumed their interborough war to begin September. A Billy Jurges homer off Clyde King propelled the New Yorkers to a 5–4 win. Branca started for Brooklyn and allowed four runs in six innings. The kid from Mount Vernon, New York, had traveled to a Giant tryout in 1942 at the age of sixteen. It rained that day and the following day he did not get to pitch. Eventually the scrawny kid impressed the Dodgers who signed him in June 1943. He would become a part of Giant tradition but not as he had hoped.

On September 2, a season high crowd of 54,740 (49,204 paid) maneuvered their way into the Polo Grounds for a doubleheader. The Cubs held a two game lead over St. Louis in the National League while the Dodgers were in third place a half game ahead of the Giants. Van Lingle Mungo, the ex–Dodger, started for New York. Mungo was a hard-drinking, fun loving, six-foot two inch right-hander from Pageland, South Carolina. With Brooklyn he had been a star hurler, winning 102 games before coming to New York in 1942. Mungo possessed a fiery temper and paid out approximately $15,000 worth of fines in his career, which matched his highest Brooklyn salary. One day he lost a game with two out in the ninth when Tom Winsett dropped a routine fly. Mungo was irate and tore up the clubhouse. The next day he sent a telegram to his wife, "Pack your bags and come to Brooklyn. If Winsett can play in the big leagues, it's a cinch you can too."[11] Al Lopez would later state "Mungo was a nice fellow. When he had a few drinks in him, he just went crazy, but he wasn't a bad guy."[12]

The first game dragged on for three hours and eleven minutes and boiled over in the seventh. Leo Durocher, the consummate bench jockey, was incessantly needling the Giants' pitcher. By the seventh, Mungo had enough and began to walk towards Durocher near the first base coaching line. A brawl was thwarted when umpire Beans Reardon held Durocher while arbiter Larry Goetz held back Mungo. Other players lingered around. After nine innings the teams were knotted at four. Mungo left in the eighth when he slipped and injured his left shoulder on an Augie Galan grounder. Adams followed and Maglie worked a perfect tenth. He lost the game in the eleventh when Brooklyn scored three. Years later Maglie recalled the way the Dodgers shelled him in that game and feelings it provoked: "For some reason that made me resent the Dodgers. All the time I pitched for the Giants I hated the Dodgers."[13] The Giants got their revenge in the nightcap as Gardella and Ott each hit two-run homers. Voiselle won his fourteenth.

If Mel Ott was the "gentle Giant," a nice guy who played with grace and style, then Durocher was the antithesis. He was crude and controversial on the field and impeccably tailored off of it. He had been a brilliant defensive shortstop with the New York Yankees of Ruth, Gehrig, Meusel, and Lazzeri. Later he played with the Gas House Gang Cardinals, employing every trick in the book to win a game. In 1939, Larry MacPhail gave Leo his first managing job in Brooklyn. The two had a combative relationship throughout the years. The league quickly learned to hate Durocher's Dodgers. Leo's main weapon was the beanball, prompting six NL teams to complain to Commissioner Landis in 1942 suggesting that the Dodgers were headhunters. The beanball was used to intimidate and force the opposition into submission or retaliation. He got under the opposition's skin with verbal abuse till they were ready to kill him. In 1942, his pitcher, Les Webber, tried to hit every Cardinal in the lineup. The reserved Stan Musial broke down and charged the mound for possibly the only time in his career. Pitchers who threw at batters' heads found $100 bills in their locker. Dodger Pete Reiser recalled, "Christ, in those days all you heard was 'Stick it in his ear,' adding "There were times I thought we should've got combat pay, playing for Leo."[14] Reiser should know; he had the skills of a Willie Mays but ruined his career by running into rock solid outfield walls at top speed. Eleven times he was carried off on a stretcher and nine times regained consciousness in the clubhouse or in the hospital. He took beanballs in the head and always came back for more till his body had nothing left. Concerning Mel Ott, Durocher told a reporter, "A nicer guy never drew breath than that man there." Regarding the Giant players, "Walker Cooper, Mize, Marshall, Kerr, Gordon, Thomson. Take a look at them. All nice guys. They'll finish last. Nice guys. Finish last."[15] Off the field Leo whored around, and incessantly cheated on his wife when married. He hung around with reported thugs and gamblers. He wasn't a nice guy. He came to win, he came to kill you.

On September 3, a total of 265,336 spectators watched games in big league parks, the largest turnout since the war began. New York attracted 21,567 at the Polo Grounds for a Labor Day doubleheader. The crowd put the Giants over the million mark for the first time in their history. Harry Feldman hurled a four-hitter in the opener to defeat Ben Chapman's Philadelphia Phillies by a 3–2 score. New York took the second game 9–0, as Maglie pitched a four hit shutout to improve to 4–2. Roy Zimmerman, who had been recently acquired from the Yankees organization, hit an inside the park homer and Rucker had two triples within the expansive ballpark. The Phils would finish the season with a 46–108 record in last place. While wartime baseball allowed a few perennial losers such as the St. Louis Browns and the Washington Senators to become competitive, the Phils continued to lose in large numbers. Harry Cross wrote in the *New York Herald Tribune*, "The Phils in their present status look sad. It isn't difficult to beat them. The brace of games yesterday were just about exciting as the Russian-American cable chess match."[16]

The Giants traveled to Chicago and promptly lost three straight to the front running Cubs before Maglie stopped the bleeding with his third shutout, a 2–0 win. Sal was sharp in the contest, allowing six hits, one walk, hitting Mickey Livingston, and recording eight strikeouts. He had to be on top of his game since Chicago's ace Hank Wyse, an eighteen game winner, was the opposing hurler. Sal's stuff was not overpowering, but he worked to spots and kept them off-balance. Ernie Lombardi discussed Sal's success in '45 as follows: "He puts the ball just where it should be and, while it is not an attractive pitch, the hitter still must swing at it."[17] Maglie was what some would call a "junk pitcher," meaning that he relied on off-speed pitches and deception instead of the fastball. At this point of his career he only threw from a three-quarters arm slot.

At Sportsman's Park in St. Louis on September 11, New York lost their fourth straight as their Western trip continued. Maglie left during the eighth inning, allowing four runs on seven hits and one walk. Zimmerman and Gardella hit homers early to give New York a 4–0 lead. The Cardinals scored five runs in the last three innings to emerge victorious, 6–5. Adams took the loss. Pittsburgh overtook New York for fourth place. By the 16th they were fifteen games behind first place Chicago and two and a half games behind the fourth place Pirates. The Giants ended the road trip by splitting a doubleheader in Forbes Field. They failed to hit in the clutch, losing the opener 3–2. Maglie took the loss, allowing ten baserunners in the game. Preacher Roe, who was in the early stages of experimenting with the wet one, worked for the Pirates. Jack Brewer led the Giants to a 9–2 win in the second game.

Mel Ott's team stumbled to the finish line dropping two games to the Braves on the 23rd. Maglie lost his fourth in a quick hour and forty-five minute contest. He allowed three runs in seven innings. Between games Ott was honored by National League President Ford Frick. He accepted a lifetime pass to league parks for his meritorious service with one club. Horace Stoneham honored him in his own way four days later by tearing up his contract which had one more year remaining and giving him a five year pact with a sizable raise. The last two games at the Harlem horseshoe were won by the Dodgers. New York closed out the season by outlasting Boston 1–0 in thirteen innings at Braves Field. The second game ended in a 2–2 tie, as it was called after sunset. Maglie pitched well enough to win the second game, allowing two runs on five hits and two walks in seven innings. However the real story of the day was the batting race. Phil Cavarretta of the Cubs had been battling Boston's Tommy Holmes for the crown. Maglie pitched Holmes high and tight down the stretch and particularly in the last game. Holmes was knocked down unceasingly with the high heater. Sal was not merely trying to take away the inside corner, he was also helping his fellow Italian ballplayer Phil Cavarretta win a batting title. Maglie stated, "If you were Italian," referring to Holmes, "I wouldn't have decked you so many times."[18] Tommy went 0 for 2 with a walk in the second game. Cavarretta won the batting title at .355. Holmes finished at .352.

New York finished the season in fifth place with a 78–74 record. Maglie had been impressive, albeit against wartime competition. He sported a 5–4 record with a 2.35 ERA, including three shutouts. He worked 84.1 innings, gave up 72 hits, walked 22, and struck out 32. The talent pool in 1945 was grossly inferior to prewar standards and many characterized Maglie as merely a wartime pitcher. Voiselle slumped to 14–14 with a high 4.49 ERA as he lost confidence in himself. Feldman was 12–13. Mungo weighed in at 14–7 with solid 3.20 ERA. Adams appeared in a record sixty-five games and contributed an 11–9 mark with a 3.42 ERA. Mel Ott managed to hit .308 with 21 homers and 79 RBIs. Lombardi batted .307 with 19 homers and 70 RBIs while Gardella drove in 71 with 18 homers. Brooklyn finished in third place. The '45 Dodgers were not Durocher's type of team; he preferred a veteran more experienced contingent. Arthur Daley wrote concerning wartime baseball, "It's not easy, to discern that the current center fielder missed catching the ball by the extra step a Joe DiMaggio would have taken or that the batter missed making a hit by the fraction of an inch which would not have eluded a Ted Williams or a Stan Musial. The spectator takes what he gets, asks no questions, and seems eminently satisfied with it."[19]

The war was over and the boys were coming back, which spelled trouble for many wartime players. A surfeit of talent would overflow big league camps in '46, as players competed for the fixed number of jobs available. Some players who went overseas such as Hank Greenberg and Bob Feller had come back and helped their teams down the stretch. It was going to take a while for the veterans to refine their skills despite the fact that many had played military ball. Greenberg had helped the Tigers win the pennant, which he climaxed with a grand slam homer on the final day of the season. Sportswriter Warren Brown best summed up the World Series between the Cubs and the Tigers. When asked who would win, he answered "Really, I can't conceive of either team winning a single game!"[20] It was poorly played and when 42 year old Chuck Hostetler tripped as he rounded third trying to score the winning run for Detroit in the seventh inning of the sixth game it represented the way in which both teams had played the series. Baseball was also stumbling home after years of ineptitude. The Tigers belatedly won in seven games to end years of inferior play.

THE BASEBALL WAR, THE BLACK LIST, AND THE MEXICAN JUMPING BEANS

At the conclusion of their final series in Boston, the Giants traveled back to the Polo Grounds where the players engaged in the pedestrian act of cleaning out their lockers. Horace Stoneham was a magnanimous owner whose favorite pastime besides the Giants was alcohol. Despite his reputation he kept his players hungry with meager salaries while he pocketed the revenues like the rest of the owners. Tom Yawkey of the Red Sox may have been the lone exception. The Giant players were promised a bonus after the season, but instead they received two autographed baseballs.

Dolf Luque, one of the Giant coaches, slammed his locker shut and walked over to Maglie to inquire about his winter plans. Luque had just finished his final year as a major league coach. It consisted of a four-year stint under Bill Terry (1935–37, 1941) and four years under the reign of Mel Ott (1942–45). He was affectionately known as the "Pride of Havana," in his native Cuba and had been the first Latin American star in the majors. After a brief cup of coffee with the Boston Nationals in 1914–15, he starred in Cincinnati during the roaring '20s. His best year was 1923, when he compiled a 27–8 record with a 1.93 ERA. He completed his career with the Brooklyn Dodgers and the New York Giants finishing with 194 victories.

A great developer of talent, Luque would return to Cuba during the winter where he played and managed in the prestigious Cuban Winter League. In eight different seasons he would manage his Cuban League team to a championship. Maglie had planned to return to Niagara Falls during the winter and work. Luque urged him to come to Cuba. He told the pitcher that he would have fun, the fans were crazy about baseball, and the tropical sun would help his arm. He would also earn $400 a month. Maglie wanted to go but he first needed the approval from his wife Kay. That evening they sold the idea to her over dinner. An idyllic picture was painted, and Maglie insisted that it would be like a second honeymoon. Kay informed her husband that they never had a first one before agreeing to the proposal. In later years Sal talked about the support she gave him, "With Kay, my wife, I went down to Cuba. She was a wonderful woman. She'd watch me pitch and never say a word. We never talked baseball at home, except once. After a bad call I threw my glove down ... She told me later, "Sal, that was bush. You should never act like that again." I never did."[1] Sal was getting old and he had a lot to learn if he was going to master the craft of pitching a baseball.

The 1945-46 winter league season was instrumental for a number of reasons. It was the first full professional season since the conclusion of World War II. The league had a high number of quality players. It consisted of Cubans from organized ball and the Mexican League (the term "organized ball" is used to represent U.S. baseball which is sanctioned by the major league owners in this discussion), returning American veterans, and Negro Leaguers. The four circuit clubs were particularly strong this year: Marianao, Habana, Almendares, and Cienfuegos. Luque's Cienfuegos squad included Roland Gladu, a Canadian outfielder belonging to the Dodgers and Luis Tiant, who was one of the greatest Cuban pitchers to toe the slab (his son with the same name would have a brilliant major league career). Negro League great Martin Dihigo was on the team. Luque's connection to the majors was particularly evident as 28 percent of his team was composed of major leaguers. Adrian Zabala, Nap Reyes, Ray Berres, Maglie and Luque himself were from the Giants. Jose Zardon was from the Senators. Miguel Angel Cordero Gonzalez (Mike Gonzalez) a former big league player and a coach for the Cardinals during the Gas House Gang era managed Habana in the Cuban circuit. The big rivalry in the league was between the Habana Reds (or Lions) and the Almendares Blues (or Scorpions). Both franchises had existed since the 1860s.

During the 1945-46 season games were played at the spacious La Tropical park. Strong cigar smoke hovered over the stadium on game day as the predominantly male audience watched the action in the pasture.

Betting was rampant. Cuban baseball was usually played by the so-called "book." This was scientific baseball or small ball, little ball. Execute the fundamentals, bunt a runner over, and play for a single run. It was not unique for a cleanup hitter to lay down a bunt.

Dolf Luque worked hard imparting his knowledge on the young ballplayers through the years. He had learned to throw a decent curve from the great Christy Mathewson while Mathewson was managing the Reds. He had been a master of "shaving" hitters, throwing the heater in the batter's kitchen a little too close for comfort. The intimidated batsman would be remiss to dig a solid toehold in the box and would be bailing out when Luque nicked the corner with the curve. In Luque's eyes, Maglie had pitching skills but not pitching finesse. So with his fertile baseball mind he began to transform Maglie into a pitcher, an intimidator and not merely a thrower. With the help of his tutor, Maglie began to develop his trademark style which would frighten hitters for years to come. Any psychological advantage he could find would be used to intimidate a batter. A scowl, a menacing laugh, or a fastball at the head. Fear plays a significant factor when hitting a baseball. The uncertainty of velocity, action, and the destination of a pitch are exacerbated by noticeable aberrations in a pitcher's control. Luque believed that the inside corner of the plate belonged to the pitcher. He believed in protecting his bread and butter and Maglie would become his most dogmatic student in his philosophy of pitching.

The Cuban League was a rough circuit. In one contest Herrera who was pitching for Almendares nailed Roland Gladu. Herrera pitched with his left hand but batted right-handed. When he came up Maglie knew what to do, impart revenge. Maglie hurled the sphere towards home plate and nailed the pitcher on the shoulder. He later stated, "I had to protect my team, and I had to protect the plate. This is the way things are in baseball."[2] Maglie stubbornly would protect his teammates through the years and if someone wanted to retaliate they could certainly do so when he went to the box with the stick. To hit Maglie may not have been the best strategy because you would merely hasten the wrath of the Renaissance Assassin. Maglie was not a bench jockey, a holler guy, like Leo Durocher. If he got angry he usually didn't retaliate with his mouth but instead a fastball at your skull.

Dick Sisler tore up the Cuban League, batting .301 with an astonishing nine homers in the huge park. On January 23, 1946, he belted a mammoth shot to right-center, clearing the two fences. The next day he hit three Ruthian shots off Maglie. He singled his next time up and was passed intentionally by reliever Colorao Roger his fifth time up. Luque did not care about a possible record and walked Sisler in an ideal situation.

Cienfuegos lost to Habana, 9–7. Maglie and the Cienfuegos team had the final laugh as they took the championship. Sal led the club with nine wins along with Zabala who also weighed in with nine. Nap Reyes batted a solid .269 with six triples. It is reported that Maglie defeated Mike Gonzalez's Havana team, their chief rival, seven times. Sal was treated like a hero by the Cuban citizenry. The season was a financial success for the league. A new bastion of Cuban baseball was being built, Gran Stadium, to replace the archaic La Tropical for the following year. La Tropical did not seat a lot of fans and was far from the city.

The most significant event that took place over the winter did not happen on the field. In February, Luque introduced Maglie to Bernardo Pasquel. They met at the Sevilla-Biltmore hotel in Havana. Bernardo was the brother of multimillionaire Jorge Pasquel, who would attempt to raid the major league rosters during spring training. He was in Cuba on a scouting trip hoping to lure big name players to the Mexican League. Bernardo offered Maglie $7,500 to jump his Giants contract. This was the same salary he was earning with New York, but the $3,000 bonus made the offer enticing.[3] Sal asked for double that amount, and Bernardo declined but left his business card as he departed. He urged Sal to call him collect if he changed his mind. Maglie was content with his Giants contract and felt he had a future with the organization but things would quickly change.

The landscape of organized ball was slowly changing. On October 23, 1945, in a press conference between officials of the Montreal Royals and the Brooklyn Dodgers it was announced that Jackie Robinson had signed a contract to play with the Royals in 1946. With Happy Chandler as commissioner instead of Landis the move was accepted by baseball's highest official. The newspapers hyped Robinson as the first "Negro" in organized ball but like other baseball myths such as Abner Doubleday inventing the game and Ruth calling his shot it was not necessarily true. Men of color had played in the big leagues throughout its history. Moses Fleetwood Walker endured incredible abuse when he played in the American Association, a big league circuit, in 1884. Adolfo Luque, Maglie's tutor, a light-skinned Cuban, enjoyed a long big league career while a dark-skinned Cuban with similar ability, Martin Dihigo, was forced to ride undetected through the night on rickety buses for Negro League clubs. Jill Barnes wrote, "In race-conscious North America, at a time when dark-skinned Latinos had trouble breaking into baseball, Luque's light skin was to his advantage. A newspaper story of the period describes him as "looking more Italian than a full-blooded Cuban."[4] Just as in Caribbean slave societies where light skinned blacks were allowed a small amount of social mobility, Luque was "tolerated" by the bigots who ran organized ball. Clark

Griffith, owner of the Washington Senators, had sent his scout Joe Cambria to sign Latin Americans during the war. He was a skinflint who signed Latins for meager wages and hoped that the government would not take them for military service. The government eventually threatened conscription and many of his players returned to their home countries. Olive-skinned Armando Marsans and Rafael Almeida had played under Griffith when he managed the Reds. Despite this he had the audacity to criticize Rickey for signing Robinson. Hypocrisy was rampant among ownership. Black sportswriter Art Rust Jr., wrote "The Washington Senators in the mid-thirties and forties were loaded with Latin players of darker hue (than Jackie Robinson), who because they spoke Spanish got away with it."[5] Tommy de la Cruz pitched for the Reds during the war, and Pirate scout Howie Haak said, "Hell, Tommy de la Cruz was as black as they came!"[6] Hi Bithorn was a light-skinned black who pitched for the Chicago Cubs during the war. He would die mysteriously in 1952 when policemen shot him in the stomach as he tried to sell a car. These are just a handful of players of color who put on big league uniforms before Robinson. This discussion is not to diminish Jackie's role in any way for he symbolically integrated baseball. He was burdened with every racist gesture imaginable and strived in the face of it. If he failed the cause might have been pushed back a decade, but the history books fail to give notice to those persons of color who also played and were burdened with abuse before Jackie.

The New York Giants were busy during the off-season. First they purchased the contract of Clint Hartung from the Minneapolis Millers and declared him the next Babe Ruth. Ted McGrew, the head of the Boston Braves farm system, lauded Hartung. "I'd have given a whole ball club to get Hartung. And swim a river to get his name on a contract."[7] He had seen him play and was obviously impressed. Newspaperman Tom Meany commented sarcastically, "Hartung's a sucker if he reports to the Giants. All he has to do is sit at home, wait until he's eligible, and he's a cinch to make the Hall of Fame."[8] On January 5, Horace Stoneham gave the Cardinals $175,000 for the services of Walker Cooper. He was still in the Navy but had almost accumulated the requisite discharge points to leave. All the skills were there: the arm, great speed for a catcher, and a prodigious bat. In 1943 and '44 he batted .318 and .317 respectively and had helped the Cardinals to the World Series three times: 1942–44. With the boys returning from the war, competition was going to be stiff during camp. It was uncertain which players on a roster could be counted on. By early January, the Giants had already mailed out forty-nine contracts.

In late January, Mel Ott told reporters about his pitching plans for spring training. Sal Maglie's name was conspicuously missing. By early

February, twenty-nine hurlers were expected in camp. Ott was particularly looking to three men to carry the load: Hal Schumacher, Dave Koslo, and Bill Voiselle. Schumacher's arm was well rested from his last big league season in '42. The Giants' manager had received reports that Koslo was one of the two best pitchers in the European Theater along with Ewell Blackwell. Voiselle had looked sharp in a recent USO trip through the South Pacific.

In 1946 the major league teams no longer had to endure cold winters in the north and were allowed to train in the south. On February 8, the Giants boarded the Sun Queen and headed for Miami. When they began training under the hot Florida sun, fifty-one players were already in camp. Management was uncertain concerning how the opening day rosters would look. Stoneham attempted to sign his players to small contracts. However an exceedingly high number of players had returned their contracts unsigned. The questions were numerous: Which wartime players could perform well against the returning players from the service? Did a young player mature during the war while playing service ball? What was the skill level of the returning players and how long would it take for their skills to become sharp if they ever will? To exacerbate the situation, the clubs ran a very ineffective camp. There simply were too many players and too few games to give everyone a proper look. In this air of uncertainty, Jorge Pasquel stepped into the breach and began to conduct the first raid of the majors since the old Federal League.

Jorge Pasquel was born into wealth on April 29, 1907, in Veracruz, Mexico. His father, Fransisco, had become rich through a cigar factory and later a customs brokerage. Jorge was the oldest of five brothers, and also had three sisters in the large family. Bernardo, twins Alfonso, Gerardo and Mario followed him in age. In 1914, the U.S. Navy bombarded and seized Veracruz, a Mexican port city. Jorge and his friend Migel Aleman would remember the incident vividly and help the young boys develop visceral emotions towards the United States. In July 1932, Jorge married the daughter of former Mexican president Plutarco Elias Calles. The marriage helped him make political connections and benefited the customs brokerage. Shortly after, the marriage would dissipate but Jorge would benefit greatly from the nuptial arrangement. By 1940, the Pasquel family fortune was estimated at $60 million.

Jorge bought the controlling interest to the Veracruz Blues of the Mexican League by 1940 and later the Mexican City Reds. He was majority owner of Mexico City's Delta Park. This provided him with control over the league since most of the teams wanted to play there. Pasquel's influence is best illustrated by the example of black players Quincy Trouppe and Theolic Smith. Both sought a draft exemption to play ball in Mexico but were turned down by American officials. Pasquel successfully arranged to send 80,000 war laborers to the U.S. in return for their services.[9] Tensions between the Latin American countries and organized ball were particularly prevalent by the 1940s. Clark Griffith had assigned scouts, most notably Joe Cambria, to go to Cuba and sign players for his Senators. He also signed Mexicans. The players were encouraged to jump contracts and their respective clubs were not compensated. Yet when Rickey had signed Robinson, Griffith insisted that he compensate the Kansas City Monarchs which had Jackie under contract. In 1944, Rogers Hornsby, who was unable to find work in the U.S., managed in the Mexican League. That same year Jorge toured U.S. parks spending $285,000.

During the winter of 1945 Jorge Pasquel accidentally became acquainted with Danny Gardella at Roon's Gymnasium in New York. Gardella was a successful wartime player. He could hit but defensively there was much to be desired as he ran circles around routine flys trying to catch them. Dan Parker wrote, "the more casual fans hoped that Danny wouldn't drop the ball, while connoisseurs prayed that he wouldn't get killed."[10] Danny was a prankster who was tolerated by the Giants during the war, but that ended when the veterans returned. He ate dandelions in the outfield to entertain fans, performed tightrope acts on Pullman cars and had once scared Nap Reyes to death when he wrote a suicide note and stated that he had jumped out the window. During the '45 season he had injured his ankle while chasing a kid who took his cap. Jorge was shocked to learn that Gardella had to work during the off-season to get by. He realized that the 1946 spring training was the opportune time to lure players to his Mexican League. The baseball establishment would be shaken, not only by Pasquel but also by Robert Murphy, a Boston lawyer, who formed the American Baseball Guild and attempted to unionize the players.

On February 14, Gardella was kicked off the Giants. He had refused to sign his '46 contract and had arrived at spring training without money. When he walked into the team dining area, he unknowingly broke a team rule calling for players to wear a jacket and a tie. He found Eddie Brannick, the club secretary, and asked him for money. Eddie informed the late arrival that he first had to sign his contract and harsh words were subsequently exchanged. Four days later, Ott and Gardella each held separate press conferences. Danny declared that the Giants were an "autocratic aristocracy" and he could not deal with them. As far as the club selling his contract to another team, he declared "The Giants will never get any money selling Gardella."[11] Pasquel gave him the astronomical sum of $15,000 for his services. New York had offered $5,000. Gardella would stay around the

Giant camp and act as an agent for the Pasquels recruiting players such as Adrian Zabala, Maglie, George Hausmann, and Roy Zimmerman for the Mexican League.

Sal Maglie arrived at the Giants camp late because of his sojourn in the Cuban Winter League. Ott initially thought he was a holdout but on February 19, Maglie and Ray Berres called the team and informed them they would arrive as soon as they could book plane reservations. Three days later they were in camp eager to prepare for the season. Sal was in great shape just off his winter league season and was extremely optimistic when Ott greeted him with a big hello stating "We're depending on you, boy."[12] On the 23rd the paper reported that he signed his contract.

Among the returning serviceman in the Giants camp were position players Dick Bartell, Mickey Witek, Johnny Mize, Sid Gordon, and Babe Young, while Willard Marshall and Walker Cooper were due to be discharged in early April. Mize's last season before joining the Navy was 1942 when he posted a career low .305 batting average. In camp he did not look sharp. The fate of the '46 Giants would rest on veterans like Mize and everyone watched carefully if he could return. The G.I. Bill of Rights required employers to give veterans their old jobs back for at least a year unless conditions prevented their doing so. The baseball owners attempted to circumvent the rules by offering 15 days' pay at the previous salary level and a 30 day spring training trial or 15 day regular season trial. Maglie would be competing with a number of capable moundsmen for a spot on the roster: Koslo, Schumacher, Warren Sandel, Rube Fischer, Voiselle, Tom Gorman, Marv Grissom, Jack Brewer, Monte Kennedy, Harry Feldman, Mike Budnick, Mike Seaward, Frank Joyce, Bob Carpenter, Van Lingle Mungo, Warren Pickel, Ken Trinkle, and Ace Adams. This is a partial list.

The New Yorkers defeated the Boston Braves in their first exhibition game before 6,300 fans at Miami Field. Koslo, Sandel, and Brewer looked impressive. On March 1, Maglie saw some action in an intrasquad game. As training dragged on, he was used merely as a batting practice pitcher, as if this were a reoccurrence of the '42 camp. On the 3rd, the Giants and Braves fought to a 4–4 tie in seventeen innings. Maglie would have to sit patiently through four more games before he got to pitch again. While he was sitting on the bench, Pasquel found success in signing American players. Happy Chandler was forced to act and stop Pasquel's pilfering of his talent. He announced that players who reneged on their contracts or did not abide by baseball's reserve clause by jumping to Mexico would be suspended for five years unless they returned to their major league clubs by opening day. The reserve clause was a provision in the players' contract that allowed that team to sign the player for the following season. It represented a "perpetual contract" where the player was property of the club until he was sold or traded. The Cubans were shocked and feared that their homegrown players would not return to their winter league, afraid that playing with or against outlaws would kill their chances of major league glory. Those who jumped to the Mexican League were blacklisted. They were branded as "outlaws" by the press and referred to as the "Mexican jumping beans."[13] Mike Guerra, Gil Torres, Lou Klein, Dick Sisler, Fred Martin, and Maglie were warned not to play in Cuba during the winter of '45–'46. Chandler did not take action against these players at the time and had traveled to Cuba to warn the players against jumping. The great baseball war of 1946 was well under way.

In Maglie's first exhibition game against big league competition, he looked sharp as New York defeated Boston 8–3. In five innings as the starter he yielded two runs on five hits and one walk to earn the win. As late as March 20th, the New Yorkers had used fifteen pitchers in exhibition games while another half dozen had not been given the opportunity to pitch. Many of those who had pitched, like Maglie, had done so only by a limited amount. Al Lancy summed up the dire situation in the *New York Herald Tribune*, "It is an unsatisfactory situation and may lead to one or more serious errors of judgment because of insufficient knowledge regarding the ability of individual pitchers. For the time is close when some must be sent elsewhere, and those who will make up the regular staff must begin to pitch more than two or three innings."[14] Maglie was knocked around by Connie Mack's Athletics on the following day as New York lost 11–7. He took the loss allowing six runs in the eighth inning on three hits and four walks. He also balked.

Towards the end of March, Jorge Pasquel persuaded Vern Stephens, the St. Louis Browns' star shortstop, to head south of the border. He agreed to a five-year contract for the astronomical sum of $175,000.[15] Vern was immediately dispatched to Mexico, where Pasquel treated him like royalty. Everything was done for him. The defection had sent shockwaves through organized baseball. This was not a fringe player such as Luis Olmo and Gardella that Pasquel had signed but a young wartime star who had excelled at his craft. Pasquel's coup frightened the baseball owners and intensified the war.

Against Philadelphia on March 30, Maglie redeemed himself to win his second game of the spring. Little did he know that it would be the last game he would pitch as a Giant for nearly four years. Despite his good work Maglie recalled, "Ott just ignored me."[16] The word was out that Pasquel was paying ridiculous sums of money for marginal players. Most major leaguers earned more money then the average American worker, but not much more, as their salaries were modest. The demises of great players like Jimmie Foxx who retired broke despite a great career were well known by people close to the game. This situation was much too frequent with ex-big leaguers. Salaries for the big stars like Ted Williams, and Joe DiMaggio were large and heavily publicized in the press to give the impression that this was the norm to an unknowing public.

George Hausmann and Roy Zimmerman were not getting much of a look during camp. Buddy Blattner, Mickey Witek and other returning servicemen were garnering more attention. They had heard that Maglie had received an offer from Pasquel. The two ballplayers asked Sal how they could get in touch with the Pasquels. Maglie had remembered the card Bernardo had given him in Cuba, which was currently located in his hotel room. In the evening they fished out the card and Sal offered the players the opportunity to call from his phone when they asked. Hausmann and Zimmerman were signed up right away as they accepted offers. Maglie again asked for double his salary before hanging up. Pasquel did not budge on the proposed terms. Sal shook hands with Hausmann and Zimmerman and wished them luck in Mexico. Maglie had just walked into the center of a storm and did not know it. He recalls, "That's what fucked me up with Stoneham and Ott. I suppose the switchboard operator told somebody about the call, and since it came from my room the club figured it was me who made it. You know how word gets around a ball club."[17]

When Hausmann and Zimmerman left Sal's room he called his wife in Niagara Falls. He told her what transpired that night and asked what he should do if Bernardo met his terms. Sal was anxious, knowing fully that fifteen thousand dollars was a lot of money, particularly with the cheap living expenses in Mexico. He would turn 29 years old in April and only had a few more years before his arm would give out. Maglie and his wife finally concluded that if Bernardo met his terms he would bolt.

The following day you could have heard a pin drop in the Giants clubhouse. Something was wrong. Mel Ott had received word concerning the phone call in Maglie's room and acted immediately. Sal was summoned to the skipper's office and was asked if he was working as an agent for the Pasquels. This was something which Danny Gardella was actually doing. Ott berated his pitcher with a verbal tirade and accused him of stealing his players. Maglie attempted to explain himself but was not given the opportunity. The normally amiable Ott, the "Gentle Giant," was livid and called Maglie a double-crosser. Maglie was now hot himself, and when Ott asked who the other jumpers were, Sal suggested he find out for himself.

The manager stormed out of his office and lined up his players asking each one if they were jumping. Sal was disturbed and upset by the lack of preparation he had received during camp and now he was upset that Ott chewed him out. Maglie was indeed going to Mexico. As the tension mounted in the clubhouse, Bill Voiselle, who had difficulty hearing, sang a popular song of the day, "South of the Border, Down Mexico Way." He was unaware of the events that were transpiring in the clubhouse. A teammate rushed in and told Voiselle to cut it out.[18] Maglie traveled to Mexico City by train when he could not book plane reservations. Pasquel paid his fare. He succeeded in getting his salary doubled by Pasquel and also received a bonus.

The newspaper accounts the following day were particularly sympathetic to the Giants ownership. Maglie was one of the players who reneged on a signed contract; others had merely jumped the reserve clause (a club's option to sign a player for the following season). *The Sporting News* articles served as a voice for the plight of organized baseball. Jumpers ridiculed their former teams, while owners minimized the importance of such players and suggested they were un–American for jumping the entity of organized ball. They were branded as "outlaws," and blacklisted from organized ball. Stoneham took offense when his former players stated that he reneged on bonuses after the '45 season. He denied the other accusations as well. Maglie insisted that a number of Giants had signed their contracts for a minuscule $2,500. *The Sporting News* contended that Maglie believed a minimum salary of $10,000 should be in effect for big league players. Stoneham discussed previous attempts at unionization in his propagandist manner: "Then some of them [the players] who were a little better than the others, wondered if it wouldn't level off all the salaries so that all the first baseman would be making so much and all the catchers would be making so much. The better players decided baseball was an unusual business and so they rebelled against the idea and broke it up."[19] Mel Ott's headaches did not end with the jumpers; during batting practice before a game on April 9 he was beaned by young right-hander Mike Budnick and spent the night in the hospital.

In the end Jorge Pasquel proved relatively successful in drawing big leaguers to Mexico. The Giants were the hardest hit. Besides Maglie, they lost Adrian Zabala, Nap Reyes, Hausmann, Zimmerman, Gardella, Ace Adams, Harry Feldman, along with lesser-known commodities such as Tom Gorman, Charlie Mead, and Andres Fleitas. Gorman's salary with New York called for $2,500. His last club was with Clinton in the Three I League. Pasquel offered him an $8,000 bonus and $12,000 for three years of service.[20] The Giants had let him go early in the spring and he hooked up with Billy Southworth's Boston Braves. Southworth was dumbfounded by Pasquel's offer and helped Gorman out of his contract with the club. The St. Louis Cardinals were also hit hard, losing Lou Klein, Max Lanier, and Fred Martin. The Dodgers lost Mickey Owen and Luis Olmo. Vern Stephens, Pasquel's big catch, eventually came back to the Browns by opening day. Owen had wanted to return but missed the deadline. Pasquel did not land a megastar such as Bob Feller, Ted Williams, Stan Musial, Terry Moore, Joe DiMaggio, or Pete Reiser but he tried. An absurd sum of $500,000 was reportedly offered to Feller and Williams. Hank Greenberg was offered $360,000 for three years of work.[21]

The characters that Maglie caroused with in Mexico would have made that great baseball fan Ernest Hemingway proud. When the Dodgers were training in Cuba for a couple of games in '42 Hugh Casey engaged in a boxing match with the writer. Casey got the best of him but Hemingway wanted more suggesting they duel in the mourning. Pistols, knives or swords, Casey was to pick the weapon. Hugh's teammates got him out of there before the bloodshed began.[22] In the eight-team Mexican circuit, the best players were assigned to Pasquel's Veracruz Blues and the Mexico City Reds. Games were played on Thursday, Saturday, and Sunday. Ninety-eight for each club. Maglie's low standing was represented by the fact that he was assigned to Puebla, a small city 7,000 feet up into the Sierra Madre. It was one hundred miles from Mexico City. Dolf Luque would be his manager in Puebla. Sal's wife flew down to live with her husband. The Pueblans treated Maglie like a king, and he became a local celebrity during his time there. Pasquel paid the expenses such as rent for a furnished apartment. The Pueblans were rabid baseball fans who incessantly attempted to shake Maglie's hand as if he were the best baseball player who ever walked the earth.

Castor Montono, a banker and Chevrolet dealer, was the owner of the Puebla Parrots. He quickly told Pasquel that he could not afford any more Americans on his team. Counting Maglie's lucrative salary, his payroll had already reached $80,000. This was approximately the revenue he would generate for the season. He would try to cut expenses the best he could, but he stated that there was no chance for his club to become profitable. It was reported that attendance receipts were pooled and apportioned equally among the teams after 45 percent had been taken out for the reserve fund. In addition, the exorbitant salaries that Americans garnered brought about dissension among Mexican players. Mexicans were not paid nearly as much as the foreigners. The American blacks enjoyed their situation especially because they were treated as equals in Mexico unlike the discrimination they faced in the United States and to a certain extent in Cuba.

Baseball was a carnival in the Mexican circuit. Delta Park was the only respectable facility, seating 23,000. The remaining parks were in atrocious condition. All the infields were skin with no grass infields in the league. Balls moved quickly which put a premium on fast infielders. The outfield ground was as hard as a brick due to the Mexican clay underneath the surface, which baked in the heat. The park in Tampico had a railroad track going through the outfield. Games were temporarily halted to let the trains through. One American reporter expected to see the following bulletin, "Game called end of 8th. Slow freight."[23] Maglie's team actually lost a game in Tampico when a scorching liner ricocheted off one of the rails and sailed over the outfielder's head.[24] Games were chaotic. Gambling was rampant throughout the park, as one reporter described it, "Betting is illegal, plentiful but unorganized," adding "Gamblers shout their odds on a pitch or an inning."[25] Home run celebrations delayed games. Routine plays were celebrated with fireworks, as a lucky customer may have won money on a mere strike. Fans crawled over each other to get to their seats since aisles were nonexistent. Vendors sold their goods outside the parks, including a variety of Mexican foods which U.S. players were best advised to avoid. Riots were frequent occurrences at the parks. Jorge manipulated the rosters to his benefit and ruled the league as the ultimate dictator. He always carried a pistol. Tom Gorman had witnessed Jorge's brother Bernardo kill a guy one night. When Gardella arrived in Mexico he spotted a pistol in Jorge's office. He picked it up and fired. "I wanted to see if it worked."[26] It did. Pasquel would overrule umpires, official scorers, and when he fired his manager, Mickey Owen, he went down to the field and managed himself.

The Americans were not accustomed to the Mexican food. Restaurants were excellent in the big cities but food in the countryside was suspect. Maglie found a solution to his problem. Kay would shop at the market and cook their meals at home. The other players weren't as lucky to have a spouse with them. The ballplayers did not speak Spanish and really did not need to. The umpires spoke English and the game of baseball was a known language in Mexico. Nonetheless Maglie did pick up a little Spanish which also helped him adjust. Travel was a nightmare. Teams usually traveled by buses over dangerous terrain. Some players shared seats with goats and other livestock. Maglie decided he could no longer endure the soul searching bus rides and traveled by plane. It is estimated that he spent $1,500 in two years on airplane travel. Maglie recalls, "What the hell, in those days the planes were safer than the buses."[27] The favorite expression of bus riders in Mexico was "people always get on, but nobody gets off."[28] Sal states, "The buses were driven by madmen. They used to push those old wrecks as hard as they could on the narrow, winding roads in the mountains."[29] When American sportswriters visited Mexico, they had much to lampoon in their papers back home.

With Puebla, Maglie began the season auspiciously, breezing to a 9–0 victory. He struggled thereafter and by late May his record stood at 3–3. Dolf Luque stepped in and gave Maglie a lesson in climatic conditions. The ball was flying in the Mexican highlands. In Mexico City, Bobby Estalella hit a home run that traveled an estimated 500 feet off Maglie. Puebla and Mexico City were at 7,000 feet above sea level, while Veracruz and Tampico were located down on the coast. One day Maglie would pitch in sweltering 110-degree heat on the Mexican plains and the next game work in the rarefied mountain air. Tampico was right on the Gulf of Mexico where it got unbearably hot and humid. Maglie recalls his time there: "We stayed in a hotel that must have been a warehouse. I'd get so tired there I'd walk seven or eight in a game."[30] His curve would drop off the table in Tampico. In Puebla it would hang. When throwing a curveball to the plate it meets a natural resistance of air that causes it to swerve erratically in flight. In the mountains there was not enough air resistance to act on a spinning ball. Luque advised Maglie on how it should be used. He shortened up on it and threw it like a slider in the mountains. Instead of getting it to break on the inside corner forcing the batter to back away, he broke the curve over the outside edge. The inside curve would hang over the inner portion of the plate or in the middle and get hammered in Puebla. Luque advised him to throw fastballs more often. Maglie also realized he could get three different curves depending on his release point: an inshoot, outshoot, and a curve that breaks across the plate. He threw from three different arm slots, which kept the batters off balance. The batter had to contend with an overhand, sidearm and underhand arm slot. The other curveball pitchers in the circuit complained about the rarefied air and the hanging hammer. Maglie no longer did, and realized that the atmospheric pressures could be to his benefit if utilized appropriately. As for Estalella's homer, a batted ball travels further in the mountains because of the lesser air resistance.

On September 26, he won his twentieth game defeating Veracruz 8–1. When he defeated clubs like Veracruz and Mexico City the fans would put him on their shoulders and carry him out of the park. Many American players performed poorly throughout the year, leaving them bitter from the Mexican experience. Despite the fact that Pasquel's teams stockpiled the best players they failed to finish in first place. Mexico City finished second, while Veracruz finished a disappointing seventh place out of eight teams. Puebla finished the year in third place as Maglie compiled a 20–12 record with a 3.19 ERA.

The season was certainly not lacking excitement. Luque possessed a temperamental personality. While pitching for the Cincinnati Reds he dropped his glove in the middle of an inning and charged after Giant heckler Bill Cunningham who disparaged his Latin background. Luque swung at the bench jockey and missed but nailed Casey Stengel squarely in the jaw.[31] In Mexico he carried around a .22 calibre pistol. Maglie was sitting next to one of his fellow pitchers one day when Luque took out his pistol and fired between the man's legs to get his attention.[32] He ran a strict team, and even implemented a curfew. Sal noted "Luque was all business and worked me constantly."[33] On another occasion, Roberto Ortiz hit a homer off Sal and laughed mockingly around the bases. Maglie made him eat the baseball whenever they faced him again. Hitters around the league took exception to Maglie's duster. Against former teammates he could be accommodating. George Hausmann and Maglie were friends and would often get together with their wives. Hausmann contends that Sal took it easy on him when he came up to bat.

Jorge and the baseball establishment were at war with each other throughout the summer. The New York Yankees, the Brooklyn Dodgers, and the New York Giants took Pasquel to court hoping to stop his raids through a court injunction. The Mexican magnate had threatened to build larger ballparks but it never happened. His dream of bringing Mexican baseball to the same level as the major leagues never materialized. Mexicans and Cubans had viewed the sanctimonious posturing of baseball officials as hypocritical. Wasn't it Clark Griffith who succeeded in getting National League players to jump their contracts when he helped form the American League? His scouts later were able to cajole Cubans and Mexicans to jump their contracts and come to the Senators. Branch Rickey and other owners refused to compensate Negro League owners for the players they signed in the following years. When Rickey had lost Olmo he called the Mexican circuit "illegal."[34] It was grossly inferior, but not illegal. He had strong beliefs in the values this country should espouse and would often give his "Americanism" lecture to players so they would submit to his position.[35] Jumpers were made to look un–American. Pasquel's Mexican League was attacked by the entire machinery of organized baseball and conjured up similarities with the old Players' League of 1890, which was saddled with the nickname Bolshevik League. The Mexicans railed at organized ball calling it an unfair monopoly. Pasquel stated, "When our league was struggling to get started, major league scouts came down here and stole our players. Why? Because they offered them more money. We're giving those people a dose of their own medicine."[36] The Mexican League along with Murphy's union was a direct threat to organized baseball's monopolistic power and the moguls reacted as such. They even brought their disputes into the courts, which Judge Landis had avoided during his reign. The owners survived the threats of 1946 but had to make small concessions to the players. A 5,000 dollar minimum salary, meal money and a weekly stipend during spring training were among them.

Nationalism had been one of Jorge's primary motivations in upgrading his league and luring Americans to jump contracts. The other reason may have been the presidential campaign of childhood friend Miguel Aleman. Aleman won his election on July 7, 1946, with Jorge's help. Max Lanier recalled, "Now the people of Mexico loved baseball. It was worked out so Aleman got credit for us coming down there. They figured he'd get some votes out of it…. After the election Pasquel started cutting everybody. He cut me from $20,000 a year to $10,000. That's when we started jumping back to the States."[37]

Mexican League players headed for the Cuban Winter League for the 1946-47 season. A mini war in Cuba was the ancillary effect of the Mexican League fiasco. Players who would play against ineligibles or outlaws would be banned or fined from major league baseball. This meant that Cuban players in the majors could not play in their winter league because they would compete against outlaws and be blacklisted. Mike Gonzalez, the renowned star in the Cuban circuit and owner of the Havana team, had to make a tough choice. He was a coach with the St. Louis Cardinals and shortly after they defeated the Boston Red Sox in the World Series he resigned.

A new league called the Liga de la Federacion (National Federation) was established to compete with the traditional Cuban Winter League circuit. Players in new league would be free of connections from the Mexican League and other outlaws. Initially the three teams included Havana (the English version of the name was used to avoid legal problems with the Habana team in the traditional circuit), Oriente, and Matanzas. Later on, Camaguey joined up. A few players who had played with an "outlaw" circuit managed to sneak into the National Federation. The teams played in the older park, La Tropical. The surrounding area was known for "old Cuban money."[38] The park had been built by Don Julio Blanco Herrera in 1930 to host the Central American games.

The traditional Cuban Winter League had a new park, called Gran Stadium, for the 1946-47 season. All four clubs played there, even the Elefantes of Cienfuegos. Cienfuegos was located on the southern coast of Cuba; it was a beautiful city known as "The Pearl of the South."[39] The stadium had a roofed grandstand that stretched all the way down both foul lines. Dimensions were spacious: 340 feet down the lines, 375 in the power alley, and 450 feet to dead center. The scoreboard contained an advertisement for Hatuey Beer. Cuban baseball also had a carnival atmosphere. It was a place for celebrities to be seen. When the contest concluded many fans would go to nightclubs like the Tropicana. People dressed nicely, particularly women because the league took place during the winter.

Maglie once again pitched for Cienfuegos but this time Luque was not the manager. He would skipper the Almendares ball club while Martin Dihigo, who is enshrined in three baseball Hall of Fames, managed Cienfuegos. Other notable players on the squad included Silvio Garcia (a brilliant Cuban shortstop), Roy Zimmerman, Danny Gardella, Napoleon Reyes, and Rafael Noble who would later play for the New York Giants. On the hill were Luis Tiant, Dihigo, Zabala, Alejandro Carrasquel (who played for Griffith's Senators) and Max Manning (a star pitcher for the Newark Eagles). Cienfuegos began the year slowly as Almendares and Habana took the early lead.

Cubans rallied around the traditional Cuban League at the Gran Stadium, drawing big crowds, showing their displeasure with major league baseball for tinkering with their traditions. On October 26, the stadium was christened as 31,000 packed their way into the park to watch the opener. Almendares defeated Cienfuegos by a comfortable margin, 9–1. The following day packed 37,000 fans into the stadium to watch Mike Gonzalez's Habana Lions take on Luque's Almendares ballclub. The pennant race came down to Almendares and Habana. On February 25, 1947, Max Lanier pitched Almendares to a victory over Habana in one of the most memorable games in Cuban baseball history. Cuba's national director of sports called major league baseball a "commercial, imperialistic monopoly."[40] He threatened to form a Latin American Federation to combat the American monopoly. After the 1946-47 season the structure of the Cuban League would change dramatically.

The Mexican League was drastically different in 1947. Most Americans had regretted jumping although they were paid well. They had very few options except to return to Mexico. When the rosters were first released on March 20 most Americans were not listed: Lanier, Klein, Martin, Gardella, Zimmerman, Adams, Feldman, Hausmann, Murray Franklin, and Chico Hernandez. The big leaguers on the rosters included Carrasquel, Olmo, Reyes, Estalella, Maglie, and Hayworth. Only six teams would begin the season because of the financial loses incurred during the '46 season: Veracruz, Mexico City, Monterrey, Tampico, Torreon, and Puebla. Before the '47 season began Jorge called a meeting with the U.S. players and admitted he had lost an exorbitant amount of money. He declared that '47 salaries were to be cut in half and expenses no longer be paid. The string had been cut.

Max Lanier tried to find work in the U.S. but was unsuccessful. Mickey Owen and Gardella played for semi-pro clubs but ran into trouble when several opposing players and teams refused to play against the outlaws fearing they would be blacklisted. Lanier remarked, "Financially, I have no regrets," adding "but I miss the major league life now, and I'd give anything to be back." Ace Adams was living it up on his 650-acre farm in Georgia. He had earned three times his Giant salary in Mexico. He was happy not to return in '47 and stated "being on the black list is sorta like being a criminal."[41] Maglie would later tell reporters that he had no regrets in jumping to Mexico. He was paid all the money that was coming to him, unlike some other players, and used it to purchase a house. Most of all he had learned how to pitch under the keen eye of Dolf Luque. Years later Sal would say that pitching for Luque was the "best thing that ever happened to me."[42] In high altitudes he showed his curve and made them hit the fastball. At sea level, in places like Tampico, the curve broke wickedly. The experience hardened Maglie mentally and physically. He played in the savage heat on terrible fields in rickety ballparks in front of wild fans with hazardous travel conditions and suspect food and water. When he made it back to the big show, minor problems that would affect other ballplayers would not affect Sal. Maglie later would discuss his escapade away from big league baseball as follows: "From the start, I made up my mind that I would do just one thing and that was to learn all I could about the art of pitching. I honestly didn't think we'd ever get a chance to return to the big leagues, but I was determined that if the door ever swung open and the chance did come, I wasn't going to muff it."[43] When the Cuban winter league had finished, Maglie returned to Niagara Falls where he broke his hand when he fell during a basketball game. He played the sport to stay sharp during the off-season. The activity was particularly effective in keeping his legs strong. When he reported to his Mexican League team, Luque told Sal that Pasquel would not pay him until he started pitching. He promptly unwrapped his hand and declared that he would pitch with three fingers. On April 17, 30,000 fans attended the first night game at Delta Park. San Luis defeated Mexico City, 10–7. They stirred in semi-darkness because the electric company only allowed 50 percent of the required power. On that same day, Puebla defeated Monterrey by a 3–0 score as Maglie tossed a one-hitter. He walked four and struck out five while allowing only a second inning single to Carlos Blanco. By April 21, Puebla was in fifth place with a 5–11 record and continued to struggle as the season progressed. They slowly began to turn things around behind Maglie's pitching and after the tenth week they were in third place at 20–19.

Veracruz received a boost when Max Lanier ended his holdout and declared he would come south on June 5. Puebla began to get strong pitching from Adrian Zabala, Sandalio Consuegra, and Maglie as they took three of four from San Luis. Afterwards, "Luque formally solemnized his previous civil wedding at Santiago Parish in Puebla," according to the *Sporting News*.[44] By the twelfth week, little Luis Olmo was leading the circuit in homers. Maglie tossed a six-hit shutout over the Mexican City Reds. Nap Reyes was hitting well for Luque's fourth place club and they were only two and a half games back. Luque was later afflicted with a "bilious" attack and replaced by Santos Amaro as skipper. The team was hindered by poor weather as a four game set between Puebla and San Luis Posto was cut short. Maglie improved to 14–9 winning the opening game. He scattered seven hits as his club won by a comfortable 18–1 margin. Zabala won the second game. His record was also 14–9. In the middle of September, Puebla took three of four from fifth place Veracruz. Maglie, Agapito Mayor, and Consuegra were the winners. It was Sal's eighteenth victory in the 6–1 win. Monterrey had virtually secured first place by taking four games from Puebla at the end of the month. Maglie lost a heartbreaking 2–1 contest in the opener. He pitched courageously in the fourteen-inning affair allowing nine hits while getting two hits at the plate with a run scored. Puebla finished the season with a 63–56 record, in third place. Maglie won twenty games for the second straight year, 20–13, 3.92 ERA. Zabala recorded a 19–14 mark with a 3.40 ERA and Consuegra was 10–10, 3.36 ERA. Bobby Avila led the team with a .346 batting average to win the league title.

Cuban baseball was turned upside down for the 1947-48 season. The Cuban Winter League at Gran Stadium prospered during the previous season and afterwards the baseball moguls moved in to control the Latin American market. On June 10, 1947, the Cuban League signed a pact with the National Association of Professional Baseball Leagues. This entity regulated the minor leagues in organized baseball. Cuban ownership realized that their best young talent was already connected to big league teams. Their players could not play in their own league during the winter of '46-'47 because the threat of an organized baseball blacklist. The Cubans cut a deal with the American baseball establishment. They gave up a great degree of control but were now under the umbrella of organized ball. Their best players could play in the league without penalty. In '46-'47 the league had worked closely with Pasquel's Mexican circuit but now the situation was reversed.

The ineligible players formed a new league called the Liga Nacional to follow in the tradition of the Liga de la Federacion. They played in La

Tropical. It was a four-team league consisting of the Alacranes or Scorpions, the Leones or Lions, Santiago and a team called Cuba. Luque managed the Scorpions who had most of the traditional Almendares players. The league had the most famous Cuban players who had built their reputation at La Tropical. The Leones took the championship. Roland Gladu won the batting championship at .330. Gardella hit the most homers. Maglie put together another great year. He led the circuit with fourteen victories and twenty complete games. The sponsors of the clubs pulled back their invested money when they realized that the league was losing the battle with the Gran Stadium league. Players did not receive their last paychecks.

Pasquel had lost the baseball war and a fortune in his misguided attempt to make the Mexican league like the majors. Before the 1948 season began he told the Americans that their salary would be cut to a minimum of $1,000 a month. His league would be down to four teams by July 1948 and eventually collapsed on September 19. In late October Jorge resigned as president. It is estimated that he lost $362,000 in three seasons.[45]

The American players who had jumped to Mexico hit rock bottom. Some of them wanted to go home and simply wait until the five-year ban was lifted. Others had agreed to form a barnstorming team that would tour the United States playing against semipro and Negro League teams. The barnstorming team was named the Max Lanier All Stars. Maglie agreed to Lanier's plan. He was getting old, needed the money and had no other viable options. About fourteen players chipped in to purchase a bus and the requisite equipment. The roster included Harry Feldman, Hayworth, Red Steiner, Zimmerman, Klein, Gardella, Homer Gibson and for a short period of time George Hausmann. The good news was the team won all 81 games it played. The bad news was they were unable to use any of organized baseball's parks. The better teams and players were unwilling to play against the barnstorming contingent fearing they would be punished by Commissioner Chandler. Competition was weak. Maglie and Lanier would pitch one day and play the outfield the next. The venture was a financial disaster and the barnstorming tour ended in Madison, Wisconsin. Lanier lost $8,000; Maglie lost approximately $2,000. The outlaws were out of options as their entrepreneurial plan ended in failure. Maglie was thirty-one years old and had no place to go but home.

If there was any consolation for Maglie in the lowest part of his life, it was that his former employers the New York Giants had gone south after he left in 1946. They finished in last place that year and the rotation lacked a quality starter. They followed with a fourth place finish and had two years in fifth place. When Leo Durocher, the hated Dodger, became manager of the New York Giants in mid-season 1948 loyalties were challenged. It would take a long time before Leo was fully accepted in Harlem.

While Maglie gloomily proceeded with his life back in Niagara Falls, he opened a gas station at 56th and Pine. He pumped gas most of the time and hated it. Maglie lost interest in life and wandered around like a lost soul. He had earned his money in Mexico but at a great price. A successful major league career was virtually lost. The jumpers were blacklisted not for being communists as others would be during the '50s, but merely because they had failed to play by organized baseball's rules. Maglie would roam his house, pacing back and forth thinking. Always thinking. His wife Kay could only watch and pray. Sal would rise before dawn and travel to the gas station and return around eight or ten o'clock at night. The cold weather stiffened his back and shoulders as he became inured to the shooting pains in his joints. He worked the grease pits on cold floors, fixing cars. Maglie was at the nadir of his life and needed an opportunity. He needed to be saved.

His first break came in the spring of 1949 when he was asked to come to Drummondville to pitch in the Quebec Provincial League. It was an outlaw circuit like the Mexican League. Sal was ecstatic when he told his wife the news. A couple more months in the grease pits would have stiffened his muscles to the point where he could no longer pitch. Now he could pitch until the ban was lifted in 1951 and maybe get an opportunity afterwards. He sold the gas station, content on earning $600 a month in Canada. To prepare for the season he took whirlpool baths and warmed his arm under lamps.

Some good black players and many Americans who had jumped to Mexico found their way to Canada. Alfred Molini, the owner of the Drummondville squad and president of the league, had already signed jumpers Max Lanier and Danny Gardella. Later he added Maglie, former big leaguer Tex Shirley, Negro League star Quincy Trouppe, a young Vic Power, and Roy Zimmerman. Molini recognized that by signing big leaguers the gate would increase. During World War II, Americans needed a diversion, a form of recreation, and they turned to baseball. Now Quebec needed the diversion as they were embroiled in political and social unrest when 5,000 asbestos industry miners went on strike.[46] Maglie joined Drummondville in May and won his first game.

In 1947, Danny Gardella through his attorney Frederic Johnson had filed a lawsuit against major league baseball for suspending him. Intrinsically this was a direct challenge to major league baseball's reserve clause. Gardella called it illegal and unconstitutional. He purported that the recent rise of televised games across state lines had brought baseball into interstate commerce. His argument added that baseball should be subject to antitrust laws, from which an earlier court decision had exempted it. Gardella also stated that the reserve clause allowed baseball to operate in a monopolistic way and therefore should be invalidated. As the Gardella suit proceeded, Max Lanier and Fred Martin also pursued a lawsuit against organized baseball for 2.5 million dollars. Their attorney John L. Flynn later filed a million dollar damage suit against organized baseball on behalf of Sal Maglie. The Southern Federal District Court initially dismissed Gardella's case. He then took his grievance elsewhere. The Second Circuit Appellate Federal Court in New York ruled on February 11, 1949, that the case merited a trial. It was set to commence in November 1949. The baseball moguls were nervous. To rail against the validity of the reserve clause may have been the worst sin a player could ever do in the eyes of the baseball establishment. A year before Joe McCarthy made his famous speech in West Virginia, Branch Rickey asserted that people who opposed the reserve clause had "avowed Communistic tendencies."[47] Commissioner Chandler was forced to react, for a trial could bring down the entrenched system that benefited the owners at the expense of the players. It was time to compromise. On June 5, he lifted the ban on the players who had jumped to the Mexican League about a year and a half before it was set to expire. Maglie received the good news in the fifth inning of a game. Later while still in uniform, Gardella put his hand around Sal and Lanier joined in as they read about the news.

Maglie called his wife to tell her the good news. She listened patiently with tears in her eyes. Although overjoyed, Maglie was smart as he pondered his next move. He had recently joined up with the Drummondville team where the cold weather was making it hard for him to loosen up. He was not at peak form. Horace Stoneham still bore a grudge against him believing he had acted as an agent for the Pasquels, stealing his players. The Giants would give him a short look, only because they had to, and banish him to the minor leagues and implement part two of the blacklist. The jumpers were certainly not wanted back. For they had wreaked havoc on the system. Maglie would have one chance to stick in the big leagues and he wanted to make it count. When the Giants called the next night, Sal told them that he was not in shape and would simply cost them money for wearing out the pine. The Giants saw his point of view and would wait for his return at a later date. Molini gave Sal a $15,000 bonus to finish out the season in Canada. The President's intentions were later made clear, as he hoped to earn the money back through gambling and fixing games.[48]

Most of the jumpers went directly back to their respective big league clubs. Lou Klein pinch-hit for the Cardinals two days after being reinstated but batted only .219 in 58 games. Adrian Zabala, Harry Feldman, and Fred Martin had left the Sherbrooke squad together. Max Lanier had been manager of Drummondville but he also left for the Cardinals taking his 8–1 mound record. Except for Lanier and Martin most of the players proved ineffective down the stretch with their big league clubs. Those who did not rush back included Maglie, Zimmerman, Reyes, Olmo, and Gardella. Zimmerman and Gardella also received bonuses from Molini. Those who had expedited their return to the show regretted it. At least most of them had, like George Hausmann. The jumpers received one opportunity to stick as Maglie predicted, and when Hausmann failed to perform he was sent to the minors never to return.

After the games of June 19, Maglie sported an 11–2 record while Lanier was still with the club at 7–1. At this point Lanier was holding out for double his 1945 salary. When St. Louis capitulated he immediately left Drummondville. Maglie's team was gliding to a playoff spot as they paced the league at 24–7, seven and a half games ahead of second place Farnham. On August 7, Maglie pitched a 4–3 victory over second place Granby. He allowed only six hits. A few weeks later Drummondville assured themselves of first place when they picked up Tex Shirley who had been released by the Granby Red Sox despite a 11–3 record. Manager Stan Beard, who had taken over for Lanier, led the club to a first place showing down the stretch. They finished eight games ahead of second place Granby. The starting pitching was led by Maglie, Shirley and Joe Tuminelli. Maglie claims to have won 23 games during the regular season but records show only fifteen. Vic Power paced the offense with a .341 average. Drummondville dispatched of last place St. Hyacinthe in the first round although the series went the distance. They played nine games, winning five. Sal was showered with gifts and money after winning the clincher in front of the home fans. Drummondville played Farnham for the championship and again found themselves the overwhelming favorite. They repeated their earlier performance, squeaking out five games as the series went the distance. Maglie won three games in the playoff including the 5–1 clincher to win the championship. If it appeared strange that a powerhouse like Drummondville would go to the final game of a series against inferior competition on two different occasions, there was a reason. The fix was in, as gambling served as the impetus behind their performance. Contines Tarte of Farnham stated, "We think they gave us a break so that the final game would be held in Drummondville." In both playoff series Molini got a full gate and reports circulated that $20,000 had been wagered on the final game.[49] It was the Black Sox scandal on a smaller scale with success. His teams brought in the money by going the distance, games were manipulated so gamblers made their share and when they needed to close out the series their best hurler Sal Maglie did the job. If others threw games, Maglie certainly did not. His performance was excellent throughout. His exile from major league baseball ended under suspicious circumstances.

BACK WITH THE GIANTS

The Giants' organization had changed dramatically from Maglie's first year in the big leagues. Mel Ott had failed to bring home a pennant during his tenure as manager. He led a power-laden, slow footed lineup year in and year out which had managed to break the major league record for homers in 1947 when they belted 221. Ott had been the epitome of the organization as a player but as a manager he had not fulfilled expectations. Horace Stoneham had seen enough losing in the famed ballpark. In 1948, he asked Branch Rickey for permission to talk to Burt Shotton with the intention of making Shotton the Giants manager. He had been the field general of the Philadelphia Phillies (1928–33), the Cincinnati Reds (1934), and had managed the Dodgers in 1947 when Durocher was suspended from baseball for a year. Leo hung around with high stakes gamblers. He upset the Catholic Youth organization until they were ready to boycott games as he flaunted his loose life style. In 1945 he beat a recently discharged war veteran to a pulp with the help of a security guard. These things propelled Commissioner Chandler to suspend him for actions "detrimental to baseball." Chandler stated that "Durocher has not measured up to the standards expected or required of managers of our baseball teams."[1] It was nice to know that the grand old game now had standards. In retrospect the action seemed arbitrary. Even for Durocher the punishment was probably not justified for one of the incidents that got him into hot water involved gamblers that were actually in Larry MacPhail's suite during a game. Nonetheless Rickey wanted to get rid of him. He had been backing him up his entire career beginning with the Cardinals but not anymore. In the traditional Rickey style he offered Stoneham his choice between Durocher and Shotton knowing full well that Stoneham would jump for Durocher. Rickey made it appear as if he really wanted to keep Leo. Fortunately for him it did not backfire. On July 15, 1948, the announcement sent shockwaves around baseball. Leo Durocher was now the manager of the New York National League Giants.

The Giants had a record of 41–38 under the leadership of Durocher in 1948. Earlier in the season under Ott they compiled a 37–38 record. Durocher wanted to assemble a scrappy club in his own image but Stoneham was not receptive. The Giants were a traditional Irish-dominated organization run by the Sheehans, Schumachers, Feeneys, and Brannicks. Stoneham felt a sense of loyalty to his fellow Irishman. Shortstop Buddy Kerr and utility infielder Bill Rigney were among his favorites. Leo was handcuffed as he managed Mel Ott's slow, powerful players watching impatiently as the Giants finished in fifth place in '48. Durocher implored Stoneham to make changes. "Horace, you're throwing your money away when you pay me. A little boy can manage this team. All you do is make out the lineup and hope you get enough home runs. You can't steal, they're too slow. You can't bunt. You can't hit and run. I can't do anything. I can only sit and wait for a home run."[2] Stoneham believed that his defense was good, Leo had other thoughts. Durocher characterized Buddy Kerr who Horace loved as follows: "He didn't make errors but he didn't make plays either."[3] Leo wanted a daring, quick, intelligent, scrappy, aggressive ballclub that took many chances. He began to drink with Stoneham and implemented the strategy of playing players who Horace liked until they had failed. The Giants owner was always after Leo to drink with him and Leo obliged so he could get what he wanted. Durocher recalled, "To say that Horace can drink is like saying that Sinatra can sing."[4] Stoneham acted as his own general manager and finally gave in, agreeing that changes needed to be made. He moved quickly in dismantling his ballclub.

Johnny Mize, "The Big Cat," was a prodigious home run hitter but a defensive liability. In August 1949, he was sold to the New York Yankees for $40,000 cash. Walker Cooper had been traded to Cincinnati in June of that year for Ray Mueller. Durocher had even suggested that they dump Bobby Thomson. He was a great young ballplayer but didn't necessarily have the killer instinct, the ferocity in which Leo admired. By 1950, New York had twenty-four farm clubs resulting in a staffing problem. They looked to the Negro Leagues to fill the void and on July 5, 1949, Hank Thompson and Monte Irvin became the first two blacks to play for the Giants. When the Giants pulled off a blockbuster trade with the Boston Braves, Leo had his kind of team. Willard Marshall, Sid Gordon, Buddy Kerr, and Red Webb were sent to Boston for the middle infield combination of Alvin Dark and Eddie Stanky. Stoneham had not been a big fan of Stanky. Durocher pleaded with him to pull off the deal and he finally consented. Marshall, Gordon, and Kerr were likable ballplayers, admired by the fans. The trade was not received well as the sporting press and the fans were not enthused.

Eddie Stanky was hated around the National League. He was a rough, cruel ballplayer between the white lines who would do anything to beat you. I'd "spike my mother if it meant being safe on a close play," he remarked.[5] Eddie had limited skills but made the most of them by utilizing every advantage to gain the edge. He'd perform distracting antics in the batter's box, slide viciously into second and slap the ball out of the fielder's glove. He'd flip a handful of dirt into a shortstop's eyes as he went into the bag. Later in his career he stood in the batter's line of vision and jumped up and down to distract the hitter. Durocher had once stated "Stanky can't hit, can't run, can't throw, can't field, but he's the best second baseman in the business."[6] From 1944–46 he had played under Leo in Brooklyn and when sold to Boston before the 1948 season he thought that Durocher had concocted the deal to get rid of him. Stanky was Leo's type of player; he came to kill you. He was as tough as they came. Ironically off the field, Eddie lived life as a good Catholic and was even a role model in the community.

In 1949, Stanky had an acrimonious relationship with his manager Billy Southworth in Boston. Billy had piloted the '48 Braves to the pennant but inside he was tormented. His pride and joy, Billy Southworth, Jr., had died in 1945 when his bomber crashed into the Flushing Bay. He hit the bottle and began to show up in the clubhouse drunk as the club went south in '49.[7] This did not sit well with Stanky. Stanky and Southworth had numerous run-ins throughout the season and a Boston newspaper story had written that Eddie had usurped power and actually put on a hit-and-run play on his own. Billy left the team two-thirds into the season due to an illness and Johnny Cooney managed down the stretch. Alvin Dark also joined in the anti–Southworth clique. Dark was a deeply religious man, a former bonus baby, and a smooth shortstop who had won the Rookie of the Year award in 1948. He had mastered the execution of the hit and run play and was considered to be an ideal number two hitter. Stanky and Dark were friends off the field and shared a competitive spirit that burned deep in their inner souls. Stanky wore his emotions outwardly; Dark would mask his desire. These were the players that Durocher needed for the baseball wars to come. Leo later stated, "we had two guys who could do things with the bat, could run the bases, and who came to kill you."[8] The later point was an attribute which Durocher particularly liked.

Major league teams trained in three states as they prepared for the 1950 season: Florida, California, and Arizona. The Giants were based in Phoenix, Arizona. Sal Maglie walked cautiously into the clubhouse not knowing what kind of reception he would receive. He wanted no special favors, but merely a fair evaluation of his talent to determine if he would make the team. Sal was encouraged when Durocher saw him and said, "I'm very happy to have you. I see you want to pitch."[9] Horace Stoneham on the other hand was not forthcoming. The Mexican raids of '46 were still fresh in his mind and he thought that Sal had attempted to steal his players getting them to sign with Pasquel. Horace took Maglie back only because he had to. When the jumpers were reinstated by Commissioner Chandler in 1949, Stoneham told Durocher, "That dirty jumper's not going to be around here long," adding, "He isn't going to be getting my paychecks."[10] The odds were long for the soon to be thirty-three year old righthander. If he failed to produce right away he would wilt in the bullpen and then be banished to the bushes.

As camp opened, Leo was looking for a fifth starter. Larry Jansen, Sheldon Jones, Dave Koslo, and Monte Kennedy were assured of a spot in the rotation. The recently acquired Jack Kramer was favored to fill the void. Kramer had fallen into disfavor with Red Sox manager Joe McCarthy and took a parting shot at his old manager before coming to New York. "I was very much surprised to find out that the Red Sox had let McCarthy railroad me out of the American League."[11] Leo would have his own problems with the pitcher. To promote competition in camp Durocher declared that every position on the team was open as training commenced. Kramer's competition for the fifth spot would include Maglie, Clint Hartung (after all the accolades his career had been a major disappointment, but he did have one thing in common with Babe Ruth. He could pitch and play the field), Roger Bowman, and George Bamberger.

One of Leo's pet projects in camp was Jack Harshman. He was relying on the raw busher to be the regular first baseman in 1950. The real showstopper turned out to be little Davey Williams. Davey was ticketed for Minneapolis because of the solid middle infield combination of Stanky and Dark. On March 5, Maglie gave up a run in two innings of work during an intrasquad game. When the players were separated into an A and

B squad for exhibition games, Maglie was initially placed on the B team. This was extremely discouraging since Leo put what he considered his best nine pitchers on the A team. Sal would quickly prove that he belonged on the A team and play with the first squad.

The Giants impressed the writers with their hustle and hard work. Bobby Thomson stated, "There's an intangible something which hasn't been evident in other years."[12] The training sessions were intense and the players conditioning outstanding. Durocher was even showing some restraint during press conferences instead of reverting back to earlier form and popping off with exaggerated statements, which he had done in previous years. Freddie Fitzsimmons, a coach, was managing the first team as Leo stayed with the second squad. He compared this spirited group of Giants to the '33 team and added, "it's something you can feel. These kids just won't quit."[13] Against the Cleveland Indians on the 11th at Randolph Park before an overflow crowd of 4,459, the Giants clicked on all cylinders, winning 5–3. Jansen, Maglie, and Hartung each worked three innings. Sal kept the Indians scoreless during his stint. He did run into trouble with home plate umpire Bill Summers and was called for three balks in his first inning of work. Maglie was not hesitating in the stretch position before delivery. In Mexico, the umpires had been more lenient in enforcing the rules that allowed him to cheat ever so slightly. Even though this was an early exhibition game, Sal had the razor sharp, throwing inside to the batters and even nailing Luke Easter.

Two days later, Maglie was the winner in a 3–2 decision over the Indians. He relieved Lou Sleater in the sixth and finished out the game. Frank Shellenback, the Giants' pitching coach, told Durocher that Maglie could become a good reliever. Durocher began to realize that he might have a true find on his hand despite the protestations of Stoneham. Leo later said "I'll play an elephant if he can do the job, so why shouldn't I play a jumper?"[14]

The Giants traveled to California and on March 20 won a 9–8 contest from Pittsburgh at Perris Hill Park. Whitey Lockman hit four singles and Don Mueller drove in four runs to pace a seventeen hit attack. Thomson and Harshman broke out of minor slumps. Maglie was the only Giant pitcher who proved effective during the afternoon allowing one hit, a homer by Dan O'Connell in the ninth. Dave Koslo was hammered on the following day and his recent failure may have brought Durocher down to three quality starters. Dave showed some resilience by bouncing back on the 22nd with five strong innings to lead New York to a 6–2 win over the Pirates. Maglie followed Koslo with four scoreless innings and went two for two at the plate with a double. Leo wanted to find out if Sal could last a full nine innings and prove to be more then a reliever. The New Yorkers took a 9–6 decision from the Oakland Acorns on the 26th. Hausmann blasted a homer and Koslo worked five strong innings. The next day, the Giants concluded their California tour with a 5–3 win over St. Louis.

Back home in Phoenix, Maglie was knocked around for three runs on seven hits in five innings and took the loss in a game against the Chicago Cubs. Phil Cavarretta who had won the batting crown in 1945 with the aid of Maglie had a great game that included a single, double, and a homer off Sal. Ironically Cavarretta was being rumored to be traded to New York as Durocher sought a left-handed pinch-hitter, "A guy on the order of Don Mueller. A guy who doesn't strike out, who gets a piece of the ball all the time and can hit."[15] Maglie weathered his first rough outing of the spring as he worked with runners on base in every inning. He worked an inning against Pittsburgh on the final day of March allowing a homer to Stan Rojek. Durocher's club lost their third in a row on April 2 against Pittsburgh on a beautiful cloudless afternoon. The final score was 8–3 as 3,559 fans watched the last game at Municipal Stadium in Phoenix before the team barnstormed north. Sal again was hampered by the gopher ball as Jack Phillips went deep. He worked one and two-thirds of an inning allowing three hits and hitting a batter (Ted Beard).

New York was scheduled to play fourteen games on their barnstorming trip north going through Texas, Louisiana, Oklahoma, Kansas, Missouri, Indiana, and Ohio. The sojourn was a ritual among big league clubs as they prepared for the season. The Giants and the Indians had a strong barnstorming tradition. Writers and players would get to know each other in two or three private cars. Jack Lang recalls, "We would eat and drink, and play cards. It was before TV or movies on a train. You really got to know the ballplayers." Arthur Richman who worked for the *New York Mirror* described it as follows: "Clubs would print up their own menus.... There would be barbershop quartettes. Kenny Smith of the *Mirror* would bring along his accordion. Sometimes the train would stop at some God-knows-where waterhole and Eddie Brannick and myself would run out in the middle of the night to get some sandwiches. The dining room was closed on the train ... we'd all stay up all night, throwing the bull."[16]

As the team barnstormed north the starters began to go the distance. Jansen was the first hurler to work nine innings and he was followed by Jones. On April 7, the teams stopped in Shreveport, Louisiana, as a large contingent of 8,421 fans watched the Indians pound the Giants by a 16–12 score. Bob Feller was the winner; Kennedy took the loss allowing five runs in an inning and two-thirds. He had been blasted during the spring and had not proven to the Giants' brass that he deserved to be a starter. Maglie looked impressive as he worked the final four innings, allowing one run on two hits while fanning three. Three days later New York returned the favor as they pounded Cleveland in Tulsa, Oklahoma, 15–8. A crowd of 7,369 fans came out to watch their heroes. Fans in these cities may have been able to read about the players in the newspapers and maybe lucky enough to listen to telecasts during the regular season but the barnstorming trips were the only time they got to see the players perform in person on a green pasture. Maglie gave up three runs in three innings as the game was called at the start of the ninth so the players could catch the train. The damage could have been much worse but the Giants turned two double plays behind Sal. The crowds continued to turn out even in the cold weather. In Topeka, Kansas, 8,645 of them watched Cleveland defeat New York, 9–4. New York methodically reduced their roster; this time Bobby Hofman fell victim and was sent to Minneapolis. In Kansas City, 8,645 spectators showed up at Blues Stadium as Cleveland won 4–2 behind the fine hurling of Bob Lemon. Kramer took the loss. After the first eleven games of the tour the two clubs had already attracted 84,457 paid customers, 7,600 a game. To put this into perspective, the St. Louis Browns of the American League had once drawn fewer than 85,000 for an entire year.

Sal Maglie put together a fine spring and had earned a spot on the club. In his first nine appearances he worked 32 innings, allowing only 22 hits and 10 runs. Freddie Fitzsimmons stated that Maglie was no "mourning-glory" and noted that he may become the best Giant relief pitcher since Dolf Luque.[17] Maglie liked being compared to the man who made him a pitcher. *The Sporting News* published an article sympathetic to organized baseball's plight as they continued to rail against the Mexican League. Arch Murray wrote concerning Maglie, "Though he was probably the best-treated of all the big leaguers who fled the cloistered confines of Organized Ball for the vast gobs of crisp lettuce dangling under their noses by the plutocratic Pasquels, the lord high chieftains of the Mexican League, Maglie has always felt that he took the wrong turn in the road that March day in 1946."[18] Going to Mexico was probably not the best decision he ever made, but he did learn to pitch there and was paid well. If he did not go his career might have been drastically different, one way or the other. He accepted his decision, made the most out of it, and moved on.

Durocher settled on Larry Jansen to start the opener. Leo was impressed by the improvement of Don Mueller and Wes Westrum. Jack Harshman had been inconsistent at the plate. Leo sounded ambivalent, "Harshman will start the season there, but I don't know. I hope he can make it."[19] Another problem for Leo was Bobby Thomson's bat. Kirby Higbe, Maglie, and Andy Hansen were slated to be relievers. Their exhibition schedule concluded with two games at Cleveland's Municipal

5. Back with the Giants

Stadium. New York took the first game 9–0, but dropped the second 2–1. Maglie was the loser in the second contest, giving up a run in the ninth inning on a couple of cheap bleeders. Most of the baseball prognosticators picked Brooklyn to win the pennant. The Cardinals, Phillies, and Braves seemed poised to compete. Not much was expected from the Giants.

The curtain raiser of the 1950 campaign was played on a gloomy, gray day at the Polo Grounds. Before the contest, the old-timers discussed the opening day ritual in quixotic fashion as they broke out some of the good stories. When a reporter told Boston Braves coach Bucky Walters that he looked fit to pitch he remarked, "I'd love to," adding, "Greatest job there is. Right out there in the middle is the best place in the world. There's no life like that of a twenty-game winner. He's the American aristocracy."[20] A crowd of 32,441 spectators had congregated at the tradition filled ballpark to watch the combatants go after each other in the green pasture below Coogan's Bluff. The spectacle of opening day was played out as Major Francis W. Sutherland and his 7th Regiment band led the players out to raise the flag. The Polo Grounders cheered their heroes: Marshall, Gordon, and Kerr but now they wore the uniform of the opposition. When Eddie Stanky and Alvin Dark were announced the park echoed with the disconcerting mixture of cheers and boos. Their loyalty was tested seeing the enemy; their hated rival Eddie Stanky now donning the uniform of the black and gold. When the scoreboard showed that Philadelphia had scored seven early runs against Brooklyn the Polo Grounds erupted in excitement.

Alvin Dark, the captain of the Giants, led the squad on the field. Durocher had given him the title of captain because he knew it would make the young ballplayer develop into a leader and take on more responsibility. Jansen put the side down in order in the first, which included a strikeout of a trembling Sam Jethroe who was making his major league debut. The hurler was starting his third consecutive opening day and would have the same fate as the previous years. New York scored a run in the bottom of the first but Boston roared back with two in the third. Larry was knocked from the box in the fifth inning when Boston put up a five spot to take a 7–2 lead. Maglie relieved him, and allowed the final run of the inning. Sal was through after the inning and so were the Giants. Higbe and Hartung followed him to the mound. The final score was Boston 11, New York 4.

The worst part of the day for New York was that Marshall, Gordon, and Kerr each played a key role in the Braves' victory. Stanky was 0 for 2 with a couple of walks and Dark went 2 for 4. The arbiters were heckled throughout the contest. Lee Ballanfant behind the plate and Al Barlick at first were berated by Durocher and Boston skipper Billy Southworth on a couple of close calls. Giants fans took solace in the fact that the Philadelphia Phillies defeated the Brooklyn Dodgers by a 9–1 score before a record opening day crowd of 29,074 at Shibe Park.

Durocher was booed unceasingly the following day as Boston again defeated New York, 10–6. The baseballs seemed livelier as they flew out of parks at an accelerated pace. Once again the old Giants came back to haunt their former employers. Sid Gordon hit two homers including a grand slam. Kerr hit his second triple of the season in the expansive ballpark and Marshall drove in two.

The Brooklyn Dodgers humiliated their hated rivals by an 8–1 score to open their home schedule at Ebbets Field. Don Mueller was hitting well in the cleanup slot and contributed with two hits for New York. After Koslo was knocked out of the box, Maglie had another unsuccessful relief appearance. He worked two innings giving up two runs on three hits and two walks. Jackie Robinson reached Sal for a two-run double to left field. When Maglie faced the Dodgers catcher, Roy Campanella, it wasn't the first time they had met, "I had pitched against Campy before he was in organized ball. That was in Welland, Ontario—when he was with the Baltimore Elite Giants—and I struck him out four times. When I came back to the Giants I said to him, 'Hey, remember me?' He said 'Sure do. Welland, Ontario.'"[21] Campanella would remember Maglie all too well during his career, for his head would became one of Sal's favorite beanball targets. Durocher's squad lost its fourth in a row the following day as two costly errors by Hank Thompson and Jack Harshman did them in.

After Maglie's first two miserable appearances, he sat in the bullpen waiting for his impending release to the minors. He was insecure about his future and therefore did not get a permanent apartment in New York. Instead he lived with his wife Kay in a temporary residence. New York compiled a 2–3 record in their next five games. Durocher's biggest problem had been the lack of consistency by Jack Harshman at first base. The youngster was not hitting the long ball as hoped for. By May 5 he had seen enough and handed the first base job to Tookie Gilbert. In Pittsburgh's Forbes Field in front of 31,785 reserved spectators Gilbert hit a home run in his big league debut. Despite the rookie's performance, New York found a way to lose, dropping a 5–4 decision. They squandered a rally in the ninth as Jack Maguire grounded into a game ending double play. Sheldon Jones dropped his record to 0–3. Maglie looked sharp in two innings of scoreless relief. He did not allow a hit, walked two and struck out three. The Giants scratched out a win the following day by a 9–8 score salvaging the final game of the three game set in Pittsburgh. Bobby Thomson's grand slam in the eighth put New York up 9–7. Maglie earned the win in relief, giving up one run in two innings, but he needed some great relief help from Andy Hansen in the ninth to survive. The contest dragged on for three hours and nineteen minutes.

New York traveled to Chicago and promptly swept the Cubs in a doubleheader. Tookie Gilbert had impressed Leo since being purchased from Minneapolis. The pitching had come around as well. Maglie, Jack Kramer, Sheldon Jones, and Andy Hansen had recently produced fine efforts. On May 9 the Cubs ended New York's three game winning streak with a 6–0 win at Wrigley Field. Tempers flared in the seventh when Hank Sauer lined to Dark who threw to Stanky to double up Preston Ward who was caught off the bag. Frank Dascoli immediately called the runner out, but when Ward crashed into Stanky, dislodging the ball and knocking the second baseman to the ground, he reversed his ruling. Durocher and Stanky boiled over, arguing with the umpire, and they quickly got tossed. Shortly after, Lou Jorda, the home plate umpire, ejected Sheldon Jones who was barking from the bench. Larry Jansen's record fell to 1–3 as he surrendered three gopher balls. He had already allowed seven home runs in twenty-six innings of work. Maglie gave up an unearned run in one inning and two-thirds of work. Hank Thompson's error led to the run. Sal allowed one hit and a walk and struck out two.

During the early stages of the 1950 season, rain was wreaking havoc around the major leagues as a exceedingly high number of games were canceled. On May 10, New York dropped a contest to the Cardinals at Sportsman's Park by a 5–1 score. Max Lanier, one of the old Mexican jumping beans, went the distance. Stan Musial led the way at the plate with four hits. The word had circulated around the league that the Giants struggled against southpaws. Their vulnerability hindered them on numerous occasions. In fifteen games the Giants had faced seven lefties; all but one had gone the distance and emerged victorious. The offense was anemic. Right-handed batsmen Bobby Thomson, Wes Westrum, and Alvin Dark were not hitting. The starting pitching was suspect. Jansen, Kennedy, Kramer, Jones, Koslo, and Hartung had all been used as starters as Leo searched for the right combination to establish a set rotation.

After completing their unimpressive Western trip the Giants traveled back east to take on the Philadelphia Phillies in Shibe Park. The Fightin' Phillies were wearing flashy new uniforms and were anchored in first place with a 14–8 record. Durocher's stumbling ballclub was in seventh place at 5–11. The change in Philadelphia was more than aesthetic; they had assembled a legitimate pennant contender and were no longer the doormat of the National League. The history of the ball club was appalling. From 1917 to 1948 the Phillies finished in the first division only once, when they accomplished the modest feat in 1932. In 1949 they had climbed to third place behind their capable manager Eddie Sawyer and were now poised to seriously compete for a pennant.

Before Eddie Sawyer became the manager in Philadelphia he had managed in the bushes where he was known for his ability to handle and develop young talent. Richie Ashburn, Puttsy Caballero, Stan Lopata, and Granny Hamner had played under him at Utica. Sawyer was a brilliant, intelligent man, but he could also be tough when necessary, putting wiseguy ballplayers in their place. Sawyer believed that the game of baseball should be simple, unlike Durocher who made it complex and convoluted. Eddie did not have pregame meetings. The signs were remarkably uncomplicated and he rarely came out to the mound.

Harry Grayson, a sports editor, is given credit for calling the 1950 Phillies the "Whiz Kids."[22] A large number of fans began to attend games at Shibe Park watching this young, enthusiastic contingent of ballplayers perform. Eddie Waitkus was the first baseman. He became famous in 1949 when Ruth Steinhagen shot him in a hotel room. She was one of the so-called "Baseball Annies" who obsessed over players and in most cases were more than willing to please them sexually. This was a time when sexual escapades were frowned upon by ballclubs as they used bed checks, curfews and fines to combat such behavior. Marty Marion once said "dames wrecked more teams than bad liquor, big bonuses, or all the sore arms."[23] In Steinhagen's case she would watch Waitkus religiously when he had played with the Chicago Cubs and decided if she couldn't have Eddie then nobody else would either. In 1950 he would bounce back, bat .284 with 102 runs scored to win the comeback player of the year award despite periods of shooting pain. He played in all the games. The Phillies' second baseman was Mike Goliat. A tough, scrappy kid named Granny Hamner played short. Willie "Puddin' Head" Jones was the third baseman. The outfield from left to right consisted of Dick Sisler, Richie Ashburn, and Del Ennis. Andy Seminick was the catcher, backed up by Stan Lopata. The pitching staff included Robin Roberts, Bob Miller, Bubba Church, Russ Meyer, and Curt Simmons, while Jim Konstanty was the main reliever.

On May 13, the Giants were shot down by yet another southpaw, Curt Simmons. He tossed a three-hitter in the 7–1 win over New York before 12,596 Shibe Park spectators. Simmons was one of the numerous bonus babies which the Phillies had signed in their attempt to become competitive. He had been paid $65,000 to sign. Dave Koslo was roughed up for the loss. Maglie gave up two runs on two hits and one walk in two innings of relief. As the home runs continued to fly out of the parks, Sal contributed to the trend by serving up a gopher ball to Del Ennis. Jansen came back the next day to lead New York to a hard fought 4–3 win. The second game was suspended after eight innings because of Pennsylvania Blue Laws with Philadelphia up 9–7.

The New Yorkers traveled back home and split their first four games of the homestand with the Cubs and Pirates. After the first month of play, the Giants were tied for last in the National League with twenty double plays turned. The combination of Stanky and Dark had failed to produce, while coincidentally Buddy Kerr and his Boston Braves led the circuit in that category. Stanky had made up for his suspect fielding with the bat. He reached base safely by the way of a hit or a walk in twenty-eight straight exhibition games and followed that with twenty-two regular season games before he failed to reach base in a game. On May 21, they dropped a doubleheader to the Pittsburgh Pirates before a large Polo Grounds crowd of 34,972. Jansen pitched admirably but lost a 4–2 contest in the opener. The Pirates came back and took the second game, 8–6. The Giants used seven pitchers to fall one short of a National League record as the game dragged on for two hours and fifty-three minutes. Maglie was one of the seven hurlers who trudged despondently to the center of the diamond where he tossed an uninspiring two-thirds of an inning. In dealing with his pitching staff, Leo was the first manager in big league history to routinely employ several pitchers in a game. If a starter was not working well, he was not afraid to pull them early and use several pitchers to finish up a contest. He was advanced in the theory of the game, for he was the first manager to bring in a left-hander out of the bullpen to face a big left-handed bat on a regular basis. Or a right-hander to face a big right-handed bat. He believed in the aggressive use of his bullpen.

Another significant move that Durocher made in May was to bring up Monte Irvin from Jersey City. He had batted a mere .224 in 1949 during a short stint with the Giants and Leo had soured on him by spring training. Irvin was rumored to be the player who would break the color line but Robinson was chosen instead, and it began to look as if the great Monte Irvin had left his best days behind him in the Negro Leagues. In the first three weeks at Jersey City he batted .510 and Leo clamored to get him back to New York. That good right-handed bat helped New York defeat left-handers Johnny Schmitz and Ken Raffensberger. After a good start he would begin to slump again and Leo's confidence in him waned but in June, Irvin would hit his stride and show the major leaguers what they had been missing for all those years when blacks had not been allowed to play in the show.

New York ended their homestand by losing five out their last six. They pitched poorly, hit poorly, and played defense poorly. Stanky and Dark were kicking the ball around in the field. On the 27th they were fourth in team batting average but only sixth in club fielding. Durocher frequently juggled his lineup. Leo was not one to stand still and watch a ballclub lose. If things were not working right he would change his lineup and see if it improved. If it didn't he would change it once again. Some of the more recent changes included Irvin in right field and Bobby Thomson batting cleanup. The starters were not finishing ball games. Utility and bench players Bill Rigney, Jack Lohrke, Spider Jorgenson, Jack Maguire, and Sam Calderone would make an occasional appearance in a game. Mueller was the only Giant batting over .300 at .309. Irvin sported a .290 average while Thomson, Dark, Stanky, Lockman, and Thompson were all in the .270s. Maglie had a good performance against Philadelphia on May 27 working two scoreless innings. He was beginning to pitch more consistently in mopup roles. More importantly he was regaining his confidence.

They ended May by splitting a doubleheader with Boston at Braves Field. The park was located on the corner of Commonwealth, Gaffney, and Babcock streets. When it opened in 1915 it was the first concrete and steel ballpark to be erected. At first the dimensions were huge but by 1950 they stabilized at 337 down the left field line, 390 feet to dead center, and 319 down the right field line. The outfield wall was plastered with signs for "Maloney Motors," "Gem Razors and Blades," "Baylight Television," and "Peters for Used Cars."[24] Boston took the first game of the doubleheader by a 7–2 score. Kennedy got knocked out of the box early. Maglie followed him to the hill working five and a third innings, giving up three runs on six hits and three walks while fanning two. Durocher once again juggled the lineup, batting Mueller third, Thompson fourth, and Thomson fifth. Dark had a tough day as he failed to cover second on a double steal in the opener. He went 0 for 4 and after striking out in the fourth inning he broke his bat as he slammed it into the ground violently. New York's frustration continued to mount as Kennedy nailed Sid Gordon and Jack Kramer hit Sam Jethroe. Gordon and Jethroe were minorities, and they stuck out in a game played by white country boys. Gordon was Jewish and Jethroe an African American. Since Jackie Robinson "integrated" baseball, the throwing of beanballs, which was already a frequent occurrence, rose significantly. Larry Doby recalls, "I once checked statistics to find out whether there was any truth in the rumor that Negro players were being thrown at more than whites. The statistics prove it's true, no matter what some of us say. I was knocked down in many games. I was hit by more pitched balls than any player of equal power in the league. Jackie, Campy, and Minnie Minoso were also hit repeatedly. We were hit 75 per cent more than Joe DiMaggio, Ted Williams, or Stan Musial. If a guy wants to brush you back, that's baseball. But head-hunting Negroes isn't baseball."[25] The reality was that "head-hunting Negroes" occurred more frequently then the history books tell us.

Jansen went the distance for a 10–3 win in the second game. Mueller, Roy Weatherly and Thompson each had a good day. Dark went 1 for 5 and his bad day continued when he watched a third strike go by with the bases loaded in the ninth. Umpire Frank Dascoli banished him to the clubhouse. The Braves retaliated for the beanings in the opener by plunking Stanky and Mueller.

The New Yorkers went on a Western trip to start June. They began the month by splitting a doubleheader with the Cincinnati Reds at Crosley Field. The club scored four runs after two were out in the ninth to win the opener 8–7. Maglie got the last out in the eighth and received credit for his second victory as he watched his club score four runs in the ninth. Dark made a fine play on a sharp bounder by Peanuts Lowrey to end the game. Cincinnati came back to win the second game, 5–2. Maglie also saw action in the second game, this time working a scoreless inning. On June 2, the Giants won ugly taking a 7–6 decision. Cincinnati committed five errors while New York committed one (by Dark). Kennedy started but was ineffective and did not figure in the decision. Willie Ramsdell lost his control in the ninth as he walked four consecutive batters after two were out to force home the winning run. Maglie pitched scoreless baseball for an inning and a third.

After a postponement in Cincinnati, New York traveled to Pittsburgh where they swept the Pirates in a three game set. They took the opener by a 4–3 score as Maglie won in relief improving his record to 3–0. It was a short two-thirds of an inning appearance as he was one of seven hurlers to toe the slab for New York. Sal was becoming a workhorse relief pitcher, appearing for the fifth time in the last six games. Kramer exploded in the ninth when he questioned a called ball from home plate umpire Frank Dascoli. He came off the mound and was immediately thrown out of the game. The pitcher went after the ump and had to be physically restrained as he mouthed a verbiage of harsh words at Dascoli. Players and umpires swarmed around the participants. Higbe finally succeeded in convincing him to leave the premises.

While the Giants were in Pittsburgh, President Frank McKinney of the Pirates talked with Horace Stoneham about making a trade. Frank wanted what he judged as quality players: Thomson, Dark, Lockman, Jansen, Jones, and Koslo. Names were discussed as both teams desperately tried to make a deal. At one point Stoneham griped, "Well, we might let him have the jumper."[26] He was referring to Maglie but fortunately for the

Giants, Pittsburgh was not interested in the hurler and the deal fell through. McKinney noted in the paper concerning Stoneham and his proposed deals, "but all he wanted to offer was second-rate players." When the deal failed to materialize Horace stated "We spent an hour crying on each other's shoulder."[27]

The offense came alive in Chicago as they swept the Cubs to extend their winning streak to seven. Stanky, Lockman, Mueller, Thompson, Thomson, Westrum, and Dark each produced at the plate during the three game series. Mueller was seeing most of the playing time in right field as Irvin usually sat. Lockman extended his hit streak to fourteen, while Eddie Stanky, the pesky second baseman nicknamed "The Brat," continued to find a way to beat you. He would bat an even .300 for the season while drawing a major league leading 144 walks and scoring 115 runs. He'd stand in the batter's box and incessantly fidget, call time, perturb the pitcher till his timing was off and he walked him. After beating up on second division ballclubs, the St. Louis Cardinals humbled the Giants with a 6–2 victory at Sportsman's Park on June 10. Clint Hartung was the surprise starter and was knocked out of the box in the third. Jones, Hansen, Maglie, and Higbe followed. Sal recorded the final two outs in the seventh after Hansen had yielded two runs. The Cardinals swept a doubleheader the following day as Koslo and Kramer lost as starters. Durocher's club featured a 20–24 record and had moved up one notch to sixth place.

Jansen and Jones contributed solid performances to lead New York to victories in their next two games. On June 17, Chicago won by a 9–7 score before a ladies' day crowd of 11,781 at the Polo Grounds. Maglie kept the New Yorkers in the game by working six and a third innings of strong relief. He allowed one run on four hits and two walks. At the plate he smashed a double in three at-bats. The Giants rebounded on the following day by taking two from Chicago.

Ebbets Field was one of those early ballparks that were built up in urban areas consisting of a large population. The park was forced to conform to the configuration of the city block. This gave the structure its unique architectural shape and resulted in the short right-field fence that ran adjacent to Bedford Avenue. Ebbets Field was encircled by Sullivan Place, Bedford Avenue, Montgomery Street, and McKeever Place. The park was a bandbox, a pitcher's nightmare. The dimensions were claustrophobic: 348 down the left field line, 389 to dead center, and 297 down the right field line. In right field the wall was 19 feet tall and included a similar length screen above the wall. Opposing right fielders had a tremendously difficult time of it because the wall was bent in the middle, which resulted in wicked hops which caromed in every possible direction. To

5. Back with the Giants

Aerial view of Ebbets Field. Notice how the park fits nicely within the surrounding city streets. (Author's collection)

exacerbate the situation, the scoreboard was located between right field and center field. Ebbets Field was the location of some of the most heated baseball wars to ever take place on a diamond. When the Giants and Dodgers played it was war and people flocked to the ballpark to watch them go for the jugular.

Carl Furillo was a hardworking professional with a cannon for an arm who had mastered the skill of playing the right field wall in Ebbets Field like no one else ever had. He knew all the idiosyncrasies and how to play every angle. From 1946 until the Dodgers left for Los Angeles, Furillo was the mainstay in right field. At the base of the scoreboard stood the famous Abe Stark advertisement, "Hit Sign, Win Suit."[28] Furillo's presence assured that very few suits were won and it was rumored if nobody hit the sign during the season Carl took home a suit. "I loved the game, I wanted to be there in right field. It was my job like someone goes to an office every day. It was my job to take care of right field and I tried to do my job with all the ability I had."[29] He was a great hitter as well, batting over .295 or better eight times in his career. Carl was unfortunately known for being hit by far more pitches than he cared to count. In 1950, he was the target of beanball pitchers once again as they were throwing at batters' heads at an alarming rate in the grand ballparks of the major leagues.

There was no love lost between the Giants and Dodgers. Players did not fraternize before games. Fans at Ebbets Field would pelt the Giants players with food and bottles. If you were sitting in the visiting bullpen, which was a bench near the reserved seats in the left field corner, you were an easy target. The fans were close to the action and there was no place to hide. Monte Irvin recalled that Dodger fans would yell, "You'll never get back to New York alive. If you try and win today, we'll be waiting for you outside the ball park."[30] The Cardinals also had a vicious rivalry with Brooklyn and Terry Moore recalled "Firecrackers, bottles, anything they had handy. And it seemed like every time we'd come in there something would happen."[31] The umpires were scared to work such games. The borough of Brooklyn rallied around their "Bums" but the rest of the baseball world looked upon the Dodger fans as second class citizens. John Lardner described the Dodger fans' attraction to their team to be "brash, low, even buffoonish."[32]

Furillo hated the Giants but most of all he hated Leo Durocher. Leo urged his pitchers to throw the duster and "Stick it in his ear." There were several willing participants to this philosophy such as Maglie and Ruben Gomez. Others like Sheldon Jones and Larry Jansen were not as willing, but they eventually fell under the spell of Durocher, and whether under threat of a fine or some other reprimand, they threw the beanball. When Carl played under Leo in Brooklyn the two of them had an acrimonious relationship. During the 1950 season he would be skulled by a Sheldon Jones pitch at the urging of Leo (numerous baseball books erroneously state that Jones' skulling of Furillo took place in 1949). Before the game Durocher poked his head into the Dodger clubhouse and shouted at Furillo, "We had you skipping rope with the left-hander last night. Tonight we got the right-hander. You'll be ducking." Carl told Leo to "Go fuck yourself," then a minute later Herman Franks (one of Durocher's coaches) yelled, "Tonight we get you, dago."[33] Sheldon Jones was the right-hander, and he skulled Furillo that night. While Furillo was in the hospital with a severe concussion Jones made a weak attempt to apologize: "I just did what Durocher told me to do."[34]

Bill Starr wrote in his book *Clearing the Bases*, "Brushback pitches do not harm. It's the knockdown pitch, a pitch at the batter's shoulders, that is dangerous. It's the rare pitcher who will use the batter's shoulders for a target."[35] Sal Maglie was that rare pitcher. He used not only the shoulders but the batter's head for a target. He would employ every physical and psychological advantage to record the out. He did not shave before games and came out to the mound with a thick growth looking like he was ready to execute somebody. The batter would step into the box and Maglie would scowl at him. He looked angry. The batter would tremble in the batter's box, at which time Maglie might turn his back to the hitter, laugh, and slowly rub up the ball. While time elapsed the hitter would wonder if the next pitch would be thrown at his skull. The petrified batter would not dig into the box solidly; instead he would be ready to bail out making him vulnerable for the pitch on the outside corner. The choices were clear: Survival or success. Does he bail out with his foot in the bucket and come to the clubhouse with his head attached to his shoulders or does he try to hang in and put forward the extra effort to attempt to get a hit? Throughout the history of baseball there were those players who were willing to risk their life while attempting to catch or hit a baseball (Pete Reiser for example).

Maglie knew full well what he was doing on a baseball field. Only a handful of people are born with the capability to throw a Walter Johnson fastball. Sal, not blessed with great natural skills, was a control pitcher and would get the batters chasing pitches outside the strike zone. High and tight, low and away was his mantra. His nickname added to his persona and reputation. He was Sal "The Barber," a name in the tradition of a mafia gangster such as Tony The Knife. Other nicknames included "Sinister Sal" and "The Renaissance Assassin."[36] Maglie transformed the art of pitching into an act of terror. Ballplayers were rock solid men who looked more like cowboys or coal miners during this era. If you didn't go all out on every play there was always someone waiting to take your place.

Maglie did not throw brushback pitches; he threw unmistakable beanballs that sailed behind the batter's head. The hitter's first reflex is to move backward on an inside pitch and if the ball is behind him it can result in a "serious skulling."[37] He delivered a pitch that could literally kill. Carl Mays had once skulled Ray Chapman. Chapman died. This was the only death that occurred on a major league field as a result of a beaning but there were many close calls. The beanball was widely employed during Maglie's time to intimidate the batter. This was a time before the development of sturdy batting helmets and batters had to play in some parks that did not have a batting eye. The white ball came out of the white shirts from the bleachers. That split second which the batter lost as a result, not only hindered his ability to hit a baseball but increased the probability of getting hit by a pitched ball.

Roy Campanella and Carl Furillo were Maglie's special projects, his favorite beanball targets. When thrown at they would lose their tempers and lose their concentration making them easier to get out. Maglie stated, "Of course, I was hated in Brooklyn. At Ebbets Field they booed at me, yelled at me and I loved it. The whole scene made me competitive. The first time Campanella would come to bat I'd put the ball about two feet over his head. Down he'd go, and all the Dodgers would start screaming. They'd get so damn angry that they'd try to kill me with home runs—be the big heroes—and they'd break their backs swinging at bad balls. They didn't get anything. I had their number."[38] Other pitchers threw at Campy: Jansen, Gomez, and Hal Gregg among them. In a team meeting before a game against the Dodgers, Campanella's name would come up and Maglie would announce, "Campanella's going down on the first pitch."[39]

Monte Irvin states in his autobiography that Maglie was fairly even handed in his application of the knockdown pitch. When they discussed the opposing lineups in meetings, the leadoff batter would be announced and Maglie would say, "Well, the first pitch I'll come in high and tight and knock him down. Then I'll start to work on him." Sal would subsequently describe how he would pitch to the batter during the rest of the at-bat. He'd go down the entire lineup saying that the first pitch would be high and tight. The entire order would be knocked down and Irvin recalls, "Everyone got the same treatment and the Barber was known to shave all the batters real close—not just a once-over job."[40] Aside from Maglie's so-called "special projects," Irvin is correct in stating that Maglie didn't care who you were, he'd knock you down if he felt like it. When Sal went over to the Dodgers late in his career he faced his old teammate Willie Mays, and threw high and tight knocking him down.

If the Brooklyn Dodgers did not know much about Sal Maglie during the early stages of the 1950 season, they certainly were introduced to him on the night of June 19 as 19,208 fans congregated at Ebbets Field. Brooklyn won 8–5 as Ralph Branca struck out ten batters in the first five innings and sailed to the win. Hartung and Hansen worked the first two innings as Brooklyn scored five runs in the second inning to take the early advantage. The inning was highlighted by Furillo's fourth homer of the season. Maglie came in to pitch beginning in the third and Gil Hodges narrowly escaped with his life. The count went to no balls and two strikes. This is the ideal spot to throw the beanball since the pitcher can afford to waste a pitch and loosen the batter up. Maglie delivered a vicious duster behind Hodges' head. Gil was visibly shaken as was the home plate umpire Larry Goetz. Goetz later admitted, "My heart was in my throat," adding

"I didn't think Hodges could get away from the pitch."[41] On such a pitch the batter's first reaction is to move backward which results in a life threatening act if the ball is behind him. In 1949 a bulletin was issued stating that the umpire should warn the pitcher after such a pitch and kick him out if he does it again. The arbiters around the game were not prepared to become mind readers and thus the edict had fallen on deaf ears. Carl Furillo stepped into the box later in the game, and Maglie nailed him in the back. Sal gave up three runs in three innings of work but the Dodgers had been warned that Sinister Sal would torment them for years to come.

Beanballs were being thrown frequently early in the 1950 season. Bob Miller of Philadelphia nailed Ray Mueller of Cincinnati. Ray was sent to the hospital, carried off the field on a stretcher. Paul Minner almost took off Jim Russell's head in Chicago. Pittsburgh's Cliff Chambers threw a beanball at Earl Torgeson. Earl threw his glasses down and went after Chambers. Torgeson was banished to the clubhouse for his action, while Chambers was allowed to finish the game. Major league hitters knew full well that hitting a baseball could be dangerous to your health. National League president Ford Frick had declared, "Brushing a batter back is part of the game, but a bean ball has no place in baseball."[42] Unfortunately it is often difficult to distinguish between a brushback pitch used to back the hitter away from the plate and a beanball which is meant to intimidate and injure.

The Giants traveled home where they won three out of four from St. Louis. Westrum hit his eighth homer in the first game to lead the way as Jones won his fifth. Jansen and Koslo won the other two games. Maglie faced one batter in the second game when Kirby Higbe was the surprise starter as the New Yorkers lost 14–6. Cincinnati visited the Polo Grounds and split a four game set. On June 24, the Giants hit seven home runs. Westrum hit three of them. The following day they dropped a doubleheader by scores of 6–3 and 6–4. Two consecutive errors by Hank Thompson in the fifth inning led to five unearned runs as Kramer took the loss in the opener. Maglie was given his first start of the year in the second game. He was not up to the task as Ted Kluszewski, Johnny Wyrostek, and John Pramesa hit homers. Pramesa's homer was inside the park, misplayed by Don Mueller. He was not much of a fielder at this point of his career but with hard work he would later improve. Maglie yielded six runs in six innings on ten hits, no walks, while fanning three. Ewell Blackwell hit Thomson with a pitch in the opener, while Frank Smith nailed Stanky in the second game. The belligerent "Brat" would be hit twelve times on the year. By the time the sun began to set, most of the 22,464 fans had left the Polo Grounds. The baseball was horrific, as eleven errors were committed on the day. In the second game, Cincinnati made four and New York three.

For years Maglie had waited patiently for his opportunity to start a big league game and now had squandered it. He was excited before the contest began, felt fresh physically and mentally ready to pitch a quality game. Afterwards he was demoralized. That evening he began to pace and think. Suddenly it hit him, he realized that he had not been throwing his way, the way Luque had taught him. Before the game Durocher and Westrum went over the hitters, and Sal pitched according to the Giants "book." From that moment on Maglie made his own book on the hitters and pitched his way regardless of what the manager and coaches said to him. He would watch the action intently on off days and try to recognize the strengths and weaknesses of batters. When he pitched he would remember what pitch they hit, and what he got them out on and store the information in his memory.

After an exhibition game against the New York Yankees, the Giants traveled to Ebbets Field where Larry Jansen improved his record to 8–4 with a victory in the opener. Thomson hit an inside the park homer which was surrounded by controversy. It was a liner down the left field line. Gene Hermanski raced after the ball and had to fight his way through the Giants bullpen members to find it while they laughed at him. He realized that Thomson was going to have more than two bases and according to Andy Hansen yelled to a fan "pick up the ball, pick up the ball," and acted as if it were a ground rule double. Hansen tried to dislodge the ball from the fan but "All I did was knock the beer out of his other hand."[43] There were other theories to what happened such as the ball being lodged between the bench and the fence. The umpire thought Hermanski was pretending the ball was lost and gave Thomson four bases.

The next night, June 28, Preacher Roe won his ninth game for Brooklyn as they defeated the New Yorkers 5–3 before a modest Ebbets Field crowd of 15,492. Furillo hit a two run homer in the fourth. In the eighth inning, after one out had been recorded Sheldon Jones was urged on by Durocher to throw high and tight to Carl. To "Stick it in his ear." Jones heeded his manager's request and skulled Furillo. It was a glancing blow off his left ear. Carl was out cold, lifeless. All activity suddenly stopped to watch the stricken man lying on the ground. They carried him off on a stretcher, first to the clubhouse, later to the hospital. Furillo had been hitting the baseball with tremendous results over the past two years against New York and he paid the price. In the dressing room he lay on the stretcher, surrounded by teammates as doctors looked into his dazed eyes. He managed to smoke a cigarette as he waited for the ambulance.

Fortunately the x-rays turned up negative, but if not for his quick reflexes, the beaning very easily could have resulted in a fractured skull. National League president Ford Frick had witnessed the incident in the park. This was one of six "skullings" that Furillo was stricken with in his career. In addition, he was hit far too many times to count in other parts of his body. He would exacerbate the situation by crowding the plate. He wore his anger outwardly when thrown at which made him a visible target for many pitchers. Furillo would be skulled and always come back for more, not showing any plate shyness when he returned. Tommy Holmes wrote an article in the *Brooklyn Eagle*, poignantly entitled, "The Loosening Up of Carl Furillo."[44] As for Sheldon Jones, in one three year period under Durocher (1948–50) he would hit 23 batters, including 10 in 1949. He was no headhunter, like Maglie. His control was not actually great either but on certain occasions the man who had resisted throwing the duster was forced to abide by the dictatorial requests of Leo Durocher. Durocher approached the game like a war, and expected his players to do so as well.

New York ended June by losing to Boston, 8–4. Sibby Sisti hit a pinch-hit grand slam homer in the ninth off Sheldon Jones to win the game. Jones was probably still shaken by the beanball he delivered the previous night. He walked three batters and recorded only one out before serving up the grand slam and exiting the premises. Kennedy was knocked out in the first, and Maglie followed and kept them in the game by working six and one third of an inning in which he allowed one run on four hits and two walks. After his poor start against Cincinnati, Maglie was once again relegated to bullpen work. Irvin was beginning to play regularly and hit well as Lockman left the club for an emergency appendectomy. *The New York Herald Tribune* reported on July 1st that Larry Jansen, who was having a stellar year, had been offered in a trade during spring training to Brooklyn for Ralph Branca, Erv Palica, and a reserve player. Branch Rickey held out for more and failed to pull the trigger.[45] If he had, Brooklyn surely would have won the pennant in 1950 and 1951.

On July 2, Maglie worked in the opening of a doubleheader against Boston before 32,862 Polo Grounds customers. Boston took both games, 11–5, 6–3. Koslo started the opener but left after recording only one out. Hansen, Higbe, and Maglie followed. Sal worked two innings, giving up two runs on three hits and one walk. He had taken exception to the quality pitching of Johnny Sain and nailed him in the later innings. Jones took the loss in the second game as Sid Gordon hit a three-run homer in the ninth. Umpire Scotty Robb was harassed by the Giants throughout and when Stanky heaved buckets of water out of the dugout to criticize his calls, he was banished to the clubhouse. Durocher was kicked out after he gave a curse-laden speech to the umpire and the typically reserved Bobby Thomson was tossed when he threw a towel out of the dugout.

Larry Jansen won his ninth against Brooklyn on July 3. On the 4th of July, 49,316 fans packed their way into the Polo Grounds for a doubleheader between the interborough rivals. Maglie tossed a scoreless inning in the opener to earn the win in a 5–4 New York victory. His record improved to 4–1. The Giants scored three in the eighth against Don Newcombe to put the game on ice. Dark was swinging a hot bat and hit a homer in both games. Brooklyn won the second game, 5–3, as Koslo took the loss. Maglie worked in this contest as well, allowing a run in two and two-thirds innings. Koslo hit Furillo in the second game. Furillo ran towards right field and crossed Durocher who was running to the first base coach's box. Words were exchanged and Carl went after the Giants skipper but a fight was averted as the umpires stepped in. Leo was the leader who gave the orders to throw at Carl. Furillo later remarked, "See, I knew Durocher, I knew how he talked, 'Don't let that son of a bitch beat you.' That's the way he talks. 'Don't let that son of a bitch beat you, stick it in his Goddamn ear. Don't let him take the bread and butter out of your mouth.' I knew how he talks. To me, I didn't hate the [Giant] ballplayers, I hated Durocher. I hated his guts."[46] Before the games had begun that day, thirteen-year-old Otto Flaig Jr., was killed by a stray bullet as he sat in the bleachers. It occurred just after noon, 12:35 p.m.[47] The stadium at the base of a bluff with a lot of high ground that looked down on the park and which made this tragedy possible.

In Philadelphia, they finished the suspended game from May 14 and the Phillies held on to win 9–7. New York lost the regularly scheduled contest as well, 10–8. Maglie relieved Hartung in the first and worked five and two-thirds innings, allowing two runs on five hits and one walk. The 17,771 fans fought off large bugs that infiltrated Shibe Park. The severe thunderstorm that halted play for an hour and ten minutes did not help matters. Durocher, who usually went on the field to a coach's box when his team hit, decided to watch the entire game from the dugout. Stanky, Thomson, and Gilbert produced at the plate. Jones lost his tenth the following day.

The Braves swept three games from New York in Boston. Maglie worked a scoreless eighth inning. Tempers flared the next day when Durocher's boys lost a heartbreaking 3–2, thirteen-inning game. Kramer pitched seven strong innings before handing the ball to Maglie. Sal worked five and two-thirds innings and surrendered the winning run. Sam Jethroe led off the final frame with a double. Earl Torgeson was walked intentionally and Bob Elliott popped up. With two strikes on Sid Gordon, Jethroe stole third and was called safe by umpire Lon Warneke. The Giants exploded with rage, and boiled over. One Giant threw water out of the dugout as Durocher cursed Warneke from the dugout. Maglie finally went back to work and induced Gordon to hit a tailor made double play ball, a comebacker right to the pitcher. His throw pulled Stanky off the bag, as Jethroe scampered home with the winning run. Durocher and umpire Jocko Conlan went after each other, arguing vociferously as they left the field. When they reached the clubhouse steps in center field they jostled one another in sight of the remaining spectators. New York ended the first half of the season with a 34–40 record at the All-Star break. They were in sixth place; ten and a half games behind first place Philadelphia. Maglie's record stood at four wins and two losses. It was impressive. The second half would be tremendous for he would win fourteen games during that stretch to finish the season with eighteen victories. It was a majestic feat.

The National League won the All-Star game by a 4–3 score in fourteen innings at Comiskey Park. Red Schoendienst of St. Louis hit the game-winning homer. Blackwell earned the win, pitching the final three innings. Larry Jansen was the only pitcher to work over three innings, he worked five. They were of the scoreless variety and included six strikeouts. Jansen was allowed to bat for himself two times; when he came up in the tenth Durocher muttered to himself in front of his television set, "What the hell is going on here?" He was not particularly pleased that Brooklyn manager Burt Shotton, who skippered the National League, kept him in there for so long.[48]

New York opened the second half in Pittsburgh winning 7–5. Maglie looked impressive in eight and two-thirds innings of relief as he won his fifth game of the year. Jones was not pitching well and received the early hook. Two days later, they lost their third straight game after Maglie's win, losing a doubleheader to Cincinnati. Maglie lost the second game in relief as his record fell to 5–3. He worked five scoreless innings before giving up an unearned run in the twelfth as Hank Thompson committed an error. He had lost his last two games as a result of defensive miscues, although his poor throw in Boston was not officially ruled as an error. In their next five games, New York would play to a 2–3 mark. Durocher needed pitching and on July 10 had purchased Jim Hearn from the Cardinals for cash. He won his first game wearing the black and gold uniform. From 1947–49 he had a 21–16 record with St. Louis but had slumped badly in 1950 going 0–1 in only six games with the Cardinals. Coaches Frank Shellenback and Freddie Fitzsimmons immediately got him going in the right direction. He had been throwing straight over the top and featured a nice rainbow drop curve. Shellenback told him to change his arm slot and throw from a three-quarters position. With this advice Hearn developed a good sinkerball and his fragile personality was slowly built up. He became a new pitcher and would finish the season with an 11–3 record with New York and a 1.94 ERA. His aggregate 2.49 ERA would lead the National League. With the emergence of Hearn and Maglie in the second half to complement Jansen, the Giants had three excellent pitchers by season's end. This would allow them to leave the second division behind.

In St. Louis, New York dropped a doubleheader to the Cardinals on the 20th by scores of 10–3 and 18–4. Jansen's record fell to 9–7, Jones's to 6–11. The pitchers were getting hammered. The Giants had lost eleven out of its last thirteen games. Don Mueller and Tookie Gilbert were benched for the night game as Leo shook up the lineup. Jack Maguire played first but he wasn't the answer in the long run, batting only .175 in limited time for the year. Hartung left his pitching behind, and played left field. Irvin played right. After the day's games, Leo told his players to go out and have a good time: chase women, drink, do anything to relax. It worked as they bounced back with a 13–3 win behind Koslo who improved to 9–8 on the year.

Leo was still looking for the right combination of starting pitchers. Once again he turned to Maglie, and gave him the pill. In the last game of the Cardinals series at Sportsman's Park, he walked to the center of the diamond as the starter before over 11,000 spectators. Eddie Dyer, the Cardinals' manager, turned to Cloyd Boyer as his starter. Both pitchers had worked predominantly in relief and were making their second starting assignment.

St. Louis took the early advantage as Stan Musial drove home Rocky Nelson in the bottom of the first. Nelson walked, stole second, went to third as Gilbert booted a grounder and scored on Musial's hit. Leo's confidence in Gilbert was running thin; this was the second straight game in which he would be charged with an error. He wasn't the answer at first base either, for he would bat only .220 on the year and eventually be replaced by Irvin. The Giants clawed back and scored three in the third, but could have had more when Gilbert flied out with two runners in scoring position. Maglie gave the two runs right back in the bottom half to knot the game at three. Walks to Musial and Enos Slaughter came back to haunt him, as they scored on Tom Glaviano's single. New York took the lead in the fourth as Dark hit a triple, and came home on Stanky's double play grounder. When Maglie came out to work the fourth, he was scowling at the hitters in a menacing way with his heavy-bearded appearance. He shook off Westrum several times, and decided to pitch his way: high and tight. Sal broke off a number of curves and retired the side in order. In the fifth and sixth innings he was in complete control.

5. Back with the Giants

In the seventh, Stan Musial stepped into the box. The count went to two and one, as Maglie came into Musial's kitchen with the heater. He tried to sneak a curve over the outside corner, but it hung in the middle of the strike zone and Stan crushed it over the right field wall to knot the game at four. In Sportsman's Park it was 310 feet down the right field line, but there was an 11 and a half foot fence which became 33 feet in front of the right field pavilion. Despite the mistake to Musial he stuck with the curve the rest of the way and didn't make any more mistakes. The game went into extra innings, tied at four. Maglie began to tire, and take more time between pitches as he rubbed up the ball, scowled at the hitter, and walked behind the mound. The two combatants battled until the eleventh. Boyer walked Gilbert to start the inning but a botched hit and run retired him. Dark doubled up the left center field gap and Maglie moved him to third with a grounder to the right side of the infield. Then Eddie Miller, the Cardinal shortstop, booted Stanky's grounder to allow Dark to score.

Roy Weatherly, playing left field, made a fine running catch off the bat of Glaviano to begin the Cardinals half of the eleventh. Freddie Fitzsimmons came to the mound to see if Maglie could finish. This was the Barber's game, to win or lose, and he was not leaving the mound. Miller singled and went to second on Rice's grounder to third. The bullpen was active. Westrum and Fitzsimmons visited the mound to discuss strategy. Eddie Kazak, pinch-hit for Boyer, and the count quickly went to 0 and 2. Maglie stepped off the slab, rubbed up the ball and stared in at Westrum who was flashing out the sign. The high heater sent Eddie spinning in the dirt. Then he put him away with a curve, low and away. Kazak swung and missed the pitch. It was a great win for Maglie as he had trudged to the center of the diamond for eleven innings, and emerged triumphant. This despite the fact that he was a relief pitcher for most of the year.

Maglie's record improved to six wins against three defeats on the year. He allowed the four runs on six hits and four walks while striking out six Cardinals on the day. He hit Del Rice with a pitched ball. From that moment forward, Maglie became the hottest pitcher in the National League. Stan Musial had gone three for four against him in the contest. That evening at the Chase Hotel, Musial bumped into Russ Hodges, the Giant broadcaster, as New York was leaving to board their train. Musial said, "Where have you been keeping that guy?" adding, "He's got the best curve I've ever seen."[49] Wes Westrum stated "Sal had three types of curves, one broke four inches, the second six inches, and the third was a big, breaking curve that moved eight inches. He wrapped the ball differently for each one and he wasn't afraid to pitch inside. He would throw a high, inside pitch to a batter, shave him close. Then when he got the ball back from me he would play this little game. He'd say, 'This ball is slippery. Give me a new one.' As if it was the ball's fault that it came in tight."[50] The win lifted the spirits of the team as they headed to Chicago. Eddie Brannick, the traveling secretary, let the newcomers know when they had arrived. It was Eddie's birthday, and he gave the biggest piece of the cake to Maglie.

Sal contends that after this game, Jim McCulley of the *New York Daily News*, began calling him "the Barber," in tribute to the way he shaved the batters' chins, and threw high and tight. There are numerous other claims to the origin of the nickname. Some contend that Durocher during the 1950 spring training told reporters that Maglie looked like the barber in the third chair at the hotel. Another theory is that Durocher called him the Barber because he was an uncommunicative man off the field and thus the term was used in a joking manner. According to *The New Dickson Baseball Dictionary*, a "barber" is "A garrulous player; one who engages in chatting and joking during a game, in the manner of an extroverted barber; a willing and eager conversationalist; the American League equivalent of bag puncher."[51] Other theories contend that McCulley began calling him the Barber as early as the 1950 spring training because he gave "close shaves." Some credit Frank Shellenback, saying that he gave him the nickname for the way he shaved the corners. Regardless of the true origin, the name was apt as Sal the Barber was the master of applying close shaves to batters.

The pitchers' use of the beanball during the 1950 season may have been in response to the growing offensive productivity in the majors and the escalation of the home run ball. Simply put, their profession was in serious peril. Throughout the decade the game would become more and more dominated by the home run, as baseball became one-dimensional. The stolen base was becoming rare. Strikeouts were on the rise. There were exceptions, such as Durocher's Giants who still employed scientific baseball, or small ball. In 1950 home runs were flying out of parks at a record pace. By year's end a new National League, American League, and major league home run record was established: 1,100 homers were hit in the National League, 973 in the American League, for 2,073 total. Yankee coach Bill Dickey stated, "It's making a joke of the game."[52]

Many suggested that the ball was livelier as several agencies conducted tests on the 1950 baseball. Ford Frick and Branch Rickey advocated for the return of the spitball and Frick also suggested a wider plate. Writer Red Smith suggested that the quality of pitching had eroded. Since the spitball had been banned in 1920, the changes to the game had favored the hitters. Owners had witnessed the home run explosion led by Ruth during the '20s and the fans that flocked to the ball yards as a result. The changes in the rules that benefited the hitters did not look like they would be reversed despite the protestations of Frick and Rickey.

The Giants began to play extremely well after Maglie's win in St. Louis as they swept a three game set in Chicago. Hearn and Jones tossed shutouts; Sheldon's performance was a one hitter. Jansen went the distance for his tenth win in the other game. They traveled to Cooperstown to play the Hall of Fame game at Doubleday Field and lost to the Red Sox, 8–5. Back against regular competition they defeated Cincinnati 7–6, as they opened an eleven game homestand. On the 26th they extended their winning streak to seven when Maglie pitched a complete game before only 4,852 customers as New York won 3–2. His record improved to 7–3. The last time Maglie started a game against the Reds earlier in the season, he was knocked around. He wasn't going to make the same mistakes. Sal pitched to them his way, using his own book. Instead of working the left-handers on the inside corner of the plate, he worked them on the outside edge with that great curveball of his. He was in command throughout the game using an assortment of curves and excellent control to keep the enemy off balance. The only time he faltered was in the fifth inning, as two runs scored. In the Giants' half of the inning he tripled into the left center field gap. Lockman hit a fly ball, and as he tagged up, he left early and was doubled up for the out. In the seventh, he redeemed himself by driving in Dark with what proved to be the winning run. The Barber yielded six hits in the game, two of them were infield hits. Maglie, Jansen and Hearn were putting together the nucleus of a fine rotation. Lockman's bat was coming around as he was recently moved into the second position in the lineup, replacing Mueller who was batting seventh.

The winning streak extended to nine games before it ended on July 30. Irvin replaced Gilbert at first base and continued to hit the ball with authority. Around the first base bag he was adequate but his bat kept him in the lineup as he sprayed the ball to all fields instead of going for the seats as he had done earlier in the year. He cut down his swing out of desperation, "I knew that I had to do something drastic or I was a goner. I knew it was my last chance."[53] Over the final two months he hit at a .353 clip to bring his average to .299 on the year with 16 homers and 66 RBIs. The Cardinals defeated the Giants by a 6–3 score before a sentimental Polo Grounds crowd of 35,073 as the streak ended. It was old-timers day, and the old time Giants defeated the aging Cardinals by a 2–1 score. Carl Hubbell, Freddie Fitzsimmons, and Hal Schumacher pitched an inning apiece in the three-inning game. In the regular contest, Sheldon Jones surrendered three runs in the sixth to end his scoreless inning streak at fourteen. His record fell to 7–12 as the loser. The Barber started the ninth but was ineffective, yielding three runs in two-thirds of an inning. He stood on the hill menacingly in the sweltering heat that beat down on him and intensified his appearance. What Maglie did succeed in accomplishing on this day was nailing hitters. He hit two, Del Rice and Tom Glaviano. It was the second time in little over a week that Maglie had nailed Rice. On the Giants' side, Dark was hit by Gerald Staley. This was not a demotion to the bullpen for Maglie, but instead Leo would use the pitcher in short relief between starts.

New York had won eleven of twelve after sweeping a doubleheader from the Cubs on August 2. Jansen improved to 12–7 in the opener. Chicago hurlers showed their frustration as they hit Irvin and Stanky and lost 11–1. The second game was competitive as Maglie went the distance to win 8–6. It was his eighth win as he allowed six runs on nine hits while striking out six. He had a hit at the plate and scored a run. Andy Pafko had his number, hitting three homers with two outs each time. For as hot the Giants were playing, the Cubs were that cold as they lost their twelfth game out of their last fourteen.

Billy Meyer's Pittsburgh Pirates were swept in four straight at the Polo Grounds in early August. Hearn won the second game with a shutout. New York swept a doubleheader on August 6 by scores of 5–0 and 3–0. Jansen and Maglie applied the whitewash. Giant pitchers ran their scoreless innings streak against the hapless Bucs to thirty. Sal won his ninth, allowing seven hits, four walks while striking out seven. He started slowly, working out of a bases loaded jam in the first, and Stanky ranged far to his left to make two excellent plays in the fifth and ninth innings. New York was on a six game winning streak and had won fifteen out of their last sixteen games. The pitching had been superb while the batters were hitting well in clutch situations. The only potential downside to these recent developments was that all the success had come predominantly against second division competition. The upcoming series with Boston and Philadelphia would test their abilities. They won two out of three in Boston to begin the road trip.

Throughout the 1950 season, the Giants and the Phillies engaged in a heated rivalry that boiled over one late summer afternoon at Shibe Park. It began early in the year, when Eddie Sawyer accused Durocher's pitchers of throwing intentionally at the Philadelphia batters. Leo accused Sawyer's catcher, Andy Seminick, of blocking home plate when he did not have the ball, which made his players vulnerable to possible broken legs. "And your pitchers aren't too careful where they throw the ball either," he added. The Philadelphia skipper called the Giants "bushers," pouring more fuel on the fire.[54] These two clubs hated each other in a way that rivaled the Dodger/Giant wars. Monte Irvin recalls, "We always had trouble with the Phillies, and the worst fans in the world at that time were in Philadelphia. They hated Durocher and Durocher hated them. They hated the Giants and we hated the Phillies."[55]

In Boston, Stanky had been his typical irritating self, living up to his nickname, "The Brat." He concocted a plan to distract opposing hitters. On August 9, Bob Elliott requested that umpire Al Barlick move to a different location so that he would not be impeding his line of vision. Barlick obliged, but Stanky immediately moved into the location where the umpire had been originally. Elliott became distracted by Stanky's presence and struck out.

Philadelphia had a five game lead over second place Boston as they played host to the Giants in the second game of the series on August 11. Maglie faced Curt Simmons. Curt had been the first major leaguer drafted for the Korean War and was waiting to be called on active duty. He had a 14–6 record and the Phils would milk as many games as they could out of him before he left. The Fightin' Phils stranded opportunities all day as they hit into three double plays. Sal the Barber was wild, but he sharpened his razor in the pinch and stranded 11 base runners. He had worked fourteen scoreless innings before he yielded a run in the fifth. New York won 3–1. Maglie won his fifth in a row and his tenth on the year as he gave up seven hits, seven walks and struck out three. Andy Seminick did not reach base, walking four times and being hit by a pitch.

The trouble started in the eighth inning when Stanky began to bother Seminick the same way he had bothered Elliott in Boston. Eddie moved into his line of vision and began performing jumping jacks or what the players call "hop straddles." Seminick complained to home plate umpire Al Barlick, "He can't do that." Barlick was in a bind since there was no rule in the book stating that such an act was illegal. Stanky continued his performance. Now Maglie was fuming, having taken umbrage to the fact that Seminick had the audacity to complain. Sal spun out of the windup and nailed the batter on the elbow. Andy took his beaning like a man, indicative of the way many players reacted to a hit ball in a hostile situation during the time. He didn't rub it; he simply went down to first base. In the clubhouse after the game, the elbow became severely swollen and discolored but he played the next day. Seminick later was recorded as saying, "So I was really boiling about that. In addition, they had a history of throwing at me. Maglie, in particular, was always throwing at me or behind me, and in the eighth inning of that game he hit me in the elbow."[56] Earlier in the season, the Barber had thrown high and tight to Seminick. Andy bunted the ball down the first base line hoping to draw Maglie to the bag and get even. Maglie didn't want any part of the tough catcher and hovered about the security of the mound. The game of August 11 wasn't the end; Seminick tossed and turned all night trying to think of a way to get the Giants back.

The sickening irony of it all was that the following afternoon was "kid's day" at Shibe Park. A crowd of 23,741 settled in to watch the combatants go after each other. The violence that flared up had not been witnessed in the ballpark since Ty Cobb sharpened his spikes and went in high against third baseman Frank (Home Run) Baker in 1910. The fans were enraged as the citizens of Philadelphia threatened to take his life. One letter read, "I'll be on the roof of a house across the street from the ballpark with a rifle and in the third inning I'm going to put a bullet right through your heart!"[57] The last riot at Shibe Park ensued on August 21, 1949, when the Phillies fans rioted with the Giants in town. Umpire George Barr had ruled that Richie Ashburn had trapped a ball instead of catching it. The fans threw bottles and any other objects they could find on the field as the game was forfeited to New York.

Sheldon Jones faced off against Robin Roberts. Tensions had seemingly been quelled when Durocher promised to keep Stanky in line and quit his activities until Ford Frick could rule on the appropriateness of Stanky's behavior. Things quickly fell apart as Seminick was out to get the Giants and "the Brat" would continue to act as an unruly child who was out to misbehave. Durocher would later issue this statement: "This is professional baseball. This isn't a sissy game. Sure I wouldn't like it if I was the batter and it was done to me. But what could I do about it? Nothing. And if we can win a ball game by distracting a batter, I say do it. That's what I'm here to do, win, and nobody makes it easy for me."[58]

The Giants got a run off Roberts in the second to take the lead. With two outs in the bottom of the second, Granny Hamner doubled bringing up Seminick as the next batter. Durocher either wanted to upset the catcher or believed he would not pull the ball as he ordered his infield to shift to the right side. Stanky was now located behind second, in the batter's line of vision. He began his distracting routine: bending down and folding his hands around his knees and then standing straight up with his arms folded. Seminick worked a walk, bringing up Mike Goliat. Jones was becoming inured to the throwing of the beanball and sent the second baseman spinning in the dirt, delivering a vicious beanball at his head. Goliat took a step towards the mound but thought better of it and hit the next pitch to left field, scoring Hamner. Seminick was looking to nail someone and rounded second, heading towards Hank Thompson at third. Just as Lockman's throw reached the third baseman, Seminick gave Thompson a forearm shiver to the face. His teeth that had been firmly in place were now scattered around the third base bag. It was a vicious blow. Richie Ashburn recalls, "He just cold cocked him."[59] Thompson was unconscious lying on the ground, with blood streaming from his mouth while Durocher and Fitzsimmons tried to bring him back. While he lay inanimately on the ground, the Phillies players mocked the Giants from the dugout. As they escorted the injured third baseman from the field, he hit his head on the concrete overhang in the dugout when he failed to duck. Thompson was knocked out again. Seminick had scored when he knocked over Thompson, as the Phillies pushed across three runs in the inning.

In the fourth inning, Jack Kramer replaced Jones as the hurler. With two outs and the bases empty Seminick came up for the second time. Whatever Durocher had promised before the game to the umpires was now definitely off. He implored Stanky to wreak havoc behind second base. "The Brat" waved his arms above his head in a windmill fashion. The distracting act intensified and he began to wave his arms wildly. Kramer delivered his second pitch and the Philadelphia catcher deliberately missed, throwing his bat at the hurler. Umpire Lon Warneke had seen enough and tossed Stanky out for "making a farce of the game."[60] In the meantime, Seminick retrieved his bat and waded through hostile territory. Several Giants hovered around ready to pounce, but did not. Durocher ran on the field and argued Warneke's decision vigorously. He declared that the Giants were playing the game under protest. Bill Rigney replaced Stanky at second, while Jack Lohrke manned the hot corner. When Tookie Gilbert dropped Lohrke's throw on a grounder, Seminick was safe at first. Goliat followed and grounded to Dark who flipped the ball to Rigney for the force. Seminick went into the bag with his spikes high trying to put Rigney out of action. Rigney went after Seminick and the fight was on. The Phillies catcher pulled him down by the shirt and started pounding on him. Both benches cleared as a riot broke out. Some players tried to break up the pair who had started the ruckus, but other fights broke out. Bubba Church and Monte Irvin paired up, each wielding a baseball bat as a weapon. Church tossed Durocher into the outfield. Irvin recalls, "They were trying to get to Durocher and I was fending them off with that bat.... Well, I didn't hit anybody, but that melee was unbelievable."[61] Jimmy Bloodworth made contact with a couple of his punches. He went after Jim Hearn and Rudy Rufer and threw a punch at Durocher. The *Philadelphia Inquirer* reported, "one unidentified Phil swung at an umpire, but missed."[62] Tookie Gilbert went wild and was almost arrested for not listening to a police officer's orders. Umpire Lee Ballanfant dissuaded the officer from taking Gilbert away in handcuffs. The riot lasted for nearly ten minutes.

The Phillies won the game 5–4 in eleven innings. Jim Hearn got revenge the next day by throwing a shutout. Eddie Stanky had not violated any rule in baseball, but had been kicked out for his antics. Red Smith wrote in the *New York Herald Tribune*, "The umpire was wrong. It was an abuse of authority to act as though Durocher's indulgence had the force of a rule."[63] National League president Ford Frick backed up his umpires and forbade any more shenanigans similar to Stanky's from occurring. He disallowed Durocher's protest. Such behavior as Stanky's in the future would result in banishment to the clubhouse. Frick met with Stanky and Durocher privately in his office to rebuke them.

The Giant fans who rooted for their team openly at Shibe Park were harassed throughout the game by the Philadelphia spectators. One fan wrote Frick saying,

> We went to Shibe Park in a party of four. During the Stanky rumpus, and the ensuing fight between Rigney and Seminick, the Philly fans near us, who knew we were pro–Giant, threw soda pop at us in paper cups. They also tossed rolls and mustard on us. One member of our party was wearing a light gray suit. It looked as though it had been tailored by Gulden after the fourth inning.
>
> I always thought that Ebbets Field fans were supposed to have the reputation for untoward actions but there's no comparison. There was no police protection and the female ushers they have in Shibe Park couldn't do a thing although they tried to help. In addition, with ladies in our party, we were subjected to insulting remarks just because they knew we were rooting for the Giants. You can bet that we're not going back to Shibe Park for a while.
>
> Your witness, Mr. Frick.[64]

After their contentious series with the Phillies, New York hosted the Dodgers at the Polo Grounds. Jansen lost a heartbreaking 1–0 game to Preacher Roe in the opener. On the 16th they exploded for a ten hit, nine run first inning to propel them to a 16–7 victory. Maglie went the distance for his eleventh win. He allowed seven runs on eight hits and four walks. He hit one batter, Dan Bankhead. Gil Hodges touched the Barber for his second homer in the eighth inning with the Giants well ahead. This would be the last run scored off Maglie in nearly a month during four starting and three relief appearances. Hank Thompson hit two inside the park homers while Mueller hit one of the traditional kind. Sam Calderone caught because Westrum was missing time as a result of a broken finger. The following day saw Brooklyn sweep a doubleheader from New York.

The first game was a beanball war as three New Yorkers were hit and Jones nailed Jackie Robinson.

Over their next twenty-four ballgames New York continued to play great, going 17–7. Maglie continued to add to his scoreless innings streak and pitch with a ferocity, which was becoming well known around the National League. On August 23, Sheldon Jones won his fifth game of the year over the Cubs as he won his tenth overall. Maglie relieved him in the eighth and gave up three hits while recording only one out. None of his runners scored due to the excellent pitching of Monte Kennedy. Maglie came back the following day in St. Louis and shut the door for a 3–2 win. With the winning runs on base in the ninth he saved the day by recording the final two outs in a pressurized situation. With Durocher's team becoming more disliked around the majors, Giant batters expected opposing pitchers to throw at them with great intensity. The Cardinals and Giants traded brushback pitches all year. Philadelphia and Brooklyn were also involved in this conduct.

In St. Louis on the 27th, Sal shut out the Cardinals 3–0. He scattered eleven hits, walked two, and struck out two for win number twelve. This was his thirty-sixth game of the season. He had worked 135 innings, given up 110 hits, 61 walks, and struck out 64. Maglie threw another shutout on the 30th, this time against Pittsburgh, his fifth win over the Pirates on the season. His scoreless innings streak was extended to twenty with his second straight shutout. He allowed five hits, two walks, and threw one wild pitch while fanning four. He also doubled and drove in a run. One of Sinister Sal's inside fastballs got away from him in the fifth. Danny Murtaugh was skulled as a result and taken from the field on a stretcher. Stanky had reached base nine times in a row, including seven straight walks before he made an out.

After splitting two games with the Dodgers, the New Yorkers visited Shibe Park for the first time since the riot. The Giants not only swept a doubleheader from the Phils, but also shut them out in both games. Hearn led the way to a 2–0 win in the opener. Maglie needed only 98 pitches to dispose of the opposition in the second game, 9–0. Stanky was booed throughout the day by the hostile Philadelphia fans. Someone unleashed a black cat that scampered on top of the Giants dugout but did not prove unlucky for the visitors. The win was Maglie's fourteenth and his ninth straight, each of which had been a complete game performance. He gave up nine hits, walked one and fanned one while contributing with a sacrifice at the plate. Russ "The Mad Monk" Meyer hit Maglie in the fifth inning, but Sal did not retaliate, thus possibly averting another free-for-all.

Maglie had a bruised right bicep as a result of the Meyer beaning, but he still made an appearance against Boston on September 8. He worked a perfect ninth inning but Warren Spahn put them down in the bottom of the ninth to win 4–3. Hearn's five game winning streak came to an end. Against Brooklyn on September 9, Maglie tossed his fourth straight shutout as a starter at the Polo Grounds. Alvin Dark hit two solo homers to provide the offense as New York won 2–0. Sal won his tenth straight as his record stood at 15–3 for the year. Seven Dodgers reached base while he fanned five. His scoreless innings streak had reached thirty-nine. He was poised to enter the record books. Carl Hubbell held an eighteen-year-old National League record for tossing forty-six and one-third consecutive scoreless innings. Maglie became only the fifth man in league history to pitch four straight shutouts. The others included Mordecai Brown (1908), Grover Alexander (1911), Ed Reulbach (1908), and Bill Lee (1938). Brown, Reulbach, and Lee each achieved the feat with the Cubs; Alexander pitched his with the Phillies. Hubbell did not share in the four shutouts record because one of his games was an eighteen inning, 1–0 victory. In his next start, Maglie would attempt to tie Doc White's major league record of five straight shutouts which was achieved in 1904 with the Chicago White Sox. The man that nobody wanted, who was almost traded to the Pirates earlier in the year but had not been wanted in Pittsburgh, was now tempting fate, trying to break one of the game's sacrosanct records which were achieved by immortals.

The New York Giants played their home games in the green pasture called the Polo Grounds. It was the third park to bear such a name. The park was located in North Harlem on Eighth Avenue between 157th and 159th streets. Home plate was beneath a craggy cliff known as Coogan's Bluff. In 1883, John B. Day constructed the ballpark below the bluff. Coogan's Bluff was named after New York landowner, James J. Coogan. Giant fans were considered classy, compared to the unruly Dodger fan. Businessmen were often seen at the park wearing shirts and ties in the same box seat game after game. Political figures, financiers, society leaders, film stars, and the rich would be seen carrying on in the ballpark.

The Polo Grounds looked like a bathtub from above. The double-decked roofed grandstand went all the way around the infield. In center field a single deck bleacher section was divided by the players' clubhouse and the Giant offices. The upper deck hung over the lower deck in left field. The dimensions were 279 feet down the left field line, 483 feet to the clubhouse in center, and 257 feet down the right field line. A memorial in honor of Eddie Grant was situated a few feet in front of the clubhouse in fair territory. Grant was a former Giant who was the first big leaguer

5. Back with the Giants

The Polo Grounds with its horseshoe shape sat against Coogan's Bluff with home plate almost directly below the craggy cliff. (Author's collection)

killed in World War I. In left field the concrete wall was 17 feet high, in right field 12 feet high. Because of the overhang, balls only had to travel 258 feet to left field and 259 feet to right field for an upper deck homer due to the 34 foot trajectory. Two green "batting eyes" were placed at the bottom of the bleachers, flanking the clubhouses. Seating capacity was about 55,000.

Sal Maglie awoke on the morning of September 13, knowing full well what was at stake. He carefully studied the opposing hitters and knew how they would be worked. Ralph Kiner gets a steady diet of low and away pitches. Throw Gus Bell inside and low, avoid the fastball. Move the ball around on Danny O'Connell. He had plenty of success against Pittsburgh in his short major league career and knew how to work them. Sal said good bye to his wife at the Polo Grounds before entering the clubhouse. Kay promised to pray for him on this historic day. Inside, the clubhouse smelled of liniment and alcohol. It was a bleak day, already drizzling outside. They were scheduled to play two, but now that was in doubt. Durocher informed Maglie he would work the first game instead of the scheduled second contest. Westrum would catch.

Westrum was having a breakout year with the Giants in 1950. A great backstop but not much of a hitter, he would bat .236 on the year with a career high 23 homers and 71 runs driven in. At the urging of Durocher he formed close relationships with the pitchers. They bonded. When they were ridiculed, he knew how it felt for he was the object of such behavior for years. Westrum had been Leo's scapegoat, shouting to clubhouse reporters within earshot of Westrum, "If only we had a Campanella on this club!"[65] He persevered despite little job security and helped bring divergent pitching styles together to form a quality rotation. Larry Jansen remarked, "You didn't have to worry with Wes back there. He did the job."[66] Offensively he was outclassed by Campanella and Yogi Berra, but defensively he was just as good. His fingers were often bruised and broken to the point that he could barely grip a bat, but he played through the pain.

The wind was howling and the sky was threatening but 11,684 customers braved the elements in hope that history would be made below the craggy cliff called Coogan's Bluff. Maglie started quickly putting Bob Dillinger, Tom Saffell and Ralph Kiner down in order in the first. The cold weather usually made Sal's arm stiffen which could cause him to lose control. As he trudged to the dugout, the streak had reached forty. It almost unraveled in the second. Gus Bell led off with a walk. O'Connell followed with a smash through the box. Sal was fortunate to get the runner at first base as he slipped on the muddy surface. Bell advanced to second. Ed Stevens bounced one towards the right side but Irvin who was playing first could not reach it. Stanky raced over and speared it, as runners were now at the corners. Johnny Berardino flied to Lockman. Bell tagged at third and faked going home. Lockman came up firing nonetheless, and the ball skipped by Thompson at third and ricocheted towards the dugout. Maglie was backing up the play, and pounced on the ball, throwing a perfect strike to Westrum. Bell was called out at home. Maglie's streak was extended due to his own vigilance.

After six innings Maglie had held them scoreless to extend the streak to forty-five. He was out there in the center of the diamond, the loneliest place on earth, chasing the great Carl Hubbell. Hubbell, the man blessed with great intrinsic gifts, and the ability to throw a tremendous screwball. Maglie was merely getting by on junk: cunning and craft, intelligence and guile. He threw from different arm slots, at different speeds to varying locations. To some spectators the event was almost sacrilegious. Red Smith wrote in his column, "To an incurable worshiper of Hubbell the idea was—well incongruous not to say outrageous and downright obscene."[67] Smith was not putting Maglie down, but merely commenting on the irony of it all.

The drizzle became a steady downpour. The field became drenched, full of mud as the game progressed. Gus Bell, a rookie outfielder, led off the seventh. Maglie was within four outs of tying Hubbell's record. With the count 0 and 2, Sal decided to waste one. It was designed to be a low, inside curve. The ball headed towards its desired location, and swerved inside at the knees of Bell. The batter had been temporarily fooled. At the last moment, Bell swung off balance and hit a liner down the right field line. The ball ricocheted off the foul pole. The spectators became quiet; they were stunned by the blow. Bell hit what was known as a "Chinese homer." In fact he had hit what was the shortest possible homer in the National League, 257 feet.

The game was called after seven innings, as New York won 3–1. The win was Maglie's sixteenth and eleventh in a row. In the clubhouse Maglie was not down, but relieved and glad it was over. "Now, maybe I'll get some sleep." Regarding the fateful pitch he said it was "a curve, inside low," with which he had "been getting Bell out every time he faced him."[68] Carl Hubbell, who was the head of the Giants' farm system at the time, told reporters that he had wished that Maglie had broken the record. Reporters reminded Sal in the clubhouse that the last run he had allowed before the streak had been the homer to Hodges in the blowout against Brooklyn. If that game had been close he might have tried to bear down and pitched Hodges tougher and broken Hubbell's record. The reporters suggested that the breaks had gone against him. He disagreed, protesting, "You guys have it all wrong. You talk about the bad weather and the breaks against me. You say I'm unlucky. It wasn't so many months ago that I was an outcast, branded a Mexican League Jumper, washed up in baseball. It wasn't very long ago that baseball to me meant riding in rattletrap busses from town to town, playing in 110-degree heat in Mexico, or in freezing cold in Canada for nickels and dimes."[69]

On September 17, Sal Maglie was given his own "day" at the Polo Grounds. About 1,000 citizens of Niagara Falls were on hand to honor the pitching exploits of their hero. The festivities commenced before the game in which Sal was showered with gifts: a $2,500 war bond, a radio from his teammates and a watch from the Polo Grounds fans. On special "days" for the players the Polo Grounds bleacher fans would contribute money to buy the player a watch. After all the pre-game excitement, the Barber may have been trying too hard in front of his hometown residents as he allowed four runs in the first inning. Durocher almost pinch hit for him in the second but did not and Maglie responded with the first of two hits on the day. He also drove in a run, stole a base, and executed a sacrifice. He worked eight innings, yielding five runs on seven hits and four walks. He recorded five strikeouts. Tommy Glaviano was hit by a Maglie pitched ball for the second time on the season. New York scored three runs in the ninth to pull out a 7–6 victory. Kennedy earned his fifth win. Another streak of Maglie's came to an end on September 21, against Cincinnati. He was saddled with a loss, as his winning streak ended at eleven. He yielded eight hits and two walks as his record fell to 16–4. Irvin and Mueller hit homers in the 8–5 loss. An error by Thompson at third led to two Reds runs in the third. New York was firmly anchored in the first division. Their second half surge brought them into fourth place with a 77–66 record by the 21st.

Jackie Robinson faced great indignities during his first year with the Brooklyn Dodgers in 1947. Opposing ballplayers incessantly yelled racial slurs at him, as did the fans who taunted him. Beanballs were flying at his head and the opposition tried to cripple him with malicious take-out slides, with spikes that cut. The St. Louis Cardinals even threatened to strike when he came to town. A large contingent of southern boys resisted integration by their actions on the ballfield. Ben Chapman, the Phillies' manager, was what writer Roger Kahn appropriately called a "Klansman without a hood."[70] To say that Chapman hated Jews was an understatement. As a player with the New York Yankees he would give the Nazi salute to umpires and fans.[71] He also hated blacks. Chapman would yell at Jackie, "Hey you, there. Snowflake. Yeah, you. You heah me. When did they let you outa the jungle." "Hey, black boy. You like white poontang. Black boy? You like white pussy? Which one o' the white boys' wives are you fucking tonight?"[72] Every racial slur imaginable was hurled in his direction. During the game many of the Philadelphia players pointed their bats at Robinson and made machine gun noises, knowing full well he had been besieged with death threats. Chapman's actions unified the Dodgers around Jackie. As the years progressed this was certainly true with the Dodger starters, though several of the bench players were not entirely hospitable towards him. Eddie Stanky was one but even he came to Robinson's defense when the Phillies verbally and physically assaulted him.

Robinson had promised Branch Rickey that he would not fight back until things stabilized. This was extremely difficult for the man, because he had a fiery personality, which was exacerbated and intensified by racial abuse. By 1949, the gloves were off. He began to verbally retaliate against ballplayers who had tormented him through the years. He argued with umpires. When he saw Ben Chapman after he ceased being the Phils manager, Jackie said, "You SOB.... If you open your mouth one more time, I'm gonna ... kick the shit out of you."[73] The baseball establishment frowned upon this new aggressiveness. If Durocher, a white man, acted in such a way he had spirit. If Robinson did it, he was a problem. Jackie remarked that "as long as I appeared to ignore insult and injury, I was a martyred hero to a lot of people who seemed to have sympathy for the underdog. But ... the minute I began to sound off—I became a swell-head, wise guy, an "uppity" nigger."[74]

It was not surprising when the two combative personalities, Jackie Robinson and Leo Durocher, developed an intense feud on the field. Leo hated Robinson. It wasn't a hate of a racial nature but merely a personal one. By 1950, the feud was intense. Durocher would taunt Robinson putting his hands around his head from the coach's box, indicating that Jackie was a "swellhead." Jackie would yell, "Heh, Leo, are you still using your wife's perfume?"[75] or "Leo I can smell Laraine's perfume!" He was referring to Laraine Day, Durocher's wife. Durocher would give a crude gesture and retort, "My dick to you." Robinson answered, "Give it to Laraine, she needs it more..." They challenged each other's manhood, and Robinson would call Leo a "pussy" to his face repeatedly.[76]

New York traveled to Boston and disposed of the Braves in two games. On September 25, they took on the Dodgers in claustrophobic Ebbets Field in a day-night doubleheader. Brooklyn had won the day game by a 3–2 score as Preacher Roe won his nineteenth. Durocher was kicked out for arguing and Stanky objected to an umpire's call by throwing a towel out of the dugout and was also banished. In the night game, Maglie won his seventeenth contest before the howling, hostile crowd. He surrendered two runs on four hits and six walks in seven innings. Carl Erskine nailed Stanky. The Barber had some close shaves but did not bring home a scalp.

After dropping another game to Brooklyn, the Giants prepared to play consecutive doubleheaders with the Phillies. New York was nine games off the pace in fourth place. Brooklyn was within striking distance, only five games back. The Whiz Kids' comfortable lead had eroded down the stretch. Curt Simmons was finally taken by the military. Bob Miller, a right-handed pitcher, hurt his back when he slipped on some steps. Bubba Church, another starting pitcher, had been hit in the face by a vicious line drive. The staff was decimated, not to mention overworked. To make matters worse for the Phils they had to play the Giants in four games in two days at the Polo Grounds. Durocher's club was poised to play the role of spoiler. They were also in retaliation mode, out to get Seminick for what he had done to their team.

On September 28, Robin Roberts worked in the opener trying to win his twentieth game for the fourth time but was hammered early and often. New York won by an 8–7 score in ten innings. They enjoyed a 7–2 lead until the Phillies began hitting New York's starter, Monte Kennedy, hard.

Three consecutive singles in the eighth prompted Durocher to replace him with Maglie. The Barber immediately nailed Andy Seminick in the ribs to load the bases. Philadelphia followed with two hits and Koslo was summoned from the bullpen. Koslo allowed a hit to Waitkus before closing the door with the game tied at seven. Alvin Dark drove home Monte Irvin with the winning run in the tenth inning. As Irvin rounded third, Seminick prepared to block the plate despite the fact he did not have the ball. Just as the ball arrived he reached away to catch it and Irvin slammed into the catcher, sending him flying into the air. "He slid in fairly high on me but I just didn't get turned around in time."[77] The ankle was broken and the Giants got their revenge. It wasn't a dirty play, just a hard clean slide. They wanted to carry the catcher off the field, but he refused and walked the 500 feet to the clubhouse in center. Seminick played the rest of the season despite the injury, while Stan Lopata saw time as his backup. It wasn't until the season had concluded that they realized he had broken the ankle; initially they thought he sprained it. Jim Hearn threw a five hit shutout in the second game.

The Giants humiliated their rivals on the following day, winning the doubleheader by identical 3–1 scores. Maglie won his eighteenth game in the opener. It was his last appearance of the season and he finished strong retiring the last fourteen Phillies batters. He went the distance, giving up five hits, and two walks while striking out three. Bobby Thomson hit two home runs. Sheldon Jones won his thirteenth in the second game. Durocher's club had come alive in the second half and coalesced into his type of team. In September they compiled a 22–11 record and closed out the year with a 5–1 win over the Braves on October 1. Their third place finish was impressive, with an 86–68 record. The Phillies defeated the Dodgers on the last day of the season to win the pennant thanks to Richie Ashburn's throw in the ninth inning to cut off Cal Abrams at the plate and Dick Sisler's three run homer off Don Newcombe in the tenth.

Maglie was 18–4 for the season with a 2.71 ERA and led the National League in winning percentage at .818. He appeared in 47 games and pitched 206 innings, gave up 169 hits, walked 86, and struck out 96. His five shutouts also led the National League. Against the Dodgers he was masterful, finishing with a 4–0 record. As a hitter, Maglie batted .121. Maglie secured his reputation around the league by hitting ten batters. Hard throwing Larry Jansen was the perfect complement to Maglie's soft stuff. Hitters were challenged by his excellent fastball. Jansen finished at 19–13 with a 3.01 ERA. Sheldon Jones was 13–16, 4.61 ERA. The Cardinal castoff, Jim Hearn, went 11–4 for the season with a league leading 2.49 ERA. Maglie finished second to Hearn in the ERA department. Hearn and Maglie, two pitchers who did not get going till the second half, ranked one and two in overall performance. Sal's eleven game winning streak was the longest in the league. Koslo finished at 13–15, with a 3.91 ERA. New York had the second best ERA in the league behind Philadelphia at 3.71. New York's pitchers hit 31 batters, a third of which came from Maglie.

Irvin tore apart the league during the final two months after replacing Gilbert. Hank Thompson hit at a .289 clip with 20 homers and 91 runs driven in but committed 26 errors, which led National League third basemen. Thompson had broken the Giants' color line with Monte Irvin in 1949. In 1947 when Jackie Robinson debuted with Brooklyn, Thompson and Willard Brown got an opportunity to play with the St. Louis Browns. St. Louis was considered a Southern city in its attitudes towards racial issues. The fans berated the two players with catcalls and racial slurs and Thompson eventually broke down. The rumor was that the Browns signed the two players as a publicity stunt. Thompson took the hostility hard and lost his composure. Now he turned to the bottle. As a youth, he had run-ins with the police. He had beaten a man to death. Garry Schumacher, publicity director of the Giants, said "The way things worked in the South then, when one colored guy killed another colored guy, it didn't count. The white cops wouldn't even make arrests."[78] He had a few good years with the Giants and many bad ones but his talent never came to the surface. The bigotry he encountered enraged him. When he showed up sober he played well; when he was hung over he didn't. He became a recidivist, and after the 1956 season was arrested for armed robbery at the age of 31. When he came out of prison, Stoneham found him a job working with refractory youngsters. It looked as if he was turning his life around when he died of a heart attack.

Stanky batted .300 and collected 144 walks. With Brooklyn in 1945 he walked 148 times and 137 the following year. Don Mueller solidified himself as the regular right fielder, batting .291 with 7 homers and 84 driven in. He possessed a "seeing eye bat" and like Wee Willie Keller hit them where they weren't. At this point of his career he was still fighting whether he should pull the ball and hit homers or spray the ball around and hit for average. Bobby Thomson hit .252 with 25 homers and 85 RBIs. Whitey Lockman batted .295 with 6 homers and 52 driven in. Westrum batted only .236 but powered 23 homers and his .999 fielding percentage broke an eighteen year record previously held by Pittsburgh's Earl Grace. He made one error in 680 chances. A groin injury hindered him down the stretch as he began to catch every game when Sam Calderone was taken by the military. He was hitting around .280 when he injured himself but declined sharply as the season closed out. Dark batted .279 with 16 homers and 67 RBIs. The Giants finished third in club fielding behind only Brooklyn and St. Louis.

6

THE AMERICAN ARISTOCRACY AND THE MIRACLE FINISH

Shortly after the season ended Walter O'Malley won a power struggle in the Brooklyn front office and Branch Rickey moved on to the Pittsburgh Pirates to become the general manager. O'Malley quickly fired third base coach Milt Stock and manager Burt Shotton. Stock was second-guessed for waving Cal Abrams home in the ninth inning of the final game with none out. He paid for the mistake with his job. Shotton was criticized throughout the season, and particularly for the way he managed the final contest. Burt was a veteran, laid back skipper, who managed from the bench in civilian clothing, and kept score of the game's proceedings. O'Malley took a departing shot at Shotton and stated that he was not even welcome to manage in the Brooklyn Dodgers minor league system but should carve out another position for himself. "People like to see the manager in uniform," stated O'Malley.[1] He wanted someone who was intense and would light a fire under his team. He handpicked Charlie Dressen for the job.

Dressen was the supreme egotist. When Leo Durocher became manager of the Brooklyn Dodgers in 1939, Dressen was soon hired as one of his coaches and stayed for eight years. In 1934 Larry MacPhail hired him

6. The American Aristocracy and the Miracle Finish 117

to manage the Cincinnati Reds but four years later he was fired for lack of success. When MacPhail went to Brooklyn he hired Dressen. Durocher always surrounded himself with good coaches and with the Dodgers, Charlie was his right hand man. In 1951 Dressen was out to prove that he had been the brains behind Durocher during his tenure in Brooklyn. Carl Erskine, one of Dressen's pitchers, remembers it as follows: "Charley felt that a lot of the strategic moves Leo made when he managed the Dodgers were actually his decisions. So when Charley became manager of the Dodgers, he was obsessed by a drive to show Leo and the world that he was the brains and always had been. While the rivalry between the two teams intensified when Leo went to the Giants, the undercurrents of the rivalry were further enhanced with Dressen's appearance on the scene."[2] Another ancillary effect was the intensification of the beanball war on the Dodgers side. Under Burt Shotton the Dodgers did not retaliate aggressively when their batters were thrown at. That changed under Dressen as pitchers Joe Black, Billy Loes, Clem Labine, and Don Newcombe threw continually at Giant batters. However, the Giants threw at the Dodgers with greater intensity as Durocher continued to implore his pitchers to throw the beanball at their heads.

On December 26, the same day in which Commissioner Chandler signed a historic television contract, Sal Maglie signed his 1951 contract for a modest $15,000. He asked for $20,000, but in the end was content with what he received, "I've got no kicks. Of course, I'm getting from the Giants now what I got in Cuba and Mexico five years ago, when nobody even heard of me."[3] The other main hurler on the staff, Larry Jansen, was estimated to receive $30,000 for 1951.

When the National League schedule was released a record total of 209 night games were scheduled, an increase of four from the previous year. The owners realized that more fans could attend games at night and thus continued to increase after dark contests. The St. Louis Cardinals led the way with fifty-three night games scheduled. The traditional New York Giants organization resisted the trend and scheduled a league low fourteen night games. The Giants opened spring training on February 18 at Sanford, Florida. They worked out there for ten days with pitchers and catchers and then moved on to St. Petersburg. The Yankees and the Giants were trading spring training sites in 1951. Casey Stengel's squad trained under the Arizona sun at Phoenix.

Coming into camp, Durocher was seeking dependable starters to complement Jansen, Maglie, and Hearn. Jones was scheduled to be the fourth starter, leaving one spot available. Allen Gettel, a veteran purchased from Oakland of the coast league was to get a look. He had once played for the Yankees and came to the Giants on the recommendation of Dressen. Charlie Dressen managed Oakland before being named the Dodgers manager. Younger pitchers such as George Bamberger, Norman Fox, Charlie Bishop, Oswald Kolwe, Roger Bowman, and Frank Fanovich were to be evaluated. Leo's other problem would be finding a reliable first baseman. Before leaving for Florida, he told reporters that Lockman would be tried at first. He was hoping that this move would be similar to the one he made with the Dodgers when he moved Gil Hodges from behind the plate to first base. If the Lockman experiment worked out, Irvin would be back in the outfield were he preferred.

In the second day of camp, Bobby Thomson crushed three balls over the left field fence as New York had a productive workout. Durocher had already soured on his young hurlers after a couple of days. Jansen, Hearn, Maglie, and Jones were all right-handers. Durocher hoped that one of his left-handers would develop into a competent pitcher: Dave Koslo, Monte Kennedy, Frank Fanovich, and Roger Bowman. Kennedy's problem was that he always tried to be too fine with his pitches and lacked confidence. He seemed to be turning the corner during camp. Koslo also looked sharp.

Freddie Fitzsimmons and Frank Shellenback were the Giants' pitching coaches. Experienced men who knew what they were doing, they molded the pitchers into a formidable rotation. When they discussed young pitchers they sounded the same. Fitzsimmons noted, "Once in a blue moon you'll see a young feller come along and make good in the big leagues real quick: but it's rare. He's got to have experience pitching." Shellenback added, "I figure it takes a pitcher five years to learn how to pitch, to know exactly what he can do with what he's got."[4] They knew pitching like the back of their hand. Shellenback in particular was gifted in spotting mechanical flaws in a pitcher's delivery and correcting them. He believed in putting a lot of action or movement on a baseball and even someone like Maglie who did not possess a great fastball could get people out by pitching this way. Maglie would snap the ball off his fingers with a sharp turn of the wrist and elbow. Shellenback realized that every pitcher had his own style and approach to setting up a hitter. For Maglie it was the assortment of curves and the high heater. For Jansen it was a good slider and fastball. Certain managers like Charlie Dressen insisted they knew about pitching when he did not and would not listen to anybody's advice on the subject. To Durocher's credit he took Shellenback at his word. "I take Shelly's word on anything about pitching. If he says a fellow is ready, he's ready. He's the best. He has a genius for spotting when a pitcher is doing something wrong. I may sense it. But Shelly sees it immediately–and has the answers."[5]

Fitzsimmons had a fine big league career, which included a stint under Durocher in Brooklyn. From 1943–45, Freddie managed the lowly Philadelphia Phillies. Frank Shellenback was the old spitballer who played briefly with the Chicago White Sox in 1918–19. When the spitball was banned beginning in the 1920 season, seventeen noted spitballers were allowed to continue throwing the pitch until the end of their careers. Shellenback had inadvertently been left off the list and relegated to play in the Pacific Coast League from 1920 to 1938 where he won 296 games by loading up the baseball legally. He called the spitball, "the perfect pitch for the man with a good fastball and no curve."[6]

When Maglie first came up it was Shellenback who kept whispering in Durocher's ear that he might be a good pitcher. Frank was a great teacher. He had turned around the career of Jim Hearn when he came over from St. Louis. Maglie and Jansen were taught how to throw a good slider under Frank's guidance. He also believed greatly in throwing a change of pace and varying the speed of deliveries. On the 1951 team Maglie, Jansen, and Koslo were the best when it came to pulling the string. As for the spitball, Jim Brosnan had once described the Shellenback-taught Giants as "a club that annually leads the National League in denying that its pitchers throw spitballs." Since there is no wrist turn, the spitter does not put as much strain on the arm. Shellenback notes, "The slippery part of the ball takes the place of violent wrist and arm twist."[7] Wes Westrum denies that any of the pitchers were ever taught to throw a spitball or actually threw one in a game. It is a very difficult pitch to control. The fact remains that the New York Giants were probably the most accused team when it came to throwing a spitter. If they were going to load up the ball they had the best teacher, a guy whose spitball was compared to Burleigh Grimes and who, had he not inadvertently been kept off the infamous list of 1920, would have spat his way into the Hall of Fame.

Maglie was accused of throwing a spitball throughout his career but denied doing so and no evidence has come forward to suggest he did. When his career ended he gave several interviews in which he openly discussed his application of the beanball and his headhunting tactics. One article with *Cavalier* was entitled, "I Always Threw Beanballs." Concerning the spitball he said, "If I had used the spitter, I'd admit it now. I have no secrets." Maglie was one of the most honest players to be found when it came to describing his on the field activities. According to Maglie, the opposition thought he was loading up the ball because of his tremendous curve and the fact that he would put his fingers in his mouth. In addition the opposition would often ask the umpire to look at the baseball to try to upset the pitcher or his rhythm and get him to break his concentration.

Maglie would make his hands sticky by mixing resin and olive oil. For each of his different curveballs, the amount of time he held onto the ball determined how the curve would break. The resin would make his hands stiff and dry throughout the course of a game, at which time he would moisten his fingers with his tongue. Before he delivered the ball he would dry them off on his shirt. "As a matter of fact, I didn't like having to lick the fingers, because the smell of the resin made me want to gag. On the Giants, a couple of times when I started gagging, Eddie Stanky ran over from second and asked "What's the matter? Starting to choke up?" Eddie's a joker. I took care of him later when he was on the Cards."[8]

Catcher Rafael Noble was brought into the Giants organization to put some pressure on Westrum. With Oakland he batted .316 and hit 15 homers prompting Durocher to predict that Westrum would soon be relegated to warming up pitchers. Unfortunately for Leo, Noble was not the savior he was looking for behind the plate. Clint Hartung's days as a pitcher were over, as he would concentrate solely on his outfield play. The Giants left Sanford just in time and headed for St. Petersburg for they had become irritated with the cloistered atmosphere of the barracks. On March 1 they conducted their first workout at Miller Huggins Field. Jim Hearn who had been holding out finally signed his contract for an estimated $16,000. Jack Kramer was the remaining holdout.

Fans flocked to the park to watch Durocher put on one of his trademark infield practice exhibitions. When Leo's wife, the beautiful Laraine Day, made an appearance it added to the excitement. Lockman, Stanky, Dark, and Thompson were the expected starters on the inner garden. Infielders Bobby Hofman, Davey Williams, Pete Pavlick, Artie Wilson, Rudy Rufer, Jack Lohrke, and Bill Rigney were competing for reserve spots.

On March 10, the Giants opened their exhibition schedule by losing to the St. Louis Cardinals by a 4–2 score before 6,654 spectators. Kennedy allowed two runs in three innings to take the loss. They rebounded the following day, winning 4–3. Maglie was the winner, allowing one hit (no walks) in three innings. Sal's next start came against Philadelphia as he was pounded for five runs on six hits in three innings. New York scratched their way back and won 6–5 as Allen Gettel won in relief. That was the first of four straight wins for the Giants as they followed with a three game sweep of Charlie Dressen's Brooklyn Dodgers.

The Boston Red Sox defeated the Giants, 2–1, on the 19th. Jansen worked five scoreless innings to start the game. Maglie followed and lost it when he allowed single runs in the seventh and eighth innings. The Red Sox order was impressive: Dom DiMaggio, Jim Piersall, Johnny Pesky, Ted Williams, Lou Boudreau, Walt Dropo, Bobby Doerr, and Billy Goodman.

6. The American Aristocracy and the Miracle Finish

The previous day, Ted Williams, the $125,000 slugger of the Red Sox, made headlines saying "I'm sick and tired of these spring exhibition games. We don't need this much to get in shape. I spent the winter fishing off the Florida Keys. My left elbow feels good. It needed rest and that's what I did for it."[9] The "Splendid Splinter" was never afraid to speak his mind.

On March 20 the bats came alive as New York pounded the Detroit Tigers, 16–7. Noble was putting together an excellent spring and hit a homer. Spider Jorgensen was purchased from Minneapolis the following day as Rudy Rufer, Davey Williams, and Tookie Gilbert were sent down. New York began to slump and compiled a 4–6 record over their next ten games. During that stretch Maglie gave up three runs in six innings against Detroit. Vic Wertz drove in two with a single. Sal would have trouble with the powerful left-handed swinging Wertz for his entire career whenever they met.

In their last game in St. Petersburg before barnstorming north, the Giants defeated St. Louis by a 12–8 score. Maglie surrendered five runs in five innings on eight hits and one walk. Sal was being hit hard. However Durocher told reporters he was not particularly worried about his pitcher's progress and added, "He'll be all right when the bell rings."[10] Artie Wilson had apparently earned himself a spot on the roster as the extra infielder by this point of spring training. He batted at a .480 clip over his first twenty-five at-bats. In 1949 he had played under Charlie Dressen in Oakland where he batted .312.

The Giants went 7–4 the rest of camp, playing mostly against the Cleveland Indians, with a couple of contests against the Boston Braves. The Indians/Giants contests drew huge crowds in Alabama, Texas, Arkansas, Tennessee, Georgia, and North Carolina. Since the two clubs were in opposite leagues, players fraternized and got to know each other well. It was not uncommon to see a veteran ballplayer help out a youngster on the opposing club. Such was the case in 1946 when Joe Gordon of the Indians taught Bobby Thomson how to play second base in a couple of days. Mel Ott eventually moved Thomson to the outfield where he could best utilize his great speed. The barnstorming tradition between the Giants and the Indians began in 1934, and at the conclusion of the '51 spring training schedule, Cleveland held a 101–98 advantage (there were six ties).

On April 7, a crowd of 9,531 fans showed up in Dallas, Texas, to watch the Cleveland Indians defeat New York by an 8–7 score in eleven innings. Bob Lemon faced off against Sal Maglie. Maglie allowed six runs on ten hits and six walks in nine innings. He was pitching well until the seventh when Cleveland scored four runs. In the eighth inning he drove in a run off Lemon. Bobby Avila's double in the eleventh off Allen Gettel scored

George Stirnweiss with the game winner. Maglie's last warm-up before the regular season came in a 6–6 tie before 9,857 fans at Norfolk, Virginia. Sal allowed three runs on five hits and five walks in five innings of work. The big news of the day involved a fire that erupted in the bleachers where 2,000 fans were packed in like sardines. Play was halted for twenty-two minutes as people were forced onto the field when the wooden bleachers went up in flames. The thick black smoke made its way onto the field, as people began to panic when they realized there was no visible exit. Serious danger was prevented when the wind suddenly changed course and the police did a good job of crowd control. There were a few minor injuries. After the fire department got the flames under control, play was resumed and the fans returned to the unburned sections of the bleachers.

As the season was about to open, Durocher's Giants looked poised to make a run at the pennant after their great finish in 1950. The Giants received favorable press throughout camp, partially due to the new attitude of Durocher. In 1941 Durocher's Brooklyn club had a tough time winning the pennant because he enraged every team in the league. Every team hated the Dodgers and they were out to beat them. Rud Rennie wrote in the *New York Herald Tribune* that Durocher was showing signs of mellowing and toning down his irascible behavior. "He appears to have finally put into practice something he must have learned years ago as a player for the Yankees: Never arouse a sleeping enemy. Let him sleep and kick his brains out."[11] John Drebinger wrote in the *New York Times*, "Leo Durocher seemed more confident than ever that his club would make that quick start so vital to success in the 1951 National League flag race."[12] The memories of that horrendous first half in 1950 were still fresh in his mind. Charlie Dressen's Brooklyn Dodgers were favored by most of the writers to win the pennant. Their lineup was overpowering and struck fear into the hearts of opposing managers: Carl Furillo, Duke Snider, Jackie Robinson, Gil Hodges, Roy Campanella, Pee Wee Reese, and Billy Cox.

The Giants were bursting with enthusiasm on opening day and the game could not have gone much better for Durocher's team. It was April 17, and Douglas MacArthur had returned to the mainland and been given a hero's welcome in San Francisco. Leo was anxious to have a good start. The position players were the same as in 1950 except for first base; Irvin was at the gateway. Larry Jansen did not disappoint, throwing a five hit shutout before 6,081 frigid fans at Braves Field. He exorcised the jinx of years past and finally won a game on opening day. The final score was New York 4, Boston 0. After the game Leo astonished the writers by his remarkably good mood: "I'm so happy, I'm frightened, I've never had a club going so well and it scares me."[13] All fourteen hits in the game were singles. Philadelphia defeated the Dodgers by a 5–2 score in their opener. Carl Erskine was the surprise starter, as Don Newcombe complained of arm soreness.

New York lost the following day by an 8–5 score. Alvin Dark unleashed a bad throw and Bobby Thomson dropped a fly ball, which led to two unearned runs for Boston in the first inning. Maglie got out of more trouble by getting a double play grounder and striking out Walker Cooper. He held them scoreless over the next four innings before Cooper drove home two in the sixth. Sal left the game for a pinch-hitter after the sixth. Maglie allowed four runs on five hits and two walks. He also hit a batter, Earl Torgeson. Cooper continued to do more damage later in the game. This was the type of ballplayer which Durocher disdained when he was with the Giants. In the eighth, he hit a homer off George Spencer. Sam Jethroe hit a dramatic three run homer off Koslo in the bottom of the ninth to win it. Gettel took the loss. Maglie was not particularly sharp and the cold weather did not help matters. Johnny Sain, Boston's starter, nailed Sal Yvars with a pitched ball in the contest. Brooklyn won their game, 4–3, as Robinson drove home the winning run in the ninth.

On April 19, New York was scheduled to play a Patriots' Day doubleheader with the Boston Braves. The Dodgers were set to play host to the Phillies at Ebbets Field but the game was mysteriously canceled. The casual observer may have been confused to why such a game was canceled since the weather was not threatening. The Dodgers were headed into the Polo Grounds the following day and Charlie Dressen wanted to win those Giant games more than anything. Roscoe McGowen wrote in the *New York Times*, "By calling off yesterday's series final with the Phils at Ebbets Field, Dressen now had big Don Newcombe ready to toss at the Giants. Pitching plans and lack of attendance must have influenced the cancellation, because it was rather a nice afternoon with some sunshine and a mild temperature."[14] Protocol dictates that the home team starts a game and then the umpires take over. This is how deep the Giant/Dodger rivalry penetrated: the Dodgers purposely canceled a game while their rivals would struggle in a doubleheader before traveling back home. Dressen wanted to win, but most of all he wanted to humiliate the Giants.

The doubleheader in Boston was a nightmare for Durocher and his team. The first game started at 1:30, while the second game did not end until 8:10. Things went smoothly in the opener as Jim Hearn scattered seven hits to defeat Warren Spahn, 4–2. The second game was a wild three hour and thirty-nine minute contest, won by the Braves, 13–12 in ten innings. Durocher used six pitchers. Jack Kramer started and was followed by Spencer, Bamberger, Gettel, Kennedy, and Koslo. Kennedy had been with the club since 1946. He was a hard throwing left-hander who never quite lived up to expectations. Koslo first played with the Giants in 1941 and had been the victim of poor run support over much of his career. In 1949, he had led the National League in ERA while posting an 11–14 record. Koslo blew the lead in the eighth and lost it in the tenth when Torgeson drove home the winning run. Durocher was upset because he had sent Jansen and Maglie back to New York to rest for the Brooklyn series. Jansen recalls, "When Leo saw us he said, 'Boys, you got out of your uniforms for the last time this year. If I had either one of you in Boston we'd have won that second game.' From that point on we were always ready. Either one of us could have helped because you can always come back and throw an inning or two."[15] Durocher's happy demeanor after a successful spring training and opening day now turned sour.

Little did the Giants know at the time that the last game they played in Boston would be the first of eleven straight games they would lose. On April 20, New York City was buzzing as General Douglas MacArthur went up Broadway during a tickertape parade. The previous day he had addressed a joint session of Congress and explained the military situation in Korea. He closed the speech saying, "Old soldiers never die; they just fade away. And like the old soldier of that ballad, I now close my military career and just fade away — an old soldier who tried to do his duty as God gave him the light to see that duty. Good-bye."[16] He faded away about as well as Leo Durocher stopped arguing with umpires. A crowd of 30,870 showed up for the Giants' home opener at the Polo Grounds. Dressen and Durocher flanked Marine Pfc. Walter Townsend, Jr., a three time wounded Korean veteran from Jackson Heights, who threw out the first ball. The Dodgers won the game handily, 7–3, behind Don Newcombe. Charlie Dressen was out to prove he was an intelligent baseball man and humiliate the Giants in the process. The ostentatious behavior in which he engaged in during the seventh inning would have made the disobedient commander which the city was cheering proud. Artie Wilson had been smoking the ball all spring; he came up to pinch-hit for George Spencer. Dressen had managed the left-handed hitting Wilson in Oakland and believed he could not pull the ball off Newcombe. Bill Rigney recalls, "As far as I'm concerned, Charlie Dressen put on the biggest act I had ever seen."[17] Dressen called time and climbed out of the dugout. He brought Furillo in from right field and put him at second base. Robinson moved over to his right to become a second shortstop. Snider came in from center into shallow left field. Cox was playing right on the line at third and Reese was moved deep into the third base hole. Don Thompson, the left fielder, played close to the line. Virtually the entire right side of the diamond was vacated except for Furillo at second base. In the meantime

Durocher was going nuts, cursing Dressen with every name imaginable. After the "grandstanding" had been completed, Dressen rubbed his hands together as if he had performed some great work and looked at Wilson with pity. With the pressure on, Wilson bounced back to the mound. Artie was humiliated by the incident, and afterwards became helpless at the plate. This was only the beginning of a season long war between the two clubs. Ballplayers have long memories and these kinds of humiliating theatrics are not forgotten. Dressen would be engaged in the theater of the absurd all year. The beanballs were flying throughout the game. Newcombe threw at Irvin while Carl Furillo was the main target for Giant pitchers. In the fourth inning, Eddie Stanky insisted that Gil Hodges had been doubled off by Whitey Lockman's throw but umpire Augie Donatelli called him safe. Durocher argued vigorously and showed up the umpire holding his palms apart to indicate by how far the runner was out. In 1950, Stanky had been booed throughout the opening game at the Polo Grounds. The man whom Giant fans had hated with a religious fervor had won them over, and now they cheered him enthusiastically. Sheldon Jones took the loss. Irvin and Dark made errors as the Giants were not playing strong fundamental baseball. Lockman led the team with two hits.

Douglas MacArthur was among the 32,445 fans who witnessed a serious beanball war at the Giants' home ballpark the following afternoon. Once again, the Dodgers won by a 7–3 score. The game almost turned into a backroom brawl. Under Burt Shotton, the Dodgers were less willing to retaliate for the beanballs. Dressen on the other hand had a two for one rule. If they hit one of our batters we hit two of theirs. Coincidentally, Durocher had the same rule. Larry Jansen was a gentle man playing a hostile game who for years had given up far more homers than he should have allowed. Hitters took a firm toehold in the box with the knowledge that Jansen was unlikely to brush them back. Like Sheldon Jones he had resisted Durocher's orders to throw the beanball, but like Jones he would submit and heed Leo's order of "Stick it in his ear." In the fifth inning Durocher gave Jansen a direct order. It was time for Campanella to go down. He ignored Leo's orders and threw the first two pitches for strikes. Campy was bailing on the second pitch, concerned that the ball was coming at his head. Durocher implored his pitcher to brush the batter back and this time he threatened him with a fine: "It'll be a C-note if you don't!" Campy was confused; he stepped out of the box bent down to rub some dirt on his ,hands and asked Westrum if Jansen was going to throw at him. Westrum replied, "Who, Larry? He wouldn't throw at Adolf Hitler." With Jansen under a threat of a fine, he unleashed a pitch at Campy's head but took a little off so the hitter could get out of the way. Campanella was livid, arguing with umpire Donatelli that the ball hit his shirt sleeve and therefore he should be awarded first base as a result. He told Westrum, "you gonna pay for that."[18] Westrum was in a bind because he had just told Campanella that Jansen would not throw at him. Durocher had been grinning at the Dodger catcher the whole time and Campanella finally looked at a third strike on the outer edge of the plate.

In the sixth, Chris Van Cuyk threw at Westrum. Westrum went sprawling into the dirt and came after Campanella but a fight was averted as the umpire stepped in. In the eighth inning, Jansen pitched close to the Dodgers catcher once again. Campanella went after Westrum, shoving him back into the umpire. Westrum retaliated and shoved Campy towards the pitcher's mound. Westrum began shedding his catching equipment, the "tools of ignorance" as they say, and preparing for an all out fight with Campy. Both benches emptied before the hostilities finally settled down. When Ralph Branca came into the game he nailed Bobby Thomson. Branca was not shy about throwing inside and would protect his players. The other events of the day included Stanky knocking the ball out of Reese's hands when he stole second. Rocky Bridges throwing a shoulder block at Bobby Thomson during a pickoff play. Van Cuyk knocked Hank Thompson down. Thompson took offense and had some words with the Dodger hurler. The season was not even a week long but the Giant/Dodger war was already in mid-season form. When the teams exited the premises after the game Dressen taunted Durocher. Leo responded by giving him the finger.

For two days Maglie watched the proceedings from the dugout and was not entirely pleased at how his team was treated. On April 23, he got his chance to face the Giants' hated rival for the first time during the season. The Dodgers won the game by a 4–3 score in ten innings to sweep the series as 32,954 spectators watched intently. A total of 96,269 fans witnessed the three game series. Maglie lost his first game of the season. He worked all ten innings, allowing the four runs on seven hits and four walks while striking out six. After Maglie put the Dodgers down in the first inning, Dressen asked umpire Lee Ballanfant to inspect the baseball. Durocher gave the ball to the umpire only after a long argument at which time Ballanfant found nothing wrong with it. When Stanky led off the Giants' half of the inning he demanded that the umpire throw the ball out of the game. An argument broke out and Durocher once again was involved. Brooklyn took the early lead when Hodges hit a homer off Sal in the second inning. The Giants scored two runs in the fourth and Bobby Thomson hit a homer in the sixth to put New York ahead 3–1. It looked as if Maglie had all the runs he needed. However Sal tired late, giving up a run in each of the last three frames. Nevertheless Durocher decided to stick with his veteran right-hander throughout the entire game, even when Maglie was visibly tired. He gave up a two out RBI single in the eighth to Gene Hermanski. In the ninth Maglie retired the first two batters, and needed only one more out for a 3–2 win. Hodges walked and the struggling Roy Campanella singled. Maglie had owned Campy all day with fastballs below the chin and curves low and away. The Barber was throwing a number of sidearm curves to keep the hitters off balance along with the intimidating brushback pitch. The fact that Campanella reached base with a hit should have been a sign that Maglie was drained. Pee Wee Reese tied the game with a single before Maglie recorded the final out of the inning. Furillo hit a 0 and 2 pitch for a homer to win the game in the tenth. Durocher refused to go to his bullpen, possibly because he did not have confidence in his relief pitchers. The Dodgers had swept their hated rivals and humiliated them. How badly Dressen wanted to win that final game is indicated by the fact that he used Don Newcombe out of the bullpen. He was overpowering, getting all nine hitters he faced to earn the win.

The Giants visited Philadelphia and lost three straight as the losing streak extended to seven. Hearn, Bowman, and Jansen were saddled with loses. Hearn had defeated the Phillies nine times in his career without a loss before the Phils knocked him out of the box. The third game of the series was particularly disheartening as Jansen, Jones, and Gettel held the Phils to five hits but still lost by a 2–1 score. They out-hit the added Phillies but stranded twelve base runners. The consecutive doubleheaders the Phils had dropped to the Giants' towards the end of 1950 were still fresh in their minds. During spring training, Eddie Sawyer stated that the Giants' excellent finish was an accomplishment of a team "that had no pressure on them," implying that the Giants would have choked if they had been competing for the pennant.[19] When some baseball writers picked the Giants to win the pennant, Sawyer dismissed their chances and said that the Dodgers were a much better club. The Giant/Phillies rivalry was alive and well.

The Boston Braves won two games from the Giants at the Polo Grounds. Sal Maglie lost his second game of the season as he dropped a 3–0 decision on April 26. All three runs scored in the eighth as Roy Hartsfield and Sam Jethroe hit homers after Johnny Sain reached first on a catcher's interference. This was the second game in a row in which Maglie faltered late in the contest. Sal allowed seven hits, three walks, and struck out one in his nine innings of work. Sain won his first of the year and his one-hundredth of his career. The game proceeded in a swift manner and took one hour and fifty-five minutes to complete. Durocher benched

Stanky and replaced him with Artie Wilson who went one for three. During spring training, Leo attempted to anger Stanky by insisting that youngsters such as Wilson, Bobby Hofman, or Davey Williams might replace him in the regular lineup. It was a typical Durocher ploy — build up one of the younger players to get the regular to play harder and make him think that his job was in jeopardy. Stanky was a good player when he was angry. New York dropped a 7–3 decision to Boston on the following day.

The Giants were reeling and after the Braves series they prepared to enter hostile territory, Ebbets Field. Walker Cooper recalled what it felt like to enter that ballpark as a visitor. "It was a rough place to play. They had that band, the Sym-Phony, and they would razz you all the way back to the bench. And if you beat them, the fans would follow you to the clubhouse, cussing and yelling at you, telling you how they would get you next time. That could only happen in Brooklyn because they had that runway back to the clubhouse."[20] To get to the dugout, players had to walk down a long dirt runway. A fence on each side separated the fans from the players. When Leo was managing the Dodgers he would take a triumphant journey down the runway. With the Giants it became a dangerous excursion. "They spat on you. They threw dirt at you, rocks, hot dogs covered with mustard. Anything. They sprayed you with Coca-Cola. They called you every filthy name they could think of."[21]

The Giants were desperate for a win as the once optimistic ball club was in danger of being buried early. The tailspin continued when they lost their tenth in a row to Brooklyn by an 8–4 score on the 28th. The Giants were in last place at 2–11, already seven games behind first place Boston. The losing streak reached eleven when the disconsolate Giants lost a 6–3 decision in the second game of the series. Jansen nailed Robinson with a pitch in the sixth inning and Hodges followed with a homer to break a 2–2 tie. Robinson had words for Jansen from the time he reached first base until he was in the dugout. He continued the verbal assault from the bench. The Giants offense had done poorly during the losing streak as they failed to hit in the clutch. The game felt like a funeral for the visitors, and the Dodgers taunted them throughout. It continued into the clubhouse. At Ebbets Field a single wooden door separated the two clubhouses. Furillo and Robinson yelled, "Eat your heart out, Leo, you sonofabitch. You'll never win it this year."[22] The Giants were now 2–12, seven and a half games behind Boston. Brooklyn was 8–4, only a half-game back. Durocher needed to do something drastic to wake up his dormant ball club.

When the team settled into the clubhouse Durocher exploded and began tearing into everyone. For a team with such great talent as the Giants had, to lose eleven in a row was almost unfathomable. No one was immune to his manic tirade. The tension had been building for a week: the frustration, disappointment, and anger. It started in the second game of the doubleheader in Boston and continued for ten more days of losing. During that stretch, the Dodgers had emerged triumphant five times against them. Durocher called his club every vile name he could think of, and ripped into individual players. Bill Rigney recalls, "He'd been going on for about ten minutes — motherfucking this, cocksucking that — you know how he talked. Everybody was hanging their heads, a lot of them wincing at the same time." Some of the players felt uneasy taking the language Leo threw at them. As he was informing Hearn that he couldn't hit a barn door from five yards away, the bat boy came in and asked Shellenback where the batting practice balls should go. When Shellenback failed to answer he asked Leo. Durocher exploded and tossed a glove at the kid from about six yards away, and missed the door by about two feet. Then Alvin Dark spoke, "Hey, Skip, five yards." Stanky added that the follow through wasn't too good either. The clubhouse suddenly erupted with laughter. The Dodgers were only separated by that single wooden door. They heard Leo's tirade and suddenly they heard uncontrollable laughter. Rigney recalls, "They must have thought we were all gone crazy, like maybe we murdered Leo and were all celebrating over his body."[23] Leo implored the players who were staying in at night to go out and for the players who stayed out late to stay in. They hadn't won a ballgame but the tension had been lifted.

On the night of April 30, the Dodgers could see the dying carcass in front of them and they were out for blood. The Giants needed to end their losing streak right now, so they could stagger out of Ebbets Field with a shred of dignity still in tact. A howling, hostile contingent of 33,963 fans were there to taunt the opposition. Salvatore Anthony Maglie was on the hill and his razor was sharp. For what was thought to be a baseball game became an all out war. The Giants came out swinging, scoring six runs in the first inning as they hammered Chris Van Cuyk and Earl Mossor before Joe Hatten put out the fire. The Dodgers were not prepared to lie down and die as they scored two runs off Maglie in the bottom half of the first. Gene Hermanski led off the inning with a homer. Furillo followed him to the box and was almost beheaded on the first pitch. After Furillo and Snider recorded outs, Robinson hit a solo homer. Maglie did not feel loose and told Durocher that he was going to the bullpen to warm up some more while the Giants batted. He had to wait a long time in the dugout while the Giants scored their six runs and it may have affected his sharpness. New York scored two more runs in the second but would be held to only two hits for the remaining seven innings. In the second inning Maglie knocked down Pee Wee Reese. Reese hit a double, which led to a Brooklyn run. In the third inning, Sal avoided damage by getting Snider to hit into a double play. Despite the deterioration of the Giants' hitting as the game progressed and the Dodgers' resilience to chip away at the lead, New York managed to win the game by an 8–5 score. Maglie gave up four runs on eight hits and two walks in five and one-third innings. He struck out three. It was Sal's first win of the year. Sheldon Jones did a great job in relief. Stanky, Lockman, and Thompson led the hitters.

The real trouble occurred in the third inning, as the heated atmosphere almost erupted into violence. On Jackie Robinson's first time up, Maglie threw a vicious beanball at his head. In the third inning, Sal brushed Robinson back with the first pitch. Jackie stepped out of the box, rubbed some dirt on his hands and stepped back in. Maglie spun out of the windup and again threw close to Robinson's head. He had been thrown at a little too much for his own liking. After throwing two straight heaters, high and tight, Maglie took something off and tried to break a slow curve off the outside corner. The batter bunted down the first base line. Robinson did not burst out of the batters' box and held up his gait slightly. It was a purposely concocted strategic move; not necessarily to get a base hit but designed to get the pitcher to cover first base so he could run up his back and nail him. As Maglie approached first, Robinson sped up barely within the baseline and rammed into the pitcher's backside sending him flying into the air in the opposite direction. Maglie went after Robinson but was restrained as the two exchanged heated words. Durocher argued his case to the umpires insisting that Robinson had left the baseline as he tried to inflict bodily harm on the pitcher. The manager's curse laden tirade was directed towards each of the three umpires. Leo tried to settle his pitcher down. "I told Maglie, to stick to his pitching, that Robinson was trying a bush-league trick to get his goat."[24] Later in the clubhouse Robinson would respond, "If it was a bush stunt he is a bush manager, because he taught me to do it."[25] The ball that Jackie had bunted had gone foul. In the batter's box, Westrum tried to explain the situation by saying, "Sal wasn't throwing at you, Jack…. He was just trying to brush you back." Robinson was not having any of it, replying, "That's too fine a difference for me."[26] On the next pitch, Jackie singled to left field. In the fourth inning Robinson, who played second, covered the bag on a double play grounder; Westrum went in hard and rammed him.

The war of words continued after the game. Robinson had insisted that Maglie was deliberately trying to hit him. Maglie responded, "That's almost like accusing a guy of attempted murder…. Look, let's get this straight once and for all. I pitch like this: throw 'em high inside and low outside. I got to figure that every guy up there batting is trying to belt my brains out. So I pitch him tight, he can't get set. He has to stay loose — can't get that toe hold on the ball. Then when I come back with the low, breaking stuff on the outside, he really has to reach for it. That's the only way to pitch and win."[27] Sal told the writers that pitchers are not perfect and occasionally one will get away and hit a batter. Leo added that Maglie needed to pitch Robinson high and tight or else Jackie would hit the ball with great authority against his pitcher. The Giants were exhausted after their hard fought win, and were looking forward to a good night of sleep. The attitude in the clubhouse was very reserved as the Giants dressed with a somber look on their faces, except for Lockman who was still celebrating the recent birth of his child. The baseball prognosticators had already written the Giants off after their slow start. Arthur Daley wrote in the *New York Times*, "It would take a miracle for them to win the championship now."[28]

During this era players were always talking in attempt to motivate their team or upset the opposition. When the pitcher walked up the small rise in the middle of the diamond and faced a batter, he was urged on by his teammates. Bobby Thomson recalls that Durocher told his infielders to, "Get on Maglie! Get on Jansen! Tell 'em to bend their backs." If the pitchers got upset, the Giant infielders would yell "Let 'er rip!, Let 'er rip!"[29] This would develop into the Giants' battle cry during the second half of the season. Bench jockeying or heckling opposing players was an art form during the times. Little used players such as Bill Rigney excelled at the craft. His nickname was "The Cricket" for his ability to assault players verbally. Rigney was among a handful of Giants who idolized Durocher and wanted to be like him. In addition to his verbal skills, he was also proficient at stealing signs from the opposing team. Dick Williams was the twenty-sixth man on the Dodgers in 1951. It was his rookie year and he would bat an even .200 in 60 at-bats. He was the ultimate bench jockey and made himself useful in that capacity. He was one of those second string Dodger ballplayers who were opposed to Jackie Robinson's presence on the team. He once responded to a question concerning the black ballplayers by answering, "Yeah, they're gonna run us all right out of here."[30] Williams and Rigney had a great view from the bench as they showed off their vocal skills during a game. Their extra "skill" was not taken for granted by their respective managers. When the Giants played the Dodgers, they incessantly taunted Dressen's club and suggested they were "gutless." Don Newcombe was a particular target as the jokes made their way to reporters by the end of the season. "What has two arms, two legs, and no guts?" the Giants joked. Maglie put it crudely when he said, What did Newcombe and a homosexual have in common? "They both choked on the big one."[31]

The Giants had done exactly what they had guarded against, to get off to a bad start. They ended April with a 3–12 record but would play excellent baseball for the rest of the season. New York defeated the Chicago Cubs by a 5–3 score to begin May as Alvin Dark hit his first big league grand slam. Hearn earned his second win while Jones pitched well in relief for the second straight night. When the Cubs heckled umpire Frank Dascoli after a called balk and shouted, "You wouldn't have the guts to call that in Brooklyn," the umpire cleared the entire Cubs bench to the clubhouse.[32] New York won the next day, 8–1, behind George Spencer. They won a psychological battle as well. National League President Ford Frick admonished Jackie Robinson for bumping Maglie in the last game of their series. Frick declared, "What I did, was notify the Brooklyn ball club that if it could not control Jackie Robinson, I would. I am sick and tired of his popping off."[33] Robinson responded, "And I'm getting tired of being thrown at. Let Mr. Frick change the color of his skin, put on a baseball uniform, and go out and hit against Maglie."[34] With that one statement, Robinson implied that Maglie was acting in a racist manner when he was thrown at. Maglie read the story in the Polo Grounds clubhouse, and smiled. He had Jackie right where he wanted, venting his anger and hopefully losing his concentration.

Pittsburgh came into the Polo Grounds and won the first game of their three game series, 7–4, in ten innings. Durocher and Fitzsimmons were kicked out for arguing a pitched ball. Maglie came back the following day and spun a masterful one hitter as New York won 5–1 before a small Ladies Day crowd of 4,926. The no-hit suspense was lacking as Pete Castiglione led off the game with a triple. When Monte Irvin momentarily bobbled Gus Bell's grounder, Castiglione scored. Irvin was having a difficult time of it early in the year. Maglie walked the bases loaded in the second but escaped without damage when Bobby Thomson made a fine running catch and his throw to the plate cut the runner off. Except for two walks, Maglie was in full control for the rest of the game and retired the final eighteen Pirates in succession. Sal improved his record to 2–2. It was his third complete game of the season and improved his lifetime record against Pittsburgh to 8–1. He walked five and struck out five. Thomson, Thompson, Jorgenson, and Irvin each hit home runs. On the same day, the Dodgers entertained the Reds at Ebbets Field but lost 5–4. Dascoli indicated during the first game of the Cubs/Giants series that he was not going to tolerate excessive abuse. In this contest, he banished Don Newcombe and Dan Bankhead from the Dodger bench. It wouldn't be the last time that the Dodgers and Dascoli would come to loggerheads.

6. The American Aristocracy and the Miracle Finish   133

On May 5, Dark hit another grand slam as New York defeated Pittsburgh 8–3. After splitting a doubleheader with Cincinnati, the Giants swept three from St. Louis. In the opener against Cincinnati, Lockman fell victim to the old hidden ball trick as Connie Ryan tagged him out in the tenth inning. Durocher argued violently and was kicked out of the game but he was partially to blame for he did not warn Lockman from the third base coach's box. The Giants routed St. Louis by a 17–3 score on May 9. Maglie was the recipient of all those runs and improved his record to 3–2. New York collected twenty-one hits. Maglie went the distance, giving up three runs on five hits and three walks. He had two singles in five at-bats, scored a run and drove in two. Every starting Giant weighed in with at least one base hit. This was an inferior Cardinal lineup Maglie was facing because many of the Redbirds were sick in bed with the flu. Marty Marion, the Cardinals skipper, had eight left-handed hitters in the starting lineup against the right-handed pitching Maglie.

The Giants ended their thirteen game homestand with a 10–3 record that culminated with a doubleheader sweep of Philadelphia on May 13. Jansen won his third game of the season in the opener. Maglie improved his record to 4–2 by winning the second contest. He gave up two runs on eight hits and three walks while striking out two. Noble was handling most of the catching since Westrum had broken one of his fingers on the last day of April. Ray was swinging a hot bat, going 3 for 5 in the opener and 2 for 4 with a homer in the nightcap. Richie Ashburn gave Maglie fits as he went 4 for 4 in the second game. Irvin stole home with two outs in the fourth to electrify the crowd. When he tried to score in the sixth on Maguire's double he was out at home as Del Wilber put an exceedingly hard and unnecessary block on him. The Polo Grounds crowd booed the catcher loudly. Several of the Giants, including Durocher, were fighting the flu.

New York followed with an eleven game road trip, in which they compiled a 7–4 record. Durocher's rotation was set with Jansen, Maglie, and Hearn but after that he tried a number of pitchers to find the right combination. Kramer, Jones, Bowman, Spencer, Kennedy, and Koslo had all started at least one game. If things were not going Leo's way, he would change, change, and change some more before they finally did. They received a boost on the 19th when Monte Kennedy went the distance in a 3–2 victory. The Giants were now only a single game below .500 at 16–17. Brooklyn was at 16–13 and Boston at 17–14. Maglie had won his fifth straight on May 18 against Cincinnati. He worked seven and two-thirds innings, giving up three runs on eight hits and three walks while striking out three. The thirty-four year old Maglie took on the thirty-three year old Ken Raffensberger. These were two crafty veterans who knew how to pitch. Joe Adcock tripled off Maglie in the fourth and came home on a balk. It was the first time a Giant pitcher had been charged with a balk since 1949. Thompson was caught flat-footed on a bunt and charged with an error. With two runners on base and two outs in the inning, Maglie struck out the opposing pitcher. Raffensberger left in the sixth when the Giants scored all four runs as they went on to win 4–3.

On May 20 at Sportsman's Park, the Cardinals defeated the Giants by an 8–7 score. Hearn made his first appearance in the ballpark since the Cardinals had let him go. He was knocked out of the box in the third inning. Bowman took the loss. Stanky was kicked out of the game. Durocher argued ferociously when Red Schoendienst had a long argument with umpire Lon Warneke in the eighth inning and was not banished to the clubhouse. After the game concluded, Durocher and Warneke exchanged heated words. Reporters circulated a story insisting that Leo took a punch at the umpire but it was unfounded. Nonetheless Warneke filed a report with Ford Frick and the Giants manager was fined $100 for using "vile and abusive" language that was directed at the umpire. The umpire expressed regret for not kicking out Schoendienst and added, "However, Schoendienst did not use abusive language. Durocher's was pretty rough."[35] If this was the criterion to determine if ballplayers would be fined, then Leo was in jeopardy every game he managed. Another story developed in Cincinnati where three anonymous letters threatened Jackie Robinson's life. The FBI and local authorities took the letters seriously and took precautions including checking several buildings which looked down upon Crosley Field.

Monte Irvin had not been doing a good job defensively at first base during the early part of the season, although his bat had been active. He had never enjoyed the gateway position and was originally a third baseman with the Newark Eagles in the Negro Leagues. An inner ear problem exacerbated the situation and made it difficult for him to react to balls hit on the infield. The outfield gave him time to recover from his mistakes and still catch the ball. Irvin had not made it to the big leagues until 1949 when he appeared in 36 games for the Giants. He became bitter in reaction to the racist attitudes he encountered and his exclusion from organized ball due to the color of his skin. As Jackie Robinson played in the big leagues in 1947 and 1948, Irvin was still denied his opportunity. He had a great final two months in 1950 and was producing with the bat ever since. On May 21, Durocher made Irvin a happy man when he put him in left field and switched Lockman to first base. Lockman had played first base during spring training and was somewhat familiar with the position.

The Lockman/Irvin switch was one of the moves made by Durocher that would propel the Giants forward for the rest of the season.

After dropping another game to St. Louis, the Giants traveled to Chicago. Maglie continued to pitch well, winning his sixth straight in a hard fought 2–1 victory on May 23. He pitched out of trouble all day, as he scattered ten hits and one walk while fanning four. Alvin Dark lost his cool when he slammed the ball to the ground and was banished from the game in the first inning when Dee Fondy stole second and Dark objected to Augie Donatelli's call. The umpire subsequently listened to Durocher give a long tirade. The Cubs had a runner on base in all but two innings. Sal's last three wins were all close games. Maglie went hitless but helped his club out with two sacrifices. He was always willing to do the little things to help his team win.

All season long Durocher had been imploring Horace Stoneham to bring up a kid from Minneapolis of the American Association. His name was Willie Howard Mays. Mays was a natural, a precocious talent that does not come around often. From 1948 to 1950 he had played with the Birmingham (Black) Barons of the Negro Leagues while encountering Jim Crow racism in the deep south as the team traveled. Roy Campanella had once urged the Dodgers to sign him but they did not. When Artie Wilson was playing with Birmingham he surreptitiously scouted talent for the Brooklyn Dodgers. He urged them to sign Willie but the Dodgers balked. Eddie Montague, a Giant scout, had gone down to Birmingham to scout their first baseman. He issued the following report to the Giants front office, which eventually reached farm director Carl Hubbell: "I saw a young kid of an outfielder I can't believe. He can hit, run, and throw like — like nobody. Don't ask questions. Just grab the boy."[36] Willie was a five-point player and excelled at each tool: hit, hit with power, run, field, and throw. There was nothing he couldn't do. Nothing.

His first year in the Giants chain was at Trenton of the Interstate League where he batted at a .353 clip in 81 games but hit only 4 homers. Then in 1951 he tore up the American Association during his short time there, and batted a gaudy .477 in 35 games. Durocher knew the numbers. He had seen Willie perform during spring training and wanted him at his side right now. Leo pleaded with Stoneham until he finally gave in. It is reported that Stoneham's reluctance to bring Willie up is attributed to several reasons: He was afraid that the military might take him. Secondly, he had a good working arrangement with Minneapolis and did not feel comfortable taking their star player. In fact when he did come up Stoneham took out a full page ad in the Minneapolis paper so he could explain his situation and apologize. The Minneapolis fans did not want to see their great star leave so early. The third reason was racial. He already had four blacks on the roster: Thompson, Irvin, Wilson, and Noble. Besides the Dodgers and the Giants, only the Boston Braves had a black man on their roster in the National League during 1951. Sam Jethroe was the one black player on the Braves and was targeted frequently by racists and beanball pitchers. The possibility of five blacks and four whites going on the field together did not sit well with Stoneham. Fan reaction might be adverse as would league reaction. It was even a possibility that ballparks could explode with violence at such a sight. This was a legitimate concern during the times, considering how tough the first couple years had been for Jackie Robinson as well as the other black players. Monte Irvin states in his autobiography, "Although nobody wants to admit it, there was an unwritten quota system at the time that limited the number of black players on the ball club."[37] Stoneham wanted a quid pro quo. Artie Wilson goes down, Mays comes up. One black for another black. Some say that Durocher initially resisted but eventually gave in. Others say that Leo was going to send Wilson down anyway because he couldn't pull the ball. Nonetheless, the move was a bitter pill for Wilson to swallow. The man who had once suggested that the Dodgers sign Mays was being sent down to make room for him. He never was given the opportunity to reach his full potential as the 19 games he played with New York in '51 represented his entire big league career.

Another prominent black player at Minneapolis was Ray Dandridge. One of the greatest players in Negro League history, he became a member of an organized baseball team but was denied the chance to play in the big show. If the Giants were disappointed in the erratic play of Hank Thompson at third base their answer may have been at Minneapolis. In 1949, Dandridge batted .363. Two years later he won the Most Valuable Player award. He had been thirty-five years old when he signed, but the skills were still there. The Giants braintrust said he was too old but Satchel Paige was nearly ten years older and he pitched effective major league ball up through the 1953 season. In fact the Giants could have picked up Paige in 1950 when they needed a relief pitcher. After playing with the Indians in 1948 and 1949 he did not pitch in the big leagues in 1950. He found work with the St. Louis Browns from 1951 to 1953. Essentially Paige had one employer, Bill Veeck. There is some evidence to suggest that major league scouts tended to avoid players who were old, even if they performed superbly. Ollie Carnegie was an example with the Buffalo Bisons.

Willie Mays arrived in New York while the Giants were traveling from Chicago to Philadelphia. When Garry Schumacher, who was the head of publicity, saw the boy he thought he was another kid looking for a tryout. He wore a strange cap and brought only the clothes he was wearing along

6. The American Aristocracy and the Miracle Finish

Manager Leo Durocher and his precocious young star Willie Mays. (Author's collection)

with some baseball equipment. Before Horace Stoneham sent him to Philadelphia they bought him some new clothes. Willie joined the team in Philadelphia. As he stepped into the batter's box, everyone on both teams stopped what they were doing to watch. Mays put on a hitting show that impressed all of the spectators. Bob Cooke began an article in the *New York Herald Tribune* by stating, "Willie Mays, a preposterous rookie outfielder, reputed to be so skilled that his play may make Leo Durocher forget about the frailties of an umpire, was acquired by the Giants yesterday."[38]

With the arrival of Mays, Bobby Thomson's days as the Giants' center fielder were apparently over. Willie went 0 for 5 in his first game as New York won 8–5. Thomson played left field. Irvin played right. Mueller, who was still slumping with a batting average under .200, sat on the bench. Jansen tossed a shutout the following day against Philadelphia. New York swept the series when Maglie threw a two-hit shutout to win his seventh consecutive game. Granny Hamner and opposing pitcher Russ Meyer accounted for the two hits. Maglie faced only two batters above the minimum as the Giants turned two double plays. He walked one and struck out two. Dark made an error on Ennis's grounder in the ninth. He made another high throw as he tried to turn a double play but got the force at second. New York led 2–0 but the Phillies had the tying run at the plate. Once again Maglie found himself in a tight ballgame. He reached back and got Ashburn to hit into a double play to end the game. Sal's record improved to 7–0 lifetime against the Phillies. Durocher's club had won eighteen of their last twenty-five games. They weren't buried after all. Thomson was playing with added vigor, but his average was in the .220's and his job in jeopardy. Mays had gone 0 for 12 in the series. He had a confidence problem when he first came up and admitted years later that he was "scared shitless."[39]

Willie didn't believe he belonged after his dismal start and begged to go back to Minneapolis. Durocher realized that some of the players performed better if they were angry. Sal Maglie was one of them. Leo would push his buttons and verbally assault him until Maglie was fuming and took it out on the enemy. "So I get him mad," says Durocher. "I say, 'Whatsa matter, you stupid wop, you choking?' He gets so mad he wants to kill me, but he don't. He takes his dago temper out on the fucking hitters."[40] Durocher compared Sal to his old teammate with the Yankees, Tony Lazzeri. In the case of Willie Mays, Leo coddled him and constantly reminded him that he would be the Giants' center fielder no matter what happened. He had a meeting with the club to make sure they understood the situation. "He's a young boy, he's a baby. But he's got more talent in five minutes than the rest of us will ever have in our lifetime. It doesn't mean that I don't like you fellows equally well. But I think it does something for Mays if I keep telling him, 'You're the greatest, no one can carry your glove, nobody can put your shoe on.' I think it makes him a better player, and as long as it does, buddy, he puts money in your pocket and mine."[41] In later years players would regret the way Leo favored Mays while ignoring others, but not in 1951. Not when they were playing this well. Monte Irvin benefited greatly by Willie's presence and took him under his wing. Irvin taught Willie how to play the outfield and molded his great talent into a phenomenal ballplayer. Eventually Mays would hit. The Giants pulled for one another as a team. The black players got along with the white players extremely well. There was never that eerie feeling that Hank Thompson experienced when he walked into the St. Louis Browns clubhouse in 1947. Other teams with blacks in 1951 had problems, even the Dodgers. The regular players got along fine with Jackie and the others, but many of the second tier players did not. The Giants bonded in a way that was truly unique for the times.

6. The American Aristocracy and the Miracle Finish 139

The Giants ended May by losing two of three to Boston. In the fourth game of Willie Mays' career he got his first major league hit, a home run off Warren Spahn. Durocher described the shot using his own special vernacular: "I never saw a fucking ball go out of a fucking park so fucking fast in my fucking life."[42] The Dodgers ended the month in chaotic fashion as Ebbets Field almost erupted in violence. Russ (The Mad Monk) Meyer was on the hill for the Phillies. With Hodges on second and Robinson on third the Ebbets Field crowd was howling. Meyer yelled at Jackie, "Go ahead you nigger, try to steal."[43] This was a big mistake. A squeeze play failed and Jackie was hung up. The Phillies threw the ball back and forth until Meyer dropped it and refused to get out of the baserunner's way. Jackie shouldered his way through Meyer and crossed home plate. Meyer followed and shoved his face into Robinson's chest as they exchanged words. The explosion which Branch Rickey originally feared was imminent. The two ballplayers headed underneath the stands to settle the issue as fans scurried to get a good look at the action. Robinson's teammates forcefully brought Jackie back to the dugout. Several Phillies players hovered near Meyer just in case something broke out. When things settled down, Brooklyn won the game by a 4–3 score.

On June 1, the Giants were in fifth place with a 21–21 record. After their horrendous start they had climbed back to respectability. The Dodgers were in first place at 24–15. Dark led the New York hitters with a .335 average after the month's first game. Thompson was at .254, Bobby Thomson at .250, and Mueller was floundering at .197. Maglie won his eighth in a row on the first day of June. It was an 8–2 victory over Pittsburgh before 16,875 Polo Grounds spectators. Maglie gave up two runs on five hits and three walks while striking out four. He did not have to sweat this game out in the ninth inning. The Barber was in full control until Danny Murtaugh touched him for a homer in the fifth. Pete Reiser led off the eighth with a triple past Mays and scored on an outfield fly. That was all the scoring for Pittsburgh. Maglie had a single and a double at the plate and scored a run. Mays couldn't buy a hit, going 0 for 5, and was now 1 for 26 to start his career. Thompson also took the collar in four at-bats. The win was the Giants' twentieth in their last twenty-eight games. Throughout the month of June, Sal the Barber was on top of his game.

New York pounded the Pirates 14–3 as they scored twelve runs in their final two at-bats. Hearn won his fourth and Mays had two hits. On June 3, Koslo pitched a two-hit shutout as New York defeated St. Louis in the first game of a doubleheader 1–0. He was masterful facing only thirty batters. The Cardinals came back and won the second game, 4–3. Stan Musial always hit the Giants hard and he went 4 for 4 in the game. Harry Brecheen welcomed Mays to the National League by hitting him. Musial's performance incensed Leo and he exploded in the clubhouse, "Whatever you guys did today don't do it again!"[44] Maglie was constantly studying hitters and their respective habits. He knew the next time he faced the Cardinals he would have to send a message to their star hitter. Musial needed a close shave and the Barber was aptly skilled in its application. Stan the Man killed them the following day as well, hitting two homers off Jansen as St. Louis won 7–2. Larry did pitch inside and nailed Nippy Jones.

Maglie extended his winning streak to nine against the Cincinnati Reds and won a difficult 3–2 contest before 12,119 fans under Coogan's Bluff. He did not have his best stuff but pitched like a great warrior, reaching down for a little extra and finding a way to win. The Reds hit safely in seven out of their nine times at bat. Bob Usher led off the ninth with a triple that Mays misplayed and scored on a fly ball. Grady Hatton grounded out and Maglie fanned Connie Ryan to end the game. Mays was making a lot of fielding mistakes: throwing to the wrong base, missing the cutoff man, and trying to catch every ball in sight. The raw talent was apparent to everyone, but the skills needed to be refined. Maglie allowed nine hits and two walks while striking out two. He had one hit and scored a run. In 12 games, he had pitched 101 innings and given up 75 hits and 32 walks.

Alvin Dark's ninth inning error led to a loss on the following day. Hearn won his fifth as the Giants opened a series against Chicago. Larry Jansen improved his record to 6–5 by defeating the Cubs in the first game of a doubleheader on June 10. Sal the Barber pitched the second game but New York lost 7–4. It was Maglie's first defeat since April 26 and the first time he was taken out since May 18. After the first two batters reached in the fourth he was taken out. He gave up four runs on nine hits and one walk while throwing one wild pitch. The damage could have been much worse but he started double plays in the first two innings to get out of trouble. The Cubs scored single runs in those innings. In the third, Randy Jackson and Andy Pakfo touched Maglie for homers. It was the first time the Cubs defeated the Giants that year and Maglie's first defeat lifetime against them.

After an exhibition game against the Red Sox, the Giants traveled to Cincinnati. Allen Gettel in his nineteenth relief appearance of the season earned his first National League win on the 12th. Durocher once again was kicked out for arguing. Maglie made his first relief appearance of the season the following day and recorded the final five outs as the Giants won 5–2. He pitched out of a tough jam in the eighth by getting the two men he faced to record outs with runners on base. Jansen, Hearn, and Maglie won the next three games to extend their winning streak to five. Sal became the first National League pitcher to win ten games as he led his team to a 6–1 victory before a sparse Forbes Field crowd. He held the opposition to three singles and walked four. The Pirates managed only a hit and a walk over the first six innings. Pete Castiglione, who got the only hit in Maglie's one hitter on May 4, led off this game with a clean single. Pittsburgh pushed across a run in the seventh as Maglie walked a batter with the bases full. He lost his control temporarily by giving up three walks and a single in the frame. Sal hit his first major league home run in the fourth inning over the left field wall. Left hander Paul La Palme gave up the gopher ball that traveled over 400 feet. Maglie improved to 10–1 lifetime versus Pittsburgh while Jim Hearn was 13–2. Willie Mays had two hits and drove in two while making two good catches. With the encouragement of Irvin and Durocher, Willie had come around and had batted safely in eleven of his last twelve games. New York was in second place at 32–26, five games behind Brooklyn, 35–19.

In St. Louis on June 18, the Giants opened their series by playing sloppy baseball but still managed to win 5–4 in twelve innings. Dark made two errors in the sixth that led to a run, Stanky messed up a double play ball in the ninth and Mays also contributed an error. Koslo pitched effectively as the starter and enjoyed a 4–2 lead heading into the ninth but was taken out after surrendering a leadoff single to Del Rice. Maglie entered and after getting Peanuts Lowrey to pop up, Stanky booted a double play ball that should have ended the game. Sal worked out of the inning but not before Wally Westlake hit a two-run single to tie the game. New York pushed home a run in the twelfth as Sal held them scoreless the rest of the way. It was his eleventh win as he gave up one run on four hits, three walks, and fanned two in four innings of work. In addition to the four errors, the Giants stranded thirteen base runners. Maglie pitched Musial tight, as he only managed one hit in six at-bats. St. Louis won the final two games of the series.

They traveled to Chicago where New York defeated the Cubs 9–6 in ten innings. Maglie was taken out in the sixth when Spencer got Hank Sauer to hit into a double play to end the inning. Sal stood to be the winner as New York led 6–4. He would have won if Thomson had caught Bob Ramazzotti's fly ball in the ninth, but he misplayed it. Hal Jeffcoat followed with a homer to tie the game. Willie Mays hit a three run homer in the tenth to give New York the victory. Maglie did not have his good stuff. He pitched five and one-third innings, giving up four runs on seven hits and four walks while fanning three. He was charged with a balk. George Spencer worked a solid four and a third innings of relief to earn the win. When the Cubs won the following day it was the first time since May 9,

1950, that they had defeated the New Yorkers at Wrigley Field. Jones won his first game during a relief stint in the last game of the series.

Back home, playing against the Dodgers, New York won two of three only after they played another exhibition against the Red Sox. On June 26, Sal the Barber sharpened his razor and gave Brooklyn hitters a close shave throughout as he tossed a three-hit shutout leading the Giants to a 4–0 win before 45,732 fans. National League President Ford Frick still remembered all too vividly the last series in which the Giants and Dodgers played. The series had been a harsh beanball war, which almost boiled over when Robinson and Maglie went after each other. Frick told both managers to prohibit pitchers from throwing at opposing batters heads and ordered them to play "hard and clean." Umpires Augie Donatelli, Al Barlick, and Lee Ballanfant were told to keep things under control. They discussed the situation with Dressen and Durocher at home plate. The game was full of theatrics and the two pitchers Preacher Roe and Sal Maglie were accused of throwing the spitball all night. Roe was a noted spitballer and confessed to it after his career ended. Harold Rosenthal wrote in the *New York Herald Tribune*, "The umpires spent a good portion of the evening conversing with Maglie, meanwhile rubbing the ball in their hands, probably to restore circulation."[45]

Maglie was a notorious slow starter and threw the first six pitches out of the strike zone before settling down and getting out of the inning without any damage. New York scratched a run across in the bottom half as Dark singled, Mays doubled, and Westrum singled home a run. In the second inning the game became remarkably serious as another war developed in the proud tradition of Giant/Dodger contests. Maglie fired a ball over Andy Pafko's head that sailed to the screen. Donatelli walked the new ball out to the mound and had words with Maglie. Durocher was not happy that Donatelli bothered his pitcher, and had words with the umpire. Lockman led off the second inning for New York, and Preacher Roe threw a pitch at his head as the ball sailed all the way to the screen. Third base umpire Al Barlick warned Roe and Lockman followed by hitting an opposite field homer to give New York a 2–0 lead.

The umpires were watching the pitchers closely, maybe too closely. When Maglie threw an inside fastball to Campanella at the letters in the fifth inning, he was warned by Donatelli. Durocher objected to the call and argued with the umpire. When Maglie came up in the bottom of the inning with one out, he asked for a new ball. Barlick had a couple words with Preacher Roe as the ball was checked carefully. Maglie followed with a single. Eddie Stanky stepped into the box and took a half swing at a pitch but Donatelli rung him up for a strike. "The Brat" argued violently to the

Maglie completes his delivery. (National Hall of Fame Library, Cooperstown, N.Y.)

point where he was about to get kicked out of the game. Durocher came out of the dugout and instead of yelling at Donatelli, he rebuked Stanky. He stood the bat on its end and ordered the belligerent "Brat" to stand back in the box. Durocher wanted Stanky on the field and not in the clubhouse during another competitive Giant/Dodger game. Stanky was so infuriated that he hit a two-run homer. The Dodgers heckled him all night. "Here's your bat, Eddie dear," yelled Pee Wee Reese. "Don't get thrown out of the game sweetie." Ralph Branca scoffed, "Durocher the peacemaker, How do you like that? He sure did protect his little boy, Eddie."[46] A couple of minor debates took place when Durocher called a meeting with Barlick and Donatelli. In the middle of the sixth, Donatelli spoke to Roe.

Maglie improved his record to 12–3 on the year. Duke Snider was the only Dodger to reach second base in the masterful pitching performance. He gave up two walks and struck out four. Preacher Roe lost his first game of the year, falling to 10–1. Douglas MacArthur and his wife attended the game and enjoyed the battle that took place on the field. Bill Rigney played third base instead of the slumping Hank Thompson. During the recent road trip Thompson had batted only .189. Two days later he would make three errors at third base. Leonard Koppett succinctly summed up the first game of the series, "By midnight, Maglie had his second shutout, the Giants had beaten the Dodgers, and no one had been skulled."[47]

The Boston Braves pounded the Giants by a 19–7 score on the last day of June. They scored eight runs in the seventh and seven runs in the eighth. Tommy Holmes was making his first appearance at Braves Field since replacing Billy Southworth as manager. Maglie was touched up for four runs in the first inning, highlighted by Sam Jethroe's triple and Sid Gordon's two-run homer. Leo showed confidence in his hurler and let him stay in the game. Over the next five innings he held Boston to two hits before the floodgates opened in the seventh. The Giants rallied to take a 7–4 lead. Sal faced five hitters in the seventh and they all reached base before Jones replaced him. Sheldon gave up four hits before Koslo belatedly got out of the inning. Maglie lost his fourth game of the season; he had never defeated the Braves and had lost to them four times. He pitched six innings, giving up nine runs on eight hits and four walks while striking out five. In the first inning Vern Bickford threw a pitch at Mays' head. Willie raised his right hand to protect himself and the ball hit him there. Maglie later hit Jethroe in retaliation. When Maglie felt like nailing someone he did. Sal Yvars recalled one day when Maglie kept shaking off Yvars with a 2–2 count on Jackie Robinson. Maglie wanted to bring some heat, and Yvars angrily stormed to the mound. Yvars barked, "Throw your goddamn curve!" Maglie responded, "Forget it, I feel like knocking him on his ass."[48] Mueller had broken out of his slump and had hit in nineteen straight games. It was the longest Giant streak since Fred Lindstrom batted in twenty-four straight in 1930. Earl Torgeson hit two homers for Boston, while driving in seven runs.

The Brooklyn Dodgers apparently wrapped up the pennant with a 18–10 record during the month of June. On the eve of the trading deadline on June 15, the Dodgers solidified an already potent lineup by acquiring Andy Pafko, Johnny Schmitz, Wayne Terwilliger, and Rube Walker from Chicago in exchange for Bruce Edwards, Joe Hatten, Gene Hermanski, and Eddie Miksis. Pakfo was the left fielder the Dodgers had long sought after. In 1950 he batted .304 with 36 homers and 92 driven in. Many baseball men believed that Pakfo's presence in left field would assure the Dodgers of a pennant. Leo Durocher had made an offer for Pafko but Frankie Frisch, the Cubs general manager, turned him down. Durocher and Frisch had a very quarrelsome relationship dating back to their time on the St. Louis Cardinals. Frisch was the manager and Leo thought he could be a better field general than Frisch was. He implored Branch Rickey to get rid of him. Frisch in turn told Rickey to get rid of Leo, and that's actually what he did after the 1937 season. It's been suggested that this trade may have been payback for Frisch.

Brooklyn had a murderous lineup: the infield included Hodges at first, Robinson at second, Reese at short, and Cox at third. The outfield from left to right consisted of Pafko, Snider, and Furillo. Campanella was behind the plate. The pitching staff was formidable with Newcombe, Roe, Carl Erskine, and Branca. This was a pushbutton team. That is used not to denigrate the lineup but merely because very few changes were needed for them to be successful. It wasn't like the Giants where Durocher was always searching for the right combination. Charlie Dressen felt suffocated. He couldn't show off his great baseball acumen by using a number of tactics and varying strategies throughout the course of a ballgame. All he had to do was write those nine names down and the Dodgers won. Eventually his ego would take over and he would begin to make illogical and foolish decisions. He wanted to take all the credit when they won and let his players take the blame when they lost. His self-centeredness led to irrational judgments. Durocher surrounded himself with good baseball men whom he listened to: Freddie Fitzsimmons, Frank Shellenback, and Herman Franks. Dressen refused to take advice from those around him. Clem Labine recalls, "Leo certainly understood that you had to pump a player up sometimes and give him confidence. I never felt that Charley could do what Leo did in terms of making a player truly confident in what he could do. In fact, he was just the opposite, which is not a very complimentary thing to say. But I really think he was more apt to tear a person down than build him up."[49]

The Giants continued to play well in July as Maglie, Jansen, and Hearn won consistently while Spencer became a stabilizing force in the bullpen. In Philadelphia, Hearn won his seventh. On July 3, New York needed thirteen innings to defeat Philadelphia 9–8 in a three hour and fifty-two minute game at Shibe Park. Durocher wanted this game badly and used Jansen in relief who won his tenth. Leo used five pitchers while Maglie and Hearn warmed up in the bullpen. Eddie Sawyer selected Giant pitchers Jansen and Maglie for the National League All-Star squad. Dark was also on the team. The Phillies were having a tough time of it. The Whiz Kids' mastery had eluded them, as they would finish in fifth place in '51. At the end of June, Sawyer tore into his team for their lackadaisical play. He sent Mike Goliat to the minors and informed his club that others may follow, "I wouldn't sell that kind of player. I'll send him back to the minors and let him stay there until he realizes that we're in the game to win."[50]

Durocher's pitchers were a slightly overworked group as they headed into the 4th of July doubleheader with the Dodgers at Ebbets Field. The 34,640 Brooklyn fans who attended the game celebrated two Dodger victories by scores of 6–5 and 4–2. The opener took over three hours as Preacher Roe squeezed home the winning run in the eleventh inning. He had worked a full nine innings two days earlier, but Dressen did not hesitate to use him in relief as he worked two innings to tie Maglie with twelve victories. Noble's throwing error allowed Robinson to advance to third and set up the squeeze bunt. Maglie was working on a four-hit shutout until the eighth when he allowed three enemy runs. Campanella touched him for a two run homer while Reese hit a solo shot. Sal pitched eight innings (he got the hook in the ninth) giving up eight hits, one walk, while striking out two. He hit Gil Hodges with a pitch. Jones was the losing pitcher in relief as his record fell to 2–6. Ralph Branca won the second game for the Dodgers, while Koslo took the loss as the starter. Dressen was kicked out. Erv Palica, coach Jake Pitler, and Don Newcombe were also tossed. Durocher exploded when he saw Dressen in the owner's private box. Umpire Scotty Robb told Leo that Dressen could stay there as long as he stayed off the field and did not give signals to his team. It appeared that Dressen was sending signals. Earlier in the season, Dressen had infuriated Cardinals manager Marty Marion when he was kicked out and appeared in the dugout with a groundskeeper's cap. Marion protested the contest. One writer suggested that the Dodgers decided to play the nightcap without their brains. The long day ended in controversy as pinch runner Hank Schenz was called out for going out of the baseline to avoid Robinson's tag. It resulted in a game ending double play. Durocher argued the call of umpire Babe Pinelli as did several other Giants. Leo's confidence in the hard drinking Thompson having faded, Rigney played both games at third base. The Dodgers won the following day 8–4 as Newcombe won his twelfth. Jansen hit Furillo in the bottom of the first. John Lardner poked fun at the Dressen/Durocher battles in *Newsweek*. "The chances are that Durocher and Dressen are roughly equal intellectually. It's a tribute to Dressen's brain that he uses Jackie Robinson every day, but, if he didn't, he'd be back in Oakland, Calif. It speaks well for Durocher that he pitches Sal Maglie whenever he can, but, if he didn't, a man from the state hospital would come and drop a net over him. Call it a good, clean draw."[51]

In the last game before the All-Star break, New York lost to Boston by a 6–5 score in ten innings. Maglie held the Braves scoreless before allowing two runs in the fourth and getting knocked out of the box in the seventh. He worked six and one-third innings, allowing five runs on six hits, two walks, and one hit batsman (Luis Marquez). Sal collected two singles in three at-bats. Sid Gordon won the game off Koslo when he smashed a homer off the left field upper deck façade. Davey Williams was recalled from Minneapolis as rumors circulated that Stanky would become manager of Bill Veeck's St. Louis Browns. In 1952 he would replace Marty Marion as the manager of the St. Louis Cardinals. Williams played in 13 games in 1949 and in 1951 he would play in 30 as he prepared to become the regular second baseman. He was not a prolific hitter but could play the field extremely well. Brooklyn had an imposing 50–26 record at the break, good enough for an eight and a half game lead over the Giants. New York's second place record was 43–36. Brooklyn's team batting average was .282 while New York was batting at a .258 clip. Maglie had a tremendous first half appearing in 21 games and compiling a 12–4 record for a .750 winning percentage. He pitched 153 innings, gave up 123 hits, 50 walks, and struck out 65.

The eighteenth All-Star game was played at Detroit's Briggs Stadium. The Dodgers' supremacy in the National League was apparent as seven Dodgers were on the squad: Hodges, Robinson, Campanella, Snider, Reese, Newcombe, and Roe. The American League was favored heading into the contest but Eddie Sawyer's squad handed them an 8–3 loss. Stan Musial, Bob Elliott, Gil Hodges, and Ralph Kiner hit homers for the Nationals, tying a record for most homers hit by one team. Vic Wertz and George Kell went deep for the American Leaguers. Sawyer wanted to win badly and even pulled his own pitcher Robin Roberts after two innings of work. Maglie followed with three innings in which he allowed two runs on three hits and one walk while striking out one. He served up solo homers to

Wertz and Kell. The left-handed batting Wertz continued to hit Maglie hard. After the fifth inning, the Nationals had a 4–3 lead which they never relinquished making Maglie the winner of the game. Newcombe followed Sal with three scoreless innings and Ewell Blackwell pitched a scoreless ninth. Ashburn was the outstanding player as he hit a single, double, scored two runs, stole a base, and played an excellent center field. The gate was announced at $124,000, which was $2,000 short of the record set in the 1950 contest at Comiskey Park. The players' pension fund received the money. Briggs Stadium was a hitter's park and this game did not tarnish its reputation.

After the midsummer classic, St. Louis took two of three from the Giants at the Polo Grounds. Two Pirate killers pitched on July 15, Maglie and Hearn. Pittsburgh won the opener in twelve innings, 7–6, as Maglie did not figure in the decision. The Pirates got two runs off Sal in the second inning. George Strickland slugged a homer, Pete Castiglione singled and Gus Bell tripled. New York scored five in the third as Mueller hit a homer and Mays drove home two with a triple to highlight the inning. Maglie had a 6–2 lead when they scored one in the sixth but couldn't hold it. Sal was taken out in the seventh when he gave up a homer to Joe Garagiola, two walks and a single. Allen Gettel came in and got Kiner to pop up with the bases loaded as New York held to a 6–4 lead. Pittsburgh tied the score in the ninth and won it in the twelfth when Erv Dusak singled off Koslo. Maglie gave up four runs on seven hits and two walks while fanning four. In the second game Hearn went the distance for his eighth win of the year as New York won 8–3.

Bobby Thomson was the son of a Scottish professional soldier who emigrated to the United States with his family when Bobby was two years old. He first made the New York Giants team in 1946 and would not leave until after 1953. He hit at least 24 homers in six of the seven full seasons he played in New York. A great low ball hitter, he possessed a fluid graceful running stride and a batting stance that drew comparisons to Joe DiMaggio when he first appeared on the green pasture below Coogan's Bluff. He may have been the fastest man in the National League, even faster than Willie Mays when he joined the Giants. His speed was deceptive due to his loping strides. Despite Thomson's speed and natural gifts he never became a complete ballplayer. The little things were not part of his game: bunting, baserunning, and the correct sliding techniques. Thomson's career high for stolen bases was ten in 1949, which was a sad commentary on his ability to read pitchers and his willingness to steal. Although during the times he played, the stolen base was being employed less often as a weapon. Bobby was never Durocher's type of ballplayer. He did not have the fire and intensity that Leo insisted upon.

Thomson started the '51 season slowly, went on a home run spree, and then began to slump again. Durocher called Thomson into his office. Bobby was nervous and was expecting the worst; either he was going to be sent down or traded. He stood in front of Leo with an indifferent look on his face while he was dying inside. Leo tore into Bobby and told him he should be a much better ballplayer with the skills he had. Thomson was dumbfounded and as the conversation ended he headed for the door at which time Leo informed him that he was the new third baseman. He had played the position early in his career and Leo thought that he could make the adjustment in the middle of a season. Durocher also persuaded Thomson to change his batting stance. He previously held the bat very high in a vertical position. Bobby began to bend his knees and hit out of a crouch and explode after the ball. He would have his problems at third but once he became acclimated to the position he settled down.

Hank Thompson had not done the job at third and found it difficult hitting under an "alcoholic haze." Eventually he was farmed out to Ottawa with his batting average in the low .200s. His 1951 numbers with the Giants were troubling to the front office: .235, 8 homers, and 33 runs driven in for the season to go along with 15 errors. Perhaps if they could get him away from the bars in Harlem he would regain his batting eye.[52] Thompson received the news of his demotion shortly after he had been spiked by Chicago Cubs pitcher Frank Hiller. He needed stitches as his right toe was cut open. Circumstances allowed him to stay with the club a little longer than expected but in early August he was sent down temporarily. Al Corwin, a young hurler with an awkward delivery from their Ottawa farm team, eventually replaced him on the roster.

The Giants won the final game of the Pittsburgh series by a 7–6 score as a season low 3,390 spectators showed up at the Polo Grounds. Frankie Frisch, manager of the Cubs, took pleasure in defeating Durocher in the two games that followed. Frisch was ending a 16-year career as a big league manager, which included stints with the St. Louis Cardinals and the Pittsburgh Pirates. These were his last games managing against his old rival. Phil Cavarretta would soon replace him as manager. Irvin was hit by a pitch in the opener. In the second game Frank Hiller nailed Stanky and Westrum. He also cut open Hank Thompson. Frisch lost both of his shortstops to injuries, Roy Smalley and Jack Cusick. Durocher and Frisch battled each other to the very end. On July 20 a rejuvenated Bobby Thomson played third base and went three for five at the plate with two RBIs. New York defeated Cincinnati 11–5 as Sal Maglie finally won his thirteenth game in his fifth try. It was his first victory since June 26 when he tossed a three hit shutout against Brooklyn. He was working on another three hit shutout until the Reds scored three in the seventh. Ted Kluszewski hit a two run homer off Sal in the ninth. Durocher had Sal Yvars behind the plate hoping that he would get after Maglie to work harder. He gave up the five runs on eleven hits and three walks while striking out four. Horace Stoneham gave Leo a two-year contract extension through 1952. It was a vote of confidence and gave Durocher one less thing to consider down the stretch.

Larry Jansen won his twelfth when Stanky hit a two run inside the park homer to put the Giants up for good as New York defeated the Reds 3–2. Two days later, on July 24, Maglie won his fourteenth as the Giants defeated Pittsburgh 4–3 in ten innings. Pittsburgh scored all their runs in the fourth inning, but two of them were unearned as Dark made an error. He redeemed himself with three hits including a double in the tenth and scored the winning run on Mays' single. Maglie was in full control after the fourth inning as he held the Pirates without a hit while Gus Bell was the only batter to reach base with his walk. Sal allowed four hits and two walks (one was intentional) while striking out ten. He unleashed one wild pitch. Larry Jansen earned the win in relief as the two teams completed a suspended game from June 17 on the following day. Al Corwin made his major league debut in the regularly scheduled game and looked impressive before being knocked out in the seventh. The Pirates won 5–4 as Spencer took the loss.

Against Cincinnati the New Yorkers swept a four game series. Hearn, Jansen, Maglie, and Spencer picked up victories. Maglie went the distance in the first game of a doubleheader on July 28 for his fifteenth win. He allowed one run on seven hits and two walks while striking out six in the 3–1 victory. Sal had a single and drove in a run at the plate. On the last day of July, Maglie recorded the final four outs to secure a New York victory over Chicago by a 4–3 score. He relieved Jones in the eighth with two men on and two out and immediately gave up a hit to new manager Phil Cavarretta. Eddie Miksis grounded to Dark to end the inning. Hearn won his tenth. Dark was charged with two more errors. He would lead the major leagues with 45 for the season.

The Dodgers stumbled after the All-Star break going 3–6 but rebounded by winning their final ten games of the month to finish with a 21–7 record. When they dropped a 13–12 game against Pittsburgh on July 18, they had lost six of seven. Erv Palica was the losing pitcher. He had pitched well in 1950 with a 13–8 record and a 3.58 ERA but had not lived up to expectations in '51. Charlie Dressen had declared when he became the Brooklyn manager that there would be no doghouse under his leadership but he would not follow what he preached. After the game Charlie told the press, "I never saw a fellow with so many alibis," adding, "If it isn't his groin, it's his arm, or something else." Palica was stereotyped as an immature kid and this character assassination was sanctioned by the Dodger management. Dressen told the press concerning his pitcher, "When you're ready to throw the ball hard you can pitch for me again. Until then, no. It's all up to you."[53] Buzzy Bavasi, the Dodgers' vice president, also attacked Palica. Dressen suggested the kid was "choking."[54] The reality was grossly different from how the Dodgers wanted to portray it. They attempted to perpetuate a myth that baseball was played by dumb inarticulate men. Palica had won two courageous games against Philadelphia down the stretch in '50. In 1951 he twisted his ankle and continued to pitch until his arm hurt. When a pitcher came to Dressen complaining of an arm ailment he believed it was all in the pitcher's head. "Go soak your head in the whirlpool."[55] The verbal abuse by his employers tormented Palica. His pregnant wife walked down the street as people yelled, "your husband hasn't got any guts."[56] Erv Palica's career was over before it started and he would never again be an effective big league hurler.

Dressen's antics were over the top, even more so because his club was way out in front. Charlie told reporters, "We've lost six of our last seven, and where are we? Eight games in front yet. If Newk and Branca had been all right we'd be ahead by eleven, at least."[57] When the Dodgers won the final ten games of July it seemed almost certain that the pennant was in grasp. However, the pitching staff was beginning to show signs of overwork as Clem Labine was called up from St. Paul. As the season dragged on Dressen would continue to behave illogically and try to prove he was a superior manager. Dressen seemed to be setting up alibis as if the Dodgers would collapse. The daily newspapers helped the Dodgers typecast their ballplayers. In early August, Bob Cooke wrote an article in the *New York Herald Tribune* defending the Brooklyn manager. "In the interests of accuracy, it should be reported that Dressen never called Palica 'gutless' as has been said in some quarters. He merely referred to Palica as a man of many alibis."[58] What Dressen actually did was stand in front of reporters with his hands around his neck suggesting that his pitcher choked up.

New York began August by losing three of four. Al Corwin pitched a shutout over Chicago to earn his first major league victory. On August 3, Sal Maglie's record dropped to 15–5 as St. Louis defeated the Giants by a 5–4 score at Sportsman's Park. He was working on a four hitter and had a 1–0 lead before the Cardinals scored five in the seventh to knock him out of the box. Previously the Cardinals had runners in scoring position in the second, fourth, fifth, and sixth innings but failed to score. In the seventh he issued three hits and two walks before departing. Kennedy the left-hander was brought in to face the left-handed hitting Musial. Musial drove in three with a bases loaded triple. Maglie had kept the Cardinals' star hitter scoreless in three at-bats. Sal gave up seven hits and three walks while striking out two. Earlier in the season Durocher had boiled over when Musial went on a rampage against Giant pitchers. In later years Maglie recalled in an interview with Robert Boyle how he pitched Musial: "Several weeks later I started against the Cards, and I figured I had better deliver the message to Musial. He was the kind of gentleman who understood. To hit Musial you had to throw the ball two feet inside, and I hit him in the hip. He put the bat down and went to first base and never said a word. You have to respect a gentleman like that." Maglie went on to call Stan the "best hitter I ever pitched against."[59] Sal's memory was a little off because he didn't hit Musial in that game, nor did he hit Musial in 1951. Nonetheless he provided a succinct statement on how the game was played during the time. Hitters expected pitchers to throw inside and many of them accepted it as a part of baseball strategy. When Maglie threw at Musial in his career, the Cardinals slugger would be unperturbed. When Maglie did hit Stan he behaved actually as was stated, by simply running to first base.

Koslo tossed his second two-hit shutout of the year against St. Louis on the 4th. New York won the final game of their Western swing defeating the Cardinals by an 8–4 score. Corwin won his second game of the year and received some help from Maglie out of the bullpen. Sal relieved Corwin in the eighth with runners on second and third. Sal Yvars could not hold one of the Barber's offerings and was charged with a passed ball as a runner scored. Maglie shut the door after that. He drove in a run with a single as well. Gerald Staley took the loss: he had defeated the New Yorkers in five straight games including two successive shutouts before this game. In Thomson's first seventeen games at third base he batted .345 with 5 homers and 18 RBIs. The Giants finished the Western trip with a 10–5 record, but their interest began to wane towards the end.

Rain postponed a Giant/Dodger game on August 7 and set up a day-night doubleheader the following day at Ebbets Field. The Giants were nine and a half games behind Brooklyn. They would play six games against the Dodgers in eight days. At the beginning of July, the Dodgers swept the Giants in three straight at which time Dressen declared that he no longer had to worry about the New Yorkers. As they headed into a crucial series in early August, Leo told reporters that he had not conceded anything to their hated rivals. If the Giants were going to mount a surge their time was running out and they had to move now.

Many of the Giant fans who dared to enter Ebbets Field were upset that Dodger management was charging two admissions for the August 8 doubleheader. The tension gripped the small ballpark, as fights broke out in the stands like wild brushfires. The Brooklyn fans watched the action unfold on the diamond like a bunch of untamed jackals ready to pounce at any moment. Brooklyn won the game by a 7–2 score behind Carl Erskine's stellar relief pitching. Monte Irvin was nailed by a pitched ball from Erskine. In the seventh inning Sheldon Jones sent Pee Wee Reese into the dirt with a vicious knockdown pitch. Later in the inning, Campanella went down. Durocher and umpire Jocko Conlan had a heated exchange, which included several bombastic gestures by the Giants' manager.

Whatever tension and hatred that griped the stands in the first game was now fully evident on the playing field in the second. Brooklyn won 7–6 in ten innings to extend their lead over New York to eleven and a half games. The Renaissance Assassin was on the hill for the Giants and the Ebbets Field fans were howling for his scalp. The Maglie/Robinson feud was heightened to another level as they ferociously competed against each other. The gloomy weather only added to the ominous feeling that hovered over the ballpark. Maglie enjoyed the edge over Robinson whenever they met in these kinds of battles. On this night Jackie humiliated the proud Giants hurler. He beat him with his mouth, his bat, and his legs. When Robinson stepped into the box his first time, he went down. Jackie started to walk towards the mound and cursed the Barber throughout. The Barber grabbed his crotch in response and turned his back, as he gazed out into the green pasture towards center field. He was scowling at the hitter, with his heavy beard and threatening persona. One runner was in scoring position. Maglie spun out of the windup and threw a curve that started at Jackie's head and broke low and away. Robinson hung in and slashed the ball to right field driving in a run. He taunted Maglie at first base. Jackie danced off the bag and stole second while mocking the pitcher for the whole time. Furillo had led off the inning with a homer. Brooklyn had a 2–0 lead after the first frame.

Duke Snider drew a two out walk in the third. When Robinson came up for a second time he bunted down the first base line hoping to draw Maglie over and nail him as he had done earlier in the year. The Barber refused to come close to the bag, hovering around the safe haven of the pitcher's mound. Jackie danced off the bag using disturbing gestures in an attempt to unnerve the pitcher. Maglie threw over to first four times but the runner got back easily. The crowd yelled every vulgarity they knew in his direction as a cascade of boos reverberated throughout the claustrophobic ballpark. The Barber was a slow worker with runners on base and umpire Bill Stewart told him to hurry up his deliveries. Sinister Sal surreptitiously gave Stewart the finger in reply as the crowd made even more noise. He threw over to first once again in a contemptuous manner. Maglie began to stall as Robinson had invaded his confident demeanor and implanted some doubt in his head. The Dodgers scored two more runs when Pafko singled, Robinson and Snider stole bases and Yvars helped out with a couple of wild throws.

In the fourth inning Reese drove Newcombe home with a two out single. When Jackie came up with two men on base the Barber threw two wicked knockdown pitches. The crowd was fixated on the action. Maglie had enough humiliation for one day and looked towards the bullpen but nobody was up. Ebbets Field erupted when he belatedly got out of the inning. The crowd marked his departure by throwing beer cups, hot dog rolls, peanuts and anything else that seemed convenient in his direction. Sinister Sal tipped his cap and extended his middle finger before disappearing into the dugout. He had lasted only four innings, giving up five runs on seven hits and two walks. He welcomed Andy Pafko to the Dodgers by hitting him. Mueller and Rigney were nailed by Dodger pitchers. New York was trailing 6–3 heading into the ninth but they rallied for three runs to tie the game. Billy Cox's RBI single in the tenth off Koslo won it for the Dodgers. It was a line shot off the left field wall. Yvars' poor defense had prompted Durocher to replace him with Wes Westrum. He had been charged with two errors and gave up a couple of stolen bases. Earlier in the game when Robinson bent down to grab some dirt, Yvars threw a handful of it in Jackie's face. Robinson cursed him out and informed him what would take place if it happened again. Yvars understood. Jackie was 3 for 5 as he beat the enemy using every skill he had. The Dodgers stole seven bases in the doubleheader, and Robinson had three of them. Rube Walker recalls that after Robinson tormented Maglie he'd come back to the dugout "practically frothin' at the mouth."[60] Clyde King, the Dodgers' relief pitcher, threw over to first base several times in the tenth inning. Durocher also charged from the third base coach's box and declared that King was making quick pitches. The game had all the theatrics characteristic of a great Dodger/Giant game. It appeared as if the Dodgers had assured themselves of a pennant with the doubleheader defeat.

The lead was extended to twelve and a half the following day as Brooklyn defeated New York by a 6–5 score to sweep the three game series. Charlie Dressen and his Dodgers held a 12–3 record against the New Yorkers for the season. The two teams broke a major league record by walking twenty-four batters in a nine-inning game. The five Dodger pitchers walked fifteen while the four New York pitchers walked nine. After the game the Dodgers rubbed it in and taunted the Giants. They kicked a sleeping dog right in the mouth. A single wooden door separated the two locker rooms in Ebbets

Field and if you spoke loudly your voice could be heard on the other side. The Dodgers taunted the opposition without mercy and banged their bats against the door. "The Giants are dead! The Giants are dead!" the Dodgers shouted. "Roll out the barrel, we got the Giants on the run!"[61] They taunted them, teased them, and cursed them. Reports had Newcombe, Branca, Furillo, and Robinson at the door berating Durocher's team, leading the tirade. Some of the Dodgers urged their teammates to leave them alone but they continued. Furillo and Robinson yelled, "Eat your heart out, Leo, you sonofabitch. You'll never win this year."[62] The Giants just sat around until blood began to boil and their hatred of the Dodgers became more ensconced. Bill Rigney recalls, "Because they had kicked our butts we had to sit there and take it. But we didn't forget." Alvin Dark reportedly stated, "Human beings can only take so much and we had a bellyfull. You just can't treat human beings like they treated us and get away with it."[63] Stanky lost it and began cursing across the wooden door in retaliation. His cursing tirade pierced the air, while throwing in some racial epithets along the way. "Stick that bat up your ass, you black sheepfucker!" Stanky finally realized that Monte Irvin was standing behind him. "That's good enough for me, Eddie."[64] When a reporter asked Leo if he would make more lineup changes, Leo "the Lip" blew up, "This is my team," adding "There will be no changes in the lineup. If they go down, I go down with them."[65]

The Giants lost the opener of a four game series to the Phillies on August 11. Eddie Sawyer's ball club had suddenly awoken and won ten of twelve. When Brooklyn won their first game of their doubleheader against Boston the lead was at thirteen and a half. This was an insurmountable margin for any team to overcome, particularly against the mighty Brooklyn Dodgers. When Durocher's clubs were not in the pennant race, he would begin to lose interest and allow his coaches or even the players to manage games. The players whom he did not hold in high regard, as far as their abilities were concerned, were given an opportunity to perform. This way he could go to Stoneham and ask to get someone better. Bill Rigney recalls, "Anyhow, I think I 'managed' that day, and of course it was like trying to manage a bunch of robots. Nobody cared any more — well, almost nobody. Everybody was playing for themselves, for their next year's salaries."[66] The following afternoon was Wes Westrum day at the Polo Grounds. The players vowed to play hard and not to embarrass Wes on his day before the good folks of Poughkeepsie.

Sal Maglie got the call the following day and faced Russ Meyer in the first of two. Once again the Barber got off to a tough start. Waitkus and Ashburn led off the game with singles and Jones sacrificed to move them along. Del Ennis hit a little roller in front of the mound; Maglie fielded it and cut Waitkus down at home as Westrum applied the tag. With two outs, Sisler singled, scoring Ashburn to give the Phillies the early advantage. In the bottom half of the first, Meyer was spiked by Dark as he covered first base. Both of the players converged on first base bag simultaneously and Meyer fell to the ground in agony. The spiking did not appear to be intentional. Russ was carried off the field on a stretcher and needed seven stitches. Eddie Waitkus touched Maglie in the third for his first homer of the year off the right field overhang. Irvin hit a three run homer in the third to give the Giants the lead. Jocko Thompson and Maglie threw up zeroes for the next five innings. The heat was unbearable, enough to put anyone in a bad mood — particularly the Renaissance Assassin. He needed one more out to win the game. Eddie Waitkus stood in the way of his sixteenth victory, with two outs in the ninth. Eddie had tacked on two singles to his homer and was hitting the Barber extremely well in '51. Maglie recalls, "He always hit me pretty good, but he was a loudmouth, you know. He always liked to let everybody know about it." Sal gave the batter a menacing look, the look of an expressionless executioner about to put the man in front of him out of his misery. Thomas Kiernan wrote that he looked at you "like an undertaker silently estimating your coffin measurements." Waitkus was a low ball hitter and Maglie was a low ball pitcher. He was also left-handed which gave him a slight edge on the right-handed pitcher in that he would have a better view of the ball when it was delivered. With the count at no balls and two strikes, Maglie considered "hitting the bastard." The Giants were playing out the string of a long disappointing season so if he unleashed the beanball and put him at first it would not jeopardize their pennant hopes if he came around to score. The crowd implored Sal to "Knock the fuckin' bastard down." Waitkus sensed that a ball was about to be thrown at his skull and therefore stepped out of the box. He felt a stabbing pain in his side, only two years removed from the shooting episode in Chicago. When Eddie stepped back in, Sal's threatening gaze was fixated on his skull. He looked at the batter as a fox looks at lamb chops. The Barber made Westrum go through the signs once again and flash a dummy signal as if something special was in store for the batter. Eddie had the audacity to upset the Barber by yelling, "Go ahead, you fuckin' wop! Go ahead, I'm ready for it!"[67] The Barber scowled and gave a contemptuous smile. Durocher implored Sal to deliver a pitch. Maglie decided not to put the tying run on base and tried to get him with a pitch on the outside corner instead of hitting him. Waitkus hung in and slugged the ball down the right field line but it went foul. As Waitkus retrieved his bat he gave the pitcher the finger and then Sal put him away for the final out. His record stood at sixteen and five. He allowed seven hits, one walk and struck out three. Maglie was masterful against this club, 8–0 lifetime. Al Corwin went the distance in the second game to improve to 3–0. It was another close game as New York won 2–1 and it rained throughout. It had rained on the Giants all year but little did the 17,072 fans who attended the doubleheader know that their Giants had just won the first two games of sixteen straight they would win to get them back in the pennant race.

New York won the final game of the Philadelphia series by a 5–2 score as Jansen won his fifteenth. The Giants than proceeded to sweep the Dodgers in three games. Erv Palica came out of Dressen's doghouse and made his first appearance since July 4. It was a start he wished he never made as Mueller hit a two run homer in the first and Lockman added a solo shot. Palica was done after the first and so were the Dodgers. George Spencer came out of the bullpen to start and went the distance for his seventh win as New York won 4–2 before 42,867 Polo Grounds fans. The following day's score was 3–1 as Hearn tossed a six hitter for his eleventh victory. Westrum, who was in a mighty slump, won the game with a two run homer in the eighth, his sixteenth of the year. The Dodgers had runners on the corners with one out in the eighth inning as Furillo stepped into the box. He lifted a drive towards right center and Billy Cox went back to the third base bag to tag up. Mays made a fine running catch towards the right field stands. He had no chance to throw the runner out. At least that's what most of the spectators thought but this was the great Willie Mays. He completely spun around, 360 degrees, and unleashed a bullet towards home plate in a single motion. Lockman ducked out the way so he wouldn't get killed as Westrum caught the strike and nailed the runner. Harold Rosenthal wrote in the *New York Herald Tribune*, "It was the finest double play seen in the Polo Grounds in a long time."[68] Willie was the first man up in the bottom of the eighth and got a single before Westrum hit his homer.

On August 16, fans and players at the Polo Grounds stood for a moment of silence to honor Babe Ruth who had died three years earlier on the same day. Maglie faced Newcombe. It was strength versus strength. The irresistible object versus the immovable force. Each of them had a 16–5 record heading into the contest. This would be the Barber's day, as he became the first National Leaguer to win seventeen games in the hard-fought 2–1 win. He allowed four hits, did not walk a batter and struck out three. Billy Cox broke up the shutout with a leadoff homer in the eighth. New York made three errors, of which Dark made two. The heart of the order faced the Barber in the ninth: Robinson, Campanella, and Pafko but they each grounded out meekly. The Giants had won six in a row and cut the lead to nine and a half games. Charlie Dressen's club was finally humbled by the Polo Grounders.

Going into the weekend series with the Phillies, Leo was thinking more about holding off the third place Phillies than catching the Dodgers. Despite the fact that Leo had not verbally conceded the pennant to the Dodgers, his mannerisms suggested otherwise. During the sixteen game winning streak he allowed Dark and Stanky to manage some games. New York swept the series as Spencer, Jansen, and Corwin won games.

Back at the Polo Grounds against Cincinnati they won two games. On August 21, Maglie was looking to win his eighteenth game of the season. The Giants' early performance was not characteristic of a team that had won nine straight. New York scored a run in the second to take the early advantage. Bobby Adams and Connie Ryan hit back to back homers in the fourth to put the Reds in the lead. Maglie got Virgil Stallcup to hit a grounder in the fifth, but Thomson booted it and threw it away for a double error. John Pramesa went the other way for a home run into the right field stands. Rigney pinch-hit for Maglie in the bottom half of the inning. Spencer and Jones each worked two scoreless innings the rest of the way to keep them in it. Trailing 4–1 in the eighth, the Giants exploded for six runs to win 7–4. Sal gave up only three hits and did not walk a batter but each one of the hits was a homer. Spencer earned the win as his record improved to 9–4. The following day, Lockman hit a double to chase Dark home with the winning run in the eighth to win 4–3. The streak was at eleven. A reporter boldly asked Leo if he thought they could catch the Dodgers. Durocher exploded and rebuked the writer for what he considered a stupid question: "I'd rather beat those guys than anything else in the world." He added, "Of course I think we can catch 'em."[69]

The excitement began to build in the Giants' clubhouse. They were playing hard, one game at a time. It's an old baseball cliché sometimes rendered trite, but that's how the Giants played. They had already failed by their early season debacle. The team had nothing to lose, and looked relaxed in their fluid execution. Sometimes they played ugly, but they found a way to win. On August 24, they scratched out two runs in the bottom half of the ninth to defeat St. Louis by a 6–5 score. Thomson's error in the eighth allowed St. Louis to take the lead. Williams hit a grounder to Solly Hemus at short with the bases loaded and Thomson rammed into the catcher to score the winning run. It was the fourth game in a row in which they rallied late to win. On the 26th and 27th the Giants won consecutive doubleheaders from the Cubs to extend the streak to sixteen. On the first day, Westrum won the opener with a homer coming with two out in the ninth to give New York a 5–4 win. Every day the hero was somebody different. Maglie started and looked as if he would win his eighteenth. In the ninth he served up a three run homer to Chuck Connors that tied the game. He worked eight and one-third innings, giving up four runs on nine hits and two walks while striking out nine. Spencer recorded the final two outs of the ninth and earned his tenth win.

The streak ended when Pittsburgh defeated New York by a 2–0 score. New York played sloppy defense as Jones, Stanky, and Mueller committed errors. Only 8,803 fans showed up at the famed Harlem ballpark to watch a club that had won sixteen straight. Many thought they had been watching an illusion for the past two weeks. The streak was nice but to beat the mighty Dodgers was asking too much. During the streak the Giants continually came from behind. Eight of the sixteen victories were decided by one run. They split their final two games of August. Their record for the month stood at 20–9. For the season they were 76–53 but still seven games behind the Dodgers. Brooklyn had not faltered much in August, recording a 19–13 record.

The Giants and Dodgers were set to play the Labor Day weekend with two games at the Polo Grounds to begin September. If Durocher's club wanted to keep a flicker of hope alive they had to win both games. Maglie enjoyed a 3–1 record against the Dodgers on the season and he toed the slab in the opener. The Dodgers countered with Ralph Branca. Charlie Dressen was home in bed with the flu; therefore coach Cookie Lavagetto ran the team in his stead. Despite the manager's absence the game was a typical Dodger/Giant war, filled with beanballs, bench jockeying, and arguments. The Dodgers looked helpless in the contest as New York won easily by an 8–1 score behind the exploits of Maglie, Mueller, and Stanky. The Barber finally won his eighteenth game as he limited the Dodgers to seven singles. He did not walk a batter and struck out seven. Mueller hit three home runs and drove in five. Thomson hit his twenty-fourth homer. In the fifth inning, Reese lined into a triple play as Dark speared it, flipped to Stanky for the second out and "The Brat" tagged Furillo for the third out.

The day started out hot and muggy but by the time the 40,794 persons began to take their seats below Coogan's Bluff, it was overcast, windy, cold, and dreary with the threat of rain. When the Brooklyn batting order was announced the crowd booed powerfully to make sure that the enemy knew they were not welcome guests. New York took the early lead as Mueller hit a solo shot in the first and Thomson hit a two run homer in the second to put them up by a 3–0 score. Tensions were high right from the start. In the first inning the moody but reserved Duke Snider exploded when Lee Ballanfant, the home plate umpire, punched him out on a 3–2 pitch. Robinson and Lavagetto ran towards Snider and tried to calm him down. In the second inning, Sinister Sal sharpened his razor and threw close to Campanella a couple of times. Jackie Robinson faced Maglie with the bases loaded and two outs in the third inning. Maglie broke off an inside curve that didn't break as he had expected. Jackie hung in and then ducked away at the last moment, raising his hand to protect his face, but the ball glanced off his left wrist. It forced home a run. Maglie was hot and trotted towards the umpire insisting that the ball hit his bat not his wrist. Westrum was also arguing, as was Durocher. Despite the ill feelings that Maglie felt towards Robinson, it was extremely doubtful that Maglie nailed him on purpose. He wanted to win and if he were going to hit Jackie it would have been a fastball between the shoulder blades. The argument raged for several minutes, at which time the four umpires huddled to discuss the situation. There were four umpires instead of the customary three because of the combative nature of Giant/Dodger games. Ballanfant told Durocher and Lavagetto to make their pitchers cease throwing at each other, despite the fact that Maglie's pitch was a hanging breaking ball. Pee Wee Reese later stated that nobody was throwing at anybody. Robinson and Lockman had no complaints. This was baseball, a rough and tumble sport that employed the beanball, the brushback, and the knockdown as a part of baseball strategy. Durocher suggested that the umpires should stick to umpiring instead of mind reading.

In the bottom of the third Mueller hit his second homer as New York took a 5–1 lead. The Giants killed a Brooklyn rally with a triple play in the fifth inning. Maglie was in full control after that as he held Brooklyn to only two singles. Mueller hit another two run shot in the seventh to put New York up 8–1. The Barber held down the big Brooklyn bats all day. Snider went 0 for 4 while Hodges and Robinson did not hit the ball out of the infield. Before the game one of the spectators in the grandstand yelled at the writers, "Hey, tell the truth for a change today!" Harold Rosenthal wrote in the *New York Herald Tribune*, "The truth is that the Dodgers were as outclassed as if the world championship Little Leaguers from Stamford, Conn., watching the game from behind home plate, had taken their places. Maglie's mound mastery baffled Brooklyn, and every time the Giants got one of their eight hits it raised a large welt."[70] In addition to Maglie hitting Robinson, Lockman was hit twice each time by a different Brooklyn pitcher.

The lead was cut to five on the following day as New York won 11–2. The game was full of knockdown pitches, arguments, and even bench clearing incidents. Hearn was shaving the batters close and won his fourteenth game. The Dodger pitchers retaliated by knocking down Thomson and Mays. Mueller continued to swing a potent bat by hitting two homers to tie a National League record of five in two games. Right before he hit his second homer in the eighth, Mueller was informed that his wife had given birth to a boy. Thomson hit his twenty-fifth homer and was nailed by a pitch. The Dodgers did not play with the expected class of a first place ball club. When home plate umpire Al Barlick called a strike on Pee Wee Reese in the fifth inning the Dodger bench verbally assaulted the umpire. Barlick kicked out Branca and the young, bombastic Dick Williams. Williams had done his job for the day as the consummate bench jockey. Newcombe objected to a balls/strikes decision by Barlick in the sixth. He was banished to the clubhouse, along with Labine and Robinson. Maglie was conducting some bench jockeying of his own, suggesting that Newcombe was "choking." The large Dodger right-hander was fuming at the suggestion. Dressen subsequently emptied his bench and ordered his players to the clubhouse so they would not get kicked out. The problem was that the clubhouse at the Polo Grounds was in dead center field, about 500 feet from home plate. It took them several minutes to walk out there. When Cal Abrams was called to pinch-hit it took over three minutes for him to come to home plate. Barlick also had to ask the public address announcer to order the Dodgers to shut the clubhouse door, not once but twice. This was actually the third time during the season that Dressen had sent his players to the clubhouse. Any objective observer of the national pastime could see that these tactics were bush, certainly not worthy of a first place ball club like the Dodgers. Dressen was fined for "failure to control his bench." Red Smith wrote in the *New York Herald Tribune*, "Charley Dressen, manager of the best National League club in years, has been making a spectacular ass of himself."[71] The Dodgers were cracking and feeling the pressure.

New York won four out of their next five games to keep the pressure on. On September 5, New York took a doubleheader from the Braves in Boston by scores of 3–2 and 9–1. The inconsistent Sheldon Jones went the distance in the opener to improve his record to 5–10. Maglie went the distance to earn his nineteenth win in the second game. He allowed one run on six hits. New York scored five runs in the fourth to bust the game open. Irvin hit a three run homer in the inning, his eighteenth. Brooklyn had won all four of its games during the same stretch. Despite this, the Dodgers were feeling the pressure and began watching the scoreboard to see how the Giants were playing. For the first time all season they began to care about what the Giants were doing in their games. A rumor circulated that Newcombe and Hodges had gotten into a fight. They denied it of course but the Dodgers were beginning to bicker and have inner squabbles while the Giants played like a team with everyone helping each other out.

On September 8, the Dodgers pummeled New York by a 9–0 score. Their victory suggested that talk of a Giant comeback may have been premature. Newcombe was overpowering, throwing a two hitter. The lead was now six and a half. Before the game many of the Dodgers peered into the stands, expecting a sellout but only 23,171 persons packed into Ebbets Field. The park held about 32,000 seats but could hold more. Hearn took the loss for New York. In the fourth inning, Robinson danced off the bag and so unnerved the Giants pitcher that Durocher came out of the dugout to calm him down. Jackie scampered home on a wild pitch. Ed Sinclair buried the Giants the following day in the *New York Herald Tribune*. "Well, Sir, the Giants got caught up yesterday just as many expected they would be and they now must wait till next year to bring their carefully nurtured pennant hopes out of their hope chest. They gave it a good run after a bad start, but the law of averages finally tagged them and through the medium of the team which figured to win all year long, the Dodgers."[72] The Dodgers tried to put the nail in the coffin the following day. The Giants were clinging to a 2–0 lead in the eighth but Maglie was in trouble. Snider singled and Robinson tripled, scoring the first Brooklyn run. Dressen held Robinson up at the third, but the ball got away from Dark and through Stanky's legs. Robinson could only watch from the vicinity of the third base bag. The Giants' bullpen sprang into action. The count went to one and one on Pafko and Durocher came out to talk to Maglie. At that moment 30,000 white handkerchiefs waved through the air as the Brooklyn faithful taunted Durocher derisively. Home plate umpire Artie Gore told the public address announcer, Tex Rickart, to tell the crowd to stop waving the handkerchiefs. The fans waved them with increased intensity as a cascade of catcalls and boos reverberated around the park. When play resumed, Pafko slashed a grounder down the third base line. Thomson made a great backhand stab, tagged Robinson and fired it across the diamond to complete the double play. Durocher later declared, "That's the greatest play I've ever seen a third baseman make."[73] The play saved the game and a chance at the pennant. Maglie got pinch-hitter Jim Russell to bounce into a double play to end the game in the ninth. He became the first twenty game winner in the National League, joining what Bucky Walters had once called the "American aristocracy."[74] He allowed the one run on seven hits and four walks while striking out four. Irvin produced the offense with a two run homer in the fourth, his twentieth. Durocher later lauded Maglie saying, "Sal's a great pitcher, and I'll tell you why—three curves and the guts of a burglar."[75] If the Dodgers thought their rivals were going to lie down and die they were mistaken.

New York traveled to St. Louis where they lost two out of three. On the 11th they won the opening game of a doubleheader before 28,348 fans at Sportsman's Park by a 10–5 score. New York scored four in the ninth to pull away as Koslo won his eighth game in a relief stint. Westrum hit his third grand slam on the year. Gerald Staley shaved the Giants close and hit Dark and Irvin. Jansen started the second game but had nothing, allowing twelve hits and two walks for three runs in seven innings. His record fell to 18–11 as the Cardinals won the game by a 4–3 score. Rain postponed the following day's game but they gained a half a game as Brooklyn lost to Cincinnati. History was made the following day. St. Louis defeated New York by a 6–4 score in the makeup game during the day. At night, the Cardinals played host to the Boston Braves and lost 2–0. It was the first time since 1883 that a team played two other teams in the same day. Only 4,160 showed up for the Giants game. Maglie was knocked out of the box in the second inning. He recorded only four outs, allowed five runs on three hits and two walks and hit Solly Hemus with a pitch. St. Louis had a six run second inning and never relinquished the lead. Sal's record fell to 20–6.

After the St. Louis series, New York won five straight before losing to the Reds on September 20. At Wrigley Field for the last time, New York defeated the Cubs in two games. In Pittsburgh, the Giants swept a doubleheader by scores of 7–1 and 6–4. Jansen won his nineteenth game by throwing a three hitter in the opener. Maglie had nothing in the second game, but showed the guts of a veteran pitcher and hobbled to victory, his twenty-first. Durocher needed him out there, despite the fact he was working on two days' rest. He gave up four runs on twelve hits and three walks while striking out twelve. At the plate he laid down two sacrifices. Durocher, Thomson, and Herman Franks were banished in the fourth inning for arguing balls and strikes with Augie Donatelli. Pittsburgh first baseman George Metkovich was kicked out for arguing a call at first base in the seventh. Maglie blew a 4–1 lead in the eighth to allow Pittsburgh to tie it and worked a shaky ninth inning. New York scored two in the top of the ninth to take the lead. They defeated Cincinnati in their next game before only 5,448 Crosley Field fans but lost on the 20th as Hearn dropped his ninth.

Brooklyn split two games with the Pirates on the 14th and 15th and split two with the Cubs the following two days. Clem Labine had improved his record to 4–0 on the 16th. He had given the Dodgers a much needed boost since being recalled from St. Paul. They dropped a 5–3 decision the following day as Clyde King's record fell to 14–7. Turk Lown accidentally beaned Roy Campanella in the head. As Campy fell to the ground in agony his teammates rushed to his aid. They feared the worst as he bled profusely out of his left ear. Campy was removed from the field on a stretcher and would miss the next four games. The loss was particularly bitter because Gene Hermanski, who had gone to the Cubs in the Pafko deal, hit a two run homer to decide the game. Brooklyn won two of their next three from St. Louis.

The Dodgers traveled to Philadelphia and lost two of three to the Phillies. Clem Labine was knocked out in the second inning. He gave up seven runs including a grand slam to Willie "Puddin' Head" Jones. The young Brooklyn hurler who had saved their tired rotation suddenly found himself in Dressen's doghouse. When Jones came up with the sacks full, Labine opted to pitch out of the stretch position because he felt it would give him better control, particularly because he wasn't getting the curveball over. Dressen yelled at him from the dugout and demanded that Labine take a full windup. The cocky pitcher ignored the manager's directive and Jones hit a grand slam homer. Dressen rebuked his young pitcher and virtually ignored him for the rest of the season. He made one relief appearance for the rest of the regular season. Labine later recalled, "After that he wouldn't talk to me, wouldn't even recognize I was on the team.... Charlie was a vindictive guy. He wanted to make sure I paid the penalty for not listening to what he said."[76]

While the Dodgers played a three game series in Philadelphia from September 21–23, New York swept Boston in three straight from September 22–24. Jansen won his twentieth in the first game to give the Giants two twenty game winners for the first time since Carl Hubbell and Cliff Melton had done it in 1937. The Giants had won thirty-one of thirty-eight games and were only three games behind the Dodgers. Maglie won his twenty-second on the following day and finally emerged victorious against the Braves. It was "Sal Maglie Day" at the Polo Grounds as he was on the field well before game time. The Loyal Order of Moose organized the event as a train full of friends traveled down from Niagara Falls. He made a speech beforehand and received several gifts, most prominently an automobile. New York won the game 4–1, but the innings of a long season were beginning to add up and the fatigue began to show. Maglie pitched out of trouble all day as he allowed thirteen hits and struck out seven. Five times the Braves had two hits in an inning. Only Bob Addis' dying quail single to center which scored Sid Gordon in the sixth proved crucial. Maglie had a single at the plate while Irvin, Mays, Lockman, and Thomson drove in the Giant runs. Irvin was leading the National League in RBIs at this point with 113. New York swept the series the following day as Stanky hit a two out single in the ninth to win the game 4–3. Attendance was poor throughout the series as they drew 11,925, 17,774, and 6,059 for the three game set. New York was two and a half games behind Brooklyn with four left to play.

One of the reasons for the Giants' late season surge was attributed to the fact that they were stealing the other teams' signs. They had a powerful naval telescope pointing out of one of the windows of the clubhouse in dead center field. A spotter watched the game from behind the telescope and relayed the type of pitch through a buzzer system that had been hooked up and connected to the Giants' first base dugout and the right field bullpen. Sal Yvars usually watched for the signal and relayed the sign to the batter. If there wasn't a buzz it meant a fastball was coming, one buzz indicated that a breaking ball was on the way. Yvars told the batters to watch the baseball in his hand as they batted. If he tossed the spheroid into the air it meant a breaking ball was coming; if he held it, a fastball. Some players took advantage of the intricate system while others preferred not to.[77] The two days in which Mueller feasted on Dodger pitching and hit five homers it was suggested that he knew what pitch was coming. Bill Rigney stated that the Giants stole signs from second base. The first runner to advance to the midway would find out the sequence from the catcher and give it to Rigney. The runner at second would also flash the signs to the hitter. Former Giant Willard Marshall recalled, "There was a lot of sign stealing going on back then. When I was with the Giants we had Bill Rigney in the clubhouse with a spyglass."[78] Dark and Stanky were particularly skilled in stealing the opposition's signs and relaying them from second base. The Dodgers complained about the intricate sign stealing system at the Polo Grounds, but the truth was that just about every team stole signs to some degree. Sometimes the batters would perform badly if they knew what was coming. The fine art of sign stealing went back as far as the nineteenth century, so this was nothing new. John McGraw had a guy raise or lower a venetian blind in center field to signal the batter which pitch was coming. Durocher like many other managers did anything to get an edge. Wes Westrum, who later became a coach and a big league manager after his playing career finished, stated "I must have helped Willie Mays to at least another twenty-five homers in his career by letting him know what pitch was coming."[79]

On September 25, a crowd of 7,219 fans showed up at Shibe Park as the Phillies played host to the Giants. In Boston, the Braves were playing a doubleheader against the Dodgers. Jim Hearn was given an early 3–0 lead and he shut out the Phils through the first six innings. The Dodgers were the most hated team in the National League by the players and in many quarters by the fans. In the fourth inning, the sparse crowd erupted in cheers as they stared at the scoreboard. The numbers told the story. All the Giants turned around in amazement and became mesmerized by the digits on the scoreboard. Boston had won the opener 6–3. Willie Jones touched Hearn for a homer to lead off the seventh. The Giants' bullpen sprang into action and began warming up at a ferocious pace. Maglie, Koslo, and Spencer were throwing. Hamner popped up but Waitkus and Wilber singled in succession. Durocher wasn't messing around; he went with his best. The thirty-four year old right-hander, Sal Maglie, trudged in from the bullpen. Hearn came off the field and began to cry, thinking he had disappointed the team and robbed Maglie of a day's rest. Sal had gone the distance two days earlier and Hearn was only thinking about the team. Maglie worked Del Ennis carefully but fell behind as the count went to 3 and 1. He broke off a perfect pitch. Ennis swung and beat the ball into the dirt. Dark fielded it, flipped to Stanky, who turned it over to Lockman. A 6-4-3 tailor made double play and the Giants were out of the inning. Maglie put the Phils down in the eighth and ninth to secure the victory. He allowed only one hit and did not walk a batter. Hearn won his sixteenth. In Boston, the Braves completed the doubleheader sweep by winning the second game 14–2. Brooklyn played like a team under immense pressure. They played sloppy baseball, committing three errors. Then they threw inside. Sid Gordon had been hit twice while Robinson and Furillo were hit by Boston hurlers. The impenetrable thirteen and a half game lead was now down to one. Brooklyn had five games remaining while the Giants had three. The Dodgers began to argue with one another, and Dressen's odd behavior only exacerbated the situation. One writer had noted that the Dodgers looked like a "tired old fighter, a little punch drunk, who occasionally brings one up from the resin to stay in the scrap."[80]

The Giants won easily the following day in Philadelphia by a 10–1 score as Jansen won his twenty-first. Brooklyn woke up and humiliated Boston by a 15–5 score. In the eighth inning the Dodgers had a 13–3 lead with Robinson dancing off third base. Jackie showed up the opposition when he quickly stole home. Whether he had done it intentionally to humiliate the opposition or had seen an opportunity and taken advantage of it, the steal violated one of baseball's unwritten rules. Manager Tommy Holmes stated, "They needed that run like a hole in the head. All I know is it made my guys mad and they're really gunning for them now."[81] Only 2,244 showed up at Braves Field for the game. Furillo was hit by another pitch. When Boston played the Giants to end the season they wouldn't actually lie down and die but they certainly weren't going to play as hard as they did against Brooklyn. They played a congenial contest. As for Holmes, he lived in the Bay Ridge section of Brooklyn and received death threats from neighbors.

The Giants were off the next two days while the Dodgers dropped two games. On the 27th Brooklyn lost a 4–3 decision to Boston and lost their cool in the process. Only 2,086 fans bothered to show up. The game turned ugly in the bottom of the eighth. The Dodgers had their infield drawn in with runners on the wings. Torgeson bounced a chopper towards second. Robinson swept in and fielded the ball and fired to Campanella at the plate. It was a bang, bang play. Umpire Frank Dascoli called the runner safe. Campy exploded like he never had before and was thrown out of the game, as was Cookie Lavagetto, thrown out for the first time in his career. Gordon grounded into a double play when play resumed. As Cooper wielded his bat at the plate, Dascoli sent all the Dodgers to the clubhouse except Dressen and coach Jake Pitler. Robinson was nailed by a Chet Nichols pitch in the contest. The Dodgers continued to harass the umpire after the game. Robinson cursed Dascoli as he left the field. The umpires' door was located next to the visiting clubhouse and as the Dodgers went by they kicked it viciously and continued to curse the umpire. Preacher Roe kicked a hole through the door, Robinson was there as well. Robinson was fined $100 while Roe was fined $50 for the incident. Even if Dascoli had blown the call, it wasn't Dascoli who had lost all those ballgames down the stretch as the Dodgers choked in the pinch. The Giants were euphoric when they heard the news about Campanella. If the mild mannered Dodger catcher blew up they knew the Dodgers were feeling the heat. Many of the baseball writers chastised Dascoli in their respective papers. Bob Cooke did not, and said it best, "If you examine the tableau closely you'll see how unsavory it actually is. The Dodgers, still a pennant possibility as this is written, should be ashamed of themselves. They're old enough to know that baseball is a game in which pennants are won with a bat, or a right arm, or left, but never with the aid of an umpire."[82] A coin toss was held in Ford Frick's office in order to determine where the three game playoff would be held in the event of a tie. The Dodgers won and opted to have the first game in Ebbets Field and the following two in the Polo Grounds. Brooklyn had won nine of eleven from the Giants in Ebbets Field and Dressen wanted to take the early advantage before going into enemy territory. Durocher was not disappointed by their choice. When the Dodgers dropped a 4–3 decision to the Phillies the following day, the Giants were in a first place tie. Philadelphia starter Karl Drews nailed Hodges and Pafko as the Dodger hitters were being hit at an accelerated rate down the stretch. When the Giants visited Shibe Park the fans had cheered, but when the Dodgers came in they booed them without mercy. Not only were tempers short in the clubhouse but everywhere they went they faced small, but hostile crowds. The opposing players were not too friendly either.

The two teams were tied with identical 94–58 records with two games remaining. New York traveled to Boston to finish out the season while

Brooklyn had two more games in Shibe Park. On Saturday, September 29, the Giants played a day game at Braves Field while the Dodgers played at night. Sal Maglie was given the pill for New York. Warren Spahn, arguably the best left-hander in baseball, pitched for Boston. He had already compiled twenty-two wins, which equaled Maglie's total. It was a game that tested the heart of a man. Salvatore Anthony Maglie was a tired pitcher who reached down deep for something extra and pitched a magnificent game. It was cold and windy, not the conditions which the Barber preferred. New York took the lead in the second. Mays walked with one out and promptly stole second. As Spahn held the ball he stole third. Mueller hit a dying quail that dropped softly onto the grass just over second base. In the fifth, Maglie singled with one out, went to third on Stanky's single and scored on Dark's fly to left field. The final run came in the ninth as Lockman tripled off reliever Vern Bickford and scored on Westrum's single.

The 7,091 fans who braved the cold weather were cheering the Giants loudly and providing encouragement all through the game. Maglie took a long warmup because of the cold weather, which tended to make him stiff. He was also a slow starter and wanted to make sure he was breaking off his curve properly. Boston managed only two scratch hits in the first six innings. In the fifth, Bob Addis hit a ground ball towards right field. Lockman made an unsuccessful dive and the ball eluded his grasp. Stanky knocked it down and threw to first where Maglie recorded the out. In the seventh the Braves had runners on the wings but Sibby Sisti hit a comebacker to end the frame. In the ninth, Boston threatened with runners on first and second and one out. The bullpen was working quickly. Maglie induced Cooper to hit a little dribbler in which the Giants got the force at second. Marshall popped up to Lockman at first to end the game as New York won 3–0. The Giants played errorless ball behind their ace right-hander. Maglie improved to 23–6. He allowed five hits, walked one and struck out one. With Brooklyn not scheduled to play until that night, the Giants were a half game in front. Durocher gave all the credit to his players, "These guys have been great. You can't put your finger on any one guy and say he did it. It has been a team job, and each and every one of them is entitled to the credit. If there's any justice at all they'll win it because they deserve it."[83]

Sal Maglie was a pitcher who was dead tired. So were the rest of the starting hurlers. In Philadelphia he had injured his shoulder throwing out Richie Ashburn but he pitched even when hurt. He'd come to the park with an aching shoulder practically every day and the trainer had to work on him for at least twenty minutes. Jim Hearn recalls the predicament of the

6. The American Aristocracy and the Miracle Finish 169

staff, "We were just plain worn out, our arms were hanging dead."[84] They weren't sleeping well either, if at all. When Sal walked from the hill after his game in Boston, his teammates quickly congratulated him. Afterwards Durocher said, "When you beat Spahn, you beat the best left-hander in both leagues. Terrific game, Barber." The Braves lauded him as well. Walker Cooper stated, "I never saw a better exhibition of control by anybody. He put the ball exactly where he wanted it."[85]

That night in Philadelphia, the Dodgers won by a 5–0 score to pull even before 28,408 hostile Shibe Park fans. Newcombe threw a seven-hit shutout for his twentieth win. The following day Charlie Dressen was quoted in the *Brooklyn Eagle* making illogical statements that would have baffled any normal human being, "The Giants can't hurt us," Dressen said "Let me explain about the Giants. They are a flash in the pan. You'll see, when they come down the stretch, they'll crack. It isn't that I have anything against the Giants personally. I admire the Giants, in a way. They are so lucky. For a team that has no class, they have been very lucky. But in the long run, you know yourself, class will tell." Dressen continued to disparage the Giants, even saying they had "no class, no ability, no talent."[86] To put it bluntly, Dressen had cracked.

The season came down to one game. Both teams were tied with identical 95–58 records. The Giants' pitching staff was overworked, tired, haggard, pitching with only a wing and a prayer. The tall Oregonian Larry Jansen toed the slab in the all-important game. It was another cold day at Braves Field as 14,209 persons showed up to cheer the Giants on. In the first inning Bob Addis doubled and Sid Gordon singled to drive home the first run of the game. For the next seven innings Jansen pitched with the heart of a champion and held the Braves hitless and allowed only a walk. In the second inning, Thomson had tied the score with a homer off the left-field scoreboard. When the scoreboard showed that the Phillies had a 4–0 lead over Brooklyn, the Braves Field fans stood and cheered the news. New York scratched out another run in the third with three singles. The Giants closed out their scoring for the day in the fifth when Irvin's single scored Dark. When Jansen walked a runner in the sixth, Durocher told Maglie to grab his glove and walk down to the bullpen. Sal the Barber strode out triumphantly in a long black coat and the fans acknowledged his gutsy performance from the day before and cheered him. Sal loosened up slowly just in case his weary arm was needed one last time. After five innings, the Phillies had an 8–5 lead. It was the ninth inning in Boston as the Dodger game moved into the sixth. Addis led off the ninth for Boston with a double to right field. Jethroe hit a cheap single and Addis moved up to third. Torgeson tapped one towards short. Dark swept in and thought about throwing to first but flipped the ball to Stanky at second for the force. Jethroe, who was a very swift runner, slid in a second too late. The score stood at 3–2. Stanky had been inadvertently spiked on the play but stayed in the game. Jansen bore down and got Gordon to make an out. His back was aching and he was dead tired just like the others. Durocher came out of the dugout but Jansen met him halfway. Larry definitively told Leo he was staying in. This was his game to win or lose. One more out and the Giants looked like they had the pennant. Marshall flied to Irvin in left and the game was over. Players and fans rushed onto the field and mobbed Jansen as he strode exhaustedly from the center of the diamond.

When the Giants boarded their train headed for New York, the Braves and Dodgers were still playing. The champagne was on ice. Russ Hodges was on the phone relaying the play by play to the players. Brooklyn was fighting for their lives in Philadelphia. Jackie Robinson single-handedly rose to the occasion and kept his team in the game. The Dodgers rallied and tied the game at 8–8 in the eighth. In the twelfth, the Phils had the bases loaded with two outs and Eddie Waitkus up at the plate against Newcombe. The batter tore into a pitch and sent a low liner headed for right field. Robinson fully extended his body as he dove and speared the ball. When he crashed to the ground his left elbow jammed into his stomach. He lay on the ground unconscious for a couple seconds, feeling the stabbing pain in his side. Umpire Lon Warneke signaled that the batter was out. In the fourteenth inning Robinson hit a solo homer off Robin Roberts and cautiously circled the bases still shaky from the earlier blow. Brooklyn won the game, 9–8, as Jackie Robinson personally lifted the club to victory. On the Giants' train, Durocher walked over to Hearn and without emotion informed him that he would start the first playoff game in Brooklyn. The Dodgers came back from the clutches of defeat and pulled one out. The game took four hours and thirty minutes of nerve-racking baseball till it came to its conclusion. The tension was temporarily lifted and they celebrated as if they were given a reprieve from the governor. When the Giants got off their train they were mobbed by well wishers. Nothing had been decided after 154 games; both teams stood at 96–58. New York City and the rest of the country were transfixed by the pennant race.

The first playoff game was on October 1 at Ebbets Field. The Giants' battery rode to the ballpark together: Wes Westrum and Jim Hearn. Hearn's confidence was fragile and he was nervous. Westrum tried to calm his hurler down. Westrum recalled, "With him, it was a matter of confidence. If he was feeling confident, there wasn't a better pitcher in baseball."[87] Westrum would have to take charge and lead the pitcher in this crucial game. Hearn had a strained ligament in his left side but wouldn't dare tell anyone about it. Ballplayers simply played hurt back then and were not quick to complain about an injury. Doc Bowman worked on it before the game. A crowd of 30,707 hostile fans jammed their way into Ebbets Field. Hearn pitched a marvelous ballgame, a five hitter, as New York won 3–1. After Ralph Branca hit Irvin in the fourth, Thomson hit a two run homer. Branca and Thomson would meet again. Irvin added a solo shot for New York. Branca gave up three runs on five hits and five walks in eight innings. As they had done all season the Giants scraped and hustled for the entire game. Since August 12, they had won an unreal thirty-eight of forty-five ballgames. This was the team to which Charlie Dressen said would crack a day before the regular season ended. After the game, the Giants sat around, drank beer and talked. Hearn was hurting badly, but he had never been happier in his life. Branca wandered around the Dodger clubhouse angrily, "one pitch, just one pitch." Ed Sinclair wrote in the *New York Herald Tribune*, "He was just a heart-broken young man and in a little while the dressing room was full of heart-broken men."[88] If Branca was disconsolate, in two days he would be left without a pulse.

Durocher told reporters he was uncertain if he would use Jones or Maglie the following day. Leo got together with Maglie and Jansen when the players arrived at the park. Leo openly declared, "Boys I want your help and suggestions."[89] Sal wanted the extra day's rest and opted to pitch the third game in the Polo Grounds if it was necessary. Leo followed the player's advice. Jones pitched the second game while Maglie and Jansen were available in game three. A crowd of 38,609 spectators showed up at the Polo Grounds on October 2 as the Dodgers won a must win game by a 10–0 score. Robinson, Hodges, Pafko, and Walker hit home runs. Who saved the Dodgers on this day? None other than Clem Labine who threw a shutout. The pitcher who was forgotten after he failed to listen to Dressen's orders and surrendered a grand slam homer to Willie Jones. He kept New York off balance with his curve and a fast sinker. Jones was knocked out of the box in the third and Spencer and Corwin followed. Dressen accused Jones of throwing a spitter in this one. One game would now decide the pennant. No longer could they draw this out for yet another day. Maglie would face Newcombe. Strength against strength like it should be. Maglie had tortured the Dodgers in his career and enjoyed a 5–1 record against them for the season.

On Wednesday, October 3, the pennant race would come to its ultimate conclusion. Only 34,320 fans made their way into the Harlem horseshoe below the craggy bluff. There were many empty seats, about 20,000 of them. The Giants fans may have thought that this quixotic dream of theirs was only an illusion. The 10–0 Dodger victory the previous day may have brought them crashing back to reality. Maglie had nothing left, the long season had taken its toll. He would trudge to the mound with a tired old arm and a heart as big as California. While he warmed up, he realized that his arm was not responding as he would have liked. Maglie recalls, "I just couldn't get anything on the ball. I usually wouldn't have said it, but this time I told Leo to get me out of there the first sign of trouble."[90] The Dodger lineup had a notable absence. Campanella had a torn hamstring and would be replaced by Rube Walker. He had played the first playoff game, but Dressen opted to go with the healthy backstop in the next two. As the game began, Durocher was already imploring Maglie to "Stick it in his ear," as Furillo led off.[91] Maglie worked the count to two and two and then struck Furillo out. He walked Reese and Snider. Maglie's curveball was hanging, and he couldn't find the plate, missing high in the strike zone. Sal was a low ball pitcher so this was a sign that something was wrong. Robinson singled to left, driving in Reese with the first run of the game. Maglie got Pafko and Hodges to end the inning but Brooklyn had struck first against the notoriously slow starting Maglie. Newcombe made quick work of the Giants in the first and looked sharp.

In the bottom of the second, Thomson made a deplorable base running mistake. It was so atrocious that fans might have discussed it for generations to come if the Giants had lost as a result. Thomson would have been branded as the goat in the tradition of Merkle and Snodgrass. Lockman singled with one out. Thomson pulled a Newcombe offering down the left field line. He put his head down and plowed needlessly towards second base not looking at the play develop in front of him. When Pafko fielded the ball, Lockman who had rounded second retreated to the bag. Cox took the throw at third and fired to Robinson. Thomson was startled to see Lockman at second, when he finally looked up. He was embarrassed when Robinson tagged him for the out. He literally ran the Giants out of a rally in the biggest game he would ever play. Freddie Fitzsimmons, the first base coach, had tried to stop him and he cursed Thomson in the dugout. Newcombe escaped the inning without any damage. It became dark and overcast early in the game and the lights were turned on at 2:04 at the start of the third inning. The game developed into a pitching duel as Maglie and Newcombe looked like two great prize fighters, a little dazed, trying to get through the last round by throwing everything they had at each other. Maglie had nothing but pitched with guile and intelligence to get by. He kept the Dodgers off balance and wouldn't let them dig in, throwing the curveball inside, where it started at the head and broke away at the last second. His demeanor was as dark as the weather and he meant business. The fastball had nothing on it as he went to the curve and used good control to locate it.

Irvin touched Newk for a double to left in the seventh. Lockman bunted. Rube Walker fielded the ball and threw to third but Irvin was safe. Billy Cox tried to catch Irvin sleeping with the hidden ball trick, but Irvin wasn't buying it. Newcombe got ahead of Thomson at 0 and 2 and Bobby was suddenly fighting for his life. Bobby was swinging at anything close. He hit a fly ball to center, which was deep enough to bring Irvin home with the tying run. When the Dodgers faced the Barber in the eighth, they were no longer bailing out but set themselves firmly at the plate. They knew that Maglie couldn't afford to hit anyone. Maglie tried to compensate, making every pitch perfect, trying to be too fine. Westrum recalls, "Now they were setting up with authority. It was like they'd made a pact among themselves in the dugout. They were no longer afraid of Maglie."[92] Westrum noticed this by the way they dug into the box. Furillo made an out to start the inning. Reese and Snider singled. Jansen was up in the bullpen. Robinson stepped into the box and exchanged words with his old rival. Maglie lost his control and bounced a curve in front of the plate that got by Westrum. Reese scampered home with the Dodgers' second run to take the lead. Snider moved to second on the wild pitch. With first base open Robinson was passed intentionally setting up a possible double play. Pafko was the next batter. He hit a grounder towards third, Thomson tried to hurriedly backhand the ball, step on third for the force and throw across the diamond for an inning ending double play but instead the ball grazed his glove and went towards left field. Snider came home and Robinson went around to third. It was a play that a good third baseman should have handled but it was not routine. Maglie reached down and fanned Hodges for the second out. Cox subsequently hit a hard bounder towards Thomson. The ball once again eluded his grasp and went into left field scoring Robinson. Walker made the last out and Maglie came off the diamond in a bad mood as the Dodgers had virtually wrapped up the pennant and led 4–1.

Newcombe had been breezing along with his overpowering fastball. Despite this, it's been reported that he began asking out of the game as early as the seventh inning. Reese, Robinson, and Campanella yelled at him and succeeded in getting him to continue. Newk was bringing the heat in the eighth, blowing it past the Giants. It did not look as if he had lost anything. Rigney pinch-hit for Westrum, and Newk blew him away as if he were throwing to a little leaguer. Rigney recalls, "Newcombe was throwing aspirin tablets."[93] In the baseball vernacular, that meant he was throwing extremely hard. Hank Thompson pinch hit for Maglie and hit a comebacker for the second out. Stanky struck out to end the inning as the Dodgers headed into the final frame with a comfortable 4–1 lead. Maglie had pitched courageously giving up four runs on eight hits and four walks.

While Jansen came out of the bullpen to pitch the ninth, Erskine and Branca were throwing hard in the Dodger bullpen. The Dodgers heckled the Giant pitcher. Giant fans could already hear Dressen tell reporters how they had it all the way and that the cream always rises to the top. He would suggest that the Giants had choked in the pinch. Jansen tuned out the hecklers in the Dodger dugout and retired the side in order. The Giants had risen from the grave all season long and now they had to do it one more time. Durocher wasn't conceding anything and before running out to the third base coach's box he yelled at his club, "we come this far, you guys, we come this motherfuckin' far and it ain't over yet. We still got a motherfuckin' chance, so get out there and do somethin' with it!"[94] Leo told Dark, "It's up to you to get it started."[95] The Giant players showed a myriad of emotions as they prepared to prolong their final three outs: anger, disappointment, and sadness were emanated by the players demeanor. Maglie had already taken the long walk to the clubhouse. Horace Stoneham, the man who had tried so hard to get rid of the "jumper," now embraced him. "Sal you had a hell of a year. The game's not over yet. Have a beer."[96]

Newcombe whispered to Robinson that he had nothing left. Jackie cursed his pitcher and implored him to do his job. Alvin Dark strode to the plate and dug into the box, holding the black bat just off his shoulder. He hit a bounder towards the right side and the ball eluded the grasp of Hodges and Robinson for a base hit. Dressen was pacing incessantly in the Dodger dugout, his nervous energy dripping off him. During the final two innings he impulsively called Clyde Sukeforth in the Dodger bullpen to see how Branca and Erskine were doing. All year he refused to ask anyone for advice but now he turned to Sukeforth as if in the final hour he had all the answers. Mueller came up next, the batter who hit 'em where they ain't and could punch a ball through any hole. Don was going to try to hit the ball right up the middle, but he saw Hodges close to the first base bag almost holding Dark on. The Dodgers on the bench wouldn't dare tell Dressen that Hodges was out of position, knowing the manager would have exploded and rebuked them. Instead they stayed silent. Mueller instinctively saw the big hole on the right side of the infield between Hodges and Robinson. He bounced one through the vacated hole for a single and Dark raced around to third base. When Dressen realized the mistake, instead of accepting responsibility, he cursed Hodges. Irvin came up and was trying to tie the game with one swing of the bat; instead he popped up to first. Newcombe tried to sneak the second pitch over the outside corner against Lockman. Whitey went with it and hit a liner down the left field line. Dark scored and Mueller headed towards third, but he twisted his ankle on the bag and fell to the ground in immense pain. The Polo Grounds erupted; the Giants had risen from the dead once again. It took a little while before someone realized that Mueller was hurt. The score was 4–2, runners on second and third with one out. As the Giants surrounded Mueller and eventually removed him from the field on a stretcher, Dressen came out to get Newcombe. Branca was firing hard in the bullpen while Erskine was bouncing his curve. Dressen huddled with Newcombe and his infield and for the first time asked for their advice. Big Newk had pleaded to be taken out as the game progressed into the later innings and now he was granted his wish. Branca was summoned from the bullpen to face Thomson. Bobby had hit Branca well; in fact in the first game of the playoff he hit that two run homer. Earlier in the game he stood to be the goat but now he could be the hero. Clint Hartung came in to run for Mueller at third, Lockman was at second. This was the ballgame, someone was going to celebrate wildly. Someone else was going to die.

Before the "Flyin' Scot" made his way into the batter's box Leo grabbed him by the shoulder and said, "If you ever hit one, hit one now." Branca finished his warmups and Thomson stepped in. Dressen had opted to pitch to Thomson, instead of putting the winning run on and pitching to the trembling rookie Willie Mays who was on deck. Bobby told himself to wait and watch and he blocked out everything else in the park except the man holding the baseball. Thomson watched a fastball go right down the heart of the plate. A batter may get one good pitch in an at-bat and Thomson had just let it pass him. "Watch the damn ball!" Thomson said to himself.[97] Branca came with a another fastball, this time up and in. Thomson sprung out of his crouch and made solid contact, lashing the ball down the left field line. Pafko went to the wall as if he was going to catch it but watched it carry into the lower left field stands. Russ Hodges called the game on radio, "There's a long drive ... it's gonna be ... I believe ..." He then paused for what must have felt like a year, "The Giants win the pennant! The Giants win the pennant!" The Giants win the pennant! The Giants win the pennant!"[98] Snider fell to his knees in anguish in center field. The Polo Grounds erupted like it never had and the fans and players went crazy. Bobby Thomson, the son of Scottish immigrants, raced around the bases like a gazelle. Stanky jumped on Durocher at third base. Leo jumped on Thomson as he rounded third. Bobby fought his way through a crowd and jubilantly jumped on home plate. The Giants picked the "Flyin Scot" onto their shoulders and carried him around. The place went mad. The million to one shot had come in; the impossible dream was indeed a reality. Jackie Robinson stood at his second base position as Thomson rounded the bases to make sure he tagged each one. Then he began the long walk to center field. Thomson and the other players ran towards the clubhouse as fans tried to tear their clothes off. Everyone had gone mad. A girl was on her knees down the first base railing giving oral sex to a man. A couple of people noticed including newspapermen but the pictures of course were never published.[99] In the Dodger clubhouse the place was a morgue. Branca lay on the steps crying his eyes out. The fans stayed for hours after the game as their heroes came out of the clubhouse and were cheered. The Giants had miraculously won the pennant which they had no business winning.

The Giants' clubhouse was full of varying emotions. Herman Franks cried unrestrainedly. Westrum and Hartung tried to pour champagne into Stanky's mouth. "You're gonna get drunk now," they shouted.[100] Stanky lived a clean life off the field and preferred milkshakes to alcohol. In Philadelphia when Maglie had a couple more victories then Jansen, he said to him, "You catch up to me and we'll win the pennant."[101] They both finished with 23 wins. Charlie Dressen bowed out with some class and came to Durocher's office still fighting back the tears, "I told you last spring in Miami that we'd finish 1–2, and we did. I am number 2. Now the only thing I want you to do is to win four more."[102] Jackie Robinson acted like a true professional in defeat. He shook Maglie's hand in the Giant clubhouse and said, "It's all over. No hard feelings."[103] The baseball writers tried to describe what they had witnessed. One Chicago newspaper described how people reacted in a North Side tavern, "Tough men, hardened to most emotions by years of observing the frailties and triumphs of men, were crying.... Years from now, when we tell our grandchildren about this, you know what they'll do? They'll sneer and walk away and say that we're nuts. They'll never know how these guys have reached deep inside us and grabbed our hearts with both hands."[104] Red Smith said it best when he wrote in the *New York Herald Tribune*, "Now it is done. Now the story ends. And there is no way to tell it. The art of fiction is dead. Reality has strangled invention. Only the utterly impossible, the inexpressibly fantastic, can ever be plausible again."[105]

New York finished the season with a 98–59 record. The playoff games counted in the regular season statistics. Maglie tied Jansen with 23 wins to lead the National League. Sal was 23–6 with a 2.93 ERA. Only Boston's Chet Nichols had a better ERA in the league, and Maglie pitched 142 innings more then the Boston hurler. He appeared in 42 games, pitched 298 innings, gave up 254 hits and 86 walks while striking out 146. He had three shutouts and batted .152 at the plate. He hit six batters. Against Brooklyn he won five, lost once. Jansen was 23–11 with a 3.04 ERA. Hearn 17–9 with a 3.62 ERA. Koslo was 10–9 with a good 3.31 ERA. Spencer was

6. The American Aristocracy and the Miracle Finish

The 1951 New York Giants. The Giants miraculously came back from a thirteen and a half game deficit on August 11 to defeat the Brooklyn Dodgers for the National League pennant. (Author's collection)

10–4 and Jones 6–11. Al Corwin had gone 5–1. Lockman batted .282 with 12 homers. Stanky batted only .247 with 14 homers but walked 127 times. Dark hit .303 with 14 homers. Mueller batted .277 with 16 homers. Irvin had a breakout year with an impressive .312 average, 24 homers and a league leading 121 RBIs. Thomson batted .293 with 32 homers and 101 RBIs. Mays batted .274 with 20 homers. Westrum battled injuries and hit only .219 with 20 homers but led the league catchers in fielding average at .987. The pitching staff led the league with an aggregate 3.48 ERA. Brooklyn led the league in batting (.275), runs scored, doubles, home runs, slugging average, and stolen bases. New York batted 15 points lower then Brooklyn at .260. The numbers did not even begin to tell the story.

The World Series would be anticlimactic as Durocher's club took on Casey Stengel's New York Yankees who had won the American League pennant with a 98–56 record. After their delirious final game to win the pennant, the Giants had to begin the World Series at Yankee Stadium the very next day. Ford Frick had recently been picked to replace Happy Chandler as Commissioner and was there to throw out the first ball. A crowd of 65,673 packed into Yankee Stadium and were shocked to see their Yankees lose by a 5–1 score. It was the first time since 1936 they had been defeated in the opening game of the fall classic. The Giants' pitching staff was dead tired. Koslo worked the opener and did not disappoint throwing a seven hit complete game. Allie "Superchief" Reynolds pitched for the Yankees but left after giving up five runs in six innings. He had compiled a 17–8 record for the year with a 3.05 ERA and had pitched two no-hitters. Monte Irvin shocked the crowd in the first inning when he stole home. He had done this five times during the regular season. The country saw Irvin at his best. Now they knew what they had missed all those years when he had wilted away in the Negro Leagues. Monte had four hits in the game. Dark hit a three run homer in the sixth. After playing the last few weeks under great tension, the Giants found the first game relaxing compared to the Giant/Dodger wars down the stretch. Joe DiMaggio was playing his last games as a Yankee for he would retire at the end of the season. He went 0 for 4 and took the collar. The Yankee Clipper was always an introvert but as the season progressed he moved inward even more, secluding himself from his teammates and not even talking to Stengel. To further exacerbate the situation a Dodger scouting report was published in *Life* magazine after the season and the comments on DiMaggio were damning. The distinguished ballplayer who took so much pride in what he did was embarrassed. He broke down and cried.[106]

On October 5, the Yankees brought the Giants back down to earth as they defeated them by a 3–1 score before 66,018 fans. The crafty left hander Ed Lopat tossed a five hitter. Jansen did not pitch badly for the Giants, giving up two runs on four hits (no walks) in six innings. He gave up a run in the first with the help of two Yankee bunts and in the second Joe Collins hit a wind-blown home run. Mickey Charles Mantle was a rookie right fielder for the Yankees in 1951. He batted a modest .267 with 13 homers and 65 RBIs in a tumultuous rookie season in which he was even sent down to the minors. Mantle was the heir apparent to DiMaggio in center field. A switch hitter who could do everything, he was indoctrinated into the fine game of baseball by his father. Mickey knew that if he didn't succeed in this game it was off to the coal mines. Before the second game, Stengel told his right fielder to catch everything he could for DiMaggio had a heel problem. Three of the game's greatest center fielders took part in the most unfortunate of plays in the fifth inning. Mays led off with a fly ball towards right-center. Mantle and DiMaggio converged on the ball and at the last possible moment the Yankee Clipper yelled, "I got it." Mantle tried to stop but tripped over a wooden sprinkler cover and fell to the ground in great pain. Mickey already had a leg condition and this only made things worse, draining his legs of life for the rest of his career. Years later Mantle said, "You (just) don't run into Joe DiMaggio."[107] They removed him from the field on a stretcher and he remained bitter at the incident for years after his career had ended saying, "I was never right again."[108]

6. The American Aristocracy and the Miracle Finish 179

The third game was played before 52,035 fans at the Polo Grounds. The Polo Grounds and Yankee Stadium were within walking distance of each other separated by the Harlem River. The Giants took a 2–1 edge in the series as they won 6–2. Hearn was the winner while Jones recorded the final four outs. Thomson hit a double to score Mays in the second but the real explosion came in the fifth inning when the Giants scored five runs. The game turned on one aggressive play, which epitomized Leo Durocher's type of baseball. Stanky worked a walk with one out in the fifth off Yankee starter Vic Raschi. Dark stepped into the box and the hit and run sign was flashed in his direction, but the Yankees were also watching and pitched out. When Phil Rizzuto caught the throw from Yogi Berra, Stanky wasn't even close to the bag. Stanky went in hard and literally kicked the ball out of Rizzuto's glove with his right leg. When the ball caromed into center field, Stanky ran to third. Rizzuto was charged with an error on the play. The Yankees were about to kill a rally by catching the Giant runner at second but now the tables were turned and "The Brat" was standing on third base with one out. The floodgates opened. Dark singled. Thompson singled. Irvin was safe on an error and Lockman topped off the inning with a three run homer. After the game, Durocher jubilantly shouted to reporters, "Listen, gentlemen. You cannot tag Mr. Stanky with the ball held nice and easy in your glove. You got to hold it in your bare hand and go for him like that and maybe you get spiked but maybe you get him out. It ain't a fucking tea party out there. Not against my guys."[109]

The Giants were set to play the following day as Sal Maglie was ready to pitch on three days' rest, but rain postponed the contest. Years later players such as Irvin, Dark, Rigney, and Thomson would agree that this broke their momentum. Stengel was planning to pitch either Johnny Sain or Tom Morgan but with the cancellation, Allie Reynolds could come back with three days' rest. Rizzuto also needed an extra day of rest as he sported two injured wrists. One was courtesy of Eddie Stanky; the other injury came when Hearn hit the Yankee shortstop on the wrist with a pitched ball. While the rain came down at the Polo Grounds, Maglie relaxed inside. He wore a suit and had his legs up on a chair, his hands behind his head, smoking a good cigar. After all the great games he had pitched with an exorbitant amount of pressure, tomorrow's game certainly would not be any more difficult. He felt ready. That night he went to an Italian restaurant and loaded up on spaghetti and macaroni. The following day he felt heavy and later said, "I hate to admit it, but to this day I believe I ate us out of that Series."[110] He was also accustomed to working every fourth day and on three days' rest. Pitchers are creatures of habit and the extra day of rest broke the cycle.

Stengel's club evened the series at two games apiece when they won game four, 6–2, in front of 49,010 spectators. Hank Bauer worked a four-pitch walk to lead off the game against Maglie. Rizzuto struck out. Berra lined out to Mays in center. Rizutto had battled The Barber before striking out, and DiMaggio did the same thing but Sal got him with a fastball. DiMaggio was hitless in the series up to this point, going 0 for 12. The Giants scored a run in the bottom of the first and Maglie gave it right back in the second. As Sal came to the dugout, Durocher needled him and tried to anger the thirty-four year old pitcher so he would pitch better. "C'mon, you son of a bitch. Pitch like you can."[111] Maglie's control was gone, and the Yankees had no problem with the ailing pitcher. In the third, DiMaggio got his first hit of the series and in the fifth he hit a two run homer on a hanging curve. The Yankee Clipper took the grand tour around the bases for the last time. It was his eighth World Series homer and his last. Durocher continued to curse at Maglie, but it was no use, the old man had nothing left. Sal worked five innings, giving up four runs on eight hits and two walks while striking out eight. He was the losing pitcher as Jones and Kennedy followed him to the mound. Hank Thompson led off the ninth with a walk and Irvin followed with a single. Lockman flew out and Bobby Thomson singled home a run. There would be no miracle this time; Mays grounded into a 6-4-3 game ending double play. It was the third double play in which the twenty-year-old center fielder had grounded into during the day. Dark hit three doubles for New York. Allie Reynolds pitched an eight hit complete game for the win. After the game, Maglie claimed that he threw only three good pitches in the contest. Westrum grudgingly admitted that he had never seen Maglie's control that bad before. The Giants had the Yankees backed into a corner before the game, a little shaky, but now it was the Giants who were on the defensive.

The Yankees won the next two games to wrap up the series. Stengel's squad crushed the Giants in Game Five by a 13–1 score. Game Six shifted back to Yankee Stadium. Stengel's club won their third World Series in a row, as they put down the Giants by a 4–3 score in the final game. Hank Bauer hit a bases loaded triple in the sixth to lead the way. Koslo started for the Giants and was followed by Hearn and Jansen. For the Yankees, Raschi started followed by Sain and Bob Kuzava. The Giants entered the final inning three runs down and just like they had all season they put up a fight. Stanky, Dark, and Lockman singled to load the bases. Kuzava came in and got Irvin to fly to left as Stanky scored and the other runners moved up. Thomson flied to left as well and Dark scored. Sal Yvars was called to pinch-hit with the tying run on second. He had batted .317 on the year in only 41 at-bats. Yvars explained his predicament as follows: "I hit .317 that year, and Durocher didn't use me up to then for the whole Series. We had an incident during the season. I ended up taking a swing at him. I got a hot Italian temper, but you better know, too, that Durocher was a vulgar, filthy guy who treated me and Maglie like dirt. When I ask why he ain't using me in the Series, Durocher says, 'I'm teaching you a lesson. Now get the fuck away from me.' He hated me. I got so mad I went and broke all my bats, six Louisville Sluggers. Now, finally, Durocher's got to use me. He's got nobody else. And I gotta borrow a bat."[112] Yvars flew out to Bauer to end the game and the series. The Giants' World Series share was $4,951.03, a record for the loser of the series up until that time. Irvin had starred in the series batting .458 while Dark batted .417. No other Giant batted above .250. The tired Giant pitching staff was hit hard. Jansen was 0–2 with a 6.30 ERA and Maglie lost his game. Defensively the Giants committed ten errors while the Yankees booted only four. Despite the loss, the Giants could hold their heads high for they had won the ultimate battle against the Dodgers.

7

PITCHING IN PAIN

In 1950, Sal Maglie had proved the naysayers wrong and not only returned to the big leagues but excelled. He compiled an 18–4 record and led the league in winning percentage and shutouts. In 1951 he was even better at 23–6. In those two years Jansen and Maglie carried the staff, Jansen winning 42 games and Maglie winning 41. The Barber was thirty-four years old and realized he did not have many years left to play in the big leagues. When it came time to negotiate his salary, he was prepared to take a firm stance. Horace Stoneham called Sal during the winter to ask what salary he would like for the '52 season. Maglie dropped the bombshell, and told him $50,000. He was asking for a $35,000 increase from the previous year's salary. The Barber did not necessarily think that Stoneham would give him such a sizable raise, but he was expecting something close. When the contract came in the mail, New York offered $27,000. Maglie was outraged, and returned the contract unsigned. In January, while in New York to attend the annual Baseball Writers' dinner, he met with Stoneham at the Giant offices. Sal came down to $40,000 while Stoneham offered $33,000. Maglie told reporters, "You see, I don't think they're keeping their word with me. When I was reinstated in 1950, they told me if I did okay they would take care of me. Well, they're taking care of me to a certain extent but it doesn't seem quite enough." He added, "Last year I was one of the first to sign up, and I kept my word with them. I never refused a manager anything in my life because I always was and always will be a team man. I pitched out of turn. I worked in the bullpen with a sore arm. Anything they wanted of me I did and we made out pretty good, didn't we?"[1] As spring training approached, it looked as if Maglie would be conspicuously missing in Phoenix. In preparation for the season he was running and playing volleyball at the First Street Y.M.C.A in his hometown.

When spring training started in Phoenix, Arizona, on February 18, Maglie was still among the missing. Four days later, Maglie agreed to a $37,500 contract, although the papers stated that he had accepted $35,000. Since Jansen had signed for $35,000, the Giants reported to the papers that Maglie had signed for the same amount so Larry would not get upset. Jansen had been with the Giants much longer then Sal, and his performances justified that his salary be a benchmark for how high the Giants should go. In 1946, Larry had won thirty games in the coast league with the San Francisco Seals, while sporting a 1.57 ERA. He made his big league debut with the Giants the following year and compiled a 21–5 record. That was followed by 18–12, 15–16, 19–13, and his '51 performance of 23–11. In those five seasons his ERA was never above four. In his first five big league seasons he had nearly averaged twenty wins a season, compiling 96 of them. Jansen threw a curve, a live fastball, and a deceptive slider. He was another of the Giant pitchers who benefited greatly from the presence of Frank Shellenback. Frank successfully persuaded him to move the ball around, to pitch in and out to the batters. When the Giants offered to fly Maglie down to Arizona, he declined, opting to take a train. Durocher heard the news and couldn't have been happier since the salary squabble did not go on any further, "I'm glad he signed. I'm glad he's comin' in. He needs to work a lot every year at this time. He's a slow starter."[2]

The 1952 Giants began camp facing several significant changes. Eddie Stanky had moved on to become the manager of the St. Louis Cardinals. The slick fielding Davey Williams would take his place. Willie Mays was scheduled to be drafted by the Army in May. Leo planned to use Lockman in the leadoff spot and put Dark in the two spot. However once the season began Williams would bat leadoff and Lockman would be placed in the two spot after the first game, while Dark batted in the lower half of the batting order. With the absence of Stanky, Leo looked to Dark to take on more responsibility as a team leader. Leo stated "Sure, Davey Williams is just as good defensively. Maybe better.... But nobody is going to take Stanky's place as far as morale is concerned."[4] Leo was still looking for that left-handed bat off the bench. James Lamar "Dusty" Rhodes would make his debut in '52 and eventually fill that void. At first glance Rhodes wasn't Leo's type of player because he was one-dimensional. He was a horrible fielder but excelled at drinking people under the table and hitting the ball with some authority. Leo was giving another left-handed bat a look in camp, the old American League castoff Dick Wakefield. As far as the pitching staff was concerned, Leo was looking to seven pitchers to lead the way: Jansen, Maglie, Koslo, Hearn, Jones, Kennedy, and the recently acquired Max Lanier.

In Phoenix, the locals treated every Giant like a celebrity. Willie Mays had never been west of Kansas City and the brilliant sunshine of Arizona fascinated him along with the mountains and the cactus. There was always a party being thrown for the Giants. Bobby Thomson was the biggest hero of them all, in camp ten pounds heavier after he made the rounds of the winter banquets. Durocher was in a good mood as he shouted words of encouragement at his players, taught them, and drove them to perform better then they thought they could. In the off hours, Leo played cards with his players and provided some good-natured criticism.

Durocher was planning to use Maglie differently in 1952. Since Sal tired down the stretch in 1951 he wanted to use him every fifth day instead of every fourth. This was contingent on whether the rest of the staff could pick up the extra work and be successful. Durocher always worked his best pitchers very hard, and such suggestions often did not come true once the regular season began. Especially because of Leo's inclination to make lots of changes. He also wanted the pitchers to make only one full nine-inning start before the season opened. Leo contended that the high number of innings his pitchers threw during the previous spring played a role in the eleven game losing streak at the beginning of the season. The pitching staff was one area where it appeared that Leo did not have to worry based on the results of the previous year when New York led the league in five pitching categories and tied in another. They compiled the lowest ERA, and allowed the least number of hits, runs, earned runs, and walks. They tied the Dodgers with 64 complete games.

Maglie looked impressive in his first intrasquad game, working three strong innings. On March 9, the Indians defeated the Giants by a 5–4 score at Phoenix's Municipal Stadium. The Cleveland Indians played hard and drank hard in '51. They boasted three twenty game winners (Mike Garcia, Early Wynn, and Bob Feller) yet failed to take the pennant from the Yankees. Hearn tossed three scoreless innings and was followed by Jansen who gave up three runs in his three innings of work. In the seventh Maglie was touched for two runs as he took the loss. Harry Simpson singled. Larry Doby tripled off the center field wall driving in the first run and Dale Mitchell's single brought Doby home. Sal allowed six hits and struck out two in three innings. Cleveland won their third straight over New York on the following day. On the 13th, the Barber bounced back and pitched two hit ball for five innings in a 6–0 victory over the Chicago Cubs. The players fought the wind and dust before the rain ended the game early. Sal was beginning to approach top form as he kept the Cubs off balance with a sharp curve and mixed his pitches well. Leo was still upset over a couple of mental lapses his players made earlier in the week. Durocher was satisfied with Sal's performance and lauded his pitcher, "if I had to pick one guy in the league to win twenty games, it would have to be Maglie."[4] One thing that Leo was extremely pleased about was the progress of his pitchers.

When Maglie hurled five scoreless innings in a heartbreaking loss to Pittsburgh in San Bernardino, California, he extended his scoreless innings streak to twelve and had not allowed a walk all spring. Jansen allowed a run the following day, and it marked the first run scored off Jansen, Maglie, and Hearn in twenty-six innings. The hitting was slow to come around. On March 20, Willie Mays had the highest Giant batting average at a modest .297. Sal won his second contest of the spring on the 23rd, extending his scoreless innings streak to nineteen as he tossed seven scoreless innings against the Oakland Oaks to end their successful California trip where they won six of seven. Jansen and Maglie in particular were pitching well, while Hearn and Kennedy combined to throw a no-hitter on the trip.

Back at their home base in Phoenix, Maglie won his third game of the spring in a 9–6 win over the Cubs. The scoreless innings streak ended at nineteen when Ron Northey connected for a home run in the seventh inning. He allowed three hits in three innings, walked his first batter of the spring and struck out one. Some of the Giants hitters were breaking out of slumps. Bobby Thomson hit a homer for the second consecutive day while Dark and Lockman also went deep. Davey Williams was pressing early in camp and trying to do too much but now he was hitting the ball with authority as he collected two hits. The following day Williams hit two homers as New York played its last game in Phoenix. The Giants traveled to Los Angeles where they would begin to travel back east with the Cleveland Indians. This was a disastrous trip home for New York and not simply because the Indians won the first seven games. Red Smith wrote in his column that the New Yorkers could ill afford anything to go wrong. "If a fatal weakness develops, chances are it will be lack of a sustained attack. Although the Giants have been winning their exhibition games, they have difficulty getting a big inning started and more difficulty keeping a rally alive."[5]

On March 30 in Los Angeles, Bobby Avila hit a two run homer with two outs in the ninth to lead Cleveland to a 6–5 victory before 19,239 fans. Maglie pitched well, allowing three runs on eight hits and one walk in seven innings of work. He fanned four Indians and threw a wild pitch. Al Corwin took the loss. Corwin was being hit hard during the spring as the opposing batters had been sitting on his fastball, realizing that his curve was nonexistent. He would be sent down to Minneapolis before the season began, but eventually returned. The Giants entourage traveled towards the mountains of Denver, Colorado. This was a trip they would later wish they had avoided. They were a dispirited group, having been within one out of defeating the Indians two days in a row before the roof fell in. Thomson and Mays were doing the job offensively but the rest of the club left much to be desired. Westrum was batting .093 after thirty-two at-bats. Kennedy and Jones were driving Leo mad with their inconsistent pitching. On April 2, the Giants' pennant hopes were essentially dashed. Irvin led off the second inning with a walk. Mays followed with a single to center. Irvin rounded second looking to take the extra base. Monte was unaware that Mays was caught in a rundown between first and second. When the Indians shortstop Ray Boone caught the relay throw from center fielder Pete Reiser (Pete was a mere shell of his earlier self and would play his final season in '52) Irvin tried to hold up at third. His spikes caught and he fell to the ground in anguish. A bone had torn through the skin, while the foot was turned in an unnatural inward position. Willie Mays was down on his knees by the second base bag, beating the earth with his fists, crying his eyes out. No one else on the club was closer to Irvin then Willie. Irvin was his roommate, his mentor, and their relationship was like that of close brothers. Durocher took a quick glance at his player's gruesome injury and became nauseated, returning to the bench. Herman Franks had put his arms up from the third base coach's box, signaling Irvin that he could slow down. He also turned away sick. Monte had a broken right ankle. Irvin would return for 46 games at the end of the season, but his bat would be sorely missed. Over the second half of 1950 and the entire 1951 season, you would be hard pressed to find a better clutch hitter then Monte Irvin.

On April 6, the Indians continued to manhandle the Giants, winning by a 9–4 score before 11,302 spectators at Burnett Field in Dallas, Texas. Maglie was hit hard. He allowed nine runs on nine hits and four walks in seven innings. The Giants received some good news two days later when Bob Elliott was acquired from the Boston Braves for Sheldon Jones and $75,000. He had batted .285 with 15 homers and 70 RBIs the previous year. Elliott would replace Irvin in left field. Boston manager Tommy Holmes stated, "Bob is one of the greatest clutch players I have seen. I hated to part with him but we are rebuilding and I figure the youngsters should be given a chance."[6]

A pinched nerve in Maglie's elbow bothered the right-hander as spring training began to wind down. In his final appearance before the regular season, Sal gave up one run in five innings. His fine performance prompted Durocher to name him the opening day starter against Philadelphia. Hearn, Jansen, and Maglie each finished the spring strong with quality outings. Durocher was impressed by the work of Davey Williams, Hoyt Wilhelm, Roger Bowman, and Hank Thompson as well. Wilhelm was a twenty-eight year old knuckleballer who had bounced around the minors before finally getting his chance. Many times he had been available in the draft, vulnerable to be picked up by another team. With the recommendation of farm director Carl Hubbell the Giants finally protected him. "Willard Ramsdell hung around the majors with a knuckler. Wilhelm has a better one," said Carl.[7] For years baseball men had looked skeptically at those who threw this spinless pitch. It is extremely difficult for catchers to handle and it is hard for pitchers to control. Giants coach Freddie Fitzsimmons threw the knuckler at three different speeds during his playing career. He called it the "dry spitter." Durocher had in Wilhelm a bonafide relief specialist.

As the '52 campaign was set to open Leo was content on the way he had brought his players along during camp for they were beginning to peak at the right time. He was also happy to see Happy Chandler leave the commissioner's post. This was the man who had suspended him for a full season in '47 and he had other run-ins with him as well. Among the owners Chandler became known as the "Hillbilly Commissioner," and the "Bluegrass Jackass."[8] There was one story early in spring training which did not get that much publicity but seemed quite disturbing. The new commissioner, Ford Frick, denied reports that a "police" system was put in place to monitor the players before games so they would not mingle with fans. Umpire Bill Summers told the St. Louis Browns that this new system was supposed to keep players from coming into contact with gamblers. Frick talked to the respective league presidents and directed them to caution their players when it came to talking with strangers. The system would be implemented as follows: the third base umpire would watch the players before the game while the second base umpire would watch the stands looking for suspicious activity. Despite Frick's denial to such an elaborate system, the fact that Summers warned the Browns and provided details suggests that it was seriously considered. The umpire went so far as to tell Browns manager Rogers Hornsby that his players were forbidden to fraternize with opposing players.[9]

Unlike the two previous years when the Giants got off to miserable starts, they played excellent baseball to begin the '52 campaign. By May 28 they boasted a 26–8 record. That was also the day on which Willie Mays left for the Army and the Giants' fortunes precipitously declined afterwards. Sal Maglie baffled the hitters early in the season. Through the hazy sunshine that beat down on the green diamonds in '52, a spectator may have mistaken Maglie for Dizzy Dean as it appeared he had a legitimate chance to win thirty games. Eventually the bottom dropped out, and his thirty-five year old body began to break down.

After a rainout, the Giants opened their season on April 16 in the first night game opener at the Polo Grounds before a modest crowd of 17,472. Maglie defeated Robin Roberts of the Phillies by a 5–3 score. The Barber allowed his runs in the fifth inning. Connie Ryan led off with a single. Waitkus hit a line drive through the box; Maglie knocked it down but threw to the wrong base and was charged with an error. Forrest Burgess hit a triple over Mueller's head in right that Don misplayed. Hamner's fly ball scored Burgess with the third run. Sal surrendered just one earned run on four hits and two walks while striking out eight. Bob Elliott was the hitting star, smashing two homers off Roberts. Manhattan borough president Robert F. Wagner Jr., threw out the first ball. John McGraw's widow and National League president Warren Giles were among the spectators.

The Brooklyn Dodgers were prepared to redeem themselves after losing the pennant on the last day of the season two years in a row. They won their first five games of '52, collecting 43 runs and 69 hits in the process. They looked invincible to everyone except Salvatore Anthony Maglie. Since he had returned to organized ball in 1950, he had posted a 9–1 record against the Brooklyns. The Barber toed the slab before 29,266 enemy fans at Ebbets Field on April 20. The Dodgers had been sporting a .374 average before the game, but Maglie stopped them cold and tossed a dazzling two-hitter in a 6–0 win. It was the first time the Dodgers had been shut out in their own ballpark since August 25, 1949, when Johnny Schmitz of the Cubs turned the trick. For 176 straight games the mighty Brooklyn lineup was able to push across at least one run in their own ballpark till this game. Campanella's single in the fourth and pinch hitter Cal Abrams' quail shot in the eighth were the only hits he surrendered. When he temporarily lost his control and walked the bases loaded in the third, he induced Robinson to ground out. In the ninth with two out and a no balls, two strikes count on Gil Hodges, Maglie showed contempt for the Dodgers. The next pitch turned Hodges around, and as he brought his left hand up to protect his face the ball hit him on the hand. He then humiliated Carl Furillo once again, and struck him out for the fourth time to end the game. The Barber had never lost in Ebbets Field. Maglie walked six batters, struck out eight and threw one wild pitch. Tommy Holmes wrote in the *Brooklyn Eagle* concerning the Barber, "But yesterday he was able to keep what the ball players call his "Gillette" in its handy carrying case and let the Dodgers defeat themselves by their own imagination."[10] Maglie had the Dodgers reaching all day for his tantalizing curve and they often went out of the strike zone trying to make contact.

Hoyt Wilhelm put together a stellar season in 1952 as opposing batters were perplexed as to how they should approach hitting the knuckleball. He set a Giant record by appearing in 71 games, while compiling a 15–3 record. Wilhelm was the National League leader in appearances, ERA (2.43) and winning percentage (.833). On April 23, he won his first major league game and hit a homer in his first major league at-bat. That was his only homer of his career, he would fail to go deep in his next 431 at-bats.

Maglie's third victory came against the Cincinnati Reds before 19,531 spectators at Crosley Field. He tossed a three hitter, walked one and struck out seven as the Giants won by a 2–1 score. Ewell Blackwell was the tough luck loser for Cincinnati. The Reds hurler was nicknamed "The Whip," and after winning 17 in 1950 and 16 in 1951 he would never win more then four games in a season for the rest of his career. He stepped with his left leg towards third base and pitched sidearm. The wicked crossfire delivery made right handers tremble at the plate as the ball came at them from the third base side of the rubber. His 6'6" frame only exacerbated the situation for hitters, as the ball would be right on top of them before they could react. Mays got nailed by a pitch in this game. Maglie gave up two singles in the first inning. Hank Edwards touched him for a homer in the fifth to tie the score. The Barber then retired the next fourteen batters as he had the Reds eating out of the palm of his hand. The game was tied at 1–1 headed into the ninth. Dark worked Blackwell for a walk to lead off. Westrum grounded out, and Dark advanced to second. Maglie followed with a single to left field, which brought across what proved to be the winning run.

The Giants won their fifth straight behind the Barber. They defeated the Pirates by a 3–2 score at Forbes Field. It was his seventh win in a row, dating back to the previous season and his twelfth straight win over Pittsburgh. He gave up two runs on seven hits and four walks while striking out six. His record stood at 4–0 to start the season. Maglie singled in the seventh and scored what proved to be the winning run. George Strickland was unable to avoid one of Maglie's vicious inside pitches in the fourth inning and was skulled. Knocked unconscious, he was removed from the field on a stretcher and taken to the hospital. There were real repercussions to the Barber's utilization of the brushback pitch, the knockdown pitch and the beanball. Years later he would state that, "Beaning (Danny)

Murtaugh and (George) Strickland was no fun. I felt sick when I saw them go down." The anatomy to his beanballs was as follows: "Why didn't I throw at, say, batters' chests, instead of their heads? I threw at the head because I knew that a batter could see a pitch up around his face better than he could see a pitch to any other spot. It's no trick to hit a batter in the ribs. Any pitcher with decent control can do it. It's a bigger target than the head and, besides, it's a lot tougher for a batter to move his body than his head. So I aimed at the head. The pitch served my purpose. It kept the hitter loose. It made him move. But at the same time there wasn't much chance of my beaning the batter. The pitch was effective without really being dangerous."[11]

Sal won his fifth in a row against the Cardinals at Sportsman's Park on May 7 winning another close one, this time 3–1. Maglie's only disappointment was that he could not finish the game. He worked eight and one third innings, giving up one run on six hits and three walks while striking out seven. The Barber recorded the first out of the ninth before Musial doubled for his only hit of the game and Wally Westlake drew a walk. Leo took the tired old man out and brought in a fresh arm in Larry Jansen. Enos Slaughter's double play ball to Davey Williams ended the game. Don Mueller who was originally from St. Louis drove home two runs for New York. Sal's ERA stood at 1.02 after pitching forty-four and a third innings.

On May 14, the Giants defeated the Cincinnati Reds by an 8–3 score before only 6,366 spectators below Coogan's Bluff. Maglie went the distance for his sixth win, giving up three runs (two earned) on six hits and four walks. Bobby Thomson hit a triple in the opening frame. On the second pitch to Elliott he electrified the crowd by stealing home. Mays and Westrum hit homers in the second. New York scored two in the fifth and then two in the eighth on Thomson's bases loaded single. Almost every Cincinnati batter in the early innings asked umpire Augie Donatelli to inspect the baseball implying that Maglie was throwing a spitball. They were urged on by Cincinnati skipper Luke Sewell, whose primary intention was to get Maglie to become angry and lose his concentration. He insisted that the Giants' pitcher was wetting the ball in the palm of his glove before throwing. The charge was made incessantly to the point that the Barber became infuriated. Sewell made the charge pitch after pitch. In the sixth inning, Maglie unleashed his first pitch and once again the charge was made, but this time he had enough. Donatelli motioned for the ball and Sal threw the ball over his head to the grandstand. Durocher wasn't going to let his pitcher get harassed without retaliating. When the Cincinnati hurler threw his first pitch in the bottom of the inning, Leo accused him of loading up the ball. He did this three times until the home plate umpire yelled, "This is going to stop right now, Durocher!" Leo "The Lip" yelled back, "You're darn right it's going to stop!"[12] When Sewell came out to complain in the seventh, Donatelli stopped him and told the manager to inform his players that Maglie was getting them out with curveballs, not spitballs. The Reds scored single runs in the third, fifth and seventh. Cincinnati had the bases loaded with no outs in the third but scored only one run. In the seventh they managed to score an unearned run due to Dark's first error of the year. His defense was greatly improved in '52, his errors dropped from 45 to 27. Dark's approach to the ball was often awkward, for he lacked the eloquent grace of a Marty Marion or a Phil Rizzuto. Dark made a lot of tough plays that Buddy Kerr was unable to make, but he had the tendency to commit errors on routine grounders. Towards the end of the season he would be placed in the two hole where he was best suited because of his ability to bunt, and get the runner over when needed. The Yankee Clipper, Joe DiMaggio, had once called him a "Red Rolfe type of hitter."[13] Things were going great for the New Yorkers. They were in first place, two games ahead of the Dodgers, and had won twelve of their last thirteen games.

On Sunday, Giant fans were shocked to find out that the day's game had been canceled at the Polo Grounds. The Giants/Pittsburgh doubleheader was mysteriously postponed. The Pirates were easy prey, in last place with a team batting average of .167. It had rained a little in the morning. The drainage system at the old ballpark was atrocious, and a morning shower could easily cancel an afternoon game. However that wasn't the case here; the cancellation had more to do with Horace Stoneham's ego than anything else. He was a big drinker and liked to stay out late. As the Giants prepared for the game in their locker room, Stoneham stumbled in and suggested to Durocher that he was thinking about calling the game. Leo exploded at such a suggestion and yelled "You can't call the game."[14] Stoneham insured Leo that he could, simply because he was the owner and he did. The previous year the Dodgers had canceled an early season game so they could prepare for the upcoming series with the Giants. On May 19, Louis Effrat of the *New York Times* wrote, "Someone guessed wrong. That is why there was no action yesterday at the Polo Grounds, where the Giants and Pirates were listed for a doubleheader. And that is why some 3,000 to 4,000 fans who wended their way through sunshine to Coogan's Bluff between the hours of 11 A.M. and 2 P.M. ran into locked gates."[15]

Maglie's victory total reached seven with a 4–0 shutout over the Pirates on Monday. The Barber put in another professional performance, giving up seven hits, one walk, and striking out six. Only one Pirate got past first base. Even though Maglie had just tossed his second shutout of the season, he seemed disturbed in the locker room afterwards. "Something's wrong," he told Shellenback. "I'm not loose. I don't have all my stuff."[16] Shellenback looked at him as if he was crazy. This was the pitcher who had won seven straight games to start the year and had completed all but one of his games. That was the game against St. Louis in which Jansen finished and he had worked eight and one-third innings. He was feeling stiffness in his back, which was exacerbated by the damp weather they had encountered. Maglie had first felt the stiffness on May 7 in St. Louis. The Barber was as tough as nails and not one to complain. Shellenback shrugged off Maglie's concerns and kiddingly suggested he was getting too much sleep.

On the 23rd, the Barber weathered some early trouble to win his eighth game as New York defeated Boston by a 5–3 score before the largest Polo Grounds crowd of the year up till that point at 24,812. Maglie started slowly. He retired Roy Hartsfield to start the game but subsequently walked Jethroe. Eddie Mathews hit a single towards right field and Jethroe scampered to third. Sid Gordon hit a bleeder down the third base line, Thomson swept in, bare handed the ball and got the runner at first but Jethroe scored on the play. The Braves had two on and one out in the second but Maglie worked out of the jam. In the third they had two on and again failed to score. In the ninth Ebba St. Claire touched him for a two run homer. The Giants scored all their runs in the fourth, which was highlighted by Dark's two run homer. Maglie gave up the three runs on eight hits and three walks while striking out three. The Giants played errorless ball behind the Barber and turned three double plays to give them thirty-four on the season.

Four days later he tossed his second shutout of the year in Ebbets Field, and his third for the season as the New Yorkers defeated Brooklyn 3–0. Maglie did not have his best stuff but he was able to escape trouble all day. Sal walked Bob Morgan, the Brooklyn leadoff hitter in the first. Reese hit into a 1-4-3 double play, which was started by Maglie. Thomson was charged with an error on Snider's grounder but he fielded Robinson's grounder cleanly and made the throw to end the inning. Brooklyn threatened in the sixth with runners on the wings but Andy Pafko popped up to retire the side. Robinson led off the ninth with a double but Maglie retired the next three Dodger batters to win the game. Mueller and Mays hit homers while Reese's error allowed an unearned run to score in the ninth to account for the New York scoring. Maglie gave up four hits and four walks while striking out six. The Barber's record stood at 9–0 and it was only May 27. After the game the Dodgers accused Maglie of cutting the ball and throwing an emery ball. When throwing the emery ball or what is better known as the scuffed ball, the intention is to rough up the ball on one side to increase air resistance. The ball will break erratically to the opposite side of the scuff mark. It's a pitch that does not put as much strain on the arm. The pitcher doesn't necessarily have to mar the surface; one of the infielders can do it for him. Durocher used to manipulate the surface of the ball for Dizzy Dean. The Dodgers had a lot to complain about, as Maglie had an 11–1 record against them since 1950. With Maglie pitching so well the accusations were flying insisting that he was throwing beanballs, spitballs, and now emery balls. Of course the beanball accusation was legitimate. Jackie Robinson had connected for two hits in the game and scoffed at his teammates' accusations. "You can't take anything away from Sal today. He pitched a whale of a game, and I'm not going to accuse him of anything." Robinson grinned and then added, "Except maybe having a hex on us. We just can't seem to beat that Barber."[17] Maglie's mastery over Brooklyn was already beginning to take on legendary proportions.

With Maglie going so good, he took time to discuss pitching with Arthur Daley. "Anyone can get the ball over the plate, it's learning to nick the corners that makes such a big difference. Control comes only from experience and from work. Most young pitchers make the mistake of exceeding their gait, which means throwing too hard. They lose control. You have to find what your proper gait is and stick to it. Then, when you have the batters used to your proper gait, you can slow down or speed up, perpetually keeping them off balance." He sounded remarkably like Frank Shellenback in that statement. "I'd say that five of seven pitches I throw are curves. Yet I might throw nothing but fastballs at a batter, merely to cross him up. I watch every hitter. If I catch him leaning over the plate, waiting for a curve, I'll fastball him. If he's standing back for the fast one, I'll hook him. Of course, I've studied every batter and never give him what he likes to hit — if I can help it, I mean." One of the tricks he picked up playing for Luque in Cuba and Mexico concerning his curve was as follows, "I had been in the habit of letting it go high on the downsweep of my arm. But now I throw it from in front of me so that it comes out from my uniform. The batter can't see the ball until it's on top of him." Maglie threw a slider, a rainbow drop curve, and an outshoot, all at different speeds and arm angles. As far as opposing hitters, Jack Merson of Pittsburgh and "the new fellows" were giving him trouble this year. Maglie added, "Naturally I have certain difficulties with Stan Musial and Jackie Robinson. Who doesn't? They don't guess. They hit with the pitch, pulling an inside pitch and slicing an outside one to the opposite field. But that's why they are such great hitters. Pee Wee Reese bothers me more than he should. I know he's a high-ball hitter, but I never seem able to get the ball low enough on him. ...There are days, though, when my curve isn't worth a damn. Sometimes it's when the atmospheric conditions are bad. For instance, when the wind is blowing in, the curve won't break properly. Other days I just don't have it. However, I always know right away and I also know I'll be getting an early shower." Essentially that was Maglie's approach towards pitching, excluding the anatomy of the beanball. Former pitcher Dutch Ruether compared Sal to Grover Cleveland Alexander in that, "He never makes the same mistake twice."[18] Maglie was someone who not only studied the art of pitching in theory but could apply it even when his skills were limited.

While Maglie was compiling his nine game winning streak, the rest of the squad was also performing well. By the end of May, Hearn, Jansen, and Wilhelm were each 4–1. Koslo, Kennedy, Lanier, and Bowman were the second tier pitchers who had started games for Durocher. Lockman was among the league leaders in batting average at .333. Willie Mays had struggled. He had dazzled the spectators down in Phoenix during spring training but when he asked for a draft exemption the military turned him down. Mays' unspectacular performance may have had to do with his impending military conscription, the devastation he felt when he saw his roommate Monte Irvin get injured or both of these. When Willie left for the Army on May 28, he had compiled a .236 average, 4 homers and twenty-three RBIs. The Giants were leading the National League, two and a half games in front of Brooklyn. Despite Willie's subpar performance his mere presence in the lineup lifted up the entire team. This is not usually said of a twenty-one year old ballplayer but it was true in Willie's case. With Mays in the lineup they had a 27–7 record. Once he departed the Giants dropped eight of their next ten games. Mays' ebullient personality lifted any tensions that may have been lingering around the clubhouse and also counterbalanced Durocher's irascible persona. Before long Charlie Dressen would be taunting the Giants once again, "The Giants is dead! The Giants is dead!"[19] Surely Mays' departure wasn't the sole reason why the Giants would head south. Their pitching staff would be the main culprit, particularly the unfortunate precipitous decline of Sal Maglie. The hitting and defense also became poor.

In St. Louis against Eddie Stanky's Cardinals, the Barber should have won his tenth game but two errors in the field allowed the Cardinals to escape with a 5–4 win. "The Brat" took great pride in sweeping the Giants. Stanky was surrounded by controversy throughout the season. During spring training he got into it with the Yankees' second baseman, Gil

McDougald. Eddie told reporters, "they want to cry and bellyache. I tried to knock the ball out of McDougald's hand." Stanky added "That's what happened and he didn't like it" and sharp words were exchanged.[20] It was during the previous fall that he had kicked the ball out of Rizzuto's glove in the fall classic and the Yankees were still on the defensive. When the Dodgers came into St. Louis in early June, the Cardinals' bench called Jackie Robinson "nigger" and "black bastard." Stanky lied to a reporter, "Didn't hear a thing.... Of course there was the usual jockeying, but that was just routine riding."[21] In the following year Stanky's bench jockeying of Robinson fell to a new low. In the June 2 game against St. Louis, the Giants had a 3–0 lead headed into the bottom of the third. They had pushed across a run in the first. Williams hit his fifth homer in the third, and Lockman followed with his sixth homer. In the bottom half, Dark made an error on a double play ball which led to two Cardinal runs, one of which was unearned. In the sixth, Mueller misplayed a line drive off the bat of Peanuts Lowrey with two out, which led to three runs. Maglie was fuming on the hill, visibly upset by his club's poor defense. Mueller in particular seemed to perform poorly in the field whenever Maglie took the ball. Lockman made an error in the game although he was now tied with Hank Sauer as the National League leader with a .335 average. Maglie allowed five runs (four earned) on eight hits and three walks and hit Billy Johnson with a pitch. He worked six innings while Max Lanier pitched the final two. Maglie had pitched eighty-six and one-third innings on the season, allowed fifty-five hits and thirty-one walks for eighteen runs. He had fifty-one strikeouts. Ed Sinclair wrote in the *New York Herald Tribune*, "Three runs usually are plenty for the Barber, but, after all, he can't play the infield and the outfield, too."[22]

His back continued to bother him but he didn't say a word to anyone. The hapless Pirates finally defeated the Barber, after losing to him thirteen straight times. Sal was given an early shower, lasting only four innings for his second loss in a row. He gave up five runs (three earned) on six hits and three walks while striking out three. Pittsburgh won easily by an 8–1 margin. Lockman, Mueller, and Westrum committed errors as the New Yorkers continued to play poor defense. Every facet of their game had collapsed. On June 10, Cincinnati defeated Durocher's club by a 6–5 score in fourteen innings at Crosley Field. The game took four hours and twenty-one minutes to complete. Maglie pitched respectably for seven innings, before being taken out in the eighth. He allowed four runs on eight hits and four walks while striking out five. Lanier, Spencer, Koslo, and the eventual loser, Wilhelm (4–2), followed him to the mound. Hal Gregg was purchased from the Oakland Oaks on the following day in an attempt to stabilize the staff. He had one flash of brilliance in the big leagues, winning eighteen games for the Dodgers against inferior competition in 1945.

The Giants' recent reversal of fortunes couldn't have been more apparent than on June 15, when 41,899 fans packed their way into the Polo Grounds and watched the Giants blow an eleven run lead in the first game of a doubleheader. They scored five in the second and six in the third to give Maglie an eleven run cushion. The Cardinals started their comeback by scoring seven runs in the fifth inning as Tommy Glaviano and Enos Slaughter hit homers off the Barber. Once again Maglie got the early hook, lasting only four and two-thirds innings, giving up seven runs on nine hits and one walk while fanning one. The once impenetrable Barber was not finishing games anymore and more importantly was suddenly having great difficulty getting batters out in the clutch. Loyal followers of the Giants' National League ballclub must have felt that something was amiss. St. Louis collected eighteen hits as the final score stood at 14–12. The Cardinals and Giants each committed errors, Maglie was charged with one. Koslo continued his domination over Stanky's club by pitching a five hit shutout in the second game as New York won 3–0. He had beaten them eleven times in a row. Gerald Staley continued to work New York inside and nailed Williams with a pitch. New York was now three and a half games off the pace in the National League. Some of the skeptics blamed Durocher for letting Maglie pitch deep into the fifth inning of the opener. The Barber was frank with reporters afterwards. "With that big lead, I was sure we had this one stowed away, so I just let up. Then I couldn't get going again."[23]

The following day it looked as if the Giants were going to drop another one to Stanky's Cardinals. New York squandered early homers by Williams and Dark, wasted five double plays, and fielded poorly behind Maglie and Lanier. Kennedy started but was taken out in the sixth. Maglie followed with an ineffective inning and two thirds in which he allowed two runs. Lanier and Spencer followed him. New York trailed by a 7–4 score heading into the bottom of the ninth. They managed to load the bases with one out. Stanky played the percentages and brought in the right-handed Willard Schmidt to pitch to the right-handed Bobby Thomson. One out, last of the ninth in the Polo Grounds, the Giants down by a couple of runs. Thomson was familiar with the situation. He lifted a fly towards left field that went into the upper deck portion of the left field stands for a grand slam homer that won the game. Cardinal catcher Del Rice argued violently, insisting that the ball had gone foul, but umpire Lee Ballanfant disagreed. Stanky did not engage in any theatrics but simply picked up his glove and walked to the clubhouse while his players followed. With one swing of the bat, Thomson erased the Giants' sins on the day. Again they had committed three errors. The game was another beanball war with pitchers working inside consistently. The aging southpaw, Harry Brecheen, hit Elliott. Kennedy nailed Dick Sisler while Maglie nailed Glaviano who had hit a homer off him the previous day. Maglie's struggles continued against Chicago as New York won, 4–3, in ten innings. He started but left after two innings, allowing three runs on four hits and one walk. Max Lanier, the thirty-seven year old southpaw, followed with eight shutout innings to earn the win (2–4). Lanier was a close friend of Maglie going back to their Mexican League days and was also his roommate. After the game, Maglie downplayed his performance and told reporters that he was not worried.

In five starts and one relief appearance, Maglie had failed to win a game. He was unable to finish any of his starts during that stretch. Many began to wonder if the thirty-five year old right-hander was through. During the 1951 regular season he had pitched an exorbitant 298 innings and his excessive workload may have begun to catch up to him. On June 26, Maglie proved the prognosticators wrong, and summoned up the energy to hurl a three hit shutout against the hated Dodgers before 32,767 captivated witnesses at the Polo Grounds. He stood below the craggy cliff, sweating profusely in the 100-degree heat and put down the Dodgers in an economical fashion. Dressen's team was dumbfounded by any rumor suggesting the Barber had nothing left. To Brooklyn such rumors were premature and unfounded. Maglie had walked to the center of the diamond three times against the Dodgers this year; three times he had tossed shutouts. In twenty-seven innings against them, Sinister Sal had allowed only nine hits and not even an unearned run. In 1950 he was 4–0 against them. In 1951, 5–1 and now in 1952, 3–0. He became the first National League pitcher to win ten games, just like he had done in 1951. This was truly amazing since his last win came on May 27, almost a full month ago. The shutout was his fourth of the year. It was another inspiring performance, for he used only 85 pitches to dispose of Brooklyn. He walked three and struck out three.

New York scored three runs in the game. Elliott hit a two run triple in the first. Hank Thompson hit his own triple in the third and scored on Elliott's long fly ball to left center field. Maglie retired the first nine Brooklyn batters before Furillo walked to lead off the fourth. Sinister Sal continued to mow down the opposition as the Dodgers failed to scratch out a hit. Maglie had a no-hitter going into the seventh. The suspense filled the Polo Grounds as the spectators were well aware what was transpiring. Jackie Robinson stepped into the box, and pulled his body into a crouch, waving the bat back and forth, anticipating the pitched ball. It was two old warriors competing against each other once again. Maglie knew how he liked to pitch him, how he liked to pitch everybody in fact, high and tight. The count went to 1 and 2, an ideal time to knock Jackie down. Maglie spun out of the windup and Robinson got hold of it, knocking a clean single to center field. The crowd applauded the Barber, recognizing his fine effort. When Campanella followed with a walk it looked like he was in trouble, but he would bear down and get the next three batters, pulling another Houdini act. In the ninth, Cox led off with a single to left and Chuck Diering who had replaced Elliott for defensive purposes as he often did scooped it up and threw back to the inner garden. Robinson grounded into a 6–4–3 double play. Campanella singled before George "Shotgun" Shuba grounded to Lockman to end the game. The Renaissance Assassin would haunt the Brooklyn Dodgers like no other pitcher ever did. Maglie recalled after his playing days ended, "When I was pitching for the New York Giants in the early 1950s, my friends used to warn me never to walk across the Brooklyn Bridge.... Dodger fans hated me then the way they hate Walter O'Malley now. They believed that when I pitched against Brooklyn, I threw at the heads of the Dodgers. This was their belief and I can't really blame them for it. They were 100 percent correct."[24]

The injury to Irvin and the departure of Mays devastated Durocher's outfield alignment. He would have had one of the best outfields around, but now they were nothing more than a mediocre contingent. Hank Thompson replaced Mays in center and left much to be desired. For the season he batted .260 with 17 homers and 67 RBIs with a .956 fielding percentage which included time in the outfield (72 games), third base (46 games), and second base (4 games). Thompson caught the routine balls but balls that were a little more difficult were beyond his grasp. The spectator sat in the Polo Grounds and attempted to ascertain if Mays would have caught the ball that Thompson missed by several steps. Maglie and the other pitchers knew that with Willie in center, all they had to do was to keep the ball in the expansive Polo Grounds center field and Mays would certainly catch it. Durocher contended shortly after Mays left the team, "However, we must not judge Thompson too hastily. I can't expect him to make the plays Willie made, because there's no one like Willie."[25] Mueller batted .281 for the year with 12 homers and 49 RBIs. Bob Elliott was supposed to replace Irvin in left but he proved to be a disappointment, batting .228 with 10 homers and 35 RBIs. Chuck Diering, who had a good glove but no bat, was a late-inning defensive replacement but his batting average dropped 85 points from the previous year to .174. Durocher cringed at the idea of putting Dusty Rhodes in the outfield; his fielding average was .917 but he batted .250 with 10 homers and 36 RBIs. He spent the first half of '52 at Nashville in the Southern Association where he batted .354 with 18 homers and 68 RBIs. By the end of the year Bobby Thomson vacated third base and returned to center field. Thompson and Rigney manned the hot corner. Despite Leo's problems, he kept the squad fighting all year and remarkably finished in second place.

On June 27 and 28, the Phillies took two games from the Giants at Shibe Park. Curt Simmons threw a shutout in the first game, which marked Eddie Sawyer's last game as manager. The Phils were struggling in sixth place and Bob Carpenter decided a change was needed and fired him. Steve O'Neill, Maglie's old manager at Buffalo, was named the new skipper. Eddie would return to manage the Phils in 1958–59 and retire after losing the first game of the 1960 season. Jansen failed to last through the second inning as his record fell to 6–4. Larry was also having his problems in '52. The following day they lost by a 7–2 score as Hearn's record fell to 8–2. The Giants' frustrations came to the forefront in this game. Mueller hit a fly ball to Del Ennis in left field during the second inning. Ennis came in and speared it as umpire Bill Stewart signaled that the batter was out. Elliott was doubled up off the second base bag. Durocher blew sky high, arguing that Ennis had actually trapped the ball. Durocher argued violently and kicked dirt on home plate, and umpire Stewart. He also nailed the umpire in the shins with his leg. The Giants continued to heckle the umpires as Kennedy and George Wilson were kicked out. Leo's actions earned him a four-day suspension. Monte Irvin recalled, "Durocher developed a style of his own that rubbed off on the Giant teams. He used to draw fans to the ballpark. They loved to see him go toe to toe with teams we played against."[fg] The irascible Leo Durocher was linked with John McGraw at the hip in so many ways. They both drew fans to the park because of their pugnacious behavior. They challenged umpires, fans, anyone who got in their way. Off the field, their acquaintances were dubious members of society. When Durocher argued with umpires there was a method to his madness. In later years he stated, "Whenever I argued with them, I'd try to get them near the line. Then I'd kick the lime off the line onto their pants. If they didn't get the lime off pretty quick, it'd burn a hole in their pants. They always tried to get out on the grass."[27]

Without their peerless leader, the Giants won their third in a row, sweeping the Braves in a doubleheader at Braves Field on June 30. The opener was a close 8–7 win while they relaxed in the second game, winning 4–0. Maglie became the first eleven game winner in 1952, improving his record to 11–2 in the opener. It was his eighth win at night. Sal put in another shaky outing, working seven innings, while giving up six runs on eleven hits and three walks and fanning five. He got the hook in the eighth when he walked Eddie Mathews and Jack Daniels hit a double. Sal Yvars was hit by an Ernie Johnson pitch. The next day he would he involved in a violent outburst. Jansen pitched a five hit shutout in the second game to improve his record to 7–4. The rhubarbs continued to break out everywhere as Braves manager Charlie Grimm and pitcher Vern Bickford were kicked out.

New York ended June with a 15–11 record in spite of all the chaos. On the first day of July only 5,442 spectators entered Braves Field and watched the Giants win by a 6–3 score. The tension began to mount in the first inning when Earl Torgeson took a vicious cut at a Hal Gregg offering and nailed Sal Yvars on the shin with the backswing. Heated words were exchanged. Torgeson managed a single to right field and as he vacated the home plate area, Yvars picked up Torgeson's bat in retaliation and slammed it on top of the plate causing the bat to split. Torgeson stayed out on the field and took his position in right field as the Giants went down in the top of the second. As Lockman passed Torgeson at the end of the inning, he informed him that his bat was broken. After viewing the evidence himself and seeing his bat broken in the bat rack, the enraged player threw off his glasses and began sprinting towards the Giants dugout. Yvars was oblivious to what was going on as he worked on his equipment, bending over and putting on his shinguards. Torgeson dove into the Giants dugout and sucker punched the unsuspecting catcher with a ferocious left hook cutting a deep gash above the catcher's right eye. Several other Braves jumped into the enemy dugout, as an explosion seemed imminent. Most of the players tried to pull the enraged Torgeson off Yvars. The tough New York catcher was patched up by the doctor and allowed to continue. Westrum was already hurting and the Giants didn't have anyone left. After the contest, Yvars' eye became discolored and he needed stitches in the hospital. Torgeson and Bickford were kicked out of the game. The irony of it all was that the ex–Giant, Sheldon Jones, was on the mound for Boston. He had become inured to the throwing of the knockdown pitch under the guidance of Leo Durocher. He hit Hank Thompson with a pitch while Gregg hit Jethroe. The only two blacks in either lineup paid the price for the earlier battle and were hit. Jethroe was amazingly playing his last full major league season. In 1950, his rookie year, he had batted .273 while leading the league with 35 stolen bases and winning the Rookie of the Year award. The following year he batted .280 and again led the league with 35 steals. His numbers would drop in '52 but certainly they could have used such a talented ballplayer. The black players were unfairly expected to act in a more dignified manner than the white players. When Charlie Grimm and other players called him "Sambo," he reacted with the threat of violence. "Watch it. I'll get a bat and there'll be no one left in this clubhouse but me," he informed his teammates.[28] White players of lesser ability found big league jobs, but Jethroe was through after the '52 season except for a cup of coffee with the Pirates in 1954. Playing in Boston, a profoundly prejudiced town, exacerbated the situation. In three seasons with Boston he was hit by a pitched ball 25 times, including 11 in 1951. As for Torgeson and Yvars they would go at it again with different teams. Ballplayers have remarkably long memories and payback is a bitch.

The Brooklyn Dodgers finally figured out Sal Maglie and handed the Giants a 5–1 loss on the fourth of July before 49,443 spectators in Harlem. It was the first time the Dodgers defeated the Barber since April 22, 1951. He walked four batters in a row in the first frame, throwing only two strikes during that stretch as Brooklyn took a 1–0 lead. In the second Cox singled and Reese hit a homer into the lower right field stands. Sal lasted only two innings, giving up three runs on three hits and four walks while fanning one. Bobby Thomson failed to hit in the clutch, including one time with the bases loaded. The Giants stranded twelve baserunners on the day. Yvars popped out with the bases loaded in the sixth inning. A twenty-eight minute rain delay halted play with the Dodgers batting in the same inning. The game was called after eight innings on account of rain. Ed Sinclair called the game "one of the most futile exhibitions Leo Durocher has yet to witness as the New York manager."[29] The Barber's record fell to 11–3. Maglie was selected to the All-Star team for the second year in a row. Durocher was the manager of the National League squad. Lockman and Thomson were the other Giants selected.

In their last day of baseball before the All-Star break the Giants split a doubleheader with the Phillies. After losing the opener, 2–0, the Phillies bounced back behind Russ Meyer in the second game and won 4–1. Maglie had a 9–0 lifetime record against the Phillies before he dropped his first game. It was his fourth loss of the year as he allowed three runs on five hits in seven and one-thirds innings. The Giants committed three errors on the day, as their defense was still shaky. The 1952 All-Star game was played at Shibe Park in Philadelphia as the National League won a 3–2 five-inning rain shortened game. Jackie Robinson and Hank Sauer hit homers for the Nationals. Maglie did not pitch in the contest as Curt Simmons and the eventual winner Bob Rush handled the pitching chores. Lockman led off and went 0 for 3 while Thomson went 0 for 2.

The Giants lost their third in a row and sixth out of seven when they dropped a 6–2 decision to the Pirates on July 11. Billy Meyer's Pirates were on their way to a 42–112 last place finish in '52 and losing to such a club was particularly disheartening. It was the second straight day they lost to them. Maglie lasted seven innings, allowing all six runs on ten hits and one walk and hitting Ralph Kiner with a pitch. His record fell to 11–5. He had failed to go the distance in nine out of his last ten starts. Merson continued to hit the Barber well, getting two hits. Durocher had removed himself from the third base coach's box and was replaced by Herman Franks. After the game Leo was disconsolate. "I made a few boots and so did the players." Dusty Rhodes was called up from Nashville. "I'm not sure exactly where Rhodes will play," Leo said, "but he'll be in the line-up. I can lose just as well with new men as the ones I've been playing. This team can't live on last year's reputation. I'm going to build a fire under somebody."[30]

Sal Maglie had put up with the pain for too long. He went to the mound injured, and suffered alone on the hill doing the best he could. On July 16 the bottom dropped out, as the Giants held on for an 8–7 win in ten innings at Sportsman's Park. The Cardinals scored five runs with two out in the ninth to tie it before Dark's double chased home Williams in the tenth with what proved to be the winning run. The game took three hours and fifty-six minutes to complete. It was a "duster" war with pitchers on both teams knocking hitters down. Stanky, Buzzy Wares and Solly Hemus were kicked out of the game at various times. The Barber knew he had nothing, as the pain overwhelmed his aching body. If he was going to have any success he would have to keep the Cardinals hitters off balance by pitching high and tight. Rookie pitcher Wilmer (Vinegar Bend) Mizell struck out the side in the first inning. Soon after that, the early innings developed into a beanball war between Maglie and Mizell. Mizell was a southpaw who took an exaggerated windup that included a high leg kick. He featured a live fastball and a roundhouse curve. In the second inning he sent left-handed batting Dusty Rhodes into the dirt. His fastball was blazing, really popping the glove hard. Maglie came in high and tight to Billy Johnson and nicked him with a pitch. The Barber's back was killing him, and his troubles were only made worse when Mizell nailed him on the left arm in the third inning. When umpire Babe Pinelli rebuked the Cardinals pitcher, Durocher yelled at the umpire. If they wanted to have a knockdown war, so be it, Durocher's men could take care of themselves. Stanky also discussed the situation with the arbiter. Maglie was sweating profusely as he tried to reach down and defy his pain filled body by pitching a ballgame. In the fourth he got the first two batters before Mizell tripled to center field. Leo had seen enough and went out to get his pitcher. He was not charged with a run but gave up four hits and two walks. He never complained of an injury, but Leo could read from the pain in his mournful eyes that something had gone amiss.

In their last trip to Cincinnati, Shellenback realized that Maglie had been pitching under excruciating pain. By this point Maglie figured it was to late to complain and he simply tried to pitch through his problems. For one quarter of the season he had pitched like Dizzy Dean in his best year, for the other quarter of the season be looked like a raw busher. Sal Maglie was catching fungoes in the outer garden at Crosley Field when he felt shooting pain in his back and could barely bend over. He threw the ball in an unorthodox motion back to the infield. When the Barber took his turn on the hill he threw junk. Slow curves, change-ups and a nothing fastball and he did so with an awkward delivery in which he did not follow through with his pitches. Somehow he got by for it took the Reds on that June 10 day till the seventh inning before they hit the Barber hard. When he got the hook, he walked off the field in an awkward, vertical, stiff-backed posture and threw his glove disgustedly into the corner of the dugout. Shellenback followed him down to the clubhouse. Maglie tried to surreptitiously untie his shoes, concealing the act from his pitching coach. He bent his body and pulled himself forward so that he would do minimal bending to untie the laces. Shellenback had been watching and talked frankly with Maglie about his ailments. The Barber was the ultimate competitor and consummate team player. He managed to cajole Frank not to tell Durocher, at least not yet. For nine more games he trudged to the mound with nothing and tried to pitch. His team was still in the pennant race and the Barber wasn't going to miss anything. With Mays and Irvin already gone, Maglie knew if he left the rotation their chances might be dashed. So he pitched with the "guts of a burglar," before the masquerade ended in St. Louis.[31] He tempted fate and threw caution to the wind.

In St. Louis, Shellenback watched him like a hawk. Durocher knew something was wrong—you don't have a precipitous decline like Maglie had without something being amiss. For six weeks, Leo waited for the old Barber to return but except for that contemptuous performance against Brooklyn when he tossed a shutout he did not. Leo's fourth and fifth starters were shaky regardless of whom he threw out there and he needed Jansen, Hearn, and Maglie to carry the club. By the third inning Maglie was hurting bad. The bullpen was working quickly. By the fourth inning, the Barber was crippled yet somehow he retired the first two batters. He was throwing the old prayer ball, standing on the hill with nothing but a glove and a prayer. Mizell hit the triple and Leo had seen enough. In the annals of baseball history you would be hard pressed to find a man who had pitched with greater pain than Salvatore Anthony Maglie, with barely even a whisper of a complaint. Durocher took the long walk that he had dreaded for so long. His head was down and his hands in his back pocket. Westrum walked despondently to the mound to join in. Durocher knew that old man Maglie had given him everything he had, and then some. He had gone the extra mile for Leo. The two men walked back to the bench together. Some of the Giants found themselves looking away, knowing that the end might have arrived for the thirty-five year old right-hander. He had fallen so far and so fast from his lofty perch. In the dugout, Shellenback went to get a drink of water, hiding his face, holding back tears. The old man was broken but not beaten.

Maglie failed to get better on his own volition and was subsequently sent to the Chicago Medical Center. He kept asking the doctors when he could pitch again as he took diathermy treatments for nearly two weeks. The recovery process was excruciatingly slow for the anxious Barber. He was eventually transferred to the Harkness Pavilion in New York's Columbia Presbyterian Medical Center. He lay on the bed stricken, wondering when he could pitch again. Even more disturbing was that the Dodgers were increasing their lead. He had a lump on the lower end of his spine which doctors called a strained ligament. When taken off the treatment, the doctors cautioned him against doing too much, too fast and said it would take two weeks before his back could take the strain of pitching. If he disregarded the doctors' orders, permanent damage was a possibility. He went home to his apartment to be with his wife Kay and the next day he was at the Polo Grounds. Sal was allowed to work his way back into shape slowly and began throwing some batting practice after a short time. Durocher shocked Sal by asking him if he could pitch in the big series against Brooklyn at the beginning of August. Sal's back wasn't ready but New York managed to win two of three. He tried to pitch and even took his regular pregame warmup but the back stiffened. The next day he couldn't bend his back.

On August 7, the Giants split a doubleheader with Brooklyn at the Polo Grounds. New York won the opener by an 8–2 score as Corwin improved his record to 2–0. Corwin had found his rhythm once again after a miserable spring and earned a trip back to the big show, despite winning inconsistently in the American Association (8–11). With New York still in the running and the Dodgers haunted with the memory of their season ending failures of the two previous years, Durocher concocted a brilliant psychological ploy. He arranged to have Leo Durocher Night at the Polo Grounds while celebrating their miracle of Coogan's Bluff from the previous year. The Dodgers had to sit and bear it. He had a positive attitude with the press suggesting they could make a run at the pennant even when they were behind by a sizable margin. New York reporters wrote stories in the general vein of, "Can Leo Do It Again."[32] Leo was honored before the second game of the day-night doubleheader. He was given several gifts, most prominently a Cadillac. His speech went as follows: "Usually I'm not at a loss for words, but I am tonight. I don't have to tell you what a wonderful evening this is for me. I can think of only one thing I would trade it for — another 16-game winning streak. I don't consider it a tribute to Leo Durocher, but a tribute to the Giants. If John McGraw — the greatest manager baseball has ever known — were here I'm sure he would say that this was his kind of a Giant team. Joe DiMaggio once said that it was great to be a Yankee. It's also great to be a Giant, Joe."[33] George Spencer started the second game but got nobody out as Campanella hit a grand slam before he got the hook. Brooklyn had a 6–0 lead when Cox and Robinson hit solo shots in the second frame off Hal Gregg. Campanella, batting cleanup, followed Jackie to the plate and Gregg unleashed a duster that sailed over his head. Snider was knocked down in the next frame. With the Giants at bat, Durocher constantly asked the umpire to examine the ball. Dressen began doing the same thing to Giant pitchers. When Yvars was saying unsavory things to Cox when he was batting, umpire Babe Pinelli warned the Giant catcher. New York rallied for five runs in the fifth, highlighted by Lockman's three run homer. Brooklyn had a 7–5 edge in the ninth. With two out, Lockman singled off Joe Black to bring the tying run to the plate. The count went to 3 and 2 on Thompson before Black threw a blazing fastball right down Broadway to end the game. Leo had exhausted his pitching staff in the series and his club was still five and a half games back.

Boston swept four games from New York on August 8, 9, and 11. On August 13, the Giants split a doubleheader with Brooklyn at Ebbets Field. Wilhelm won his tenth game of the year. Hal Gregg continued to impress Durocher by throwing inside. He nailed Robinson in the first game. Leo had put pressure on Maglie to come back and pitch, but now Sal realized he had to pitch not for Leo but for himself. Kay was worried that he would succumb to the idea prematurely. The Giants were barely staying alive in the pennant race and they needed to win the next day's game. The back still wasn't good, and to pitch risked serious injury. Sal told his worried wife that he would pace himself and cut loose only in tight spots. The following day, Maglie found Leo in the clubhouse and told him he was ready. Leo was shocked; he shook his head, telling Sal he wanted him to pitch but not at the expense of crippling his ace hurler. Maglie told Leo that he would do the same thing under similar circumstances. "Cripple yourself. Sure, you'd do it. You'd throw till your arm came off if they'd let you — and then start throwing with your other one. You wouldn't ask somebody else to do it. But if you thought it would win a game or help the team, you'd do it yourself."[34] Leo was accustomed to managing tough ballplayers. He had managed Pete Reiser in Brooklyn and they didn't get much tougher then him. It was settled, the Barber would toe the slab in hostile territory on August 14. While Maglie was gone, the Giants had barely stayed alive in the pennant race. Like Mays, he brought an intangible to the team that lifted everybody up. He was the enforcer, who imbued a ferocious competitive spirit among his teammates. New York was 11–12 during his absence.

A small crowd of 16,592 curious fans paid their way into Ebbets Field to see if the old Barber had anything left. Hank Thompson doubled home Dark in the first inning to give the Giants the early lead. Maglie walked out to the small rise in the middle of the diamond for the first time in nearly a month. He toed the right side of the slab and threw a called strike to Billy Cox. Thompson crept in at third and the rest of the infield was ready for a bunt. The Dodgers could bunt the Barber out of the ball game if they wanted to and if they knew he couldn't bend down to field a ball. Maglie spun out of the windup, and delivered the pitch which Cox grounded to short. When Reese and Robinson stepped back into the box, Maglie reintroduced himself to each of them and threw two unmistakable beanballs at the general direction of their skull. Tommy Holmes who always wrote graphically and honestly about the beanball wrote in the *Brooklyn Eagle*, "There are rules against the beanball but the umpires ignore them, being the only ones in the park who do not recognize a duster when they see one. Umpires never do anything about this until the other side fires back and proceedings begin to resemble a duel."[35] Reese and Robinson hung in, and each of them reached for singles. Sal was pitching with artfulness and the only thing he could bend was his curve. The bullpen was already active. Jackie was dancing off the first base bag taunting the Barber like he always did, and Reese was hugging third base. Campanella, Sal's favorite target, stepped into the box. The first two pitches were of the brushback variety, and on the third pitch Campy waved at an outside curve and popped to Lockman. Shuba walked to load the bases and Leo came out to talk to Maglie. Snider took a home run cut on the second pitch, hoping to bury the Barber early but missed. Durocher had always been lenient as far as letting Maglie work through his jams and not pulling him early but in this game he would not hesitate to bring the early hook. Sal bore down and with shooting pain running up his back, he managed to get Snider to go out of the strike zone to punch him out.

For the next four innings, Maglie held them scoreless. When the Dodgers would bunt, Sal came off the mound feigning that he could pick up the ball when he could not. Brooklyn hurler Johnny Rutherford held

New York scoreless in his next four frames as well. In the sixth inning, the Giants had the bases loaded with no outs. Thomson hit into a force play at the plate, and Hartung popped to short. Wes Westrum, another courageous fella, stepped in, barely able to grip the bat because of his injured thumb and his beat-up hands. He hit a double to clear the bases and give the Giants a 4–0 lead. Maglie had hurt his back while swinging at a pitch in the fifth inning, and he eventually struck out. He had kept the Dodgers off balance with the inside fastball and off-speed stuff. He was pitching junk but his hatred of the Dodgers had encouraged him to persevere despite the stabbing pains.

Maglie sat in the dugout before the bottom of the sixth started, trying to buy some time, knowing that he had nothing left. The Barber had left everything he had on the field and was done. Home plate umpire Tom Gorman yelled at him to hurry up. Robinson waited to the side of the batter's box as Maglie walked to the mound. Jackie Robinson like many ballplayers had his own particular quirks and superstitions. He would never step into the box, until the catcher was in his position. Wilhelm was up in the bullpen. Jackie ripped a single to left field and took second when Dusty Rhodes bobbled the ball. Durocher came to the mound. The pain had racked the Barber, but he refused to go out giving Wilhelm time to warm up. "Hang on. Pitch to one more man" he told himself.[36] Maglie fell behind Campanella and then threw one over the plate. Campy lined it to center, and Robinson scampered home with the first Dodger run. Durocher came out of the dugout and returned without his pitcher. Maglie threw one pitch to Shuba, and Durocher came out again. Gorman implored Leo to stop stalling. During one stretch, only three pitches had been thrown in thirteen minutes. As Maglie walked to the dugout, every Giant stood and applauded the Barber for his inspiring performance. Shuba hit Wilhelm's first pitch for a double, putting runners on second and third. Snider's single scored Campy and Shuba went to third. Pakfo grounded to Thompson who threw home. Westrum exploded when the runner was called safe. "I felt Shuba hit my shinpads, as I tagged him. He probably did touch the plate later, but I wasn't interested in that." Westrum pushed the home plate umpire. Leo came out to restrain his catcher from hitting the ump. Westrum incessantly kicked dirt on home plate. Wilhem did not record an out and Corwin worked the final four innings as the Giants won 4–3. Durocher continued to do anything to disrupt the Dodgers, in his strategy of psychological warfare. He threw balls into the stands, which he was forbidden to do, and called off a police officer who tried to retrieve the ball from a fan. "Billy Cox gave away two of our baseballs at the Polo Grounds. For every ball the Dodgers tossed to the crowd I made up my mind it would cost the Brooklyn club two. I'm two up on 'em now."[37] Leo was the ultimate "two for one" guy, whether it was beanballs or something else. He wanted to retaliate in these baseball wars and of course anything that Durocher did, Dressen copied and did himself.

The Barber couldn't have been happier after the game as he shouted to reporters "We're not dead yet!" When Leo was asked if his pitcher would take his next turn he said, "Sal's the boss. I can't tell him how bad his back hurts. I do know this. If Sal thinks he can throw even one inning, I won't be able to keep him out of there."[38] The Giant infielders along with Wes Westrum did a good job covering on bunts.

Maglie won his twelfth game of the year. He allowed two runs in five innings on seven hits and one walk while striking out three. The game took three hours and eleven minutes to complete. It took them two hours and sixteen minutes to play six innings. Games in 1952 and throughout the decade in general were becoming longer and longer, particularly Giant/Dodger contests. The average National League contest in 1951 took 2:22 to complete. In 1952 it took 2:24, and in 1953, 2:26. The average Giant/Dodger games were 2:47 in 1951, 2:57 in 1952 and 2:49 in 1953. The two teams engaged in every imaginable delaying tactic one could think of. Arguments and inspections of baseballs were especially time consuming. Other unspectacular incidents such as the batter stepping out of the box, the pitcher talking to the catcher, and relief pitchers coming in from the bullpen also took up time. In 1952 the Giants and the Dodgers played a nine-inning game that took three hours and thirty-eight minutes to complete. Maglie, like many other hurlers, pitched very slowly with runners on base: adjusting his cap, rubbing up the ball or asking for a new one, picking up the rosin bag, and shaking off the catcher's sign. The home run ball also contributed to longer games, as did television. Managers came out of the dugout to dramatize events, with grandiose gestures so they could look good in front of the viewing audience. Unlike the International League, managers could visit the mound as often as they wanted to. Managers were not automatically kicked out for arguing balls and strikes in 1952. John Lardner wrote about this growing phenomenon in *Newsweek*: "Critics, including this one, have been brooding lately upon the strange forces that have replaced the two-hour baseball game with the three-hour baseball game. It may be that the three-hour game is here to stay, and it may be that we will get used to it in time. Right now, it occurs to me that present-day baseball has, at least for us older hands, something of the twisted, troubled, frustrating quality of a long dream on a summer night."[39]

Leo Durocher was suspended for five days and fined $100 for a violent incident with umpire Bill Stewart on August 17. He apparently rubbed an illegal substance off the ball or manipulated the ball in some way when Hal Gregg came into pitch. When Stewart asked to inspect the baseball, Durocher blew up. He brought his hand back as if he were going to punch the umpire, but players and umpires successfully stopped him from doing so. Durocher was having a plethora of incidents with umpires in '52. In Chicago the Giants took a doubleheader by scores of 5–0 and 3–1. Maglie threw his fifth shutout in the opener to gain his thirteenth win on the year. It was the first time he had finished a game since June 26. Each inning he went out onto the mound expecting the pain to reoccur, but it never did. He allowed eight hits, walked two and struck out two. New York scored four runs in the first inning to give him the early lead. The Barber said he "felt strong" after the game.[40] "Just like my old self! I didn't feel a thing. No pain, not a bit!"[41] Wilhelm won the second game in relief, improving his record to 11–2. The erratic knuckleball baffled National League batters. Someone noted that the pitch, "swerved like a moth in a hallway, and plumbed feebly into the catcher's glove."[42]

On August 24, 23,207 Crosley Field spectators saw their Reds defeat the Giants by a 5–4 score in the first game of a doubleheader when Davey Williams committed a bases loaded error in the last of the ninth. Maglie started but did not receive a decision. He gave up three runs (two earned) on eight hits and two walks in five and one thirds innings.

In Maglie's last game of the month he defeated the Dodgers in Ebbets Field as New York won by a 4–3 score. He had a 5–1 record against them on the year, including four wins in Ebbets Field where he had yet to lose in his career. It was an encouraging performance for he allowed only four singles over the last five innings to finish strong. Davey Williams hit a three run homer in the fourth inning to lead the offense. Sal's record improved to 14–5. He gave up ten hits, struck out eight and did not walk a batter. The Giants held an 11–5 advantage over their rivals for the season. The Dodgers were hearing footsteps even though they were eight games in front. They were haunted by the collapse of 1951. Most of the experts regarded the Dodgers as "the best eight-man team in baseball."[43] Columnist George Will called the '52 Dodgers, "one of the great teams in history."[44] The lineup was unchanged from 1951. Newcombe was taken by the military for the 1952-53 seasons. Carl Erskine led the way in his absence compiling a 14–6 record while Billy Loes (13–8), Ben Wade (11–9), and Preacher Roe (11–2) proved to be capable starters. The staff was buoyed by the performance of rookie phenom Joe Black. He compiled a 15–4 record with a 2.15 ERA and 15 saves in 56 games to win the Rookie of the Year. If necessary, he would knock down a batter. Dressen told him during spring training, "When I want you to brush a hitter, I want you to go right at his head. I want to see his bat go one way, his cap go another and his ass go somewhere else." If someone threw at one of the blacks on the Dodgers, Black would retaliate. When the Dodgers visited Crosley Field early in the season, the Reds bench began singing "Ol' Black Joe."[45] Wally Post was petrified as the ball flew past his skull, and he was forced to pick himself off the dirt. The singing stopped, but Black knocked down a few more of the Reds hitters for good measure. Brooklyn defeated the New Yorkers by a 9–1 score on the final day of the month. In August, the Giants were 16–14. They were prepared to assault the Brooklyns' fragile ego in the final month and try to pull off another miracle.

Maglie became a workhorse once again in September, appearing in nine games as Durocher tried to get all that he could out of the Barber. New York split a doubleheader with Boston to begin the month, and then won five straight to put the pressure on the Dodgers. On September 3, Catholic War Veterans honored Horace Stoneham before the Giants/Phillies game at the Polo Grounds for allowing servicemen in uniform to attend games free of charge. The Giants then proceeded to defeat the Phillies by a 4–3 score in ten innings. Maglie shut the Phillies out over the first four innings. In the fifth inning, he allowed three enemy runs but only one of them was earned. Bob Elliott, who was playing third base, made a throwing error, while Maglie made a fielding error. This was added to three singles, a sacrifice and an intentional walk. He was removed for a pinch hitter in the bottom half of the inning.

Two days later Maglie closed the door on a 5–4 victory as the Giants swept the three game series over Philadelphia. He replaced Corwin with runners on first and third in the ninth inning. He struck out Johnny Wyrostek and Richie Ashburn on eleven pitches to end the game. The Phillies were certain that Sal was throwing spitballs—those curves surely couldn't have been of the honest variety, they thought. They complained loudly as they entered the clubhouse where Steve O'Neill, the Phils' skipper, informed them that they were indeed honest curves. George Wilson was becoming a good clutch hitter for Durocher, batting .406 in thirty-two at-bats as a pinch-hitter. The Dodger lead was down to six games, and they were feeling the pressure. The events that took place in early September seemed to indicate that the Dodgers were set for another monumental collapse. This happened just before the Giants were scheduled to play five straight games against them.

Durocher told reporters, "If we can pull this one out, there will be 100,000 suicides in Brooklyn." An article in the *Saturday Evening Post* in early September declared, "The Dodgers Won't Blow It Again!" Dressen told reporters that his "boys" would prove that they were not "chicken-hearted bums." Arthur Daley did not hold back when he wrote, "What's that Charley? Speak a little louder please. It almost sounds as though you said that your staggering heroes cannot miss this time."[46] Right before the Dodgers were set to play the Giants, Jackie Robinson and Roy Campanella were fined by National League President Warren Giles. Joe Black threw a ball to Johnny Logan that umpire Frank Secory said nicked the batter on the right shoulder in the eleventh inning. The bat was knocked out of Logan's hand. Campanella and Labine were kicked out of the game for arguing. Robinson later exchanged words with umpire Larry Goetz after Logan had scored the winning run. Rocky Nelson had first assaulted the umpire asking, "Did you shake his (Logan's) hand when he crossed home plate?" Robinson joined in the taunting. Warren Giles was an unmistakable bigot. He fined Campanella $100 for the incident even though he did not even utter one curse word. Robinson was fined $75. If Giles was going to fine these players how about Rocky Nelson who verbally assaulted the ump? How about Labine who heckled the umpire and was tossed out? Robinson was sick of the double standards and declared, "I won't pay until I get a hearing with Giles."[47] Jackie wrote in his autobiography, "I went to O'Malley and protested. He said he didn't want the matter to get out to the press and gave me the impression that he would look into it. The story did show up in the papers, however, and although I was not responsible for it, O'Malley promptly blamed me."[48] The rift between Robinson and Dodger management was wide. Warren Giles' wire to Robinson practically declared his hostility towards blacks, "Your remarks to Umpire Goetz ... cannot be disregarded simply because neither name calling nor profanity was used." Here was the kicker, "Reviving or condoning an argument after the conclusion of a game when leaving the field can incite serious trouble and cannot be condoned or pardoned by this office."[49] How many times had Durocher continued an argument after a game and nothing happened? Countless times but Giles had no problem with his skin color. Early in the season Giles had summoned up the energy to honor Jackie before a game. Roger Kahn recalled, "I watched Robinson's face ... and his smile was hate."[50]

The Giants were only four games behind Brooklyn when they swept a doubleheader on September 6 before 49,011 fans at the Polo Grounds. The first game took three hours and thirty-eight minutes to complete, a major league record for a nine-inning game. The Dodgers had lost nine of their last twelve while the Giants had won eleven of fourteen. Bill Connelly (4–0) and Hearn (13–6) earned the victories. Maglie was once again honored with his own "day" by the citizenry of Niagara Falls. Since he wasn't scheduled to pitch he was able to enjoy this one a little bit more than the others. They gave him a gold ring and a check for $700, which he gave to the boys' club in Niagara Falls.

The following day was one that challenged the collective manhood of the Dodgers. Warren Giles was at the game and said he would be receptive to a hearing with Robinson. Jackie said, "It's a matter of principle with me now," and threatened to retire and hang up his spikes.[51] Dressen was up to his usual chicanery, announcing that the little used right hander Joe Landrum would start. He hoped that Durocher would load his lineup with left-handers and at the last possible moment Dressen declared Preacher Roe as the starter. The Giants touched Roe for a run in the first inning. Carl Prince had written, "That was the Dodgers' low point of the season — probably the low point of the postwar decade."[52] Hodges tied the score in the second with a homer off Maglie. Reese and Shuba hit solo shots in the third to give the Brooklyns a 3–1 lead. After Reese's homer, Sinister Sal knocked Robinson down. In the next frame, Roe hit Irvin between the shoulder blades. The umpires got together with Dressen and Durocher to discuss the situation. Maglie gave up his fourth homer in the seventh to Billy Cox as Brooklyn went up 4–1. Hodges sent a message to the Giants in the eighth inning when he took out Davey Williams at second with a malicious slide. He virtually cut him in half. Davey was hindered by a bad back and these incidents didn't help the situation. He was helped off the field and would miss a week of action. Ultimately it would be a Dodger who would end his career prematurely. Brooklyn held on to win 4–1 behind Roe. Maglie lost his sixth game, allowing seven hits; four of them were homers. He struck out five.

On September 8, the Dodgers won the day portion of the doubleheader by a 10–2 score while the Giants won at night under Coogan's Bluff, 3–2. The first game turned ugly, highlighted by beanballs, several hit batsman, a spiked infielder, and the removal of a pitcher from the game for throwing at the batters. The trouble began in the fifth inning when Hoyt Wilhelm hit Gil Hodges with a pitch, in retaliation for Hodges' vicious body block take-out slide on Davey Williams the previous day. Furillo hit into a double play grounder and Hodges cut open a "three-inch gash" in Bill Rigney's leg with another take-out slide. Rigney would miss some action, like Williams, and was replaced by Bobby Hofman in the game. Hodges, an ex-marine with a relative mild disposition, had taken two players out in consecutive days. The Dodgers were trying anything they could to bury the Giants and redeem themselves for the "choke" label hung on them.[53] Carl Furillo recalls, "I roomed with Gil Hodges for six years, and he was a nice person, a real nice person, but anybody says he never got mad is a lot of baloney. He'd get mad when he would see that somebody

Maglie sits in the dugout, awaiting his next start, with the stubble of his beard several days old. (George Brace photo)

was out to harm somebody. Take a guy like Durocher. Gil knew Durocher was a louse, that he was trying to harm people, and then he would get mad. Gil would say, 'He's a no good bastard.' Guys on the Giants like Rigney, they were dirty ballplayers. A guy like Alvin Dark, who was another dirty bastard, and Gil would say, 'Hi, Alvin, how are you, Alvin?' and under his breath, 'You son of a bitch.'"[54] The hostilities continued into the later innings. In the seventh, Monte Kennedy threw at Hodges and Joe Black. In the following frame, Larry Jansen nailed Andy Pafko. Joe Black retaliated and threw at the Giants. Jansen was kicked out in the last inning. He walked off the mound towards the Giant dugout before pitching to Billy Cox. The benches had already been warned in the eighth inning about throwing at batters. Umpire Lee Ballanfant ordered him to return to the hill. Jansen hit Cox with the next pitch and was kicked out. Durocher cleared his bench as he picked up the argument with the umpire and he was banished as well.

Don Mueller's two out double in the ninth chased home the winning run as the Giants won the night game. Maglie pitched three scoreless innings of relief to earn his fifteenth win. He allowed two hits, walked two and struck out two. Snider and Dark hit homers in the game, which was free of the nasty incidents that occurred in the opener. This was the last meeting between the combatants for the season with the Giants enjoying the upper hand. They defeated Brooklyn fourteen times and Maglie won six of those games. The Dodgers would play good baseball the rest of the season and would not have to sweat out another thrilling pennant race on the final day. Durocher was suspended for the third time in the season for his participation in the beanball war and fined $100. Kennedy was fined $50 and Jansen only $25 because of his "excellent conduct record."[55] Giles stated that the manager should be held responsible for all beanball incidents. Concerning Jansen's pitch that nicked Billy Cox, Durocher retorted, "You call THAT a bean ball?"[56]

The Giants won a close game on September 11 by a 5–4 score over Pittsburgh before only 3,094 spectators at the Polo Grounds. Maglie was not sharp but struggled through five innings to earn his sixteenth win of the season. He allowed two runs on six hits and two walks. The Dodgers lead was cut to three and a half games as the Brooklyns lost to Chicago by a 11–7 score. Ed Sinclair wrote in the *New York Herald Tribune*, "the noose gets tighter and tighter around the necks in some quarters."[57]

It looked as if the Giants were prepared to sweep a doubleheader from the Reds on the following day. They won the opener 4–2, but dropped a heart breaking 8–7 contest in the second game in which they had ample opportunities to win. Corwin improved his record to 6–0 in the opener as Wilhelm closed it out. Maglie came out of the bullpen in the eighth inning of the second game, and retired the Reds successfully. In the ninth, he allowed doubles to pitcher Frank Smith and Bobby Adams as the Reds took the lead and held on to win. It was the Barber's seventh loss of the season. He surrendered two hits and one walk in two innings. The Giants squandered homers by Thomson, Hofman, Yvars, and Mueller. Ed Sinclair declared in the *New York Herald Tribune* that the loss was "critical and perhaps the most disastrous reversal of the year."[58]

Maglie pitched the first complete game for the overworked pitching staff since September 6 when he led New York to a 12–1 victory over St. Louis on the 15th. They collected eleven hits while Lockman and Thomson hit homers. Enos Slaughter hit a triple over Mueller's head in right field in the seventh and scored on a Del Rice fly ball to break the shutout. The Cardinals failed to get more then one hit in a inning against the Barber. New York scored nine runs in the sixth inning to assure the victory. Maglie improved his record to 17–7, allowing six hits and two walks while striking out four. Monte Irvin had provided an infusion of productive offense since he had returned to the lineup. He was batting .346 in his first 107 at-bats. The pitching staff was hurt by the fact that Jansen and Maglie won 17 fewer games then they had the previous year, but some of the other pitchers had respectable years to compensate for the loss. After the September 8th game against Brooklyn, Jansen was shut down for the rest of the year because of a lame back. Down the stretch Leo turned to a number of pitchers to start a game. In addition to Maglie and Hearn, he used Max Lanier (7–12 for the season), Bill Connelly (5–0), Al Corwin (6–1), Dave Koslo (10–7), Mario Picone (0–1), and Jack Harshman (0–2). That was the same Jack Harshman who began the 1950 season as the Giants' first baseman. He was converted to a pitcher and put together a respectable career as a hurler. In 1953, he compiled a 14–8 record with a 2.95 ERA with the Chicago White Sox. His wife had encouraged him to resist the position change, but when he divorced her he was suddenly receptive to the idea.

One of the disturbing trends in baseball was the alarming decline in attendance that continued to plague big league clubs. In Maglie's last three games while the Giants were still in the running for the pennant, the Giants had drawn 3,094, 8,706, and 4,316 fans to the Polo Grounds. In fact the Giants failed to draw one million customers to their ballpark in '52 for the first time in years. More people stayed home, and watched games on the new medium of television. When Philadelphia swept the Giants in three straight games their pennant hopes were virtually dashed. New York lost a shameful game at Shibe Park to the Phillies on September 18 by a 1–0 score. Maglie and Curt Simmons hooked up for a classic pitcher's duel. Maglie retired leadoff hitter Connie Ryan in the first inning. Richie Ashburn followed with a walk and Mel Clark hit a lazy, routine fly ball in the direction of Clint Hartung in right field. Every big leaguer should put a ball like that in his back pocket but Hartung missed it and the ball caromed off his knee. Maglie did not conceal his disgust as he cursed his outfielder. Ashburn came around to score on Del Ennis' single before Maglie retired the side. Curt Simmons deserved to win, pitching a nine hit shutout and working out of small jams when needed. Elliott pinch-hit for Maglie in the eighth. He was saddled with his eighth loss of the year, despite working seven strong innings, and giving up seven hits and one walk.

Only 3,018 fans bothered to show up below Coogan's Bluff on September 24 as the Giants took a doubleheader from Boston by scores of 11–8 and 8–2. Maglie started the first game but retired only one batter before he got the early hook. It was his shortest start of his career. He allowed three runs on three hits and one walk. The two teams still harbored some animosity from their rhubarb earlier in the season. Boston hurlers hit Mueller and Williams. Koslo went the distance in the second game as Thomson, Dark, and Rigney hit homers. Koslo plunked Sam Jethroe, who got hit very frequently by Giant pitchers. Maglie pitched seven shutout innings in his last start of the season against Philadelphia to finish the year with an 18–8 record. He gave up six hits and three walks, while striking out three. The Phillies managed to load the bases against him twice, but the Barber escaped without harm. Wilhelm worked the final two innings so he could tie Ace Adams' 1943 Giants record of 70 appearances. He would appear in one more game to establish a new mark. The Polo Grounds attendance for this game was 1,684.

The Dodgers finished the season with a 96–57 record, four and a half games in front of the second place Giants. The World Series went seven games but the Yankees emerged triumphant to win their fourth straight world championship. Billy Martin made a great running catch on the infield with the bases loaded in the seventh inning of the final game to save the Series. Billy Loes had enraged Dressen before the series when he told reporters that the Yankees would win in seven games and then told Dressen he was misquoted and changed his prediction to six games. When he committed a balk, he told reporters that the ball slipped from his hand because it had "too much spit on it." When he missed a grounder the excuse was "I never saw the ball at all. I lost it in the sun."[59]

Leo Durocher may have done the best coaching job of his career in '52 as New York finished in second place with a 92–62 record. Officially this is six wins less than the previous year, but it was actually only four wins less because two of the victories in '51 came in the playoff against Brooklyn. Surely if Mays and Irvin were in the lineup all year they would have made up the five games and won the pennant. Things were only exacerbated by Jansen and Maglie's back problems but to Leo's credit he kept them in the pennant race right to the end. They had compiled a 18–11 record for the month of September and only in one month did they dip under the .500 barrier (July, 13–14). Brooklyn led the National League in homers with 153. New York finished second with 151. The third place team, the Boston Braves, lagged way behind with 110. Brooklyn had a .262 batting average. New York batted at a .256 clip. Both clubs compiled a .399 slugging average. New York led the league in double plays turned with 175 while Brooklyn was second at 169. New York led the circuit with 56 triples in the expansive Polo Grounds while Brooklyn led in stolen bases with 90. The Dodgers team ERA was 3.53 while New York had a comparable 3.59 ERA. One category where the Dodgers clearly out performed New York was on defense where Brooklyn committed a league low 106 errors for a .982 percentage. The Giants committed 158 errors for a .974 percentage. The Dodgers led the league with 775 runs scored, New York was second with 722.

In his three seasons since returning to the big leagues in 1950, Sal Maglie had compiled a 59–18 record. Up until June 2, 1952, when he lost his first game of the season, he had an unbelievable 50–10 record since returning to organized ball. His 1952 record stood at 18–8 with a 2.92 ERA as he fought through adversity all season because of the bad back. He pitched 216 innings, gave up 199 hits, walked 75 and struck out 112. Sal hurled five shutouts and had a 6–2 record against the Brooklyns. He hit six batters and batted .072. Hearn was 14–7 with a 3.78 ERA. Jansen dropped from 23–11 the previous year to 11–11 with a 4.09 ERA. Koslo and Wilhelm also pitched very well. Offensively Lockman batted .290 with 13 homers. Williams hit .254 with 13 homers as well. Dark batted at a .301 clip with 14 homers and 73 RBIs. Bobby Thomson batted .270 with 24 homers and 108 RBIs. Mueller hit .281 with 12 homers. Hank Thompson bounced back from his '51 debacle and batted a respectable .260 with 17 homers. Westrum only managed a .220 average with 14 homers. Monte Irvin batted .310 in his late season return with 4 homers and 21 RBIs. This team lacked a prodigious home run hitter such as a Ralph Kiner, Hank Sauer, or Gil Hodges but everyone contributed. Nine of the Giants hit home runs in the double digits. They had fought the good fight in '52 but came up a little short.

8

A Season to Forget

Sal Maglie did not squabble over his 1953 contract, signing early for an estimated $35,000. Due to Larry Jansen's mediocre performance in '52, the Giants provided an offer that called for a substantial pay cut. Larry took umbrage to the suggestion and did not see eye to eye with Giants management. Despite his uncharacteristic performance the year before, he still had an outstanding 107–68 record for his career. As the Giants' entourage headed West for spring training, Maglie boarded the team train in Buffalo. Many of the players boarded the train at different locations. In Chicago, Dave Koslo joined them as the Giant cars were hooked onto the Rock Island's Golden State run, which took them into Phoenix. The Dodgers opted to fly most of their players to Vero Beach on a DC-3. The Giants' outlook was uncertain. Leo's main concerns centered on the health of Monte Irvin's ankle and Jansen and Maglie's recuperation from back injuries. Durocher exaggerated his team's expectations as he had done in previous camps and writers were more than accommodating when writing about such unrealistic statements. Leo declared he had "more good players in this camp" than he ever had since becoming the Giants manager.[1]

Alvin Dark was a holdout, upset that management was considering moving him to second base or maybe third. He received a $27,000 salary in '52 and insisted upon an $8,000 increase. Durocher saw the future in Daryl Spencer who had played most of the season at Minneapolis before receiving a cup of coffee with the Giants at the end of the year, batting

.294 in 7 games. The insistence that Spencer was the shortstop of the future may have been another Durocher ploy, its purpose to light a fire under Dark. Dark's nickname was "Blackie," supposedly because he used a black bat, but it has been suggested that Jackie Robinson had pinned the name on him because of his reputation for heckling black players.[2] Dark's racist views were largely in line with those in the south and would get him into hot water in the early 1960s as manager of the transplanted San Francisco Giants. Pitcher Ruben Gomez immediately impressed Durocher at his first practice. When the press came around, he lauded the youngster. Frank Shellenback was more restrained in his analysis, "He wasn't trying, you know, after all it's his first day here. But he looked awful good. He's very quick, fields well and his control is very good. His screwball and curve are excellent."[3] Gomez was purchased from the Puerto Rican League for $15,000. If Maglie or Jansen faltered, Leo needed someone else to pick up the slack.

Things got off to an auspicious start for Maglie as he won his first exhibition game, 9–4, over the Chicago Cubs. Sal pitched three scoreless innings, but did not feel that his back was particularly strong. He had a small tendon knot and was a bit apprehensive of cutting loose. Luckily for Maglie he was not seriously injured when Frankie Baumholtz hit a comebacker and Maglie instinctively stuck out his right foot to stop the ball. The ball did not hit him squarely and grazed off his foot. In his next start against Cleveland, once again his back tightened but he managed to throw three scoreless innings. A Hank Majeski leadoff homer off Gomez in the eleventh gave the Indians a 7–6 win and broke New York's four game winning streak. Maglie surrendered three hits and two walks in the game. The tendon knot in his right hip was still bothersome and it did not look like he would cut loose and throw as hard as he could for a while.

Maglie had mixed results in his next start and was the losing pitcher as the Cleveland Indians won by a 3–2 score before 17,225 fans at Los Angeles's Wrigley Field. The park was named after William Wrigley, Jr., who also owned the Chicago Cubs. This was the first park named Wrigley Field for Chicago's Wrigley Field was not given such a name until 1926, and was previously known as Cubs Park. L.A.'s Wrigley Field was a beautiful little coast league park, with ivy growing on the left field wall, holding about 20,500 spectators. The popular television show "Home Run Derby" was later shot from this location.[4] Maglie was the first Giant to work five innings, giving up three runs on seven hits and one walk while striking out three. Larry Doby hit a tremendous homer over the ivy covered left field wall off the Barber. Bobby Thomson was nailed on the right hand by a Mike Garcia fastball, suffering a severe bruise, and was taken to the hospital for X-rays. Garcia was another pitcher who was not shy about throwing inside. Frank Hiller, who had been acquired from the Cincinnati Reds shortly after the season, pitched two scoreless innings for New York and struck out five of the seven batters he faced.

The Alvin Dark situation hovered over the Giants camp like an ominous dark cloud. He belatedly signed a two-year contract calling for $30,000 a season. He played a lot of second base in exhibition games, while Spencer played short. Dark did not look sharp and the papers suggested that he wasn't putting out his best effort because of the frictional relationship with management. Durocher held a press conference to discuss the situation and Dark showed up to express his concerns. They tried to quell the rumors that they were feuding with one another. Dark noted, "I told Leo last fall that I would play second base if he wanted me to. Why, that's an old man's job. It's real easy. I've told Spencer the same thing, too." Leo said he was confident that Dark was putting out but seemed to send a message when he noted, "However, if he or any player didn't give me that, he wouldn't be on the field ... I'd sit him on the bench and tell him, 'See how much money you can make there.'"[5]

When the Giants took on the San Francisco Seals on March 21, Durocher was still in a bad mood over the friction with Dark. The Giants won 12–0 behind homers by Irvin, Mueller, and Yvars. When the Giants moved West they would play their first two seasons in this pitcher's park, Seals Stadium. Maglie won his second game, working five scoreless innings, giving up three hits but walking none. He went 2 for 3 at the plate with two runs scored. Maglie was like many pitchers who took pride in their batting and were willing to do the little things to help the club such as laying down a sacrifice bunt. Five days later, Sal was the loser in a 6–5 St. Louis Browns victory. He worked six innings, gave up seven hits which included three two run homers. Sal walked one and struck out four and drove home a run at the plate. His spring record stood at 2–2.

Durocher's mood was soured even more as result of several injuries the club incurred. Davey Williams injured his back when Ferris Fain of the Chicago White Sox crashed into the second baseman's backside. He suffered a badly bruised spine, just when he was feeling better over a pinched nerve condition. This was not the first, and would not be the last time a collision severely crippled his back. He told reporters, "It doesn't feel good, that's all I can say. I can't bend it or twist it as I would on a double play, without sharp pain. And I can't throw, except by using only my arm. Gee, I don't know what to think."[6] Williams' back problems went as far back as 1950, while playing for Minneapolis when their right fielder inadvertently rammed his knee into the lower portion of Davey's spine as

8. A Season to Forget

Williams drifted back on a fly ball. Davey was certainly not a combative personality as Stanky had been. He was not really intimate with his teammates and was soft spoken. Dark and Williams combined to form a competent middle infield combination. Another injury that Durocher had to deal with was Sal Yvars' sprained left ankle suffered in the game against the St. Louis Browns. Ray Katt, Rafael Noble, Sam Calderone, and Westrum were the other catchers in camp.

As the Giants barnstormed back East, they revisited Denver, Colorado, the site of last year's demoralizing injury to Monte Irvin. This time Irvin decided not to tempt fate, and sat out the game. A crowd of 16,640 fans watched the Indians' Bob Feller face Maglie. The Indians pulled out a 12–11 victory when Dave Pope hit a bases loaded two out single to bring home the winning tally. The Giants had tied the game with four runs in the top of the ninth that included a Davey Williams three run homer. Maglie was hammered for eight runs on eleven hits and one walk in five innings. Larry Doby, Al Rosen, and Wally Westlake hit homers off the Barber. Doby's was a tremendous shot over the right center field scoreboard. Of course the climatic conditions in Denver provided a salubrious background for hitters. Maglie was accustomed to pitching in such conditions dating back to his days in Puebla of the Mexican League. Roger Bowman was saddled with the loss.

New York's nine game losing streak came to an end when they scored five runs in the tenth inning to defeat the Indians by a 13–8 score in Lubbock, Texas. Two days later Maglie improved his record to 3–2 for the spring in a 7–2 win over the Indians in Austin, Texas. The Barber looked sharp up until the fifth inning when he slipped and fell off the mound. A Dusty Rhodes catch in left field precipitated a lengthy rhubarb and Maglie left the game shortly after. He held the opposition scoreless in four and one-third innings, giving up three hits and two walks while striking out five. His early departure was due to his stiff back and he did not wish to force the issue in a mere exhibition contest. After playing on rickety bush league fields since leaving Phoenix, they finally played on a respectable playing surface at Disch Field. Maglie won in his final appearance of the spring, to improve his record to 4–2. New York was finishing the training session strong, winning seven of eight with that April 10 victory. Sal was shaky as he allowed seven runs on eleven hits and three walks. He nailed Wally Westlake with a pitch. His spring totals were not impressive. Maglie worked thirty-three and a third innings, while allowing 44 hits and 24 runs (19 of them were earned). He walked eleven and struck out seventeen. Most disturbing was that Maglie had failed to throw the ball with pinpoint accuracy, which he was accustomed to doing in the past.

He was able to get by with junk because his control was so good, but now it had eluded him.

Durocher gave the opening day nod to Jansen so he could save Maglie, the ultimate Dodger killer, for the home opener against Brooklyn. Jansen had a 1–3 opening day record on four previous occasions. Daryl Spencer would begin the season at third despite incurring a severe facial beaning sustained when one of Mike Garcia's fastballs got away from him in Nashville. The youngster had his lips stitched closed and was living on a diet consisting of mainly soup. Durocher was not changing his plans to start him at third base. "You can go a long way on soup. Besides I like hungry ballplayers."[7]

Jansen gave up one run in the opener at Shibe Park as New York won 4–1. Philadelphia rebounded the following day, 8–1, as Corwin was knocked out of the box. A small crowd of 18,307 attended the first game of a day-night doubleheader at the Polo Grounds on April 17. In the Giants' home opener, New York took the day contest by a 6–3 score. Johnny Podres, the twenty-year-old left-hander, started in place of Preacher Roe who was ill. These two left-handers joined Carl Erskine, Billy Loes, Russ Meyer, Bob Milliken, Clem Labine, and Ben Wade as the most reliable Dodger pitchers in '53. Meyer and Robinson had gotten into several ugly incidents with each other when Meyer played in Philadelphia. When he walked into the Dodgers clubhouse the first person he saw was Jackie who said to him, "Monk, we've been fighting one another, now let's fight 'em together."[8] Sal Maglie looked unhittable as he threw six and two-thirds innings of no-hit ball to begin the game. The last Giant pitcher to throw a no-hitter below Coogan's Bluff was Carl Hubbell on May 8, 1929. Jackie Robinson hit a little dying quail that died softly on the grass in left field for the first hit. Robinson took a wide turn at first and made Irvin make the throw, which is an intelligent fundamental baseball play. Irvin threw the ball away and Robinson scampered all the way to third. Campanella hit a tremendous drive for a triple scoring Robinson with the first Brooklyn run but the Giants were up by a 3–1 score. New York scored three runs in the eighth that included a two run single by Maglie to give the Giants a 6–1 lead. Maglie couldn't loosen up in the ninth, as his back stiffened. The outlook did not look good since his back had bothered him during the spring and now it was a nuisance on the first day of the season. He retired one batter in the final frame and allowed four singles before Wilhelm was summoned from the bullpen to shut the door. New York held on to win 6–3. Maglie allowed all three runs on six hits while striking out three for his first victory. His control was sharp for he did not walk a batter. Harold Rosenthal declared in the *New York Herald Tribune*, "Sal Maglie, who ran the gamut of looking first indomitable and then looking like a fellow seeking a place to sit down, scored his first victory..."[9] Westrum hit a homer. Spencer collected his first hits of the year, a double and triple, but committed two errors. Podres pitched well in his major league debut, but took the loss. Westrum said that Maglie looked "just as good as at the same time last year." The Dodgers won the nightcap, 12–4, before 29,406 freezing spectators. Hearn gave up six runs in the fifth inning to take the loss. It was a sudden, unexpected collapse, for Jim had only given up two hits in four shutout innings prior to the fifth frame. He threw three wild pitches in the game as he became unnerved by the Dodger baserunners. Lockman booted an easy grounder and the Dodgers tormented the Giants by stealing four bases. It was an ugly exhibition of baseball. The other big baseball news of the day was Mickey Mantle's homer estimated at 565 feet at Griffith Stadium that literally cut the baseball open. Durocher was dumbfounded when he heard the news. "He must have been hitting from third base."[10]

The Barber couldn't continue his mastery over the Pirates as he lost his first game of the year at Forbes Field as Pittsburgh pulled out a 5–4 victory before a freezing contingent of 6,273 fans. He worked four and one third innings, giving up five runs on nine hits and two walks while striking out four. Cal Abrams touched him for a homer to lead off the fifth. The loss was costly as Wes Westrum jammed his index finger and Davey Williams aggravated his back when he made a futile dive at Joe Garagiola's liner. The Pirates' management and the local baseball writers were having a major contentious battle, and manager Fred Haney made the press wait fifteen minutes before they could be admitted to the clubhouse.

"'Bean ball,' a game Dodgers and the Giants sometimes play instead of baseball, made its annual debut at Ebbets Field yesterday while the Giants were squaring the three-game series with a 7–5 victory."[11] That's how Roger Kahn started his article in the *New York Herald Tribune* after the April 25 war between the two teams. Maglie's control was off. Campanella was sent sprawling into the dirt as a fastball shaved him close in the second inning. George Shuba followed with a double and Furillo drove him home with the first run. The Dodgers scored four runs in the following inning and the Barber became enraged, as he scowled at the next hitter with his heavy beard. "I didn't shave the day of a game because when you perspire your face burns." Maglie added that, "I didn't know how I looked out there. I knew I had a dark beard. When I went out there I stared the batter down. It was him or me."[12] Furillo came to the bat. Maglie was stomping around the mound, kicking at the dirt, staring menacingly at the enemy batsman. The first pitch sailed over Furillo's head and went all the way back to the screen. Furillo took two steps towards the mound, and gave Maglie a dirty look, while the Barber slowly rubbed up the baseball. The Barber would intimidate the batter when he felt like it, regardless of the count, but he did have his theories on the subject and liked to throw the ball at the batter's skull when it was least expected. "You have to make the hitter afraid of the ball. A lot of pitchers think they do that by throwing at a hitter when the count is two strikes and no balls. The trouble there is with that count, a knockdown is routine. It's expected. You don't scare a guy knocking him down when he knows he's gonna be knocked down." Maglie added, "A good time is when the count is two and two. You knock him down two and two, he gets up shaking. Then curve him and you have your out. Of course, you have to be able to get your curve over the plate on a three and two count. Not every pitcher can do that."[13]

Maglie's second pitch to Furillo was a slow curve, low and away. He missed the pitch and the bat sailed out of his hands at Maglie. The bat, now transformed into a weapon, missed the pitcher and rolled to the edge of the outfield grass. Furillo walked slowly to the mound while Sal Yvars walked alongside of him. "C'mon, Carl, let it drop. Sal didn't throw at you. The ball slipped." Furillo yelled back, "So'd my bat."[14] For years Furillo had been thrown at and now the situation seemed to come to a head, as Maglie walked slowly down the small rise in the middle of the diamond

Bill Mazeroski hits the dirt avoiding a vicious knockdown pitch. (National Baseball Hall of Fame Library, Cooperstown, N.Y.)

in the direction of Furillo. Both benches cleared as the players rushed onto the field. A human wall suddenly blocked Furillo from the menacing Barber. Umpire Larry Goetz and Gil Hodges restrained the batter. Things seemed to simmer down until Furillo saw Durocher and absolutely lost it. Only Hodges' strong armlock prevented the situation from becoming ugly. Play was halted for several minutes before order was restored and the surfeit of players left the field. The Ebbets Field fans became hostile and booed Maglie vigorously until he left, while they cheered Furillo. One writer said that, "... it is evidently more sporting in the public mind to throw a bat at a person than a ball at him."[15] Maglie allowed five runs in five innings on eight hits and three walks while striking out four. Wilhelm was the winner in relief and Joe Black who would have a horrendous year after his superb showing in '52 took the loss.

After the game both Furillo and Maglie denied any wrongdoing. The beanballer often denies any wrongdoing after a game by saying, "It just got away from me."[16] Maglie denied that he was throwing at Furillo, "That's ridiculous. If I was going to throw at him I would have come a lot closer. Harder and truer, I would have thrown it." Sal Yvars added, "That's right. He didn't throw at him. The pitch was so high Furillo didn't even go down. That Campanella, he went down." Furillo said, "The bat just slipped out of my hands. It slipped." A reporter asked, "And did you slip out to the mound?" Furillo replied, "I was just going out to get the bat, that's all." Walter O'Malley, the Dodgers' president, gave Furillo an envelope containing $50 for his tactics. "It's for catching the largest bass in Vero Beach this spring," O'Malley told the press.[17]

On the last day of April, Maglie looked like his old self, tossing a shutout against the newly transplanted Milwaukee Braves. Bobby Thomson hit a home run in the ninth inning to send the 4,109 Polo Grounds fans home happy. The Barber worked out of two one-out bases loaded jams. He allowed six hits, four walks and struck out five. The Braves pulled off a rare 8–2–3 double play in the game. Wes Westrum, already hurting from injuries, bruised his knees when he collided with the fence behind home plate as he tried to corral a popup. Yvars replaced him but he was also hobbled with various ailments. Maglie's record stood at 2–1. As the month ended New York found itself in sixth place with a 5–9 record. The rotation had not come around. Hearn and Jansen each sported a 1–2 record and Corwin was 0–2.

Sal looked shaky in his first start of May in an 8–5 New York win over Chicago in the vacuity of the Polo Grounds. A crowd of 3,356 hearty souls attended the game. The ballgames under Coogan's Bluff were beginning to resemble bush league contests where you can hear the players' voices echoing around the park as they call for fly balls and other idle chitchat such as bench jockeys and infield chatter. Maglie worked four innings, giving up four runs on six hits and one walk while fanning one. He threw one wild pitch. Corwin earned his first win of the year against two losses in relief. The New Yorkers equaled a National League fielding record for having only one assist in a nine-inning game. It was credited to Maglie as he caught Paul Minner's pop bunt and doubled off Roy Smalley at first. Minner, the opposing pitcher, hit a homer off Sal in the game.

After May 7, New York ranked third in team batting (.276), fifth in fielding (.972) and fourth in pitching (4.18). Sal Yvars was batting at a .357 clip, playing more often due to the various injuries to Wes Westrum. Williams was at .317, Lockman at .304, and Thomson at .293. If Durocher's men were going to compete, the pitching had to come around. The little used Bobby Hofman hit a pinch-hit homer in the nightcap of a double-header at the Polo Grounds to enable the Giants to sweep a twin bill from Pittsburgh by scores of 4–0 and 3–2. Hofman had hit two homers earlier in the season to win a game. Maglie tossed his second shutout in the opener to improve his record to 3–1. He allowed only three hits, walked six and struck out nine. After six games he was sporting the second best ERA in the National League at 1.18. Hearn stumbled through eight and one-third innings in the nightcap, allowing sixteen baserunners but only two runs. In six starts, Jim had yet to finish a game. Frank Hiller got one out in the ninth to earn a cheap win. Mueller and Williams hit homers.

Wilmer Mizell led St. Louis to a 5–2 victory over New York on May 16 before 13,187 fans at what was formerly known as Sportsman's Park but now was called Busch Stadium. Anheuser-Busch was the new owner of the team and its president August Busch had purchased Sportsman's Park from Bill Veeck and renamed it. Maglie went the distance in the game but was hit early and often to lose his second of the year. He allowed five runs on twelve hits and three walks. Durocher kept changing his lineup trying to find the right combination. Yvars made a mental error when he failed to take the force play at home with the bases loaded. He should have touched home and thrown to first for a double play. Instead he chased the runner down the third base line to the amazement of the spectators. There was a steady downpour before the game as Leo probably had wished it rained all night. Against Brooklyn in front of 46,778 Polo Grounds fans, New York pulled out a 7–2 victory. While Maglie warmed up before the proceedings, he strained a left lumbar muscle and pitched through considerable pain in the first inning. He retired Jim Gilliam but then Reese singled, Snider hit a homer, and Robinson doubled. Maglie was given the hook after recording only one out, as Corwin came in from the bullpen to replace him. Corwin was the winner, improving to 4–2 as Koslo pitched the final five innings to close it out. This was a contest that epitomized the dangers of umpiring. When Furillo unleashed a bullet from right field it hit umpire Tom Gorman squarely in the face and he needed stitches afterwards. The unsuspecting umpire did not see it coming. They didn't call Furillo the "Reading Rifle" for nothing.

After missing two starts in the rotation because of a pulled muscle in his back, Maglie climbed on top of the hill on June 4 against the Cincinnati Reds. He had nothing as Cincinnati scored three runs off him on six hits and four walks while striking out three. The Barber nailed Gus Bell with a pitch. The pinpoint control that was characteristic of Maglie's performances throughout the years was missing. Harold Rosenthal wrote, "Maglie scarcely looked overwhelming."[18] New York won the game, 11–3, as Wilhelm emerged triumphant. The Giants were in fifth place with a record of 21-20. Ruben Gomez won his first big league game on the following day as the Giants defeated Chicago, 11–1. The pitcher who had impressed Leo during spring training had found himself in the rotation. He scattered fifteen baserunners and struck out eleven. Dee Fondy was hit by a pitch. Gomez was similar to Maglie in one way: they were not afraid to employ the beanball. Unlike Maglie, Gomez was often not willing to back the beanball up with intimidating actions after delivering such a pitch and standing his ground when needed.

The Milwaukee Braves defeated the Giants by 12–8 score on June 8 before 7,998 Polo Grounds fans. New York dropped to the .500 mark (23-23) and so did Maglie whose record fell to 3-3. It was his third consecutive loss as he allowed eight runs (four earned) in seven innings of work. Milwaukee collected six hits against the swarthy right-hander and four walks. Sal fanned three batters. The Giants defense was inept as they committed three errors in the sixth inning to lead to four unearned runs. Irvin, Thompson, and Williams were the culprits. Durocher was banished from the game for one of his dirt kicking episodes, as was Dark, when they insisted that Braves catcher Ebba St. Claire blocked his path to the plate in the ninth inning. After the game the Barber was optimistic about his performance. His injury did not bother him. "I really felt fine," said Maglie, "better, in fact, than at any time this season."[19]

Warren Spahn improved his record to 7–1 by defeating the New Yorkers on the following day. Durocher was kicked out of the game for questioning a ball call from home plate umpire Frank Secory. He insisted that all he said was, "Frank where was that pitch." Leo made the following statement in the locker room: "Don't tell me they [the umpires] don't get together before the game and decide the first time a certain person says something he is going to be put out of the game. They do the same thing to Stanky." The statement seemed to have more than a semblance of the truth to it. In fact umpire Larry Goetz publicly admitted that he gave Durocher and Stanky the quickest thumb in the game. Warren Giles took offense to Leo's premise that the umpires were "ganging up" on him. Under the threat of indefinite suspension, Durocher was forced to retract his statement and was fined $50. "There's one thing I want to stress," he told reporters, "In all my years in baseball, I've never questioned the integrity of the umpires."[20] The fact that he managed to say that with a straight face should have earned him an Oscar. This incident is illustrative of the sensitivity the baseball establishment had when a relatively innocuous statement was made which also happened to be steeped in truth. The mere fact that they threatened banishment from the game for making such a statement shows one the lengths organized baseball would go to keep its ironfist domination over the game.

On June 14 the Giants fell prey to two Cardinal southpaws, Harvey Haddix and Wilmer Mizell, as the New Yorkers dropped a doubleheader by scores of 1-0 and 9-4. Maglie lost a heartbreaker in the opening contest as his record fell to 3-4. It was the first time his record had dipped below the .500 barrier since he had returned to the Giants in 1950. He allowed the one run on seven hits and two walks while striking out five. Three consecutive hits in the fifth scored the only Cardinal run. Maglie had no run support from the anemic offense, which managed only five safeties. Dark had three infield hits while Maglie and Williams collected the other two singles. Haddix threw a good curve to supplement his other pitches that had the Giants' hitters baffled. Ruben Gomez lost the second game as his record fell to 1-3. Dark had been recently moved to third base while the slumping Daryl Spencer was moved to short.

Lou Perini, owner of the Boston Braves, received permission to move his franchise to Milwaukee before the '53 campaign began. Boston was shocked that their Braves, a charter member of the National League in 1876, were leaving town with very little notice. Perini had insisted that, "I definitely feel that since the advent of television Boston has become a one-team city, and the enthusiasm of the fans for the Boston National League Club has waned." Attendance figures supported the owner's conclusion. By 1952 they drew only 281,278 fans which prompted manager Charlie Grimm to say, "We were playing to the groundskeepers."[21] The St. Louis Browns had planned to move to Los Angeles for the 1942 season but Pearl Harbor terminated those plans. Abysmal attendance figures had the owners frightened and they soon realized there was an untapped resource out West. A club record 1.8 million fans went through the turnstiles at Milwaukee's

County Stadium in 1953. The rest of the owners were salivating. Perini turned a profit of $637,798. Walter O'Malley watched the situation closely.

The Barber's first appearance in County Stadium was a sterling performance as New York humiliated the home team, 15–1, before 34,348 spectators. This was a competent Milwaukee team that would finish second to Brooklyn in '53, accumulating 92 victories. Maglie went the distance to improve his record to 4–4. He allowed the one run on four hits, no walks, and struck out four. The Giants attack was deadly as they collected sixteen hits in the scorching heat, which had the fans in anguish. Maglie had three singles, scored two runs, and drove home four. He was batting at a .320 clip for the year. He had retired ten in a row before relief pitcher Dick Cole touched the Barber for a homer in the sixth to end the shutout. Maglie subsequently retired the last twelve batters to face him. He was efficient, throwing 91 pitches in the game and he went to a full count on only three batters.

Sportsman's Park, now called Busch Stadium, was a beautiful big league park located in northeast St. Louis. It was a double-decked facility all the way down the foul lines, with a covered pavilion. Dimensions were spacious but the ball tended to carry well in the scorching summer heat. The new owner of the Cardinals, August Busch, took down all the advertising on the outfield walls and replaced them with a sole ad for Budweiser beer. The scoreboard now had an eagle that flapped its wings after a Cardinal homer. June 24 was one of those hot St. Louis days; the temperature was hovering around 96 degrees and Sinister Sal Maglie was scowling at the hitters on top of the hill. He baffled the Cardinals with an eight hit shutout, his third shutout of the year and his fifth victory. Sal walked two and fanned six. The Giants gave him excellent defensive support and collected ten hits, including one by Maglie. When Maglie walked Steve Bilko in the seventh it was the first walk he surrendered in eighteen and two-thirds innings. In Sal's last three starts he had only given up two runs and was beginning to find his stride. Koslo had pitched poorly the previous night and Durocher set his rotation with Maglie, Hearn, Jansen, and Gomez. Leo noted, "I can't afford to give Maglie and Jansen any additional rest by dropping in a fifth starter. They'll have to work every four days because I simply haven't any more starters."[22] Koslo had been a major disappointment with a 1–8 record. Kennedy couldn't be counted on and Wilhelm was needed in relief.

Sinister Sal, the living nightmare, proved to be a menace once again to the Brooklyns as New York humiliated the Dodgers by a 20–6 score before 36,733 gloating customers below the craggy cliff in Harlem. This was a Dodger team that would cruise to the pennant with 105 wins. Roger

Kahn called the '53 Dodgers lineup "the most gifted baseball team that has yet played."[23] The saturnine Barber started slowly as the first two Dodgers he faced scored, but as always he found a way to beat the Brooklyns. The Dodger pitchers were trounced. The first three Giants to face Clem Labine scored. Labine had not thrown a complete game since the second game of the '51 playoff. Labine, who had developed arm problems which hindered his performance, was belittled by management. Dressen treated his players as if they were essentially robots that were impervious to the slights of a manager. Dressen told a reporter, "It ain't his arm. I happen to know after Labine got borned in Rhode Island, he was put in a incubator. That's the problem. Them incubator babies can't never last nine innings."[24] The first two batters who faced Joe Black scored. The first six to face Branca scored and the first batter to face Wade scored. Maglie was having a good year with the stick as he went 3 for 5, scored two and drove in two. The Barber improved his record to 6–4, as he allowed the six runs on nine hits and one walk while fanning three. He was 2–0 versus the Dodgers. New York batters walked seven times, had eleven singles, and five homers. Thompson was the hitting star with two homers and seven RBIs. Umpire Frank Secory, who called the balls and strikes, was heckled by the Dodgers throughout the contest. Jim Hughes and Robinson were tossed out of the game. Robinson noted, "All I yelled was, are you sure Frank? But I suppose he'll report that I cussed him."[25] As for Durocher he just folded his arms in the third base coach's box and laughed incessantly at the opposition.

Seven years after Jackie Robinson had debuted in the majors he was still taking abuse. On August 30, 1953, the Dodgers hosted the Cardinals and Jackie stumbled around with a bad leg. Eddie Stanky, the Cardinals' skipper, imitated an ape and suggested Robinson had the characteristics of one. Stanky's vile routine took place within full view of many of the Ebbets Field fans. Stanky had once called Robinson a "black bastard," as Monte Irvin sanctioned his words during the ugly episode in '51 when Jackie and the Dodgers banged on the wooden door in Ebbets Field.[26] Stanky called Ray Noble "Bushman," referring to the "big ape that's appearing at the circus."[27] The Dodgers had internal race relations exacerbated in '53 with the appearance of Jim Gilliam in the lineup. Robinson was to move to third and replace Billy Cox, while Gilliam played second. Several of the white Dodgers objected to the move. Jackie's antagonistic behavior resulted in a lot of players hating him, not because he was black but because he treated people in a hostile manner. The line became blurred as far as his ability to recognize the difference between a racist gesture or an innocuous statement. He had been abused so much that he jumped on people for harmless comments. It was difficult for Robinson to handle the transformation from a target, which he still was by many, to being accepted by many as an equal. His rage was understandable considering the abuse he had taken and his intensity on the field was unmatched. Durocher declared that Robinson "didn't just come to play, he came to beat you. He came to stuff the goddamn bat right up your ass."[28]

Maglie started his second consecutive game against Brooklyn on July 10 in Ebbets Field. Over 32,889 rabid fans packed their way into the Flatbush bandbox, the largest crowd in two years, and they left disheartened as Maglie tortured them once again as New York won by a 6–1 score. The Barber's domination over the Brooklyns was legendary. He sported a lifetime 18–5 record against them, and had never lost in Ebbets Field (8–0). Durocher would juggle his rotation to allow Maglie to face the Dodgers, particularly in Ebbets Field. Larry Jansen recalls, "Because it was a small ballpark, I always had a tough time pitching there. I threw too many long flies and just didn't get enough outs. Maglie was great at Ebbets, and Leo sometimes juggled the rotation so I wouldn't have to throw when we were in Brooklyn."[29] To pitch well in the Dodgers' small ballpark you had to be willing to throw inside at a ferocious pace. Maglie was willing to do that and he succeeded. In addition, the Barber developed a hatred of the Dodgers dating back to 1945, a ravenous desire to beat the Brooklyns at any cost. On July 10, he allowed the one run on six hits (no walks) while striking out six and driving in a run at the plate. The Dodgers' only run came on a Roy Campanella homer in the second. Brooklyn's prodigious offense was exemplified by the fact that they had now hit at least one homer in twenty-four straight games. The Giants had won seven games in a row, as they were working on a streak of their own. Umpire Artie Gore called Robinson out on a bang bang play in the seventh. As the inning ended, the Flatbush faithful threw beer cans at the umpire in another ugly moment at Ebbets Field. The Giants' winning streak reached eight the following day when rookie Al Worthington pitched his second straight shutout to begin his major league career.

Charlie Dressen was up to his old tricks in '53, but this time he had the audacity to go after the Renaissance Assassin, Salvatore Anthony Maglie. He needled the Barber without mercy all year, telling reporters he could see "white spots" on his curve, which is a disparaging term. After the game he said that Maglie was relying on his fastball, and was abandoning his curve. Charlie insisted that Sal used the fastball "ten times to every one time he throws the curve." Campanella's homer came on a sidearm curve that hung in the middle of the plate. Dressen mistakenly thought it was a fastball. It was true that Maglie was getting older. There were days when the bender was hanging but there were other days when he could still bring the hammer when needed and polish off a hitter. Even if the curve had deserted him, he still found ways to win through intimidation and brains. Dressen added an illogical statement as he was known to do: "He better be able to beat more than one club." Durocher told reporters, "I don't know whether it's the way Charlie Dressen needles him or not, but Sal pitches against the Dodgers like it means life or death." He added, "Did you notice him out there, concentrating on the sign for every pitch. Every time he looks for the sign, it's life or death with him. He comes to pitch, not to fool around. I don't know whether he's more determined or not, but he gets results." As Maglie strode to the clubhouse victoriously with a staid demeanor, the fans shouted outside the dressing room, "The Maglie of '51." Maglie mumbled to himself, "Tell that to Dressen."[30]

Maglie won his fifth in a row in Wrigley Field on July 16, to improve his record to 8–4. He allowed three runs on four hits, two walks while striking out five. Sal also contributed a single and a sacrifice and scored a run. Dark and Irvin extended their hitting streaks to ten games while Lockman had a nine game streak. The Giants were streaking as well as they won 10–3 for their ninth win in their last ten. Sal got off to another slow start as Hank Sauer touched him for a three run homer in the first frame. The Barber did not surrender a hit in the final five innings. Tom Sheehan, former pitcher, was now a Giant superscout. When discussing the new phenomenon of pitching, the slider, he said, "I start wondering if we old-timers could have made a mistake in thinking that a curve ball had to break two or three feet to be effective. But then I think of Sal Maglie and hesitate. Stan Musial once told me that Maglie was the only curve-baller he ever faced who tipped off his curve and still left the hitter helpless to do anything about it. The Barber's curves have so much variety that knowing a curve is coming is no help. The $64 question always is: Which of his curves will it be?"[31] According to *Sporting News* estimates, the slider was being thrown by 80 percent of the big league hurlers in 1952. The slider was one of Maglie's main weapons and Charlie Dressen described the pitch as, "either a fastball with a very small slow break or a curveball with a very small fast break."[32] The slider is thrown to give the appearance of a fastball and its late break upsets the rhythm of the batter. Al Lopez suggested that Maglie's mentor Adolfo Luque was the best curve ball pitcher he ever saw and an amazing fielder.[33]

The season went downhill for Maglie after his performance in Chicago. His last three outings in July were disastrous. On July 21 he managed to retire only one batter and lost his fifth game of the year. He allowed four runs on five hits. St. Louis won 10–6. In the second inning, Dark's throw to first on a grounder hit Red Schoendienst squarely in the face and cut him open above the left eye. The Cardinals' second sacker left the game and required ten stitches. In his next start Sal received a no-decision as he worked four and two-thirds innings, allowing five runs (one earned) on seven hits, no walks while fanning three. Maglie was charged with a fielding error. He was developing a proclivity to give up homers to his opposite number. Cincinnati's Joe Nuxhall touched him for a homer in this game. On the 30th, Maglie again lasted only a third of an inning and lost his sixth of the year, 5–0, against Milwaukee. He allowed three runs on three hits and two walks. Maglie's shoulder had been giving him problems. He told reporters he couldn't "break off" the curve. Concerning his shoulder, "I hurt it in that July 10 game in Brooklyn and it's been bothering me since. I'm going to take some heat treatments and see whether they do any good."[34] The series was particularly disheartening, as they were shut out by Milwaukee hurlers in three of the four games: Warren Spahn, Bob Buhl, and Lew Burdette turned the trick. In the last game, Monte Irvin grounded into three double plays to tie a National League record.

Despite their poor finish for the month of July, the Giants managed to stay in the race by playing well in the beginning of the month and compiling an 18–10 record. As of July 29, the Giants were leading the league in batting with a .285 average. Irvin was smoking the ball. He was second in the league with a .334 average and had hit 17 homers with 79 RBIs. Hank Thompson was at .317, with 19 homers and 55 driven in, Lockman at .319, and Dark at .303 with 10 homers and 47 RBIs. Ruben Gomez had emerged as the stopper of the pitching staff with a 9–4 record. Jansen was 10–7, Koslo 3–8, Worthington 2–3, Hearn 6–6 and Wilhelm 6–5. Things completely fell apart in the final two months as they watched the Dodgers take the flag.

The bottom dropped out in August as New York compiled a 10–25 record for the month that included six defeats to Brooklyn. Durocher was less combative and easier to deal with when his club was losing. He would often lose interest in his team when things went bad. When he was winning, he was always irascible, ready to explode at a moment's notice in an attempt to light a spark under his club. Leo was an emotional manager who could be extremely difficult to get along with and often made moves based on his personal hunches. Durocher did not care much for second place; he wanted to come in first and it meant everything to him. When things were going badly, he allowed some of his players to manage games including Dark, Westrum, Rigney and Lockman. In fact, twenty-seven of his former players went on to become big league skippers. This included his managerial stints with the Dodgers, Giants, Cubs, and Houston Astros. Leo would sit in the dugout, relax, and hardly watch the game when he allowed one of his players to manage. This is not to suggest that Leo did not become intense when needed. He would sporadically awake out of the doldrums and become the competitive personality that he embodied, particularly when they played the Dodgers.

Hitting was not the problem with the New Yorkers in '53, it was pitching. On August 5, Irvin was still second in the NL in batting at .335. Thompson, Lockman, Mueller, and Thomson were all over .300. Their .283 team batting average ranked first in the circuit. Brooklyn was second at .282. The pitching became unglued. Maglie, Jansen, and Hearn were shaky but reinforcements such as Gomez and Worthington had done well. Despite their problems, by August 26 the pitching staff ranked third in the National League with a 4.14 ERA. Something was wrong and many people were expecting Stoneham to fire Leo. After an abysmal Western trip that ended in early August with New York losing twelve of fifteen, John Drebinger wrote in the *New York Times*, "It's perhaps the most mystifying plunge ever noted in Durocher's career."[35] The ax never did drop on Durocher's head; instead he was given a vote of confidence in the form of a two-year contract extension through the 1955 season. Stoneham wanted to circumvent any more talk that suggested Durocher's imminent departure. The magnanimous owner of the Giants told reporters, "I'm well satisfied with Leo." He added, "It's not his fault that the club is not winning. It's just a combination of circumstances."[36]

Maglie's record fell to 8–7 as he lost to Chicago on August 4 at Wrigley Field. Chicago hit him hard before and after a rain delay and knocked him from the box in the fourth inning. The Barber's shoulder was still causing problems. He pitched three innings, gave up two runs on four hits and one walk while fanning one. The previous night in Milwaukee a riot was averted between the Dodgers and Braves at County Stadium. Campanella was knocked down twice by Lew Burdette in the eighth inning. When Campy came to the bat Burdette called him a "black mother-fucker." When he was knocked down for a second time he yelled, "Nigger, get up and hit."[37] The Dodger catcher struck out and Burdette yelled another racial slur. Campy started towards the mound and both of the benches emptied. The Milwaukee players harbored racist feelings towards blacks. Burdette and Spahn threw at black players to a much greater proportion than whites. Carl Prince called Milwaukee an "oddly ironic German heritage: a community with both a strong socialist egalitarian constituency, on the one hand, and a deeply ingrained white supremist, neo-fascist element, on the other. The latter seems to have dominated at the ball park."[38]

Tom Gorman, the plate umpire, did not eject anyone from the game because he had to be 100% certain that Burdette was throwing at the batter. The very next day, Walter O'Malley announced a campaign to discourage beanballs. He told reporters that at the next National League meeting, "I'm going to press for a new rule along these lines: That an umpire who believes a pitcher is sufficiently wild to endanger hitters can eject him from the game." He added, "The close pitch, is part of baseball but there is not much difference between a close pitch and a pitch at a batter's head. If the umpire thinks the pitcher doesn't have enough control to pitch batters tight without coming dangerously close to their heads, he'll be employed to eject the pitcher under the proposed rule."[39] The new campaign would lead to greater powers for umpires to eject beanball artists. The problem is that the beanball and brushback pitch are so similar that a couple of inches can transform one sort of pitch into another. Therefore again it is indeed difficult to differentiate between the intention of certain pitches, and unless they took away the pitcher's right to throw inside no major changes seemed on the horizon. Sal Maglie's craft was still intact.

The Dodgers and Giants opened a three game series at the famed Polo Grounds on August 11. A crowd of 45,604 spectators entered the park and watched Carl Erskine get his first career win and complete game in the Harlem horseshoe when he threw a two-hitter to lead the Brooklyns to a 4–0 win. While warming up as he prepared to work the fifth inning, Maglie felt shooting pains in his shoulder and after a discussion on the mound and a few warmup throws he was taken out. He gave up two runs in four innings and lost his eighth of the year. Hodges hit a homer off him. Robinson was bench jockeying the Giants throughout the game. In one game in '53 he needled Tookie Gilbert so intensely that Gilbert threw his bat and cap at the bench and gave Jackie a crude gesture. What he had done to provoke the outburst was to tell Gilbert what pitch was coming from third base. Gilbert decided not to take the advice and struck out.[40]

The umpires took control of a knockdown contest at Ebbets Field on August 18. Billy Loes knocked Daryl Spencer down in the second inning. In the bottom half, Robinson dodged two heaters aimed at his ribs. Al Worthington sat Campanella down with a fastball at his head. Gorman warned both benches at which time Durocher thought he should lecture the arbiter on the customs of the National Pastime. With the pitchers and managers realizing that the next incident would result in a fine and possible suspension, no more incidents took place. The batters would dig into the box comfortably and despite this, both clubs went scoreless for nine full innings before Brooklyn scored in the thirteenth to win, 4–3. The Dodgers would go on to sweep their second three game series from the

New Yorkers for the month. Tommy Holmes wrote about the beanball in the *Brooklyn Eagle*, "It is well known, of course, that the specific bean ball is an accidental pitch. That is, to hear the pitcher tell it. If he bounces one off a batter's skull, he wears an air of innocent concern. A fastball sailed ... a curve didn't break ... the hitter must have lost sight of the ball and fell into it."[41]

Philadelphia's Shibe Park had been renamed Connie Mack Stadium prior to the start of the '53 season. On August 22, the Phillies took a doubleheader from the Giants at Connie Mack Stadium by scores of 7–1 and 6–5 before 22,955 spectators. Maglie was given a "test" start in the opener but was grossly unsuccessful. The Barber couldn't field his position and the Phils reached him for two bunt hits in the first inning. Earl Torgeson, now playing with Philadelphia, hit a looper that went for two bases as Mueller let the ball get past him. The Phillies scored two more runs off Maglie in the second. The highlights included an error by Lockman, a single off Hank Thompson's glove at third and a bunt that got past Maglie. Sal gave up four runs (three earned) in one and one-third of an inning. He allowed six hits and his record fell to 8–9. In addition to the ball Mueller misplayed for Maglie, he made an error later in the game.

Five days later, Dusty Rhodes hit three consecutive homers off three different pitchers as New York defeated the Cardinals by a 13–4 score. This rare feat was accomplished despite his .167 batting average entering the game. By August 30, Maglie was in the bullpen as New York split a doubleheader with Chicago. He did not surrender a run in one and one-third innings of relief. Five Giants hit homers on this August 30 day, which saw balls flying out of parks at a near record pace. Dark, Westrum, Spencer, Thomson, and Rhodes went deep. Thirty-one homers were bashed around the major leagues, six short of the record. The Boston Braves themselves scored thirty runs against the Pirates in a doubleheader. Maglie started against Chicago on September 1 before the smallest Polo Grounds crowd of the year, 1,406 fans, and was lit up like he very rarely had been before. He was shelled from the mound as he gave up six runs in two and one-third innings. He allowed eight hits, three homers including one to the opposing pitcher, and walked one. Koslo won the game in relief as the Giants came back and won it 10–9 to get Maglie off the hook. Dusty Rhodes hit a homer. Harold Rosenthal wrote that Maglie demonstrated "nothing except an unfortunate penchant for pitching to the Cub batters' strength."[42]

The Giants were all but eliminated from the pennant race and the only reason 29,746 fans bothered to show up at the Polo Grounds was to witness the old interborough rivalry flare up once again. Brooklyn emerged triumphant for the eighth straight time against New York on September 4 as they won, 8–6. The game was a quintessential Giant/Dodger war marked by umpire baiting, beanballs, and long balls. Wes Westrum and Durocher were ejected from the contest for arguing balls and strikes. Bobby Hofman ducked out of the way of a high, inside pitch in the seventh. Larry Jansen knocked Duke Snider down in the eighth. Both Snider and Robinson bunted towards first base with malicious intentions, hoping to draw Jansen over and get a piece of him but Larry avoided the runners. Jansen made Campanella take a seat and both benches were warned. Robinson had been hit by Worthington earlier in the game. New York hit three consecutive homers in the third as Westrum, Corwin and Lockman took the grand tour around the bases. Hodges and Dark also hit homers in the game. The Dodgers won the following day by a humiliating 16–7 margin. Durocher had one more game against the Brooklyns in 1953. One more day to strike at the enemy and it would certainly be memorable.

Ruben Gomez was the rookie pitcher from Puerto Rico who was putting together a fine season already at 13–7 as they headed into September 6. Like Adolfo Luque he helped fuel the stereotype of the hot-tempered Latin American ballplayer. He did not shy away from knocking batters down. In his six years with the Giant organization he nailed a healthy forty batters. Leo Durocher used to say, "give me some scratching, diving, hungry ballplayers who come to kill."[43] Gomez certainly was capable of killing someone as he obeyed Leo's orders to "stick it in his ear." A baseball was not his only weapon of choice. In 1956 Gomez hit Joe Adcock of the Braves and unleashed a second beanball after Adcock charged the mound. Gomez refused to stand his ground and ran into the dugout and came back with a switchblade in his hand, ready to stab someone if needed. Maglie was outraged at Gomez's cowardly behavior, stating "He showed he wasn't willing to back up the knockdown." Adcock packed a heavy punch and was capable of breaking Gomez's ribs with one blow. Bob Buege had called Adcock, "a six-foot-four-inch stationary target."[44] Other memorable beanball incidents with Gomez involved Carl Furillo and Frank Robinson. He even aroused the ire of the affable Willie Mays on January 11, 1955. They got into a skirmish during batting practice and Mays landed a vicious right hand punch that dropped Gomez. Both players had been in Puerto Rico for the winter league season.

Giant hurlers had thrown at Carl Furillo for years, a virtual standing target for the man holding the baseball. So when the inevitable happened and Furillo boiled over in one of the most memorable fights in the history of the National Pastime it was not surprising to many. On July 20, Bob Rush of the Cubs skulled Furillo for the sixth time in his career. The impact was not as severe as some of the others for he was wearing a flimsy protective helmet. Many times he had been skulled with only his baseball cap on. However it was still an ugly scene as Furillo was taken from the field on a stretcher. Dressen had been his insensitive self, saying, "Fuckin' dumb outfielder." He added, "Furillo shoulda ducked."[45] These kinds of pronouncements from his own manager tended to make the man take things into his own hands. For years he had heard Durocher's voice from the dugout imploring his pitchers to throw at him. It was not a concealed gesture; Leo made damn sure that Furillo heard it. Carl was at the breaking point. In the second inning Furillo came to the plate. Carl heard that familiar voice perk up from the Giant dugout, as Leo instructed Gomez to "stick it in his ear." Gomez missed his head as he failed to skull the batter but hit Furillo on the wrist instead. Furillo started towards the mound in a hostile manner as he exchanged words with the pitcher but then decided to go to first base. The umpires had intervened to prevent an incident. The first base bag was adjacent to the Giant dugout and Furillo and Durocher exchanged words. "I know that was you, Leo. You told him to do that." Durocher yelled out, "That's right, you Dago prick, and the next time you come up I'm going to have him to do the same thing."[46]

Furillo's blood was boiling. The count went to two and two on Billy Cox when Carl called time and began pointing at something in the Giants dugout. The Giants' skipper motioned with his finger and invited him to come over. Furillo suddenly took off and met Durocher in front of the dugout where they tried to kill each other. Irvin tried to restrain Furillo but he got away. The rest of the Dodger players ran over to the scene while the Giants thought they wanted to turn this into a full fledged riot. They did not, the Dodgers yelled, "Let them fight. Let him kill him."[47] Umpire Babe Pinelli had taken a break from his objective position for the day and yelled, "Kill him, Carl. Kill him." For a moment it looked as if Furillo might choke Leo to death. While the fracas continued, one of the Giant players, supposedly Jim Hearn, accidentally stepped on Furillo's hand and broke one of his fingers. After the contest Furillo told reporters, "I'm gonna get him. I'm gonna get him the first time I see him … He has crossed me once too often."[48] Durocher replied, "…whenever or wherever he wants to try I'll be ready."[49] There were conflicting reports to whether any punches were landed. After Leo was kicked out of the game, Furillo made the long walk to the clubhouse in center field. Along the way the Polo Grounds customers showered him with bottles and paper cups. One fan took a swing at him with his umbrella but missed. Gomez was allowed to stay in the game despite the fact the umpire heard Leo's provocation. Throwing beanballs was an accepted part of baseball strategy but when the batter retaliated that was something different all together. Furillo also

Maglie spent seven seasons with the Giants compiling an excellent 95–42 record. (National Baseball Hall of Fame Library, Cooperstown, N.Y.)

stated that "I wasn't worried about the other players ganging up on me. A lot of the Giants hate him too."⁵⁰ Furillo would miss the rest of the regular season but as a result batted .344 to win the batting title. Many of the baseball writers had the audacity to suggest that Furillo's hand injury was a good break. Arthur Daley wrote, "It's quite possible that the most fortunate swing Carl Furillo made all season was the one he took at Leo

Durocher the other day."⁵¹ The Dodgers won that final game against New York, 6–3. The following year Campy informed Irvin that Furillo "hates your guts." Irvin was confused since he had served as a peacemaker in the fracas. "Why?" he asked. Campy replied, because "you kept him from killing Durocher."⁵²

As Maglie was relegated to bullpen duty down the stretch he turned inward. He had always been an amiable personality off the field, but now his poor performances had driven him from the ballpark in silence. On the field he was angry, crude, and dangerous. Off the field he had always been agreeable and pleasant. Despite the fact he was thirty-six years old, he refused to believe that he was washed up. The body had broken down. The previous year his back had crippled him and the injury still lingered in '53. Tightness in his shoulder hindered his ability to follow through and break off the curve. The Barber had lost his confidence and his control. While Maglie pondered his situation in the bullpen, he told Arthur Daley of the *New York Times*, "I've been doing a lot of figuring. I'm convinced I took things too easy last winter. I thought by resting I'd give my back a chance to heal completely. Now I know better. At my age, laying off for six months gets your muscles so badly out of shape you can't get them to react the way they would in a younger guy."⁵³ He planned to do some work every day in preparation for the season. Maglie wanted to take a lot of sulfur baths, go to Florida and prepare for the season after the new year and report to Phoenix ten days early for spring training. Things would not go actually as planned. Sal had never been much for conditioning and getting himself into shape before. He didn't kill himself when it came to running and exercising. Maglie told Durocher, "Hell, you can't run the ball over the plate."⁵⁴ Now he was rethinking his conditioning habits.

The Barber's last two games of the year were inconsequential. Maglie pitched four scoreless innings of relief against Chicago and gave up three runs in three innings of relief against Philadelphia. During September, he appeared in only three games. Durocher had lost all interest. In the game Maglie pitched against Chicago on September 11, Alvin Dark was the acting manager as Leo was allowing several of his players to manage down the stretch. The newspapers even knew that Leo had given up his managerial responsibilities as the *New York Herald Tribune* declared, "Dark 'Manages' to Lose Even With Gomez, 5–2."⁵⁵ Horace Stoneham certainly wasn't pleased by these turn of events and the fact that the entire baseball world knew about them.

The Giants finished the '53 campaign in fifth place with a disappointing 70–84 record. Ruben Gomez (13–11, 3.40 ERA) and Hoyt Wilhelm (7–8, 3.04 ERA, 15 saves) were the most reliable pitchers. Maglie finished with a discouraging 8–9 record and a 4.15 ERA. His highest major league ERA before this season had been 2.93 in 1951. He pitched 145.1 innings, gave up 158 hits, walked 47 and struck out 80. He pitched three shutouts and had a career high .271 batting average. Jansen finished at 11–16 with a 4.14 ERA. Hearn was 9–12 with a 4.53 ERA. Koslo was 6–12 with a 4.76 ERA. Corwin went 6–4 with a high 4.98 ERA. Worthington posted a 4–8 record with a 3.44 ERA. The starting eight had four players who hit .300 or better. Dark batted an even .300 with 23 homers and 88 RBIs. It was the third straight season he had batted .300 or better. Hank Thompson batted .302 with 24 homers and 74 RBIs. He had another tough season off the field in '53, as he got into an argument with a taxi cab driver who took a sawed off bat and slammed it on top of Thompson's head. "It's a mighty good thing I've got a strong head," he observed.[56] Don Mueller batted .333 with only 6 homers as he began to resist the temptation of pulling the ball down the right field line at the Polo Grounds and as a result his average skyrocketed. He declared, "I'm wasting my time trying to be a fence buster."[57] Monte Irvin had another strong year, batting .329 with 21 homers and 97 RBIs. Lockman batted .295 with 9 homers. Williams hit .297. Bobby Thomson batted .288 with 26 homers and 106 RBIs. Daryl Spencer was a disappointment as he managed only a .208 average with 20 homers. His fielding average was an abysmal .933 as he committed an exorbitant 32 errors. Westrum was besieged with his usual assortment of injuries and batted only .224 with 12 homers and 30 RBIs. New York's ERA skyrocketed from a respectable 3.59 in 1952 to 4.25 in 1953. In the previous two years they had led the league with the best home record but now they slipped to 38–39.

Brooklyn lost another World Series to the Yankees in '53. As the Giants and Dodgers went after each other's throats all year, the Yankees took part in the ugliest fight in the junior circuit and in the major leagues for that matter. On April 28 against the St. Louis Browns things turned ugly quickly. The Browns' catcher Clint Courtney had been feuding with the Yankees for two years. In the tenth inning, Gil McDougald rammed into Courtney at home plate on a close play. When Courtney came up he hit a single but turned for second where he cut Phil Rizzuto open with a spikes high slide. The Yankees swarmed on the catcher as Allie Reynolds pinned his shoulders down so Billy Martin could pummel him with punch after punch until Courtney was bloodied up. The fracas lasted for seventeen minutes. Browns fans threw bottles and garbage at the Yankees. American League baseball was just as rough as the senior circuit. Another disturbing trend in '53 was the dwindling attendance, which fell to 14.4 million, a drop of 6.5 million in five years. The attendance numbers would have been about 1.5 million less if not for the Braves' move to Milwaukee. After the Giants concluded their season they embarked on a one-month tour of Japan, Korea, and the Philippines. They played exhibition games and entertained the servicemen. Maglie stayed home so he could rest his aching body. Durocher was the center of controversy in Japan when he scoffed at their baseball etiquette and called the umpire a "slant-eyed idiot."[58]

9

Return to Glory

The Giants, in desperate need of pitching, pulled off a blockbuster trade with the Boston Braves as spring training approached. New York sent Boston their entrenched hero, Bobby Thomson, along with Sam Calderone in return for left-handed pitchers Johnny Antonelli and Don Liddle, infielder Billy Klaus, and catcher Ebba St. Claire. Jansen, Maglie, and Hearn were aging veterans and declining rapidly. Antonelli, a 1948 bonus baby, had not lived up to expectations but would blossom with the Giants. Left-handers Koslo and Kennedy had been major disappointments and were no longer with the club in '54. The last great left-hander to toe the slab for the Giants had been the old meal ticket himself, Carl Hubbell. Antonelli had broken in with the Braves in 1948 when they competed for and eventually won the pennant. His presence on the team was like a cancer. He was ignored by his teammates to the point where the batboy received more attention. Veteran Brave players resented his big bonus and they resented the fact they had to give him a full World Series share. He appeared in only 4 games in '48 and received little action the next two years before entering the Army. When he came out, Charlie Grimm was the manager and he was given a clean slate. In 1953 he compiled a mediocre 12–12 record and a 3.18 ERA. With New York in '54 working under the critical eye of Frank Shellenback he went 21–7 and led the league in winning percentage (.750), ERA (2.30) and shutouts (6). Antonelli threw a live fastball, a curve, and an excellent change of pace. Liddle, the other left-hander in the deal, featured quality breaking stuff and control. This trade, just like the 1949 trade that brought Stanky and Dark to New York which helped them win a pennant in '51, would prove instrumental to the Giants' chances in '54.

Sal Maglie, the man everyone thought had made the biggest mistake of his life by jumping to the Mexican League, had not only made it back to the show against heavy odds but had put together an excellent career. However his body was disintegrating. He was going to be thirty-seven years old, coming off an atrocious 1953 campaign. Many people thought he was washed up, that there would be no more shining moments in the Barber's career. The Giants braintrust could no longer count on him to come through. He was a relatively old man in baseball years with a bad back and shoulder. The Barber had been shelled off the mound too many times the previous year. Chub Feeney, the Giants Vice President, said, "For right-handed pitching, we're counting on Ruben Gomez, Al Worthington, and Jim Hearn. Give Larry Jansen and Marv Grissom enough rest and they'll do a fine job. We aren't counting on Sal Maglie. If he comes through, wonderful. But he's thirty-seven and even though his back seems to be better, we just can't count on him."[1]

The Barber's physical problems went deeper then his back and shoulder. During the winter he visited a chiropractor, Dr. Vincent Konschaft, three times a week. X-rays were taken and revealed a slight curvature of the spine and a tilted pelvis. This had the effect of making his left leg three-eighths of an inch longer than his right leg. It was a miracle that he was able to pitch with any success in '53. To alleviate the problem a leather pad three-eighths of an inch thick was placed under his right heel. Maglie told reporters in February, "How could I pitch in that sort of shape?" He added, "My arm was fine but I was throwing with just my arm. I couldn't get my body behind the pitches."[2] Maglie would finally be pitching with his legs under him, which would take the added strain off his back and shoulder.

Maglie signed his 1954 contract for $28,000, a pay cut of about $7,000 from the previous year. He reported to camp a week late because he was opening his new liquor store in Niagara Falls and waiting to obtain a liquor license. Horace Stoneham had given him permission to report late, but evidently Durocher did not receive the message. Leo was trying to anger Maglie, so he would perform better on the field just to spite his manager and prove that he still could. Durocher blasted him in the press. "Maglie should have been the first man to get here. Of all the guys he should have been the first. How do I know he can pitch at all? Maybe he thinks he's got a job won and he can do what he wants. Well, I had enough of that last year. I'm through with it." Durocher continued his tirade. "What's

Maglie more interested in? The liquor business or baseball? ... I never had a better spring camp than this. There's some enthusiasm here. Well, Maglie's fighting for his job. Right now he isn't doing very well."³ The Barber arrived in Phoenix on February 27. He put his belongings into his room and headed for the ballpark. A reporter cornered him and showed him the paper with the headline "Durocher hits Maglie for reporting late." Sal was shocked by such pronouncements. "What's Durocher talking about? I got permission from the boss to report today," he said to himself and to explain the situation to the inquisitive reporter. Maglie was oblivious to the storm that was brewing in camp and when asked another question he gave a curt "no comment" and walked away disgusted and confused.⁴ Not only had he opened a $20,000 business but also his father had a heart attack. He felt that his absence was justified. When Sal read the full story in the paper he became filled with anger.

The Barber went through a workout at Municipal Stadium after which reporters crowded around him. Durocher hovered nearby. One question inquired to whether the leather pad under his heel would make him a better pitcher. Sal replied, "I don't want to talk about that, because I don't want to sound like I'm popping off." As far as his conditioning, "The outfield grass is going to look burned, I'm going to run so hard. Don't worry about the date I reported, I'll be ready April 13."⁵ The photographers brought Maglie and Durocher together to pose and shake hands while feigning a smile. After the pictures were taken they took off in opposite directions with little regard for what the other was doing.

The prospects looked bright for the Barber early in camp as he cut loose with authority. After a particularly good workout on March 1, Durcoher, Fitzsimmons, and Irvin were each impressed with what they saw and lauded the Barber. Leo was not counting on Maglie but after seeing him perform he was overjoyed. "He had just great stuff out there. He was cutting loose harder, no just as hard, as he did any time in 1953. If only his back holds out, we'll have a staff leader." Irvin had hit against him in practice. "Sal was better than I've seen him in a long time. A real long time. He was throwing good curves and throwing hard." Fitzsimmons was the most precise. "Boys, he was firing." Maglie himself said "I was cutting loose and I feel better than I did last spring. Much better."⁶ The Barber was well conditioned and prepared to pitch early in camp. Shellenback had designed a new pickoff play in hopes of keeping opposing runners from stealing on the Giants at a frequent pace. The best news of all, excluding the 80-degree temperature was that Willie Mays had been discharged from the Army and was on his way.

The Giants became an instant pennant contender when Willie Mays arrived in camp on March 2. He had kept his skills sharp during his absence, playing service ball for Fort Eustis, hitting .420 in 1952 and .389 in 1953. Mays arrived after taking an all-night flight and immediately thrust himself into an intrasquad game where he dazzled the spectators with a monstrous homer and made two spectacular catches. He instantly lifted the spirits of the entire camp, as the rumor circulated that "Willie's here." Maglie stepped out of the shower in the clubhouse and saw his center fielder in front of him. The saturnine Barber became enthused by the development and quickly shook his hand. Mays asked in an innocent manner, "Where ya been?" Maglie answered, "In the shower." "That's what I thought," Mays responded with a boyish laugh. When Irvin asked him how his game was, Mays responded "You mean pool."[7] Indeed Willie was back and was his old ebullient self. As a result Durocher's mood became better as well. Mays was Leo's favorite kid again and the fans flocked to the ballpark to watch the two of them play fast paced pepper games that would have made the Gas House Gang proud.

The usual preseason statements by Durocher were steeped in unrealistic quixotic notions of grandeur used to pique the interests of baseball fans and writers. Unlike previous springs, this year's statements were more then hyperbole. Durocher called his first two weeks of workouts "the best ever, the greatest, just the greatest, and even better than I expected." After a workout by Maglie on March 5, Wes Westrum declared he's "throwing harder and looser than he did at any time last year."[8] The Barber was certain that Mays' presence would help his pitching. "It's different pitching with the kid in center field. All I gotta do with Willie there is keep the baseball in the park."[9] The Giants looked healthy, even Davey Williams' back had not acted up yet. As Maglie prepared for his first exhibition games, trainer Doc Bowman was one man who was cautious about the Barber's return stating, "he looks great now, but there isn't a medical man in the world who can tell what's going to happen when he starts the stress and strain of games."[10] The New Yorkers put on an abysmal exhibition of baseball on March 7, as Cleveland won 23–10. Maglie made his debut two days later as the Baltimore Orioles defeated New York, 10–9. He allowed four runs in three innings on seven hits and one walk. The Barber was satisfied with how he felt physically and so was everyone else. "I'm satisfied," he declared. "A couple of little things were wrong, but nothing serious." "The big sweeping (curve) one was fine, a couple of times I got it inside and they popped it. The little one (slider) was just spinning. When they hit me it was because I wasn't getting the ball right where I wanted to...."[11] The Barber gave up a couple of doubles which the Giant fielders had difficulty catching because of the strong wind. He was excited about pitching once again and his gloomy disposition from the previous year had changed to excitement.

In Sal's second spring start he tossed four shutout innings to earn the win as New York defeated Cleveland by a 16–6 score. He was breaking off the old hammer in fine shape. The curve was dropping off the table, breaking low and away. After the game Maglie was elated over his performance. "I could have gone another inning, maybe two, but I got another month. First time I pitched I couldn't throw just where I wanted. After the first couple of men today, I had the sharp curve — that's my baby — low, real low." He said there is "no comparison (to the previous year), I feel that good." Durocher said, "He looked like the 1951 Maglie."[12] Ray Katt got two hits including a homer in the contest. Katt was slated to replace Westrum behind the plate after two cups of coffee with the New Yorkers in '52 and '53. To Westrum's credit he did not sulk and even helped out the youngster after accepting a significant pay cut. New York's five game winning streak came to an end on the 19th as Cleveland won, 2–1, in what was supposedly the first big league exhibition game played in Las Vegas, Nevada. Maglie worked three scoreless innings in the 50-degree temperature before departing. He told reporters concerning his back that he had "an occasional twinge, but nothing serious." Maglie added, "I just need a little bit of work getting my control down, that's all." He was gunning to start the opener against Brooklyn, but Durocher retorted that he wished to see the Barber work deeper into games before he could make such a decision. A crowd of 9,088 curious spectators attended the game at Cashman Field. One observer said, "This will rank with the (Jim) Jefferies-(Jack) Johnson fight," which took place in Reno in 1910.[13]

On March 24, only 791 people showed up at Municipal Stadium in Phoenix to watch the Baltimore Orioles defeat the Giants, 4–3. Bill Veeck had been what some called "purged" from the game and forced to sell his St. Louis Browns. Shortly after, they moved to Baltimore and became the Orioles for the '54 season. Some suggested that Veeck's ouster was a "baseball version of the witch hunts that Senator Joe McCarthy was launching..."[14] This may have been a little strong but there was no doubt the baseball owners were out to get the iconoclastic Veeck. Cold War tensions were indeed hot, for in 1953, the braintrust of the Cincinnati Reds decided to change their name to the Redlegs. The publisher of the *Cincinnati Inquirer* declared, "Let the Communists change their name. We were here first."[15] Against the newly transplanted Orioles, Maglie shut them out as he surrendered only two hits over the first five innings. In the sixth he issued three runs and was the eventual loser. After the game Maglie was once again enthusiastic. "I don't hurt and I wasn't tired and if I keep on this way I'll be ready to open against Brooklyn. I made a few mistakes in the sixth, but nothing much. I'll go seven next time. I could have gone seven today. I don't want to rush things."¹⁶ Sal was the first Giant hurler to work over five innings and his scoreless innings streak ended at thirteen.

New York began to barnstorm East and play on the dusty plains cities such as Tulsa, Oklahoma City, Wichita Falls, Houston, Fort Worth, Dallas, and Beaumont. They would play a game a day on a bush league diamond, get on a train and go to another city. Durocher was up to his mischievous tricks. He took advantage of Luke Easter's gin rummy abilities and swindled $3,000 from him on the trip. Leo whored around during camp and imparted some advice on a young Roger Kahn who was covering the Giants. "Pick 'em up at seven o'clock. Sit down next to her on the couch." Durocher coz·231'

ntinued, "Now five minutes \into your date, at 7:05, put your hand on her crotch.... If she leaves your hand there, you know all you gotta know. You're gonna get laid. If she knocks it off, well it's early yet, just after seven o'clock. You got plenty of time to call up someone else.... A whole lot of famous and beautiful broads don't knock your hand off their snatch."¹⁷ Willie Mays had been the talk around camp since he had arrived. Irvin and Dark performed well. Williams did his best to play through the back injury. Maglie, Jansen, Hearn, Antonelli, and Gomez each looked strong on the hilltop. Overall Leo was optimistic as they headed East.

Willie Mays hit a wicked comebacker in Oklahoma City that nailed Maglie on the right forearm during batting practice. The X-rays turned up negative and rumors circulated that Sal would miss a turn in the rotation. The Barber quelled any fears in his next start, three days after getting hit, as the Indians pulled out a 2–1 win in Wichita Falls. He allowed a lone hit (no walks) in five scoreless innings. His back did not bother him despite the cool temperature that was hovering around 40 degrees. Durocher was cautious, and ready to replace the Barber with Grissom whenever the bruise began to bother him. Rocky Nelson's single in the first frame was the only Cleveland hit, as Maglie baffled the Indians with his curve. Of Sal's last nineteen innings, eighteen of them had been scoreless.

On April 3 in Dallas, Willie Mays continued to excel hitting two singles, a double, and a homer to boost his batting average to .420 as New York won, 6–1. In twenty-three games, he had hit nine homers while driving in twenty-four. The Giants were also hot, winning nineteen of their last twenty-four exhibition games. Despite Mays' performance, there were those skeptics who still failed to believe that Willie was the genuine superstar that others had pronounced him to be. The following day Maglie allowed four runs in seven innings as Cleveland won 8–4. George Spencer took the loss in relief. New York and Cleveland gave the 3,740 fans at

Parkway Field in Louisville, Kentucky, an excellent pitchers' duel as the Indians won, 1–0. It was the Barber's last tuneup before the regular season and he looked impressive allowing three hits and one walk in five scoreless innings. Maglie worked thirty-three innings in the spring and had an even 3.00 ERA. The previous year he worked a third of an inning longer and had a 5.79 ERA. New York finished the exhibition season with a 16–13 record, good enough for fourth place in the National League. The Dodgers led the major leagues with the best exhibition record at 22–11. Durocher seemed more confident, more focused then the previous year when he kept switching players from different fielding positions and the players performed as erratically as Leo's lineup changes. Durocher said that Hank Thompson was the biggest surprise of the spring. For once, Thompson knew what position he was going to play. With Bobby Thomson's departure to Milwaukee he knew he was the third baseman and therefore could concentrate solely on that position. As camp ended, Davey Williams' back condition may have been the biggest worry.

Baseball is an evolving game in which new rules are made and old ones modified. As the 1954 season opened two new rules had been implemented around the major leagues. A player who drove in a run with a sacrifice fly would no longer be charged with an at-bat. The second rule proved controversial among the players and stipulated that defensive players had to take their gloves off the field when they came to bat. When an inning ended the players would gracefully toss their gloves on the grass and run into the dugout. Now this old practice was disallowed. It had been a grand sight to see a player make a great defensive play and in one motion throw the glove on the outfield grass. The American League voted 7 to 1 to ignore the rule. Clark Griffith said that "only once have I seen a batted ball hit a glove lying out there. And that time it didn't affect the play. The ball was a single and ended up a single."[18] Commissioner Ford Frick quickly warned teams and players that failure to follow the rule would result in "reprimand, fine, or even forfeiture of the game."[19]

Everything came together for the New York Giants in 1954 as they brought home the world championship. The Dodgers finally fell apart under the new leadership of Walter Alston. After the '53 World Series, Charlie Dressen made the mistake of asking Walter O'Malley for a multi-year contract. Durocher had received a two-year contract through the '55 season and whatever Leo got Dressen had to have. His huge ego and stubbornness got in the way of logic. He should have sensed that O'Malley wanted to get rid of him because of his failure to defeat the Yankees in the Series and the Dodgers' debacle in '51. O'Malley held a press conference and explained his policy of not giving multi-year contracts. Dressen was

The 1954 World Champion New York Giants. (Author's collection)

reassigned to manage Oakland in the coast league. Ignore the euphemisms, he was not reassigned but fired. Walter Emmons Alston, an obscure minor league manager, was named the skipper of the Brooklyn Dodgers. For some reason he arrived in town with an assumed name as reporters wondered why that was needed. One headline declared "Alston (Who's He?) To Manage Dodgers."[20] Dressen had been pretentious to a fault, but he was also open, affable, and talkative. The dour, sullen Walter Alston was accustomed to managing in the minors where he had seventeen players he needed to direct. He did not know how to handle the eight extra players on a major league roster. Many of the Dodger players had played under Alston in the bushes but the bushes and the show were worlds apart. His players lost confidence in him during '54. He was not sure in his abilities to make a good decision. Alston antagonized veterans such as Robinson and Newcombe. By season's end, the Dodgers found themselves in the unaccustomed position of watching the Giants win the pennant without being in the race until the bitter end.

New York collected only four hits in the lidlifter at the Polo Grounds but they made them count as they defeated the Brooklyn Dodgers by a 4–3 score before 32,397 fans. Willie Mays hit a monstrous homer, over 400 feet into the left-center field upper deck. Dark and Thompson also ripped homers. The fourth hit was a Maglie single in the second. It was not wasted, for Williams hit into a fielder's choice and Dark followed with his homer. The Barber wasn't particularly sharp but he kept the Dodgers off balance with his various assortment of curves. Campanella touched him for a homer in the second frame. The Dodgers threatened in the third with two runners on base but Dark made a fine running catch in short left on Snider's fly ball and Robinson hit into a double play. Campanella hit his second homer off the Barber in the fourth. This was one of those rare days when Campy got the best of Sal and was able to focus his attention on hitting a baseball instead of worrying about being skulled. Robinson's single drove home Snider in the sixth. Campanella came up again but this time Maglie would bear down and struck him out. The Dodgers loaded the bases against the Barber in the seventh after one out. Marv Grissom was called into the game and promptly got Snider to pop up and Robinson to hit into a force to end the inning. Grissom worked the final two frames to secure the victory. Maglie did not have his best stuff but he found a way to defeat the Brooklyns as he usually did. He allowed three runs on seven hits and four walks in six and a third innings while striking out five. Furillo took the collar for Brooklyn, going 0 for 4 but he should have been thankful for the Barber was in a magnanimous mood and did not throw any heaters at his skull.

After the game the Dodgers gave Maglie mixed reviews. Walter Alston said Maglie looked fine to him. It was a diplomatic response, one which Charlie Dressen would not have given. Pee Wee Reese conceded that Maglie wasn't throwing as hard as he did during '50 and '51, but added "he's still the best curve ball pitcher I ever saw and plenty smart. They talk about the way he brushes us back and let's say he does, but he also can give you that sharp-breaking hook that makes you pull back even while you're reaching for it." Reese also stated "Nobody throws a curve like Maglie. It stays in the same plane. Most curves drop. Not his. It stays level and just shoots off at an angle." It was a gracious statement from the Dodgers' captain. Gil Hodges said Maglie is "still real good." He added "Maglie still nibbles the outside corner with his curve and he has pretty good stuff. He's not as fast but it's good enough." Snider's assessment was right on the mark, saying the Giant pitcher had "good stuff. He's not going to win 20 but he'll win his share." Furillo and Cox concurred with these remarks. The combative Jackie Robinson was among those players who thought Maglie had nothing. "He beat us but I hope he pitches the same way from now on. He's not going to get out of those jams all the time. Not with the junk he was throwing me."[21] The relationship between Maglie and Robinson was like two Cold War countries always heightening the tension, building up their arsenal, never willing to compromise and admit when the other side has the upper edge.

One of the reasons why Sal was able to defeat the Dodgers and other teams when his stuff was poor was because he studied the hitters, and pitched to their weaknesses while avoiding their strengths. Maglie worked Furillo and Hodges with breaking stuff. Of course he also knocked them down to intimidate them and back them off the plate. Duke Snider did not know the strike zone very well and was vulnerable to breaking balls in the dirt. Maglie got the hitters waving at pitches out of the zone and worked the corners. Against Robinson he would throw an assortment of pitches. "I think he would have been a better hitter had he gone to the opposite field against me. Robinson held his arms high. When I wanted to move him back I'd throw at his left elbow instead of aiming under his chin, as I did with most batters. I think he batted the way he did because he couldn't hit the inside pitch. When he was rambunctious or lively — stepping out of the box, asking to see the ball — you had to fight him, move him back."[22] Pee Wee Reese would have some success against Maglie because he would shorten his swing and hit to the opposite field instead of trying to kill the ball. Sal was always studying hitters and watching the action intently when he was not playing. In one instance he noticed that Billy Loes of the Dodgers was tipping his pitches. When he threw a curve, Loes brought the glove past the top of his cap and when he threw a fastball he brought it to the bill of his cap. Later on when he became a Dodger, he deciphered the signs of the Cincinnati Reds. Maglie read in the paper one day that Charlie Dressen wanted his players to take more pitches, and be more patient. The next game, Maglie came right at them with strikes. The Barber was a pitcher in the true sense of the word. The secondary definition of "pitcher" in *The New Dickson Baseball Dictionary* is "A term of distinction for a pitcher with great control, finesse, deceptive moves, and knowledge of the hitters, as opposed to a pitcher who depends solely on speed or power."[23] Sal Maglie fit the definition.

Five days after the opener Maglie toed the slab in Flatbush, in that small park bounded by Sullivan Place, Bedford Avenue, Montgomery Street, and McKeever Place. Maglie shaved the Dodgers close and New York won 6–3 before 23,757 belligerent fans. It was his twentieth win against Brooklyn in his career and ninth in Ebbets Field. Maglie worked high and tight when needed and then dropped the curve low and away. New York was leading 5–0 when the Dodgers scratched out a run in the third and had the bases loaded with no outs. Campanella, Hodges, and Furillo were due up, all capable hitters. Maglie kicked the slab and scowled at the Dodger hitters. He always worked from the right hand side of the rubber, sending the ball in on an angle to the right-handed batter. Maglie had very little wasted motion when he pitched, and knew how to pace himself. With Campanella up and the sacks full he needed to reach back for a little extra. He did. Campy popped up. Hodges fouled out and

Furillo struck out on three pitches. Snider and Hodges hit homers off Sal in the game while Mays and Irvin went deep for New York. The Barber did a masterful job of moving the ball in and out, up and down. He went the distance, allowing the three runs on eight hits and four walks while striking out seven. Sal nailed Campanella with a pitch. Maybe it was payback for the two homers he hit in the opener. Maglie would later say "The Dodger I threw at most often was Roy Campanella. Roy was a great ballplayer and a good guy but I found out that he wasn't the same hitter after you brushed him back.... Sometimes with Campanella, I could see that he was so sure I was going to knock him down that he'd practically be backing away before I pitched."[24] Campy became nervous and outwardly frightened in the batter's box, making him an easier out. In this game Campy took the collar, 0 for 3.

After losing three of four to the Pirates, the Giants swept the Phillies in three straight at the Polo Grounds. Leo Durocher could never stand still when it came to lineup decisions. He would let someone play a certain position for a few weeks and if he didn't perform he would soon be replaced. Ebba St. Claire had started the season behind the plate, and he soon switched to Ray Katt whom Durocher had originally expected to replace Westrum during camp. After that tough series against Pittsburgh, Leo made another move and put Westrum back in for the Philadelphia series. Not only did the Giants sweep the series but they also shut them out in all three games. Marv Grissom tossed a 1–0 shutout on Saturday, April 24. The following day, New York took a doubleheader by 3–0 and 5–0 scores as Maglie and Antonelli applied the whitewash. Philadelphia managed only eight singles on the day and six walks. Maglie allowed five singles and three walks. Antonelli surrendered three singles and three walks. The Barber struck out five. Mays continued to sparkle as he collected two hits in the opener and made a great catch off Stan Lopata's bat in the second game. Irvin and Thompson hit homers in the second contest. Westrum's presence behind the plate served as a stabilizing force. What he lacked in offense, he certainly made up for with his glove and determination. He was an intelligent man who could speak about world affairs, literature, or other topics outside the realm of baseball. Maglie had nothing but praise for his backstop. "If you haven't got your stuff, it's hard to win, but your receiver can help you immensely when you're in trouble. In that respect Westrum gives a pitcher 100 percent cooperation."[25] In an interview after his career with Robert Boyle, Maglie said, "I always wanted the catcher to work to the outside of the plate. Westrum was the best catcher who ever caught me.... I know Campy was good, but when I went to the Dodgers later he'd been hurt and he couldn't move around too well.

Westrum was flexible. With Westrum you could bounce the ball. You could do anything. The hitter never knew what was coming."[26] Westrum also had praise for Sal, as he stated "Maglie was the greatest oldest pitcher I ever caught and Antonelli the best youngest pitcher."[27]

New York split two games with Milwaukee before traveling to the Windy City to play some day baseball on Chicago's southside. Maglie went to Durocher and asked for the ball despite having only two days rest. He put on a gutsy exhibition of fortitude and perseverance as he pitched all fourteen innings of New York's 4–2 win over Chicago on April 30. The Cubs had been hammering the ball. They had five hitters in the starting lineup with batting averages above .300. The Barber was hittable early, as he gave up two runs in the first four innings on six hits. Randy Jackson hit a homer off him in the fourth inning into the left field bleachers. The curve wasn't working in the early innings and he relied on the fastball for the rest of the game. For the last ten innings Maglie pitched shutout ball, giving up only four singles and an intentional walk. Mays hit a homer in the fourteenth and Irvin drove in a run with a sacrifice fly. Maglie had pitched courageously for thirteen innings and persuaded Durocher to let him pitch one more. The Cubs went down and the Barber strode from the mound, dead tired, but triumphant. It was his longest outing of his career. He struck out four in the game and let his defense earn their paychecks as well. Davey Williams made an error in the eleventh and then Sal walked a batter before he got Jackson to hit a comebacker which he turned into a double play. When his defense let him down, he kept his composure, and did not become unnerved. Wes Westrum was astounded by Maglie's performance. "Sal was missing with his curve ball in the early innings, and I told him he would have to rely more on the fast ball. That's all there was, and in most cases, that can mean disaster to a pitcher, because the hitters can wait for the fast one. But Maglie has such extraordinary control with the fast ball that he was able to go through that long, tough game without letting them see enough of the ball for a good clout when they needed it. He is a remarkable pitcher because he not only has control, but has that invaluable sense of pace which enables him to put forth reserve strength when needed. You seldom see him, when he is right, burn out in an early-inning jam."[28]

The Barber had been spectacular in his first four starts, three of which were complete games, as his record stood at a perfect 4–0. In thirty-eight and one-third innings, he had allowed thirty hits, thirteen walks and struck out twenty-one. His ERA stood at 1.87. The winning streak ended at four, as Maglie was humbled on May 5 when Cincinnati defeated the Giants, 7–1, at Crosley Field. Maglie survived some trouble in the first inning and then the Reds teed off on the thirty-seven year old right-hander. He allowed seven runs on thirteen hits in six innings of work. Six of the hits were for extra bases, including homers by Gus Bell and Ted Kluszewski. Fred Baczewski, a big left-hander, who had defeated the Giants four times in '53, was the winner.

New York swept a two game series at Pittsburgh's Forbes Field, taking the second game by a 5–1 score to even their record at 11–11 on the season, which tied them for fifth place. The old ballpark was quickly deteriorating in the 1950s and one writer called it "as joyless as a prison exercise yard."[29] The Barber went the distance for his fifth victory but he had to work for it. Maglie put the Pirates down in order in the final two innings. He allowed six hits, two walks and struck out six. Dark, Thompson, Mueller, and Mays were the hitting stars. At this juncture of the season Mueller was the only Giant batting over .300. Leo's club had not yet hit its stride.

When the Giants defeated the Cubs by a 9–6 score at the Polo Grounds on May 14 they had won their sixth straight and moved into second place. Maglie got knocked around allowing three runs on seven hits in five innings of work. Billy Gardner pinch hit for Sal in the bottom of the fifth and walked to start a five run rally in which ten hitters came to the plate. The Giants were up 6–3 and Maglie stood to be the winner despite his shaky performance. Marv Grissom could not hold the lead. He surrendered a two run homer to Gene Baker and a solo shot to Ralph Kiner. New York scored three in the seventh to take the lead and Wilhelm held the Cubs scoreless in the final two frames to earn his first victory of the year. Alvin Dark went 5 for 5, including a homer, scored two runs, drove in two runs, and stole two bases. Mueller continued to spray the ball around the park in an efficient manner as he went 4 for 5, scored a run and drove in two. The pitchers were brushing batters back throughout the contest. Bob Rush nailed Thompson. Grissom hit a young Ernie Banks and Wilhelm plunked Joe Garagiola.

Batters were being hit over 200 times a season on average during the 1950s, a staggering increase from prewar figures that hovered around 130. There were several factors that can be attributed to the rise in hit batters. Race served as a motivating factor to many pitchers in their judgment as to which batter they wished to nail or knock down. Black players were hit at a disproportionate rate compared to white players. Hank Thompson characterized the plight of the black player in the big leagues as follows: "We spent a lot of time flat on our backs."[30] Another factor was the use of protective batting helmets. In 1952, Branch Rickey mandated that all of his Pittsburgh Pirate players wear a helmet when hitting. By 1953 most clubs encouraged voluntary use of helmets which became mandatory in a couple of years. When the batter had a helmet, the pitcher was more inclined to throw inside because the chances of killing a man or injuring him severely were significantly decreased. There were certain rivalries such as the Giants/Dodgers or Dodgers/Cardinals that were inclined to have beanball wars because of the hatred both teams exhibited towards each other. Another frequent occurrence was pitchers throwing at batters who hit a home run off them, or at the next batter. God help the hitter who showed up the pitcher when he went deep. Maglie claimed the outside three inches of the plate as his own and if the batter encroached on that territory he was going down.

Vic Raschi, the old Yankee castoff, and Sal Maglie got together for a pitchers' duel at the Polo Grounds on May 19. It was a gloomy, overcast day, which prompted the lights to be put on in the beginning of the fourth inning. A steady rainfall forced a ten-minute rain delay in the fifth which the Giants probably had hoped would continue considering the way Raschi was pitching. The sun broke through the clouds and play resumed. Raschi won his fifth game without a defeat and tossed a five hit shutout to lead St. Louis to a 3–0 win. Maglie's record fell to 5–2. He pitched well, giving up three runs on eight hits and one walk while fanning six in eight innings. The Barber continued to pitch Musial tough and plunked him with an offering. Musial, the consummate professional, took his beaning like a man and simply dropped his bat and made his way over to first base. Red Schoendienst hit a homer off Sal in the first inning. Raschi went the other way with an outside pitch in the second and hit a wounded duck into right field for a RBI single. Rip Repulski closed out the scoring with a homer in the seventh. Bobby Hofman who was batting only .111 replaced the slumping Davey Williams at second who himself was batting .153.

Willie Mays stole the show on May 24 in a 5–4 win over Philadelphia before a sparse crowd at Connie Mack Stadium. New York took three of the four games in the series. The Giants took the lead for good when Mueller doubled and Mays hit a homer in the eighth frame. Steve O'Neill, the Philadelphia skipper, decided to pitch to Mays with first base open and he paid the price. There were two outs when Mueller doubled and O'Neill did not follow the advice of many baseball experts that suggests that you shouldn't let the opposing club's best player beat you. Mays drove in four runs on the night with a single and two homers to help extend New York's winning streak to three games. Maglie started but did not figure in the decision. He allowed four runs (two earned) on four hits and four walks in six innings. He contributed to his own downfall with an error that allowed the Phils to pick up two unearned runs. Wilhelm won his second game with three scoreless innings of relief. Mueller had one hit and scored two as he continued to smoke the ball, batting at a .374 clip. Mays was hitting for power and driving in runs while boasting a .282 average. Dusty Rhodes was the premier pinch-hitter, and was batting .364 in limited duty. Antonelli and Maglie were both pacing the staff with 5–2 records.

Carl Erskine hurled a five-hitter to snap New York's six game winning streak on May 29 at the Polo Grounds. The first three times Maglie faced the Dodgers in '54, he was matched up against Erskine. The Barber lost his third game of the year. However he still enjoyed a 20–7 lifetime record against the Brooklyns and with a little run support he would have won his twenty-first. Brooklyn snapped their four game losing streak with the victory. Campanella rejoined the club after missing three weeks due to an operation on his left hand. Dodger management had pushed Campy to have the operation and Walter O'Malley even promised to pay for the $9,500 procedure. However the Dodgers owner reneged on his offer and stuck Campy with the bill, which resulted in the Dodgers' catcher being sued by the surgeon.[31] It was another incident which showed how the Dodger management failed to back up their players and manipulated them for their own benefit.

Hank Thompson had a tremendous game on June 3 in St. Louis. He collected four hits, including three homers, scored four runs and drove in eight. He had been sidelined with an injury since May 25 when he hurt his knee sliding into home plate. Hank had a chipped kneecap and the initial diagnosis said he might be out for thirty days. On June 2 he was back in the lineup. Thompson was a stocky diminutive left-handed batter who stood at 5'9", 174 pounds. He fielded well in the beginning of the year and his offensive numbers were solid in '54, his last decent big league season. He batted .263 with 26 homers (a career high) and 86 RBIs. Despite his small stature he was as strong as an ox and was one of those players who could pull the ball down the right field line in the Polo Grounds. Willie Mays accounted for the other five Giant runs as he hit two homers, a double, scored two runs and drove in five. Dark had four hits and scored four runs. Maglie started but left early, allowing six runs in one and two-thirds innings. The Giants gave him a two run lead in the first, but he couldn't hold it and Grissom earned the win in relief (3–1). New York won by a 13–8 score.

While Thompson and Mays were hammering the ball at Busch Stadium, the Dodgers were washed out. They were still feeling the fallout from the previous night when they proved that the Walter Alston regime was not immune to controversy. Umpire Lee Ballanfant was heckled all night as the Dodgers questioned the umpire's ability to call balls and strikes. The tension came to a climax when he cleared the entire Dodger bench. As Jackie Robinson made his way into the batter's box he was kicked out and threw his bat towards the bat rack in utter disgust. The bat apparently missed its target and struck two of Milwaukee's season ticket holders in the head. It was raining throughout and the bat slipped out of Jackie's hands. The Milwaukee crowd, many of whom held ill feelings towards blacks, booed and jeered Robinson. An attorney happened to be sitting in the same box seat as the couple who was struck and he threatened legal action.[32] Lew Burdette threw at the Dodgers' hitters frequently and the Brooklyns imparted some revenge when two different pitchers nailed Burdette. One of the pitchers was Newcombe, back from a two-year stint in the Army. He would have a subpar year in '54 (9–8, 4.55 ERA). He was never shy when it came to protecting his hitters as he stated in Peter Golenbock's book *Bums: An Oral History of the Brooklyn Dodgers*. "So I would do it. I would throw at them, because they were throwing at our guys. I don't deny it, and I never did. The way they knocked our guys down, the way they hit Roy in the head, the way they hit Carl Furillo, the way they knocked down Duke Snider, if you don't protect your men, you're just not gonna get any runs, and they're not gonna have any respect for you.... Sal Maglie would throw at guys, and he never denied it, just like I don't. You do whatever's necessary to help your players."[33]

Maglie bounced back with seven strong innings against Milwaukee for his sixth win as New York emerged victorious by a 4–2 score. He was pitching a two hit shutout until the seventh inning when he allowed a run but escaped further trouble by getting out of a bases loaded jam. Durocher had noticed that Maglie had been pacing himself too much so he could pitch the entire nine innings of a ballgame. Leo told Sal to cut loose from the first pitch of the game and when his arm got tired he had Wilhelm, Grissom, Windy McCall, and Liddle to back him up in the bullpen. Mueller's ten game hitting streak was broken while Irvin's quiet bat finally came alive for three hits. Lockman had two hits including a homer, scored two runs and drove home two. Burdette took the loss in front of the home crowd. He plunked Billy Gardner with a pitch. Besides knocking people down Burdette was a notorious spitball pitcher. He liked to say "My best pitch, is the one I don't throw."[34] The spitball rule, or the stipulation in rule 8.02 that banned the pitch, was rarely enforced. Therefore many advocated the legalization of the spitter such as Ford Frick and Joe Cronin. It would have helped the pitchers at a time when baseball was becoming more and more a power dominated offensive game. Billy Evans, a former umpire and general manager of the Detroit Tigers, had once stated "Heed the cries of the hurlers in their desert of dire need by letting them use the spitter."35 Frank Lane, the general manager of the Chicago White Sox, argued vigorously against the unsanitary pitch. "It would be a return to the dead ball days.... Besides, the spitter is a foul and unsanitary pitch. When some of the old spitball pitchers loaded the ball with saliva and slippery elm, it would be splattering all over the place. It can be seen from the stands, and the feminine clientele we have developed would find it objectionable."36 The "feminine clientele" and children saw beanball wars and heard vile language from the stands so it was arguable if this would have kept them away from the park. In addition, the spitter was surreptitiously used in the majors as pitchers circumvented the rules. Thus to legalize the pitch would have been to sanction an offering that was already widely used in tight situations. Gil Hodges offered his opinion as far as the ubiquity of the pitch. "Everyone knows that 90% of the pitchers in our league have thrown a spitter at one time or another."37

The Giants climbed into a first place tie with Brooklyn when they shut out the Cubs 5–0 on June 12 at Wrigley Field. Maglie, following the advice of Durocher, worked as hard and long as he could in the 90-degree heat before wilting away. His record improved to 7–3. He worked seven scoreless innings before his arm went dead, giving up seven hits (no walks), while fanning two. Sal threw one wild pitch. Willie Mays saved him with an outstanding catch in the sixth inning when the Giants were in front by only a run. The Barber had one hit at the plate, scored a run, and was credited with a sacrifice. Wilhelm retired the last six men in order to close out the game. It was a nifty combined shutout by Maglie and Wilhelm as the Giants played sound fundamental baseball. The pitchers did not walk a batter and the Giant fielders did not commit an error. The previous day they kicked away a game to the Cubs when they made six errors and lost 5–4.

Back at the Polo Grounds on June 18, the Giants' six game winning streak was broken when they ran into the hottest pitcher in the National League. Harvey Haddix of the St. Louis Cardinals collected his eleventh win, and his third straight shutout, when he applied the whitewash and led his club to a 5–0 victory. The large Polo Grounds crowd of 31,093 acknowledged the man's performance and applauded him as Haddix extended his scoreless innings streak to thirty-two. Maglie got two strikes on the Cardinal leadoff hitter Rip Repulski, before the Cardinal left fielder touched him for a homer. Maglie worked three and two-thirds innings, gave up three runs on six hits and four walks as he lost his fourth game of the season. Sal left the game after he tripped and pulled his left thigh muscle while covering first. The injury would result in him missing a turn in the rotation. It was a tough day for the Giants on the infield for Alvin Dark was struck in the face on a bad hop but continued to play.

When Maglie came back from his injury it was against Brooklyn before 51,464 rabid spectators at the Polo Grounds on June 29. Homers by Irvin and Williams gave Maglie a slim two run lead. Duke Snider hit a booming two out triple in the first inning but it wasn't until the eighth frame before the Brooklyns got another player to second base. The Barber held the 2–0 lead as he entered the ninth. After recording the first out, Robinson singled to start the Brooklyn rally. Maglie threw an inside pitch to Hodges and then knocked him down with the second offering before he struck him out. He got two strikes on Campanella and was one out away from pitching a shutout. Maglie came with a curve, but it hung in the middle of the zone, and Campy knocked it over the fence for a two run homer that tied the game. The Barber fanned Don Hoak to end the inning. Maglie worked nine innings in which he allowed the two runs on seven hits (no walks) and struck out seven. The Dodgers loaded the bases against Grissom in the tenth but Robinson popped up. Brooklyn broke through in the top of the thirteenth and scored a run. The Giants loaded the bases in the bottom half and Dusty Rhodes was sent in to pinch-hit. Rhodes exploded after home plate umpire Frank Secory called the first pitch a strike. After a second called strike, Rhodes argued violently and his departure from the game seemed imminent. Durocher came out, not to argue the calls, but to calm his hitter down. "You can't do anything about those pitches. They're gone. Go back there and forget about 'em and get that hit we need."[38] That's exactly what Rhodes did, in the form of a two run single. Grissom was the winner in relief and his record improved to 8–2.

Durocher was a changed man in '54, no longer getting thrown out of games or being suspended frequently as he had done in the two previous seasons. Stoneham had privately rebuked him before the season began. He was particularly perturbed at the fact that Leo was managing only about 140–145 games a year while his players piloted the remaining contests. It was not too much, he thought, to expect his manager to pilot all 154 games. The Giants started the year poorly as Durocher incessantly changed the lineup, seeking the right combination. In their first twenty games he used twelve different lineups but things stabilized after May 7 and the Giants played better. Alvin Dark said, "When you pass out credit for the way we are winning, cut Durocher in. He is doing a great job keeping us pulling together, and I don't think you could ask better judgment than he has shown in selecting pinch-hitters and in handling pitchers, particularly from the bullpen."[39]

New York extended their longest winning streak of the season to eight and took a five game lead over second place Brooklyn when they defeated Pittsburgh by a 9–5 score on July 2 at Forbes Field. Ramon Monzant started for New York in his major league debut but left in the fourth and surrendered four runs. He was followed by Alex Konikowski, John "Windy" McCall, Wilhelm, and Maglie. Wilhelm recorded two outs in the sixth and was the beneficiary of a five run seventh inning for New York as he improved his record to 7–2. Maglie pitched three scoreless innings to end the game and held the opposition to two singles while striking out four in the process. Everything was coming together for the Giants. They had won twenty-six out of their last thirty games. Dusty Rhodes collected another pinch hit and his batting average stood at .440. Mueller was hitting above .350 while Mays was at .327. The staff was led by Antonelli's 11–2 record. Grissom was 8–2 as he pitched predominantly out of the bullpen. Maglie and Gomez were 7–4. Wilhelm also had seven wins. Hearn had five. Jansen pitched poorly and was the main disappointment of the staff. The pitching was well-balanced and received help from several different hurlers.

Two old warriors got together for the last time on July 6 at Ebbets Field when Sal Maglie faced off against Preacher Roe. Elwin Charles Roe was playing out his last big league season in 1954. He pitched his first full major league season in 1944 with Pittsburgh. After two good years in '44 and '45 he collapsed the next two seasons and boasted ERAs over five. The Dodgers traded for him in the winter of '47 along with Billy Cox and Gene Mauch. The trade turned out brilliantly for Brooklyn but initially it did not look good as they gave away Dixie Walker, Hal Gregg, and Vic Lombardi. Roe had suffered a serious head injury in his home town and Cox had been badly shaken by his stint in the military during World War II. Roe and Maglie were similar in many ways. Preacher did not possess a great fastball, like Maglie, but he compensated for it by finding another way to gain the edge over the hitters. Maglie relied on intimidation, pinpoint control, and a great curveball. Roe turned to the spitball, deception, and control. "I commenced thinking about pitching to spots, changing speeds, fooling them hitters instead of overpowering them, and, of course, I commenced to develop my wet one."[40] In 1950 he was 19–11 followed by 22–3, 11–2, and 11–3 seasons before the bottom fell out for good in 1954. Roe discussed his ubiquitous use of the spitter after his career in a frank manner. Maglie himself openly discussed his pitch of choice, the beanball, after his career. While Maglie was breaking in with the Giants in '45, Roe was experimenting with the spitter in Pittsburgh while leading the circuit in strikeouts. Maglie was asked by a writer at one time if he loaded up the ball. Sal replied "Well, I don't throw it. I know one pitcher who throws it a lot. I won't tell you who he is, but his first name is spelled P-r-e-a-c-h-e-r."⁴¹ Roe was furious. He later fired back at Maglie in his revealing article in *Sports Illustrated* when he implied that Maglie threw a spitter by stating that Durocher and Dark did not complain about his spitter when the Barber was pitching. Roe said, "they never hollered at me when I pitched against Sal Maglie."⁴² Maglie and Roe were two grizzled veterans who knew how to get the edge and strive in the baseball wars of the 1950's.

New York won that last ballgame in which they pitched, by a 5–2 score before 33,616 hostile Ebbets Field fans. Maglie was one out away from being taken out in the first inning after Snider hit a two run double. The Dodgers were going for the jugular, to achieve the unthinkable, and knock Maglie out of the box in their home ballpark in the first frame. Durocher made the walk to the mound and asked Sal how he felt. "I haven't got anything," he told his skipper but Durocher let him stay in the game for one more batter. Robinson hit a comebacker and Snider hit a little looper which was turned into a double play as Maglie pulled another Houdini act and escaped from the lion's den once again. When the Dodgers had the Barber on the ropes they had better do as much damage as they could for once Maglie found his rhythm he was tough to get to. In the ninth Hodges, Campanella, and Furillo singled and forced Maglie from the box. Grissom got the next three hitters without allowing a run to shut the door. While Maglie had mastered the curve, Grissom was a screwball specialist. Sal's record improved to 8–4 and 3–1 against the Dodgers as he gave up nine hits, two walks and struck out four. Tommy Holmes wrote in the *Brooklyn Eagle*, "Maglie may never get to Cooperstown except by automobile but, in good times and bad, he is rough on the Dodgers."⁴³ Roe took the loss as he left the game in the fourth frame. The hourglass was almost on empty for Elwin Charles Roe.

On July 11, Maglie won the opening game of a doubleheader as New York routed Pittsburgh by a 13–7 score. He pitched eight and one-third innings to earn his ninth win of the year. The Pirates scored seven runs (six earned) off him on eleven hits and one walk. Once Maglie had a comfortable lead he eased up and coasted the rest of the way. After Bob Skinner tripled in the ninth he was taken out and Grissom struck out the final two hitters. The Giants offense exploded for eighteen hits, including six homers, three doubles and a triple. Irvin, Lockman, Dark, Thompson, Mays, and Mueller hit homers. Mays was pacing the major leagues with thirty-one circuit clouts. Mueller hit for the cycle in the game. Maglie contributed with a single and two sacrifices. There were a total of nine homers in the contest of which Pittsburgh hit three. The Pirates bounced back in the second game, 5–1, as Hearn's record fell to 6–5. Five days later in St. Louis, Mays hit his thirty-second homer but New York stranded thirteen men and lost 5–4. Maglie started but did not figure in the decision as he allowed four runs on six hits and four walks in three and two-thirds innings. Musial hit a homer off him to open the second. The tension that hovered over the Dodgers like a dark cloud was beginning to become apparent to the casual observer. They dropped a game in Milwaukee and Walter Alston was ejected for the first time as the Brooklyn skipper.

Maglie pitched two scoreless innings of relief on July 18 to close the door on a 3–1 win in the second game of a doubleheader. Johnny Temple singled and Wally Post doubled with two out in the ninth as Cincinnati got the tying run to second base but Maglie struck out pinch hitter Bobby Adams to end the game. Cincinnati hammered six New York pitchers in the opener as they won by a 14–4 score. The real action of the day occurred in St. Louis where a riot broke out between the Phillies and the Cardinals in the second game of a doubleheader. The first game was a long drawn out affair, won by Philadelphia in the tenth inning by an 11–10 score. A total of eleven pitchers were used and each team collected eighteen hits in the three hour thirty-one minute game. The scorching heat hovered near 110 degrees as the catchers discarded their chest protectors in the middle innings before a violent storm cooled things down and delayed the game. Sal Yvars, the former Giant, found himself behind the plate for St. Louis in the second game. Philadelphia held an 8–1 lead in the fifth inning when Cardinal hurler Cot Deal threw close to Earl Torgeson, the former Brave, probably at the urging of Yvars. The two players had words and precipitated an all-out brawl between the clubs. Two years had passed since Torgeson had sucker punched Yvars in the Giant dugout on July 1, 1952, and now Yvars paid him back in full. Torgeson had reluctantly offered an apology at the urging of Warren Giles but Yvars wanted nothing of it. "I don't want any apologies," he retorted.[44] During the rhubarb, Cardinals manager Eddie Stanky tackled the Philadelphia skipper, Terry Moore. There were only a couple minutes of daylight when play resumed and the game was not official for they still were in the bottom of the fifth inning. The lights were not turned on when the second game started at 6:48 because of a misinterpretation of league rules. After Deal walked a batter, Stanky came out to the mound and umpire Babe Pinelli forfeited the game to Philadelphia because of the Cardinals' apparent delaying tactics. It was the first forfeited game since August 21, 1949, when the hostile Philadelphia fans threw a barrage of bottles at players and umpires. In Stanky's first two seasons as the manager of the Cardinals he led his team to third place finishes but in 1954 they dropped to sixth place. There was no apparent dissension on the team but there was plenty of grumbling. Stanky was a strict family man off the field and he tried to impart his ideals on the rest of the players and openly frowned at those who chased women and drank. In addition his antics on the field such as kicking dirt on umpires and acting in other overly theatrical ways embarrassed many of his players. Durocher was the opposite of Stanky; he grew up virtually fatherless and sought father figures his whole life. He had no bed checks and let his players do whatever they wanted into the wee hours of the morning as long as they performed on the field. He wasn't there to hold their hands, acting more like a big brother to his players, and did not try to manage their personal lives.

Willie Howard Mays was putting together a remarkable year in '54 and everyone was taking notice. Hal Jeffcoat, a pitcher for the Chicago Cubs, noted "He's out there all the time stealing your ballgame. He makes the kind of plays that win ball games, and he'll do it every day."[45] A *New York Times* book review stated that "Topic A (these days) is either the hydrogen bomb, sex, where-shall-I-go-on-my-vacation, or Willie Mays." An advertising agency declared that Mays "has become the hottest thing for us since Babe Ruth."[46] The accolades were coming from everywhere. When New York traveled to Minneapolis for an exhibition contest, the fans stayed in line all night for tickets. Mays' ascendancy to the Giants in '51 from Minneapolis brought visceral feelings of anger and disappointment to the fans, for their hero was taken away. Now Willie was returning a legend, in only his first complete major league season. During the times Roger Kahn's elaborate praise of Mays during the spring training of '54 may have sounded like hyperbole but it was not. After Mays went hitless in an exhibition game he wrote, "Non-candidates for the Hall of Fame played more important roles than Mays today."[47] Willie was inundated with endorsements, and television and radio requests. Durocher may have said it best. "Look, there are only five things a man can do to be great in this game. He can run, throw, hit, field, and think. Willie does them all, better than most and as good as the best of them. So what else can you call him but great?"[48] When Mays made a seemingly difficult catch look relatively easy, someone replied, "Spectacularly routine."[49] Willie Howard Mays had come of age in 1954.

Mays' early season home run barrage put him on a pace to break Babe Ruth's sacrosanct record. On July 28 Willie hit his 36th homer but would only hit five more for the rest of the season, which included two inside the park jobs. It took him seventeen days before he connected on his 37th circuit clout. As the Giants began to slump at the end of July, Leo asked Mays to raise his batting average by making a concerted effort to hit the ball to right field. Durocher contended that Mays would produce more runs if he accumulated more hits and therefore would be more inclined to help the club. He promptly put together a twenty-one game hitting streak during which he hit very few homers. Instead he sprayed frozen ropes around the park, filling the box scores with doubles and triples. The young man had matured as a hitter and had become more patient. He was a professional hitter now, laying off the high hard one that gave him trouble when he first came up and taking the low, outside curve the other way. He made the necessary adjustments when needed. On July 17, Willie was devastated by the news of his aunt's death. She had been like a mother to him. The Giants themselves went south as they compiled a 3–8 record over their next eleven games, which included a six game losing streak.

In many ways the improvement of the Giants in '54 was directly correlated with the improvement of Willie Mays. He led both leagues in batting (.345) and slugging percentage (.667). He scored 119 runs and had 110 runs batted in. He led the National League in triples (13), collected 33 doubles and hit 41 homers. Spectators were amazed, not merely by the outstanding numbers, but by the grace and style in which he played the game. When Mays chased down a fly ball his cap would come flying off to give the appearance that he was running faster then he actually was. In fact Mays concocted the artifice on his own and wore large caps knowing full well it would fall off when he chased a ball. Many people became familiar with Willie's innovative basket catch. He was not showboating when he corralled the ball down by his waist; it allowed him to get rid of it quicker. Most outfielders brought the ball all the way behind their ear before they threw it, but Mays did not. Willie threw from the lower part of his body, almost sidearm. He therefore caught the ball at his waist and got rid of the ball in a low launching position without wasting time. If he caught the ball at his shoulder he would have to bring his arm downward to his favorable throwing position, which wasted time. Rabbit Maranville, who would be inducted into the Hall of Fame in 1954, also utilized the basket catch, also known as the "bread-basket" and "belt-buckle" catch.

After experiencing unbearable heat in St. Louis and Cincinnati, the Giants traveled to Chicago where an overnight storm cooled things down considerably for the following day's game on July 21. Mays was attending his Aunt Sarah's funeral, and Dusty Rhodes took his place in center field but went hitless. New York took the lead on pinch hitter Billy Taylor's two out RBI single in the ninth inning. In the bottom half of the ninth, Maglie retired the Cubs in order to win his tenth game as New York won by a 2–1 score. Sal allowed four hits and three walks while striking out seven.

The Giants had lost four in a row and had a mere four game advantage over Brooklyn when they prepared to play them on July 26 at Ebbets Field. Maglie's record was a perfect 10–0 lifetime in the small Flatbush ballpark. When the Barber was on the mound, the Giants found a way to win as they elevated their game to match Maglie's intensity. Sal recalls "I pitched better at Ebbets Field, the fans there made a lot of noise, but I didn't hear what they said. It just kept me awake. I was more careful and deliberate pitching there. I made sure I kept the ball down and had them hit it on the ground."[50] He was particularly tough on the powerful right-handed batters in the Dodger lineup: Cox, Reese, Hodges, Robinson, Furillo, and Campanella. As the hostile crowd of 33,251 made their way into the park, Maglie and Erskine warmed up for fifteen minutes before the rains came. The rain may have taken the edge away from the Barber for it was fifty minutes before they were allowed to take their second warmups. He had already given up four runs when Gilliam led off with a walk in the sixth and Reese followed with a single. Sinister Sal was taken out and left the game to a chorus of boos as the crowd waved handkerchiefs to celebrate his exit. Wilhelm came in and couldn't find the strike zone and bonus baby Paul Giel had to shut the door on the three run inning. Each time the Barber had pitched poorly against Brooklyn, the Giants got him off the hook, but not tonight. Tonight the deity came back to earth as the citizenry of Flatbush found out that Maglie was indeed human. He allowed six runs on eleven hits and three walks in five innings of work as he lost his fifth game. Tales of the "FBI" man had terrorized children in the borough for years. The "F.B.I. Man" stood for "full-blooded eye-talian," Maglie's new nickname among the Ebbets Field press corps.[51] Erskine, the master of the overhand curve, pitched a five hitter to win his twelfth. Brooklyn won the game, 9–1, but the damage could have been much worse for they stranded fourteen runners in eight innings.

Two days later Antonelli won his tenth straight as he improved his record to 15–2. Rhodes paced the New York attack by hitting three homers. On the final day of July, New York defeated Cincinnati by a 7–0 score as Maglie won his eleventh. At the start of the game the temperature stood at 106 degrees in the press box. Maglie pitched seven and one-third innings before tiring and allowing Grissom to close out the game. He scattered three hits and three walks and struck out one. Thompson hit two homers, drove in two and scored four runs. Don Mueller helped Maglie out when he made a fine running backhanded catch in the second inning. Bob Cooke wrote in the *New York Herald Tribune* "Don has a knack of making a play look impossible before completing it."[52] Despite his .333 batting average in 1953, Durocher threatened to replace him with Billy Taylor at the beginning of the year. Once in the lineup, Mueller continued his success from the previous year. Baseball was an integral part of the Mueller family. He grew up in Cardinal country and his father, Walter Mueller, had played with the Pittsburgh Pirates in the 1920s.

New York weathered a minor slump in July and finished with an 18–14 record for the month. Larry Jansen retired as an active player at the beginning of the month and Al Corwin was called up from Minneapolis to replace him on the roster. Larry had battled shoulder and arm trouble the previous year and in '54 he failed to pitch seven innings in any game and finished with a 2–2 record and a 5.98 ERA. He would remain with the club as a coach. In 1956 Jansen made a brief comeback with the Cincinnati Reds before retiring for good. Another interesting highlight of the month included a heated argument between Durocher and Whitey Lockman during a game with the Cardinals. It occurred on a hot, steamy day at the Polo Grounds, at the end of the month while the Giants were slumping badly. Durocher was in a foul mood and so was his team. Lockman failed to run out a grounder at first base and was shocked to find Bobby Hofman replacing him in the field. The mild mannered Lockman suddenly became filled with rage and went after Durocher. He had slipped as he exited the batter's box and fallen to the ground and was unable to make a legitimate effort to beat the throw but everyone was following the ball and not Whitey. Directly in view of the patrons under Coogan's Bluff, Lockman and Durocher argued violently. The incident did shake the team up, for they won their next six games. One of the players stated "It may hurt one player but it helped the other 24. We needed something to stir us up. We were getting careless."[53]

During the middle of the season Maglie usually worked every fourth day, with three days rest. Maglie approached Durocher and told him he would like to deviate from that setup and work every three days, with two days rest. The experiment backfired on August 4 against Chicago, but New York still managed to win the ball game by a 4–3 score in eleven innings. Maglie allowed three runs on six hits in one and one-third innings.

Antonelli's eleven game winning streak ended on August 6. Johnny came to the Giants with a fastball, curve and changeup. Freddie Fitzsimmons taught the young pitcher a screwball, which accounted for much of Antonelli's success in '54. New York dropped its fourth in a row as Milwaukee swept a three game series at the Polo Grounds on August 8. Admirers of Willie Mays honored their favorite center fielder with his own day. As he accepted awards, people held signs behind him that said among other things "Say Hey Willie Is Our Boy," and "Say Hey Watch Willie Go! Go! Go!"[54] The two star hurlers from Western New York, Warren Spahn and

Sal Maglie, hooked up. Spahn was a graceful southpaw who recorded 363 wins in his career, including thirteen seasons in which he compiled twenty wins or more. He threw a fastball and two different curves early in his career and later on turned to other pitches such as the screwball, changeup and slider. Spahnie was a moralist and did not necessarily believe in manipulating the ball.[55] When he first came up to the Braves in '42, Boston manager Casey Stengel decided to find out what kind of pitcher he was. Stengel ordered Spahn to throw at Pee Wee Reese, but he refused. Casey came to the conclusion that Spahn had no guts and sent him back to the bushes.[56] He did not return to Boston until 1946. Spahn got the better of Maglie on August 8 as Boston won, 5–2. Maglie allowed three runs in seven and one-third innings on eight hits and three walks while fanning four. Brooklyn humiliated the Cincinnati Reds by a 20–7 score in Ebbets Field as the lead was down to three games. Durocher and his men were still hearing footsteps.

New York opened a crucial series with the Dodgers on August 13 at Ebbets Field and as usual Sal the Barber toed the slab. He did not figure in the decision as he allowed one run on four hits and one walk while fanning three in six innings. Once again he was matched up against Erskine who pitched well and won his fifteenth. The deciding blow came in the seventh inning when the hot hitting Carl Furillo hit a two run homer to propel Brooklyn to a 3–2 win. Furillo would get some key hits in the series including a grand slam the following day to start the comeback when the Dodgers were down 5–0. He was always straightforward when discussing Maglie's headhunting with his Dodger teammates. "If that son of a bitch Maglie throws at my head again, I break my bat across his fucking dago head."[57] After Maglie had shaved the Dodgers, the sensitive Brooklyn players complained when Grissom threw close to Campanella in the seventh, which resulted in the pitcher being warned. Erskine was given a close shave when he followed Campy to the plate. Brooklyn swept the three game series from the Giants and the lead was down to a half a game.

The Giants' reserves helped them snap their losing streak. Bobby Hofman hit two homers on the 17th to lead the New Yorkers to a win. The following day, Dusty Rhodes hit two homers himself as New York defeated Philadelphia by a 6–2 score. Maglie did not relinquish an early lead courtesy of a three run homer by Rhodes in the first. He scattered ten hits, walked none and struck out three to improve his record to 12–6. Richie Ashburn, a proficient contact hitter, fouled thirteen pitches off Maglie in the fifth inning, and eleven of them came after the count went full. Ashburn recalls that "I think my record was against Sal Maglie when he was still with the Giants. One afternoon I fouled 18 or 19 pitches off of him on a 3 and 2 count. He had excellent control and so did I. After a while he just started laughing. Then he would throw me another pitch and I would foul it off. That was the only time I ever saw Maglie laugh on a baseball field."[58] Ashburn finally hit a comebacker and both players were laughing uncontrollably by that point. Richie could place the ball anywhere he wanted; he had great bat control. One time he hit a lady in the stands and hit her a second time while they carried her away on a stretcher.

Brooklyn dropped a doubleheader on August 22 while New York took two games from Pittsburgh to increase their lead to four. Antonelli took his 18–3 record to the mound in the opener but was knocked out of the box in the first inning. John McCall, the fifth Giant pitcher, won his first major league game as New York rallied for five runs in the ninth to win, 5–4. Maglie started the second game but looked shaky. He escaped two bases loaded jams before succumbing in the fifth frame when he allowed five singles for three runs. Durocher gave him the hook in that inning and brought in Wilhelm who went the rest of the way to collect his ninth win. The Barber surrendered eleven hits and one walk in four and one-third innings. New York committed three errors in the game while Pittsburgh made four errors which helped them lose, 5–3.

On August 27, Maglie led the New Yorkers to a 3–1 win over the Milwaukee Braves before a record breaking crowd of 46,944 fans at County Stadium. The Barber was impressive, hurling a five hitter for his thirteenth win. He walked one and struck out six. Sal was bruised up when Gene Conley nailed him on the left shoulder in the sixth inning while at bat with the sacks full. In the eighth frame Maglie was hit on the right thigh with a line drive. Joe Adcock's single in the first frame drove in the only Braves run. Adcock was having a tough year, he hit four homers and a double off Brooklyn at the end of July and Clem Labine beaned him the next day. His batting helmet was dented and saved him from serious injury, possibly death. After the game he stated, "When they throw me high and tight, I can duck, but when they throw behind your head I have to believe they mean business."[59] In September, Don Newcombe ended Milwaukee's pennant hopes when he struck Adcock on the hand, an injury that sidelined him for the rest of the year.

As New York traveled home from their crucial Western swing in which they went 6–4, the Giants prepared to open a three game set with Brooklyn. Maglie had been sent home early from St. Louis to rest in preparation for the big contest. He worked the first six innings with mixed results in front of the home crowd, allowing four runs on six hits and three walks while striking out three. Hoyt Wilhelm followed and despite some wildness in the eighth inning managed to keep them scoreless the rest of the way and earn his tenth victory. Durocher used his two best pinch-hitters in the sixth inning when New York knotted the game at four. With runners on the wings and two out in the seventh, Wilhelm was forced to bat for himself and produced a fortuitous single that drove home the lead run. The Barber got off to another slow start, as Brooklyn scored two runs in the first inning. He blamed his early problems on too much rest. "I hadn't thrown a ball in a week and I couldn't get loose at first."[60] The win improved his record to 4–4 at night, for he was pitching much better in day games.

The Giants split a doubleheader with the Cubs on September 9 at the Polo Grounds. Maglie started the opener but received a quick shower after recording only four outs. He did not have his pinpoint control as he allowed three hits, walked two and hit a batter (Walker Cooper). Sal was only charged with one run as George Spencer who was recently called up from Minneapolis successfully worked out of a bases loaded jam in the second inning. Hank Thompson gave New York the lead when he hit a two run homer in the third and squeezed home the winning run in the ninth as the Giants won, 7–6. Grissom won his tenth game in relief. Chicago won the second game by a 3–0 score. Durocher's club had a four game lead over Milwaukee and a five and a half game edge over the Dodgers. Brooklyn won their game over St. Louis by a 10–1 score despite a prank that cost them Jackie Robinson for seven innings. Someone had imitated the voice of Jackie's wife, Rachel, and told the club that his children were very sick. Robinson had to leave the game as he rushed to a telephone and called his wife where he was relieved to find out that his children were in perfect health.[61]

In Maglie's next start, New York defeated Milwaukee, 2–1, on a Billy Hofman pinch single in the eighth before 31,331 Polo Grounds spectators. He pitched an excellent game, giving up the one run on seven hits and two walks in seven innings of work. Sal fanned five batters and contributed with a hit at the plate. Mays made a one-handed catch in the first inning. Willie made a great throw to the plate in the second to stop Andy Pafko at third after Johnny Logan's double. Maglie walked George Metkovich on purpose before getting out of the bases loaded, one out jam, with no damage. In the fifth, Maglie pounced on a bunt by Gene Conley and cut down Metkovich at third. Wilhelm with the use of his unpredictable knuckleball won his eleventh game in relief. Four days earlier, Ray Katt set a new major league record when he was charged with four passed balls in one inning as he tried to catch the old bob-and-weave unsuccessfully. Hofman hit his pinch single in the eighth as one run scored. Dusty Rhodes was cut down at the plate trying to tally a second run. Durocher was beside himself, arguing that shortstop Johnny Logan had bumped the base runner and therefore slowed his progress towards the plate, which should have resulted in an interference call. After the game Leo said "that was interference if I ever saw it, Logan pulled a smart play — and got away with it. After the ball went through, he stepped right back into Dusty's path. That's got to be interference." Durocher had been pulling off smart plays for years, and could appreciate the implementation of such a stratagem. Someone yelled at Maglie in the locker room "You were great. It (the win) should have all been yours." The Barber responded, "That would have been nice, but the main thing is we won. All I care about is this," and he pointed to the letters across his uniform: G-I-A-N-T-S.[62]

On September 20, a crowd of 26,982 spectators assembled at Ebbets Field to watch the funeral of the Brooklyn Dodgers as the hated Giants were poised to clinch the pennant. Once again, the Barber would start the opener of the three game series and Carl Erskine would be his opposite number. Durocher, a very superstitious manager, became nervous when he saw Maglie. He had decided to shave so he could look good for the photographers. "What the hell did you do that for?" yelled Leo. As they discussed the opposing lineup Leo asked "Sal, you got anything to say to the boys?" Maglie responded "Yeah, Campanella's going down on the first pitch."[63] Sal got off to another shaky start as he walked the first two batters while throwing only one strike. He wasn't bending his back and Durocher came out to provoke his pitcher into a fit of anger, so he would take it out on the opposition. Leo yelled, "Let's go! You're through, Maglie! Out." Sal refused the order. Durocher fired back "Like hell I'm not (taking you out). I don't need you. I got eight other guys out here who want to win this game. Out." Leo didn't want Maglie out of the game, but he wanted to get his blood boiling. Snider hit into a double play and Hodges struck out as Maglie escaped the inning without damage. Sal was in a frenzy, overcome with anger towards Durocher. As he walked to the dugout he put his hand on his crotch and gave Leo the "Italian salute." The Barber wasn't finished, he went directly to the water fountain, filled his mouth with water and spit all over Durocher's shoes. Maglie yelled "How do you like it?" Durocher had accomplished his intention and cursed the Barber for good measure for the rest of the game.[64]

Sal allowed a hit in each of the next four innings and Brooklyn scored their lone run on a RBI single by Hodges in the third. Campanella went down his first time up just like Sal had told his teammates and he wasn't the only one. Maglie got better as the game progressed. Hodges led off the sixth with a single, which was the Dodgers' last hit. The Giants' bats came alive and built a 7–1 lead as they entered the ninth. Robinson walked with two outs in the ninth, the first Brooklyn baserunner since Hodges had singled in the sixth. Campanella hit a bouncer that Maglie fielded and threw to Lockman for the final out as New York won the pennant. The Barber had given up only five hits, walked five and struck out five to improve his record to 14–6. He was a money pitcher, always willing to take the pill in the crucial games. As he came off the hill and tried to make his way to the clubhouse, he was mobbed by well wishers, some of which tried to rip his shirt off. Unlike 1951 when the champagne was not even chilled because of their unexpected miraculous victory, a barman handed out the chilled champagne as they entered the clubhouse. Durocher embraced his pitcher. Maglie told him "You get me so mad I could kill you. I know what you're doing, and that's what makes me so mad. I tell myself I'm not going to let you do it to me again, and then I still let you get under my skin."[65] Horace Stoneham, the Giants owner who truly loved the game, wandered around the locker room congratulating his players. He deserved much of the success for the Giants turnaround, for hiring Durocher and making Carl Hubbell the farm director who in effect turned the organization around. Walter O'Malley, Buzzy Bavasi, Walter Alston, and Pee Wee Reese came in and wished Leo good luck in the upcoming series against the Cleveland Indians. Maglie had started nine games against the Dodgers in '54 and compiled a 4–2 record. He might have lost a game in Ebbets Field but his reputation as a Dodger killer was firmly intact. As far as Sal's clean shaven look, a photographer took an eerie picture which caught the Barber in a dark light, with the whites of his eyes showing, and an angry look on his face. Maglie recalls "The s.o.b. won a prize for that picture."[66]

After finishing 35 games behind Brooklyn in 1953, the Giants had completely reversed their fortunes. The Dodgers still put together a good year (92–62) but they could have gone much further if not for injuries, internal arguments, and the lackluster leadership by the dour Walter Alston. Newcombe returned from the Army but his record was less then spectacular, 9–8, as he battled a sore arm, alcohol, and the fear of flying. Johnny Podres was 11–7 in his second year despite the fact he was hindered by an appendicitis problem. Carl Erskine (18–15) and Billy Loes (13–5) led the staff. Offensively, Carl Furillo dropped 50 points from his league leading 1953 batting average to .294. Campanella battled injuries and betrayal by management while Billy Cox was benched in favor of Don Hoak. The Dodgers were still a potent offense as Snider, Robinson, Reese, and Hodges each hit over .300. Hodges hit 42 home runs and Snider hit 40. They tied the Giants for the league lead in home runs with 186 and produced a .270 batting average. Their ERA was 4.31 while New York led the league at 3.09.

Maglie made his final appearance before the World Series in a 2–1 loss to Philadelphia, which took eleven innings before a sparse crowd at Connie Mack Stadium. He started and worked two innings, allowing one run on two hits and one walk while striking out two. Mueller collected two hits and Mays went hitless as they battled for the National League batting championship along with Duke Snider. Durocher said he was inclined to go with his veteran pitcher, Maglie, in the World Series opener instead of the youngster, Antonelli. The Barber had turned in a fine year. He compiled a 14–6 record with a 3.26 ERA. He appeared in 34 games, pitched 218.1 innings, allowed 222 hits, 70 walks and struck out 117. Maglie hit three batters and batted .127.

The batting race came down to the final day of the season with Mays, Mueller, and Snider in a virtual three way tie. Willie knocked Robin Roberts around as he collected a single, double and triple in four at-bats. Mueller went 2 for 6 while Snider went hitless. Mays emerged as the batting champion with a .345 average. Mueller finished at .342 and Snider at .341. The '54 Giants compiled a 97–57 record. Antonelli paced the staff with a 21–7 record and a league leading 2.30 ERA. Gomez was 17–9 with a 2.88 ERA. Grissom was 10–7 with a 2.35 ERA, mostly out of the bullpen. Wilhelm was 12–4 with a 2.10 ERA. Liddle was 9–4 with a 3.06 ERA. Hearn dropped to 8–8 with a 4.15 ERA. Antonelli, Gomez, and Maglie formed the nucleus of a strong rotation while Grissom and Wilhelm led the way in the bullpen. This was a formidable staff, not as strong as Cleveland's pitchers, but close. Mays and Mueller led the way offensively. Lockman batted .251 with 16 homers. Williams struggled at .222. Dark dipped under .300 at .293 but hit 20 homers and drove in 70. He committed the most errors in the majors at shortstop with 36 while Lockman led the way at first base with 18. Thompson batted .263 with 26 homers. Irvin hit .262 with 19 homers. Westrum batted only .187 while Katt batted .255.

The biggest surprise was the hard drinking, womanizing, country boy named James Lamar Rhodes. Everybody called him "Dusty." In 1952, his rookie year, he compiled a modest .250 average and followed that with .233. Dusty could have come directly from a Ring Lardner novel, the 1950s version of Jack Keefe. When he saw little playing time during spring training he told the writers that he disliked his life with the Giants and he began to appear defiantly in public places with a drink in his hand. During spring training as the team bus prepared to go to the airport in Las Vegas, Dusty boarded the vehicle with a glass with his favorite alcoholic beverage. Nobody thought he would stick once the season began. Leo even implored Stoneham to get rid of him.

Luckily, Rhodes stayed and collected 56 hits including 15 homers, 7 doubles, and 3 triples for a .341 batting average. He produced in the clutch when a timely hit was desperately needed and drove in 50 runs. Rhodes batted .333 as a pinch-hitter. When New York began to struggle it was reserve players Rhodes and Bobby Hofman who got them going in the right direction. Rhodes was always imploring Leo to let him hit in tight spots. Hofman kidded Leo, "Put us in there. We'll get you seven in front again … then we'll go fishin'."[67] Hofman and Rhodes were close friends off the field. Hofman insisted upon Leo that Rhodes was in shape as he arrived for spring training by saying, "He brought his own under-wear." Dusty originally played organized ball with the Chicago Cubs organization in 1947 but it became apparent that he would never make it in that town. He would be miscast, a 12 o'clock guy playing in a 9 o'clock town. Rhodes' infectious personality permeated the clubhouse during the season and the World Series. When a reported asked him if he ever played high school ball he replied "Heck, no, I was in the eleventh grade and three months later I wound up in the ninth grade so I quit."[68] Dusty could whack the ball with the best of them but Durocher called him "the worst fielder who ever played in a big league game." As far as his reputation Red Smith wrote, "In baseball, as in war, a man's reputation follows him around. The Giants' Leo Durocher and Horace Stoneham occasionally hear tales about Rhodes like those Abraham Lincoln heard of General Ulysses S. Grant. They make the same answer Lincoln did."[69]

The New York Yankees won 103 games in 1954 and to the casual observer of the history books, one would suspect that they played the Giants in the World Series. They did not of course since the Cleveland juggernaut amassed a remarkable 111 wins. After the All-Star break, the Indians went 55–16 to end the year. Four of their pitchers would later be inducted into the Hall of Fame, as would their manager and general manager. The staff was led by Early Wynn, Mike Garcia, and Bob Lemon with Art Houtteman and Bob Feller filling in as the other starters. The bullpen contingent included Ray Narleski, Don Mossi, and Hal Newhouser. Their staff led the major leagues with a 2.78 ERA. Wynn and Garcia had a reputation for throwing vicious knockdown pitches. Wynn, in particular, was a fierce competitor who hated to lose: "Every hitter I face is a man trying to take money out of my pocket. Every hitter is an enemy."[70] He also declared, "When a damn sales-man loses a sale, he doesn't laugh. When I lose a ballgame, keep the hell out of my way."[71] Mickey Mantle declared "that son of a bitch is so mean he'd fucking knock you down in the dugout."[72] In fact, he once knocked down his own son because he was crowding the plate. The Indians had a professional staff that performed their task in a business like manner; there were no theatrics. General Manager Hank Greenberg boasted "They don't showboat, they don't stall, they don't complain, and they don't often argue with umpires—they just pitch."[73]

Al Lopez was the Indians skipper and unlike Durocher he did not engage in theatrics or coddling of ballplayers. He treated each of his players like men and regardless of what they did off the field as long as they arrived on time and kept in shape, he didn't quibble. Many of his players liked to drink heavily and chase skirts. Al had been a terrific big league catcher, had gone through all the wars, and he knew how big leaguers wanted to be treated. Lopez treated his players with respect. He did not give his players elaborate pregame speeches, but when the bell rang his men were ready to perform.

The Indians were plagued by injuries throughout the year but remarkably they continued to win. When Al Rosen injured his finger, Vic Wertz was acquired from Baltimore to take his place. When Bobby Avila went down, Hank Majeski filled in. George Strickland broke his jaw and Sam Dente filled in and did a good job. Cleveland batted .262 for the year and led the American League with 156 homers. Avila took home the batting championship with a .341 average. Larry Doby led the league in homers (32) and RBIs (126). Rosen contributed with a .300 average, 24 homers and 102 RBIs. Lemon and Wynn led the American League with 23 victories apiece while Garcia won 19 and led the junior circuit in ERA (2.64). Cleveland and New York had a strong barnstorming tradition and were accustomed to playing each other during spring training but now they would be meeting in the biggest stage on earth. The Indians were favored going into the series but their 111 victories belied their weaknesses. The American League was unbalanced in '54 with only three good teams. While the Indians feasted on second division ballclubs they had trouble with the Yankees and White Sox.

Bob Lemon took the pill in the opener. He featured a sinking fastball, an excellent curve and a slider in his repertoire. Maglie toed the slab for New York and as he warmed up in the bullpen he was noticeably off his game. On numerous occasions, the Barber had found out that he had nothing as he warmed up before a game only to find his rhythm later on. He looked confounded as the curve hung in the strike zone and his fastball missed its desired location. Perry Como performed the national anthem before 57,751 Polo Grounds spectators and Sinister Sal walked slowly to the mound. Once on the mound Maglie continued to miss his location, as his first three pitches to lead off man Al Smith were out of the strike zone. The frustration on Maglie's face was evident and he nailed

Smith in the ribs with the fourth pitch. "If I'm going to walk you, I might as well hurt you," the Barber declared.[74] Avila followed with a poke to right field that died on the grass and Smith scampered to third when Mueller fumbled the ball. Don Liddle began to throw in the Giants' bullpen. Doby and Rosen popped up before the powerful left-handed slugger Vic Wertz hit a triple, driving home two runs. The top half of the first ended when Dave Philley hit a long drive that Mueller caught for the out. Maglie had been hit hard in the first frame as the Indians took the early advantage.

New York threatened in the bottom of the first, but with runners on first and third and one out, Mays and Thompson failed to produce. Maglie settled down in the next two innings as he found his control that had previously eluded him. The Indians were hitting the balls off Maglie to the opposite field while the Giants were pulling the offerings off Lemon. The Indians' pitcher was flirting with trouble, for the Polo Grounds is fertile ground for pull hitting which could result in short homers. New York knotted the game at two when a run scored on Mueller's fielder's choice and Thompson's single in the third inning. The Giants had two runners on base but Irvin struck out and Davey Williams grounded out to end the threat.

Both teams were held scoreless in the middle innings. Except for Vic Wertz, the Indians were not hitting the ball with a lot of authority in the first four innings. The Barber was particularly tough on the right-handed batters who were backing away from the inside pitch and chopping at the ball when they swung. Only one ball reached the outfield in the first twelve outs Maglie recorded. Despite the fact that Maglie and Wertz played in opposing leagues, the left-handed slugger always hit the Barber hard whether it was in exhibition contests or All-Star competition. New York threatened in the fifth, while Cleveland made some noise in the fifth and sixth innings. Mueller's inept defensive play continued to haunt Maglie, as he inaccurately threw behind the runner Wertz in the sixth inning in an attempt to pick him off. It was his second error of the game and allowed the runner to advance an extra base when the throw eluded the first baseman. Wertz was the one Indian batter who had figured out the Barber, for he had collected a triple and two singles off him.

Maglie slowly labored at his job in the fifth and sixth innings and the Giant bullpen was active. He began to take more time before delivering pitches. He had a menacing disposition as a ferocious scowl adorned his sullen face. In the seventh, he managed to settle down and put the Indians down in order for only the second time in the game. Lemon, Smith, and Avila were the victims. Just as the Barber began to tire, Lemon had settled down. As Sinister Sal walked despondently to the center of the diamond to pitch the eighth inning it became all too clear that the hourglass was on empty. Maglie had pitched a hell of a ballgame, getting by with cunning and craft and keeping the contest tied at two. The heart of the Cleveland lineup was due up: Doby, Rosen, and Wertz. Sal reached back for a little extra and sent a message to Doby, knocking him down to the ground. Larry picked himself up and worked a walk. Liddle and Grissom were warming up quickly in the bullpen. Rosen, who was crippled by injuries, hobbled to the box, as the Dark and Williams pinched towards the middle of the diamond hoping to turn a double play. Maglie threw a curveball that did not have bite to it, and Rosen hit it hard into the hole between third and short. Dark ranged to his right and stabbed at the ball with his bare hand as he often did. The ball glanced off his flesh into left field and he quickly pounced on it, holding Doby at second while Rosen had himself a single. Freddie Fitzsimmons was sent to the mound with orders to bring the old warrior back to the dugout. Sal was drenched with perspiration. It was another inspiring performance by the thirty-seven year old right hander. The crafty left-hander Don Liddle was summoned from the bullpen. When the Polo Grounds fans had first seen the Barber hours earlier they encouraged him to "Stick it in their ears today, Sal."[75] Now he exited and the applause filled the ballpark. The old warhorse trudged towards the clubhouse in center field and Maglie waved to the people as if to say thanks.

    The left-hander Liddle came in to face the left-handed Wertz who had owned Maglie in his career. Liddle was tough on left-handed hitters while Wertz had difficulties against southpaws. However this time the slugger tore into an offering and hit it viciously into the deepest reaches of center field. An eerie feeling overcame the patrons at the Polo Grounds for many of the seasoned fans thought for certain that was the ballgame. Willie Mays was sprinting, head down, towards the runway between the two bleacher sections. It was as if Mays knew exactly where the ball would land. He possessed an uncanny ability to get a great jump on the ball and instantly knew whether he should come in or run back from the sound that the wooden bat made when it hit the ball. As Mays approached the unyielding wall he did not flinch and caught the ball over his left shoulder. Many an outfielder had misjudged his location on the outer diamond and smashed into the outfield wall only to find himself regaining consciousness in some hospital later on. Willie had outrun the baseball. The play was not over and he was fully cognizant of the situation. On plays such as this, a baserunner could tag up from second base and score. The real estate in center field at the Polo Grounds was huge: 460 feet to the bleachers and 483 feet all the way to the clubhouse. Willie turned hard to his right and unleashed a prodigious throw to the infield. There was no wasted motion; he caught the ball low and threw the ball from the same position. Doby only advanced to third while Rosen held at first. The catch by Mays was the most publicized of his career and mistakenly characterized as his best because it happened in the World Series. The catch was outstanding but the throw was miraculous. In the press box, the visiting reporters were dumbfounded.

There are certain moments that can be pointed to as a turning point of a ballgame or even a World Series. Willie Mays' catch was such a moment in time. If he had failed to catch the ball the Indians would have scored two runs and most likely won the game and had the momentum in their favor. Baseball is a game of inches. A pitcher's success in a game is in large part determined by a few inches. If a hurler is missing the outside corner by a few inches with his curveball, the ball may hang in the middle of the plate and the hitter should take advantage of such an offering. How many times during a game does the ball miss the chalk, down the foul lines by inches? Or does the fielder miss catching the ball or scooping it by inches? If Mays had misjudged the ball as he tried to corral it over his shoulder and it glanced off the edge, the World Series certainly would have progressed differently.

Marv Grissom, the thirty-six year old right-hander, replaced Liddle on the mound. As Don departed he said to Grissom, "Well, I got my guy." Grissom had possessed a blazing fastball when he was younger but like Maglie he adjusted with age and relied on other ways to get batters out. For Grissom it was the screwball. Maglie smoked cigars, Rhodes drank alcohol, and Grissom took vitamin B injections. He was ahead of his time in realizing the importance of taking care of his old body. The Giants were relying on a couple of old arms in '54 with several young ones as well; it was a good balance. Grissom got the Giants out of the inning without any damage. Irvin and Mays ran in from the outfield and Irvin told the young prodigy, "That was the greatest catch I ever saw." Willie responded rather nonchalantly "Had it all the way. Had it all the way."[76] It must have been "Spectacularly routine."

The game stayed knotted at two into the tenth inning. Cleveland got a runner to third base but they could not push him across. In the bottom half, Mays worked a walk off Lemon with one out. Lopez had pinch-hit for his starting catcher in the tenth, and was forced to put Mickey Grasso behind the dish. After the warmup pitches he did not make the customary throw down to second base. Willie concluded that his arm was not sound and stole second easily. Hank Thompson walked and Durocher sent up the left-handed pull hitting Dusty Rhodes. Lemon tried to break off a curve but Rhodes pulled it gently down the right field line. Second baseman Avila and right fielder Dave Pope chased the fly but it carried just above the 257-foot marker in right field and caromed back on the field. Pope made a futile leap at the wall but the ball eluded his grasp. Baseball, like life, is unfair. Wertz hits a mighty 450-foot blast into center field that is caught while Rhodes hits a 258-foot "Chinese home run" and the Giants win the game. Rhodes' hit was a mere "pop fly." The final score read: New York 5, Cleveland 2.

Cleveland failed to produce in the clutch. Five times after they had scored their two runs in the first inning, they had a runner at third base and did not score. Maglie allowed the two runs on seven hits and two walks while striking out two in seven innings of work. Marv Grissom earned the win in relief. Lemon was the hard luck loser as he went the distance for the Indians. Mays turned the game around with his great catch but Hank Thompson also contributed with two good fielding plays at third. Wertz collected four hits for Cleveland, while Dark, Mueller and Westrum had two hits apiece for New York. The press rightfully lauded Mays after the contest. When Durocher was asked if Willie's catch was the greatest he ever saw, Leo turned on a reporter, "What the fuck are you talking about, Harold [Rosenthal]? Willie makes fucking catches like that every day. Do you keep your fucking eyes closed in the press box?" Durocher tore into him for several minutes, as Rosenthal was humiliated in front of his colleagues. Harold wrote for the *New York Herald Tribune*, and Leo felt he should have known better than to ask what he considered an inane question. Al Lopez declared the catch and the throw as "the best play anybody ever made in baseball." He added "I got no idea, no idea at all, what Durocher is talking about."[77]

Game Two started auspiciously for Cleveland as Al Smith hit a homer off Johnny Antonelli to lead off the game. Early Wynn was pitching for the Indians and the burly right-hander was in command through the first four innings. Dusty Rhodes pinch hit for Irvin in the fifth, with Mays on third and Thompson on first. Wynn sent him a message, a fastball at the skull that sent the batter sprawling into the dirt. When a reporter had asked Wynn if he would knock down his mother, he replied "I'd have to, mom was a pretty good curveball hitter."[78] The hard-drinking country boy was fearless and stepped right back in the box. He hit a dying quail single to center field that scored Mays. When Rhodes went to bat in the seventh, he was knocked down again. He got up and slammed a homer to right center to propel New York to a 3–1 victory. After the game the reporters stayed away from Wynn in the clubhouse, fearing that they too would be knocked down.

The teams traveled to Cleveland and played Game Three in front of 71,000 fans at Municipal Stadium. In the third inning, New York loaded the bases and Rhodes was sent up to pinch hit for Irvin. He drove in two runs with a single to right and the Giants went on to win 6–2. When the pinch-hitting star was asked if he was nervous he replied, "What is there to be nervous about? These games with Cleveland are like exhibitions after what we went through to beat the Dodgers. That was tough, this is fun."[79] Many of the Giants felt the same way when they played the Yankees in '51 after their exhaustive pennant thriller against Brooklyn.

With the Giants in the driver's seat, Leo had the luxury of giving Maglie some more rest and starting Don Liddle in Game Four. Lopez opted to go with Lemon instead of the well rested Bob Feller. New York won the game, 7–4, to sweep the Series from the Indians. The Giants had miraculously swept the Series from a team that had won 111 games. While the '51 season will forever be known as the "Miracle of Coogan's Bluff," their 1954 World Series performance was the "Little Miracle of Coogan's Bluff." The Giants' pitching staff had a 1.46 ERA while the Indians staff compiled a 4.84 ERA. Rhodes was the batting hero as he hit for a .667 average with seven runs driven in. He was never one for modesty as he bragged that "the guy I can't hit, I ain't seen yet."[80] Other solid contributors included Dark (.412), Mueller (.389), and Hank Thompson (.364). Durocher did not rub it in; he was gracious. "Everything we did seemed to be right. Everything they did seemed to go against them, we got every break. The Indians didn't get any."[81]

10

BANISHED TO CLEVELAND

Due to a new rule that prevented players from working out before March 1, Maglie was forced to train on his own during this critical time for pitchers in late February. Sal was also not pleased with a decision by the Giants' front office to do most of their traveling by air for the upcoming season as train travel was being phased out. Initially it appeared as if Maglie would not sign his contract until he spoke to Horace Stoneham in Phoenix. They were only about $2,000 apart. Rud Rennie wrote in the *New York Herald Tribune*, "Really, Maglie just likes to talk to the boss about his contract just as Babe Ruth always did his contract business with Col. Ruppert and not Ed Barrow, the Yankees general manager."[1] On February 16, Maglie came to terms without talking to Stoneham. Instead he spoke to Chub Feeney, the Giants' vice-president, over the phone and accepted a contract for an estimated $30,000. All the key players were signed before camp opened; the Giants had no salary squabbles in '55, which often hampered teams who had won the World Series.

Willie Mays' arrival in camp was a stark contrast from the previous year. He arrived at the hotel and intended to lie down and sleep but Stoneham ordered him to get to the ballpark. The previous year he arrived in camp after a long flight with virtually no sleep and thrust himself into an exhibition game. Mays told reporters he was not physically tired from playing winter ball in Puerto Rico. "I'm just bored with baseball," he declared.[2] He had played a grueling schedule since March 1954, which consisted of about 230 games. In Puerto Rico he got into fisticuffs with Ruben Gomez and was booed vociferously by the San Juan fans in the next game. The fight between Mays, a black player, and Gomez, a Latin American player, served as a harbinger of things to come in the early 1960s. Under Durocher, the Giants' clubhouse was a relatively harmonious place as far as race relations was concerned. Race wasn't an issue with Leo. By 1960, the Giants were a fractious unit, divided into three distinct parts which gravitated towards each other: the blacks (led by Mays), the Latin Americans (led by Orlando Cepeda), and the whites. When Alvin Dark became manager it only exacerbated the problem, with his open hostility towards blacks and Latin Americans. When Willie was booed by the San Juan fans he was shaken, unaccustomed to such treatment; he feigned a knee injury and returned home but eventually was talked into returning. Mays was not the effervescent personality people were accustomed to seeing when he arrived in camp. He seemed a bit cynical and the veneer had begun to come off.

Mays and Lockman touched Maglie for homers in an intrasquad game on March 6. Willie did not disappoint the 6,000 spectators who watched him hit a homer, a double, and make two great catches. Against Cleveland on March 13, Sal worked four scoreless innings while scattering five singles and one walk. Despite the Barber's fine performance, the Indians won, 13–6. Tempers flared between the two pennant winning ball clubs when Al Worthington nailed Wally Westlake on the side of the head. The Cleveland left fielder was not injured due to his protective helmet. When Durocher emerged from the dugout, Westlake became incensed at the sight of the peerless New York skipper. Al Rosen also exchanged heated words with Durocher. Earlier in the game, Garcia had nailed Williams with a pitch. The Indians may have thought the Westlake beaning was in retaliation for the beaning incurred by Williams. There was added tension in the air in these exhibition games, since New York had humiliated the Indians in the World Series.

On March 16, New York defeated the Chicago Cubs by a 5–3 score as Mays and Irvin propelled them to victory. Maglie allowed one run in two innings of work. In his next start, Sal became the first Giant pitcher to work five innings as New York won, 4–2. He looked sharp early, pitching four scoreless innings, before the Indians tallied two runs off him in the fifth. The Barber struck out one batter in the first and struck out the side in the second. Mays hit three homers on the day and Wilhelm earned the win in relief. On the 27th, Maglie and Hearn pitched New York to an 8–4 win over the Cubs. Mays hit his eighth homer, which is the number he hit the previous spring. Maglie was the winner despite the fact he was hit hard. He allowed three runs in five innings.

In San Antonio, Texas, on March 31, an overflow crowd of 11,649 fans watched the Indians defeat New York by a 14–11 score. The setting was reminiscent of the way baseball was played in the late 19th and early 20th centuries. The overflow crowd spilled out into the field, and helped account for the nineteen ground rule doubles. Umpire Ed Runge kicked Durocher out of the game for arguing a fan interference call when Al Smith, the Indians' right fielder, tried to catch a ball but was supposedly interfered with by a fan and the batter was ruled out. Maglie took the loss as he was shelled from the mound, giving up eight runs in three and one-third innings. Cleveland teed off against the aging Barber; they batted around in the third scoring four runs and they scored four more runs in the following frame. The arguing was not endemic to the Giants, for Al Lopez argued a call when Ralph Kiner supposedly caught a ball in the crowd, but it was ruled a double. On April 5 in Columbus, Georgia, the fans were treated to a pitching rematch of the first game of the World Series as Maglie faced off against Bob Lemon. Monte Irvin (two homers) and Bob Lennon, a rookie outfielder, hit homers to propel New York to a 5–1 win. Maglie became the first Giant pitcher to go the distance as the New York/Cleveland exhibition series was tied at eight games apiece. Maglie allowed thirteen base runners but scattered them well as Cleveland stranded eleven men on the bases. His last start before the regular season came against the Boston Red Sox at Fenway Park where he allowed two runs on five hits and two walks in four innings. He fanned three batters. New York ended their exhibition season with a 17–13 record as opening day beckoned.

The National League began the '55 season with a new rule that forced its players to wear protective safety caps. The American League would follow suit in 1956. Larry MacPhail had initially attempted to make players wear a protective liner inside the regular baseball cap but it did not catch on when proposed, during the '40s. Starting in 1952, Branch Rickey forced his players to wear protective headgear at the bat and while running the bases. Maglie had skulled two Pittsburgh players during his career, Danny Murtaugh and George Strickland. Some of the players resisted the rule because it assaulted their manhood. Others resisted it because it obstructed their view and they claimed that pitchers threw at them more often with the helmets on. A so-called "grandfather clause" allowed players to bat without the helmet if they had before. In 1956, Baltimore Orioles manager Paul Richards said, "any player who doesn't wear a helmet is crazy."[3] Other rules were designed to speed up the game such as a clearly defined catcher's box and a rule mandating that pitchers must deliver the ball within twenty seconds when the bases are unoccupied. Pitchers were finally given a break as the strike zone was enlarged in 1955 and established as the "space over home plate between a batter's armpits and the top of his knees when he assumes his natural stance."[4]

Cold weather held the crowd to 13,219 at Connie Mack Stadium on opening day as the Phillies defeated the New Yorkers by a 4–2 score. Antonelli got the call for New York. Robin Roberts was on top of his game, trying to pitch the second opening day no-hitter in major league history but Dark spoiled it with a one out single in the ninth on a 0 and 2 count. Richie Ashburn did not play due to an injury to shatter his 731 consecutive games streak.

The Giants hoisted their pennant and world championship flags at the Polo Grounds on a cold, drizzly day, as 29,124 fans watched the home opener under Coogan's Bluff. Maglie worked against his archrival but was saddled with the loss as Brooklyn won, 10–8. The Barber allowed four runs (zero earned) on four hits and two walks in four innings. He fanned three. Dark made an error in the fourth inning with two outs and Campanella followed with a three run homer. Newcombe followed Campy with a solo shot. Newcombe added another homer in the game while Furillo also hit one. Hofman and Thompson went deep for New York. Newcombe had only one major league homer before this contest. His batting totals were impressive in '55, for any player, let alone a pitcher. He batted .359 with 7 homers (an NL record for a pitcher) and 23 RBIs. The game was highlighted by a leaping catch by Duke Snider in the ninth. Mays also made a good catch in the game. Brooklyn had ended their spring training in good shape despite some friction between Jackie Robinson and Walter Alston. Walter O'Malley could not have been more pleased upon seeing his reserved manager show some emotion. Jackie was upset when he did not play in an exhibition game and his competition, Don Hoak, played instead. O'Malley said "It's great. I'm glad to see my manager at the end of spring training blow his top."[5]

New York began the season winning only one of their first six games, which culminated in a doubleheader loss to Philadelphia by identical 4–2 scores on April 17. Antonelli and Maglie were the losing pitchers and each dropped to 0–2 to begin the year. The Barber started the second game, allowing four runs (two earned) on seven hits and two walks while striking out two. Robin Roberts won the opener for the Phils to improve his record to 2–0. Roberts, a former bonus baby who signed out of Michigan State University, was the class pitcher in the National League during the early 1950s. From 1950 to 1955 he won at least twenty games a season. He led the league in wins in 1952 (28), 1954 (23), 1955 (23), and tied for the league lead in 1953 (23). Remarkably he had very few pitches. He got by with his fastball which he challenged hitters with and pinpoint control.

When the Dodgers faced the Giants on April 22, they had already pulled ahead, winning their first ten games to start the season. New York took two of three from Brooklyn, but they subsequently put together an eleven game winning streak to all but wrap up the pennant. The '55 Dodgers were a well-balanced club that excelled offensively and defensively. Don Newcombe bounced back from his mediocre 1954 campaign and compiled a 20–5 record and a 3.20 ERA. Clem Labine had a 13–5 record with 11 saves while Carl Erskine, Johnny Podres, Billy Loes, Ed Roebuck, Roger Craig, and Don Bessent also contributed. The staff led the league in ERA (3.68) and strikeouts (773). Offensively they led the league in runs scored (857), doubles (230), home runs (201), batting average (.271), slugging average (.448) and stolen bases (79). Campanella won his third MVP award while Hodges and Furillo had huge years.

The Giants defeated the Dodgers in the first game of the series by a 5–4 score to break Brooklyn's ten game winning streak. Walter Alston, showing more emotion, blew his top and was kicked out of the game for arguing a close play at the plate. Don Zimmer, the Dodgers' shortstop was hit by a Grissom pitch in the game. While in the minor leagues in 1953, Zimmer narrowly escaped death when he bore the brunt of a vicious skulling that left him unconscious for three weeks and hospitalized for seven. When he got the call to the show in '54, the Dodgers would not let him play until his special fiberglass batting helmet arrived. Don was a stocky, 5'9", 165-pound player, who would freeze when a ball was thrown at him, unable to get out of the way. Maglie said in later years that he "hated to pitch against him. I didn't dare throw at him because I knew he'd freeze." Zimmer seemed to have a death wish; besides his inability to elude inside pitches, he stood right on top of the plate daring pitchers to throw inside. Don Drysdale said that Zimmer had the following philosophy: 'If you're going to hit me, don't wound me. Get me good. I don't want to lie there quivering. Just end it.'[6] In 1956 he was beaned by Hal Jeffcoat, and was almost blinded as doctors urged him to leave the game. He refused and played until 1965.

The following day, Sal the Barber toed the slab against a hostile Ebbets Field crowd of 32,482. Monte Irvin once said "When you walked onto the grass at Brooklyn in your gray flannel road uniform with New York printed across its front, the feeling of hatred focused at you was so thick you could cut it with a knife." Andy Pafko had said "Dodger-Giant games aren't baseball — they're civil wars."[7] This was one of those games; Maglie was once again shaving them close with the high heater. Using the Dodgers' heads as a target, he showed contempt for the opposition. In the second, he threw a fastball behind Robinson's shoulders. Maglie had been throwing at the Dodgers for years and as the game progressed the Dodgers' captain, Pee Wee Reese, told Robinson that something needed to be done. Campanella was knocked down with a vicious beanball and eventually struck out in the fourth. Robinson was the next batter and vowed that he would carry the torch and impart revenge on Sinister Sal. It was a typical Robinson ploy, to draw Maglie over to first base with a bunt and run up his back and nail him. Maglie certainly was aware of Jackie's malicious intentions when the first bunt rolled foul. Jackie was determined and bunted again. Lockman came onto the infield grass and scooped up the ball but Maglie did not want a piece of Robinson and lingered around the safety of the mound. Robinson ran like a locomotive towards first, head down, ready to go after the Barber and oblivious to anyone who dared get in his way. Davey Williams, with his small 5'10", 160 pound frame, alertly snuck behind Lockman and covered first. Robinson at 5'11" and a half and 195 pounds of rock solid muscle crashed into Williams and nailed him with a knee into his lower spine. Williams went flying into the air, and was injured badly. Robinson had excelled in football, among other sports at UCLA, and to be hit by him from a running position was quite a blow. Alvin Dark, the Giants' captain, took it upon himself to go after Robinson. He raced over from his shortstop position and got into an angry exchange of words with the Dodger third baseman. Both benches emptied but a riot was averted.

When the inning ended, Durocher took his team down into the tunnel. It was like the soldiers surrounding the general in battle and plotting their next move. Leo told his club "The first man up that gets on, I want you to just keep running and I want you to give him what he gave to Davy."[8] The man who would be placed in such a position was the captain, Alvin Dark. Dark was the leader, and when he doubled up the left center field gap, he kept going towards third. Ordinarily he had no business heading towards third but these were anything but normal circumstances. Robinson got the ball well ahead of Dark and slammed it into his forehead before it popped loose. Jackie, overcome with hatred, informed Dark that the war wasn't over. The two players did not break into fisticuffs; they were two professionals who knew what needed to be done. Robinson knew they would retaliate, as it was part of the game.

Brooklyn won the contest by a 3–1 score. Maglie went the distance but lost his third game to start the year. He brought home one scalp on the day when he hit Sandy Amoros. As for Davey Williams he refused to be taken out of the game but the damage had already been done. He would be out of action for two weeks and his promising career would end with the '55 season at the age of 27. A bad back had hampered him throughout his career but this was the final nail in the coffin. Whether Jackie Robinson knew he was covering the bag or not, the combative Dodger had ended his career with one vicious blow. Maglie and Robinson would be intrinsically linked by this incident as future generations pondered who was to blame — Maglie whose beanballs and knockdown pitches had provoked Jackie and his failure to cover the bag? Or was it Robinson whose malicious intent to get somebody, anybody, had gone over the line? Carl Furillo puts the ugly incidents on the shoulders of the Giants. He says in Peter Golenbock's oral history of the Dodgers, "Listen, the Giants started it. It wasn't the Dodgers. See, they were trying to build up real friction to draw crowds [which was an old John McGraw ploy, adopted by Durocher. In one game, Leo almost started a riot when he encouraged fans to throw bottles at umpire Jocko Conlan.[9]] Rigney was no prize package. And Alvin Dark, if he got a shot at you, he took it. And Herman Franks, he did what Durocher said. Monte Irvin, he wasn't dirty, but we didn't give a shit who was dirty. You had that Giant uniform, you were out to hurt us. And we were out to get you. We didn't give a shit for Monte Irvin or anybody. These guys wore spikes, and those bastards cut. And like I said, Durocher was a dirty manager. He was a dirty ballplayer. I can see knocking a man down if they knocked your man down. But to deliberately try to hit a guy in the head or spike a guy, ruin a guy for life? Look at poor Davey Williams. He got hit because of Rigney. And the dirty ballplayers all ended up being managers for look how many years."[10]

New York hosted Chicago on May 4 in a wild game that epitomized the way in which the season would progress for the Giants. They entered the contest with a 7–9 record and Durocher who was not one to stand pat shook up his lineup. Gomez emerged from Leo's doghouse to win his first game as he pitched all eleven innings in a 4–3 victory. Willie Mays dropped a routine fly as he attempted to make one of his "waist-basket" catches. Durocher was asleep at the switch when he purposely walked Clyde McCullough, the seventh place hitter, to get to the dangerous Gene Baker. Leo lost track of the batting order and thought the pitcher was coming up after McCullough. Luckily, Baker lined into a double play and although the Giants survived this game they were not destined to win back to back pennants in '55 for the first time since Bill Terry led the way in 1936–37.

Willie Mays put together another huge year for New York in 1955. He led the league in home runs (51), slugging average (.659) and tied for the league lead in triples (13). Willie finished second in batting average (.319), RBIs (127) and stolen bases (24). He became as horrific a sight for the Ebbets Field patrons with the bat as Sal Maglie had been on the mound. In the Flatbush bandbox he hit nine homers in eleven games. Despite the incredible numbers things did not always go smoothly. In an August game at the Polo Grounds, Duke Snider hit a sinking liner to center field that Mays missed as he attempted to make a shoestring catch. The ball skipped past him towards dead center field. Mays turned around to take a quick look and refused to run after it and Snider had an easy inside the park homer in which he could have walked home. The Giant fans and the Dodger fans in attendance booed him without mercy, as the jeers reverberated below Coogan's Bluff. Joe King wrote in the paper the following day "Maybe success did come too fast for the young man. Maybe the dramatic Negro boy the Giants plucked out of deep South obscurity has failed to appreciate that last year [1954] was a freak and that baseball is a job you work at 60 minutes an hour, and that the prima donnas are hated worse than any other by the fans. That's what Willie was yesterday—a prima donna."[11]

On May 5, New York reached the .500 mark and Sal Maglie won his first game of the year by defeating the Chicago Cubs, 6–3, before the home crowd. Maglie started the game despite a stiff neck and had to endure two rain delays before leaving after six innings. After the second rain delay, Randy Jackson tripled and Bob Speake hit his first major league homer. The Barber allowed two runs on five hits and one walk. His record stood at 1–3. It was his first start since April 23, the Giants had played eight games before he was given this opportunity to start. While New York defeated the Cubs, controversy once again came to the forefront with the Dodgers. Don Newcombe refused to throw batting practice for the second time within a week and was suspended by the club. The big right-hander was labeled a "choker" throughout his career, more then any other Dodger. Brooklyn management constantly assailed Newcombe. When he first came up, Burt Shotton said he "couldn't keep his mouth shut," and that he didn't want him "spoiling it for the other two [black] fellows."[12] Charlie Dressen declared in 1951 that Newcombe was "lazy and too prone to ask out."[13] The stereotype attributed to Newcombe developed from a number of areas: Many whites wanted to reinforce the myth that blacks choked under pressure. Newcombe pitched a lot of important games in which the Dodgers lost by close scores (Game One of the 1949 World Series, the last game of the 1950 season and game three of the '51 playoff in particular). Dodger management had a policy of attacking the manhood of their players and speaking negatively about them in the press with the purpose of making them easier to handle. Finally, Newcombe had a reputation for asking out of games, and complaining about a sore arm.

Maglie made two relief appearances against Pittsburgh in a doubleheader at the Polo Grounds on May 8. He worked a scoreless ninth inning in the opener as the Pirates won, 7–5. Gomez took the loss (1–3). In the second game, Maglie came in with the bases loaded in the fifth inning and induced George Freese to fly out to Mays in center. Sal finished out the game and earned his second victory of the year as New York won by a 6–3 score. The Barber pitched four and one-third innings, giving up one run on four hits (no walks) and striking out two. Mueller collected five hits on the day, as he extended his hitting streak to twenty-one games and boosted his average to .421. Mays had four hits in the second game that included two singles, a triple, and a homer. Hank Thompson continued to struggle and made an error in the second contest. He would have a bad year with the bat and the glove.

When the Giants traveled to St. Louis on May 13, a beanball war broke out as Durocher and Stanky watched the action intently. Harvey Haddix nailed three batters in the game: Thompson, Dark, and Irvin. Stan Musial had two hits and two RBIs when he faced John "Windy" McCall in the ninth inning. McCall threw a vicious knockdown pitch that missed Musial before hitting him on the wrist with another offering. Willie Mays came up in the tenth with the game tied at three and was knocked down with a high heater delivered by Haddix. Unperturbed he promptly stepped back into the box, took a ball and then hit a homer which propelled the New Yorkers to victory.

Maglie won his final four starts in May to extend his winning streak to six games. He pitched his first complete game of the year against the Cubs on May 15, allowing four runs (three earned) on nine hits and two walks. He hit young Bob Speake with a pitch. Speake had hit a homer off the Barber in the last game in which they met. Don Mueller tied a team record by hitting in twenty-four consecutive games. Freddie Lindstrom had achieved the mark in 1930. Mueller would not break the record, as he went hitless in his next game. Frank Bergunzie, of the Giants front office, showed Maglie films that revealed he was not striding properly as he came off the mound. Maglie made the necessary adjustment. On May 22, Maglie won his fourth game as New York defeated Pittsburgh by a 3–2 score. He allowed two runs (one earned) in eight and two-thirds innings on nine hits and two walks. Wilhelm came in to shut the door but Ray Katt's inability to catch the knuckler almost cost them the ballgame. Katt was charged with a passed ball and when Wilhelm struck out Sid Gordon he failed to catch the ball and the batter reached first base. As Wilhelm left the game he was understandably upset. Grissom recorded the final out. After uncharacteristically losing his first two games against Brooklyn in '55, Sal finally defeated his archrival as New York won by a 3–1 score before 37,911 Ebbets Field spectators on May 27. The Barber got by with guile and determination instead of power and kept the Dodgers' hitters off balance with an assortment of slow curves. Only once did he throw a legitimate high and tight pitch and the ball hit off Campanella's bat for an easy out. Maglie held the opposition to seven hits and contributed with two sacrifices at the plate. On the last day of May, the Barber improved his record to 6–3 as New York won a close one from Philadelphia, 2–1. He allowed a first inning run before settling down. The Phillies collected five hits, five walks and struck out seven times against him. Maglie nailed his hated rival, Andy Seminick, with a pitch. He contributed at the plate with one hit, scored a run and was credited with a sacrifice.

New York played at an 18–13 clip in May but the bottom dropped out in June as they compiled a 10–17 record for the month. On June 5, the Giants split a doubleheader with the Cubs at the Polo Grounds. They took the opener by a 3–2 score as Maglie improved his record to 7–3 with the win. He went the distance, allowing two runs on seven hits and one walk while striking out six. Chicago scored their runs in the first and the fourth innings. After the fourth frame he held the Cubs to two hits the rest of the way. Thirty-seven year old Sid Gordon played third, and contributed with a hit. The old Giant was coming home to end his career; he had been reacquired from Pittsburgh for cash, since Thompson was not doing the job at third base. He started his career in 1941 when Bill Terry was still managing the ballclub. Gordon hit .243 for the New Yorkers in '55, his last big league season. The Cubs took the second game, 3–1, as "Toothpick" Sam Jones struck out eleven for the Cubs. Chicago hurler Jim Davis had nailed the Giants' rookie first baseman Gail Harris in the first game. A duster war broke out in the second contest. After Hofman hit a solo homer in the fifth, Jones knocked Westrum down. Hearn returned the favor and knocked Randy Jackson to the ground. Jones nailed Dark and Lockman with pitches in the contest, although the dusting never got out of hand. Durocher looked indecisive in the final frame. He made a defensive replacement in the middle of an inning, Williams replacing Hofman. With runners on first and second, Hearn, who had pitched a terrific game, threw two balls to pinch hitter Frank Baumholtz and was suddenly taken out. Grissom was called in and Baumholtz hit a three run homer on the first pitch.

St. Louis visited the Polo Grounds and split a doubleheader with the Giants on June 12. Antonelli improved his record to 6–7 as New York won the opener by an 8–3 score. Williams and Mays were nailed by pitches from Cardinal hurlers. St. Louis bounced back and won the second game by a 6–5 score in thirteen innings. Maglie started slowly as usual, giving up a first inning run while the Giants scored four in the first and one in the second to give him a 5–1 lead. St. Louis scored two in the third and in the sixth it began to rain which precipitated a 29-minute delay. In the seventh inning, Solly Hemus lined a shot towards right field that hit umpire Lee Ballanfant in the foot. Gail Harris caught the ricochet but Maglie failed to cover first base. Williams subsequently juggled a double play ball and got only one out. Musial followed with a two run homer on a 3 and 1 pitch and the lead had vanished. Maglie gave up five runs on eight hits and two walks in six and two-thirds innings. Marv Grissom nailed Musial in the back during the twelfth inning and was promptly warned. Mueller failed to cut off a liner by Paul LaPalme in the following inning and it went for a double, driving in what proved to be the winning run.

Durocher tore into Maglie concerning his failure to cover first on Hemus' liner and ripped him in the press. Leo told reporters that Sal's "carelessness" had cost them the ballgame.[14] It had been a freak play; when Hemus hit the ball Maglie thought it had gone foul and the batter momentarily held up before running to first. Nonetheless, Maglie could have recorded the out if he ran right away but Durocher's condemnation of the Barber may have been over the top. Durocher had long maintained his maniacal, dictatorial approach to managing with little rebellious activity from his players, although in 1943, while managing the Dodgers he made a big theatrical scene in which he kicked Joe Medwick and Bobo Newsom off the squad. The players rebelled and Leo lost control of his team. Arky Vaughan picked up his uniform and handed it to Durocher saying "Here. If you want his uniform, you can have mine, too."[15] Leo had made a living of publicly humiliating his players and now he did it to Maglie. Before spring training in 1954 he attacked the Barber for arriving late to camp and Maglie responded with good pitching performances. After all the great years Maglie had given Leo, one would think he would have taken him behind closed doors and ripped him in private. Leo did not and told reporters "I'm real sore at Maglie, because he blew an easy play. Real sore. But hell, that's the way it's been all year, one guy or another too damn lazy to make the easy plays. That's why we're hurting. Maybe this looks like the same club that won last year, but you can't tell me these guys are champions. The spirit is gone. It's shot. It isn't there."[16] Earlier in the season, Leo chewed out some of his players in private but not in a public forum. The incident created a rift between Maglie and Durocher for the rest of the season.

Things went from bad to worse for the stumbling Giants. While the team was traveling from their hotel to County Stadium to play the Braves on June 18, one of the Giants tried to relieve the tension by playing a practical joke on Marv Grissom. The unsuspecting ballplayer was so startled that he jumped straight up and nailed his head against the top of the bus.

He cut his head open and was taken to the hospital for stitches. The Giants then proceeded to drop a 7–4 decision to Milwaukee. Since Leo had ripped into Maglie and denounced him as "lazy," the Giants had gone 2–3. Durocher's club stood fourteen games behind Brooklyn, in third place with a 31–30 record. The Barber was ineffective on the day and did not get a decision. He allowed four runs on ten hits and three walks in five innings and was charged with an error in the field. After the game, Sal entertained reporters and discussed some of the reasons for his success. He rarely pitched to the hitter's strength and always remembered what he threw to a certain batter and the ultimate result in that at-bat. For example, Maglie handled Ralph Kiner with curveballs. One day Westrum called for the fastball and Kiner knocked it out of the park. No longer did the Barber throw him heaters. Milwaukee's shortstop, Johnny Logan, was a fastball hitter and one day asked Maglie when he was going to see some heaters. The Barber replied "When you show me that you can hit the curve." The next day Maglie faced Logan and broke off two curves for strikes and then snuck a fastball by him. Logan was infuriated and he cursed the Barber and yelled "You bastard." Sinister Sal broke into a menacing laugh.[17]

In Cincinnati, Maglie ended New York's six game losing streak as he pitched a complete game 4–3 victory. He scattered ten hits and two walks while striking out seven. Durocher's club continued to play sloppy baseball. In the third inning, Ray Katt froze at third when he should have scored on a ball which the second baseman couldn't handle. Lockman subsequently hit into a double play and the baserunning blunder cost the New Yorkers a run. Maglie extended his winning streak to eight games after losing the first three games of the season. The winning streak ended on June 28 before 30,482 Polo Grounds fans against the Dodgers. Brooklyn scored five runs (four earned) in six innings against their hated rival on six hits and two walks. The final score was 6–5. New York squandered scoring opportunities in the seventh and eighth and in the ninth a hard hit ball was turned into a double play to end the game. As July beckoned, Mueller was the only Giant regular batting over .300. Maglie had been inconsistent despite his record, while Gomez and Antonelli had dropped off their previous years' pace.

July began inauspiciously for New York as they dropped a 9–3 contest to the Phillies. Antonelli's record fell to 6–10 while Durocher and Lockman were ejected for arguing balls and strikes. Harris hit a homer off Robin Roberts. Roberts, who won his eleventh game, would set a new major league record by allowing 41 homers in '55. His insistence on challenging the hitters with the fastball led to an exorbitant amount of gopher balls hit by opposing batters. Nonetheless, the Philadelphia right-hander showed he had a sense of humor when he said, "In the long history of organized baseball I stand unparalleled for putting Christianity into practice.... No one has ever been so good to opposing batsmen. And to prove that I was not prejudiced, I served up home run balls to Negroes, Italians, Jews, Catholics alike. Race, creed, nationality made no difference to me."[18]

Sid Gordon, Willie Mays, and Ray Katt hit homers on the following day to propel New York to a 6–1 victory over the Phillies in the scorching summer heat at Connie Mack Stadium. Maglie looked like the wounded soldier who returned to the battle one last time to save his mates. Roger Kahn wrote in the *New York Herald Tribune*, "Amid the ashes of the Giant camp. Sal plays the role of Phoenix nearly every time he pitches. He refuses to fit into the current Giant scheme...."[19] The heat took its toll on the Barber as he lasted eight and one-third innings with the help of salt tablets. Players wore loose flannel uniforms that became extremely heavy and cumbersome when they soaked up the perspiration in the heat. The run that scored was unearned as the Giants fielded poorly behind Maglie. He allowed nine hits, three walks and struck out four.

On July 5, the Reds were hosting the Cardinals at Crosley Field. Cincinnati manager Birdie Tebbetts became upset, insisting the opposition was using delaying tactics when Cardinals catcher Bill Sarni frequently attended the mound to talk to his pitcher. In the ninth inning, Tebbetts came out to complain and the Cardinals' manager, Harry Walker, joined him. The two managers got into a heated argument until Tebbetts fired the first punch. Tebbetts and Walker began to pummel each other, as they fell to the ground and both benches emptied. Order was restored but not until Walker suffered a bruised forehead and Tebbetts had a bloody nose and a cut in his mouth. National League President Warren Giles gave each manager a $100 fine for igniting the ninth inning free-for-all. It may have been the ugliest fight of the year.

When the Giants and Dodgers got together they came to kill but most of all they came to win. On July 8, a crowd of 43,578 spectators packed themselves into the Polo Grounds but were disappointed to see Brooklyn win by a 12–8 score. Thirty-seven players were used, including eleven pitchers, in the nine-inning game that lasted over three hours. New York knocked Newcombe of the box in the third inning. They scored four in the second and two in the third to take an early 6–0 lead. Newcombe's suspension for refusing to throw batting practice only lasted one day and he pitched superbly after he was reinstated. He entered the game against New York with a 14–1 record so to knock him out early was no small feat. The Barber gave five runs back in the fourth and departed after the inning as he failed to hold the lead. Sal allowed four hits and two walks while striking out four in the ballgame. As he departed and took the long walk to the center field clubhouse, enemy Dodger fans who had assembled in the bleachers waved handkerchiefs at him in a derisive manner. Gomez took the loss as his record fell to 6–4.

Two days later Maglie came back against his hated rivals on one day's rest and pitched admirably. Doc Bowman massaged his right arm for nearly a half an hour in preparation for the game. This was the last time he would wear the white uniform with black and gold trim and pitch against the Brooklyn Dodgers. The last time Jackie Robinson would face him, with his blue cap and the signature white "B" in the middle. The Dodgers wore their road grays with "Dodgers" written in script across the uniform. On July 10, a crowd of 34,790 Polo Grounds fans watched the Giants score two runs in the last of the ninth to pull out a 3–2 victory. Maglie was long gone at the end but gave his club five strong innings. He allowed two runs on four hits and two walks. One of his runs scored on a balk as he slipped off the mound. Grissom plunked Robinson with a pitch. In an eleven year major league career Robinson was hit a staggering 72 times, including a career high 14 times in 1952. These numbers are truly high when you consider that no one eluded a pitched ball better then Jackie Robinson. He was accustomed to being thrown at incessantly, and had the fortunate ability to get out of the way of pitched balls that were right on top of him. Robinson and Durocher continued to battle right to the bitter end. Jackie harbored animosity towards Leo ever since Durocher humiliated him when he arrived for the 1948 spring training overweight. Russ Meyer recalls, "He hated Durocher with a Goddamn passion. He used to taunt him. He'd drive that Goddamn Durocher crazy. He'd call him, 'Hey, you, pussy,' just drive the fucking guy crazy. 'Hey, Leo, who you going to marry next?' and like 'Is Laraine taking good care of you?' Shit like that."[20] One day Leo removed his cap from the third base coach's box, and Jackie yelled from the dugout "Hey, skinhead, put on your hat before somebody jerks you off."[21] Robinson also taunted Maglie and likewise battled him to the end.

After the Brooklyn game, Maglie would go into a precipitous downward climb that ended with his banishment from the Giants. New York won its fifth in a row when they defeated Milwaukee by an 8–7 score at the Polo Grounds on July 16. Seven homers were hit in the contest but the winning run scampered home on a wild pitch in the bottom of the ninth. Maglie served up homers to Bill Bruton, Del Crandall, and Henry Aaron. He allowed four runs on nine hits and two walks in seven innings. Liddle won the game in relief as the Giants had won nine out of their last ten games. They defeated St. Louis on the 20th before 4,017 Polo Grounds spectators by a 6–5 score. The heat was suffocating and Maglie was given an early shower, allowing four runs (one earned) on four hits and one walk in one and two-thirds of an inning. Westrum had uncharacteristically been the best hitter for the Giants over the past three weeks, but he cracked a bone in his finger on a foul tip and left the game. Two days later the Giants defeated the Reds, 6–3, as Harris hit a three run homer in the fourteenth inning to win it. Maglie came back on one day's rest but was chased after serving up a two run homer to Wally Post and solo shot to Ted Kluszewski. He allowed three runs on six hits and two walks in three innings. On the 25th, the New Yorkers defeated Chicago, 6–5, at Wrigley Field but Maglie had nothing once again. He allowed three runs on five hits and one walk in two and two-thirds innings. Hank Sauer and Ernie Banks hit homers off him.

The climax occurred in Milwaukee's County Stadium on July 30 as the Braves defeated the New Yorkers by a 5–3 score. Maglie did not record an out as the starter. He was taken out after he walked the leadoff hitter and gave up three successive hits. All four of the baserunners scored as Maglie's record fell to 9–5. Sal was perplexed by his poor performances, he felt fine physically and the back had not acted up. The following day Maglie watched the game patiently as the Giants pulled out a 7–3 victory behind a fine pitching performance by Hearn. Sal felt something was up and as his teammates started for the clubhouse, Maglie sat on the bench thinking. Durocher approached the sullen Barber and informed him that he had been sold to the Cleveland Indians. In seven seasons with the Giants, Maglie had compiled a formidable 95–42 record. He was nothing but a junkballer when he came up in '45 but developed his limited skills to become a solid big league hurler. Sal had overcome tremendous odds to make it: the limited skills, a blacklist, crippling injuries, and an advanced age. The only person to thank Maglie for his service to the ball club was Leo Durocher. No one else said a word; ballplayers were commodities to a ballclub and once they thought they couldn't perform they were discarded without a short word of thanks.

Things had changed drastically under Coogan's Bluff since Sal Maglie first toed the slab in 1945. With attendance declining rapidly, Horace Stoneham suggested building a stadium near the Whitestone Bridge that would house both the Yankees and the Giants. George Weiss, general manager of the Yankees, scoffed at the idea when it was proposed in August. In 1955, the Giants drew 824,112 fans to the Polo Grounds and followed that with 629,267 and 653,903. The urban ballparks had become dilapidated, outmoded, and were located in bad neighborhoods. Monte Irvin recalls what it felt like to play in Ebbets Field: "We hated to go to Brooklyn. Since we lived at home, we would all drive to the game in our cars, whether it was a night game or day game. There was never enough parking and we had to go through all that traffic to get there.... Then when we came out of the ball park, we feared for our lives."[22] The Dodgers announced on August 16 that they would play seven night games in Jersey City's Roosevelt Stadium for the following season. Walter O'Malley played hardball and demanded a new stadium but he had his eyes on greener pastures out West.

What was happening to the ballparks and the cities can be traced back to the end of World War II, when Bill Levitt began building small communities in the suburbs for which became known as "Levittown." From 1950 through 1980, eighteen of the country's top twenty-five cities had witnessed a decline in population. The great exodus had begun and whites began to move out of the surrounding neighborhoods of Ebbets Field and the Polo Grounds while blacks began to take their place. Slowly the composition of the crowd began to change as an ever growing number of blacks and latins showed up at the park. John Belson states in Peter Golenbock's oral history of the Dodgers, "In the '40s the crowds had been all white, but by the mid–'50s, after Jackie Robinson had been there a while, you go to a Sunday doubleheader, and the dominant smell in the ballpark was bagged fried chicken."[23] Stan Lomax recalled, "The scene at Ebbets Field was one of riding on the crest of a volcano. If they didn't get a new park, they would have had a riot or some terrible disturbance. Especially at the mid-week games — there was too darn much drinking. There were narrow aisles, the seats were too close and you had a rough, tough bunch there. If somebody threw a bottle or stabbed someone — that's all that was needed — the dynamite was there ... with too many people in too small an area."[24] O'Malley was not particularly fond of the clientele that frequented his ballpark. Dick Young stated that O'Malley confided in him why he wanted to leave Ebbets Field, "because the area is getting full of blacks and spics."[25] Bill James has suggested in his *Historical Baseball Abstract* that he should write an article called "Sympathy for the Devil," to describe the predicament in which O'Malley found himself in.[26] Major league baseball is a pliable institution, and the move of the Giants and Dodgers out West did not hurt the game as some suggest. Times change, the game evolves, and we move forward but the memories persist.

Leo Durocher knew he would be gone at season's end. The old warriors had slipped. Irvin was sent to Minneapolis in June where Bill Rigney was fine-tuning his managerial skills. Durocher did not lose interest as he had in poor seasons beforehand; he guided his club to an 80–74 record, good enough for third place. This was a team whose main first baseman was Gail Harris (.232). Their main second baseman was Wayne Terwilliger (.257) and catcher Ray Katt (.215). Durocher knew he was a goner and his

Hollywood friends unceasingly made fun of Horace Stoneham, portraying him as an incompetent drunk. There may have been some truth in their parodies, but Durocher continued to humiliate people right to the end. Leo's tenure as the Giants manager ended on a triple play. Bill Rigney replaced him as the new skipper.

The defending American League champion Cleveland Indians were in the thick of the pennant race with the Yankees and the White Sox. They picked up Maglie not only in hope that he still had some magic left in his thirty-eight year old right arm but also to make sure the Yankees would not take him. Sal cleared waivers with every major league team and the Indians paid $25,000 for his services. Al Lopez guided his club to a second place finish (93–61) despite down years by several of the key hitters: Al Rosen, Bobby Avila, and Vic Wertz. Bob Lemon, Mike Garcia, and Early Wynn would have their collective win totals drop almost twenty games from the previous year. Maglie found difficulty in the junior circuit, mainly because he didn't know the players and the American League

Manager Al Lopez welcomes Maglie to Cleveland. (National Baseball Hall of Fame Library, Cooperstown, N.Y.)

umpires called a different game and would not give him the corners. The umpires in the respective leagues took different positions behind the catcher and thus had a different vantage point when calling balls and strikes. The NL umpires could move around better because they wore chest protectors under their coats while the AL umps held up a protective object in front of them. The American League umps were more inclined to call the high strike.

Maglie joined fellow beanball pitchers Early Wynn and Mike Garcia in Cleveland to form a terrifying staff. Of course he knew many of the Indians from their spring training barnstorming trips. Sal sent a warning to American League hitters, specifically to Ted Williams, that he would continue to throw inside at a ferocious pace. Williams made it a habit to take practice swings close to the batter's box so he could gauge the pitcher's delivery. Maglie insisted that if Williams stood close to the box against him, he would throw a beanball on a warmup pitch.[27] On August 5, he made his American League debut at the nation's capital as Vice President Richard Nixon, Secretary of State John Foster Dulles, and Attorney General Herbert Bronwell watched the game unfold in Griffiths Stadium. Maglie was

Maglie joins tough pitchers Early Wynn, Mike Garcia, and Bob Lemon to form a terrifying staff. (National Baseball Hall of Fame Library, Cooperstown, N.Y.)

ineffective as he allowed five runs (two earned) on six hits and one walk in two innings to take the loss. He gave up four first inning runs and the Senators went on to win, 7–5. Two days later Maglie tossed a scoreless inning in relief as Washington swept the three game series with a 9–3 win while the scheduled second game of the day was rained out. Errors by George Strickland, who Maglie had skulled in '51, Al Rosen and Early Wynn helped the Indians lose the game. Cleveland relief hurler Jose Santiago nailed two batters in one inning of work.

When Al Lopez's squad swept a day-night doubleheader from the Kansas City Athletics they increased their first place lead over the White Sox to one game. The Yankees were in third place, only a game and a half behind. Cleveland won the opener behind Lemon by a 17–1 score as Avila hit two homers while Jim Hegan and Wertz hit one apiece. Maglie worked the final three innings and allowed one unearned run on three hits and one walk. Art Houtteman was the winner in the second game as Cleveland won, 6–5. The Athletics brought their home attendance over the million mark in the opener. Arnold Johnson, a Chicago businessman, had bought the Philadelphia Athletics from the Mack family on November 8, 1954. Johnson received permission to move the club to Kansas City for the '55 season much to the chagrin of Connie Mack whose sons Earle and Roy argued over the operation of the club. The club drew over a million more fans in '55 then they had in Philadelphia the previous year. The attendance reached nearly 1.4 million. This was another financial success story that was watched closely by the other owners. St. Louis, Boston, and Philadelphia no longer had two major league clubs in their cities, nor could they support two clubs.

Maglie continued his tour of American League ballparks in Detroit as 47,553 saw southpaw Billy Hoeft toss a sparkling two-hit shutout for the home team to win easily, 7–0. Maglie hurled scoreless baseball for three and two-thirds innings of relief. The Indians were no longer in first place and were a game and a half behind New York. Back home in Cleveland on August 21, the Indians defeated Kansas City by a 9–4 score as Santiago earned the win in relief. He nailed another batter while the Athletics' Art Ditmar nailed Al Smith. Maglie pitched two perfect innings of relief.

Casey Stengel's New York Yankees defeated the Indians by a 5–2 score on August 25 before 36,945 in the expansive Municipal Stadium in Cleveland. Wynn was knocked out of the box early while rookie Rip Coleman pitched well for Stengel's club. Maglie pitched three and one-third innings of no-hit relief. Santiago nailed yet another batter in the game. Municipal Stadium was originally known as Lakefront Stadium and later changed to Cleveland Stadium. It was an expansive park that held nearly 80,000 customers. Emil Bossard was the Indians' groundskeeper and he would doctor and manipulate the field to augment the strengths of the Cleveland ballclub. He even changed the field on a daily basis if needed to meet the specifications of different pitchers. His tactics included hardening the dirt in front of home plate to allow the ball to be hit quicker through the infield, and tilting the foul lines to help the capable Indian bunters. He changed the distances down the lines, depending on how many pull hitters the Indians had. Bill Veeck recalled that they used a different tarp when it rained during his tenure as owner. "We roll one out when we're ahead and time is called for rain. It takes our ground crew two minutes to put it in place. But when the Indians are trailing we get out the second set. It's more unwieldy. Twenty minutes is the time for laying it."[28] Chicanery was rapid around the majors; anything was done to gain an edge in this game of inches.

On August 28 Cleveland dropped a doubleheader to the Washington Senators. The Senators would finish in last place in '55 but with the two victories they improved their record to 12–7 on the year against Cleveland. The Indians' inability to defeat this team consistently may have cost them the pennant. Al Lopez lost his cool and was banished in the second game. Maglie allowed four runs in two and two-thirds innings of relief. The Barber shaved them close and nailed Eddie Yost with a pitch. The junior circuit was seeing Maglie's sharp razor for the first time and his heavy-bearded visage. The Barber once said "The only time I can't look mad, is when I really want to the most. I mean if I press and try to look like a menace, it doesn't work. If I just leave my face alone, it's okay." Sinister Sal referred to the knockdown pitch as his "bread and butter." He added, "You can't let them dig in up there. I don't brush 'em any more than I have to."[29] He went up against an old rival who was now with the Senators. Charlie Dressen was the Washington skipper but his club finished in last place with a 53–101 record.

On September 2 with the Yankees and Indians tied for second place, a half game behind the White Sox, Maglie was the surprise starter against Chicago in the opener of a crucial four game series. Lopez hoped that Maglie's assortment of slow curves would keep the predominantly right-hand hitting, fastball slugging White Sox at bay. In addition Wynn had a strained elbow and could use the extra rest. Maglie opposed Jack Harshman who had started the 1950 season as the Giants' starting first baseman but had since transformed himself into a capable pitcher. The Barber was ineffective and lost his second American League game, allowing three runs in three and one-third innings as Chicago won, 8–1.

Cleveland completed their eighteen game homestand (12–6) on the 5th as they split a doubleheader with Kansas City. The Athletics won the opener, 5–4, before Cleveland bounced back behind rookie sensation Herb Score who won his fifteenth game and struck out eleven to lead the Indians to a 9–2 win in the second game. Maglie faced one batter in the opener and successfully recorded the out. In Baltimore on September 8, Maglie made his last appearance of the season as Larry Doby's two run homer propelled Cleveland to a 5–3 victory. Sal allowed one run in four and one-third innings and drove in a run with a sacrifice fly at the plate. Maglie finished the season with a combined 9–7 record and 3.77 ERA with the Giants and Indians. He sported a 9–5 record for New York in 23 games and an 0–2 record for Cleveland in ten games. He pitched 155.1 innings for the season, allowing 168 hits, 55 walks, and 82 strikeouts.

The Yankees took on the Dodgers in the fall classic and once again no one gave Brooklyn a chance. Alston's club had been carrying around the "choke" label for years. Dick Young wrote in the *Daily News*, "The tree that grows in Brooklyn is an apple tree, and the apples are in the throats of the Dodgers."[30] A harsh rivalry developed between the two clubs. In 1953, the series was tied at two games apiece when Casey Stengel tried to grasp the psychological advantage from Brooklyn. The Dodgers complained that they heard Stengel urge one of his pitchers to "stick it in his ear." After the game Stengel told reporters, "I'm not interested in what the Brooklyn players say or in their opinions.... I'm fed up. The Dodgers have been crying all year. That's what they are—cry babies.... All season long I've been hearing and reading about somebody trying to kill the Brooklyn ball players. Well, they're still alive."[31] In 1953 Jackie Robinson went on a popular television show and caused some commotion when he appropriately stated that the Yankees were purposely keeping black players off their team. Yankee management was afraid black ballplayers would attract black fans and scare off their wealthy white customers. Jackie struck out against Allie "Superchief" Reynolds, who was part Creek Indian, three times in a World Series game. Stengel responded "Before that black sonofabitch accuses us of being prejudiced, he should learn how to hit an Indian." Elston Howard became the first black to play on the Yankees in '55. Stengel told a reporter "When I finally get a nigger, I get the only one that can't run."[32] The differences between the ballclubs not only existed among players and management but among the fans. Arthur Daley had once written that the Brooklyn fan "has the brashness and ostentation of the nouveau riche while the Yankee fan has the conservatism and slightly disdainful superiority of the born aristocrat."[33] In 1955 the Dodgers finally defeated the Yankees in the series as Johnny Podres won Game Seven with the help of a fine running catch by Sandy Amoros. Joe DiMaggio, Charlie Dressen and

The 1955 World Champion Brooklyn Dodgers. Maglie joined the Dodgers the following year and led them to their final pennant in Brooklyn by compiling a 13–5 record and a 2.87 ERA. (Author's collection)

Billy Cox (who played his last big league season with Baltimore in '55) were among those who predicted a Yankee victory. The celebration in the clubhouse was unrestrained as they held nothing back. Furillo told a reporter "print it in big letters. Tell Billy Cox we didn't choke up. Tell him we won it — without him. Tell him to stay in that little town of his and rot."[34]

THE BARBER JOINS THE ENEMY

As the 1956 season closed, Sal Maglie's future as a big league ballplayer looked bleak. He looked out of place in the American League, like a ship that had lost its direction in unstable waters. The Indians had a formidable pitching staff that compiled the third best ERA (3.39) in the junior circuit the year before and was led by Early Wynn, Bob Lemon, and young Herb Score. It seemed as if Maglie would be competing against the aging Bob Feller for a permanent spot on the roster. Indians management was inclined to give Feller every opportunity to make good since he had given the organization so much through the years. The great pitcher had finished the previous season with 266 big league victories which would be his final total (0–4, 4.97 ERA in '56). Hank Greenberg, the Indians' general manager, sent Maglie a letter over the winter informing him that his salary would be cut since he was no longer considered a front line starter and he would merely be trying to win a job on the roster. Since the Barber did not fit in with the Indians' pitching plans, Greenberg tried to unload him but found no takers. Not even the two respective last place clubs, the Pittsburgh Pirates and the Washington Senators, were interested. Despite the odds against him, Maglie reported to camp several days early, determined to prove the prognosticators wrong once again. He was prepared to work harder than he ever had and even gave up smoking to increase his stamina.

Maglie would turn thirty-nine in April but felt optimistic about his chances. He told a friend, "I may be thirty-nine years old, but I have a young arm. I'm a long way from being finished."[1]

The Indians had finished second under Al Lopez four out of his first five years managing the club and the manager had not been pleased with yet another second place finish in '55. Lopez stated that only the versatile Al Smith was sure of a regular position on the team and that competition would be intense. Smith put together a breakout year with the Indians in 1955 that included a league leading 123 runs scored. The Indians were training in Tucson, Arizona, where Lopez told reporters, "When I call the players together for a meeting tomorrow I'll point out to the young fellows that they'll have as much chance as any one else of winning a place on the team."[2]

There was a storm brewing in the Dodger camp, which would inevitably have an impact on the future of Sal Maglie. Johnny Podres, the young skirt chasing, hard drinking kid, had become a hero for tossing a shutout in the final game of the World Series. His draft board had previously declared him 4-F because of a bad back but they reversed their position and reclassified him 1-A. It was another situation in which a draft board examined a ballplayer with more scrutiny then they would have an average citizen. Podres would miss the entire season to military service and his departure left the aging Dodgers one arm away from seriously competing. Ted Williams, "The Splendid Splinter," was never afraid to speak his mind and came to the defense of Podres. He rebuked the "gutless draft boards, politicians and sports writers," and stated "if Podres had lost the World Series games instead of winning them, he'd probably be with the Brooklyn club all season."[3] Williams argued that ballplayers should serve their military time during the off-season if there was no war going on. Billy Martin concurred with Williams. "Ted's absolutely right. I know. They drafted me twice. Deferred me once too. Then I do pretty well in a World Series, make a little money and they get me.... I think all draft boards should be investigated."[4] The caustic Williams continued his acrimonious relationship with the Boston press and fans in '56 which culminated in the notorious spitting incident when he expectorated on Fenway Park patrons. The Boston baseball establishment expected Williams to be a deity and when he failed to act as one they attacked him. When he returned home a war hero from Korea, Bill Cunningham wrote in the *Boston Herald*, "Williams is a competitor, but ... his blood is ice cold."[5]

Maglie appeared in six spring training games and although his overall performance was not spectacular, it was good enough to earn him a spot on the opening day roster. On March 13, Cleveland defeated the Chicago

Cubs by an 11–7 score as the Barber started and hurled three scoreless innings but did not figure in the decision. He walked the leadoff batter, Gale Wade, and then set the next nine Cubs down in order which included three strikeouts.

For years Maglie had prepared for the regular season by pitching against the Indians in the spring. Now as the two teams continued their active spring training schedule against one another, Sal would toss against the Giants in an Indians uniform. On the 18th he pitched three strong innings against his old team to earn the victory as Cleveland won, 8–6. Maglie allowed one run on two hits (no walks or strikeouts). Bill White touched him for a homer. The Barber was not throwing hard but he had good control. A crowd of 15,671 watched the game in Los Angeles and they got on Willie Mays who had gone hitless the day before and managed only one hit in four at-bats in this game. Four days later Maglie took the loss as the Giants won by a 10–1 score in Phoenix. Gomez pitched six strong innings for Bill Rigney's club while Gail Harris hit two homers and Mays and Westrum hit one apiece. Westrum's homer came off his old battery mate. Maglie gave up three runs in three innings as his control deserted him. He allowed four hits, walked three, struck out two and hit two batters (Dusty Rhodes and Foster Castleman). Jim Busby's leadoff homer in the ninth on the 27th gave the Indians an 8–7 win over Baltimore in Tuscon. Maglie was not sharp as Baltimore scored two in the first and one in the fourth off him. Cleveland was winning a large percentage of their exhibition contests. On April 1 they led the American League with a 14–8 exhibition record.

On April 6, New York defeated Cleveland by a 13–6 score before 7,882 enthusiastic spectators in Houston, Texas. Wynn gave up seven runs in four innings. Maglie followed him to the hilltop and allowed one run on four hits (no walks, one strikeout) in two innings of work. The Giants and Indians were originally scheduled to play an exhibition game on April 10 in Meridian, Mississippi, but it had been canceled earlier in spring. Both clubs feared for the security of their black players for there had been racial outbursts in neighboring Alabama. Maglie's final spring appearance came in a 3–2 Cleveland victory over Milwaukee in Indianapolis on April 13. He worked three scoreless innings in relief of Houtteman. Lopez's Indians finished the exhibition tilt with a 20–15 record.

Maglie was relegated to bullpen duty once the season began. On April 21 the Detroit Tigers won their first game of the year in Municipal Stadium as they defeated Cleveland by a 7–6 score. Garcia was knocked out of the box early and Maglie followed him to the hill with three ineffective innings. He allowed two runs on six hits and one walk while striking out two and throwing one wild pitch. On May 4 the Baltimore Orioles collected only three hits but managed to win by a 4–3 score as they took advantage of erratic fielding and catching from the starting battery of Herb Score and Hal Naragon. Maglie tossed two scoreless innings of relief in what would prove to be his last regular season game in an Indians uniform. The Indians finished in second place once again in '56 despite showcasing three twenty game winners (Wynn, Lemon, and Score). Hank Greenberg lost confidence in his manager and Al Lopez resigned at the end of the season. The congenial Lopez was too talented to stay unemployed for long and he soon signed on to manage the Chicago White Sox. He led the Sox to a pennant in '59 as the team relied on basic fundamentals, speed, and intelligence to win games.

Sal was used sporadically with the Indians. (George Brace photo)

The Barber's biggest game with the Indians came in an exhibition contest against the Brooklyn Dodgers at Roosevelt Stadium in Jersey City. The Dodgers played seven regular season games in Jersey City in 1956 and in 1957 they played eight. In addition they set up an exhibition game with Cleveland to earn some extra money on the Indians' first eastern swing. Walter O'Malley's manipulation of the Brooklyn citizenry was well under way as he surreptitiously planned to move his club out West. This was not a shock to the close observer who watched the conniving actions from the avaricious O'Malley. In 1955, O'Malley sold Ebbets Field for three million dollars and also sold minor league ballparks in Fort Worth and Montreal.

He then used that money to purchase the Los Angeles Angels franchise in the Pacific Coast League and their ballpark, Wrigley Field. The move gave him territorial rights to Los Angeles and cleared the way for a franchise to be moved into that location.

A surprisingly large crowd of 10,439 spectators braved the cold weather on April 30 to watch the Indians defeat the Dodgers by a 1–0 score in a nifty pitchers' duel. Lopez's three hurlers held the opposition scoreless in the biting cold: Feller, Bud Daley, and Maglie. The Barber was sharp as he tossed the final four innings, giving up one hit and one walk. Despite the home field presence by the Dodgers, the Jersey City citizenry treated them with hostility. Jackie Robinson was feuding with the local fans but did not play because of an injured thumb. He did suit up and made two appearances when he warmed up the starting pitcher at which time he was jeered by the fans. The fans waved handkerchiefs in his direction. The *Jersey Journal* wrote, "Robinson wasn't the only Dodger to get the bird from the spectators.... Roy Campanella got his share when he led off in the first inning, and so did Don Newcombe when he pinch-hit in the ninth...."[6]

The Dodgers were flabbergasted by all the talk insisting that Maglie was washed up. His curveball was breaking off the table and he looked like the same pitcher who had haunted them through the years. Campanella and Newcombe in particular lauded Maglie's performance in Jersey City. In the middle of May the Indians had to cut down their roster and someone had to go. They certainly were not going to dump the legendary Bob Feller, thus Maglie was chosen instead. Greenberg attempted to stir up some interest in the Barber and put in a call to Dodgers general manager Buzzie Bavasi. Greenberg explained his current predicament. "He can still help a ball club, Buzzie, I'm sure of that. But with all the young pitchers we have, there just isn't room for him here. You can have him for the asking." The Dodgers had gotten off to a good start in '56, going 7–4 in April but losing five of their first six games in May before rebounding. If they could only find one more quality arm to complement their staff, they would be a legitimate pennant contender. Bavasi first called Walter Alston who admitted "He looked mighty good to me in Jersey City. I'd say grab him. I think he can help us." Pee Wee Reese told his general manager, "Buzzie, I honestly couldn't see any difference. He looked like the same guy to me ... I'd like to see him on our side."[7] Final approval was needed from Walter O'Malley. O'Malley loved to rail against the traditional structure of major league baseball and nothing would please him more than to see the old Dodger killer in a Dodger uniform. Brooklyn paid a mere $1,000 for the services of Salvatore Anthony Maglie as the baseball world was turned on its head. The man who inspired hatred among the Flatbush partisans like no other player ever had would don their uniform. This move may have been more shocking than Durocher coming over to manage the Giants in '48. Durocher would command his players to "Stick it in his ear," but Maglie was the person who actually implemented this aggressive strategy.

There was tension in the Dodger clubhouse on May 16 when Sal Maglie entered. For years he had been sharpening his razor sending Dodger hitters spinning into the dirt with the high heater at the skull. Carl Furillo had borne the brunt of the beanball and was the most sought after target for Maglie and Durocher through the years. As the infamous Barber entered the clubhouse the Dodger players including Erskine, Reese, and Campanella looked to Furillo to be their leader in this difficult moment. They waited for a sign from the hard working professional. Maglie had compiled a 23–11 lifetime record against Brooklyn, including 11–3 in Ebbets Field. From 1950 to 1954 he was 22–6 with five shutouts. Furillo broke the ice. "Hello Dago." Maglie responded, "Lo, Skoonj." One of Furillo's nicknames was "Skoonj," for his appetite for skungilli. When Erskine was later reminded that Maglie led them to a pennant in '56, he responded "That may be, but when I saw Maglie standing in our clubhouse, wearing our uniform, I knew nothing in this world would ever surprise me again."[8]

Maglie and Furillo become close friends. They were like two lost brothers who had found each other, two kindred spirits. Furillo's approach to the game was practical, which included hard work, dedication, and perseverance. Peter Golenbock referred to him as being "coldly efficient." He was not well read and kept his distance from the better-educated players such as Snider, Erskine, and Robinson. Carl had once beaten Tommy Brown to a pulp when Brown refused to turn off the lights so he could finish what he was reading.[9] Maglie was also "coldly efficient." He was a practical pitcher who didn't do a lot of profound introspection of the game and remained relatively aloof from his teammates. Maglie said, "I never went much for that philosophy stuff. I just wondered whether I'd get good fielding or not. I remember writers used to ask me what my 'pitchin' philosophy' was. I'd just laugh at 'em. My philosophy was to shave the corners, that's all, I'd say."[10] Furillo became Maglie's best friend on the team but the Barber also got along with Robinson, Snider, Campanella, Hodges, and Reese to name a few. Maglie recalled, "Although there were players on the Dodgers who were bitter enemies, there was no trouble when I joined them. It's your job as a pitcher to win the game and all the players have to go with you. Furillo and I got along real well when I became a Dodger. But the rivalry was good. The rivalry between the boroughs was baseball."[11]

The Barber's former teammates on the Giants were stunned when they heard Maglie had joined the enemy. To many of the disbelieving Giant

Jackie Robinson, Maglie, and Carl Furillo. (*The Sporting News*)

fans it was as profound as when that American war hero Benedict Arnold joined the British and gave up the cause for independence. Of course Maglie had no choice concerning where he was sent but he did not resist. His friends on the Giants could not hate him in a few minutes but instead they wished him well. Wes Westrum said, "I think he'll help them as a relief pitcher, he's got that side arm curve. That's his best pitch and he seemed to have it this spring when we saw him." The Giants' vice-president, Chub Feeney, expressed the sentiments of the organization when he stated, "Sal is a wonderful fellow. I'm happy he landed a job, and I know Horace (Stoneham) feels the same way." He also said, "I just hope they pitch him against us. We'll sell out the ball park." Nonetheless the Giants had to be kicking themselves when they realized there was still life in the Barber's right arm after all. The Dodger players also expressed their opinions. Jackie Robinson stated, "I'm only sorry he didn't join us sooner — say about five or six years ago." Furillo said, "He'll be wearing the same uniform I'm wearing and that's all that matters, if trouble starts, I'll be right out there with him.

All that's happened in the past is forgotten." Campanella noted, "I still don't know how the Giants let him go." The captain Pee Wee Reese added, "From what I saw in Jersey City he could be more than a little help.... I've always admired Sal. He's a real fighter. I don't think he got much of a chance in Cleveland with all that pitching they got. Here we can spot him and he'll get the rest he needs between starts. Let me tell you, he's not a bad guy to have goin' for you instead of against you."[12] Walter Alston wanted to see Sal pitch before he made a judgment about the current status of his pitching abilities. The Dodgers handled what could have been an explosive situation with class.

Maglie was experiencing a myriad of emotions which was exacerbated when his father died at the age of seventy-two on May 18, only two days after Sal first stepped into the Dodger clubhouse. He immediately left the team and returned to Niagara Falls to attend the funeral services and console his family. When he returned to his uptown Manhattan apartment, his wife Kay and his newly adopted son Sal, Jr., welcomed him back. Maglie adopted two sons in his life: Sal and Joseph. His namesake later died under tragic circumstances. Despite the Barber's ominous appearance on the field, he was affable and pleasant off of it. He was well controlled off the field and did not lose his temper. Russ Hodges, the Giants' radio announcer, stated "Despite his ferocious appearance, Maglie was a gentle soul." He recalls that the only time he saw Sal upset off the field occurred when a college professor insisted that the curveball did not actually curve and that it was an "optical illusion." Unlike throwing velocity, the curveball can be taught and become an acquired skill. Through hard work, the Barber had become one of the best curveball pitchers to ever toe the slab and his pride was hurt when someone had the audacity to suggest that the pitch was a hoax. Maglie said, "I wish that guy would come up here. I'd take him across the street, and stand him behind a tree. And if I didn't break one around the tree and hit him, I'd give him my next month's paycheck."[13]

Sal tossed batting practice his first day with the club and accidentally knocked down Pee Wee Reese with his first pitch. Reese picked himself off the dirt and reminded the Barber that they were no longer enemies. He yelled, "Hey, we're on the same team, Dodgers."[14] During the first half of the season, Brooklyn was in the thick of the pennant race along with Milwaukee, Cincinnati, St. Louis, and Pittsburgh. A crowd of 16,432 fans braved the chilly weather on May 24 and assembled in Connie Mack Stadium to watch the Phillies defeat Brooklyn by a 6–4 score. Nineteen year old rookie Don Drysdale returned to the scene of his only major league victory and served up two homers to Willie (Puddin' Head) Jones as his record fell to 1–2. When Philadelphia scored two runs off Maglie in the sixth, Jones drove in a run off the thirty-nine year old right-hander who was making his Brooklyn debut. Maglie allowed two runs in two innings on four hits and one walk while striking out one.

Just as Maglie had been educated in the art of pitching by Dolf Luque and Frank Shellenback he began to impart his wisdom on some of the young Brooklyn hurlers. Maglie gave a young Sandy Koufax pitching advice, but his theories concerning the beanball would be followed by the impressionable Don Drysdale. Drysdale was an intimidating sight on the hill, standing at 6'5" and 190 pounds; he cultivated his headhunting skills under the tutelage of Sal Maglie. Maglie was more than twice his age and incessantly talked pitching with Koufax and Drysdale during his two years with the team. Don was all too willing to listen to Maglie's old war stories and implement his strategy on pitching. Maglie told the young kid that "Every time a batter gets a hit off you, it's like he picked your pocket for a dollar."[15] In later years Drysdale said, "He advised me to pitch inside, not one knockdown pitch, but two, to let the batter know you were serious."[16] When Willie Mays hit a Drysdale curve for a homer, the dejected youngster returned to the dugout and fired his glove down. Maglie said "Don, don't throw him the curveball. Let him see it now and then. Next time give him one high and inside."[17] Drysdale recalls that "Sal would give me the knockdown sign from the dugout. One time he gave me the sign with Henry Aaron up, and I knocked him down. Before the next pitch he gave me the sign again, so I knocked Henry down again. When I asked him why later, Sal said, 'You do it the second time to let him know you meant it the first time.'"[18] Drysdale owned Aaron on the hill. The Braves' slugger feared that Drysdale would skull him and terminate his career. Drysdale had excellent control and when he threw at your head it was no accident. Leonard Koppett made the following observation, "Drysdale flaunted his willingness to injure the hitter. He wanted the batter thinking, 'Hey, he's willing to kill me!'"[19] Drysdale acknowledged "I didn't give a shit what happened, as long as I got the job done."[20] He hit an astonishing 154 batters in his career, the most in the senior circuit since the turn of the century. In comparison, Maglie, a known headhunter himself, nailed 44 batters in his career. It was suspected that Drysdale would load up the ball in tight situations to get a clutch strikeout. He objected to umpires searching him on the mound. "It would have to be a private showing in the dugout. Besides, when I have fingers run through my hair, I usually get kissed." Drysdale also said, "My mother told me never to put my dirty fingers in my mouth." Gene Mauch noted that "He talks very well for a guy who's had two fingers in his mouth all his life."[21] It's reasonable to

Headhunter Don Drysdale sends Vada Pinson sprawling into the dirt. (National Baseball Hall of Fame Library, Cooperstown, N.Y.)

suspect that Maglie may have taught Drysdale to throw a spitter. A pitcher who is willing to pitch in any situation, whether he misses a day of rest or is injured, helps a club in countless ways. Drysdale was a stabilizing force on the Dodgers' rotation for years. Orlando Cepeda may have provided the best advice on hitting the Dodger right-hander when he said that the trick was to hit him before he hit you.

On May 30 Maglie made his first start as a Brooklyn hurler but it was not encouraging. He started the first game of a doubleheader against Philadelphia as 35,942 fans packed their way into Connie Mack Stadium. He allowed three runs on four hits and two walks in four innings while striking out five. Brooklyn won, 6–5. Jack Meyer nailed Junior Gilliam with a pitch in this game. In 1953 when Gilliam replaced Billy Cox in the lineup it engendered animosity and hatred by many of the southern whites who resented his place on the team. Robinson was moved to third base so Gilliam could play second and Cox was benched. Cox strongly opposed playing with that "nigger kid,"[22] as did the "bench-warming southerners."[23] Gilliam was a capable hitter with little power but a lot of speed. Philadelphia won the second game by a 12–3 score as Drysdale took the loss. He nailed one batter in the game, Stan Lopata. Brooklyn played at a .500 clip in May (12–12) and on June 1 they were in fifth place (19–16) in the crowded National League race, but only three games behind the front running Milwaukee Braves.

The Dodgers lost their first three games in June to Chicago before salvaging the final game of the series as Koufax won his first. On June 1, Brooklyn lost a heartbreaking contest at Wrigley Field by a 4–2 score in fifteen innings when Gene Baker hit a two run homer off Ed Roebuck. Roger Craig started for Brooklyn and was followed by Labine, Maglie, and Roebuck. Maglie pitched two scoreless innings and left after he walked the first two hitters in the fourteenth. He did not allow a hit but walked three. Jim Brosnan had been the starting pitcher for Chicago but he did not receive a decision. He was one the many intellectuals who slowly began to infiltrate the game, and held views that were contrary to the baseball establishment. Off the field Brosnan often wore a blazer, occasionally a beret, incessantly smoked his pipe and drank a gin and tonic. He upset baseball officials with his two revealing books on the life of a major leaguer, *The Long Season* and *Pennant Race*. His nickname was the "Professor," which became a term of ridicule as well as admiration. The press and other outlets began to unfairly criticize those players who failed to be knowledgeable in areas outside of their chosen profession of baseball. Baseball is not merely a game of instincts but one which necessitates immense mental agility. Whether it involves flashing a convoluted series of signs, stealing signs, or anticipating what the pitcher will throw next by deciphering his set sequence, if he has one, it takes brains.

The Dodgers continued their exhaustive twenty game road trip as they traveled to Milwaukee. They were set to play a four game series with the first place Braves and Walter Alston feared that a poor performance would knock them out of the pennant race. The Dodger skipper planned to use the Barber later in the week, but Maglie approached Alston the day before the series opened and told him he was ready to pitch if needed. After a fine relief appearance against Chicago, he told Alston, "Well, I think I'm ready to go nine innings."[24] That's exactly what he did in front of a hostile County Stadium crowd of 29,786 to lead the Dodgers to a 3–0 victory. He was in complete control as he tossed his first shutout since April 25, 1954. It was his first complete game since June 22, 1955, and his first major league victory since July 2, 1955. He allowed only three hits and walked one while striking out five. Eddie Mathews collected two of the knocks and Bill Bruton had a scratch single. When Bruton stole second he represented the only Brave to reach the midway in the game. Maglie did not allow a hit after the fourth inning. In the ninth, the Barber induced Hank Aaron to ground out to Reese for the final out. His control was impeccable, breaking the curve over the inner and outer edge of the plate but never coming over the middle. Tommy Holmes wrote in the *New York Herald Tribune*, "A long-time Brooklyn nemesis became a Dodger of vast distinction as Sal Maglie made it appear that Milwaukee batters were waving banana stalks through nine innings here tonight."[25] Maglie also collected two hits. After the game the Dodger players lauded the Barber and his sharp breaking curve. Campanella stated, "It sure is a pleasure to have that curve of Sal's workin' for you, instead of comin' at you."[26] The win lifted the spirits of the team as they went on to win three of the four games in Milwaukee.

Over the next six weeks Maglie made nine starts with anywhere from two to five days rest in between. His record was inauspicious at 3–3 but he received little run support. The Dodgers scored only four runs for him in the three losses. Alston used him predominantly against their top competition: Milwaukee and Cincinnati. Eight of his first thirteen starts were made against those two clubs. At Crosley Field on June 9, Maglie was spinning another shutout through seven innings. The Barber held the opposition hitless in the first four frames as the Dodgers slowly built their 5–0 lead. Maglie loaded the bases with two singles and a walk in the eighth inning to bring up big Ted Kluszewski. The batter was an imposing figure at 6'2" and 225 pounds of muscle. He refused to conform to uniform specifications and wore sleeveless shirts to reveal his bulging biceps. Maglie delivered a pitch that Kluszewki knocked into the right field bleachers for a grand slam. Sal allowed four runs on six hits in seven and two-thirds innings while fanning four. He had one hit at the plate. Ed Bailey tied the score with a solo shot off Clem Labine in the ninth but Brooklyn rallied for three runs in the tenth to win, 8–5. The Reds had a powerful team in '56 and hit 221 homers to tie the National League record set by the Giants in 1947. Rookie Frank Robinson hit 38 homers while Wally Post (36), Gus Bell (29), Kluszewski (35) and Bailey (28) also added power. They finished the season in third place with 91 victories, only two games behind Brooklyn.

11. The Barber Joins the Enemy

Brooklyn kept themselves in the race by compiling an 11–9 record over their long road trip. Back at Ebbets Field on June 15, the Flatbush faithful got their first glimpse of Sinister Sal wearing the home white uniform of the Brooklyn Dodgers. Loyalties were questioned, as they did not know how to react when their archenemy was now wearing the uniform of their beloved Bums. Maglie allowed four runs on four hits, four walks while striking out four in seven innings. He had the Gillette sharpened and threw close to the Braves' hitters all night. Lew Burdette toed the slab for Milwaukee. He had thrown at the Dodger hitters for years but now ironically it was Maglie who protected Campanella, Robinson and the rest of the Brooklyns. He sent a message to the opposing pitcher in the third inning with two brushback pitches but he subsequently walked Burdette. Danny O'Connell also walked before Bill Bruton hit a three run homer. Rube Walker hit a bases loaded single with two out in the ninth to give Brooklyn a 5–4 win. It was their fifth straight victory to move them into second place as Ed Roebuck earned the win in relief. Alston finished the game under protest when the Braves called for a relief pitcher from the bullpen to face Walker and then changed their mind. Shortly after this incident manager Charlie Grimm (24–22 record as the manager in '56) would be replaced by Fred Haney (68–40) as the Milwaukee skipper. The Braves finished the season in second place (92–62) only a game behind Brooklyn. Joe Adcock, Eddie Mathews, and Hank Aaron led their offense while Warren Spahn (20–11), Burdette (19–10), and Bob Buhl (18–8) led the pitching staff. Burdette continued to throw the spitter much to the chagrin of National League hitters. John Lardner wrote an article for *Newsweek* in September called "A Real Damp Year," in which he began, "This may go down in recent baseball history as the year of ptyalism, which is a $3.95 word for excess salivation. In other words, there has been quite a lot of spitting going on: Some of it symbolic, as in the case of Ted Williams, and some of it very practical and mighty illegal, as in the case of — to hear the boys in the National League tell it — Lew Burdette."[27]

Maglie took the loss on the 22nd as Cincinnati defeated Brooklyn by a 6–0 score at Ebbets Field. Sal was knocked around for five runs on five hits and one walk in four and one-third innings. Ed Bailey hit two homers off him while Frank Robinson hit one. On June 26 the Barber improved his record to 2–1 as Brooklyn won comfortably by a 10–5 score over Chicago before 12,362 spectators in Ebbets Field. Maglie became the first Dodger pitcher to go the distance in nineteen games as he allowed five runs on eight hits and two walks while striking out five. Rube Walker was a last minute replacement for the injured Roy Campanella and hit a double, triple, and homer to drive in six runs. Jackie Robinson hit two homers for

Brooklyn. Alston's club ended June with an 18–12 record for the month. Maglie pitched superbly on July 1, taking a 4–2 lead into the ninth inning against Philadelphia before he lost his control. He hit Solly Hemus with a pitch and threw two balls to pinch-hitter Harvey Haddix before being replaced. Clem Labine replaced Sal but gave up four runs as Philadelphia won the first game of a doubleheader by a 7–4 score. Maglie allowed three runs (two earned) in eight innings on six hits and four walks while striking out five. Brooklyn won the second game, 4–1.

On the final day of baseball before the All-Star break, the Dodgers split a doubleheader with the Phillies at Connie Mack Stadium. Brooklyn finished the first half of the season in third place, two games behind the front running Reds. Don Newcombe (11–5) threw a four hitter to lead Brooklyn to a 9–2 victory in the opener. Campanella was nailed with a pitched ball in the game. Maglie took the loss in the second game (2–2) as the Phillies scored three in the sixth and held on for a 3–2 win. The Barber was impressive early on but became wild in the sixth frame. He walked Richie Ashburn, Granny Hamner, and Del Ennis. Three runs scored on Willie (Puddin' Head) Jones' two out double with the sacks full. Maglie allowed three runs on five hits, five walks, and five strikeouts in five and two-thirds innings. Robinson was nailed with a pitch thrown by Ron Negray. It had been ten years since Jackie Robinson had broken the color barrier, yet the Phillies still hadn't employed a black man on their team. On April 16, 1957, Chico Fernandez became the first black to wear the Philadelphia Phillies uniform. The city of Philadelphia harbored hostility towards blacks and their feelings were well represented by their ballclub, which became the last National League team to integrate its roster. They were the fourteenth team to integrate their club, with the Tigers (June 6, 1958) and the Red Sox (July 21, 1959) yet to come.[28] The pace of integration had been painfully slow as a small cadre of owners misguidedly held out hope that the black players' presence in the game was a mere trend that would fade away.

The National League won the 1956 All-Star game at Griffith Stadium by a 7–3 score. Cincinnati Reds fans stuffed the ballot box and five Reds found their way into the starting lineup while three others were runners-up which perturbed fans in other cities. Milwaukee swept the Dodgers in four straight after the All-Star break as the Braves took over first place. Hank Aaron's long single in the tenth inning gave the Braves a 3–2 victory on July 14 before 39,105 County Stadium fans in the final game of the series. Alston's team battled hard but lost each game by a close score: 2–0, 8–6, 6–5, and 3–2. Maglie shaved the opposition close in the finale before a unfriendly crowd. He worked six shutout innings before Joe Adcock hit a two run homer off him in the seventh. In the second inning, Maglie had low-bridged Adcock with his first offering. The Barber allowed five hits and one walk while fanning three in seven innings. Don Bessent (0–2) took the loss. Alston tried to shake up his lineup as Reese, Campanella, and Hodges were missing from the starting lineup. Chico Fernandez, had just arrived from the Dodgers' farm club in Montreal, and made his big league debut at short going 0 for 4. Rube Walker was behind the dish while Rocky Nelson played first.

After taking two games in Chicago, the Dodgers were swept in three straight at Cincinnati. The Reds took the final game on July 19 by a 7–2 score before 20,958 spectators at Crosley Field. Gil Hodges hit his twentieth homer in the sixth to give Brooklyn a temporary 2–1 lead. Maglie served up a homer to Gus Bell in the bottom half and the Reds took the lead, which they did not relinquish. Sal's record fell to 2–3 as he allowed the three runs on five hits and one walk in six innings of work. Jim Gilliam joined those Dodgers who were nursing injuries along with Roy Campanella, Jackie Robinson, and Ransom Jackson. The series was steeped in controversy. Robinson upset the local fans when he declared that Ernie Banks should have been the National League's shortstop instead of Cincinnati's Roy McMillan. Duke Snider got into a scuffle with a fan in the second game. In addition the Reds' (officially the team was known as the Redlegs at this juncture in their history) general manager, Gabe Paul, proclaimed that he would send a bill to the Brooklyn Dodgers ballclub because the center field clock had stopped, supposedly because a Dodger player threw a ball that hit the dial. Ken Lehman declared, "Don't look at me, you know my control's not that good." Maglie added, "I've been wild lately myself."[29] On July 24 the Dodgers opened a long homestand against the Reds and defeated them by a 10–5 score. Maglie had plenty of support as he went the distance for his third win. He allowed thirteen hits, did not walk a batter and struck out six. Reese went hitless but the day before he became only the second Dodger behind Zack Wheat to collect 2,000 hits.

Duke Snider, "The Silver Fox," was putting together another great year in which he led the league in homers with 43. Nonetheless it was his off the field statements which would make him the subject of ridicule. Ever since Willie Mays returned to the Giants in '54, comparisons were made among the three New York city center fielders: Willie, Mickey, and the Duke. He was irritated by questions inquiring to who was the best center fielder. In the spring of '55 he declared, "It's just plain silly comparing us. I think the real fans know who's the better ballplayer." He paused momentarily and then concluded, "I make more money, don't I?"[30] Snider, the oldest of the three center fielders, was less spectacular and had made his debut in 1947 while the baseball world was fixated on the presence of Jackie Robinson. No one doubted that Snider was a great player, but his attitude was suspect. He was an extremely serious man, who would sulk when things didn't go his way and constantly complained. Carl Furillo recalls, "Snider was always crying whenever there were left-handers pitching, and he cried when he wasn't hitting the ball, when he was in a slump, and he would cry when the manager didn't take him out."[31] People criticized him for not living up to his potential. Dodger management made sure that the press and the fans got the impression that Snider was a spoiled brat so that he would be more tractable during contract negotiations. When Jackie Robinson first came up, Snider gave him support right from the beginning and served as an ameliorating force concerning the Dodgers racial tensions. In May of '56 he collaborated with Roger Kahn on an article for *Collier's* magazine entitled, "I Play Baseball for Money — Not Fun." Snider discussed his disillusionment with the game and stated, "The truth is that life in the major leagues is far from a picnic ... I feel that I'd be just as happy if I never played another baseball game again."[32] Red Smith was among those who tore into Snider and pointed out that he ate in the best restaurants, rode the best trains, stayed in the best hotels, had five months vacation, and earned a better salary then most people. Yet Snider had the audacity to ridicule the life of a major leaguer. Ironically Snider would outlast the rest of the Boys of Summer, and be motivated by money until 1964, his last year wearing the uniform of the San Francisco Giants.

From July 28 till the end of the season, Maglie became the Barber of old as he pitched with three days rest most of the time and compiled a 10–2 record with a 1.88 ERA during that stretch. He took the pill in crucial games and pitched superbly, reinforcing his reputation as a "money pitcher." Sal toed the slab under great pressure of the pennant race and propelled the Dodgers into the World Series. Maglie recalls, "From the time the Giants sold me in July, '55, until I started working regularly with the Dodgers, I was pretty much on vacation. Did it help me? Let's say this — it sure didn't hurt me. I came back stronger than I'd been in years. Rest, of course, strengthened my arm and my back, but I've found when my arm gets strong it gets tight, too, and then I don't have good control. Only regular work improves my control and regular work means pitching with only three or four days' rest. I can still pitch that often when the weather isn't too hot."[33]

Brooklyn won their seventh game in a row on July 28 as they defeated the Chicago Cubs by a 6–3 score in Ebbets Field. Maglie struck out Solly Drake to start the game but Gene Baker and Dee Fondy followed with singles. Then Sal started a 1-4-3 double play that got him out of the inning.

11. The Barber Joins the Enemy

With two outs in the bottom half of the first, Hodges hit a two run bases loaded single to give the Dodgers the lead which they never relinquished. Sandy Amoros and Duke Snider each hit two run homers to account for the rest of the Brooklyn scoring. Ernie Banks slammed a homer off Maglie in the fourth and hit a RBI single in the sixth. In the ninth Furillo shied away from the unyielding outfield wall and dropped Banks' fly for a three base error that led to the final run. Sal improved his record to 4–3 as he allowed seven hits, one walk, and struck out seven in the route going performance. It was his eighth straight win over the Cubs dating back to 1953.

The Dodgers ended July with an 18–13 record for the month. After losing seven in a row to the Milwaukee Braves they began August by winning the first two games from them. It was a three-way race in the National League. Milwaukee held a two game lead over Cincinnati and they were three games in front of Brooklyn. All of the games the Braves and Dodgers played were nerve wracking affairs, and there was no exception on August 1 as the two teams played as if the pennant was on the line. Dale Mitchell had been purchased from the Cleveland Indians for cash on July 29, and he won the ballgame with a pinch-hit single in the eighth inning to lead Brooklyn to a 2–1 win. He was a good left-handed bat who had put together a solid career with the Indians and always hit for a good average. Maglie faced off against Lew Burdette in an intense pitchers' duel. Maglie allowed one unearned run in six and one-third innings as he tired in the seventh. He allowed eight hits, walked three, and struck out six. Labine, the eventual winner (9–4), and Craig pitched well in relief. Joe Adcock failed to hit a homer against Brooklyn after hitting ten homers in nine straight games against them. In 1954 he went on a hitting spree against the Dodgers and paid the price with a beanball that ended his season. In '56 he would tie a National League record by hitting thirteen homers against them. Adcock had a reputation for hitting tape measure shots. He was the first player to hit the ball into the center field bleachers in the Polo Grounds during a major league game. The drive was approximated at 483 feet and landed ten rows up in the stands. Earlier in the '56 season he hit a drive at Ebbets Field that Bob Wolf characterized as follows: "No tape measures were available, and nobody seemed able to work out the necessary problem in plane geometry, so it will never be known how far Adcock's blast traveled. The roof, however, is 83 feet high and 351 feet away from home plate, so it seems safe to assume that the drive (the first ever to clear the double decked roof in left field) went 550 feet. It might even have reached the 600-foot mark."[34] As Adcock continued to murder the Dodgers, Brooklyn hurlers paid him back with beanballs at the head.

Maglie pitched a four hit shutout on August 5 as Brooklyn won the first game of a doubleheader, 7–0, over the St. Louis Cardinals. He improved his record to 5–3 as he walked four and struck out three in the process. The win was Maglie's 100th of his career. The second game was won by a 5–3 score as Ed Roebuck (4–4) relieved a shaky Sandy Koufax after the first inning and went the rest of the way. Stan Musial had possibly the worst day of his career in Ebbets Field as he went 0 for 8 in the doubleheader. The only time he reached base was in his first at-bat of the day when the usually reliable defensive shortstop Chico Fernandez committed an error. Musial had owned the Dodgers in Ebbets Field over his career. It was the Ebbets Field fans who gave him the nickname of "The Man," as in here comes that Man again. When Musial put on one of his patented hitting exhibitions, the Ebbets Field patrons would often give him a standing ovation acknowledging his achievement.

Brooklyn dropped back to third place when the Phillies defeated them by a 3–2 score on August 10 at Ebbets Field. Maglie took the loss, his record falling to 5–4. He allowed the three runs (two earned) on four hits and two walks in one and two-thirds innings. When the Phils tallied their first run in the second it was the first earned run Maglie had allowed in eighteen and one-third innings. Philadelphia skipper Mayo Smith had loaded the bases with an intentional pass in the ninth so that the left-handed Harvey Haddix could face the left-handed hitting Duke Snider. Snider struck out to end the game as the strategy worked. Four days later the Barber faced off against his former team for the first time. It was a pitchers' duel between Hearn and Maglie before they were both lifted for pinch-hitters after tossing seven innings. Maglie scattered four hits in seven shutout innings, walked two and struck out four. Sal had no problems coming in high and tight when the situation dictated. When Dale Mitchell pinch-hit for him in the bottom of the seventh, the Ebbets Field crowd booed loudly for they wished to see the Barber continue. Willie Mays hit a two run homer off Clem Labine in the eighth inning to lead the Giants to a 3–1 win. The education of the young Mays continued in 1956. In February of '56 he had married Marghuerite Wendelle Kenny Chapman in a marriage that was doomed to fail. The fear of divorce affected Mays' on-field performance while Marghuerite milked the naive Mays for everything he was worth. She bought houses, minks, shoes, a white Cadillac and when the marriage ended after five years the treasurer of the San Francisco Giants, Edgar P. Feely, stated, "I don't have the exact figures but it looks to me as if Mays doesn't have anything left."[35] What Mays did have was debt. Many of the Giants' players knew the reputation and the intentions of Marghuerite when he got married but could not dissuade Willie.

Ballplayers were targets for the opposite sex in many ways. Bo Belinsky characterized this group of baseball wives as "spoiled bitches ... sitting around ... gossiping ... drinking coffee all morning."[36]

For years people speculated to why Don Newcombe had not made a run at a thirty victory season but in 1956 he finally put it all together. Big Newk had a fickle personality and used his temper as a defense mechanism to compensate for his lack of inner confidence. Trouble seemed to follow the man where ever he went. Earlier in the season he made derogatory statements about the umpires. On August 11 he won his ninth game in a row and eighteenth of the season. He had entered the game with three consecutive shutouts and a scoreless string of thirty-three and a third consecutive scoreless innings. The string ended at thirty-nine and two-thirds innings and fell short of Carl Hubbell's 1933 record of forty-six and one-third consecutive scoreless innings pitched. The Brooklyn lineup was aging and not as potent as years past, thus Newcombe won many of those games with little run support. The streak did not reach ten games for he lost to the Giants at Jersey City on August 15 by a 1–0 score as Mays touched him for a homer. Newcombe finished the '56 season with a 27–7 record and a 3.06 ERA as he tried to redeem himself for years of perceived underachieving. However the events that took place in the World Series would take him into a downward spiral from which he would never recover. Carl Prince wrote, "Unfair as it was, Newcombe was the goat, the embodiment of male failure of nerve, and it was so fixed in the minds of the New York baseball public."[37]

Maglie won his sixth game on a humid night on August 18 before 30,168 fans at Connie Mack Stadium. Del Ennis touched him for a two run homer in the first inning but the Barber settled down and pitched shutout ball for the rest of the game to finish with a six hitter in a 9–2 win. He walked two and struck out five. The Dodgers pounded out thirteen hits and ended the seven game winning streak of left-hander Harvey Haddix. Brooklyn usually murdered southpaws but Philadelphia skipper Mayo Smith took solace in the fact that Johnny Antonelli of the Giants had shut the Dodgers out earlier in the week. On the 24th Maglie faced off against his former teammate, Larry Jansen, who was making a comeback with the Cincinnati Reds. Snider and Furillo paced Brooklyn for the second day in a row as they won by a 6–4 score for their sixth straight victory. Maglie stayed around long enough to win his seventh as he allowed four runs on nine hits (no walks) and struck out five in six and one-third innings of work. Don Bessent kept the Reds scoreless the rest of the way and had pitched twenty straight scoreless innings in relief. Snider hit a three run homer in the third inning and when he stepped into the box in the fifth,

Jansen threw a knockdown pitch that hit him on the right shoulder. Furillo hit Jansen's next pitch over the right field fence. Maglie nailed Frank Robinson with a pitch in the game as he came in high and tight on several occasions. Robinson was a target in his rookie season and was hit by a pitched ball twenty times in '56. Four days later the Dodgers split a doubleheader with the Chicago Cubs at Wrigley Field. Newcombe won the opener in relief (21–6) after pitching five innings as the starter the previous day. Brooklyn scored three runs in the ninth to win, 6–4. Maglie started against the $70,000 bonus right-hander Moe Drabowsky. The Barber allowed two runs on six hits and two walks while striking out one in six innings of work. He was followed by Ken Lehman, Ed Roebuck, and Newcombe. Chicago won the second game, 4–3, as it was halted after seven and a half innings because of darkness. Milwaukee's lead over Brooklyn was a game and a half. Alston's club put together its best month of the year in August, compiling a 20–10 record, as they poised themselves for a run at the pennant.

The Dodgers swept their hated rivals in a day-night doubleheader at the Polo Grounds on September 1 by scores of 5–3 and 5–0. Don Drysdale (4–4) won the day game 5–3, as he received some help from Clem Labine who had recently been hindered by a hairline fracture. Hearn nailed Amoros with a pitch in the game. Maglie became enraged in the second game and overcome with anger not at the opposition but towards home plate umpire Artie Gore. Before he exploded he had struck out five, walked three and given up a mere scratch hit to Jackie Brandt. In the sixth he walked pinch-hitter Don Mueller and ran the count to 3 and 1 on Foster Castleman. Maglie thought the next pitch was a strike while umpire Artie Gore called it a ball. The Barber boiled over and pounded his glove to the ground in anger and began to verbally assault the umpire. Walter Alston and Jackie Robinson were among those who surrounded the arbiter but Maglie had already been ejected. Don Bessent allowed one hit in three and two-thirds innings of scoreless relief to secure the win for Maglie (8–4). Gilliam and Amoros hit homers while Jackie Robinson, playing his last big league season, continued to terrorize the Giants as he stole four bases on the day. The Giants bounced back the following day as they took a doubleheader from Brooklyn. Despite the fact that Durocher was no longer in the Giants' dugout and Maglie was now a Dodger, the Giants/Dodger games were still intense. Robert Creamer had once written, "The quality of civil war inherent in any Dodger-Giant game generates in the huge crowds an intense, personal interest unlike that found in any other major league ballpark. Here it is not home town against visitor but neighbor against neighbor. A strikeout is more than just fine pitching; it is a chance to demolish a rival fan. An error is a chance for him to ruin his tormentor in turn."[38]

Back at Ebbets Field, the Dodgers won two of three from Pittsburgh. On September 5, Maglie had the Pirates beating his curveball into the dirt until the ninth inning. Brooklyn held a 4–2 lead heading into the ninth. Lee Walls opened the final frame with a double past third but the thirty-nine year old veteran bore down and struck out Dick Groat and Bill Mazeroski. They were the first batters he struck out in the contest. Hank Foiles hit a dying quail to center that scored Walls and put the tying run on first. Maglie still looked strong but Alston decided to bring in Bessent who promptly struck out Jack Shepard on three pitches to end the game. Sal's record improved to 9–4 as he allowed three runs on nine hits and two walks. It was his fourth straight win and over his last ten games he had compiled a 1.96 ERA. Snider and Hodges hit homers in the game. The Dodgers continued to be hampered by injuries as Campanella, who was already banged up, injured his right index finger on a foul tip by Frank Thomas.

The Brooklyns won three of four from the Giants before they prepared for their final series of the year against the Milwaukee Braves. The Dodgers, Reds, and Braves were fighting it out for the National League pennant as they headed down the stretch. The Braves came into Ebbets Field on September 11, leading the Dodgers by one game. Salvatore Anthony Maglie was set to pitch. The Barber knew how to control his nerves and strived in pressure situations. Mel Allen wrote that "A money pitcher is one whose lifetime record may not be spectacular but who has the happy knack of being at his best in the games which his team must win to stay in the race.... The money pitcher thrives under pressure which wilts the others. Relishing the taunts of his rivals and the hoots of the crowd, he finds in the fiercest competition the stimulant which rescues him from mediocrity."[39] Maglie was such a pitcher. The Barber's mound opponent in this crucial game was the hard throwing Bob Buhl who had started seven games against Brooklyn during the season and had emerged victorious each time. In addition, he defeated them three times in the exhibition season. Not since Bucky Walters toed the slab in 1939 had a pitcher won seven games from the Dodgers in a season. Maglie himself had never done it, but came close in 1952 when he won six. The Barber was as ferocious as ever, scowling at his opponents, and throwing the heater at their head. Eddie Mathews hit his thirty-fifth homer off Maglie in the second inning. The Dodgers loaded the bases in the fourth and Alston let Sal bat for himself. He battled Buhl to a 3 and 2 count and then hit a quail shot over second base, driving in his first two runs of the year as Brooklyn took a 2–1 lead. Milwaukee threatened in the fifth when Andy Pafko led off with a double but the Barber worked out of trouble. They also made threatening gestures in the sixth and the eighth but Sinister Sal worked his Houdini act. Eddie Mathews was poised to ruin his afternoon when he strode to the plate with a man on third and two outs in the eighth. Maglie was tired as Alston climbed out of the dugout to check on his pitcher while Robinson came in from third. Sal was not one to cower away from tough situations and told Alston, "I got to pitch to this guy. I got to pitch to him."[40] Mathews would not see the same pitch he jacked out of the park. Instead Maglie got him to reach at a pitch low and away and bounce to Gilliam at second. In the Dodgers' half of the eighth, Robinson opened with a single off Ernie Johnson. Jackie advanced to second on a bunt where he taunted the hurler off the midway and tried to unnerve him. A pickoff throw sailed into the outfield and Robinson raced home sliding triumphantly across the plate. Hodges hit a homer into the left field lower deck and the Dodgers took a 4–2 lead into the ninth. Joe Adcock hit a tremendous drive into the upper deck in left center to leadoff the final frame before Maglie retired the next three men for his tenth victory. Sal had risen to the occasion when the ball club needed it the most and thrown a nifty eight-hitter (no walks) much to the delight of the 33,384 spectators. One writer declared, "In his years as pitching star of the Giants, the old right-handed bluebeard was regarded in Brooklyn as a civic plague comparable to the black death. Last night almost all of the 33,384 fans who jammed into the old Flatbush ball park rose to give him a tremendous ovation as he struck out to end the eighth inning."[41] As Maglie walked out to the hill in the ninth, what once seemed unthinkable became a reality: the crowd continued their standing ovation refusing to sit down. If a baseball fan had gone overseas and returned home after a year to witness this sight, he would have thought they had all gone crazy.

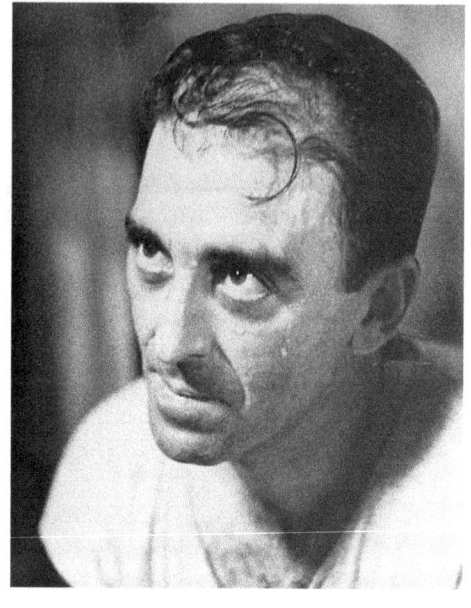

Sinister Sal with a menacing look. (National Baseball Hall of Fame Library, Cooperstown, N.Y.)

Brooklyn lost their final game against Milwaukee on the 12th and then won two games from Chicago. Maglie improved his record to 11–4 on

September 16 as he defeated Cincinnati, 3–2, before 20,714 fans at Ebbets Field. The Dodgers were now in first place, a half game in front of Milwaukee and three games in front the Reds. The Barber was on top of his game and was one strike away from throwing a shutout before the roof caved in. Wally Post hit an infield single towards Jackie Robinson at third and Smoky Burgess smashed a hanging off-speed pitch for a two run homer in the direction of Bedford Avenue in right field. After Ray Jablonski hit a single to left, Bessent replaced Maglie. The Dodgers reliever gave up one hit before he retired pinch hitter Stan Palys for the final out. Maglie allowed nine hits, walked one, hit one batter (Wally Post), and struck out five.

The Barber had risen from the dead once again and made the most out of his opportunity with Brooklyn. Whatever was left of his fastball had long vanished and he threw an assortment of curves at batters. Maglie recalled his first victory as a Dodger: "when I beat Milwaukee, 3–0, I threw 111 pitches. Eighty-nine of them were curve balls, and 85 of those curve balls were strikes."[42] Ballplayers have selective memories and even if the figures were slightly off, it exemplified his approach to pitching in his later years. Maglie said his move to Brooklyn was "the biggest and nicest break of my big-league career. I wouldn't have believed it — me the old Dodger hater — but I was made for Brooklyn and Brooklyn for me."[43] He still felt the betrayal of being traded from the Giants and said, "I got treated a hell of a lot better by the Dodgers than I did by the Giants. That was a top-flight organization."[44] The thirty-nine year old Barber would come to the clubhouse talking about his adopted son. Walter Alston admitted, "We wouldn't be up here now if it were not for Maglie." Campanella said, "When that guy pitched for the Giants he looked real mean. He never shaved. Now he looks almost handsome."[45]

The Boys of Summer had grown old and in the twilight of their career they gave the borough of Brooklyn one more shining moment in the sun. Jackie Robinson was old and gray, the pounds were starting to show, and '56 would prove to be his last season. Pee Wee Reese was a step slower and only had two more seasons left. The amiable catcher, Roy Campanella, was besieged with injuries and in January of '58 an automobile accident would leave him paralyzed. Hodges had many good seasons left while Newcombe was having his only truly brilliant year of his career. Every team had inner squabbles but the Dodgers had gone through too much to be pulled apart. Above anything else they were professionals who respected each other. When a reporter reminded Robinson that Maglie had done a great job for them, he asked Jackie if Sal was a nice guy. Robinson responded, "I don't know anything about that, but he's a helluva pitcher."[46] Pee Wee Reese said, "I don't always agree with Jack [Robinson], because sometimes he acts first and thinks second. But I admire him, everything about him. One day in Milwaukee early this year, he got excited and started arguing with some fan sitting behind our dugout. It was a tough game and some of the fellows on the bench grumbled. I didn't want to say anything there, but on the way to our positions I said maybe he ought to lay off the fan. Jack said: 'Okay, Pee Wee.' That's how it's always been with us." In many clubhouses the tensions were so high that the atmosphere became ice cold. When the Red Sox lost a game Ted Williams would selfishly declare, "I got my two hits." One photographer complained that his hardest job was "getting the Yankees to whoop it up after a win." The Dodgers were family and 1956 was their final year of success before the sun set on Brooklyn. One observer predicted the Dodgers would win their sixth pennant in ten years, concluding "They've got the pros, and this is when you need 'em."[47]

The Dodgers, having won five of their last six, traveled to Pittsburgh on September 21 and played an intense game before 10,872 Forbes Field spectators. The Pirates, managed by former Dodger Bobby Bragan, had gotten off to a surprisingly quick start but eventually faded and would finish in seventh place only six games better then the cellar dwelling Chicago Cubs. The Barber walked on top of the hill and sharpened his razor, possibly too sharp. The entire Pirate bench took notice when he sent Roberto Clemente sprawling into the dirt in the opening frame with a vicious beanball. Pirate coach Clyde Sukeforth, another former Brooklyn skipper, said, "The whole ball club got sore, I haven't seen the team so riled up all season. You don't throw at a second division club. It's not good policy."[48] Ironically the great Roberto Clemente had been originally drafted by the Dodgers. Walter O'Malley decided to hide him with the Montreal Royals in '54 instead of putting him on the big league roster, which made him vulnerable for the draft since he had been provided with a considerable signing bonus. Branch Rickey saw an opportunity to humiliate his former team and when the Pirates finished in the cellar in '54 they drafted first and took Clemente. An outfield of Clemente, Snider, and Furillo could have been a reality in Ebbets Field if not for the poor management decisions of the Dodgers.[49] Maglie shaved them close into the seventh when Frank Thomas touched Sal for a two run homer and the Pirates went on to win, 2–1. Earlier in the game Sal had hit Thomas with a pitch. When the Barber had dusted off Clemente in the first he had awoken a sleeping dog that imparted revenge on him. In the eighth Clemente made a great running catch off the bat of Duke Snider. Lee Walls jumped against the scoreboard to haul in a Campanella drive in the ninth. The Pirates bounced off the field as if they were never happier.

When Brooklyn lost three out of their next four it looked as if the Dodgers had squandered their chance for a pennant. On September 25, a crowd of 15,204 made their way into Ebbets Field on a chilly night hoping that Sal Maglie would keep their pennant hopes alive. The Braves had already won their afternoon game to open up a full game lead over Brooklyn. In the second inning the Dodgers scored three runs against Philadelphia. Jackie Robinson once again unnerved the pitcher and forced a wild pickoff throw while Campanella hit a two run homer in the frame. Brooklyn pushed across two unearned runs in the third to give Maglie a 5–0 lead. Meanwhile, the Barber was on top of his game as he retired the first eight batters he faced before walking pitcher Jack Meyer. Unperturbed, Sal retired the next thirteen batters until Willie Jones walked to lead off the eighth. The nearest thing the Phils had to a hit was Jones' hot grounder towards second in the fifth inning, but Gilliam had him played perfectly and scooped it up for the out. The Phils were hitless and the tension began to mount. Solly Hemus was doubled up in the eighth on a ball that hugged the first base line. The Philadelphia second baseman exploded, argued violently, and dropkicked his helmet. Sal Maglie at the age of thirty-nine was flirting with destiny. For eight innings he had trudged to the center of the mound, collecting his thoughts, and played catch with Campanella, mowing the Phils down. He was pitching against time, against aging, playing a young man's game in an old man's body. In the one game where time doesn't exist, Sal Maglie was able to reverse the aging process and produce the illusion that he was young again. The years had flown by. He had been transformed from a raw busher, to an outlaw, to a respected big league hurler. He had mastered the art of pitching with relatively limited skills. Now he stood on the brink of immortality. When Sal came into the dugout his teammates began to avoid him as if he had been bitten by a rat from Calcutta and the disease would spread.

The tension was heavy as they entered the ninth. On May 12, before Maglie joined the Dodgers, Carl Erskine had pitched a no-hitter against the Giants. It was the second of his career. In the ninth, Frank Baumholtz hit a twisting pop up that Campanella caught as he stepped down into the Brooklyn dugout for the first out. The Barber then struck out pinch-hitter Harvey Haddix for the second out. The count went to 1 and 2 on Richie Ashburn before Sal hit him on the left foot with a curve, low and inside. Hodges came over to remind the Barber of the situation. "Forget about Ashburn. You got five runs."[50] Maglie got Marv Blaylock to ground to Gilliam at second for the final out. "I watched the ball bounce all the way. I watched every damn hop until Gilliam got it and Hodges grabbed his throw and the ump's arm went up for the out."[51] At thirty-nine years, four months, and thirty days old, Sal Maglie had become the second oldest pitcher behind Cy Young to toss a no-hitter. As he left the mound he was pummeled by his teammates. The celebration was reserved, for the Dodgers still had more business to take care of. Erskine hugged Maglie joyfully in the clubhouse. Maglie stated, "It was one I'll always remember, but I think I was just as good the night I held the Braves to three hits in Milwaukee in June. I had a good curve ball and mixed it occasionally with the fast one. I only shook Campy off twice all night and that was against Elmer Valo."[52] Maglie threw 110 pitches, walked two, hit a batter, and struck out three. It was the last no-hitter ever thrown in Ebbets Field. Red Smith said it was the easiest no-hitter he ever saw. Dodger fan Ron Green recalls, "It was funny. There was reaction when Maglie pitched the no-hitter, but it was not like one of your own doing it. He was like a foreigner who won a game for the team you rooted for, but it wasn't like Carl Erskine pitching a no-hitter."[53]

Maglie celebrates his no-hitter with his teammates. *Left to right:* Roy Campanella, Maglie, Don Drysdale and coach Jake Pitler. (Author's collection)

11. The Barber Joins the Enemy

The Phillies defeated Brooklyn, 7–3, the following day as Roberts gained the upper hand on Newcombe. The Dodgers were not scheduled to play the next day and rain washed away the game on the 28th. Alston had planned to use Roger Craig but with the rainout, he could bring back Maglie, and pitch him in the doubleheader scheduled against Pittsburgh. Maglie appeared relaxed as he played with his sixteen-month-old son in his Manhattan apartment before going to the park. Maglie told a reporter, "I'm usually nervous until I start. You got to be. Nobody who's good at pitching isn't. But when I'm throwing I'm fine — except for this week's no-hitter. It was my first. I didn't think I got scared. But my wife was watching on television, and she said she could tell." The Barber discussed the current status of his pitching abilities, "You got to throw at [Hank] Aaron. That's the only way you're ever going to get him out on your good curve … If my curve stops breaking I can throw fastballs for an inning because, hell, the hitters still got to be looking for the curve … I'm a better pitcher than I was in '51. I throw less pitches. Almost everything is for a strike, except the close ones." Maglie continued, "I've learned, and I'm still learning and I've been getting to be a better pitcher all the time. But I think now I'm as good as I'm gonna get."[54] Maglie spotted the Pirates two runs in the first inning on the 29th, but the Dodgers stormed back behind homers from Amoros, Furillo, and Hodges to win, 6–2. Sal improved his record to 13–5 as he allowed six hits, walked one and struck out six. The Flatbush orchard almost exploded in violence in the nightcap. In the fifth inning Clem Labine bunted and the Pittsburgh catcher pounced on it, and made an errant throw to second which forced Dick Groat to jump in the air while Campanella slid into the bag. Campy was clearly safe but umpire Vic Delmore called him out and the Dodgers argued violently. Alston, coach Billy Herman, and Campanella were in the middle of the heated rhubarb. The start of the sixth inning was delayed for ten minutes as the raucous Brooklyn fans littered the field with anything they could throw. Senior umpire Jocko Conlan got on the loudspeaker and threatened a forfeiture in this important game and the crowd ceased its hostile activities. Brooklyn won the game, 3–1, behind Clem Labine (10–6). The kid who had been ridiculed by Dodger management and placed in Dressen's doghouse in '51 won this crucial game. They took a one game lead to the season's final day and Newcombe earned the victory as the Dodgers outlasted Pittsburgh, 8–6, to win the pennant by one game.

Brooklyn's final record stood at 93–61. Maglie finished the season at 13–5 with a 2.89 ERA. He pitched 196 innings, allowed 160 hits, walked 54 and struck out 110. He tossed three shutouts, plunked five batters and batted .129. Don Newcombe won the MVP while Maglie finished second.

When the Barber walked between the white lines he was all business. (George Brace photo)

Brooklyn had the second best ERA in the senior circuit (3.57) although they were quite a distance behind Milwaukee (3.11). Roger Craig was 12–11 with a 3.71 ERA. Erskine compiled a 13–11 record. Labine was 10–6 with 19 saves and a 3.35 ERA. Drysdale was 5–5 with a good 2.64 ERA. Roebuck went 5–4 and Bessent 4–3 with 9 saves. Offensively Duke Snider led the way with a .292 average with 43 homers and 101 RBIs. Furillo batted .289 with 21 homers and 83 runs driven in. Amoros contributed at .260 with 16 homers. Hodges batted .265 with 32 homers and 87 RBIs. Gilliam batted an even .300 with 21 stolen bases. Reese batted .257. Randy Jackson hit .274. Jackie Robinson batted .275 with 10 homers, 12 stolen bases and 43 RBIs in his last season. Campanella struggled with injuries, hitting .219 with 20 homers while his backup Rube Walker batted only .212. The offense had slowed a little but was still potent. They batted .258 as a team with 179 homers.

Casey Stengel's New York Yankees won the pennant easily in the American League by compiling a 97–57 record. "The Old Professor" had seen Maglie pitch a game on television towards the end of the season and had been impressed with what he saw. He analyzed Brooklyn's situation as follows: "They had trouble in three places this spring. They lost Podres to the Army. Spooner had trouble with his arm. Loes was no help at all. It looked like Alston might be in real trouble. Taking Maglie was almost a desperation move. They were willing to try anything that might help them out of the jam. And look what happens. He not only helps them, he saves their life. You sure have to give him a lot of credit."[55] The World Series was played a month before the presidential and congressional elections and therefore President Eisenhower was on hand for the opening game at Ebbets Field to throw out the first ball. Maglie gave up a two run homer to Mickey Mantle in the first and a solo shot to Billy Martin in the fourth as he pitched the Dodgers to a 6–3 win. Robinson and Hodges went deep for Brooklyn. It was Sal's first and only World Series victory as he allowed nine hits, four walks, and struck out ten batters. He pitched out of trouble all day and on two occasions Alston considered taking him out. Stengel had opted to pitch southpaw Whitey Ford (19–6) in the opener. Ebbets Field was a nightmare for left-handers because of its short dimensions and the powerful right-handed bats of the Dodgers. He lasted three innings, allowing five runs. Ford manipulated the ball in a variety of ways and threw every illegal pitch he could get away with. He threw a spitball, mud ball, and cut the spheroid with a steel ring so he could throw an emery ball. Ford stated, "Whenever I needed a ground ball, I'd cut it good. It was as though I had my own tool bench out there with me."[56] He also threw an assortment of honest curves and fastballs for good measure. Eisenhower was impressed with the pitching skill of the Barber and asked O'Malley to "tell Sal that I thought he pitched one hell of a ball game."[57] The Yankees were also impressed. Hank Bauer said, "Maglie fights you on every pitch."[58] Jerry Coleman once admitted, "When Maglie was right, he might've been as good as any pitcher that ever lived."[59]

An underachieving pitcher named Don Larsen would play center stage in the '56 series. Larsen had all the tools at 6'4" and 215 pounds but had never applied himself to the task of becoming a great pitcher. He threw hard, could field his position and could hit. In 1953 he debuted with the St. Louis Browns and when they moved to Baltimore the next year he led the league with 21 losses. In 1955 he moved on to the Yankees where he compiled a 9–2 record and followed that with an 11–5 mark (3.26 ERA) in '56. Larsen was a heavy drinker and liked to stay out to the wee hours of the morning. His former manager in Baltimore, Jimmy Dykes, said, "the only thing Larsen fears is sleep."[60] During spring training in '56 he crashed his car into a telephone pole at 5:30 A.M. and destroyed a mailbox. Stengel told reporters that he would not fine his pitcher and said, "Anybody who can find something to do in St. Petersburg at five in the morning deserves a medal, not a fine!"[61] Mickey Mantle who was an alcoholic himself wrote that "Larsen was easily the greatest drinker I've known, and I've known some pretty good ones in my time."[62] Don's estranged wife had gone to court in hope of forcing Larsen to support her child. Her attorney argued, "While this baseball hero is enjoying the luxuries of life and the plaudits of the public, he is subjecting his fourteen-month-old baby girl and his wife to the pleasures of starvation existence."[63]

In Game Two, Larsen failed to make it past the second inning due to poor pitching and shaky fielding as the Dodgers went on for a 13–8 victory. Adlai Stevenson, Eisenhower's Democratic opponent, showed up for the second game at Ebbets Field. The Yankees used seven pitchers to set a series record while Brooklyn used three. Yogi Berra, whose mother had a leg amputated earlier in the week, hit a grand slam. Snider hit a three run homer for Brooklyn. Newcombe also failed to make it past the second inning and reaffirmed his reputation as a choker. He left the park early and when a parking lot attendant noticed he was disconsolate he needled him, "What's the matter, Newcombe? Can't you take it when it gets rough?" Newcombe decked him with a vicious blow. Whitey Ford told a reporter, "I tell him that he does [choke], but I don't believe it. I mean I'll yell 'choke' at him to try and get him mad but how the hell could he win all those games … this season if he's got so much trouble swallowing."[64]

A crowd of 77,977 fans showed up at Yankee Stadium for Game Three to watch Whitey Ford go the distance in a 5–3 victory. Roger Craig took the loss for Brooklyn. Enos "Country" Slaughter at the age of forty hit a three run homer in the sixth to lead the way. Martin hit a solo shot in the game. The Yankees evened the series in Game Four, 6–2, as Tom Sturdivant pitched a six hitter. Mantle and Bauer hit homers. Mantle put it all together in '56 and became the first Triple Crown winner since Ted Williams in 1947. He batted .353, hit 52 homers, and drove in 130. Mantle was besieged by injuries throughout his career and exacerbated the situation by not taking care of himself physically. Enos Slaughter called him "the greatest one-legged player I ever knew."[65] The early career of the Oklahoma kid had been far from idyllic. He suffered from osteomyelitis and was classified 4-F. The fans could not understand how such an imposing physical specimen could be a 4-F. They came to the park and taunted Mantle, called him a coward and a communist.[66] Mickey escaped the pressures like many ballplayers and turned to the bottle.

The night before the fifth game of the World Series, Don Larsen went out for drinks with several of the Yankees. There are varying accounts to how long Larsen stayed out. In Roger Kahn's book *The Era: 1947–1957 When the Yankees, the Giants, and the Dodgers Ruled the World*, Bob Cerv, a backup outfielder who had gone out with Larsen that night is quoted as saying, "I am not going to say much, I left him at four A.M."[67] Larsen did not think he was going to pitch the following day since he had pitched poorly in the '55 series and was knocked out of Game Two in '56. Although he told his friend Artie Richman, a writer for the *New York Mirror*, that "Maybe I'll beat Maglie tomorrow and hit a grand slam…. What the hell, I might even pitch a no-hitter."[68] Larsen was in disbelief when he walked into the clubhouse and found a ball in his shoe that indicated that he was the starting pitcher. Hank Bauer witnessed Larsen's reaction. "You had a

11. The Barber Joins the Enemy

look of shock and disbelief on your face. And then you took a big gulp. It was like you had an apple stuck in your throat."[69]

On Monday, October 8, a crowd of 64,519 fans showed up at Yankee Stadium to witness the pivotal fifth game of the World Series. Larsen had turned to a no windup delivery towards the end of the season because he was tipping his pitches. As a result it also improved his control. He mixed fastballs and sliders, high and low, and struck out Junior Gilliam looking to start the game. Reese worked the count full before he was caught looking and Snider flew to right field to end the first inning. Now Salvatore Anthony Maglie made his way out to the hill and sent a message right away. His second pitch sailed behind Hank Bauer's head. Bauer was not amused and stared out at Maglie with a malicious look. The Barber had told a reporter before the fifth game that "When I'm pitching, I figure the plate is mine ... and I don't like anybody getting too close to it."[70] Bauer popped up to Reese behind third. Joe Collins bunted but Robinson threw him out, and with Reese shifted to the right side of the infield, Mantle flied to left to end the inning.

Both pitchers had retired the first nine men they faced in the ballgame as they entered the fourth inning. Jackie Robinson was robbed of a hit leading off the second frame. He hit a screamer towards the hot corner that ricocheted off the glove of third baseman Andy Carey. Shortstop Gil McDougald quickly scooped up the ball, fired to first, and got the aging Robinson by a step. Jackie had lost a step or two over the years and surely would have beaten it out a couple years earlier. Larsen retired Gilliam and Reese on two pitches to begin the fourth. Duke Snider stepped into the box, took two balls, and then missed hitting a homer by less then a foot on a long drive. He eventually struck out looking on a slider to end the Dodgers half of the fourth. When Maglie retired the first two batters in the bottom half, both pitchers had combined for 23 consecutive outs. Then Sal hung a curve to Mantle, who deposited it into the right field seats, just inside the foul pole. Snider made a great catch off the bat of Berra to end the inning but the Yankees had struck first.

There were six umpires on the field in the Series games and they came in handy for those close drives down the line. Ed Runge, who was situated down the right field line for Game Five, grew up in Buffalo and had managed Maglie in the St. Catherine League while Sal had taken a hiatus from organized ball during World War II. Babe Pinelli, the home plate umpire, was retiring after the season. After Larsen retired Robinson to start the fifth, Hodges drove a 2–2 slider to deep left center but Mantle made a fine running catch. Amoros came up next and just missed hitting a homer to right field before he grounded out and Larsen once again escaped without damage. Maglie retired the Yankees in the bottom half and a tense pitchers' duel was well under way. Larsen made quick work of the bottom of the Brooklyn order in the sixth: Furillo, Campanella, and Maglie. Hank Bauer hit an RBI single in their half of the sixth to take a 2–0 lead. The inning ended on a 3–2–5–2–5 double play. While Maglie kept the Yankees scoreless in the next two frames, Larsen kept the Dodgers hitless as he had retired 24 consecutive batters.

Everyone in the sacrosanct Yankee Stadium was fixated by the action on the pasture. Larsen kept the Dodgers off balance with fastballs, sliders, and sinking curves. He made very few mistakes and had great control. The flawed Yankee had become infallible and was aiming for perfection in the biggest stage there was. Broadcasters Vin Scully and Bob Wolff avoided the words "no-hitter" and "perfect game" as they articulated what was happening to their listeners. Wolff told his audience, "I just can't describe all that is going on as far as Larsen is concerned, but I'm sure that all who are listening are well-informed."[71] When Larsen returned to the Yankee bench, his teammates avoided him like the black plague.

As Larsen strode to the mound in the ninth he felt sick. "I was so weak in the knees I thought I was going to faint."[72] The crowd was on their feet. A nervous energy permeated the ballpark and every player felt it. Mantle recalls in later years, "I played in more than 2,400 games in the major leagues, but I never was as nervous as I was in the ninth inning of that game, afraid I would do something to mess up Larsen's perfect game."[73] The combative Billy Martin brought the infielders together. "Nothing gets through," they vowed; they would sell out their bodies on every play if needed.[74] Furillo battled Larsen, but flew out to right field on the sixth pitch. Campanella followed with a harmless grounder to Martin. With two outs, Alston called on Dale Mitchell to pinch-hit for Maglie. As fate would have it, it would be his next to last major league at-bat. Babe Pinelli, the home plate umpire, was calling the balls and strikes for the last time. With the count 1 and 2, Larsen unleashed his 97th pitch to the plate and Pinelli raised his right arm and punched the batter out on a questionable call. Don Larsen had pitched a perfect game. Yogi Berra jumped into his pitcher's arms as players and fans rushed the field. Maglie had pitched a fine game himself; good enough to win on most days but not today. He gave up two runs on five hits and two walks while fanning five. The Yankee players swarmed Larsen as they headed for the clubhouse. In the umpire's clubhouse, Babe Pinelli was crying his eyes out. His career was coming to an end and nobody bothered to thank him for a fine day's work that day. Umpires received very little, if any, recognition for their contributions to the game.

Maglie was gracious in defeat and came over to the Yankee clubhouse to congratulate Larsen. Maglie told reporters, "Everybody might have been cheering for you, Don, in the ninth, but I felt sorry for you because I know what was going through your mind. Had the same experience a few weeks ago, remember? Gee, it's tough in the ninth. Can't make a mistake, watch your control, remember what the "book" says about each batter. Hope a blooper doesn't drop in or a topper along the foul line or an accidental hit off a bat or a million and one things that can ruin you. I really felt sorry for you, Don. But you were the best and there was nothing we could do about it." Sal also said, "I wanted to see us win it without spoiling his performance."[75] Many of the Dodgers, including Maglie, believed the outcome would have been different if they played in Ebbets Field. The Barber stated, "In our ballpark I don't believe they would have beat me. Mantle's home run was 310 feet, 'cause it's only a four-foot fence there, and it wouldn't have been a home run in Ebbets Field. The ball he hit would probably have been a double off the wall, and it might have been a different game altogether. And the other one was a cheap run. Carey was on second, and the ball went out to left, and they let him go on all the way through to home, and Amoros fumbled the ball a little bit. Didn't matter anyway."[76] Shirley Povich summed up the perfect game as follows in the *Washington Post*: "The million-to-one shot came in. Hell froze over. A month of Sundays hit the calendar. Don Larsen today pitched a no-hit, no-run, no-man-reach-first-game in a World Series."[77]

On October 9, they series shifted back to Ebbets Field and the Dodgers won a must win sixth game when Enos Slaughter misjudged Jackie Robinson's fly ball in the tenth inning. The final score was 1-0 as Clem Labine went the distance. Newcombe was hammered in the final game, allowing two, two-run homers to Berra and a solo shot to Elston Howard. Big Newk failed to come through in a clutch game once again and the Yankees wrapped up the world championship with a 9–0 win. For years Dodger fans had stated "Wait till next year" when they lost the series. However, the Dodgers had played their last World Series in Brooklyn and next year would never come again.

From Dodger Blue to Yankee Pinstripes

The big news story in the off season surrounded Jackie Robinson. On December 13 he was traded to the New York Giants for $35,000 and left-handed pitcher Dick Littlefield. Many baseball traditionalists cringed at the idea of seeing Sal Maglie in a Dodger uniform pitching to Jackie Robinson in a Giant uniform. The trade appeared to benefit both clubs. Brooklyn needed a good southpaw on the hill while the Giants hoped to boost attendance with Robinson on their team and fill a void at first base. Jackie was in a bind. He recently accepted a job as the vice president of personnel with Chock Full O'Nuts and then sold the story of his retirement to *Look* magazine. When reporters asked him questions about the trade, Jackie made statements suggesting that he was going to play for the Giants in the following season. When the *Look* issue hit newsstands in early January it contained a two-page article on Robinson, entitled, "Why I'm Quitting Baseball." Jackie tried to quell the controversy that surrounded the article by saying, "I've always played fair with my newspaper friends, and I think they'll understand why this was the one time I couldn't give them the whole story as soon as I knew it."[1]

The baseball establishment was outraged by Jackie's deceptive behavior. Chub Feeney, the vice-president of the Giants, said, "I still can't believe he won't play." Buzzie Bavasi, the vice president and general manager of the Dodgers, said, "That's typical of Jackie. Now he'll write a letter of apology to Chubby. He has been writing letters of apology all his life ... This is the way he repays the newspapermen for what they've done for him. He tells you one thing and then writes another for money. You fellows will find out you've been blowing the horn for the wrong guy."[2] Jackie had rubbed a lot of players the wrong way, on his team and the opposing teams. Maglie said that Robinson was concerned with self-promotion and therefore was not liked by many of his teammates. When Sal was asked if Jackie would make a good big league manager, he scoffed at the idea, "I don't think any ball club would take a chance on Jackie, because you just couldn't get anybody to play for him after the way he's been rapping other players."[3] Shirley Povich of the *Washington Post* wrote that Jackie Robinson "was a big leaguer all the way, until his final act of retirement. And then he went out bush."[4]

The Dodgers put together a 16–17 exhibition record in 1957, which put them in last place in the National League. They began training in Vero Beach but played their exhibition games at Miami Stadium. The Barber threw batting practice on March 2. Sandy Amoros stepped into the box and Sal inquired if he had his protective helmet on. Amoros, who spoke broken English, acknowledged when he said "Si." Maglie then plunked him with a slow curve. Eight days later, the Barber was shelled in his first exhibition game as Milwaukee defeated Brooklyn by a 7–4 score in Miami. He allowed all seven runs (six earned) on six hits, no walks, while striking out one in three innings. Alston planned to take him out after three innings, but Maglie successfully persuaded him to let him pitch another inning. Aaron and Mathews opened the frame with homers, as Milwaukee scored five runs and Maglie failed to record an out in the inning. Wes Covington had touched Sal for a two run homer in the second. On the 14th, the Braves won by a 12–9 score in Bradenton. Maglie pitched well as the starter, allowing one run on three hits in two innings. Johnny Podres, back from his military service, followed him to hill and was shelled.

Brooklyn hammered the Detroit Tigers by a 8–1 score on the 18th. Newcombe, who had been complaining about arm ailments early in camp, threw without pain for the first time to earn the win. It was his first respectable outing since he was knocked around in the Series. Maglie allowed the only run which scored on a passed ball as he surrendered four hits, two walks and fanned one in four innings. Maglie and Whitey Ford, the starting pitchers in the opening game of the '56 series hooked up on the 23rd. Brooklyn won, 3–2, when Gilliam lined a single over Martin in the ninth. The Barber allowed two runs on four hits, two walks, while striking out five in five innings. Maglie was knocked around in his next start, losing his second game, as the Detroit Tigers hammered Brooklyn in Lakeland by a 18–1 score. They touched the Barber for six runs on seven hits and one walk in three innings. He pitched two scoreless innings against the Cardinals on April 1 before the game was called due to rain. In Dallas, Texas, on April 6, the Braves pulled out a 3–2 victory in the ninth. Maglie was outstanding as the starter. He allowed one run on three hits and no walks while fanning one in six innings. Maglie's final tuneup before the regular season came on the 13th as the New York Yankees defeated the Dodgers, 5–4, before 7,105 Ebbets Field spectators. Maglie lost his third game. He allowed four runs on five hits and two walks while fanning six in five innings. All the runs scored in the second inning.

For the first time in eight years the Dodgers would fail to finish in first or second place in '57. They would compile a 84–70 record, good enough for third place. As the season beckoned, Robert Creamer called the Dodgers "an old team, a collection of marvelous baseball players but old ones, past their prime, prone to injury, prone to ailments, losing slowly but surely to age."[5] Excluding his three years in the Navy, Pee Wee Reese had not missed an opening day since 1941 until this year. He had a crippling back injury. Newcombe and Erskine complained of arm ailments. Towards the end of camp, Erskine declared, "I haven't been able to throw the ball without pain this spring."[6] Snider hit 40 homers in '57, despite a bad knee. It was the fifth consecutive season he hit 40 or more homers. Furillo at .306 was the only starting player to hit over .300. While the old pitchers showed their age, young Don Drysdale led the staff with a 17–9 record and a 2.69 ERA. Podres was 12–9 and led the league with a 2.66 ERA. Brooklyn still had a formidable staff as young pitchers such as Drysdale, Podres, Danny McDevitt, and Craig stepped up. Their staff led the league in ERA (3.35) but their batting slipped to .253 with 147 homers. Two years earlier they had hit 201 long balls.

On opening day, the Dodgers needed twelve innings to defeat the Phillies, 7–6, before 37,667 spectators at Connie Mack Stadium. Sal Maglie was slated to pitch the opener at Ebbets Field against Pittsburgh. With the future of their ballclub uncertain, Dodger fans seemed apathetic and only 10,000 advance seats were sold. For the final time the ritualistic opening day festivities took place at Ebbets Field. Ironically, April 18 brought gloomy weather to the old Flatbush orchard and only 11,202 fans bothered to show up and watch the home team win, 6–1. Maglie defeated the Pirates once again and went the distance for his first win. He tossed a four-hitter, walked three and fanned five. The only run scored off him was unearned as Don Zimmer had a tough day at short and booted two balls. Maglie was scheduled to pitch against the Giants on the 24th but showed up to the ballpark with a stiff neck and Koufax got the call in his stead. Brooklyn won, 4–3, while Furillo was nailed once again by a Giant pitcher. The Barber missed a turn in the rotation and did not pitch again until April 30 against the Cubs. Don Zimmer won the game with a homer in the tenth for a 10–9 win. It was his fifth hit. Forty year old Sal Maglie opposed twenty-one year old Moe Drabowsky in the game. Sal lasted five and two-thirds innings, allowing five runs on six hits and two walks while fanning one. There was plenty of dusting in the contest as the Barber plunked Gene Baker while Jim Brosnan nailed Gilliam. Brooklyn was competitive in the first half of the season and they got off to a fast start with an 8–3 record in April.

The Dodgers continued to play good baseball in May and at the end of the month they were sporting a 23–15 record. There record for the month was 15–12. On May 5, 26,599 fans made their way into Ebbets Field and watched the Braves outlast the Dodgers by a 10–7 score. Walter Alston sent Maglie, Bessent, Rene Valdes, Koufax and Don Elston to the mound. The Barber allowed three runs (one earned) on six hits in only three innings of work as the starter. Brooklyn was in the thick of the pennant race as they traveled to the Polo Grounds on May 10 to take on the Giants. The old rivalry could still draw fans to the ballpark as 34,435 of them showed up. Willie Mays was released from the hospital at noon, for he was battling a virus, and led the Giants to a 2–1 victory with a great game at the bat and in the field. Ruben Gomez and Sal Maglie shaved the hitters throughout the after dark contest. The Barber's dusting was halted early as he left after four innings in which he allowed the two runs on six hits and two walks. It was a typical Giant/Dodger game with brushback pitches, arguments, and drunken fans running onto the field. The Giants won a wild game the following day, 6–5, that took nearly five hours. The dusting continued as two of the Dodgers (Hodges and Amoros) and one of the Giants (Red Schoendienst) were nailed with pitches. Maglie had long been criticized for going to the mound unshaven, but now he added a new twist as he grew a goatee. The Giants and Dodgers used six pitchers each on the 25th in another long game in which New York won, 8–7. Maglie scattered five baserunners and pitched two scoreless innings. Schoendienst was nailed by another pitch. Two days later both clubs were granted permission by National League owners to move out West to San Francisco and Los Angeles respectively. Duke Snider's ninth home run of the year on May 30 helped lead Brooklyn to a 4–3 win at Forbes Field in the first of two. Maglie improved his record to 2–1 as he allowed the three runs on seven hits and one walk in seven and two-thirds innings. The Pirates took the second game, 2–1.

Maglie did not pitch a game in June as he suffered from various ailments, including a sore neck, sore thumb, and sore shoulder. He hurt his thumb shagging fly balls in Philadelphia at the beginning of the month. Despite the absence of the Barber, the Dodgers stayed in the pennant race as they compiled a 14–17 record in June. As the season progressed Red Patterson, a Brooklyn Dodger official, said, "This year is a bizarre one. That's the word for it — bizarre."[7] The Reds and Dodgers developed hostile attitudes towards one another and on June 7 their pitchers dusted one another off. Snider and Gino Cimoli were nailed with pitches while Roger Craig plunked Frank Robinson. On June 13, tensions became heated between the Braves and the Dodgers at Ebbets Field before a crowd of 14,778, including 6,000 knothole gang kids. Milwaukee took the early lead, 4–0, as Bill Bruton hit homers his first two times up. In the first frame, Drysdale had hit Johnny Logan as he threw to first base to try to pick him off. Logan advanced to the midway. After Bruton hit his second homer, Logan came to the bat in the second frame. Drysdale was fuming, and nailed Logan in the back with a fastball. As the batter made his way to first base, he exchanged words with the Brooklyn hurler and then charged the mound. Drysdale landed a right hook that cut a gash above Logan's left eye. Eddie Mathews, who was on deck, came flying into the fray and knocked Drysdale to the ground with a vicious blow. Both benches emptied as the melee ensued and then settled down. Drysdale and Logan were kicked out as Milwaukee held on for an 8–5 victory.

This was not even the biggest fight of the day, as the Yankees, who got into three bench clearing brawls that week, squared off with the White Sox on June 13. New York pitcher Art Ditmar sent Chicago's Larry Doby sprawling into the dirt with a pitch at his head. Doby got up furious and yelled "If you ever do that again, I'll stick a knife in your back." Ditmar responded, saying "Go fuck yourself."[8] A fight broke out and both benches cleared. While Moose Skowron went after Doby, Enos Slaughter and Walt Dropo faced off. Country Slaughter was as tough as nails at 5'9½" and a half and 180 pounds. Dropo, a former football player, at 6'5" and 220 pounds was an intimidating force. While the other fights simmered down, everyone gravitated and watched the Slaughter/Dropo slugfest. It finally appeared as if the hostilities had ended, but Billy Martin asked Ditmar what Doby had said and then became enraged and pummeled Doby. After the fight ended, the forty-one year old Slaughter left the field with his uniform torn apart and his head down. The Yankee players were accustomed to trouble. Earlier in the season Mickey Mantle, Whitey Ford, Yogi Berra, Hank Bauer and Billy Martin went to the Copacabana nightclub to celebrate Martin's birthday and see Sammy Davis, Jr. perform. When one of the drunken customers asked Bauer what he thought of "Little Black Sambo," Bauer took exception to the racist remark. A fight ensued in the cloak room with everyone swinging. A bouncer hit a customer in the face with a blackjack.[9] The media was all over the incident and therefore George Weiss needed a scapegoat, and he quickly dispatched Billy Martin to play with the Kansas City Athletics. Two days after the fight with Chicago, on June 15, Martin was traded to the Athletics. Martin was a bad apple but so were several of the other players who constantly found trouble.

In July the Dodgers put together their best month yet, compiling a 20–10 record. After games on August 1, they were only a game and a half behind the first place Cardinals and Braves. Maglie tossed a shutout at the Polo Grounds on July 2 as the Dodgers defeated the Giants by a 6–0 score. Drysdale had tossed a shutout against the New Yorkers on the previous night. Maglie was in full control as he allowed four hits, walked none, hit a batter (Danny O'Connell) and struck out three to improve his record to 3–1. On the 7th the Phillies took a doubleheader from the Dodgers. Maglie was the hardluck loser in the opener as Brooklyn lost, 2–1. He allowed five hits, walked three and hit a batter (Harry Anderson). Duke Snider made an inexcusable mistake when he lined to the shortstop in the first inning and then began to walk to the dugout for he thought the ball was caught. The Phils quickly completed a 6–2–3 double play to the astonishment of the Connie Mack Stadium crowd.

Earlier in the season Roy Campanella and Cincinnati pitcher Raul Sanchez had exchanged heated words. On July 11 at Ebbets Field the two teams boiled over and a free-for-all brawl broke out. In the seventh inning, with the Reds up 4–3, Sanchez made Junior Gilliam take a seat with a pitch at his skull. Gilliam wanted a piece of Sanchez and employed an old Dodger trick. With the count 2 and 0, he bunted towards first but popped it up in foul territory. There was no play on the ball but Sanchez met the batter halfway up the line and they both started swinging. The benches cleared. Don Hoak, a former Dodger, was an ex-marine who had lied about his age at 16 to get into the service. He saw action at Saipan in the Pacific. He was a temperamental, cruel, vulgar, and hateful human being. Walter Alston once said, "If Hoak went out to get a bear, bare-handed, I gotta bet on Hoak." As Hoak came to the aid of his teammate, Charley Neal of the Dodgers sucker-punched him with a right hand to the jaw. Hoak picked himself up and looked for Neal but Gil Hodges, another tough ex-marine, restrained him from doing major damage. Meanwhile Sanchez and Gilliam were buried under a pile of ballplayers. Zimmer had been thrown out of the game earlier and he was joined by Hoak, Sanchez, Gilliam, and Neal. The Dodgers went on to win, 5–4, behind Duke Snider's two homers. In the clubhouse, Hoak vowed to impart revenge on Neal for the cheap blow. "I'll get him. I'll whip his hide and his wife won't know him when I get through."[10]

Gilliam was nailed by a pitch the following day as the Dodgers defeated the Reds, 3–1, in Jersey City. Bob Buhl and Sal Maglie hooked up for a pitchers' duel on July 14 at Ebbets Field. Gil Hodges hit a two-run homer in the ninth inning to give Brooklyn a 3–2 victory. Podres earned the win in relief (7–3). Maglie allowed one run on five hits, no walks, committed one error and fanned six in seven innings. The Dodgers took a doubleheader from the Cubs on the 19th and honored Gil Hodges with his own "night" between games. He was given a plethora of gifts including a Dodge convertible. Among those who sent telegrams were Vice President Richard Nixon, Admiral William (Bull) Halsey, and Mayor Robert Wagner of New York. Halsey said, "He is an outstanding ball player and also was a fine Marine and member of my team in the South Pacific."[11] Hodges was an intense, serious and relatively quiet man but did not hesitate to come to the aide of his teammates when needed. Roger Kahn once wrote, "Remembering Hodges against Sal Maglie or Allie Reynolds, I see a man hating to come to bat against such intimidating stuff and hating more the fact of his own fear."[12] Snider hit homers in both games of the doubleheader on Hodges' night. Koufax fanned eleven in seven innings of work in the opener but Labine (4–5) earned the win in relief. Maglie (4–2) won the second game despite giving up homers to Ernie Banks and Bob Speake during his six innings of work. On the 24th the Dodgers managed to get only three singles against Larry Jackson as the Cardinals won 3–0 in St. Louis. Maglie pitched well but lost his third game. He allowed two runs on seven hits and one walk in seven innings. Six days later the Barber won a 1–0 game in the opener of a doubleheader against Chicago. The Cubs took the second contest, 4–3. Maglie allowed six hits, walked one and fanned three in seven and one-third innings as Labine finished out the game in relief. Newcombe (9–9) lost the second game. It was his fourth straight ineffective outing.

Maglie's record fell to 5–4 when the Milwaukee Braves defeated Brooklyn by a 9–7 score on August 4 before 43,109 spectators at County Stadium. He allowed four runs on five hits in an inning and two-thirds. Eddie Mathews and Del Rice hit homers off him. The Dodgers dropped five games behind the front running Braves when they lost a 12–3 decision to the Giants on the 8th. Maglie (5–5) allowed four runs on three hits and two walks as he failed to survive the first inning, recording only two outs. The Barber got a no-decision in his next start, allowing two runs in only two and two-thirds innings as the starter. The Giants won the game, 4–2, at the Polo Grounds. Several fans ran onto the field with anti–Batista signs before order was restored and umpires Jocko Conlan and Vince Smith tore up the signs. Tommy Holmes wrote in the *New York Herald Tribune,* "Maybe a few American umpires would restore order in Latin-America."[13] The Dodgers defeated the Pirates, 2–1, in the first of two on the 18th. Pittsburgh took the second game, 8–6. Bob Friend surrendered only two hits to the Dodgers in the opener: a single to Gilliam that was soon followed by a Snider homer. Maglie threw a six-hitter to improve his record to 6–5. He walked two and fanned six.

The following day the board of directors for the New York Giants voted 8–1 to move the team to San Francisco for the 1958 season. The Giants initially had planned to move their club to Minneapolis where they owned the Minneapolis Millers franchise of the American Association. Then Walter O'Malley called and persuaded them to seek riches in California. The Dodgers would not announce their decision to move until October 9 during the World Series. The city of San Francisco gave the Giants a good offer and it was estimated that it would bring them annual profits of $200,000 to $300,000 once the new stadium was built. In the interim they would play their home games at Seals Stadium. Horace Stoneham, unlike most of the owners, truly loved the game and felt bad they were leaving. One reporter asked, "How do you feel about the kids in New York from whom you are taking the Giants?" While the Dodgers still drew over a million fans in '57, the Giants attracted only 653,903 to the Polo Grounds. Stoneham answered without hesitation, "I feel bad about the kids. I've seen lots of them at the Polo Grounds. But I haven't seen many of their fathers lately." Roger Angell, a Giants fan, would later write in *Holiday* magazine, "The end of the World came on Monday, August 19, 1957.... It was a funny way for the world to end: no trumpets, no clap of thunder, no fireball—just a brief announcement of the vote by a plump, pin-striped businessman named Horace C. Stoneham."[14]

The Dodgers were trying to stay in the race but slowly were losing ground and when they lost to Milwaukee on August 22, they were seven and a half games off the pace. Maglie, who had always performed his best in the big games, was showing his age as the season progressed. He allowed four runs on five hits and two walks in five innings as his record fell to 6–6. Hank Aaron belted a three run homer off him in the opening frame. Three days later, the old Barber was called in from the bullpen and struck out Ken Boyer with the bases loaded to preserve a 6–5 Dodgers victory over St. Louis at Ebbets Field. To many, Maglie's performance reminded them of when old Grover Cleveland Alexander stumbled in from the bullpen with the sacks full and struck out Tony Lazzeri to enable the

Cardinals to defeat the Yankees in the World Series. It was shaping up to be a year of reminiscing. Maglie was an old arm clinging to an old team and the Dodgers concluded he had outlived his usefulness and were trying to dump him. He was besieged with various ailments and the Dodgers put him through waivers hoping to send him to another club. It appeared as if O'Malley was waiting for a sizable monetary offer. Chuck Comiskey of the Chicago White Sox vowed that he would outbid the Yankees if they tried to obtain him. The White Sox and Yankees were fighting for the pennant when they were not fighting with each other. On August 31, the Dodgers played the last game they would ever play against the Giants in Ebbets Field. A ladies day/knothole gang crowd of more then 23,000 were on hand, of which 14,222 were cash customers. Maglie toed the slab and allowed five runs (two earned) on seven hits, two walks and one hit batter (Al Worthington) in five and two-thirds innings. Ed Roebuck (7–2) pitched scoreless relief to earn the win as Brooklyn won, 7–5.

Casey Stengel and his Yankees were in the fight of their life, trying to win his eighth pennant in his ninth year managing the team. The pitching staff was coming apart. They were led by Tom Sturdivant (16–6), Bob Turley (13–6), Bobby Shantz (11–5 and a league leading 2.45 ERA), Bob Grim (12–8, 19 saves) and Don Larsen (10–4). Whitey Ford developed a sore shoulder and fell to 11–5 with a 2.57 ERA. They would lead the league in ERA (3.00) but needed another pitcher for the stretch run. Offensively they boasted only two .300 hitters (Mantle and Skowron) but still led the junior circuit in hitting at .268. On September 1, Salvatore Anthony Maglie came full circle, being employed by all three New York baseball teams, and became a member of the New York Yankees. He was now a member of the aristocracy or at least that's how the Yankee brass thought of themselves. They gave the Dodgers a reported $25,000 and two minor leaguers for his services but because he was acquired after midnight of August 31, he was not eligible to play in the World Series. Maglie showed up ten minutes before a game and told Stengel, "Skipper, when do I work?" The old Professor was happy to have him and told reporters, "I hope he helps us win this pennant, if we win it. I didn't hire him to lose it. I've seen him pitch and I know he's a pro." Stengel added, "I don't know if he can go nine innings, but I do know that when he's in there he'll get quite a few batters out."[15] For years the Yankees had gone out and acquired themselves old veterans who were apparently washed up but had a little extra left in the tank. They included: Johnny Mize, Johnny Sain, Enos Slaughter, Ewell Blackwell, Jim Konstanty, Gerry Staley and Bobby Shantz. Now the Yankees turned to Maglie for some of his old magic. As for the Dodgers, they turned a sizable profit considering they had purchased Maglie from the

12. From Dodger Blue to Yankee Pinstripes

On September 1, 1957, Maglie was traded to the New York Yankees who were baseball's aristocracy. (George Brace photo)

Indians for $1,000. Buzzy Bavasi deliberately completed the deal after the deadline so he wouldn't come back and haunt them in the World Series.

On September 3, Maglie, wearing the famous Yankee pinstripes, relieved Tom Sturdivant in the ninth at Memorial Stadium in Baltimore and secured a 2–0 win. The Barber allowed one hit in one scoreless inning as the Yankees secured their tenth shutout of the year. He told reporters that if the White Sox were successful in acquiring him, he would have quit the game and retired to run his liquor store. His off the field interests also included an interest in a soft drink distributorship in Poughkeepsie and a small part in a TV drama. Maglie's salary that was estimated at $27,500 and the Dodgers' asking price may have scared the White Sox off. Sal declared, "It would have been Cleveland all over again; one club buying you just so you won't be able to pitch for another, without even thinking that it would probably mean the end of a man's career."[16]

Mickey Mantle went hitless in four at-bats and dropped his average to .370 as he was battling Ted Williams (.376) for the batting championship. The hustling Enos Slaughter was a defensive replacement late in the game. Slaughter made his major league debut in 1938 when the Gas House Gang was breaking up. Later he teamed up with Stan Musial and Terry Moore to make up a tremendous outfield for the Cardinals. He always hit the top step running and nobody played harder then he did. Even though he now played in the American League, Slaughter was the embodiment of the St. Louis Cardinals and still viewed himself as such. When he left the Cardinals he cried uncontrollably. He was constantly chattering and pumping players up which did not sit well with the stately Yankees. His teammates thought his hustling was pretentious and showed them up. Slaughter and Stengel grew an affinity towards one another and would often take turns lambasting the younger Yankees. With the Yankees, the old Cardinal was an invaluable pinch-hitter.

Maglie made his first start as a Yankee on September 6 against the Washington Senators before 22,467 spectators at Griffith Stadium. He pitched well until the seventh, shaving the Senators close, when he surrendered successive doubles and left the game. The Barber allowed three runs on seven hits, one walk, one hit batter (Milt Bolling) while fanning four. The Senators were destined for yet another last place finish (55–99) as Cookie Lavagetto replaced Charlie Dressen as manager early in the season. For years, people in the press box had joked, "Washington—first in war, first in peace, and last in the American League."[17] Against the Yankees they pulled out a 4–3 victory, their fifth win in their last six tries against them, as Jerry Coleman inexplicably dropped a routine throw in the ninth. Stengel was worried since the club was nursing several injuries and on the following day Mantle was hospitalized because of shin splints. He would finish second to Williams in the batting race. Mantle at .365, Williams at .388. When Mickey returned a couple of days later, they would win seven of their next eight. In his Yankee Stadium debut, Maglie tossed a 5–0 shutout against Cleveland, in the first of two on the 11th. The Barber was commanding, allowing only three hits on the day and fanned only one. He kept the opposition off balance with a slow changeup. Four days later Bob Turley and Maglie combined for a 5–3 win in the opener against the Kansas City Athletics and then Larsen tossed a 3–0 shutout in the second game. Maglie tossed two scoreless innings. The mighty Yankees were 19–3 against the Athletics during the season. They had formed a working friendship with them off the field that allowed them to acquire several of their good players in unbalanced trades. Sal got his second Yankee win on the 18th as Yogi Berra hit two homers to pace the New Yorkers to a 4–3 win over Detroit before 6,502 Yankee Stadium fans. Maglie allowed three runs (two earned) on ten hits and two walks in seven and one-third innings. Charley Maxwell hit his 24th homer of the season off him in the eighth inning. Four days later the Yankees defeated the Red Sox, 5–1, before a large Yankee Stadium crowd of 34,186. Maglie successfully got the two batters out which he faced in the game.

September 29 was a somber, gloomy day at the Polo Grounds. Sal Maglie was there, not to wear the uniform of the white, black, and gold Giants but to watch the last game the New York Giants would ever play below Coogan's Bluff. A hearty crowd of 11,606 souls showed up to watch them take on the Pittsburgh Pirates. Among those former Giants who were in attendance included Jack Doyle, Red Murray, George Burns, Hooks Wiltse, George Davis, Carl Hubbell, Billy Jurges, Monte Irvin, Willard Marshall, Sid Gordon, Buddy Kerr, and Babe Young. The assemblage sat with Mrs. John McGraw. Bobby Thomson and Whitey Lockman had recently returned to the club and they were in the starting lineup. As was Dusty Rhodes, Willie Mays, Wes Westrum, Don Mueller while Johnny Antonelli toed the slab. Very few, if any, teams had a rich history comparable to the Giants. Since entering the National League in 1883 they had won 17 pennants. Bill Rigney's 1957 Giants were entrenched in sixth place and going nowhere fast. As Willie Mays stepped into the box with one out in the ninth, the crowd urged him on with a tremendous ovation. He stepped out of the box and graciously tipped his cap in acknowledging their gesture. Then he bounced out to short. Rhodes was the last batter, and with the count at 3 and 2, he also bounced out to Dick Groat at short. The Pirates had won, 9–1, and the clock stood at 4:35 P.M. The fans rushed the field and tore the place apart. Roger Angell later wrote, "I didn't feel anything. Nothing at all. I guess I just couldn't believe it. But it's true, all right. The flags are down, the lights in the temple are out, and the Harlem River flows lonely to the seas."[18]

The Brooklyn Dodgers played their last game at Ebbets Field on September 24 and beat the Pirates, 2–0, before only 6,702 fans. Carl Furillo would later say, "O'Malley put the buck in front of everything else. The players thought only of baseball. We thought we'd never move. It seemed the whole team belonged to Brooklyn."[19] Arthur Daley of the *New York Times* was among those who criticized the two owners for moving West. He wrote, "Baseball is a sport, eh? It may be for Tom Yawkey of the Red Sox, Phil Wrigley of the Cubs, and one or two others. But the crass commercialism of O'Malley and Horace Stoneham of the Giants presents the disillusioning fact that it's big business, just another way to make a buck."[20]

Maglie was 6–6 for the Dodgers in '57 in 19 games and was 2–0 for the Yankees in 6 games. His combined 8–6 mark brought him a 2.69 ERA. He pitched 127.1 innings, allowed 116 hits, walked 33 and struck out 59. He pitched two shutouts on the year and plunked five batters. The Barber had pitched well for the Yankees down the stretch but could not participate in the World Series. Stengel's club had coasted to the pennant with a 98–56 record and were eight games in front of the second place Chicago White Sox. The Milwaukee Braves defeated the Yankees for the world championship in seven games and produced a dent into their perceived superiority.

13

THE END IS NEAR

Every ballplayer has to face that moment in his career when he realizes that he is through and can no longer hit major league pitching or get major league hitters out. Players react in different ways when they see the writing on the wall. It is a gut wrenching feeling to leave the game in which you have played since you were a kid. Some players retire gracefully such as Joe DiMaggio or Al Rosen. Others try to milk every last ounce of strength from their old bodies and play till the game has passed them by. Baseball after all, is a game dominated by youth, and one can fool father time for only so long before his body gives out. Monte Kennedy was one ballplayer who refused to believe he was washed up and went down to the minors where bush league hitters knocked him around. One day he declared in the dugout, "Now I know it. My arm's gone. I'm through!" When Enos Slaughter retired they had to tear the uniform off him; his last season (1959) he batted only .171 in 117 at-bats. There are different signs that indicate a player is fading but it is not an exact science. They include decline in performance, arm problems, injuries, lack of desire, or the legs giving out. Jackie Robinson stated, "I think a ballplayer knows when he is through by the difference he feels in his performance. True, it may be only a small difference to the fan watching in the stands, but to the player himself it's like the difference between night and day."[1] The love of the game sometimes fades away yet many players hang on to receive the healthy paycheck they command as a big leaguer. Ted Williams was 38 years old in

1957 and told reporters, "I'm playing because I need the money. If I didn't need it, I would have quit two years ago."² In 1956 Duke Snider was criticized for collaborating on an article with Roger Kahn stating that he played the game for the money, yet many ballplayers felt the same way.

After a great big league career, Sal Maglie could see the handwriting on the wall. On April 26 he would turn forty-one years old. Murry Dickson was the only big league hurler older than him. The old Barber wanted to become the first hurler to pitch in the World Series with all three New York teams and if he stayed on the Yankees the entire season he probably would get his chance to accomplish that goal. He would try to milk every inning he possibly could out of his tired right arm. When a reporter asked him when he would know he was through, Maglie responded, "I can't speak for anybody else, but in my own particular case, I think my arm will outlast my legs. My legs will tell me."³ Birdie Tebbetts, manager of the Cincinnati Reds, stated "There is no infallible way of judging when a ballplayer is through. If you doubt that, take a look at Sal Maglie. Do you think such good managers as Leo Durocher and Al Lopez made mistakes when they let Maglie go? Baloney! Both Durocher and Lopez are sound managers and nothing much escapes them. They let Maglie go because he could no longer help either one of them. Everybody thought Maglie was all done. But he proved he wasn't with Brooklyn. That's why I say there is no sure sign."⁴ Sometimes a change in atmosphere, and an opportunity to play on a new team will help an old player. Lefty Gomez once left a game because of shoulder problems, and jokingly stated, "I knew I was all done the day I threw a fastball and then had to chase after it to help push it up to home plate."⁵

When the conditioning program opened for the pitchers on February 22, Casey Stengel was not happy to find six of his pitchers missing. Bob Turley, Johnny Kucks, and Bob Grim were holdouts. Tom Sturdivant was unsigned but on his way to camp from Oklahoma while Tommy Byrne (also unsigned) and Maglie were still at home. Maglie had already signed but his business in Niagara Falls would hold him up for a few days. Stengel was pleased to see Don Larsen, who had been working out in San Diego a few weeks before camp, and appeared to be in shape. The Yankees skipper did not appear worried the first day as he took his players onto Miller Huggins Field in St. Petersburg, Florida, to begin spring training. However, things would change quickly as the Yankees compiled an unimpressive 14–16 spring training record. Casey would consume an immoderate amount of alcohol when he drank, walking the beaches until the wee hours of the morning, cogitating the poor performances from his pitchers. If the pitching worried him, at least he could find comfort in the fact that the offense was potent. The infielders included Bill (Moose) Skowron, Gil McDougald, Bobby Richardson, Tony Kubek, Andy Carey, and Jerry Lumpe. Mickey Mantle, Elston Howard, Harry Simpson, Enos Slaughter, Hank Bauer, and Norm Siebern were the outfielders. Yogi Berra was behind the plate and Howard backed him up.

The Yankees were shut out for the third time in their first six games when they dropped a 1–0 decision to the Boston Red Sox on March 13 in Sarasota. They had now been shut out more times then they had in the entire 154 game, 1957 season. Maglie pitched three scoreless innings in relief of Zack Monroe. He allowed three hits. Double plays got him out of the trouble in the fifth and sixth innings. The Barber was scheduled to pitch against the Cardinals on the 19th at Al Lang Field but it rained. He sat in the clubhouse and declared, "How can they do it? They're selling the stuff cheaper than I can buy it."[6] He was referring to liquor prices as he continuously worried about his store and examined the competition. The Barber faced Sandy Koufax on the 22nd as the newly coined Los Angeles Dodgers pulled out a 7–6 win in twelve innings in Miami. The Dodgers scored three runs off Maglie in the fourth inning. After losing four of their last five, the Yankees defeated the Athletics, 5–4, on the 27th in St. Petersburg. Maglie earned the win in relief of Johnny Kucks as he allowed three runs (one earned) on five hits in three innings of work. Bill Skowron hit two homers and drove in eight to lead the Yankees to a 15–11 win over the White Sox on April 1 in Tampa. Maglie started but was hammered. He allowed six runs on six hits and one walk in two innings. Skowron had a terrific spring and led the team with 11 homers and over 30 runs driven in. As the Yankees barnstormed north with the Phillies, a crowd of 10,059 fans showed up at Ernie Shore Field in Winston-Salem, North Carolina, and saw the Yankees drop a 12–8 decision. Maglie was knocked around as he survived six shaky innings as the starter. He allowed eight runs on eleven hits, five walks, while striking out five. Harry Anderson and Rip Repulski hit homers off him. Maglie's spring numbers were disheartening. In 18 innings, he had allowed 20 runs (18 of them earned) and 28 hits.

As the curtain rose on the 1958 season, New York city was without a National League club for the first time since 1882. A city that was accustomed to housing three tradition filled baseball teams could only find comfort by watching the majestic New York Yankees. Stengel's club got off to a tremendous start as they won seven of their first eight games while their main competition, Boston and Chicago, stumbled out of the gate. On May 26, their record stood at 25–6. At the All Star break they were 48–25, eleven games in front of the second place teams: Kansas City and Boston. They won the pennant going away with a 92–62 record; ten games ahead of the second place White Sox. *Life* magazine declared that "success had taken the suspense out of the race and made cheering for the Yankees somewhat like cheering for U.S. Steel."[7]

The reason for the Yankees' great start was attributed to the pitching. Ford, Shantz, Kucks, Larsen, Turley and a rookie named Ryne Duren all pitched well. Therefore, Stengel did not need to call on the forty-one year old Barber to pitch many games and he languished on the bench. Bob Turley, a highly intelligent, religious man, put it all together in '58 and became the best hurler in the junior circuit, leading the league in wins (21), winning percentage (.750, 21–7 record), and complete games (19). With the Yankees' five man rotation he only started 31 games. Turley was a proficient sign stealer and his inability to put together a great season in the past prompted the caustic Casey Stengel to say, "Look at him. He don't smoke, he don't drink, he don't chase women, and he don't win."[8] Turley had a great fastball but did not throw inside and batters took a good toehold in the box. Whitey Ford was 14–7 and led the league with a 2.01 ERA. Ryne Duren was a nice surprise, compiling a 6–4 record with 20 saves and a 2.02 ERA. He was notoriously wild and supposedly beaned a batter in the on-deck circle in the minors. He wore thick glasses and would often throw a warmup pitch to the screen to get the hitter thinking about his survival. Batters feared he couldn't see the plate and the fact that he could throw a 100-mile per hour fastball with little control sickened them. Stengel once said, "I would not admire hitting against Duren, because if he ever hit you in the head you might be in the past tense."[9] Detroit Tigers pitcher Paul Foytack skulled him on July 24, and Duren fell to the ground. He was a stricken figure, lifeless, with blood streaming from his face as they took him off the field on a stretcher on his way to the hospital. Yet Duren would be back. He was tough, and had once picked a fight with five men while playing in the bushes, been beaten to a pulp, and taken to jail. Offensively the Yankees led the league in batting (.268) and homers (164). Stengel no longer had patience for young players and constantly ridiculed them. He pushed his team hard down the stretch, as they became lackadaisical. In August they were 15–16 and in September 12–12, yet they coasted to the pennant. They defeated the Braves in the World Series and Stengel won his seventh world championship. Milwaukee won three of the first four games but the Yankees pulled themselves together and stormed back. Stengel declared, "We showed 'em that we were still the Yankees."[10]

With the cut down date quickly approaching when major league clubs had to cut their roster to 25 players, the Yankees entertained the Milwaukee Braves at Yankee Stadium on May 12 in an exhibition game. The Yankees' park was the first to be called a "Stadium" when it opened in 1923 and was christened with a game-winning homer by Babe Ruth. The new title was used to signify its urban setting. Steven A. Riess wrote that "The rustic titles and the layouts of earlier parks were rural metaphors, which had reinforced the agrarian ideology of baseball."[11] Yankee Stadium became known as "The House That Ruth Built," and the very structure epitomized the imposing, aristocratic, and mythological image of the team. An estimated crowd of 15,000 showed up for the exhibition game with the Braves with some of the proceeds going to charity. The Jimmy Fund for children's cancer research was among those that benefited. Stengel was not going to waste one of his regular pitchers in this game so he called on Maglie. If he pitched poorly there was a legitimate possibility he would be cut from the team. He hadn't pitched in over a month, since April 9 when he was hammered by the Phillies. Just as it looked like his career might end, he rose to the occasion and gave Stengel seven strong innings. He allowed two runs on four hits and three walks while fanning three to reassure his spot on the roster. The Barber shaved them close and he nailed Felix Mantilla with a pitch in the game. He used every pitch he knew to keep the Braves off balance. Milwaukee pulled out a 4–3 win as Kucks took the loss.

Despite the fact that the Yankees were the only team in the city, their attendance had not gone up early in the season. Maglie made his first appearance of the regular season on May 18 at Griffith Stadium before 27,704 spectators, including Vice President Richard Nixon. The forty-one year old Barber pitched eight strong innings for the victory as the Yankees won 5–2 in the opener of a doubleheader. He allowed two runs on seven hits and one walk while fanning two. Duren pitched the final inning. Sal hit his second major league homer, a three run shot, off Pedro Ramos in the fourth. The switch-hitting Mantle had opened the scoring with a "wrong field" homer to left. The juggernaut Yankees won the second game as well, and had won six in a row and ten of their last eleven. One writer called the rest of the league a "seven club second division."[12] On the 24th Maglie pitched well against the cellar dwelling Detroit Tigers but lost a 3–2 decision at Briggs Stadium as the Yankees' ten game winning streak was snapped. In the second inning he made a diving putout at first base which left him badly shaken but he continued. He allowed three runs on eight hits, four walks, while striking out three. Harvey Kuenn hit a homer off him. After winning seven games in a row to start the season, Bob Turley lost his first against Kansas City on May 27. The following night, the Athletics won again, 4–3. Maglie gave up a hit and a walk in two scoreless innings of work. Mantle, who was in a bad slump to start the year and was battling a shoulder injury, went hitless. He had hit only four homers thus far.

The Yankees were back at the Stadium on May 30 but lost a doubleheader to the Senators before 39,742 fans. Maglie was the fifth Yankee pitcher in the opener as they lost, 13–8. He allowed two runs on three hits in an inning and a third. Ken Aspromonte hit a homer off him. The Yankees and the White Sox split a doubleheader on June 5. New York won the opener, 12–5, which included plenty of beanballs. After many productive years with the Senators and Indians, Early Wynn pitched against New York for the first time in a White Sox uniform. In the second inning he nailed Yankee third baseman Jerry Lumpe on his protective helmet. Lumpe fell to the ground with a sickening thud. The fiberglass material on the right side of his helmet had cracked with the impact of the blow. Lumpe was shaken but not injured, for the helmet saved him from serious injury. Don Larsen nailed Jim Landis with a pitch in the game. The White Sox rallied to win the nightcap, 3–2. Maglie gave up two hits and one walk for one run in one inning of relief.

In 1958 a rule was implemented to discourage beanballs by fining a pitcher $50 if he was simply warned by an umpire for throwing at a batter. There were many critics of the rule including Casey Stengel. The Old Professor said, "I not only think it won't work, but I think it's all one huge joke. In fact, the umpires are going to be more reluctant to threaten beanballers because they won't want to be blamed for costing the pitcher 50 bucks." The rule seemed arbitrary and reputed beanballers such as Maglie and Wynn were probably more inclined to get fined merely on reputation. Stengel went on to explain how Cleveland rookie Gary Bell came into a game and incessantly threw at the heads of his batters, mainly because of his wildness. Stengel concluded, "After all, how much is the Cleveland club paying this kid anyway? If he gets fined $50, he probably has to give the league all his salary. They wouldn't want to do that. The boy shouldn't play for nothing, you know."[13] The Yankee skipper had a way with words and after the All-Star break he gave a grand performance of convoluted speech in front to the Senate Subcommittee on Antitrust and Monopoly.

On June 9, Johnny Kucks lost two ballgames as the Cleveland Indians won a doubleheader by scores of 14–1 and 5–4 before 40,903 Yankee Stadium spectators. Maglie was ineffective as the starter in the second game; he allowed four runs on five hits and two walks in three innings. Knuckleballer Hoyt Wilhelm, the former Giant, closed out the second game for Cleveland. Minnie Minoso, who had returned to the Indians in '58 after several years with the White Sox, collected three hits in the second game. He was a dark, black man, born in Havana, Cuba, under the name Saturnino Orestes Armas Minoso y Arrieta in 1922. Like many kids in Cuba he grew up idolizing Martin Dihigo but unlike Dihigo he got the opportunity to play in the big show but found it anything but idyllic. Minoso played the game in the gutsy style of Pete Reiser, Pepper Martin, and Pete Rose. Yet because he was black, his flashy style was frowned upon and he bore the racial taunts, beanballs, and threats just like Jackie Robinson had done in the National League. Jimmy Dykes, manager of the Philadelphia Athletics, proved to be his most vicious attacker. When Minoso stepped into the on deck circle, Dykes put a black dog on the dugout steps. Historian Peter Bjarkman wrote concerning Dykes that "It was treatment paralleling that meted out in the City of Brotherly Love against Robinson by Phillies skipper Ben Chapman only a handful of seasons earlier."[14] From 1951 to 1961, Minoso led the junior circuit in being hit by pitches, ten out of those eleven years. Minoso was fearless and exacerbated the danger he faced by crowding the plate. In 1955 he failed to lead the league because he missed time when Yankee Bob Grim beaned him and fractured his skull. In 1956, he set a new American League record by getting hit by a pitched ball 23 times. The treatment Minoso received was disturbing, yet indicative of the brutal way in which the game was played.

On June 12, the Yankees won a 3–2 decision at the Stadium after losing the afternoon game to Kansas City, 4–1. Ryne Duren closed out the nightcap in controversial style. He threw beanballs at the head of Vic Power and Joe DeMaestri making them hit the dirt. Home plate umpire Joe Paparella apparently warned Duren to cease throwing beanballs but in a postgame interview he said he had merely advised the pitcher to dry his hands before throwing the ball. Ralph Houk, the Yankees' first base coach, was kicked out of the game when he argued with first base umpire Ed Hurley for he thought his pitcher was being unfairly bothered. Duren faced five batters and fanned four of them. In twenty five and two-thirds innings on the season he had struck out forty batters. Forty-one year old knuckleballer, Murry Dickson, took the loss for Kansas City. Whitey Ford plunked him with a pitch earlier in the game. Maglie pitched an inning of scoreless relief in the opener. He gave up one hit and struck out one batter. The regal New York Yankees were accustomed to uniformity and consistency and could no longer tolerate the uncertainty and the erratic pitching of Sal Maglie. Casey Stengel called Maglie into his office and said, "Sal, we're sending you to St. Louis."[15] Thus on June 14, Maglie's dream of playing for all three New York teams in the World Series ended when the Cardinals bought him for a waiver price. Fred Hutchinson was the Cardinals manager for most of the season, excluding ten games at the very end when they had collapsed and Stan Hack took over. The pitching staff was relatively weak, led by "Toothpick" Sam Jones (14–13), Larry Jackson

(13–13), Vinegar Bend Mizell (10–14), and Jim Brosnan (8–4). The Cardinals finished in sixth place (72–82) after competing for much of the first half. In May, that St. Louis icon, Stan Musial got his 3,000th hit. At the age of 37, he batted .337 for the year with 17 homers and 62 RBIs. He became the first National Leaguer to command a $100,000 contract in 1958 and it was well deserved. St. Louis was a great baseball city, and the Cardinals a respected organization, but they were in a state of transformation and needed a change to bring them a winner. Bing Devine, who had recently taken over as general manager when Frank Lane wore out his welcome, would slowly rebuild the Cardinals, which would culminate with a world championship in 1964.

Sal Maglie reported to the Cardinals ready to do his best and hopefully help them win a pennant. The Barber once said, "It didn't matter who I pitched for. I want to be remembered as someone who tried to win all the time, as someone who tried to keep his team in the ball game."[16] He was back in the National League where he was more familiar with the players. Hutchinson immediately placed Maglie in the starting rotation. On June 22 he pitched seven strong innings to lead his new team to a 2–1 win over Milwaukee. It was the second straight day on which the Cardinals had defeated the Braves by a 2–1 score. Maglie allowed one run on five hits and five walks while fanning one. It looked like the acquisition of Maglie might pay off greatly for St. Louis, when he pitched a complete game, six days later before 11,010 customers at Connie Mack Stadium. He allowed one run on five hits and three walks while fanning two. St. Louis rookie Gene Green hit a grand slam to lead the way in an 8–1 triumph. The Phillies turned a triple play in this game. Maglie was 2–0 with the Cardinals and 3–1 for the season but as fate would have it, that game in St. Louis was his last big league victory.

When the Cardinals traveled out West, Maglie got his first opportunity to witness the institutions known as the Los Angeles Dodgers and the San Francisco Giants. Major league baseball was now a coast to coast venture and Sal wasn't particularly pleased with the long plane trip he had to take to get there. While a new stadium was built, the Dodgers played their home games in the expansive Los Angeles Coliseum. The dimensions were ridiculously awkward: 440 feet down the line in right but only 251 feet down the left field line. A 42-foot high fence was erected in left field but many feared Babe Ruth's sacrosanct home run record would be threatened by the short distance. The place became known as "O'Malley's Chinese Theater" and "The House that Charlie Chan Built," because all the "Chinese home runs" hit to left field.[17] The Chinese population in the area was not amused by such titles. The new Dodger park, aptly named Dodger

Maglie with St. Louis, where he finished his career. (George Brace photo)

Stadium, would be built in Chavez Ravine which was the home of many indigent families and marked as an area of low cost housing. The city and Walter O'Malley were in a struggle to cajole these families to leave which sometimes required a high monetary compensation. The borough of Brooklyn felt betrayed and many Dodger fans ceased to support the team out West. Writer Joe Flaherty once wrote, "I think Hemingway said it, that if you live long enough, everything you love will be sullied, and it was

O'Malley who was the first one who really put the shit into the game, the one who showed everyone that loyalty means nothing."[18] On the field the Dodgers collapsed. They were wilting away in last place when the Cardinals visited them and would finish the season in seventh place (71–83) only a few games ahead of the cellar-dwelling Phillies. Financially the move was a windfall for O'Malley as fans flocked to the Coliseum. Over 66,000 spectators showed up on July 3 and watched the Dodgers split a doubleheader with St. Louis. The Cardinals won the opener, 4–2, before losing the nightcap by a 3–2 score. Maglie hooked up with Johnny Podres in a pitchers' duel in the nightcap. He went the distance (eight innings) gave up three runs (two earned) on seven hits, three walks while striking out four. Charlie Neal and Dick Gray hit homers off him. After winning two of three in Los Angeles, the Cardinals took two games in San Francisco. Until the new park was built the Giants played their home games in Seals Stadium which had a seating capacity of only 23,900. Willie Mays felt constrained in the new park; its center field dimensions felt claustrophobic compared to the expansive Polo Grounds. In addition the San Francisco fans adopted Orlando Cepeda as their favorite son, not Mays. The Giants drew 1.3 million fans to the small park, almost twice as many as they drew in the Polo Grounds the previous year.

On July 10, the Phillies overtook the Cardinals for third place when they defeated St. Louis by a 13–3 score at Busch Stadium. Maglie took the loss as the starter as he allowed five runs on four hits and six walks in three and two-thirds innings. Most disturbing of all was that his control failed him. In the past he was able to get by with poor stuff and good control but once the control left him he was a sitting duck. St. Louis was still in the race, only three games behind the front running Braves. Milwaukee hammered Maglie five days later as they won by a 4–1 score. Sal lasted five innings, gave up four runs on five hits and three walks as his record fell to 2–3 with St. Louis. Hank Aaron hit two homers off him while Wes Covington hit one. The Barber's next start came eighteen days later. His wife Kay went into the hospital to have an operation and Maglie remained at her bedside for ten days. Fred Hutchinson told his pitcher in the middle of a pennant race, "Sal, go on home. Your family comes first."[19] When he returned, the club fell apart. The Pirates swept the Cardinals in three games at the beginning of August and were leading a fourth game before it was suspended because of a Pennsylvania Sunday curfew law. In the three of a completed games and in the suspended game the Cardinals failed to score a single run. On August 3, in his first game back, Maglie lost a tough 2–0 decision. He allowed two runs on four hits (no walks) in six innings. The time off had apparently helped the Barber. Six days later he pitched seven strong innings against the Cubs at Wrigley Field. They touched him for two runs on four hits and one walk. Phil Paine was the winner in relief when Curt Flood hit a ninth inning homer to give the Cardinals a 3–2 victory. The Cubs' Alvin Dark was nailed twice in the game. Maglie hit him once. The left side of the Cubs infield had a disastrous day. Dark committed three errors at third base while Ernie Banks booted two balls at short.

When the Cardinals woke up on the morning of August 15 they were eleven games out of first place and sinking fast. Then they went out and dropped a twi-night doubleheader to the Dodgers in Los Angeles by scores of 4–3 and 5–3. Maglie took the loss in the second game, lasting only four innings in which he allowed five runs on five hits, one walk, and one hit batter (Charlie Neal). He tried to compensate for his lack of stuff by throwing the high heater and moving the ball around but the Dodgers got the best of him. Sinister Sal nailed his 44th and final batter of his major league career. That is a high number for a control pitcher. He used the baseball as a psychological weapon to intimidate the hitter and made them put their own survival ahead of hitting a baseball. Some of the players he nicked, others he plunked in the ribs or shoulder while others he skulled. The hitters came to the plate with their knees trembling, ready to bail out of the box at a moment's notice, often swinging with their foot in the bucket. If it wasn't for this fact, he would have hit a lot more batters than he did. Ballplayers could only thank the lord that he was not given the ability to throw a Walter Johnson fastball, because if he had he would have surely killed someone. Roy Campanella would say, "Maglie's pitching tomorrow; bring your football helmets."[20] The Barber pitched as if his goal was to separate the batter's head from his shoulders. Managers such as Leo Durocher and Dolf Luque encouraged their pitchers to throw at the batter's skull. Pitching inside was an accepted part of the game. Maglie declared, "Besides knocking people down, I look like a fellow who would knock people down. They say I look sinister, and I guess I do with my dark beard, the whites of my eyes, the stare and scowl on my face."[21] He was an intimidator, an enforcer, and instilled fear into the batter. Sal did anything he could to gain the edge and get the batter out. Maglie was a headhunter, although he did not intentionally try to maim the batter. During the '50s several pitchers consistently threw at opposing batters' heads and Maglie needed to do so to be successful.

Maglie started on August 23 against Philadelphia at Busch Stadium but recorded only one out as the Phillies teed off on him. He took the loss, his sixth of the year with St. Louis, as he allowed three runs on three hits and one walk. Wally Post hit a homer off him. Fred Hutchinson, showing incredible patience, gave Maglie one more chance to start on August 31 before 16,335 spectators at Busch Stadium. This time he lasted only three innings as the Cubs hit three homers to win, 8–5. Sal got a no-decision, allowing five runs (two earned) on four hits and two walks. He committed one error in the field and struck out one. It was the final game he pitched all season, as he watched the rest of the games from the bench. In seven games with the Yankees he compiled a 1–1 record. With St. Louis he was 2–6 in ten games. His aggregate 3–7 mark included a high 4.72 ERA. He pitched 76.1 innings, gave up 73 hits, walked 34 and struck out 28. Sal plunked two batters on the year. It was by far the worst season of his career and a sign that the end was near.

After years of fielding a mediocre baseball team in St. Louis, Gussie Busch decided to make wholesale changes. No longer would he rely on advice by management employees from the brewery. He wanted to surround himself with intelligent baseball men that could be trusted. In September it was announced that Solly Hemus would become the new manager for the '59 season. Birdie Tebbetts, who had recently left his position as manager of the Cincinnati Reds, was offered a job in the front office. On the field, Hemus was a mediocre middle infielder. He had a loud mouth and the uncanny ability to stop pitched balls. In 1952 (hit 20 times) and 1953 (12) he led the senior circuit in being hit by pitches. In 1958 he tied for the lead, being hit 8 times. He broke in with the Cardinals in 1949 and spent most of his career there. From 1956 to 1958 he played with the Phillies. When he was traded to Philadelphia in May of '56 he wrote Gussie Busch a letter thanking him for the way in which he was treated by the organization. He proved incompetent during his two and a half years as manager of the Cardinals. To compensate for his poor managerial judgment he would constantly argue with umpires and excessively cheer on his players. Hemus treated the black players on the team with hostility and had no problems using the words "black bastard" and "nigger" in their presence.[22] Many of the whites objected to this bigoted language such as Stan Musial, Ken Boyer, and the highly educated Jim Brosnan. Hemus mistreated the aging Stan Musial and was probably the only manager who failed to get along with the popular superstar. When Hemus was named manager, it was reported that Sal Maglie was being considered as the pitching coach. Johnny Keane and Harry Walker had already been named as coaches.

Maglie showed up for spring training at St. Petersburg believing he could still pitch and get batters out. He prepared for the season in a slow, methodical manner, but the results were not impressive. In his only exhibition game, he served up a grand slam to Philadelphia's Dave Philley. During the winter an article under Bill Rigney's name suggested that

Maglie threw a spitter. The Barber agreed that his curve broke like a spitter but denied the accusation. "I never lie. I couldn't throw a spitter. I use too much resin." When the reporter asked him if he had any message for Rigney, he joked, "Yes, tell him I'm working on my spitter."[23] If he planned to get batters out anymore, some manipulating of the baseball certainly would not hurt. St. Louis was rebuilding and had no room on their roster for a pitcher who would soon turn forty-two years old. Instead it was time for young hurlers such as Ernie Broglio, Gary Blaylock, Marshall Bridges, and Bob Gibson to make their major league debut. Solly Hemus approached Maglie one day and said, "We're letting you go, but we want you to work in the higher minors with our pitchers."[24] The Barber felt he could still win and earn the relatively high salary that he commanded. Like many ballplayers, Maglie found it difficult to accept the harsh reality that his career was over. Everyone likes to exit on their own terms, gracefully, and it's difficult when someone shows you the door. He waited three weeks before he gave the Cardinals an answer, and then was resigned to accept his fate. As opening day was quickly approaching, the career of Salvatore Anthony Maglie officially ended on April 10 with his release.

To Maglie's credit he hung up his spikes at the right time. He could have tried to hang on with some second division team until he was a mere shell of himself and till they had to rip the uniform off him. Or he could have gone to the bushes and hoped some big league team picked him up. The minor league players would initially view him with awe but that would wear off and they'd realize he was just some disgruntled old ballplayer past his prime. Many players milk every last inning out of their bodies until they are an embarrassment to themselves and their team. Maglie did not — possibly he hung on one year too long, but he left when the era had ended. He left when the time was right. It didn't seem the same anymore with the Dodgers in Los Angeles and the Giants in San Francisco. Baseball had changed so much since he made his debut in 1945, the last year of World War II. Then came the blacklist when he jumped to Mexico. He experienced the dangerous conditions, the rabid fans, the rickety ballparks, and the unfamiliar food in Cuba and Mexico. Then he played in the biting cold in Canada before the Giants were forced to take him back. Stoneham wanted to get rid of him, but he got a break, proved he could pitch, and stuck around. If he was not given a chance, Maglie admitted in later years that he would have asked for a trade. This was something ballplayers did not do during the times, with the reserve clause firmly entrenched, and it would have probably ended his career. He was already thirty-three years old when he returned to the Giants in 1950. From 1950 through 1952 he was one of the best pitchers in the game. Then came the crippling injuries, but he pitched in pain and persevered. Again his career looked like it was over in '56 when he was sent to Cleveland but then the Dodgers saved him. His career ended inauspiciously with the Yankees and Cardinals. His final numbers won't get him to Cooperstown, nor should they, but they were impressive nonetheless. In ten major league seasons he compiled a 119–62 record for a 3.15 ERA and an impressive .657 winning percentage. He pitched in 303 games, started 232 of them and threw 93 complete games. Sal pitched 1,723 innings, allowed 1,591 hits, 562 walks and struck out 862. He tossed 25 shutouts, compiled a .135 batting average (2 homers) and nailed 44 hitters on the mound. In the World Series he pitched better then his 1–2 record may indicate and had an impressive 3.41 ERA. Some speculate as to what kind of numbers he would have compiled if he had not lost four years for jumping to Mexico and been put on the blacklist. However it's best to accept the reality of what happened; certainly Bob Feller and Ted Williams' final numbers would have been through the roof if they had not missed time to the service. They had no regrets for they served their country and Maglie had no regrets for he learned how to pitch under Luque.

Maglie became a scout and minor league instructor for the Cardinals. He said he drove 27,000 miles in three and a half months. He helped young pitchers such as Marshall Bridges, Ray Sadecki, and Bob Miller. Another pitcher that he took an interest in, beginning at spring training, was a young right-hander with a crackling fastball named Bob Gibson. Gibson spent much of the year with the Omaha Cardinals in the American Association and went 3–5 with a 3.33 ERA in 13 games with the big club. He was learning to throw a slider to complement his fastball and curve. Just like Luque had imparted his knowledge on Maglie, the Barber did the same thing with Gibson and other young pitchers. Solly Hemus would constantly insult the black players and treat them as if they didn't have a thought in their head. This included the college educated Gibson. As they reviewed hitters before a series, Hemus would say, "You don't have to listen to this, Gibson. You just try to get the ball over the plate."[25] It wasn't until Johnny Keane became manager that Gibson would blossom into a great hurler. His confidence was shattered during the Hemus years and his inability to consistently throw strikes did not help any. What Maglie and Gibson had in common was a willingness to throw inside and control the inside edge of the plate. Gibson stated, "I actually used about nine pitches—two different fastballs, two sliders, a curve, change-up, knockdown, brushback, and hit-batsman."[26] He didn't fraternize with the opposition and remained an enigma to the hitters. In his autobiography with Lonnie Wheeler he systematically breaks down the art of throwing inside. He wrote, "The knockdown is basically a brushback pitch with an attitude, the difference being that on a knockdown the batter is not supposed to be on his feet when the ball reaches the catcher's mitt. It also serves a different purpose. Whereas the brushback is a strategic device, the knockdown is a statement of retaliation. I consider retaliation to be the only necessary and indisputably valid reason for knocking a batter down, although I confess to having expanded its application to include intimidation."[27] Gibson would help carry the torch of throwing inside into the next decade. He wasn't a headhunter in the true sense of the word as Maglie and Drysdale were, but he did skull batters in his career. Richie Ashburn once said, "Gibson and I share the same loyalties to the state of Nebraska, and we had nothing against each other, but when the game started I always had the feeling I was standing there as the Grand Dragon of the Ku Klux Klan."[28] Gibson was a ferocious competitor and dominated the game like few did. He scowled at the hitter, barked at his catcher, and pitched his game. Maglie was proud of his pupil.

During that final spring training in St. Petersburg, Red Smith wrote this laudatory piece in the *New York Herald Tribune*:

> Sal Maglie looks like a Roman friar in one of those orders that specialize in jumping on grapes or maybe illuminating the parchment pages of sacred writings. There is an Old Testament cast to the elongated visage with the deep and mournful eyes. The hair, thinning a trifle more noticeably with each passing year, makes way now for a monk's gleaming tonsure behind the two dark tufts which top the lofty brow.
>
> The speech is soft and mild, the demeanor is that of a brooding scholastic, until he gets a baseball in his paw and plants his spikes against the pitcher's rubber. Then the gentle ecclesiastic vanishes. What the batter sees is a tall figure of menace, expressionless as an executioner, who throws too close.
>
> According to the book, Sal is six weeks short of his 42nd birthday. For two hours he had been out with the youngsters sweating in the sun. The nude spot on his skull glistened with perspiration. A visitor in the Cardinals club house nudged a companion.
>
> "Look at him. He was a professional pitcher before some of the kids in here were born. There are guys here who weren't two years old when he went on the voluntarily retired list."[29]

14

THE OLD WARRIOR
FADES AWAY

Midway through the '59 season, Billy Jurges became the manager of the Boston Red Sox. He asked Maglie to be his pitching coach for the 1960 season. The Barber still wanted to pitch but Jurges told him to concentrate on coaching and teaching the youngsters. Jurges, a scrappy shortstop, had played a tough brand of baseball in the '30s and '40s with the Chicago Cubs and New York Giants which included vicious takeout slides, beanball wars and an estranged lover even tried to kill him but she was a poor shot. Maglie taught the young pitchers to throw inside and this is what the Boston skipper wanted. However Jurges lasted only 42 games (15–27) into the season before he was let go. The Red Sox finished in seventh place (65–89). Del Baker (2–5) and Pinky Higgins (48–57) succeeded him as manager.

The following season was an expansion year. The Red Sox finished in sixth place in the ten team circuit as Pinky Higgins continued to be their skipper and in 1962 they finished in eighth place. Maglie left the team after the '62 season and returned to Niagara Falls to care for his wife Kay who was extremely ill. For three years he stayed away from the game before he went back to the Sox in the spring of '66. She died in February of '67. Back with the Red Sox in '66, they finished in ninth place under Billy Herman (64–82) and Pete Runnels (8–8). In '67 the Red Sox won the pennant but

14. The Old Warrior Fades Away

Sal as pitching coach with the Boston Red Sox. (George Brace photo)

lost the World Series to the Cardinals in seven games. Bob Gibson went the distance in Game Seven. The loud, abrasive Dick Williams was the manager of the Red Sox that year as he guided them to a 92–70 record and won the pennant by one game over Detroit. When they lost the World Series, Maglie was one of the coaches who paid the price with his job.

One of the players Maglie took a particular liking to on the Red Sox was Jim Lonborg. In 1966, Lonborg was 10–10 with a 3.86 ERA, a significant improvement from his rookie year in '65. Then in 1967, he blossomed into a tremendous hurler as he led the league in wins with a 22–9 record, had a 3.16 ERA and led the league in strikeouts with 246. The transformation was directly linked to his willingness to follow Maglie's advice and he began to throw inside at a ferocious pace. He nailed 19 batters as Maglie explained, "He was just protecting the plate, his bread and butter."[1] Lonborg had graduated from Stanford University and served as the Red Sox player representative for four years. Later he served as the Milwaukee Brewers' representative. Russ Gibson, a backup catcher, had played with Lonborg in the bushes. "He was the shyest guy you've ever seen in your life. Then I came here to Boston and the first night I caught him we were playing Kansas City. I said, 'Lonnie, you want to go over the hitters?' ... He said 'Campaneris is leading off. I'm going to hit him in the head with the first pitch.' He didn't miss by much, I tell you! I think the ball went between his head and his helmet. I just couldn't believe it — the change! He turned into just a complete guerrilla."[2] What happened was that he came under the spell of Sal Maglie. It had been a tough year for hitters in '67. Maglie witnessed the vicious beaning of the Red Sox Tony Conigliaro who was beaned by Jack Hamilton of the Angels. The Barber contended that Hamilton nailed him with a spitter that got away.

In 1969, Maglie found employment as the pitching coach of the Seattle Pilots expansion team. Joe Schultz was the manager and they finished last in the American League Western Division with a 64–98 record. The Seattle experiment was a disaster. The team was sold after the season and moved to Milwaukee. A knuckleball pitcher named Jim Bouton in the latter stages of his career chronicled that season in his book *Ball Four*. It was an irreverent look at the national pastime in which he told tales of his teammates and opponents concerning sex, drugs, and personal behavior. The portrait he paints of Maglie is unflattering to say the least. Maglie had been his childhood hero and Bouton was disillusioned with what he had found. Bouton shows him as a contradictory coach, a constant second-guesser who can't communicate well with his players, and doesn't understand pitching as well as he should. Sal is not a big fan of Bouton's knuckleball and tells him to mix up his pitches to which Bouton takes offense particularly since Maglie himself threw games in which he relied on one pitch, the curveball. Bouton's feelings may have been genuine or merely hyperbole but they painted Maglie as a coach who had outlived his usefulness. Maglie responded, "It was bullshit [Bouton's stories]. I'll tell you about Bouton. He was like a spoiled little brat, always had to have things his own way. I had nine or ten other pitchers to worry about and he was forever comin' around botherin' me about his knuckleball. Look, I'll say this, if he'd still been useful as a pitcher he wouldn't be writin' books, would he? ... Bouton was washed up — if it hadn't been for the expansion he'd of been in the minors."[3] In fact Bouton spent part of the season in the minors.

Maglie was among several coaches who were fired after the '69 season. He returned to Niagara Falls and faded away into the sunset. After he had left the Red Sox the first time he had done some coaching with the Buffalo Bisons. Later he did some more coaching with Newark of the Pony League. He became general manager of the Niagara Falls Pirates of

A haggard looking Sal Maglie as pitching coach with the expansion Seattle Pilots in 1969. Sal was distressed by the changes in the game since he had retired as a player. The conformity of the '50s had given way to the individualism and iconoclastic ballplayers of the '60s. (George Brace photo)

the New York-Penn League. They named a ballpark in his honor, "Sal Maglie Stadium." His off the field jobs over the years included selling mutual funds, owning his liquor store, and working in sales for a distillery. He was the deputy commissioner for the New York State Athletic Commission. After Kay died, he remarried, to Dorris Ellman. Maglie became ill and underwent brain surgery in 1982. In the late 1980s he entered a nursing home after suffering a stroke for the second time. He was an invalid in his final years and did not even recognize his own family. He died at the nursing home on December 28, 1992. Two days later a funeral mass was held at Our Lady of Mount Carmel Roman Catholic Church in Niagara Falls.

Sal Maglie was a vanished breed of a man. A man who played baseball in a tough era and excelled at his craft with limited skills. Everyone who saw him play has an image of the Barber indelibly etched in their head. Steve O'Neill, his first professional manager, recalled, "He can do [things] with the curve that I never saw before. You'd think it was a spitball, but it's an honest, on-the-level pitch." Maglie threw the curve with a fastball motion and it dropped off the table like the illegal wet pitch. Tom Meany wrote, "His appearance is formidable. He has the look of foxes to hens. He'd make a dandy heavy in a movie about the Mafia." *Look* magazine wrote, "Maglie goes about his business with the formality of an undertaker. In every city except New York, dark-bearded and sinister-visaged Maglie might receive a welcome reserved for a public hangman."[4] His wife Kay once said, "He isn't tough at all. He lets his beard grow before a game so he'll look fierce. I used to wonder what people were talking about when they said he scowled ferociously at the batters. Then I stayed home one day and watched him on TV. I hardly knew him."[5] Jim Bouton wrote in *Ball Four*, "Another thing Sal Maglie looks like (he) is the friendly neighborhood undertaker. You can just see him standing in the mortuary doorway saying, "Oh yes, we have something very nice for you in mahogany.""[6]

Vin Scully, the Dodgers' broadcaster, remembered Maglie in those Giant/Dodger wars. "In the early 1950s, Charlie Dressen managed the Dodgers, and Leo Durocher the Giants. The rivalry was feverish, lots of knockdowns ... lots of retaliations, including a sequence where Sheldon Jones and Ruben Gomez both beaned Carl Furillo, and then Durocher challenged Furillo, who broke his hand in the brawl. Sal Maglie was at the center of all this. He looked like a villain ... had a five o'clock beard ... hat pulled down ... looked mean and rough." Sportswriter Marshall Smith wrote, "When Maglie is on the mound, the enemy batter and fans see the most menacing face in baseball, with its famous blue-black 5 o'clock shadow, hawk nose, down-turned mouth, and hooded eyes. Maglie also possesses an encyclopedia knowledge of batters' weaknesses and the skill to exploit those weaknesses. He can throw the ball exactly where he wants to, and hitters complain after facing him four times in one afternoon that they never saw the same pitch twice.... When Maglie 'throws at their ear' he lets fly as if he is genuinely interested in finding out whether a baseball can penetrate a human skull." The *Boston Globe* reported one ballplayer as saying, "Maglie could look a pitch through you. He was so mean he'd get you with sliders. You'd lean forward and think you were safe, and the thing would break right off your neck."[7] Rich Westcott wrote, "He looked mean, and he was mean ... he resembled one of those gunslingers that the good guys were always chasing in the cowboy movies."[8] Wes Westrum recalled, "You could catch Sal sitting in a rocking chair, perfect control."[9] Stan Lomax remembers, "In his prime, he was sallow with sunken cheeks, black hair, black eyebrows. He looked like an undertaker coming in to pitch. He threw right under a batter's chin. He had a guy managing him who wanted him to be mean and worked on him to do it. Maglie was real intimidating. He took the fire right out of a hitter."[10]

Sal Maglie's story is one of courage, perseverance, hardships, heroism, and determination. He was a "money pitcher" who gladly took the pill in the important games and excelled. When he didn't have his stuff he kept his team in the game with cunning, craft, and intelligence. He was a professional pitcher in the true sense of the word, always taking his turn, and pitching when injured. In fact he pitched when he was crippled, until the pain was so intense it paralyzed his body, while the perspiration soaked his flannel uniform and the sweat burned his eyes. The Barber was a feared and respected craftsman of the times. Arnold Hano in his book, *A Day in the Bleachers*, writes the following, describing Maglie as he left the mound during game one of the '54 World Series: "All the great people and great things in life are failures; it is in doing what we cannot do but must try to do that humans rise to their exalted fulfillment. Maglie had tried to do with an old man's arm and back what a young man might not even have been able to do as well—of such failures is greatness made."[11] The prognosticators thought Maglie was washed up on several occasions, but each time he proved them wrong and rose from the dead, until he had nothing left.

Baseball during the '50s was a rough, intense game in which fights, beanball wars, high take-out slides, retaliation, bench jockeying, racism and untoward behavior by fans and players were rampant. Ty Cobb once said, "Baseball is a red-blooded sport for red-blooded men. It's no pink tea, and mollycoddles had better stay out of it. It's ... a struggle for supremacy, a survival of the fittest."[12] Cobb's observation that "baseball is not unlike a war" was still applicable in the 1950s.[13] The beanball was the Barber's weapon of choice and in later years he described it as a form of addiction. "I couldn't stop throwing the knockdown. That would be the same as if Marilyn Monroe stopped wearing sweaters." It allowed him to become successful, and the Barber described it as "a tool of the trade like a carpenter's hammer or a barber's scissors ... the best pitch in baseball.... The batters expected me to knock them down. I didn't want to disappoint them."[14] Ballplayers of the times are a lost breed, which will never be witnessed again. Alvin Dark once described Eddie Stanky as follows: "Stanky couldn't hit, run, or field. He couldn't do anything except beat you. He would sit on you at second base to keep you there. He would pull on your shirt, step on you .... When he got on base he immediately filled his hands with dirt.... He wanted something to throw in the second baseman's face."[15] Baseball was a war and strategic moves such as these were used to win ballgames. A player had to handle innumerable fears concerning such things as his reaction to a 95-mile per hour fastball thrown at his head while listening to the intense heckling from the opposing dugout in attempt to break his concentration. Bench jockeying provoked violence and retaliation. Hi Bithorn while pitching for the Cubs had once fired a beanball at Durocher in the dugout while Leo was managing the Dodgers. Jimmie Wilson, Bithorn's manager, fined his pitcher not for throwing the ball but because he had missed hitting Durocher.[16]

It would not be surprising if Bouton's description of Maglie in *Ball Four* had some truth to it. The game changed and passed the old warriors by. In 1973, Leo Durocher managed his last season with the Houston Astros. The new breed of ballplayer scoffed at his dictatorial managerial tactics. They ignored him, cursed him, and mocked him. Leo wrote, "It's a different breed, boy, and they're going to keep right on doing it their way."[17] As baseball entered the 1960s, Maglie stated, "I think the whole game of baseball has been sissified. The men who run the sport are trying to make it a delicate game, and it's not. I'm a pitching coach now and, when I'm working with young fellows in the Cardinal farm system, I'm not going to tell them to be polite to the batters. I'm teaching them to be tough."[18] Vin Scully once described Walter Alston as follows, "Walt was miscast. He should have been born in another time period; he would have been comfortable back in the days of the old west riding shotgun on a stagecoach."[19] Maglie was not an anachronism; he played at precisely the right time in history, but then things changed quickly, much too quickly for his own good. Much too quickly for others as well, players like Alvin Dark and Durocher.

An examination of Maglie's latter years is deliberately omitted from this book. For I prefer not to remember the deity transforming into a mortal, as Babe Ruth tragically did and faded away a mere shell of his former self. I prefer to remember the players in their prime and Sal Maglie in particular. Wearing the black and gold uniform for the New York Giants and avoiding objects thrown in his direction by a hostile Ebbets Field crowd. Facing his old rival, Jackie Robinson, and throwing the pill behind his head to the backstop. Then they battle like two Roman gladiators until Robinson waves at a curve that breaks off the outer edge. Maglie triumphantly exits the center of the diamond, drained by his Pyrrhic victory, with his back racked with pain, while the rabid Ebbets Field crowd grudgingly applauds his performance. The Barber stood in the center of the arena during perhaps the best decade of baseball. He played center stage in some of the most conspicuous games in baseball history: Game Three of the '51 playoff when Bobby Thomson hit "the shot heard round

14. The Old Warrior Fades Away

the world" to win the pennant from Brooklyn; Game One of the '54 World Series when Willie Mays made his famous catch off the bat of Vic Wertz; Game Five of the '56 World Series when Don Larsen pitched his perfect game. Some people remember Maglie as the Barber, Sinister Sal, or the Renaissance Assassin. He played in the most vibrant city in the world, on all three of its baseball teams. Many will recall his ferocity, competitiveness, or his intimidating presence. Others remember the crippling injuries, the struggles, and his perseverance to overcome them. There have been few players in the game who achieved so much with so little. Ultimately Maglie was the personification of baseball in the '50s. Theodore Roosevelt once said, "…the credit belongs to the man who is actually in the arena, whose face is marred by dust and sweat and blood … who knows the great enthusiasms, the great devotions and spends himself in a worthy cause … who in the end at best knows the triumph of high achievement and at worst fails while daring greatly, so that his place shall never be with those cold and timid souls who know neither victory nor defeat."[20] This statement is most certainly applicable to Salvatore Anthony Maglie.

NOTES

Chapter 1

1. Shapiro, *The Sal Maglie Story*, 40.
2. Meany, *The Incredible Giants*, 109.
3. Karst and Jones, *Who's Who in Professional Baseball*, 619.
4. Berton, *Niagara*, 264–65.
5. *New York Times*, 25 May 1952.
6. Maglie and Boyle, "Baseball Is a Tough Business," 15 April 1968, 86.
7. Overfield, "A Giant Among Men."
8. Maglie and Boyle, "Baseball Is a Tough Business," 15 April 1968, 86.
9. Violanti, *Miracle in Buffalo*, 11.
10. Golenbock, *Bums*, 36.
11. *New York Herald Tribune*, 19 June 1955.
12. Overfield, "A Giant Among Men."
13. Sullivan, *The Minors*, 142.
14. "Maglie, Sal," 407.
15. Scheinin, *Field of Screams*, 241–42.
16. *Sporting News*, 8 June 1939.
17. Shapiro, *The Sal Maglie Story*, 41.
18. "Maglie, Sal," 407.
19. Keyes, *Silver Anniversary*, 17.
20. "Maglie, Sal," 409.
21. *New York Herald Tribune*, 28 March 1959.
22. Honig, *Baseball America*, 241.

Chapter 2

1. Overfield, "A Giant Among Men."
2. Pietrusza, *Baseball's Canadian-American League*, 158.
3. Thomson with Heiman and Gutman, *"The Giants Win the Pennant!,"* 82.
4. Goldstein, *Spartan Seasons*, 124–25.
5. *Jersey Journal*, 15 June 1942.

Chapter 3

1. Goldstein, *Spartan Seasons*, 111.
2. Mayer, "Bill Voiselle and the $500 Pitch," 136.
3. *Hudson Dispatch*, 19 June 1945.
4. Kiernan, *The Miracle at Coogan's Bluff*, 184.
5. Shapiro, *The Sal Maglie Story*, 45.
6. "Maglie, Sal," 407.
7. Shapiro, *The Sal Maglie Story*, 47.
8. Karst and Jones, *Who's Who in Professional Baseball*, 729.
9. Westcott, *Diamond Greats*, 290.
10. Gershman, *Diamonds*, 145.
11. Karst and Jones, *Who's Who in Professional Baseball*, 687.
12. Goldstein, *Superstars and Screwballs*, 188.

13. Maglie and Boyle, "Baseball Is a Tough Business," 15 April 1968, 88.
14. Scheinin, *Field of Screams*, 229.
15. Durocher with Linn, *Nice Guys Finish Last*, 14.
16. *New York Herald Tribune*, 4 September 1945.
17. Phillips, *The Mexican Jumping Beans*, 8.
18. Gilbert, *They Also Served*, 249.
19. *Ibid.*, 189.
20. Oakley, *Baseball's Last Golden Age*, 11.

Chapter 4

1. Maglie and Boyle, "Baseball Is a Tough Business," 22 April 1968, 40.
2. Maglie and Boyle, "Baseball Is a Tough Business," 15 April 1968, 80.
3. Shapiro, *The Sal Maglie Story*, 51.
4. Bjarkman, *Baseball with a Latin Beat*, 25.
5. *Ibid.*, 203.
6. *Ibid.*, 201.
7. *New York Herald Tribune*, 12 December 1945.
8. Stein and Peters, *Giants Diary*, 96–97.
9. Vaughn, "Jorge Pasquel and the Evolution of the Mexican League," 10.
10. Graham, "The Great Mexican War of 1946," 118.
11. *New York Herald Tribune*, 19 February 1946.
12. Kiernan, *The Miracle of Coogan's Bluff*, 184.
13. Phillips, *The Mexican Jumping Beans*, 13.
14. *New York Herald Tribune*, 21 March 1946.
15. Phillips, *The Mexican Jumping Beans*, 32.
16. Graham, "The Great Mexican War of 1946," 119.
17. Kiernan, *The Miracle of Coogan's Bluff*, 185.
18. Graham, "The Great Mexican War of 1946," 119.
19. *Sporting News*, 18 April 1946.
20. Phillips, *The Mexican Jumping Beans*, 27.
21. Oakley, *Baseball's Last Golden Age*, 36.
22. Golenbock, *Bums*, 49, 51.
23. Lowenfish and Lupien, *The Imperfect Diamond*, 158–59.
24. Maglie and Boyle, "Baseball Is a Tough Business," 22 April 1968, 41.
25. Phillips, *The Mexican Jumping Beans*, 30.
26. Graham, "The Great Mexican War of 1946," 123.
27. Kiernan, *The Miracle of Coogan's Bluff*, 186.
28. *Washington Post*, 14 April 1946.
29. Graham, "The Great Mexican War of 1946," 126.
30. Maglie and Boyle, "Baseball is a Tough Business," 22 April 1968, 41.
31. Bjarkman, *Baseball with a Latin Beat*, 25–26.
32. Phillips, *The Mexican Jumping Beans*, 40.
33. *Sporting News*, 19 April 1950.
34. Phillips, *The Mexican Jumping Beans*, 13.
35. Prince, *Brooklyn's Dodgers*, 29.
36. Graham, "The Great Mexican War of 1946," 125.
37. Vaughn, "Jorge Pasquel and the Evolution of the Mexican League," 11.
38. Echevarria, *The Pride of Havana*, 17.
39. *Ibid.*, 26.
40. Phillips, *The Mexican Jumping Beans*, 64.
41. Marshall, *Baseball's Pivotal Era*, 232.
42. "Maglie, Sal," 408.
43. *Sporting News*, 19 April 1950.
44. *Sporting News*, 18 June 1947.
45. Phillips, *The Mexican Jumping Beans*, 67.
46. Humber, *Diamonds of the North*, 121.
47. Oakley, *Baseball's Last Golden Age*, 84.
48. Humber, *Diamonds of the North*, 121.
49. Clifton, *Disorganized Baseball*, 8.

Chapter 5

1. Oakley, *Baseball's Last Golden Age*, 52.
2. Durocher with Linn, *Nice Guys Finish Last*, 289–90.
3. *Ibid.*, 290.
4. *Ibid.*, 288.
5. Kiernan, *The Miracle at Coogan's Bluff*, 33.
6. Hodges and Hirshberg, *My Giants*, 70.
7. Durocher with Linn, *Nice Guys Finish Last*, 291–92.

8. Hynd, *The Giants of the Polo Grounds*, 356.
9. Maglie and Boyle, "Baseball Is a Tough Business," 22 April 1968, 42.
10. Durocher with Linn, *Nice Guys Finish Last*, 306.
11. *New York Herald Tribune*, 27 February 1950.
12. *New York Herald Tribune*, 10 March 1950.
13. *New York Herald Tribune*, 24 March 1950.
14. Durocher with Linn, *Nice Guys Finish Last*, 306.
15. *New York Herald Tribune*, 10 March 1950.
16. Frommer, *New York City Baseball*, 37–38.
17. Shapiro, *The Sal Maglie Story*, 73.
18. *Sporting News*, 19 April 1950.
19. *New York Herald Tribune*, 15 April 1950.
20. *New York Herald Tribune*, 19 April 1950.
21. Maglie and Boyle, "Baseball Is a Tough Business," 22 April 1968, 42.
22. Roberts and Rogers, *The Whiz Kids*, 215.
23. Voigt, *American Baseball: Vol. 3*, 61.
24. Ritter, *Lost Ballparks*, 24.
25. Zoss and Bowman, *Diamonds in the Rough*, 171.
26. Hodges and Hirshberg, *My Giants*, 84.
27. *New York Herald Tribune*, 5 June 1950.
28. Goldstein, *Superstars and Screwballs*, 314.
29. Frommer, *New York City Baseball*, 118.
30. *Ibid.*, 110.
31. Turner, *When the Boys Came Back*, 122.
32. Prince, *Brooklyn's Dodgers*, 107.
33. Kahn, *The Boys of Summer*, 338.
34. Golenbock, *Bums*, 359.
35. Dickson, *The New Dickson Baseball Dictionary*, 290.
36. Karst and Jones, *Who's Who in Professional Baseball*, 619.
37. Prince, *Brooklyn's Dodgers*, 50–51.
38. Maglie and Boyle, "Baseball is a Tough Business," 22 April 1968, 42.
39. Prince, *Brooklyn's Dodgers*, 51.
40. Irvin with Riley, *Nice Guys Finish First*, 134.
41. *Brooklyn Eagle*, 22 June 1950.
42. *Ibid.*
43. *New York Herald Tribune*, 28 June 1950.
44. *Brooklyn Eagle*, 30 June 1950.
45. *New York Herald Tribune*, 1 July 1950.
46. Golenbock, *Bums*, 284.
47. *New York Herald Tribune*, 5 July 1950.
48. *New York Herald Tribune*, 14 July 1950.
49. Hodges and Hirshberg, *My Giants*, 84.
50. Thomson with Heiman and Gutman, "The Giants Win the Pennant!," 72.
51. Dickson, *The New Dickson Baseball Dictionary*, 35.
52. "Dead or Alive," 56.
53. Meany, *The Incredible Giants*, 181.
54. *Philadelphia Inquirer*, 13 August 1950.
55. Irvin with Riley, *Nice Guys Finish First*, 177.
56. Roberts and Rogers, *The Whiz Kids*, 248.
57. Scheinin, *Field of Screams*, 106.
58. *New York Herald Tribune*, 13 August 1950.
59. Roberts and Rogers, *The Whiz Kids*, 249.
60. *Philadelphia Inquirer*, 13 August 1950.
61. Irvin with Riley, *Nice Guys Finish First*, 177.
62. *Philadelphia Inquirer*, 13 August 1950.
63. *New York Herald Tribune*, 15 August 1950.
64. *Ibid.*
65. Kiernan, *The Miracle at Coogan's Bluff*, 43.
66. Kelley, "Wes Westrum," 26.
67. *New York Herald Tribune*, 14 September 1950.
68. *Ibid.*
69. Shapiro, *The Sal Maglie Story*, 18.
70. Kahn, *The Era*, 49.
71. Scheinin, *Field of Screams*, 207.
72. Kahn, *The Era*, 47.
73. Oakley, *Baseball's Last Golden Age*, 93.
74. Robinson with Duckett, *I Never Had It Made*, 80.
75. Allen, *The Giants and the Dodgers*, 204.
76. Prince, *Brooklyn's Dodgers*, 49.
77. Roberts and Rogers, *The Whiz Kids*, 302.
78. Kahn, *The Era*, 88.

Chapter 6

1. *New York Herald Tribune*, 29 November 1950.
2. Thomson with Heiman and Gutman, "The Giants Win the Pennant!," 76–77.
3. Shapiro, *The Sal Maglie Story*, 89.
4. *New York Herald Tribune*, 23 February 1951.
5. *New York Times*, 21 May 1954.
6. Quigley, *The Crooked Pitch*, 158.
7. *Ibid.*
8. Maglie and Boyle, "Baseball Is a Tough Business," 15 April 1968, 87–88.
9. *New York Herald Tribune*, 19 March 1951.
10. *New York Times*, 3 April 1951.
11. *New York Herald Tribune*, 15 April 1951.
12. *New York Times*, 3 April 1951.
13. *Sporting News*, 25 April 1951.
14. Thomson with Heiman and Gutman, "The Giants Win the Pennant!," 88.
15. *Ibid.*, 90.
16. Halberstam, *The Fifties*, 115.
17. Thomson with Heiman and Gutman, "The Giants Win the Pennant!," 91.
18. Kiernan, *The Miracle at Coogan's Bluff*, 63–64.
19. *Sporting News*, 25 April 1951.
20. Thomson with Heiman and Gutman, "The Giants Win the Pennant!," 94.
21. Durocher with Linn, *Nice Guys Finish Last*, 285.
22. Thomson with Heiman and Gutman, "The Giants Win the Pennant!," 95.
23. Kiernan, *The Miracle at Coogan's Bluff*, 65–67.
24. *Brooklyn Eagle*, 1 May 1951.
25. Oakley, *Baseball's Last Golden Age*, 137.
26. Shapiro, *The Sal Maglie Story*, 93.
27. *Ibid.*, 93–94.
28. *New York Times*, 1 May 1951.
29. Thomson with Heiman and Gutman, "The Giants Win the Pennant!," 142.
30. Prince, *Brooklyn's Dodgers*, 13.
31. *Ibid.*, 74.
32. *New York Herald Tribune*, 2 May 1951.
33. *New York Herald Tribune*, 3 May 1951.
34. Kiernan, *The Miracle at Coogan's Bluff*, 68–69.
35. Thomson with Heiman and Gutman, "The Giants Win the Pennant!," 105.
36. Hano, *Willie Mays*, 44.
37. Irvin with Riley, *Nice Guys Finish First*, 142.
38. *New York Herald Tribune*, 25 May 1951.
39. Kiernan, *The Miracle at Coogan's Bluff*, 164.
40. Kahn, *Memories of Summer*, 189.
41. Durocher with Linn, *Nice Guys Finish Last*, 310.
42. Honig, *Baseball America*, 280.
43. Roberts and Rogers, *The Whiz Kids*, 53.
44. Maglie and Boyle, "Baseball Is a Tough Business," 15 April 1968, 85.
45. *New York Herald Tribune*, 27 June 1951.
46. *New York Times*, 28 June 1951.
47. *New York Herald Tribune*, 27 June 1951.
48. Robinson, *The Home Run Heard 'Round the World*, 149.
49. Thomson with Heiman and Gutman, "The Giants Win the Pennant!," 169.
50. *New York Herald Tribune*, 29 June 1951.
51. Lardner, "Razor Blades Amok," 77.
52. Kiernan, *The Miracle at Coogan's Bluff*, 82.
53. Thomson with Heiman and Gutman, "The Giants Win the Pennant!," 137.
54. Prince, *Brooklyn's Dodgers*, 70.
55. Thomson with Heiman and Gutman, "The Giants Win the Pennant!," 137.
56. Prince, *Brooklyn's Dodgers*, 70.
57. *New York Times*, 20 July 1951.
58. *New York Herald Tribune*, 5 August 1951.
59. Maglie and Boyle, "Baseball Is a Tough Business," 15 April 1968, 85.
60. Kiernan, *The Miracle at Coogan's Bluff*, 88.
61. Thomson with Heiman and Gutman, "The Giants Win the Pennant!," 147–48.
62. Irvin with Riley, *Nice Guys Finish First*, 147.
63. Thomson with Heiman and Gutman, "The Giants Win the Pennant!," 148.
64. Kiernan, *The Miracle at Coogan's Bluff*, 91.
65. Thomson with Heiman and Gutman, "The Giants Win the Pennant!," 149.

66. Kiernan, *The Miracle at Coogan's Bluff*, 91.
67. *Ibid.*, 21–22.
68. *New York Herald Tribune*, 16 August 1951.
69. *Brooklyn Eagle*, 23 August 1951.
70. *New York Herald Tribune*, 2 September 1951.
71. *New York Herald Tribune*, 5 September 1951.
72. *New York Herald Tribune*, 9 September 1951.
73. Anderson, *Pennant Races*, 212.
74. *New York Herald Tribune*, 19 April 1950.
75. Thomson, with Heiman and Gutman, "The Giants Win the Pennant!," 183.
76. *Ibid.*, 192.
77. Anderson, *Pennant Races*, 224–25.
78. Thomson with Heiman and Gutman, "The Giants Win the Pennant!," 178.
79. Gutman, *It Ain't Cheatin' If You Don't Get Caught*, 119.
80. Thomson with Heiman and Gutman, "The Giants Win the Pennant!," 197.
81. *Ibid.*, 200.
82. *New York Herald Tribune*, 30 September 1951.
83. Thomson with Heiman and Gutman, "The Giants Win the Pennant!," 205.
84. Kiernan, *The Miracle at Coogan's Bluff*, 113.
85. Shapiro, *The Sal Maglie Story*, 102–3.
86. *Brooklyn Eagle*, 29 September 1951.
87. Kiernan, *The Miracle at Coogan's Bluff*, 220.
88. *New York Herald Tribune*, 2 October 1951.
89. Thomson with Heiman and Gutman, "The Giants Win the Pennant!," 223.
90. Kiernan, *The Miracle at Coogan's Bluff*, 129.
91. Thomson with Heiman and Gut-man, "The Giants Win the Pennant!," 233.
92. Kiernan, *The Miracle at Coogan's Bluff*, 221.
93. *Ibid.*, 133.
94. *Ibid.*, 134.
95. Thomson with Heiman and Gutman, "The Giants Win the Pennant!," 243.
96. Maglie and Boyle, "Baseball Is a Tough Business," 22 April 1968, 47.
97. Kiernan, *The Miracle at Coogan's Bluff*, 144.
98. *Ibid.*, 145.
99. *Ibid.*, 148–49.
100. Kahn, *The Era*, 278.
101. Maglie and Boyle, "Baseball Is a Tough Business," 22 April 1968, 47.
102. *New York Herald Tribune*, 4 October 1951.
103. Oakley, *Baseball's Last Golden Age*, 144.
104. Kiernan, *The Miracle at Coogan's Bluff*, 150–51.
105. *New York Herald Tribune*, 4 October 1951.
106. Kahn, *The Era*, 295.
107. Honig, *Baseball America*, 277.
108. Oakley, *Baseball's Last Golden Age*, 147.
109. Kahn, *The Era*, 291.
110. Maglie and Boyle, "Baseball Is a Tough Business," 22 April 1968, 47.
111. Kahn, *The Era*, 293.
112. *Ibid.*, 294.

Chapter 7

1. *New York Herald Tribune*, 12 February 1952.
2. *New York Herald Tribune*, 22 February 1952.
3. *New York Herald Tribune*, 20 February 1952.
4. *New York Herald Tribune*, 15 March 1952.
5. *New York Herald Tribune*, 30 March 1952.
6. *New York Herald Tribune*, 9 April 1952.
7. Meany, *The Incredible Giants*, 225.
8. Oakley, *Baseball's Last Golden Age*, 150.
9. *New York Herald Tribune*, 5 March 1952.
10. *Brooklyn Eagle*, 21 April 1952.
11. Scheinin, *Field of Screams*, 288–89.
12. Shapiro, *The Sal Maglie Story*, 118.
13. Meany, *The Incredible Giants*, 73.
14. Thomson with Heiman and Gutman, "The Giants Win the Pennant!," 88–89.
15. *New York Times*, 19 May 1952.
16. Shapiro, *The Sal Maglie Story*, 120.
17. *Ibid.*, 119.

18. *New York Times*, 25 May 1952.
19. Hynd, *The Giants of the Polo Grounds*, 373.
20. *New York Herald Tribune*, 29 March 1952.
21. Prince, *Brooklyn's Dodgers*, 12.
22. *New York Herald Tribune*, 3 June 1952.
23. *New York Times*, 16 June 1952.
24. Scheinin, *Field of Screams*, 288.
25. *New York Times*, 1 June 1952.
26. Frommer, *New York City Baseball*, 87.
27. *Ibid.*
28. Thomson with Heiman and Gutman, "The Giants Win the Pennant!," 111.
29. *New York Herald Tribune*, 5 July 1952.
30. *New York Herald Tribune*, 12 July 1952.
31. Thomson with Heiman and Gutman, "The Giants Win the Pennant!," 183.
32. Prince, *Brooklyn's Dodgers*, 54.
33. *Brooklyn Eagle*, 8 August 1952.
34. Shapiro, *The Sal Maglie Story*, 142.
35. *Brooklyn Eagle*, 15 August 1952.
36. Shapiro, *The Sal Maglie Story*, 147.
37. *Brooklyn Eagle*, 15 August 1952.
38. Shapiro, *The Sal Maglie Story*, 148.
39. Lardner, "Tinker to Evers to Freud," 99.
40. *New York Herald Tribune*, 20 August 1952.
41. Shapiro, *The Sal Maglie Story*, 149.
42. Voigt, *American Baseball: Vol. 3*, 70.
43. "The Barber," 97.
44. Prince, *Brooklyn's Dodgers*, 52–53.
45. Kahn, *The Era*, 304.
46. Prince, *Brooklyn's Dodgers*, 54.
47. *New York Herald Tribune*, 6 September 1952.
48. Robinson with Duckett, *I Never Had It Made*, 116.
49. *New York Herald Tribune*, 6 September 1952.
50. Kahn, *The Boys of Summer*, 121.
51. *New York Herald Tribune*, 8 September 1952.
52. Prince, *Brooklyn's Dodgers*, 55.
53. *Ibid.*, 56–57.
54. Golenbock, *Bums*, 283.
55. *New York Herald Tribune*, 10 September 1952.
56. *New York Herald Tribune*, 6 February, 1953.
57. *New York Herald Tribune*, 12 September 1952.
58. *New York Herald Tribune*, 13 September, 1952.
59. Oakley, *Baseball's Last Golden Age*, 161.

Chapter 8

1. *New York Herald Tribune*, 23 February 1953.
2. Kiernan, *The Miracle at Coogan's Bluff*, 34.
3. *New York Herald Tribune*, 7 March 1953.
4. Ritter, *Lost Ballparks*, 201.
5. *New York Herald Tribune*, 21 March 1953.
6. *New York Herald Tribune*, 28 March 1953.
7. *New York Herald Tribune*, 13 April 1953.
8. Roberts and Rogers, *The Whiz Kids*, 53.
9. *New York Herald Tribune*, 18 April 1953.
10. *Brooklyn Eagle*, 18 April 1953.
11. *New York Herald Tribune*, 26 April 1953.
12. Frommer, *New York City Baseball*, 153.
13. Kahn, *The Era*, 292.
14. Shapiro, *The Sal Maglie Story*, 152.
15. *Ibid.*, 153.
16. *New York Times*, 13 May 1951.
17. *New York Herald Tribune*, 26 April 1953.
18. *New York Herald Tribune*, 5 June 1953.
19. *New York Times*, 14 June 1953.
20. *New York Times*, 11 June 1953.
21. Oakley, *Baseball's Last Golden Age*, 169.
22. *New York Times*, 25 June 1953.
23. Hynd, *The Giants of the Polo Grounds*, 372.
24. Kahn, *The Era*, 302.
25. *Brooklyn Eagle*, 6 July 1953.
26. Prince, *Brooklyn's Dodgers*, 11.
27. Irvin with Riley, *Nice Guys Finish First*, 129.
28. Honig, *Baseball America*, 258.
29. Thomson with Heiman and Gutman, "The Giants Win the Pennant!," 94.
30. *Brooklyn Eagle*, 11 July 1953.

31. *New York Times*, 19 July 1953.
32. Quigley, *The Crooked Pitch*, 101.
33. *New York Times*, 19 July 1953.
34. *New York Herald Tribune*, 31 July 1953.
35. *New York Times*, 12 August 1953.
36. *New York Times*, 13 August 1953.
37. Prince, *Brooklyn's Dodgers*, 17.
38. *Ibid.*, 16.
39. *New York Herald Tribune*, 4 August 1953.
40. Prince, *Brooklyn's Dodgers*, 49.
41. *Brooklyn Eagle*, 19 August 1953.
42. *New York Herald Tribune*, 2 September 1953.
43. Scheinin, *Field of Screams*, 227.
44. *Ibid.*, 267.
45. Kahn, *The Boys of Summer*, 147.
46. Irvin with Riley, *Nice Guys Finish First*, 144.
47. *Ibid.*
48. Oakley, *Baseball's Last Golden Age*, 171.
49. *New York Times*, 7 September 1953.
50. Kahn, *The Era*, 314.
51. *New York Times*, 9 September 1953.
52. Irvin with Riley, *Nice Guys Finish First*, 145.
53. Shapiro, *The Sal Maglie Story*, 155.
54. Thomson with Heiman and Gutman, "The Giants Win the Pennant!," 99.
55. *New York Herald Tribune*, 12 September 1953.
56. Meany, *The Incredible Giants*, 126.
57. *Ibid.*, 90.
58. Scheinin, *Field of Screams*, 264.

Chapter 9

1. *New York Herald Tribune*, 4 February 1954.
2. *New York Herald Tribune*, 28 February 1954.
3. *New York Herald Tribune*, 27 February 1954.
4. *New York Herald Tribune*, 28 February 1954.
5. *Ibid.*
6. *New York Herald Tribune*, 2 March 1954.
7. *New York Herald Tribune*, 3 March 1954.
8. *New York Herald Tribune*, 6 March 1954.
9. Kahn, *The Era*, 319.
10. *New York Herald Tribune*, 8 March 1954.
11. *New York Herald Tribune*, 10 March 1954.
12. *New York Herald Tribune*, 15 March 1954.
13. *New York Herald Tribune*, 20 March 1954.
14. Voigt, *American Baseball: Vol. 3*, 17.
15. Oakley, *Baseball's Last Golden Age*, 170.
16. *New York Herald Tribune*, 25 March 1954.
17. Kahn, *Memories of Summer*, 150.
18. Oakley, *Baseball's Last Golden Age*, 203.
19. *New York Times*, 5 April 1954.
20. Larsen with Shaw, *The Perfect Yankee*, 2.
21. *Brooklyn Eagle*, 14 April 1954.
22. Maglie and Boyle, "Baseball Is a Tough Business," 22 April 1968, 42, 47.
23. Dickson, *The New Dickson Baseball Dictionary*, 377.
24. Scheinin, *Field of Screams*, 289.
25. Meany, *The Incredible Giants*, 140–41.
26. Maglie and Boyle, "Baseball Is a Tough Business," 15 April 1968, 85.
27. Letter to the author from Wes Westrum, dated 6 April 2000.
28. *Sporting News*, 12 May 1954.
29. Gershman, *Diamonds*, 92.
30. Scheinin, *Field of Screams*, 262.
31. Prince, *Brooklyn's Dodgers*, 64–65.
32. *New York Herald Tribune*, 4 June 1954.
33. Golenbock, *Bums*, 240.
34. Gutman, *It Ain't Cheatin' If You Don't Get Caught*, 28.
35. Quigley, *The Crooked Pitch*, 161.
36. *Ibid.*, 162–63.
37. Gutman, *It Ain't Cheatin' If You Don't Get Caught*, 40.
38. *Sporting News*, 7 July 1954.
39. *Ibid.*
40. Kahn, *The Era*, 231.
41. Maglie and Boyle, "Baseball Is a Tough Business," 22 April 1968, 40.
42. Oakley, *Baseball's Last Golden Age*, 187.
43. *Brooklyn Eagle*, 7 July 1954.
44. *New York Herald Tribune*, 19 July 1954.

45. Oakley, *Baseball's Last Golden Age*, 209.
46. "Willie Mays: The Hottest Thing Since Babe Ruth," 74.
47. *New York Herald Tribune*, 5 April 1954.
48. "Willie Mays: The Hottest Thing Since Babe Ruth," 75.
49. Ibid., 74.
50. Frommer, *New York City Baseball*, 153.
51. *Brooklyn Eagle*, 27 July 1954.
52. *New York Herald Tribune*, 1 August 1954.
53. Meany, *The Incredible Giants*, 196.
54. *New York Herald Tribune*, 9 August 1954.
55. Quigley, *The Crooked Pitch*, 88–89.
56. Buege, "Spahn's First 'Loss' Wasn't," 62.
57. Kahn, *The Boys of Summer*, 129.
58. Roberts and Rogers, *The Whiz Kids*, 103.
59. *Sporting News*, 11 August 1954.
60. *New York Times*, 4 September 1954.
61. *New York Herald Tribune*, 10 September 1954.
62. *New York Times*, 15 September 1954.
63. Maglie and Boyle, "Baseball Is a Tough Business," 22 April 1968, 47.
64. Durocher with Linn, *Nice Guys Finish Last*, 311.
65. Ibid.
66. Maglie and Boyle, "Baseball Is a Tough Business," 22 April 1968, 47.
67. Meany, *The Incredible Giants*, 219.
68. Ibid., 220.
69. Oakley, *Baseball's Last Golden Age*, 215.
70. Scheinin, *Field of Screams*, 268.
71. Kahn, *Memories of Summer*, 183.
72. Oakley, *Baseball's Last Golden Age*, 205.
73. "Baseball: The Hot 'Hate,'" 56.
74. Kahn, *Memories of Summer*, 192.
75. Hano, *A Day in the Bleachers*, 31.
76. Oakley, *Baseball's Last Golden Age*, 213.
77. Kahn, *Memories of Summer*, 194.
78. Ibid., 184.
79. Oakley, *Baseball's Last Golden Age*, 214.
80. Ibid., 215.
81. Ibid., 216.

Chapter 10

1. *New York Herald Tribune*, 11 February 1955.
2. *New York Herald Tribune*, 2 March 1955.
3. Oakley, *Baseball's Last Golden Age*, 220–21.
4. Voigt, *American Baseball: Vol. 3*, 72.
5. *New York Herald Tribune*, 6 April 1955.
6. Scheinin, *Field of Screams*, 280.
7. Oakley, *Baseball's Last Golden Age*, 117.
8. Irvin with Riley, *Nice Guys Finish First*, 145.
9. Voigt, *American Baseball: Vol. 3*, 292.
10. Golenbock, *Bums*, 283–284.
11. Hano, *Willie Mays*, 125.
12. Prince, *Brooklyn's Dodgers*, 71.
13. Ibid., 74.
14. *New York Herald Tribune*, 14 June 1955.
15. James, *Bill James' Guide to Baseball Managers*, 120.
16. *New York Herald Tribune*, 14 June 1955.
17. Maglie and Boyle, "Baseball Is a Tough Business," 15 April 1968, 86.
18. Oakley, *Baseball's Last Golden Age*, 225.
19. *New York Herald Tribune*, 3 July 1955.
20. Golenbock, *Bums*, 340.
21. Kahn, *The Boys of Summer*, 91.
22. Irvin with Riley, *Nice Guys Finish First*, 140–41.
23. Golenbock, *Bums*, 433.
24. Frommer, *New York City Baseball*, 3.
25. Kahn, *The Era*, 327.
26. James, *The Bill James Historical Baseball Abstract*, 213.
27. Linn, *Hitter*, 284.
28. Gershman, *Diamonds*, 147.
29. *New York Herald Tribune*, 3 July 1955.
30. Kahn, *The Era*, 218.
31. Prince, *Brooklyn's Dodgers*, 58.
32. Scheinin, *Field of Screams*, 272.
33. Prince, *Brooklyn's Dodgers*, 106.
34. Oakley, *Baseball's Last Golden Age*, 231.

Chapter 11

1. Allen with Graham, *It Takes Heart*, 149.

2. *New York Herald Tribune*, 27 February 1956.
3. Oakley, *Baseball's Last Golden Age*, 238.
4. *New York Herald Tribune*, 14 March 1956.
5. Scheinin, *Field of Screams*, 276.
6. *Jersey Journal*, 1 May 1956.
7. Allen with Graham, *It Takes Heart*, 150–51.
8. Kahn, *The Era*, 330.
9. Golenbock, *Bums*, 358.
10. Kiernan, *The Miracle at Coogan's Bluff*, 190.
11. Frommer, *New York City Baseball*, 153.
12. *Jersey Journal*, 16 May 1956.
13. Hodges and Hirshberg, *My Giants*, 85.
14. Maglie and Boyle, "Baseball Is a Tough Business," 22 April 1968, 48.
15. Frommer, *New York City Baseball*, 121.
16. Overfield, "A Giant Among Men."
17. Maglie and Boyle, "Baseball Is a Tough Business," 22 April 1968, 48.
18. *New York Times*, 29 December 1992.
19. Scheinin, *Field of Screams*, 271.
20. *Ibid.*, 264.
21. Gutman, *It Ain't Cheatin' If You Don't Get Caught*, 43.
22. Voigt, *American Baseball, Vol. 3*, 34.
23. Prince, *Brooklyn's Dodgers*, 13.
24. Allen with Graham, *It Takes Heart*, 152.
25. *New York Herald Tribune*, 5 June 1956.
26. Shapiro, *The Sal Maglie Story*, 177.
27. Lardner, "A Real Damp Year," 99.
28. Bjarkman, *Baseball with a Latin Beat*, 231.
29. *New York Herald Tribune*, 20 July 1956.
30. Oakley, *Baseball's Last Golden Age*, 222.
31. Golenbock, *Bums*, 349.
32. Oakley, *Baseball's Last Golden Age*, 197.
33. Allen with Graham, *It Takes Heart*, 153.
34. *Sporting News*, 27 June 1956.
35. Hano, *Willie Mays*, 120.
36. Voigt, *American Baseball, Vol. 3*, 267.
37. Prince, *Brooklyn's Dodgers*, 75.
38. Creamer, "An Angel of Darkness Named Sal the Barber," 43.
39. Allen with Graham, *It Takes Heart*, 123–124.
40. Shapiro, *The Sal Maglie Story*, 179.
41. *New York Herald Tribune*, 12 September 1956.
42. Westcott, *Diamond Greats*, 292.
43. Maglie and Boyle, "Baseball Is a Tough Business," 22 April 1968, 47.
44. Kiernan, *The Miracle at Coogan's Bluff*, 188.
45. Oakley, *Baseball's Last Golden Age*, 240.
46. Allen with Graham, *It Takes Heart*, 125.
47. "One More World Series?" 70, 72.
48. *New York Herald Tribune*, 22 September 1956.
49. Bjarkman, *Baseball with a Latin Beat*, 149.
50. Shapiro, *The Sal Maglie Story*, 183.
51. Allen with Graham, *It Takes Heart*, 155.
52. *New York Herald Tribune*, 26 September 1956.
53. Golenbock, *Bums*, 415.
54. "The Way It Went," 82.
55. *Christian Science Monitor*, 2 October 1956.
56. Gutman, *It Ain't Cheatin' If You Don't Get Caught*, 54–55.
57. Oakley, *Baseball's Last Golden Age*, 242.
58. Allen with Graham, *It Takes Heart*, 156.
59. Frommer, *New York City Baseball*, 162.
60. Oakley, *Baseball's Last Golden Age*, 243.
61. *Ibid.*, 244.
62. Larsen with Shaw, *The Perfect Yankee*, 94.
63. Kahn, *The Era*, 331.
64. Oakley, *Baseball's Last Golden Age*, 243.
65. *Ibid.*, 237.
66. Kahn, *Memories of Summer*, 215.
67. Kahn, *The Era*, 331.
68. Oakley, *Baseball's Last Golden Age*, 244.
69. Larsen with Shaw, *The Perfect Yankee*, 35.
70. *Ibid.*, 135.
71. Quigley, *The Crooked Pitch*, 179.
72. Oakley, *Baseball's Last Golden Age*, 245.

73. Larsen with Shaw, *The Perfect Yankee*, 180.
74. *Ibid.*, 179.
75. *New York Herald Tribune*, 9 October 1956.
76. Golenbock, *Bums*, 418.
77. Kahn, *The Era*, 332.

Chapter 12

1. Oakley, *Baseball's Last Golden Age*, 248.
2. *Ibid.*, 249.
3. Dorinson and Warmund, *Jackie Robinson*, 202.
4. Oakley, *Baseball's Last Golden Age*, 249.
5. *Ibid.*, 254.
6. *New York Herald Tribune*, 2 April 1957.
7. Oakley, *Baseball's Last Golden Age*, 258.
8. Golenbock, *Dynasty*, 288.
9. Frommer, *New York City Baseball*, 140.
10. Scheinin, *Field of Screams*, 270.
11. *Sporting News*, 31 July 1957.
12. Kahn, *The Boys of Summer*, 344.
13. *New York Herald Tribune*, 14 August 1957.
14. Oakley, *Baseball's Last Golden Age*, 254.
15. *New York Herald Tribune*, 2 September 1957.
16. *New York Herald Tribune*, 4 September 1957.
17. Allen with Graham, *It Takes Heart*, 59–60.
18. Hynd, *The Giants of the Polo Grounds*, 382.
19. Frommer, *New York City Baseball*, 26.
20. Oakley, *Baseball's Last Golden Age*, 266.

Chapter 13

1. Richman, "Does a Ballplayer Know When He's Through?" 75.
2. *Ibid.*, 74.
3. *Ibid.*, 12.
4. *Ibid.*, 74.
5. *Ibid.*, 76.
6. *New York Herald Tribune*, 20 March 1958.
7. Oakley, *Baseball's Last Golden Age*, 278.
8. Scheinin, *Field of Screams*, 273.
9. Oakley, *Baseball's Last Golden Age*, 277.
10. *Ibid.*, 280.
11. Benson, *Ballparks of North America*, 269.
12. *New York Herald Tribune*, 19 May 1958.
13. *New York Herald Tribune*, 10 June 1958.
14. Bjarkman, *Baseball with a Latin Beat*, 226.
15. Maglie and Boyle, "Baseball Is a Tough Business," 22 April 1968, 48.
16. Frommer, *New York City Baseball*, 152.
17. Oakley, *Baseball's Last Golden Age*, 270.
18. Scheinin, *Field of Screams*, 271.
19. Maglie and Boyle, "Baseball Is a Tough Business," 22 April 1968, 49.
20. Larsen with Shaw, *The Perfect Yankee*, 135.
21. Overfield, "A Giant Among Men."
22. Gibson with Wheeler, *Stranger to the Game*, 53.
23. *New York Herald Tribune*, 18 March 1959.
24. Maglie and Boyle, "Baseball Is a Tough Business," 22 April 1968, 49.
25. Gibson with Wheeler, *Stranger to the Game*, 53.
26. *Ibid.*, 153.
27. *Ibid.*, 155–56.
28. *Ibid.*, 166.
29. *New York Herald Tribune*, 18 March 1959.

Chapter 14

1. Maglie and Boyle, "Baseball Is a Tough Business," 15 April 1968, 80.
2. Scheinin, *Field of Screams*, 305.
3. Kiernan, *The Miracle at Coogan's Bluff*, 182.
4. Overfield, "A Giant Among Men."

5. *New York Times*, 29 December 1992.
6. Bouton, *Ball Four*, 147–48.
7. Larsen with Shaw, *The Perfect Yankee*, 134–35.
8. Westcott, *Diamond Greats*, 288.
9. *New York Times*, 29 December 1992.
10. Frommer, *New York City Baseball*, 86.
11. Hano, *A Day in the Bleachers*, 114.
12. Scheinin, *Field of Screams*, 97.
13. Ibid., 15.
14. Ibid., 288.
15. Gutman, *It Ain't Cheatin' If You Don't Get Caught*, 119.
16. *New York Times*, 10 September 1952.
17. Durocher with Linn, *Nice Guys Finish Last*, 437.
18. Scheinin, *Field of Screams*, 289.
19. Larsen with Shaw, *The Perfect Yankee*, 3.
20. Allen with Graham, *It Takes Heart*, 13.

BIBLIOGRAPHY

Newspapers

Brooklyn Eagle
Christian Science Monitor
Jersey Journal (When researching the 1945 Jersey City Giants season, the *Jersey Journal* was now called the *Hudson Dispatch*).
New York Herald Tribune
New York Sun
New York Times
Philadelphia Inquirer
Sporting News
Washington Post

Books

Allen, Lee. *The Giants and the Dodgers: The Fabulous Story of Baseball's Fiercest Feud.* New York: G.P. Putnam's, 1964.
_____. *The World Series: The Story of Baseball's Annual Championship.* New York: G.P. Putnam's, 1969.
Allen, Mel, with Frank Graham, Jr. *It Takes Heart.* New York: Harper & Brothers, 1959.
Anderson, Dave. *Pennant Races: Baseball at Its Best.* New York: Doubleday, 1994.
The Baseball Encyclopedia: The Complete and Definitive Record of Major League Baseball. 9th ed. New York: Macmillan, 1993.

Benson, Michael. *Ballparks of North America: A Comprehensive Historical Reference to Baseball Grounds, Yards, and Stadiums, 1845 to the Present*. Jefferson, N.C.: McFarland, 1989.

Berton, Pierre. *Niagara: A History of the Falls*. New York: Penguin, 1992.

Bjarkman, Peter C. *Baseball with a Latin Beat: A History of the Latin American Game*. Jefferson, N.C.: McFarland, 1994.

Bouton, Jim. *Ball Four*. Ed. Leonard Shecter. 1970. New York: Macmillan, 1990.

Cisneros, Pedro Treto. *Enciclopedia Del Beisbol Mexicano*. 1998. ("Mexican Baseball Encyclopedia").

Clifton, Merritt. *Disorganized Baseball: The Provincial League From LaRoque To Les Expos*. Richford, VT.: Samisdat, 1982.

Dickson, Paul. *The New Dickson Baseball Dictionary*. San Diego: Harcourt Brace, 1999.

DiClerico, James M., and Barry J. Pavelec. *The Jersey Game: The History of Modern Baseball From Its Birth to the Big Leagues in the Garden State*. New Brunswick: Rutgers University Press, 1991.

Dorinson, Joseph, and Joram Warmund., eds. *Jackie Robinson: Race, Sports, and the American Dream*. Armonk, N.Y.: M.E. Sharpe, 1998.

Durocher, Leo, with Ed Linn. *Nice Guys Finish Last*. New York: Simon & Schuster, 1975.

Echevarria, Roberto Gonzalez. *The Pride of Havana: A History of Cuban Baseball*. New York: Oxford University Press, 1999.

Filichia, Peter. *Professional Baseball Franchises: From the Abbeville Athletics to the Zanesville Indians*. New York: Facts on File, 1993.

Frommer, Harvey. *New York City Baseball: The Last Golden Age, 1947–1957*. New York: Macmillan, 1980.

Gershman, Michael. *Diamonds: The Evolution of the Ballpark*. Boston: Houghton Mifflin, 1993.

Gibson, Bob, with Lonnie Wheeler. *Stranger to the Game*. New York: Penguin, 1994.

Gilbert, Bill. *They Also Served: Baseball and the Home Front, 1941–1945*. New York: Crown, 1992.

Goldstein, Richard. *Spartan Seasons: How Baseball Survived the Second World War*. New York: Macmillan, 1980.

_____. *Superstars and Screwballs: 100 Years of Brooklyn Baseball*. New York: Dutton, 1991.

Golenbock, Peter. *Bums: An Oral History of the Brooklyn Dodgers*. New York: G.P. Putnam's, 1984.

_____. *Dynasty: The New York Yankees, 1949–1964*. 1975. Lincolnwood (Chicago), IL.: Contemporary Books, 2000.

Gutman, Dan. *It Ain't Cheatin' If You Don't Get Caught: Scuffing, Corking, Spitting, Gunking, Razzing, and Other Fundamentals of Our National Pastime*. New York: Penguin, 1990.

Halberstam, David. *The Fifties*. New York: Villard, 1993.

Hano, Arnold. *A Day in the Bleachers*. New York: Crowell, 1955.

_____. *Willie Mays*. New York: Grosset & Dunlap, 1966.

Hodges, Russ, and Al Hirshberg. *My Giants*. Garden City, N.Y.: Doubleday, 1963.

Honig, Donald. *Baseball America: The Heroes of the Game and the Times of Their Glory*. 1985. New York: Barnes & Noble, 1997.
Humber, William. *Diamonds of the North: A Concise History of Baseball in Canada*. Toronto: Oxford University Press, 1995.
Hynd, Noel. *The Giants of the Polo Grounds: The Glorious Times of Baseball's New York Giants*. 1988. Dallas, TX.: Taylor, 1995.
Irvin, Monte, with James A. Riley. *Nice Guys Finish First: The Autobiography of Monte Irvin*. New York: Carroll & Graf, 1996.
James, Bill. *Bill James' Guide to Baseball Managers: From 1870 to Today*. New York: Simon & Schuster, 1997.
_____. *The Bill James Historical Baseball Abstract*. New York: Villard, 1988.
Johnson, Lloyd, and Miles Wolff. *The Encyclopedia of Minor League Baseball*. Durham, N.C.: Baseball America, 1993.
Jordan, David M. *A Tiger in His Time: Hal Newhouser and the Burden of Wartime Ball*. South Bend, IN.: Diamond Communications, 1990.
Kahn, Roger. *The Boys of Summer*. New York: Harper & Row, 1971.
_____. *The Era: 1947–1957 When the Yankees, the Giants, and the Dodgers Ruled the World*. New York: Ticknor & Fields, 1993.
_____. *Memories of Summer: When Baseball Was an Art, and Writing About It a Game*. New York: Hyperion, 1997.
Karst, Gene, and Martin J. Jones, Jr. *Who's Who in Professional Baseball*. New Rochelle, N.Y.: Arlington House, 1973.
Keyes, Ray, ed. *Silver Anniversary: Eastern League Record Book, 1923–1947*. 1947.
Kiernan, Thomas. *The Miracle at Coogan's Bluff*. New York: Crowell, 1975.
Knight, Franklin W. *The Caribbean: The Genesis of a Fragmented Nationalism*. 2nd ed. New York: Oxford University Press, 1990.
LaMar, Steve. *The Book of Baseball Lists*. Jefferson, N.C.: McFarland, 1993.
Larsen, Don, with Mark Shaw. *The Perfect Yankee: The Incredible Story of the Greatest Miracle In Baseball History*. Champaign, IL.: Sagamore, 1996.
Linn, Ed. *Hitter: The Life and Turmoils of Ted Williams*. New York: Harcourt Brace, 1993.
Lowenfish, Lee, and Tony Lupien. *The Imperfect Diamond: The Story of Baseball's Reserve System and the Men Who Fought to Change It*. New York: Stein & Day, 1980.
Marshall, William. *Baseball's Pivotal Era, 1945–1951*. Lexington, KY.: University of Kentucky Press, 1999.
Meany, Tom. *The Incredible Giants*. New York: A.S. Barnes, 1955.
Oakley, J. Ronald. *Baseball's Last Golden Age, 1946–1960: The National Pastime in a Time of Glory and Change*. Jefferson, N.C.: McFarland, 1994.
Obojski, Robert. *All-Star Baseball Since 1933*. New York: Stein & Day, 1980.
Okkonen, Marc. *Baseball Memories, 1950–1959: An Illustrated Scrapbook of Baseball's Fabulous 50's*. New York: Sterling, 1993.
Peary, Danny, ed. *We Played the Game: 65 Players Remember Baseball's Greatest Era, 1947–1964*. New York: Hyperion, 1994.
Phillips, John. *The Mexican Jumping Beans: The Story of the Baseball War of 1946*. Perry, GA.: Capital, 1997.
Pietrusza, David. *Baseball's Canadian-American League: A History of Its Inception, Franchises, Participants, Locales, Statistics, Demise and Legacy, 1936–1951*. Jefferson, N.C.: McFarland, 1990.

Prince, Carl E. *Brooklyn's Dodgers: The Bums, the Borough, and the Best of Baseball, 1947–1957.* New York: Oxford University Press, 1996.
Quigley, Martin. *The Crooked Pitch: The Curveball in American Baseball History.* Chapel Hill, N.C.: Algonquin, 1984.
Ritter, Lawrence S. *Lost Ballparks: A Celebration of Baseball's Legendary Fields.* New York: Penguin Studio, 1992.
Roberts, Robin and C. Paul Rogers III. *The Whiz Kids and the 1950 Pennant.* Philadelphia: Temple University Press, 1996.
Robinson, Jackie (as told to Alfred Duckett). *I Never Had It Made.* 1972. Hopewell, N.J.: Ecco Press, 1995.
Robinson, Ray. *The Home Run Heard 'Round the World: The Dramatic Story of the 1951 Giants-Dodgers Pennant Race.* New York: HarperCollins, 1991.
Scheinin, Richard. *Field of Screams: The Dark Underside of America's National Pastime.* New York: W.W. Norton, 1994.
Schlesinger, Jr., Arthur M., Gen. ed. *The Almanac of American History.* New York: Barnes & Noble, 1993.
Shapiro, Milton J. *The Sal Maglie Story.* New York: Messner, 1957.
Stein, Fred, and Nick Peters. *Giants Diary: A Century of Giants Baseball in New York and San Francisco.* Berkeley, CA.: North Atlantic, 1987.
Sullivan, Neil J. *The Minors: The Struggles and the Triumph of Baseball's Poor Relation From 1876 to the Present.* New York: St. Martin's, 1990.
Thomson, Bobby, with Lee Heiman and Bill Gutman. *"The Giants Win the Pennant! The Giants Win Pennant!"* New York: Zebra, 1991.
Tindall, George Brown, and David E. Shi. *America: A Narrative History.* 4th ed. New York: W.W. Norton, 1996.
Turner, Frederick. *When the Boys Came Back: Baseball and 1946.* New York: Henry Holt, 1996.
Violanti, Anthony. *Miracle in Buffalo: How the Dream of Baseball Revived a City.* New York: St. Martin's, 1991.
Voigt, David Quentin. *American Baseball: Vol. 3, From Postwar Expansion to the Electronic Age.* University Park, PA.: The Pennsylvania State University Press, 1983.
Westcott, Rich. *Diamond Greats: Profiles and Interviews with 65 of Baseball's History Makers.* Westport, CT.: Meckler, 1988.
Wright, Marshall D. *The International League: Year-by-Year Statistics, 1884–1953.* Jefferson, N.C.: McFarland, 1998.
Zoss, Joel, and John S. Bowman. *Diamonds in the Rough: The Untold History of Baseball.* New York: Macmillan, 1989.

Articles

"The Barber." *Newsweek*, May 19, 1952.
"Baseball: the Hot 'Hate'." *Newsweek*, October 4, 1954.
Buege, Bob. "Spahn's First "Loss" Wasn't." *Baseball Research Journal* 28, 1999.
Cope, Myron. "Look What's Happening to Ballplayers." *Sport*, July, 1963.
Creamer, Robert. "An Angel of Darkness Named Sal the Barber." *Sports Illustrated*, June 6, 1955.
"Dead or Alive." *Time*, July 10, 1950.

Field, Russell. "Frank Shaughnessy: International League Innovator." *Dugout*, (Vol II, Issue I), April, 1994.
Graham, Frank, Jr. "The Great Mexican War of 1946." *Sports Illustrated*, September 19, 1966.
Grosshandler, Stan. "'54 Indians: Their Pitching Staff Was One of Best Ever." *Baseball Digest*, May, 1994.
Kelley, Brent. "Wes Westrum: New York's Other Catcher." *Vintage & Classic Baseball Collector* 6, May/June, 1996.
Krah, Steve. "The Limestone League." *Baseball Research Journal* 26, 1997.
Lardner, John. "A Real Damp Year." *Newsweek*, September 17, 1956.
_____. "Imaginary Matter of Life and Death." *Newsweek*, August 12, 1950.
_____. "Razor Blades Amok." *Newsweek*, July 16, 1951.
_____. "Tinker to Evers to Freud." *Newsweek*, September 15, 1952.
Levin, Leonard. "Baseball in 1945 — The Pits." *Providence Journal*, February, 1995.
Lundquist, Carl. "Drama in Philadelphia." *Baseball Research Journal* 26, 1997.
Macht, Norman L. "Ugly Incidents on Field Have Long Cursed the Majors." *Baseball Digest*, May, 1997.
Maglie, Sal, and Robert H. Boyle. "Baseball Is a Tough Business." *Sports Illustrated*, April 15 and 22, 1968.
"Maglie, Sal." *Current Biography*, 1953.
Mayer, Bob. "Bill Voiselle and the $500 Pitch." *Baseball Research Journal* 26, 1997.
"One More World Series?" *Newsweek*, September 24, 1956.
Overfield, Joe. "A Giant Among Men." *Bisongram*, April/May, 1993.
_____. "Ollie Carnegie: Buffalo's Comeback Kid." *Bisongram*, February, 1988.
Pollack, Howard M., M.D. "The Development of the Baseball Batting Helmet: The MacPhail-Dandy Controversy."
Porter, David L. "Untold Saga of Europe's Big Leaguers." *International Pastime: A Review of Baseball History* 12, 1992.
Richman, Milton. "Does a Ballplayer Know When He's Through?" *Sport*, July, 1957.
"The Slows." *Newsweek*, September 29, 1952.
Vaughn, Gerald F. "George Hausmann Recalls the Mexican League of 1946–47." *Baseball Research Journal* 19, 1990.
_____. "Jorge Pasquel and the Evolution of the Mexican League." *International Pastime: A Review of Baseball History* 12, 1992.
"The Way It Went." *Newsweek*, October 8, 1956.
"Willie Mays: The Hottest Thing Since Babe Ruth." *Newsweek*, July 19, 1954.
Wysard, Paul L. "The World War II Years: A Re-Evaluation." (From SABR Presentation — San Francisco, 6/98.)

INDEX

Aaron, Henry "Hank" 294, 311, 314–16, 329, 337, 343, 358
Abernathy, Woody 8
Abrams, Cal 114, 116, 161, 188, 223
Adams, Ace 39, 43, 45–46, 48–49, 57, 60, 66–67, 216
Adams, Bobby 158, 214, 263
Adcock, Joe 134, 237, 269, 315–17, 319, 324
Addis, Bob 164, 168–69
Ainsmith, Eddie 26
Aleman, Migel 55, 65
Alexander, Grover Cleveland 108, 194, 343
Allen, Johnny 13
Allen, Mel 323
Almeida, Rafael 54
Alston, Walter Emmons 249–51, 257, 263, 272, 284–85, 301, 307, 310, 313–17, 322–25, 329–31, 334, 337, 339, 341, 370
Amaro, Santos 68
Amaros, Sandy 286, 301, 319, 322, 329–30, 333, 335, 337, 339
Anderson, Harry 341, 351
Angell, Roger 343, 347
Antonelli, Johnny 243, 248, 253, 257, 261, 266–67, 269, 273, 279, 284, 290, 292, 321, 347
Arnold, Benedict 309
Ash, Ken 8, 12, 16, 22
Ashburn, Richie 84, 104–5, 114, 133, 138, 148, 155–56, 168, 210, 215, 268–69, 284, 316, 327, 363
Aspromonte, Ken 354
Avila, Bobby 68, 121, 185, 275–76, 279, 297, 299

Baczewski, Fred 255
Bagby, Jim 25
Bailey, Ed 314–15
Baker, Del 364
Baker, Frank "Home Run" 104
Baker, Gene 255, 287, 313, 318, 339
Ballanfant, Lee 81, 105, 126, 142, 160, 196, 213, 257, 291
Bamberger, George 77, 118, 123
Bankhead, Dan 106, 132
Banks, Ernie 255, 295, 317, 319, 342, 359
Barker, Norbert 31
Barlick, Al 81, 103, 142, 144, 161
Barna, Babe 27
Barnes, Jill 53
Barr, George 104
Barrett, Red 33, 35
Barrow, Ed 281
Bartell, Dick 27, 30, 57
Bauer, Hank 180–81, 331–34, 340–41, 351
Baumholtz, Frankie 219, 290, 327
Bausewein, George 29
Bavasi, Buzzy 151, 272, 307, 336, 345

391

Index

Beal, Floyd 31
Beard, Stan 72
Beard, Ted 79
Beggs, Joe 3
Belinsky, Bo 321
Bell, Gary 354
Bell, Gus 109–11, 132, 148, 150, 227, 255, 314, 317
Belson, John 296
Berardino, Johnny 110
Bergunzie, Frank 289
Berra, Yogi 110, 179–80, 332–35, 340, 347, 351
Berres, Ray 51, 57
Berton, Pierre 4
Bessent, Don 285, 317, 321–23, 325, 330, 339
Bickford, Vern 144, 168, 200
Bilko, Steve 229
Bishop, Charlie 118
Bissonette, Del 43
Bithorn, Hi 54, 370
Bjarkman, Peter 355
Black, Joe 117, 205, 209–11, 213, 225, 230
Blackwell, Ewell "The Whip" 31, 93, 97, 148, 189, 344
Blanco, Carlos 67
Blattner, Buddy 59
Blaylock, Gary 361
Blaylock, Marv 327
Bloodworth, Jimmy 105
Bolling, Milt 346
Bondy, Leo 27
Bonham, Ernie 3
Boone, Ray 186
Bossard, Emil 300
Boudreau, Lou 8, 12–13, 17, 22, 38, 120
Bouton, Jim 366–68, 370
Bowman, Doc 171, 246, 294
Bowman, Roger 77, 118, 127, 133–34, 187, 194, 221
Boyer, Cloyd 98–99
Boyer, Ken 343, 360
Boyle, Robert 152, 253
Bradley, Alva 13
Bragen, Bobby 326
Bramham, William 13
Branca, Ralph 45, 92, 95, 126, 144–46, 151, 155, 159, 161, 171, 174–76, 230
Brandt, Jackie 322
Brannick, Eddie 56, 79, 100
Brecheen, Harry 43, 139, 197
Brewer, Jack 45, 48, 57
Bridges, Marshall 361–62

Bridges, Rocky 126
Broglio, Ernie 361
Bronwell, Herbert 298
Brosnan, Jim 119, 313, 339, 356, 360
Brown, Mordecai 108
Brown, Tommy 308
Brown, Warren 49
Brown, Willard 115
Brubaker, Ray 23
Bruton, Bill 294, 314–15, 340
Budnick, Mike 57, 60
Buege, Bob 237
Buhl, Bob 233, 315, 323, 342
Bunning, Jim 8
Burdette, Lew 233–35, 258, 315, 319
Burge, Les 34–35
Burgess, Forrest "Smoky" 188, 325
Burns, George 347
Busby, Jim 305
Busch, August A. (Gussie) 226, 229, 360
Byrne, Tommy 350

Caballero, Putsy 84
Calderone, Sam 86, 106, 115, 221, 243
Calles, Plutarco Elias 55
Cambria, Joe 54, 56
Campanella, Roy 82, 86, 92, 110, 122, 125–27, 135, 142, 145–47, 153, 157, 160, 163–64, 167, 172–73, 188, 198, 205–7, 211, 222–23, 225, 231, 234–35, 237, 240, 250–53, 257–58, 260, 262, 266, 268, 271–72, 284–86, 290, 307–8, 310, 314–17, 323, 325–30, 334, 341, 359
Campaneris, Bert 366
Carey, Andy 333, 335, 351
Carnegie, Ollie 8–9, 11–12, 17–18, 20, 41, 136
Carnevale, Danny (Dan) 10, 15–16
Carpenter, Robert (Bob) (pitcher) 12, 57
Carpenter, Robert (Bob), Jr. (owner) 199
Carrasquel, Alejandro 66
Casey, Daniel 31
Casey, Hugh 36, 61
Castiglione, Pete 132, 141, 148
Castleman, Foster 305, 322
Cavarretta, Phil 48, 79, 149–50
Cepeda, Orlando 282, 312, 358
Cerv, Bob 332
Chambers, Cliff 93
Chandler, Albert B. "Happy" 39, 53, 57–58, 69, 71, 74, 77, 117, 177, 187
Chapman, Ben 13, 47, 112, 355

Chapman, Ed 11
Chapman, Marguerite Wendelle Kenny 320
Chapman, Ray 91
Chartak, Mike 3
Chatham, Buster 23
Chrisman, David 11
Church, Bubba 84, 105, 113
Cimoli, Gino 340
Clark, Mel 215
Clarke, Hugh 31
Clemente, Roberto 326
Cobb, Ty 36, 104, 369
Cohen, Andy 23
Cole, Dick 229
Coleman, Jerry 331, 346
Coleman, Rip 299
Collins, Jimmy 8
Collins, Joe 178, 333
Comiskey, Chuck 344
Como, Perry 275
Conigliaro, Tony 366
Conlan, Jocko 97, 153, 287, 329, 343
Conley, Gene 269–70
Connelly, Bill 211, 215
Conners, Chuck 159
Consuegra, Sandalio 68
Coogan, James J. 108
Cook, Earl 16–22
Cooke, Bob 137, 151, 167, 266
Coombs, Bobby 29–36
Cooney, Johnny 76
Cooper, Walker 47, 54, 57, 75, 123, 128, 167–69, 270
Corwin, Al 149–52, 157–58, 171, 177, 186, 204, 207, 210, 214–15, 222, 225–27, 237, 241, 267
Courtney, Clint 241
Covington, Wes 337, 358
Cox, Billy 122, 124, 145, 154, 157, 172–73, 198, 201, 205–7, 212–14, 230, 238, 251, 261, 266, 272, 302, 313
Craig, Roger 285, 313, 319, 329–30, 332, 338, 340
Crandall, Del 294
Creamer, Robert 322, 338
Cronin, Joe 25, 258
Cross, Harry 47
Cuccinello, Tony 28
Cuccurullo, Art 44
Cunningham, Bill (columnist) 304
Cunningham, Bill (player) 64
Cusick, Jack 149
Cuyk, Chris Van 126, 129

Daley, Arthur 49, 131, 193, 211, 239–40, 301, 348
Daley, Bud 307
Dandridge, Ray 136
Daniels, Jack 200
Danna, Jesse 28–29
Dark, Alvin 76–77, 81, 83, 85–88, 96, 98–99, 101–2, 105, 108, 114–15, 120, 123, 125, 129, 132–33, 135, 138–42, 146, 150, 155–59, 162–63, 165–66, 168–69, 174, 177–81, 183, 185, 189, 191–92, 195–96, 202, 206, 213, 215, 217–21, 227–28, 232–33, 236–37, 240–41, 244, 248, 250–51, 255, 257, 260, 262, 273, 277, 279–80, 282, 284, 286–87, 289–90, 359, 369–70
Dascoli, Frank 83, 87, 132, 167
Davis, George 347
Davis, Harry 18, 21
Davis, Jim 290
Davis, Sammy, Jr. 340
Day, John B. 108
Day, Laraine 113, 120, 294
Deal, Cot 263
Deal, Lindsey 18
Dean, Dizzy 188, 193, 203
de la Cruz, Thomas (Tommy) 25, 54
Delmore, Vic 329
DeMaestri, Joe 355
Dente, Sam 275
Derry, Russ 34
Devine, Bing 356
Dickey, Bill 8, 100
Dickson, Murry 350, 355
Diering, Chuck 198
Dihigo, Martin 51, 53, 66, 355
Dillinger, Bob 110
DiMaggio, Dom 120
DiMaggio, Joe 25, 49, 59, 61, 86, 148, 178, 180, 191, 205, 301, 349
Ditmar, Art 299, 340
Doby, Larry 86, 184, 219, 221, 275–78, 301, 340
Doerr, Bobby 120
Donald, Atley 3
Donatelli, Augie 125–26, 135, 142, 144, 163, 190–91
Doubleday, Abner 53
Doyle, Jack 347
Drabowsky, Moe 322, 339
Drake, Solly 318
Drake, Tom 16, 22
Drebinger, John 122, 234
Dressen, Charlie 116–18, 120–27, 131, 142,

145–47, 150–52, 154, 157–59, 161–62, 164, 166–67, 169, 171–72, 174–76, 194, 197, 205, 208–12, 216, 230–32, 238, 249–52, 288, 300–1, 329, 346, 368
Drews, Karl 167
Dropo, Walt 120, 340
Drysdale, Don 285, 310–13, 322, 328, 330, 338, 340–41, 363
Dulles, John Foster 298
Duren, Ryne 352–53, 355
Durocher, Leo 2, 10, 29, 36, 46–47, 49, 52, 70, 75–86, 88, 90, 94–98, 100, 102–7, 109, 110–14, 116–42, 144–50, 152–56, 158–60, 162–63, 165–72, 174–77, 179–81, 183–87, 190–91, 193–96, 198–210, 212–216, 218–23, 225–35, 237–40, 242, 244–49, 253–55, 258–60, 262, 264–75, 278–80, 282–83, 286–87, 289–92, 294–97, 308, 322, 350, 359, 368, 370
Dusak, Erv 148
Dyer, Eddie 98
Dykes, Jimmy 331, 355

East, Hugh 31–34, 36
Easter, Luke 78, 248
Edwards, Bruce 145
Edwards, Hank 34, 189
Effrat, Louis 191
Egan, Jack 6
Eisenhower, Dwight D. 40, 330–31
Elliott, Bob 14, 96, 103, 147, 186, 188, 190, 197–99, 210, 215
Ellman, Dorris 367
Elston, Don 339
Embree, Red 24–25
Emmerich, Dale 40, 43
Ennis, Del 84–85, 138, 156, 166, 199, 215, 316, 321
Erskine, Carl 113, 117, 123, 145, 153, 174–75, 209, 222, 235, 257, 266, 268, 271–72, 285, 308, 327–28, 330, 338
Estalella, Bobby 63, 66
Evans, Billy 258

Fain, Ferris 220
Fanovich, Frank 118
Farrell, Perry 23
Feely, Edgar P. 320
Feeney, Chub 244, 281, 309, 336–37
Feldman, Harry 38–40, 42–43, 47, 49, 57, 60, 66, 69, 72
Feller, Bob 13, 49, 61, 79, 184, 221, 274, 280, 303, 307, 362
Fernandez, Chico 316–17, 320

Fink, Herman 22
Fischer, Rube 28–31, 36, 38, 57
Fitzsimmons, Freddie 78, 80, 97, 99, 101, 105, 118–19, 132, 145, 172, 187, 245, 267, 277
Flaherty, Joe 357
Flaig, Otto, Jr. 96
Fleitas, Andres 60
Flood, Curt 359
Flynn, John L. 71
Foiles, Hank 323
Fondy, Dee 135, 227, 318
Ford, Whitey 331–332, 337, 340, 344, 352, 355
Fox, Norman 118
Foxx, Jimmie "Double X" 38, 43, 45, 59
Foytack, Paul 352
Franklin, Murray 66
Franks, Herman 90, 145, 163, 176, 186, 202, 287
Freese, George 289
French, Larry 36
Frick, Ford 48, 93, 95, 100–1, 104, 106, 132, 134, 142, 167, 177, 187, 249, 258
Friend, Bob 343
Frisch, Frankie 145, 149
Furillo, Carl 2, 89–90, 92–96, 122, 124–25, 127–29, 145, 147, 153, 155, 157, 159, 166, 172–73, 188, 197, 212, 223–25, 227, 237–40, 251–53, 258, 262, 266, 268, 272, 284–85, 287, 302, 308–9, 318–19, 321–22, 326, 329, 330, 334, 338–39, 347, 368

Galan, Augie 46
Gallagher, Taps 6
Garagiola, Joe 148, 223, 255
Garcia, Mike 184, 219–20, 222, 274–75, 282, 297–98, 305
Garcia, Silvio 66
Gardella, Danny 40, 44, 46, 48–49, 56, 58–60, 62, 66–67, 69–72
Gardner, Billy 255, 258
Gee, Johnny 8
Gehrig, Lou 46
Gettel, Allen 117, 120–21, 123, 127, 140, 148
Gibson, Bob 361–63, 365
Gibson, Homer 69
Gibson, Josh 7
Gibson, Russ 366
Giebell, Floyd 13, 18–20, 22
Giel, Paul 266
Gilbert, Tookie 82–83, 96, 98–99, 101, 105, 115, 121, 235
Giles, Warren 188, 211–12, 214, 228, 263, 293

Index

Gilliam, Jim "Junior" 226, 230, 266, 313, 317, 322, 324, 327, 330, 333, 337, 339, 341–43
Gladu, Roland 51–52, 69
Glaviano, Tommy (Tom) 98–99, 102, 112, 196–97
Glenn, Edgar E. 44
Goetz, Larry 46, 92, 211, 225, 228
Golenbock, Peter 258, 287, 296, 308
Goliat, Mike 84, 104–5, 146
Gomez, Lefty 350
Gomez, Ruben 90, 92, 219, 227–29, 233–34, 237–38, 240, 244, 248, 261, 273, 282, 287, 289, 292, 294, 305, 339, 368
Gonzalez, Mike 51, 53, 65–66
Goodman, Billy 120
Gordon, Joe 121
Gordon, Sid 29–33, 35–36, 47, 57, 76, 81–82, 86, 95–97, 144, 147, 164, 166–67, 169–70, 192, 289–90, 293, 347
Gore, Art (Artie) 25, 162, 231, 322
Gorman, Tom 57, 60–62, 207, 227, 235
Gornicki, Henry 21
Grace, Earl 115
Graflan, Roy Van 12
Graham, Jack 34
Grant, Eddie 108
Grant, Ulysses S 274
Grasso, Mickey 278
Gray, Dick 358
Gray, Pete 38
Grayson, Harry 84
Green, Dallas 8
Green, Gene 356
Green, Ron 328
Greenberg, Hank 49, 61, 275, 303, 306–7
Gregg, Hal 92, 195, 200, 205, 209, 261
Griffith, Clark 53–54, 56, 64, 249
Grim, Bob 344, 350, 355
Grimes, Burleigh 10, 14, 30, 119
Grimm, Charlie 200, 228, 243, 315
Grissom, Marv 57, 244, 248, 251, 253, 255, 257–58, 260–62, 266, 268, 270, 273, 277–79, 285, 289–91, 294
Groat, Dick 323, 329, 347
Grodzicki, John 21
Guerra, Mike 58
Gustine, Frankie 44

Haak, Howie 54
Hack, Stan 355
Haddix, Harvey 228, 259, 289, 316, 320–21, 327
Hague, Frank 29

Halsey, William "Bull" 342
Hamilton, Jack 366
Hamner, Granny 84, 104, 137, 166, 188, 316
Haney, Fred 223, 315
Hano, Arnold 369
Hansen, Andy 39, 80, 83, 88, 92, 94–95
Harris, Bill 22, 34
Harris, Bucky 8
Harris, Gail 290–92, 295–96, 305
Harshman, Jack 77–78, 80, 82, 215, 300
Hartnett, Gabby 40, 42
Hartsfield, Roy 127, 192
Hartung, Clint 54, 77–78, 81, 83, 88, 92, 96, 98, 120, 175–76, 207, 215
Hasson, Gene 14
Hatten, Joe 129, 145
Hatton, Grady 140
Hausmann, George 38–39, 43–44, 57, 59–60, 64, 66, 69, 72, 79
Hayworth, Red 66, 69
Hearn, Jim 97–98, 101–2, 105–8, 114, 117–20, 123, 127, 129, 132–34, 139–41, 146, 148, 150, 157, 160, 162–63, 165–66, 168, 170–71, 176, 179–80, 184–85, 187, 194, 199, 203, 211, 215, 217, 223, 225–26, 229, 233–34, 238, 241, 243–44, 248, 261, 263, 273, 282, 290, 295, 320, 322
Heath, Jeff 13
Hegan, Jim 299
Helf, Henry 22
Hemingway, Ernest 61, 357
Hemus, Solly 158, 163, 202, 291, 316, 327, 360–62
Herman, Babe 9, 38
Herman, Billy 329, 364
Hermanski, Gene 94, 127, 129, 145, 164
Hernandez, Chico 66
Herrera 52
Herrera, Don Julio Blanco 65
Higbe, Kirby 80–81, 87–88, 93, 95
Higgins, Pinky 364
Hiller, Frank 149, 220, 226
Hoak, Don 260, 272, 284, 341–42
Hodges, Gil 92–93, 106, 111, 118, 122, 125–28, 139, 145–47, 160–61, 167, 171–74, 188, 212–13, 217, 225, 235, 237, 251–53, 259–60, 262, 266, 271–72, 285, 308, 317, 319, 323–25, 327, 329, 330–31, 333, 339, 341–42
Hodges, Russ 99, 170, 175, 310
Hoeft, Billy 299
Hofman, Bobby 80, 120, 128, 212, 214, 226, 237, 256, 267–68, 270, 274, 284, 290

Holmes, Tommy (columnist) 95, 188, 206, 236, 262, 314, 343
Holmes, Tommy (player and manager) 48, 144, 166, 186
Hopp, Johnny 39–40, 43
Hornsby, Rogers 56, 187
Hostetler, Chuck 49
Houk, Ralph 355
Houtteman, Art 41, 274, 299, 305
Howard, Elston 301, 335, 351
Howell, Red 35
Hubbell, Carl 27, 101, 108, 110–11, 135, 164, 187, 222, 243, 272, 321, 347
Hughes, Jim 230
Hurley, Ed 355
Hutchings, Johnny 43
Hutchinson, Fred 8, 18, 20, 22, 355–56, 358–59

Irvin, Monte 76, 85–86, 88, 90, 92, 95, 98, 101–3, 105, 110, 112, 114–15, 118, 122, 125, 132–38, 141, 149, 153, 155–56, 161–64, 169–71, 173–74, 177–81, 186, 194, 198–99, 203, 212, 214, 216–18, 220–22, 227, 230, 232–34, 238, 240, 241, 245–46, 248, 253–54, 258, 260, 262, 273, 276, 278–80, 282–83, 285, 287, 289, 295–96, 347

Jablonski, Ray 325
Jackson, Larry 342, 355
Jackson, Randy 140, 254, 288, 290, 317, 330
Jacobs, Art 14, 22
Jaeger, Norman 29–30
James, Bill 296
Jansen, Larry 77–81, 83, 85, 87–88, 90, 92–98, 101–2, 106, 110, 114, 117–20, 122, 124–28, 131, 133, 137, 140, 146–47, 150, 157–58, 163–64, 166, 169–71, 173–74, 176, 178, 180–85, 187, 190, 192, 194, 199–200, 203, 213–14, 216–19, 222, 225, 229, 231, 233–34, 237, 241, 243–44, 248, 261, 267, 321–322
Jeffcoat, Hal 141, 264, 285
Jefferies, Jim 247
Jethroe, Sam 81, 86, 96–97, 123, 127, 136, 144, 169–70, 192, 200–1, 215
Johnson, Arnold 299
Johnson, Billy 195, 202
Johnson, Ernie 200, 324
Johnson, Frederic 70
Johnson, Jack 247
Johnson, Walter 91, 359
Jones, Nippy 140

Jones, Sam "Toothpick" 290, 355
Jones, Sheldon 77, 79, 82–83, 87–88, 90, 93–98, 101, 104–5, 107, 114, 117–18, 125, 127, 130, 132–33, 142, 144, 146, 150, 153, 158–159, 161, 171, 177, 179–80, 184, 186, 200, 368
Jones, Willie "Puddin' Head" 84, 155, 164–65, 171, 310–11, 316, 327
Jorda, Lou 83
Jorgenson, Spider 86, 121, 132
Joyce, Frank 57
Jungels, Ken 34, 36
Jurges, Billy 27–28, 36, 45, 347, 364

Kahn, Roger 112, 211, 223, 229–30, 248, 264, 293, 318, 332, 342, 350
Katt, Ray 221, 247, 253, 270, 273, 289, 292–93, 296
Kazak, Eddie 99
Keane, Johnny 360, 362
Keefe, Jack 273
Keeler, Wee Willie 115
Kell, George 147–48
Keller, Charlie "King Kong" 3
Kelly, Bill 11
Kennedy, Monte 57, 77, 79, 83, 86–87, 95, 107, 112–13, 118, 120, 123, 133, 151, 180, 184–86, 194, 196–97, 199, 213–214, 229, 243, 349
Kerr, Buddy 29–30, 38, 44, 47, 75–76, 81–82, 85, 191, 347
Kiernan, Thomas 156
Kiner, Ralph 25, 109–10, 147–48, 202, 217, 255, 283, 292
King, Clyde 45, 154, 163
King, Joe 288
Klaus, Billy 243
Klein, Lou 58, 61, 66, 69, 72
Kline, Bob 16
Kluszewski, Ted 93, 150, 255, 295, 314
Knickerbocker, Austin 29–31
Kobesky, Ed (Eddie) 23, 42
Konikowski, Alex 261
Konschaft, Vincent 244
Konstanty, Jim 25, 84, 344
Koppett, Leonard 144, 311
Koslo, Dave 34, 36, 55, 57, 77–79, 82–84, 87–88,
Koufax, Sandy 311, 313, 320, 339, 342, 351
Kowalik, Fabian 8, 12, 16, 22
Kowle, Oswald 118
Kramer, Jack 77, 80, 83, 86–88, 93, 96, 105, 120, 123, 133
Krichell, Paul 11

Kritzer, Cy 40
Kroner, John 22
Kubek, Tony 351
Kucks, Johnny 350–54
Kuenn, Harvey 353
Kurowski, Whitey 21
Kuzava, Bob 180

Labine, Clem 117, 145, 151, 161, 163–64, 171, 211, 222, 230, 269, 285, 313–14, 316, 319–20, 322, 329–30, 335, 342
LaGuardia, Fiorello 29
Lancy, Al 58
Landis, Jim 354
Landis, Kenesaw Mountain 38–39, 46, 53, 65
Landrum, Joe 212
Lane, Frank 259, 356
Lang, Jack 79
Lanier, Max 61, 65–72, 83, 184, 194–97, 215
LaPalme, Paul 141, 291
Lardner, John 90, 147, 208, 315
Lardner, Ring 273
Larsen, Don 331–35, 344, 347, 350, 352, 354, 371
Lavagetto, Cookie 159–60, 167, 346
Layton, Les 42
Lazzeri, Tony 46, 138, 343
Lee, Bill 108
Lehman, Ken 317, 322
Lemon, Bob 25, 80, 121, 274–76, 278–80, 283, 297–99, 303, 306
Lennon, Bob 283
Levitt, Bill 296
Liddle, Don 243, 258, 273, 276–78, 280, 294
Lieber, Hank 31
Lincoln, Abraham 274
Lindell, John 3
Lindstrom, Fred 145, 289
Lisenbee, Hod 38, 44
Littlefield, Dick 336
Livingston, Mickey 47
Lockman, Whitey 42–43, 78, 86–88, 95, 101, 104, 110, 115, 118, 120, 125, 130–31, 133–35, 142, 157–58, 160, 164, 166, 168, 172–75, 177, 179–80, 183, 185, 194–95, 198, 200–1, 205–6, 214, 217, 223, 226, 232–34, 236–37, 241, 258, 262, 267, 272–73, 282, 286, 290, 292, 347
Loes, Billy 117, 209, 216, 222, 235, 252, 272, 285, 330
Logan, Johnny 211, 270–71, 292, 340

Lohrke, Jack 86, 105, 120
Lomax, Stan 296, 368
Lombardi, Ernie 38–39, 43–44, 47, 49
Lombardi, Vic 261
Lonborg, Jim 366
Lopat, Ed 178
Lopata, Stan 84, 114, 253, 313
Lopez, Al 46, 232, 275, 278–80, 283, 297, 299–300, 304–7, 350
Lown, Turk 163
Lowrey, Peanuts 87, 141, 195
Lumpe, Jerry 351, 354
Luque, Dolf (Adolfo) 2, 50–53, 61, 63–64, 66–69, 80, 94, 193, 232, 237, 311, 359, 362

MacArthur, Douglas 122, 124–25, 144
Mack, Connie 8, 38, 58, 299
Mack, Earle 299
Mack, Ray 14
Mack, Roy 299
MacPhail, Larry 10, 46, 75, 116–17, 283
Madura, Frank 24
Maglie, Joseph (father) 5–7, 245, 310
Maglie, Joseph (Sal's son) 310
Maglie, Kay (wife; her maiden name was Kathleen Pileggi) 24, 37, 51, 59, 61–62, 70–71, 82, 109, 204–5, 310, 329, 358, 364, 367–68
Maglie, Mary (mother) 5–6
Maglie, Sal 1–11, 13–37, 40–54, 57–64, 66–74, 77–88, 90–104, 106–15, 117–24, 126–27, 129–35, 138–44, 146–64, 166, 168–69, 171–174, 176, 179–99, 201–37, 239–40, 242–63, 265–73, 275–95, 297–348, 350–71
Maglie, Sal, Jr. (Sal's son) 310, 325, 329
Maguire, Jack 82, 86, 98, 133
Majeski, Hank 33–35, 219, 275
Maldovan, Johnny 41
Manning, Max 66
Mantilla, Felix 353
Mantle, Mickey Charles 178, 223, 274, 317, 330–35, 340, 344, 346, 351, 353
Maranville, Rabbit 24, 265
Marchildon, Phil 16
Marion, Marty 84, 133, 146–47, 191
Marquez, Luis 147
Marsans, Armando 54
Marshall, Willard 28, 36, 47, 57, 76, 81–82, 165, 168, 170, 347
Martin, Billy 216, 241, 304, 330, 332, 334, 337, 340–41
Martin, Fred 58, 61, 66, 71–72

398 Index

Martin, Joseph (Joe) 8, 12, 22
Martin, Pepper 38, 355
Mathews, Eddie 192, 200, 314–15, 323–24, 337, 340, 342
Mathewson, Christy 52
Mauch, Gene 261, 311
Maxwell, Charley 347
Maynard, Buster 29–31
Mayor, Agapito 68
Mays, Carl 91
Mays, Willie Howard 2, 47, 92, 135–42, 144, 148, 150, 157, 161, 164–65, 168, 175, 177–80, 183–86, 188–90, 192, 194, 198, 203, 206, 216, 237, 245–46, 248, 250, 253–57, 259, 261–65, 267, 270, 273, 276–79, 281–82, 284, 287–90, 293, 305, 311, 317, 320–21, 339, 347, 358, 371
Mazeroski, Bill 224, 323
McCall, John "Windy" 258, 261, 269, 289
McCarthy, Joe (manager) 8, 77
McCarthy, Joe 71, 247
McCulley, Jim 100
McCullough, Clyde 18–19, 22, 287
McDevitt, Danny 338
McDougald, Gil 194–95, 241, 333, 351
McGowen, Roscoe 123
McGraw, John J. 26–27, 43, 165, 199, 205, 287
McGrew, Ted 54
McKinney, Frank 87–88
McMillan, Roy 317
Mead, Charlie 60
Meany, Tom 54, 368
Medwick, Joe "Ducky" 29, 38, 291
Mellis, Mike 41
Melton, Cliff 164
Merkle, Fred 172
Merson, Jack 193, 202
Metkovich, George 163, 270
Meusel, Bob 46
Meyer, Billy 102, 201
Meyer, Jack 313, 327
Meyer, Russ "The Mad Monk" 84, 107–8, 137, 139, 155–56, 201, 222, 294
Miksis, Eddie 39, 145, 150
Miller, Eddie 99
Miller, Robert John "Bob" 84, 93, 113
Miller, Robert Lane "Bob" 362
Milliken, Bob 222
Minner, Paul 93, 226
Minoso, Minnie 86, 354–55
Mitchell, Dale 184, 319–20, 334
Mize, Johnny 36, 47, 57, 75, 344

Mizell, Wilmer "Vinegar Bend" 202–3, 226, 228, 356
Modak, Mike 44
Molini, Alfred 70–72
Monroe, Marilyn 369
Monroe, Zack 351
Montague, Eddie 135
Montono, Caster 61
Monzant, Ramon 261
Moore, Terry 61, 90, 263, 346
Morgan, Bob 192
Morgan, Tom 179
Mossi, Don 274
Mossor, Earl 129
Mueller, Don 78–79, 80, 82, 86–88, 93, 98, 101, 106, 112, 115, 137, 139, 145, 148, 154, 157, 159–61, 165, 168, 174–75, 177, 188, 190, 192, 195, 198–99, 213–15, 217, 220, 226, 234, 236, 241, 255–58, 261–62, 266–67, 273, 276, 279–80, 289, 291–92, 322, 347
Mueller, Ray 21, 75, 93
Mueller, Walter 267
Mulleavy, Greg 22
Mullin, Pat 18, 22
Mungo, Van Lingle 38–40, 42–43, 46, 49, 57
Murphy, Robert 56, 64
Murray, Arch 80
Murray, Red 347
Murtaugh, Danny 107, 139, 189, 283
Musial, Stan 39, 47, 49, 61, 83, 86, 98–99, 139–41, 147, 152, 190, 193, 232, 256, 263, 289, 291, 320, 346, 356, 360

Naragon, Hal 306
Narleski, Ray 274
Naylor, Earl 39
Neal, Charley 341–42, 358–59
Negray, Ron 316
Nelson, Rocky 98, 211, 248, 317
Newcombe, Don 96, 114, 117, 123–25, 127, 131–32, 145–48, 151, 154–55, 157, 161–62, 169–75, 209, 250, 258, 269, 272, 284–85, 288, 293, 307, 316, 321–22, 325, 329, 332, 335, 337–38, 342
Newhouser, Hal 38, 274
Newsom, Bobo 291
Nichols, Chet 167, 176
Nixon, Richard 298, 342, 353
Noble, Rafael 66, 120–21, 133, 136, 146, 221, 230
Nortan, Mary T. 35
Northey, Ron 185
Nuxhall, Joe 38, 41, 233

O'Connell, Danny (Dan) 78, 109–10, 315,
O'Malley, Walter 116, 198, 211, 225, 229,
 235, 249, 257, 272, 284, 296, 306–7, 326,
 331, 343–44, 347–48, 357–58
O'Neill, Steve 3–4, 7–8, 10–11, 15–16,
 18–19, 21–22, 37, 199, 210, 256, 368
Ogden, Jack 23
Oglesby, James 8, 12
Olmo, Luis 58, 61, 64, 66, 68, 72
Orengo, Joe 29, 31, 33–34
Ortiz, Roberto 64
Ott, Mel 27–30, 32, 36, 38–40, 42–50, 54,
 56–60, 74–75, 121
Outlaw, James (Jimmy) 18, 22, 33
Owen, Mickey 61–62, 67

Pafko, Andy 102, 140, 142, 145, 154, 157,
 162, 164, 167, 171–73, 175, 192, 207, 213,
 270, 285, 323
Paige, Satchel 40, 136
Paine, Phil 359
Palica, Erv 95, 146, 150–51, 157
Palys, Stan 325
Paparella, Joe 355
Parker, Dan 56
Pasquel, Alfonso 55
Pasquel, Bernardo 53, 55, 59, 62
Pasquel, Fransisco 55
Pasquel, Gerardo 55
Pasquel, Jorge 1–2, 53, 55–62, 64–69, 77
Pasquel, Mario 55
Patterson, Red 340
Paul, Gabe 317
Pavlick, Pete 120
Perini, Lou 228–29
Pesky, Johnny 120
Philley, Dave 276, 360
Phillips, Eddie 22
Phillips, Jack 79
Pickell, Warren 29–30, 57
Picone, Mario 215
Pierce, Billy 8
Pierce, Walt 41
Piersall, Jim 120
Pike, Jesse 24
Pinelli, Babe 147, 202, 205, 238, 263,
 333–334
Pinson, Vada 312
Pitler, Jake 146, 167, 328
Podres, Johnny 222–23, 272, 285, 301,
 304, 330, 337–38, 342, 358
Poland, Hugh 29, 33
Polli, Lou "Crip" 41
Pope, Dave 221, 279

Porter, Augustus 4
Post, Wally 210, 263, 295, 314, 325, 359
Povich, Shirley 335, 337
Power, Vic 70, 72, 355
Pramesa, John 93, 158
Prince, Carl 212, 234, 321
Pyle, Ewald 38

Queen, Mel 25

Raffensberger, Ken 85, 134
Ramazzoti, Bob 141
Ramos, Pedro 353
Ramsdell, Willie 87, 187
Raschi, Vic 179–80, 256
Reardon, Beans 46
Redmond, Jack 33
Reese, Pee Wee 29, 36, 122, 124, 126–27,
 130, 144–47, 153–54, 159–61, 172–73, 192,
 194, 201, 206, 212, 226, 251–52, 266, 268,
 272, 286, 307–8, 310, 314, 317, 325–26,
 330, 333, 338
Reiser, Pete 47, 61, 91, 139, 186, 206, 355
Rennie, Rud 122, 281
Repulski, Rip 256, 259, 351
Rescigno, Xavier 44
Reulbach, Ed 108
Reyes, Napoleon (Nap) 32, 38, 44, 51, 53,
 56, 60, 66, 68, 72
Reynolds, Allie "Superchief" 178–80, 241,
 301, 342
Rhodes, James Lamar "Dusty" 183, 198,
 202, 207, 221, 236, 257, 260–61, 265–66,
 268, 270–71, 273–74, 278–80, 305, 347
Rice, Del 99, 102, 141, 196, 214, 342
Richards, Paul 8, 283
Richardson, Bobby 351
Richardson, Tommy 23
Richman, Arthur (Artie) 79, 332
Rickart, Tex 162
Rickey, Branch 54, 56, 64, 71, 74–75, 95,
 100–1, 112, 116, 139, 145, 255, 283, 326
Riess, Steven A. 353
Rigney, Bill 75, 86, 105–6, 120, 124, 129,
 131, 144, 147, 154–55, 158, 165, 173, 179,
 199, 212–13, 215, 233, 287, 296–97, 305,
 347, 360–61
Rizzuto, Phil 179–80, 191, 195, 241
Robb, Scotty 95, 146
Roberts, Robin 84, 104, 113, 147, 170, 188,
 273, 284, 292, 329
Robinson, Frank 237, 314–15, 322, 340
Robinson, Jackie 2, 53–54, 56, 82, 85–86,
 107, 112–13, 115, 122–24, 128–32, 134,

400 Index

136, 138–39, 142, 144–47, 153–55, 157, 160–62, 166–67, 170–76, 188, 192–93, 195, 197–98, 201, 205–7, 211–12, 219, 222, 226, 230–31, 235, 237, 250–52, 258, 260, 262, 266, 270–72, 284–87, 294, 296, 301, 307–9, 313, 315–18, 322, 324–27, 330–31, 333, 335–37, 349, 355, 370
Robinson, Rachel 270
Robinson, Wilbert "Uncle Robbie" 9, 43
Roche, Raymond 14, 24
Roe, Elwin Charles "Preacher" 21, 48, 94, 106, 113, 142, 144–47, 167, 209, 212, 222, 261–62
Roebuck, Ed 285, 313, 315, 320, 322, 330, 344
Roger, Colorao 52
Rojek, Stan 79
Rolfe, Red 191
Rollings, Red 14
Roosevelt, Franklin 26–27, 39
Roosevelt, Theodore 371
Rosar, Buddy 3
Rose, Pete 355
Rosen, Al 221, 275–78, 282, 297, 299, 349
Rosen, Goody 10
Rosenthal, Harold 142, 157, 160, 222, 227, 236, 279
Rosso, Frank 41
Rucker, Johnny 29–32, 35–36, 38, 43–44, 47
Ruether, Dutch 194
Rufer, Rudy 105, 120–21
Runge, Ed 283, 333
Runnels, Pete 364
Ruppert, Jacob 11, 281
Rush, Bob 201, 237, 255
Russell, Jim 93, 162
Russo, Marius 3
Rust, Art, Jr. 54
Ruth, Babe 10, 43, 46, 53–54, 77, 100, 157, 264, 281, 353, 356, 370
Rutherford, Johnny 206
Ryan, Connie 28, 32, 34, 133, 140, 158, 188, 215
Ryba, Mike 21

Sadecki, Ray 362
Saffell, Tom 110
Sain, Johnny 95, 123, 127, 179–80, 344
St. Claire, Ebba 192, 227, 243, 253
Sanchez, Raul 341
Sandel, Warren 34, 57
Sandlock, Mike 44
Santiago, Jose 299

Sarni, Bill 293
Sauer, Hank 83, 141, 195, 201, 217, 232, 295
Sawyer, Eddie 84, 102, 127, 146–47, 155, 199
Scarsella, Les 18
Schacht, Al 12
Schalk, Ray 16
Scheib, Carl 38
Schemer, Mike 44
Schenz, Hank 146
Schmidt, Willard 196
Schmitz, Johnny 85, 145, 188
Schoendienst, Red 97, 134, 233, 256, 339
Schroeder, Joe 12
Schultz, Joe 366
Schumacher, Garry 115, 136
Schumacher, Hal 27–28, 55, 57, 101
Score, Herb 301, 303, 306
Scully, Vin 334, 368, 370
Seaward, Mike 57
Secory, Frank 211, 227, 230, 260
Seminick, Andy 84, 102–6, 113–14, 290
Sewell, Luke 190–91
Sewell, Rip 8
Shantz, Bobby 344, 352
Shapiro, Milton 2
Shaughnessy, Frank 8, 17, 29, 33
Sheehan, Tom 232
Shellenback, Frank 2, 78, 97, 100, 118–19, 129, 145, 183, 192–93, 203–4, 219, 243, 245, 311
Shepard, Jack 323
Shirley, Tex 70, 72
Short, Chris 8
Shotton, Burt 74–75, 97, 116–17, 125, 288
Shuba, George "Shotgun" 198, 206–7, 212, 223
Siebern, Norm 351
Simmons, Curt 84, 103, 113, 199, 201, 215
Simpson, Harry 184, 351
Sinatra, Frank 75
Sinclair, Ed 162, 171, 195, 201, 214
Sipek, Dick 38
Sisler, Dick 39, 52, 58, 84, 114, 156, 197
Sisti, Sibby 95, 168
Skinner, Bob 262
Skowron, Bill "Moose" 340, 344, 351
Slaughter, Enos "Country" 98, 190, 196, 214, 332, 335, 340, 344, 346, 349, 351
Sleater, Lou 78
Smalley, Roy 149, 226
Smith, Alfred John (Al) 12, 14–17, 22, 25

Smith, Alphonse Eugene (Al) 275–76, 279, 283, 299, 304
Smith, Clay 12, 16–17, 22
Smith, Frank 93, 214
Smith, Kenny 79
Smith, Marshall 368
Smith, Mayo 14, 18, 22, 320–21
Smith, Red 100, 106, 110, 161, 176, 185, 274, 318, 328, 363
Smith, Theolic 56
Smith, Vince 343
Snider, Duke 122, 124, 129–30, 144–45, 147, 153–54, 159–60, 162, 172–73, 175, 192, 205, 153–54, 159–60, 162, 172–73, 175, 192, 205–7, 213, 226, 237, 251–53, 258, 260, 262, 271–73, 284, 288, 308, 317–21, 323, 326, 330, 332–33, 338–43, 350
Snodgrass, Fred 172
Snyder, Frank "Pancho" 28–30, 32–36
Southworth, Billy 11, 61, 76, 82, 144
Southworth, Billy, Jr. 76
Spahn, Warren 108, 123, 139, 168–69, 227, 233–34, 267–68, 315
Speake, Bob 288–89, 342
Speaker, Tris 36
Spencer, Daryl 218–20, 222–23, 228, 235–36, 241
Spencer, George 123–24, 132–33, 141, 146, 150, 157–59, 166, 171, 176, 195–96, 205, 248, 270
Spooner, Karl 330
Staley, Gerald 102, 152, 163, 196, 344
Stallcup, Virgil 158
Stanky, Eddie 44, 76–77, 81, 83, 85–88, 93, 95–99, 102–7, 110, 112–13, 115, 120, 125–26, 128–30, 134, 141–42, 144, 147, 149–50, 155, 158–59, 162, 164–66, 168, 170, 173, 175–77, 179–80, 183, 194–96, 202, 221, 228, 230, 244, 263–64, 289, 369
Starr, Bill 90
Steiner, Red 69
Steinhagen, Ruth 84
Stengel, Casey 64, 117, 177–80, 268, 299, 301, 330–31, 344, 346, 348, 350–55
Stephens, Vern 58, 61
Stevens, Ed 45, 110
Stevens, Elmer 28
Stevenson, Adlai 331
Stewart, Bill 153, 199, 208–9
Stewart, Glen 19
Stirnweiss, George 33, 35, 122
Stock, Milt 116

Stoneham, Horace C. 27, 48, 50, 54–55, 59–60, 71, 74–78, 87–88, 115, 135–37, 150, 155, 174, 182, 191, 210, 234, 240, 244, 260, 272–74, 281, 295, 297, 309, 343, 348, 361
Strickland, George 148, 189–90, 275, 283, 299
Strincevich, Nick 3
Sturdivant, Tom 332, 344–45, 350
Sukeforth, Clyde 34, 174, 326
Summers, Bill 78, 187
Sunkel, Tom 38
Sutherland, Francis W. 81

Tarte, Contines 72
Taylor, Billy 265–66
Tebbetts, Birdie 13, 293, 350, 360
Temple, Johnny 263
Terry, Bill 27–28, 30–31, 33–34, 50, 287, 290
Terwilliger, Wayne 145, 296
Thomas, Frank 323, 326
Thompson, Don 124
Thompson, Hank 76, 82–83, 86–88, 93, 97, 104–6, 110, 112, 115, 120, 126, 130, 132, 134, 136, 138–39, 144, 147, 149, 173, 179–80, 187, 197–200, 205–7, 217, 227, 230, 233–34, 236, 241, 249–50, 253, 255, 257, 262, 266, 270, 273, 276, 278–80, 284, 289–90
Thompson, Jocko 156
Thomson, Bobby 47, 75, 78, 80, 82–83, 86–88, 93–94, 96, 114–15, 118, 121, 123, 126, 131–32, 137–39, 141, 148–49, 152, 158–59, 161–64, 169, 171–73, 175–77, 179–80, 184–86, 190, 192, 196–97, 199, 201, 207, 214–15, 217, 219, 225–26, 234, 236, 241, 243, 249, 347, 370
Tiant, Luis 51, 66
Todd, Alfred 41
Torgeson, Earl 93, 96, 123–24, 145, 167, 169, 200–1, 236, 263
Torres, Gil 58
Townsend, Walter, Jr. 124
Trexler, James 18
Trinkle, Ken 57
Trouppe, Quincy 55, 70
Truman, Harry 39, 44
Tuminelli, Joe 72
Turley, Bob 344, 347, 350, 352–53
Tyler, John 12, 18, 22

Uhle, George 10, 22
Usher, Bob 140

Valdes, Rene 339
Valo, Elmer 328
Vaughan, Arky 291
Veeck, Bill 136, 147, 226, 247, 300
Vitt, Oscar 13
Voiselle, Bill 38–40, 42–43, 45–46, 49, 55, 57, 60

Wade, Ben 209, 222, 230
Wade, Gale 305
Wagner, Robert 342
Wagner, Robert F., Jr. 188
Waitkus, Eddie 84, 114, 155–56, 166, 170, 188
Wakefield, Dick 184
Walker, Dixie 45, 261
Walker, Harry 293, 360
Walker, Moses Fleetwood 53
Walker, Rube 145, 154, 171–73, 315, 317, 330
Walls, Lee 323, 326
Walters, Bucky 81, 162, 323
Waner, Lloyd 38
Waner, Paul 38
Ward, Preston 83
Wares, Buzzy 202
Warneke, Lon 96–97, 105, 134, 170
Weatherly, Roy 87, 99
Webb, James "Skeeter" 17, 22
Webb, Red 76
Webber, Les 47
Weintraub, Phil 38–40
Weiss, George 11, 295, 341
Wertz, Vic 121, 147–48, 275–76, 277, 279, 297, 299, 371
Westcott, Rich 368
Westfall, Bob 29–30
Westlake, Wally 141, 190, 221, 282
Westrum, Wes 80, 83, 88, 93–94, 98–99, 106, 109–10, 115, 119–20, 125–26, 130, 133, 142, 149, 154–58, 160, 163, 165, 168, 170, 173, 176–77, 180, 186, 189–90, 195, 200, 203, 207–8, 217, 221, 223, 225–26, 233, 236–37, 241, 246–47, 253–54, 273, 279, 290, 292, 295, 305, 309, 347, 368
Wheat, Zack 317
Wheeler, Lonnie 362
White, Bill 305
White, Doc 108
White, Hal 18–22
Wilbur, Del 133, 166

Wilhelm, Hoyt 187, 189, 194–95, 205, 207, 209, 212, 214, 216–17, 222, 225, 227, 229, 233, 240, 255–56, 258–59, 261, 266, 269–70, 273, 282, 289, 354
Will, George 209
Williams, Davey 77, 120–21, 128, 147, 158, 183, 185, 187, 190, 195–96, 202, 209, 212, 215, 217, 220–21, 223, 226–28, 241, 246, 248–50, 254, 256, 260, 273, 276–77, 282, 286–87, 290–91
Williams, Dick 131, 161, 365
Williams, Ted, "The Splendid Splinter" 9, 25, 49, 59, 61, 86, 120–21, 298, 304, 315, 326, 332, 346, 349, 362
Wilson, Artie 120–21, 124–25, 128, 135–36
Wilson, George 199, 210
Wilson, Jimmie 370
Wiltse, Hooks 347
Wine, Bobby 8
Winsett, Tom 46
Witek, Mickey 36, 57, 59
Witting, John 29–30, 32, 34, 36
Wolf, Bob 319
Wolff, Bob 334
Wolff, Roger 24–25
Worthington, Al 231, 233–35, 237, 241, 244, 282, 344
Wrigley, Phil 348
Wrigley, William, Jr. 219
Wynn, Early 23, 25, 184, 274–75, 279, 297–300, 303, 305–6, 354
Wyrostek, Johnny 93, 210
Wyse, Hank 47

Yawkey, Tom 50, 348
Yost, Eddie 300
Young, Babe 57, 347
Young, Cy 328
Young, Dick 296, 301
Yvars, Sal 123, 144, 150, 152, 154, 165, 180–81, 200–1, 205, 214, 220–21, 224–26, 263

Zabala, Adrian 34, 41–43, 51, 53, 57, 60, 66, 68, 72
Zardon, Jose 51
Zimmer, Don 285, 338–39, 341
Zimmerman, Roy 41, 47–48, 57, 59–60, 66, 69–70, 72
Zuber, Bill 17–18, 22

www.ingramcontent.com/pod-product-compliance
Ingram Content Group UK Ltd.
Pitfield, Milton Keynes, MK11 3LW, UK
UKHW041921140426
5217IPUK00014B/256